GOOD   WINE   GUIDE

1 9 9 2

The Sunday Telegraph

in association with **WINE** Magazine

GOOD

WINE

Guide

1992

ROBERT JOSEPH

PAN BOOKS
London, Sydney and Auckland

Editor, Robert Joseph
Deputy Editor, Simon Woods
Editorial Assistants, Helen Boswell, Juliet Bruce Jones,
Justin Howard-Sneyd, Susan Low, Lyn Parry.
Editorial Coordinator, Clare Mathews

Author photograph: Christopher Hawkins

Published in Great Britain 1991
by the Sunday Telegraph
Peterborough Court, At South Quay
181 Marsh Wall, London E14 9SR
in association with Pan Books

First edition published 1982
Copyright © Robert Joseph and
The Sunday Telegraph 1991

ISBN 0 330 31968X

Designed by Peter Ward
Typeset by Jethro Probes / Word Perfect, Isleworth
Printed and bound in Great Britain by
BPCC Hazell Books
Aylesbury, Bucks, England
Member of BPCC Limited

CONTENTS

A-Z OF WINES AND WINE TERMS   33

WINE WITH FOOD   66

THE WINES   69

THE STOCKISTS   115

INDEX   267

INTRODUCTION

Where can I buy a reasonably priced bottle of wine to drink with a cheese soufflé? Or the best value fizz? Which bottles are worth looking out for in my local supermarket? What ought they to cost? What on earth is Albariño? And who would sell me a bottle?

The *Sunday Telegraph Good Wine Guide* was devised specifically to answer questions like these - to make wine drinking more interesting, better value and, above all, more fun.

With this, the ninth edition of the *Guide*, we have achieved the impossible: by shoe-horning a larger number of merchants into its pages than ever before - while still maintaining the pocket book format which has made the book such a best seller. So, we are proud to say that over 225 merchants are included, from the tiniest specialist to the most leviathan of supermarket chains.

Following suggestion from readers of previous editions, this year, we have made one or two changes to the order in which the Guide is laid out, moving the popular A-Z section to the front of the book and shifting the Merchants' Speciality and Service charts into its place just before the index. So, for that Albariño, turn to page 34 And to discover a wine merchant who could sell you wine in half bottles, have a look on page 254

As in previous years, the wines recommended in the *Guide* have been chosen from the winners at the International Wine Challenge. Organised annually by WINE Magazine, this event has become the world's biggest, toughest and most respected comparative tasting. An award won at the Challenge is arguably the one winemakers from Cahors to California most covet.

Given the recession in which this edition of the *Guide* is published, we have taken particular pains to ensure that over 200 of the wines it recommends sell for less than £5, and that 30 cost under £3. On the other hand, great wine, wine for special occasions, can never be cheap. So, we make no apology for including wines which carry price tags of £20 a bottle or more. The only criteria used to choose them is that they offer value for money - whatever they cost.

For every recommended wine, as in the past, we suggest food-and-wine combinations based on the monthly tastings held by WINE Magazine at which a team of highly experienced palates try to match hundreds of different wines with almost every imaginable style of food.

And, as always, there is advice on where to buy wine at auction, corkscrews which really work, affordable, good-looking wine glasses, made-to-measure wine racks and even computerised cellar books. All of this information will be found in the next few pages.

In short, we hope that readers of the 1992 *Guide* agree with the description by Jim Ainsworth in *Punch*: of the 1991 edition as 'An indispensable short cut to good drinking'.

ACKNOWLEDGMENTS

This year, as always, the production of the *Guide* was rather like building a skyscraper in a month. Unlike some annual reference works, each edition of the *Guide* is essentially an entirely new book. In order to make it as up-to-date and accurate as is humanly possible, we work to an incredibly tight self-imposed schedule, holding the WINE Magazine International Wine Challenge tasting in May, in order to ensure that the most recent vintages could be sampled, and publishing the book in September when the wine buying season really begins. The collation of literally thousands of pieces of information, wine names, descriptions and wine merchant addresses at this speed required a highly sophisticated computer system and the day-and-night toil of a number of knowledgeable, dedicated and extraordinary hard-working people.

Led by Simon Woods, Deputy Editor of the *Guide* and coordinator of the 1991 International Wine Challenge, the team that made it possible to produce the book in the available time consisted of Helen Boswell, Justin Howard-Sneyd, Susan Low, Lyn Parry, Juliet Bruce Jones, and Clare Mathews. They were assisted in the task of transforming well over 10,000 tasting notes into the 500 wine descriptions that appear in these pages by Patrick Porritt, trainee accountant and 1990 *Daily Telegraph* Wine Taster of the Year, and Jacqueline Moss.

Equally essential in a different way were the members of the British and international wine trade listed below who spent a week in the Tower Bridge Piazza development, tasting their way through over 4,500 wines (and half of these twice) to select 2,400 award winners.

To ensure that the right bottles of wine were placed in front of the right tasters at the right time, Charles Metcalfe led a team of wine enthusiasts consisting of: the above-listed staff plus John Stott, Byron Morrison, Mike Dentten, Mike Hinchcliffe, Michele Sandell, Cherry Jenkins, Judy Tattersall-Ryan and Nick Zalinski. But for these people, for Eric Verdon Roe and Mike Trew, publishers of WINE Magazine, Ruth Cobb, its editor, and her staff, the desktop publishing wizardry of Francis Jago of Fingal in Fulham and Nigel Ellner at Word Perfect in Isleworth, for Piers Russell-Cobb, Jas Singh, Louise Abbott, Catherine Hurley at Pan and Marilyn Warnick at Telegraph Books, this *Guide* would never exist.

THE TASTERS

Jim Ainsworth, Liz Aked, Colin Akers, Simon Alper, Guy Anderson, Keith Anderson, Christopher Andrews, P Aplin, Tim Atkin, Suzy Atkins, Angus Avery, Lucy Bailey, Richard Bailey, Chris Baker, Bill Baker, Richard Balls, Richard Bampfield MW, Anne Barlow, Ken Barlow, Andrew Barr, Stephen Barrett, Giles Bartleet, Florence Baudra, David Baverstock, Tracey Baylis, David W.R. Bedford MW, Gideon Beinstock, Charles Bennett, Rowland Bennett, Edward Berry, Liz Berry MW, John Bertaut, David Billingham, Vicky Bishop, Nick Blacknell, Peter Blackwell, David Boobbyer, Ann-Marie Bostock, Helen Boswell, Paul Boutinot, John Boys, Mark Brandon, Rodney Briant-Evans, Jane Brocket, Tony Brown MW, Juliet Bruce Jones, Chris Brunck, Mark Brunel-Cohen, Jim Budd, Richard Burgess, Nick Butler, Alistair Cameron, Hugo Campbell, Daniel Carey, David Cartwright, Guy Chisenhale-Marsh, Nick Clarke, Oz Clarke, Stephen Clarke, Philip Clive, Ruth Cobb, Hugh Cochcrane MW, Simon Cock, Pamela Collington, Dirk Collingwood, Michael Collyer, John Comyn, Matthew Cooper, David Courtenay-Clack, Michael Cox, Robin Crameri MW, Charles Crawfurd MW, Jan Critcheley-Salmonson MW, David Crossley, Amanda Dale, Robert Dale, Steve Daniel, Christophe Daviau, Martin Davis, Kimberly Dawson, Paul Day, Tom Day, Paulina de Kadt, Sergio de Luca, Mark de Vere, Simon Deakin, Demitri Demetriou, Mike

Dentten, Robert di Massimo, John Downes, Dorothy Druitt, Helen Duddridge, Paul Dwyer, Alison Easton, Michael Edwards, Julian Eggar, Nick Elliott, Jochen Erler, Sally Evans, Grant Farquhar, Simon Farr, Su-Elsa ffrenetic, Sinead Ferramosca, Alfie Fiandaca, Alex Findlater, Stuart Floyd, Luciann Flynn, Martin Fowke, Lance Foyster, Elizabeth Gabay, M Gamman, Graham Gardner, Rosemary George MW, Alastair Gibson, Alison Gibson, Dr Caroline Gilby, David Gill MW, Simon Gillespie, David Gleave, Philip Goodband MW, Nigel Gray, Peter Greet, Julie Gubbins, Bill Gunn MW, Patricia Guy, Chris Hall, Peter Hallgarten, Philip Harris, John Hart, Margaret Harvey, Richard Harvey MW, Michael Hasslacher, Peter Hastings, Peny Hearn, Harold Heckle, Tony Hein, João Henriques, Bill Hermitage, Roger Higgs, Piers Hillier, Mike Hinchcliffe, Christopher Hindle, Rosamund Hitchcock, Rodney Hogg, Pamela Holt, Mike Hooton, Terry Horton, Justin Howard-Sneyd, Ben Howkins, Ernst Hugelschafter Gebhardt, Mark Hughes, Jane Hunt MW, Colin Hynard, Lena Inger, Nicholas Ingham, K J Isaac MW, Nikki Jacoby, Daniel Jago, Nicholas James, Richard James, Andrew Jefford, Cherry Jenkins, Julia Jenkins, Brian Johnson, Robert Joseph, Rodney Kearns, Dominic Kelly, Paul Kelly, John Kemp, Bruce Kendrick, Judy Kendrick, Barry Kettle, Tony Keys, Sarah King, Simon Ladenburg, M de G Lambert, Michael Larn, Charles Lea, Willy Lebus, Peter Ledgerwood, Janet Lee, Angela Leighton, John Leighton, Nick Leonard, Alastair Llewellyn-Smith, Michael Lo, Simon Loftus, William Long, Wink Lorch, Susan Low, Liz Lucas, Debbie Lush, Katie MacAulay, Giles Macdonogh, Andrew Mackenzie, Bruce MacKenzie, Marian Macmillan, Robert Mapley, Simon March, Adrian Markwell, S Marsay, Robert Marsden, Tony Mason, Clare Mathews, Richard Mayson, David McDonnell, Kevin McKoen, Maggie McNie MW, Paul Merritt, Charles Metcalfe, Laurent Metge, Christopher Milner, Sue Moorhouse, Liz Morcom MW, Ivor Morgan, Jasper Morris MW, Jaqueline Moss, Angela Mount, Katrina Mullan, Chris Murphy, Monica Murphy, Francis Murray, Zue Newton, Grant Page, Neil Palmer, Mark Pardoe MW, Lyn Parry, Steve Parsons, Richard Pass, Diana Paterson Fox, Luis Pato, Adrian Patterson, Michael Paul, Francis Peel, J Petridis, Neil Phillips, Mike Pollard, Patrick Porritt, Vicky Power, Lynn Power, John Radford, Lewis Ragbourn, Barry Ralph, John Ratcliffe, Monique Reedman, Philip Reedman, Patrick Rennie, Gordon Ritchie, Jeremy Roberts, Liz Robertson MW, James Rogers, Christophe Rollet-Manus, Anthony Rose, Vicky Ross, Ted Sandbach, Michele Sandell, David Sandys-Renton, Michael Saunders, Hector Scicluna, Paul Shinnie, John Shortt, Joanna Simon, Pat Simon MW, James Simpson, Theo Sloot, Derek Smedley MW, Richard Speirs, Jo Standen MW, Tim Stanley-Clarke, David Stevens MW, Andrew Stewart MW, John Stott, Clare Symington, Nick Tarrayon, Christopher Tatham MW, Judy Tattersall-Ryan, Charles Taylor MW, David Thomas, John Thorn, Edward Thornton, John Thorogood, Kim Tidy, Kim Titan, Marcus Titley, Ann Tonks, J C Townend, Cheryl Trull, Michael Trull, Philip Tuck, Neil Tully, Julian Twaites, Nick Underwood, Tim Underwood, Helen Verdcourt, Roger Voss, Nicholas Wakefield, Matthew Waldin, Robert Walker, Stuart Walton, Julia Wardle, Bill Warre MW, Reece Warren, Marcia Waters MW, Simone Wedgewood, Tom Weir, Eric While, Anthony Whitaker, Paul White, Andrew Williams, Chris Williams, Laurence Williams, Marcel Williams, Douglas Williamson, Don Woossim, Rupert Wollheim MW, Melanie Wood, Arabella Woodrow MW, Richard Woodrow, Simon Woods, Thomas Woolrych, Mike Worm, Debbie Worton, David Wright, Sarah Wykes, Margaret Wysynska, Nick Zalinski.

THE AWARDS

The recommendations both of wines and merchants that form the main body of this *Guide* are taken from the International Wine Challenge tasting, held annually by WINE Magazine. Since it was launched in 1985, this event has become the biggest international competition of its kind.

The wines are entered — and judged — by representatives of every part of the UK wine trade, from the smallest English vineyard and one-man-band importer, to the most venerable of City merchants and the biggest High Street off-licence chains and supermarkets. In addition, an increasing number of overseas winemakers and trade members now make time to attend the event, contributing a truly international perspective to the judging. Following this, a full list of the wines that have received awards is sent to 1,000 retailers (whether or not they competed), enabling them to indicate to us those that they stock.

Where companies have submitted wines, we first compare the number of successful wines with the number entered into the Challenge — so the success rate of a merchant that was awarded 15 recommendations out of 25 entries is recognised as being greater than that of a firm that submitted 100, of which 30 won awards. Then we compare the total number of award-winning wines from each company with their full wine lists to see whether the recommended wines are representative of their range as a whole. Finally, we select the merchants that will feature in the *Guide*. Where companies declare that they have sufficient stocks of the award winning wines to expect to be able to supply them in the early part of 1992, the wines in question are listed.

We automatically include most of Britain's larger supermarket and off-licence chains, simply because their ubiquitous presence in the High Street virtually guarantees that most readers will shop for wine there at one time or another. Our assessment of each firm appears in their individual entries. More difficult is the task of selecting the best from Britain's wealth of independent merchants. Paramount in our considerations are the breadth of choice and the range of services offered to customers. While our regional awards reflect the national scope of the *Guide*, our category winners, for different styles of businesses, take account of the diversity of ways in which British wine drinkers may choose to shop for their wine.

THE SUNDAY TELEGRAPH GOOD WINE GUIDE/WINE MAGAZINE WINE MERCHANTS OF THE YEAR

These sought-after awards were judged this year by an expert panel consisting of: Jim Ainsworth, wine writer for *Punch*; Tim Atkin, wine writer for *The Guardian*; Ruth Cobb, editor of *WINE* magazine; Jill Goolden of BBC2's *Food & Drink* Programme; Andrew Jefford, correspondent for *WINE* and former editor of the *WHICH? Wine Guide;* Maggie McNie MW, wine consultant; Kathryn McWhirter, wine writer of the *Sunday Independent*, and former editor of both the *Which? Wine Guide* and *Wine & Spirit* magazine; Charles Metcalfe of *WINE Magazine, Homes & Gardens* and Granada Television's *This Morning* and *WINE*; Anthony Rose, wine correspondent of *The Independent*. As in the past, Robert Joseph, editor of the *Guide* excluded himself from the judging,

REGIONAL AWARDS

East of England - Adnams

In the toughest region of Britain - why are there so many excellent companies in East Anglia, Norfolk, Suffolk and Essex? - Adnams deserves particular credit for winning this award for the second year in the teeth of competition from such companies as Lay & Wheeler, Thos Peatling and T&W, all of whom were praised by the judges.

Scotland - The Ubiquitous Chip

Wine drinkers north of the border are among the best-served in the nation, each good wine merchant seemingly attracting a host of others. To win our Award for Scotland, a merchant has to be really special - which was precisely the expression used about this extraordinary Glasgow Merchant.

Wales - The Celtic Vintner

With each edition we find new Welsh merchants of whom we were previously aware. This year, twice-winner, The Celtic Vintner's pricipal competition came from Terry Platt, but when the votes were added up, the result was clear: a hat-trick for Brian Johnson's family firm and its 'brilliant' list.

North of England - Haughton Fine Wines

Taking the Award back from D Byrne, Haughton Fine Wine impressed the judges with the strength of its range, its list (which won a separate award), its sensibly down-to-earth attitude towards organic wines and its generally innovative approach to wine.

Central England - Bennetts of Chipping Campden

Until this year, Tanners seemed to have taken a lease out on this Award. It took a very dynamic effort by this young merchant to wrest it away from them - but not without a struggle from Windrush, Waters of Coventry and George Hill of Loughborough.

South West of England - Reid Wines

Although several merchants in the West Country were highly praised by the judges, it was Reid who took the prize, partly for the quality of the great old wines for which it is known and partly for the range of more affordable current drinking with which it is perhaps less associated.

London/South East - La Vigneronne

This small London merchant has long been famous among wine lovers throughout the world for its extraordinary range of mature and current wines. Described as a 'vinous reference library' by one of the judges, it beat off very tough challenges from a long list of first class companies.

Northern Ireland - James Nicholson

Direct Wine Shipments put in a tough fight, but it was this keen Ulster merchant which took this new Award. Not only is the list exemplary, but the tutored tastings and dinners are Award-worthy in their own right.

CATEGORY AWARDS

Wine List - Haughton Fine Wines

Another new Award this year, and one the judges found the most difficult of all to allocate. Quite simply, there were so many worthy candidates to judge that it would have been possible to give four or five joint winners. In the event however, the prize went to Haughton Fine Wines for a list which was described as 'small but perfectly formed' - 'worth buying in a bookshop'.

Regional Chain - Davisons

Winner for the second time, Davisons impressed the judges as much with the quality of its service, as a wine list whose range and prices benefit from the company's policy of buying wine *en primeur* and maturing it in its own cellars for sale.

National High Street Chain - Thresher / Wine Rack

Two years of evidently committed effort from Thresher and its new, up-market off-shoot Wine Rack have finally paid off. Our judges had no hesitation in recognising the way in which the chain has developed.

By-the-Case / By Mail - The Wine Society

Sometimes overlooked by observers distracted by flashier merchants, The Wine Society impressed the judges with its combination of quality wine, consistency and service. It was easy to understand, one judge said, why Wine Society members remain loyal.

Supermarket - Tesco

Winning back the Award it won three years ago, Tesco just displaced last year's Award-winner Sainsbury. While voting, the judges particularly commended the chain on its policy of innovative buying - especially in the fields of French regional, Italian and German wines.

SPECIALIST MERCHANTS

Burgundy - Morris & Verdin

It is far from easy being a Burgundy specialist, as wine merchants and drinkers know to their cost. Even so, there were several strong contenders for this prize, including most notably Le Nez Rouge, Haynes Hanson & Clarke and Howard Ripley. It was, however, Jasper Morris's company who took the prize for his in-depth knowledge and the firm's fair pricing policy.

Bordeaux - Justerini & Brooks

A long list of merchants can make very impressive claims to the Award as Bordeaux specialists. All were considered carefully before the St James's and Edinburgh merchant was declared the winner for the consistent skill with which it has approached this area and the quality of its advice.

Rhône - Bibendum

Simon Farr, whose firm was also nominated as Italian Specialist, has made the Rhône a special subject over the last couple of years and introduced a range which dazzled our judges sufficiently for them to award this prize to Bibendum in the face of strong competition from several other contenders.

German - Oddbins

Despite the excellence of the lists of several German specialists - Summerlee and The Wine Schoppen were both highly praised - Oddbins took this prize for the way in which it had covered genuinely new ground when introducing its new German range. This category needs all the support it can get, and the judges were pleased to encourage the effort Oddbins has made.

Italian - Winecellars

Winecellars, Bibendum or Valvona & Crolla? That was the question the judges asked themselves when making this Award before finally deciding that David Gleave's London shop really did deserve the prize for converting huge numbers of people to the joys of good Italian wine of every style.

Spanish/Portuguese - Moreno Wines

Few merchants have worked harder in a potentially less rewarding field. Iberian wines satisfy a great many people; they excite very few. The Moreno team has, with the firm's list and through tastings, done their utmost to convey the image of what Spain in particular really has to offer.

New World - Australian Wine Centre

It is not difficult to be an Australian specialist, but it is not easy to perform the task as comprehensively as the Australian Wine Centre. Very few good Aussie wines escape their attention or grasp, so theirs is an essential address for every keen seeker after great flavour and value.

'Fine & Rare' - Farr Vintners

If you want to buy 'Jefferson' Lafite or 1985 Lynch Bages, this prize winner can oblige - and offer almost every other wine and vintage between the two. There were other strong contenders for this prize, but Farr Vintners won itself a clear majority vote from the judges.

WINE MERCHANT OF THE YEAR

JOINT WINNERS ADNAMS / ODDBINS

So, to the big prize. When the judges' votes were counted, two companies stood apart from the rest. Adnams and Oddbins both, in their separate ways, can celebrate a richly deserved Award. We don't know whether either firm would like to be compared with the other, but the judges saw (and approved of) a direct likeness in their commitment and enthusiasm, and felt that both avoid compromises, and run businesses, which make wine drinking interesting and fun.

WINES OF THE YEAR

When selecting the Wines of the Year, our criteria are not that they should be the greatest or the most exquisite bottles on the market, but that they achieve the arguably more difficult feat of standing out from the crowd without being too esoteric; they must appeal to a wide range of tastes and suit a wide number of occasions; they must be well made, characterful, sanely priced and, in view of the rocketing sales of previous winners, widely available. In short, they are wines we would unreservedly recommend.

Red Wine of the Year : Penfolds Bin 28 Kalimna Shiraz 1987/1988

An astonishing success made by Penfolds from the Shiraz grape in one of Australia's best vineyard regions. Both vintages won Silver medals in the International Wine Challenge, dazzling tasters with their depth of spicy flavour. They are remarkable value and provide a perfect taste of Australian winemaking at its best.

White Wine of the Year: Château Haut Redon, Entre-Deux-Mers 1990

There is an Australian connection here too. Hugh Ryman (son of Nick Ryman of Château la Jaubertie, a previous winner of this Award) learned his winemaking in Australia. At Château Haut Redon, he has made an emphatically modern, refreshingly dry French wine which serves as a perfect ambassador for what used to be a woefully under-exploited region.

Joint Sparkling Wines of the Year: Lindauer; Mumm Cuvée Napa Blanc de Noirs; Salinger 1988/1989

Three sparkling wines of the year? And not one of them a Champagne? Before anyone accuses the *Guide* of making a political gesture with this Award, we acknowledge the accusation - merely countering it with the reply that nothing could have been more politcal than the decision by the Champenois to raise their prices and to make their wine a special-occasion-only drink.

Well, our main concern is value for money, so we are delighted to be able to recommend three wines made in three different countries by the Méthode Champenoise (and in one case by the distant arm of a major Champagne house).

The Lindauer is made on the South Island of New Zealand by Montana (maker of a previous White Wine of the Year) and is deliciously light, fresh and fruity. The Californian Mumm Cuvée Napa is very pale pink and full of raspberry Pinot flavour and the Salinger from Great Western in Victoria provides, in a pair of vintages, two different versions of great Australian fizz-making (the 1988 is bigger and richer, the 1989, fruitier and more pineappley).

AVAILABILITY

Among the gratifyingly large number of letters we receive from readers of the *Guide*, there is the occasional complaint that one or other of the merchants named in the book has run out of stock of particular recommended wines. We should love to be able to avoid this happening, and to guarantee availability. Indeed, when compiling the lists of wines we recommend, we specifically ask the retailers to confirm that they have sufficient stock to ensure that the wine can still be bought in the spring of 1992. They should also be selling at prices quoted in the *Guide*, though obviously merchants may be affected by currency changes when they have to bring in fresh stock

Last year, over 45,000 people bought copies of this book. If only half of those readers purchased one bottle of some of our recommended wines, cellars could literally be emptied. Were we to restrict our recommendations to wines made in huge quantities, this would be a very dull book.

HOW TO USE THE GUIDE

The *Guide* is split into three main sections. First, on p.33 is the **A-Z** which includes definitions of 1,000 wine names and terms, recommended vintages, approximate prices and suggested producers and stockists. Where a wine features elsewhere in the *Guide*, its code number will appear; otherwise a typical example and a stockist is given.

Secondly, on page 69, there is the list of 500 recommended wines (**The Wines**), divided by style and within those styles listed in order of price. With each are one or more stockist codes indicating where the wine may be bought. Every wine in this recommended wine section has a code number which features elsewhere in the *Guide*. For each wine, we list coded food styles, explained in the **Wine With Food** chapter (p.16).

Finally, the **Stockists** section (p.115) lists and describes over 225 wine merchants alphabetically, indicating the recommended wines they sell.

HOW TO READ THE ENTRIES

The Wines Listing

304[1] **ROSSO SECONDO**[2] Vinattieri[3] 1985[4] Tuscany[5] (It)[6]

   £9.65[7]   **BI**[8]   **j, k, m**[9]

   From a partnership of three of Italy's best wine experts, this is a deep purple, blackcurranty wine with dusky tannin and rich tarry fruit right to the finish - very New World style.[10]

1   The code number which refers to this wine
2   The wine name
3   The producer, though with New World wines in particular, this may already have featured as an integral part of the wine name
     - for example: **MONTANA**[3] **SAUVIGNON BLANC**[2] 1989[4] Marlborough[5] (NZ)[6]
4   The vintage
5   The region in which the wine was made
6   The country in which the wine was made
7   The price we would expect you to pay, not an average price
8   The stockists - for codes see p.16
9   Foods with which this wine might go well - for codes see p.66
10   Tasting notes

Wine names printed in red indicate particularly good quality and value.

The Stockists' Listing

Recommended wines are listed beneath each merchant thus:

354[1] **£10.75**[2] **CORNAS**[3] **GUY DE BARJAC**[4] 1986[5] Rhône[6] (F)[7]

1   The code number — refer to **The Wines** for tasting notes
2   The price which the stockist charges for the wine
3   The wine name
4   The producer
5   The vintage
6   The region
7   The country

Aglianico del Vulture (BASILICATA)[1] Full-bodied, best-known and best DOC red from this region, made from a grape used by the ancient Greeks **79 81 82 85** 88[2] £££[3] Fratelli d'Angelo 85[4] (WCE, L&W)[5]

1	Words that appear in SMALL CAPITALS have their own entry elsewhere in the A-Z.
2	Only those vintages that are good have been listed. The years that appear in bold are ready to drink.
3	Price guide: £ = under £3.50, ££ = 3.50-5.50 £££ = £5.50-8, ££££ = £8-12, £££££ = £12 and over.
4	This is a recommended example of the wine. Where possible we recommend one of the *Guide's* 500 wines, in which case it will appear as a number, for example 179.
5	Stockists — for an explanation of merchants' codes, see below. If the merchant is not featured in the *Guide*, its telephone number will appear.

Code	Name	Page	Code	Name	Page
A	Asda Stores	120	CIW	City Wines	141
AB	Augustus Barnett Ltd	125	CNL	Connollys	142
ABB	Abbey Cellars	115	CPL	Chaplin & Son	140
ABY	Anthony Byrne Fine Wines	136	CPW	Christopher Piper Wines Ltd	196
ADN	Adnams	116	CUM	Cumbrian Cellar	144
AF	Alexr Findlater & Co	152	CVR	The Celtic Vintner Ltd	139
AHC	Ad Hoc Wines	115	CWI	A Case of Wine	138
AK	Arriba Kettle & Co	119	CWM	Cornwall Wine Merchants	144
ALV	A L Vose & Co Ltd	225	CWS	The Co-op	143
AMW	Amey's Wines	118	CWW	Classic Wine Warehouses Ltd	142
AS	André Simon Wine Shops	211	C&B	Corney & Barrow Ltd	143
ASH	Ashley Scott	208	D	Davisons Wine Merchants	145
AUC	Australian Wine Centre	120	DAL	David Alexander	117
AV	Averys of Bristol	122	DBY	D Byrne & Co	136
BAT	The Battersea Wine Co	126	DLM	Del Monico Wines Ltd	146
BBR	Berry Bros & Rudd Ltd	128	DWS	Direct Wine Shipments	146
BD	Bordeaux Direct	132	DX	Drinkx plc	147
BEN	Bennetts	126	EBA	Ben Ellis & Assocs Ltd	149
BFI	Bedford Fine Wines Ltd	126	ECK	Eckington Wines	148
BGC	Borg Castel	132	EE	Eaton Elliot Fine Wines	148
BH	B H Wines	122	EP	Eldridge Pope & Co	149
BI	Bibendum Wine Ltd	128	EVI	Evingtons	150
BIN	Bin 89 Wine Warehouse	129	FAR	Farr Vintners Ltd	151
BKW	Berkeley Wines	127	FDL	Findlater Mackie Todd & Co	152
BLW	Blayneys	130	FSW	Frank E Stainton	212
BND	Bin Ends	129	FUL	Fuller's	154
BNK	The Bottleneck	133	FWC	Fulham Road Wine Centre	154
BOO	Booths of Stockport	130	G	Gateway	155
BOS	Bottles of Brock St	133	GEL	Gelston Castle Fine Wines	156
BRO	The Broad Street Wine Co	134	GEW	Great English Wines	158
BSN	Benson Fine Wines Ltd	127	GHL	George Hill	170
BTH	Booths of Preston	131	GHS	Gerard Harris Fine Wines	163
BU	Bottoms Up	134	GI	Grape Ideas	157
BUD	Budgens	135	GNW	Great Northern Wine Co	158
BUT	The Butlers Wine Cellar	136	GON	T.F. Gauntley Ltd	156
BWI	Bute Wines	135	GRT	Great Western Wine Co Ltd	159
BWS	The Barnes Wine Shop	124	G&G	Godwin & Godwin	157
B&B	Bottle & Basket	132	G&M	Gordon & Macphail	157
CAC	Cachet Wines	138	H	Hunters Food and Wine Ltd	173
CAR	C A Rookes Wine Merchants	202	HAM	Hampden Wine Co	161
CDV	Champagne de Villages	140	HAR	Harrods Ltd	164
CFW	Christchurch Fine Wine Co	141	HAS	H Allen Smith	211
CGW	The Cote Green Wine Co	144	HBR	Hilbre Wine Co Ltd	169
CHP	Château Pleck	141	HBV	High Breck Vintners	169

THIS YEAR

War, frost, recession, taxes, greedy bankers and the anti-alcohol lobby.... All in all, 1991 was a rotten year for wine drinkers, and for the wine merchants who supply them and had every reason to feel unloved. Bad weather in the Northern Hemisphere made winegrowing difficult or impossible; in Britain the financial climate compounded the wine trade's problems, which were then exacerbated by the decision of the Chancellor to raise the duty on wine for the second year running.

At the end of April, vineyards throughout France suffered the worst bout of frost since the 1940s. Typically, the immediate concern centred around the prospects for the Bordeaux Crus Classés. It was as if a man confronted with his burning home could only bring himself to worry about the fate of the family silver. Bordeaux will have been badly affected by the cold weather but, with cellars full of unsold 1990 wine, the Bordelais deserve far less sympathy than some of their neighbours in other parts of France. Besides, it is far more relevant to most wine drinkers that there is almost certain to be a shortage of 1991 Vin de Pays des Côtes de Gascogne and Muscadet.

But the situation in Bordeaux may well affect a broader range of wine drinkers after all. Many of Britain's best-known wine merchants rely on the annual *en primeur* campaign for profit and, more significantly, cash flow. How they fare when, as now, the most recent vintage on offer is not selling very briskly (largely because of the recession), and prospects of the next one seem bleak, remains to be seen.

En primeur customers who paid UK merchants in good faith for their 1990 wine in May 1991, should be aware that there are a few people in Bordeaux who are getting restive over payment for the 1989s those same merchants bought a year earlier. If the Bordelais don't get paid, the buyers of those 1989s - and 1990s - may never see their wine, a situation which customers of the now-closed Greens will readily appreciate. As we go to press, it is impossible to say whether the closure of Greens was a one-off trade failure or whether other *en primeur*-oriented merchants risk collapse. We fear the latter, and would advise readers to tread warily when buying what is always after all a very distant pig in a similarly distant poke.

Surprisingly perhaps, the one region which has regularly cried 'wolf' after frost scares in the spring, remained much quieter this year. Perhaps the Champenois finally understood that the less they said the better. After all, they had just seen sales of their wine throughout the world drop by some 30% and plummet in Britain by closer to 50% as a direct consequence of major price hikes. Recession-hit wine drinkers were unwilling to lash out £18 on quite ordinary bottles of Non Vintage fizz.

The Champenois blamed the press (including the editor of the *Guide*) for somehow deterring people from buying. Perhaps they should read the price lists of some of Britain's better wine merchants, like this comment from Bennetts of Chipping Campden: 'We have reduced the range of Champagnes on this list. After years of selling a large selection, we have decided to stock only wines we personally rate and have therefore delisted some well known names that no longer represent value for money'. Perhaps too, they should look at Victoria Wine's new list in which Champagnes are now treated alongside good New World fizz as 'Prestige Sparkling Wine'.

Elsewhere in France, the revolution continues, as a larger than ever number of regions (with none of the prestige of Bordeaux or Champagne) produce larger than ever numbers of good value, tasty wines.

Italy's revolutionaries are being similarly active, producing similarly impressive 'new' wines throughout the country, both in established denominations like Chianti and Barolo and in innumerable Vini da Tavola. Unfortunately, the price of many of these wines is so outrageously high that British wine drinkers may prefer to buy more basic examples and set aside the money they save to spend it on an Italian holiday.

Germany continued to struggle its way back into the favours of quality-conscious wine drinkers, but it's a very slow business. The Germans are finally beginning to acknowledge that we don't want tooth-strippingly acidic *Trocken* wines; indeed, at the biggest tastings of German wines, such styles (which now make up over 60% of some cellars' production) were a welcome absentee. With a set of dazzling vintages to hand, the Germans have no excuse for not offering us brilliant, classic, Kabinett and Spätlese wines. Some, as Oddbins German list shows, are doing just that. Others, including the 'big names' listed by Victoria Wine, are still producing wines that are dilute and overloaded with sulphur dioxide.

As Spain gears itself up for 1992, when Seville and Barcelona will attract millions of new visitors, the word 'mañana' remains the watchword among winemakers, all of whom are set to make earth-shattering wines...tomorrow. Every year, we look for new Spanish wines to include in the *Guide*; every year, we fall back on the ones we included last year. It is revealing that many of the most innovative developments in Spain are being made by foreigners - by the Plaimont co-operative which is making wine in the Penedés and shipping La Mancha grapes back to be vinified in France, by Nick Butler, the Sunday Times Wine Club's Australian 'Flying Winemaker' in Navarra, and by Bordeaux Blanc superstar Jacques Lurton, who is making Spanish wine under contract for a major UK buyer. It must be irksome for Spain to be treated as if it were a Third World, underdeveloped wine country entirely reliant on foreign expertise, but that's the way it appears. Fortunately, Oddbins (who else) report finding some pioneering individual estates where young Spaniards are showing what they can do.

The New World fought back this year with a vengeance. Sales of Australian wines soared by 80% at the beginning of the year, an increase rivalled only (though from a far lower base) by the New Zealanders. When we analysed over 500 merchants' lists to prepare this *Guide* we were struck by the way in which varied ranges of Antipodean wines had suddenly appeared in almost all their pages.

California, as predicted last year, tried to compete using its far heavier vinous firepower (E&J Gallo alone sell more than all of Australia combined), but it used the wrong amunition and aimed it at the wrong targets. So far, enormous efforts have been made to sell Meursault and Margaux style (and priced) wines to smart restaurants. Wine drinkers who simply want to pay £4-7 for a decent bottle of Californian wine to drink at home have had a thin time. One merchant actually stated in its list that while it was delighted with its Californian reds, it had not been able to find any Chardonnay that represented value for money. In simple terms, the Antipodeans offer wine at every price level; the Californians offer a few top class wines at special-occasion prices, plenty of cheap wines from Christian Bros, Gallo, Almaden and Wente Bros (almost none of which is as good as an Aussie equivalent) - and precious little in between.

Then there was South Africa. The British wine trade has, on the whole, not liked the ostracisation of South African wines in recent years, so the call by Nelson Mandela for an end to sanctions has been particularly eagerly awaited by merchants itching to sell Cape reds and whites alongside their Antipodeans. A small number of first class wines will thus hit UK shelves for the first time, but so too will a mass of dull, dilute German-style whites and old fashioned meaty reds.

South America continued to attract attention, but here too, it became evident that there were far too few companies making really good wine to make either Chile or Argentina a 'New Australia'. It will take considerable outside investment to improve standards.

Eastern Europe remains as confused as ever. Bulgaria seems to have lost the winemaking recipe book, and far too many current releases are tasting like dull versions of the wines we all fell in love with five years ago. But there is hope elsewhere. Hugh Ryman, the Englishman who made our White Wine of the Year was heading off to produce wine in Hungary, and Angela Muir of the Fulham Road Wine Centre side-stepped the dull Czech wines offered by the Sunday Times Wine Club to oversee the making and blending of a really good range of inexpensive whites, the first of which will be sold through Victoria Wine.

What else happens next? In the short term, wine buyers and wine drinkers will have to overcome the effects of that Spring frost in Europe. A few years ago, the prospect of a shortage of French white wine would have sent professional buyers into panic; today they know that there's plenty to be found on the other side of the world. And once wine drinkers have switched from Muscadet to a blended white from New Zealand, Washington State, South Africa or Chile, who's to say that they'll ever be as faithful to the 'classic' regions again?

And then, of course, in theory, there is the prospect of a tariff-free Europe, but in a year when the British Chancellor has defied the EC by raising the duty on wine, that day seems laughably far off. What we can be sure of, however, is the availability of a larger than ever amount of well-made wine. New plantings in the New World and the modernisation of the Old World both ensure that, very soon, a truly bad, vinegary wine will be a museum-item. Mind you, if too much of that modern winemaking is as bland as it has become in some countries, I'd predict that there will be queues of people crying out for some of that bad wine simply for want of a glassful of flavour.

WINE AND HEALTH

1991 marked yet more successes for the health fascists. Not content with lumping together wine, whisky, marijuana and heroin as similarly dangerous drugs, they announced to the world that its well-being was now at risk from crystal glasses and decanters.

Wine left 'for several months' in a decanter could apparently cause lead poisoning. Needless to say, this piece of 'news' was brought to us by scientists in North America, a continent where millions of car engines daily gush lead by the ton - and where, in some cities at least, the chances of being killed by a lead bullet while minding one's own business seem of rather more immediate concern.

All this silliness would be far less worrying if it formed part of a debate. Unfortunately, very few people anywhere in the world are prepared to plead the cause of moderate drinking. Even in France, draconian restrictions on wine advertising have now been announced.

In truth, wine represents less of a carcinogenic risk than a great many of the other substances — food, drink and air — that we consume every day. By the same token, studies in southern France (as opposed to the beer-drinking north) provide evidence that moderate wine drinking may significantly reduce the risk of coronary heart disease.

The organic movement is gathering momentum. The EC is finally to define precisely what an organic wine is and is not, and, thanks largely to the support they are now receiving from major supermarkets and from such merchants as Adnams, this year's joint Wine Merchant of the Year, organic wines are beginning to be taken seriously. We were especially pleased to see Safeway combining forces with WINE Magazine to run the first Organic Wine Challenge at Ryton Gardens. With initiatives like this, and the buying policy of companies like the Organic Wine Co, Adnams and Haughton Fine Wines, hopefully no one will need to say of a wine that 'It may not taste that good, but at least it's organic'. Would-be drinkers of organic wines should seek out the recommended 'green' wines in the *Guide*, consult our specialist chart on page 254 or contact Cornucopia Health Foods. (081 579 9431).

LEARNING ABOUT WINE

The three best wine courses in London are run by Michael Schuster, the Fulham Road Wine Centre and Leith's School of Food and Wine. The premise behind all these classes is that wine should be unpretentious, unprejudiced and, above all, fun.

James Rogers, the man behind the Fulham Road Wine Centre courses, presents his students with the wines 'blind' and encourages them to decide which they prefer (and why) before they are told the identity of what they are tasting. People who thought that they hated German Riesling discover they like it; others find that they can save a small fortune buying New Zealand Sauvignon Blanc instead of Sancerre. Similarly, those who had mocked wine writers' more fanciful descriptions discover how useful adjectives such as 'petrolly', 'oily', 'spicy' and 'peppery' can be.

These evening courses cost £12–£18 per session and succeed thanks to the enthusiasm of Rogers and his students, the quality of the wines and the small numbers present (there are rarely more than 20 at any evening). For those who want more 'classical' training, both Christie's and Sotheby's run tastings too. These are often hosted by the winemakers themselves.

Anyone wanting to join the wine trade, however, should make for the Wine & Spirit Education Trust, where they could take the simple (very simple would be a fairer description) 'Certificate', the useful 'Higher Certificate' and the testing 'Diploma'. Only once you have leaped all three hurdles may you consider trying for the real high jump, the Master of Wine written and tasting exams. But be warned; fewer than 200 people have earned this qualification in three decades.

For recommendable wine courses, contact: Michael Schuster (071 254 9734); Fulham Road Wine Centre (071 736 7009); Christie's Auction House (071 839 9060); Sotheby's (071 924 3287); Wine & Spirit Education Trust (071 236 3551); Leith's School of Food and Wine (071 229 0177).

Tastings

For many people, a course is quite unnecessary; much can be learned on a more ad hoc basis by attending tutored tastings given by wine merchants - see chart on p.242. Whether you attend a structured class or simply a tutored tasting, what you get out of it will depend on the person who is talking you through the wines. The following people are especially worth travelling to hear: David Molyneux-Berry MW, Liz Berry MW, Jane Hunt MW, Charles Metcalfe, Michael Schuster, John Vaughan Hughes MW, Maggie McNie

MW, Angela Muir MW, Richard Harvey MW, Oz Clarke, Michael Broadbent MW, David Gleave MW, Steven Spurrier, Pamela Vandyke Price, Serena Sutcliffe MW, Richard Hobson MW and Richard Mayson.

THE CASE FOR JOINING A WINE CLUB

Early in 1991, the Sunday Times Wine Club provided one of the best of all possible justifications for being a member of a wine club. Several hundred people congregated in the faded Victorian setting of the Horticultural Hall in London and had a whale of a time tasting wines from a wide range of suppliers at the club's annual festival.

Unfortunately, the evening also demonstrated two of the best reasons for not relying on a wine club for all your wine buying. The quality of the wines was very variable - far too many wines would never have found their way onto the lists of some of Britain's better specialist merchants - and prices were uniformly and in some cases, shamefully, high. Join a club by all means - but take a close look at the small print; a good wine club should give you exclusive advantages of membership; some achieve this, but only The Wine Society, which genuinely belongs to its members, truly fits the bill.

However, you may prefer a club whose raison d'être is not geared towards purchasing — a local wine appreciation society, for example, many of whom organise not only informal meetings but tastings presented by merchants and producers and social events such as theme dinners. In addition to those listed below, clubs with vacancies for new members are regularly featured in the diary pages of WINE and Decanter.

Wine merchant clubs

The Vintner (0923 51585); Vin de Garde / Vintage Expectations (0372 63251); Châteaux Wines (0454 613959); The Cellar Club of Great Britain (0734 505838). See our chart on p. 242 .

Non-merchant wine clubs

Cofradia Riojana/Gallo Nero Wine Club (081 863 2135/081 427 9944); The International Food and Wine Society (071 370 0909); North East Wine Tasting Society (091 438 4107); Northern Wine Appreciation Group (0484 531228); The Wine and Dine Society (071 274 9484); The Winetasters (081 997 1252); Evington Wine Society (Edwin Wood, 0533 416595).

BUYING AT AUCTION

Don't imagine that 'fine' clarets and ports are the only kinds of wine in which auction houses deal. Every time a restaurant or wine merchant goes bankrupt (an all-too-frequent occurrence in 1991), there is a strong likelihood that some of the contents of the cellar will end up under the hammer.

But if auctions can still be a source of bargain parcels of everyday wine, it is still worth keeping a careful check on what you may be paying per bottle. Read WINE Magazine, Wine & Spirit and Decanter's auction-price guides, consult Clive Coates' The Vine and Robert Parker's Wine Advocate newsletters for tasting notes, and bear in mind the auctioneers' own estimates. Auction fever is an infectious condition, and it is all too easy to forget that a 'bargain' £50 case of Chablis can be a little less of a snip by the time you have added on the 10% buyer's premium, 90p or so a bottle duty and 17.5% VAT, and driven to Edinburgh where it was 'lying' to pick it up.

Among fine wines today, the 1978 and 1979 clarets are still underpriced and, when compared with the prices of the 1988s, 1989s and 1990s *en primeur*, the 1986s and 1985s look positively cheap. The 1984s and 1983s are already looking surprisingly mature, but the best 1982s are holding up wonderfully and deserve to be left alone for a long while yet. The 1975s are finally 'coming round' but the 1970s are, if anything, getting tougher with age. Of older vintages, you could still pick up some affordable 1966 or 1964 Pomerols and St Emilions (rather than Médocs.)

Auction Houses

Christie's Auction House (The Wine Department, 071 839 9060); Sotheby's (071 924 3287); Colliers Bigwood & Bewlay (0789 269 415); Lacy Scott (0284 763531); Lithgow Sons and Partners (0642 710158); Phillips (0865 723524); Jean Pierre et Fils (0273 308 422).

BUYING *EN PRIMEUR* / INVESTING IN WINE

There are two ways to buy 'fine' wine: in the bottle or as a 'future' - *en primeur* - in the barrel. a few months after the harvest. There are three basic reasons for adopting this latter method. It should save you money (though possibly not in the short-term) guarantee availability of wines which might subsequently prove hard to find (older Pomerols for example) and ensure that the wine in your cellar has not been mistreated by anybody else.

If you accept the fact that your in-barrel purchase could look pricy a year or so on when merchants are offering the same vintage in bottle for less than you paid, the only problem of which you should be aware is the risk that the merchant to whom you paid for your *en primeur* wine goes bust before the bottles reach you. There are two safeguards we can suggest. First, be as sure as possible of the financial solidity of the company with whom you are dealing, remaining aware that even apparently solid UK firms can be badly affected by the collapse of a foreign supplier or a major customer. And second, ensure that any wine stored on your behalf is clearly marked with your name thus assisting you to establish ownership if the bailifs move in.

Should you treat wine as an investment? For some merchants the answer is a resounding 'no', simply because they prefer to see wine as stuff to be drunk rather than a commodity to be traded. Others take a different view, giving advice on ideal 'portfolios' and warning of the best times to buy and sell. My own view is more agnostic. The very cost of fine wine and its presence in the auction circuit makes it impossible to divorce it completely from the grubby world of finance. You have to decide today how you are going to fill the cellar you will own in 2001. Will you buy its contents at today's prices with today's money, or at 2001 prices with the cash you have then?

If you believe in following form, the experience of the last 30 years would prompt you to buy now; the value of good Bordeaux and port have risen far faster than that of money in a building society. However, markets change, reputations of vintages rise and fall, and there are times when you may not be able to sell your wine at all. In other words, unless you are a peculiarly thirsty widow or orphan, your cellar should never be more than a sideline.

If you do want to buy the kinds of wine whose value is most certain to rise, stick to blue-chip growths and vintage port from the best producers and from the 'best' vintages. I know that, by saying this, I am perpetuating the way in which a small number of wines get all the attention at auction and *en primeur* but, after years of writing, for example, that prices of fine sweet German wines are 'bound to shoot up to their proper level', I have cynically come to believe that the system is unbeatable.

The following companies should all offer good advice on wine investment: Hungerford Wine Co (see p.169), who this year guaranteed to offer the lowest *en primeur* prices in Britain, Justerini & Brooks (see p.175) who put together 'portfolios', The Wine Society (see p.232), Lay & Wheeler (see p.177) and Berry Bros & Rudd (see p.128). Pat Simon (081 455 8255)

Specialists in fine, rare and old wines

If you would like to buy your wine ready-matured, contact the companies listed on our Merchants Specialities Chart, plus: The Champagne and Caviar Shop (071 626 4912); The Old Maltings Wine Co Ltd (0787 79638); Wine on the Green (071 794 1143); Domaine Direct (071 837 1142).

WINE TOURS

Wine tours are rather like any other holiday organised for a group of like-minded people. They can be gloriously successful — or extraordinarily tedious. But earnest wine buffs are probably no more boring than earnest opera fans or train spotters. In our experience, the enjoyment of such tours depends only partly on one's fellow travellers; a much greater influence is the way in which the tour has been organised. The best wine tours I have come across are the ones put together by World Wine Tours (0865 891919), Arblaster & Clarke (0730 66883) and The Sunday Times Wine Club (see p.202).

Other tour companies

Tanglewood Wine Tours (09323 48720); Classic Wine Tours (0626 65373); Moswin Tours Ltd (0533 719922); Vacances Cuisine (010 33 94044977); Wine Trails (081 463 0012); Knights of Languedoc (071 704 0589); Vintage Wine Tours (0225 315834); Francophiles (0272 621975); Bordeaux Wine Holidays (0782 612015); Ian Dickson Travel (031 556 6777); Grants of St James's (0483 64861); Graham Faithfull Activity Holidays (0780 66280); Vinescapes (0903 744279); Citalia (081 686-5533); Spencer Scott Travel Ltd (071 494-0547).

STARTING A CELLAR

In Britain, cellars of any kind are a rare luxury and most people who want to allow even a dozen or so bottles to grow old in peace have to use their ingenuity to find a suitable corner for them. For those readers who find themselves in that situation, the following do's and don't's may be useful. Avoid areas in which the temperature varies; constant warmth is better than the variations usual in a kitchen, for example. Avoid areas which are too dry; well-insulated cupboards and attics can be ideal cellars, but be sure to keep the humidity up with a sponge left in a bowl of water. Try to find a space where there is at least some air movement; cut air holes in cupboards if necessary. If the area you have chosen is damp, remember not to leave wine in cardboard boxes. It sounds obvious, but even experienced wine buffs have lost wine by letting it fall from soggy boxes.

Purpose-built cellars and racks exist. Spiral Cellars Ltd (0372 842692) will sell you a kit (and install it, if you like) which can be sunk into the ground beneath the floor of your kitchen or garage — or in the garden. Wine racks that can be custom-built to fit awkwardly shaped areas are available from Majestic Wine Warehouses and most other helpful wine merchants. To buy direct, contact: CS Racks (0725 21858), RTA Wine Racks (032 878292), A & W Moore (0602 607012).

A cellar book provides an invaluable means of keeping track of your wines, and elegant ones have been produced by Hugh Johnson (published by Mitchell Beazley) and by Grants of St James's. These make fine Christmas or birthday presents, but for your own use a simple exercise book can perform the same function. Simply rule it up to allow space for you to indicate where and when you bought each wine; the price you paid for it; its position in your racks; each time you remove a bottle; tasting notes; and the guests to whom you served it.

For the high-tech wine lover who would rather keep his information on disk, there is now a handy, purpose-built database that can be used on IBM compatible PCs. Available from Ant Software (0524 66128), it costs around £30. Finally, if you would prefer not to store your wine in your own home, there is always the option of leaving it in the cellars of the merchants from whom you bought it (see our Merchants' services chart on page 242) or renting space at Smith & Taylor (071 627 5070) or at Abacus (081 991 9717).

GLASSES

There is so much nonsense talked about the 'right' glasses for the 'right' wine that I am tempted not to discuss the subject at all. My advice is to use any kind of clear glass whose rim has a smaller circumference than its bowl, and which is large enough to hold more than a few mouthfuls.

We would recommend the Bouquet range from Royal Leerdam; these were the ones very happily used by tasters at the 1991 WINE Magazine International Wine Challenge.

VINOUS GIFTS

An increasing range of often very silly and occasionally quite kitsch gifts is now available. For sensible selections, try Harrods or The Fulham Road Wine Centre, who also offer a range of always-acceptable antiquarian wine books. These and old maps can also be bought from Wine Arts (0264 58036). Richard Kihl (071 586 3838) is always a good source of vinous antiques and curiosities and Hugh Johnson has joined the fray with his shop opposite Berry Bros & Rudd in St James's.

CORKSCREWS

The best corkscrew of all is made by Screwpull (081847 2493) and is produced in a variety of different versions - from simple to sophisticated. These are available from most good wine shops and department stores.

WINE PRESERVATION DEVICES

The Vacuvin is widely available and has been proven to work well, as does the more sophisticated (and more expensive) Wine-keeper from Anthony Byrne Fine Wines (see p. 136) and The Broad Street Wine Co (see p. 134). 'Winesaver' from Drylaw House, Edinburgh (031 558 3666) breaks new ground in preservation technology with a heavier-than-air inert gas which sits on the wine surface and prevents oxidation. It was used to great effect in the 1991 International Wine Challenge allowing WINE Magazine readers to taste wines long after they had been judged.

By the time the 1993 Guide is published, the 'Open Market' should have made it as simple for Britons to buy wine in Boulogne as in Bognor. And the sky will be filled with elegantly airborne pigs. For the moment at least, duty-free imports are limited to just over 10 bottles of wine per adult traveller, provided those bottles were not bought in a duty-free shop, and that no fortified wines or spirits are being imported at the same time. Beyond those 10 bottles, the Chancellor gets his slice of duty — and of VAT at 17.5%, chargeable on the value of the wine and on the duty itself (in other words, he taxes his own tax). Buying at the major hypermarkets on the French coast is undoubtedly convenient; it is also a good way to end up with some pretty unimpressive wine.

The time to buy from any French supermarket is just before Christmas, when they sell some very classy wine at knock-down prices as loss-leaders to attract local custom. Otherwise, do what the French do: buy direct from the grower.

PARTY PLANNING - 30 WINES FOR LESS THAN £3

For descriptions of these wines and details of stockists, please refer to them by number in 'The Wines' section of the book.

£ 1.19	498	ST MICHAEL LIEBLING PEACH, KLOSTERHOF
£ 2.39	194	TESCO HOCK, RIETBURG
£ 2.50	499	MOSCATO FIZZ, VITICOLTORI DELL'ACQUESE
£ 2.55	477	SAFEWAY BLASQUEZ FINO CARTA BLANC
£ 2.59	400	SAINSBURY ROSSO DI VERONA FOR JS
£ 2.59	237	TESCO FRENCH MERLOT, SICA DES COTEAUX LIMOUSINS
£ 2.59	337	SAFEWAY COTES DE LUBERON, CELLIER DE MARRENON 1990
£ 2.65	453	MUSCAT DE ST JOHN DE MINERVOIS
£ 2.65	500	PETILLANT DE LISTEL
£ 2.69	209	VAL DU MONT CABERNET SAUVIGNON, VIN DE PAYS D'OC, SKALLI 1988
£ 2.75	210	ASDA ST CHINIAN, VIGNERONS DE LA MEDITERRANEE
£ 2.75	27	LA CAUME DE PEYRE, VIN DE PAYS DES COTES DE GASCOGNE
£ 2.75	238	SAINSBURY BERGERAC ROUGE
£ 2.75	26	SAINSBURY VIN DE PAYS DE GERS
£ 2.79	211	ST MICHAEL FRENCH COUNTRY RED, VIGNERONS CATALANS
£ 2.79	435	DON DARIAS RED, BODEGAS VITORIANAS,
£ 2.79	127	DONATIEN BLANC DE BLANC, DONATIEN BAHUAUD
£ 2.80	28	SAINSBURY CORBIERES BLANC
£ 2.85	454	SAINSBURY MOSCATEL DA VALENCIA
£ 2.85	239	DOMAINE DES CABANNES, COTES DU FRONTONNAIS 1989
£ 2.87	240	COOP CLARET, ESCHENAUER
£ 2.89	155	GATEWAY ANJOU BLANC, REMY PANNIER
£ 2.89	29	CUVEE JEAN-PAUL BLANC SEC VIN DE TABLE,PAUL BOUTINOT
£ 2.94	241	CABERNET SAUVIGNON, VIN DE PAYS D'OC, LUCIEN COSTE 1990
£ 2.95	242	DOMAINE BEAULIEU SAINT SAUVEUR, MARMANDAIS, UNIVITIS 1988
£ 2.99	30	ST MICHAEL DOMAINE DE PRADELLES, CO-OP BASTIDE DE COOP 1990
£ 2.99	244	CAMPO DEI FIORI CABERNET SAUVIGNON 1988
£ 2.99	245	VIN DE PAYS DE LA DORDOGNE CEPAGE CABERNET,CAVE SIGOULET 1990
£ 2.99	243	COOP BERGERAC ROUGE, CAVE DE SIGOULES
£ 2.99	212	SAINSBURY'S ST CHINIAN, CHATEAU SALVANHIAC, JEAN JEAN 1990

THE COUNTRIES

Australia

The big news in 1991 was the explosion of interest in Australian wine among huge numbers of people who had never tasted it before. In simple terms, Australia escaped from Oddbins and arrived in everyone's corner shop. Sales almost doubled and showed no signs of wanting to slow down. Australia's secret weapon, shared only with the French, is that it can offer good wine in various styles at almost any price.

The 1991 vintage was generally spectacularly good, though smaller than expected. The quality of the wines from throughout the country outclasses 1990 and probably 1988, and is certainly far better than the frankly poor, rain-hit 1989's.

For specialist stockists, see the chart on p 254, plus: The Wine Spot (061 748 2568); Bow Wine Vaults (071-248 1121); Peter Watts Wines (03765 61130); Croque en Bouche (06845 65612); Fortis Ltd (0742 642227); Domaine Direct (071 837 3521/1142).

Austria

Austria is making its comeback at last, with rich, clean and dry 1989's and 1988's; if they compete with examples from any other country, it is probably France. But the people who ought to worry are the Germans, because Austria's climate gives it every advantage over its would-be dry-winemaking neighbour - and it enables them to make great sweet wines too. Look out for examples from Hopler and Opitz (from T&W wines, see p. 214).

1990 was a mixed year in Austria because fungus affected several areas. However, some great Auslesen and Spätlesen were made.

For specialist stockists, see the chart on p. 254 plus: Alston Wines (091 384 3379); Premier Wines (0294 602409); Caxton Tower (081 758 4500).

Eastern Europe

The eagerness with which Western winemakers and investors are rushing eastwards makes it seem as though the Holy Grail had been located there. In fact, with few exceptions, the wine industry throughout the old Eastern Bloc is very like every other industry: inefficient and free of basic quality control. Bulgaria, the one country which appeared to be getting it right is now producing some very dull wine. Political problems in Yugoslavia and Rumania make the future of those industries unpredictable; in fact, the greatest hope for the immediate future lies in Hungary and Czechoslovakia, from which some very individual wines are beginning to make their way into Victoria Wine.

For specialist stockists see the chart on p. 254 plus: Bulgaria: Wines of Westhorpe (0283 820285); Czechoslovakia: Cellarworld (071 384 2588); Sunday Times Wine Club (see page 213); Yugoslavia: Teltscher Brothers (071 987 5020); Vitkovitch Bros (071 261 1770).

Eastern Mediterranean

Greece

We keep waiting for the Greek wine revolution to begin; all we hear is a distant rumbling. But there are signs that EC membership will influence at least a few younger producers to make greater use of their interest in indigenenous grapes. Try the Gentile wines from Bibendum (see p.128).

Specialist stockists: The Greek Wine Centre (0743 64636); Chris Milia (071 485 5032).

Israel

Progress is being made at last: even the Carmel winery is producing acceptable wine, but for real quality there remains only one winery - Yarden in the Golan Heights. The Muscat and Cabernet Sauvignon are the wines most worth looking out for.

Specialist stockists: Selfridges (p.209); Tesco (p.216); Peter Hallgarten (071 722 1077).

England

From 1991 English wines become eligible for 'appellation controlée' type status. Maybe this will make up for the tricky weather English winemakers have suffered this year - and finally give this slow-to-move industry the boost it needs. In the meantime, seek out some of the examples of English winemaking during the last few warm summers.

See the chart on p. 254, plus: The English Wine Centre (0323 870532); Fine English Wine Co. (0904 706386).

France

Alsace

Last year's Wine of the Year, the 1989 Pinot Blanc from Turckheim, was such a success that wine merchants throughout Britain are at last beginning to take Alsace seriously, recognising that this region arguably offers more flavour for money than any other white wine area in Europe. 1990 was a good, rather than great vintage, producing wines for relatively early drinking. For earlier vintages, the '81s, '82s, '83s and '85s are allgood bets.

See the chart on p. 254, plus: Fortnum & Mason (071 734 8040); Farthinghoe (0295 710018); Curzon Wine Co (071 499 3327); O W Loeb (071 928 7750).

Bordeaux

If the wine gurus on the other side of the Atlantic are to be believed, there have been at least two recent Vintages of the Century: 1982 and 1989. I'd beg to differ about the supremacy of either of these: 1986 and 1988 can both make a claim to be the best of the 1980's, and 1990 certainly produced some wines that were better (and cheaper) than the same properties' 1989's. This is not to say, however, that I'd necessarily advise succumbing to the blandishments of the *en primeur* merchants. Despite the prospects of a short harvest in 1991 which may raise prices of the 1990's, I still believe that some of the best buys are still to be found among the older vintages. most notably the 1978's 1979's, 1985's, and 1986's.

Similarly, it is worth bearing in mind that, as we go to press, the wine world is buzzing with rumours of imminent bancruptcy among wine merchants in the USA and Great Britain. If any of these rumours were based on fact, and if any of the yuppies who filled their cellars with claret in the 1980s feel the need to realise some cas, there would be all sorts of bargains to be had - especially of years like 1982, 1985 and 1986.

Whoever you buy from, if you *do* buy *en primeur*, beware of financially ricketty merchants. And for immediate drinking, if the price is right, grab some of the over-criticised '87s.

For specialist stockists, see the chart on p. 254, plus: Ilkley Wine Co (0943 607313); Curzon Wine Co (071 499 3327); Henry Townsend (04946 78291); Market Vintners (071 248 8382); Stephen Porter Wines (0452 618772); Andrew Gordon Wines (0306 885711); Pavilion Wine Co (071 628 8224); Classic Wines (081 500 7614); Fine Vintage Wines (0865 724866); Friarwood (071 736 2628); Kurtz & Chan (071 930 6981); Andrew Mead Wines (05476 268); Ballantynes of Cowbridge (04463 3044); David J Watt (021 643 5160); David Baker (0656 50732); Buckingham Vintners (0753 21336); Wine on the Green (071 794 1143).

Burgundy

After years in the wilderness, red Burgundy is making a comeback, partly thanks to New World successes with the Pinot Noir, to improved standards among the Burgundians themselves, and possibly thanks to sheer boredom with endless Cabernet Sauvignons. Prices of great Burgundy remain painfully high but Bourgogne Rouge and wine from lesser-known vintages is arguably a better buy than for a long time. 1988, 1989 and 1990 all produced attractive wines, though 1988 remains the greatest of the three. White Burgundies are still suffering from their international desireability. Far too often, quality and price are completely out of kilter. But here too, modern winemaking methods are helping to improve standards, though only in estates where the temptation to overcrop is resisted. Grab the 1989's when they become available; the 1990's are softer and a litle less impressive.

For specialist stockists, see the chart on p. 254, plus: Curzon Wine Co (071 499 3327); Henry Townsend (04946 78291); Market Vintners (071 248 8382); O W Loeb (071 928 7750); Classic Wines (081 500 7614); Domaine Direct (071 837 3521); Ferrers le Mesurier (08012 2660); Friarwood (071 736 2628); Ingleton Wines (0621 52421); Kurtz & Chan (071 930 6981); Andrew Mead Wines (05476 268); Ballantynes of Cowbridge (04463 3044); Domaine Direct (071-837 3521/1142); Evertons of Ombersley (0905 620282).

Champagne

What goes up, must come down. Perhaps it has been their experience of watching bubbles break this rule that has fooled the Champenois into imagining that they could fire the price of their wine into the stratosphere and expect it to remain in orbit without encountering some pretty severe re-entry problems. But sales to the UK have almost halved and prices are on their way down very encouragingly. Another triumph for people power.

For specialist stockists, see the chart on p.254, plus: Bart's Cellars (081 871 2044); Curzon Wine Co (071 499 3327); The Champagne House (071 221 5538); Champagne & Caviar Shop (071 626 4912).

The Loire

After the glorious 1989 vintage, the winegrowers of the Loire were surprised to find its quality rivalled and indeed beaten by a crop of 1990 grapes which were even more packed with flavour. The reds were generally excellent in both vintages and worth drinking young, or leaving for 5-10 years. 1986 and 1987 whites from the Chenin Blanc are worth waiting for; 1983's and 1984's are perfect to drink now.

For specialist stockists, see the chart on p. 254 , plus: Ian Howe (0636 704366); Ilkley Wine Co (0943 607313); Prestige Vintners (081 989 5084); Christopher Milner Wines (071 266 2245); F & E May (071 405 6249); Locke's (0962 60006); Mentzendorff & Co (071 222 2522); Ferrers le Mesurier (08012 2660); G E Bromley (0533 768471); Croque en Bouche (06845 65612); La Cave de Bacchus (0903 892933).

The Rhône

Rhône reds are beginning to become more fashionable, thanks in part to the enthusiastic support for them by Robert Parker in the USA. 1990 was a good year for the Northern Rhône, though less impressive in the South where the previous vintage was more concentrated in flavour. Well made 1990 Hermitages and Côte Rôties should keep well. In the meantime the 1987's and 1986's are becoming ready to drink.

For specialist stockists, see the chart on p.254, plus: Ian Howe (0636 704366); Market Vintners (071 248 8382); O W Loeb (071 928 7750); Croque en Bouche (06845 65612); Wine on the Green (071 794 1143).

Germany

It is not unknown for Germany to enjoy two consecutive good vintages; three in a row, however, is momentous. In 1990, good producers will have produced 1971-like Kabinetts and Spätlesen which should keep brilliantly. Like the '88s and '89s, the better wines of this vintage deserve to be kept. In the meantime, the 1983's and 1985's are beginning to look quite mature.

For specialist stockists, see the chart on p. 254, plus: The Wine Spot (061 748 2568); Henry Townsend (04946 78291); O W Loeb (071 928 7750); Robert Mendelssohn (081 455 9895); Douglas Henn-Macrae (0622 70952); G E Bromley (0533 768471); Dennhöfer Wines (091 232 7342).

After the disastrous 1989 vintage, Italy needed a good vintage and that is exactly what it got. Early tastings suggest that the best wines will rival the finest vintages of the 1980's. 1986 and 1987 Barolo and Barbaresco are softening well now, though the 1985's need further ageing.

For specialist stockists, see the chart on p.254, plus: The Wine Spot (061 748 2568); The Wine Shop (0847 8787); Cantino Augusto (071 242 3246); Italian Wine Agencies (081 459 1515); Continental Wine House (071 262 2126); Caledonian Wines (0228 43172); Gardavini (081-549 2779); Wineforce (071 586 5618); Organics (071 381 9924); Alfie Fiandaca (081 952 8446).

New Zealand

After bursting their way onto the international scene, with their Sauvignons, New Zealand's winemakers are now proving they can make world class Chardonnay and sparkling wines. The quality of the red wines remains questionable, however, and depends heavily on the grape-growing and wine-making skills of the producers.

Although the quality was far from even, New Zealand's wine growers were generally pleased with a 1991 vintage which was far better than the 1990 when poor weather at harvest time reduced yield.

See the chart on p.254, plus: Kiwi Fruits (071 240 1423); Fine Wines of New Zealand (071 482 0093)

Portugal

In Portugal the hot, dry conditions had less of an effect than in Spain. Even so, few people are claiming that great reds and whites were made, nor is 1990 set to be a port vintage.

The table wine vintages to look for now are 1982, 1983, 1985 and 1987. As for current-drinking port, we'd recommend 1975, 1980 and the 1982's which are coming round very quickly. For the future, the 1985's are still appreciating in value fast, as are the 1977's.

For specialist stockists see the chart on p.254, plus: D & F Wine Shippers (081 969 2277); Premier Wines (0294 602409); A O L Grilli (0580 891472); Wapping Wine Co (071-265 0448); Classic Wines (081 500 7614); Fine Vintage Wines (0865 724866); Wineforce (071 586 5618); R. S. Pass Wines (0843 584161).

Spain

The rain in Spain fell neither on the plain nor anywhere else, and the wines which were produced in Rioja and Navarra suffered the lack of acidity. In the Penedes, conditions were better, and some good quality reds and whites have almost certainly been made.

The red vintages to pick for drinking today are the light-bodied 1984's and the excellent 1985's.

For specialist stockists, see the chart on p.254, plus: The Wine Spot (061 748 2568); Premier Wines (071 736 9073); Douglas Henn-Macrae (0622 70952); Mi Casa Wines (0298 3952); Paul Sanderson (031 312 6190); Wine on the Green (071 794 1143); Bodegas Direct (0243 773474).

South Africa

1991 was the year when South Africa's winemakers readied themselves to return to the international market, showing huge ranges in both London and Bordeaux. The general consensus was that there are some tremendous Chardonnays and modern Cabernets which compare with the best of Australia and California, but far too much dilute white wine, and dull red for which there is no need at all. An end to political isolation will, hopefully, bring new, more quality-conscious attitudes towards winemaking. Producers who were ready to apply these attitudes to the potentially first class 1991 harvest should have made some very exciting wine.

For specialist stockists see the chart on p.254, plus: Chester Fine Wine (0244 310455); Edward Cavendish & Sons (0703 870171); Henry C Collison (071 839 6047); Southern Hemisphere Wines Ltd (071 731 4661).

South America - Argentina and Chile

Vintage variations are of litle relevance in countries where the climate hardly changes, and the variation from one year to the next depends principally on the opening and closing of the irrigation taps. The quality of the 1991 wines remains to be seen. But if either Chile or Argentina is to exploit its potential, far more producers will have to follow the example of wineries such as Montes, Villard and Trapiche in making fresh, concentrated red and white wines rather than over-cropped, lightweight stuff which will only ever sell on price..

For specialist stockists see the chart on p.254, plus: Eldorobo Wines (081 740 4123).

USA

It's always pleasant to feel wanted, and this year, for the first time, British wine drinkers became the object of lots of Californian attention; sales in the US were looking weak and the producers had wines to sell. But they are going to have to rethink their approach to the UK - and their prices - if they want to make real friends here. There seem to be a lot of £5-6 wines which would be worth buying for £3-4.50. A tasting of the Australian Penfolds range could teach them a lot in the Napa Valley.

Rainy weather followed the drought in 1990, spoiling the quality of some of the Zinfandel. Other varieties fared better, but acid levels were generally low and most reds will be for early drinking. The vintages to look out for at the moment are 1988, 1986 and 1984.

For specialist stockists, see the chart on p.254.

A-Z

HOW TO READ THE ENTRIES

Hermitage (Rhône) Top class northern RHONE[1] long lived wines; superb, complex, long lived reds and sumptuous, nutty whites. Also Australian name for the SYRAH grape. **76 78 79 82** 83 85[2] £££££-£££££[3] Chave 179[4] (OD YAP ADN)[5]

1 Words that appear in SMALL CAPITALS have their own entry elsewhere in the A-Z.
2 Only those vintages that are good have been listed. The years that appear in bold are ready to drink.
3 Price guide: £ = under £3.50, ££ = £3.50-5.50, £££ = £5.50-9, ££££ = £9-15, £££££ = £15 and over
4 This is a recommended example of the wine. Where possible we recommend one of the Guide's 500 wines, in which case it will appear as a number, in this example 179
5 Stockists, see page 16 for an explanation of merchants' codes. If the merchant is not featured in the Guide, its telephone number will appear.

Abboccato (Italy) Semi-dry

Abocado (Spain) Semi-dry

Abfüller/Abfüllung (Germany) Bottler/bottled by

Abruzzi (Italy) Wine region on the eastern coast. Often indifferent TREBBIANO whites. Finer MONTEPULCIANO reds **82 83** 85 88 89 £-££ Montepulciano d'Abruzzo, Tollo 1987 (AB V&C ROD)

AC (France) See APPELLATION CONTROLEE

Acetic acid The main constituent of vinegar, this volatile acid (CH_3COOH) features in tiny proportions in all wines. In excess (as a result of careless winemaking) it can turn wine to vinegar.

Acidity Essential natural, balancing component (usually TARTARIC) which gives freshness. In hotter countries (and sometimes in cooler ones) it may be added by the winemaker

Aconcagua Valley (CHILE) Central valley region noted for its CABERNET SAUVIGNON

Adega (Portugal) Winery — equivalent to Spanish BODEGA

Adelaide Hills (Australia) Cool, high-altitude vineyard region, producing top-class RIESLING, but now also growing more fashionable varieties such as Chardonnay andPinot Noir **84 85 86** 87 88 £££-£££££ 105 165 371

Aglianico del Vulture (BASILICATA) Full-bodied, best-known and best DOC red from this region, made from a grape used by the ancient Greeks **79 81 82** 85 88 £££ Fratelli d'Angelo

Agricola vitivinicola (Italy) Wine estate

Aguja (LEON) So-called 'needle' wines which owe their slight SPRITZ to the addition of ripe grapes to the fermented wine

Ahr (Germany) Northernmost ANBAUGEBIET, producing light red wines little seen in the UK Walporzheimer Klosterberg 1988 (WSC)

Aix-en-Provence (Coteaux d') (S France) Pleasant floral whites and dry rosés, and up-and-coming reds using BORDEAUX and RHONE varieties. A recent AC **80 81 82** 83 85 86 88 89 ££-£££ 230

Albana di Romagna (Italy) Usually dull white wine which, for political reasons, was made Italy's first white DOCG, thus making a mockery of the whole Italian system of denominations

Albariño (Spain) Spain's name for the Portuguese ALVARINHO. Produces often dull wine in GALICIA £££ Martin Codax (A&A Wines 0483 2746660)

Aleatico (S Italy) Red grape producing sweet, Muscatty, sometimes fortified wines. Gives name to DOCs A. di PUGLIA and A. di Gradoli

Alella (Spain) DO district of CATALONIA, producing better whites than reds 85 86 87 89 ££ Marqués de Alella (TAN)

Algeria Formerly a source of coarse, robust reds used to bolster French wine. Reds and rosés from the hilly regions are the most acceptable 85 86 87 88 £-££ Red Infuriator (PD)

Aligoté (BURGUNDY) The region's lesser white grape, making dry, sometimes sharp white wine traditionally mixed with cassis to make KIR. Also grown in the USSR where they think a lot of it 86 87 88 89 90 ££-£££ 52

Almacenista (JEREZ) Fine, old, unblended sherry from a single SOLERA , the sherry equivalent of a single malt whisky. Lustau are specialists ££-£££££ 481

Aloxe-Corton (BURGUNDY) COTE DE BEAUNE commune producing slow-maturing reds (including the GRAND CRU Corton) and whites (including Corton Charlemagne). Invariably pricy; variably great 78 79 83 85 87 88 89 £££££ Olivier Leflaive 88 (L&W ADN)

Alsace (NE France) Dry (and occasionally sweeter) whites and pale reds pitched in style between France and Germany and named after grape varieties 83 85 86 87 88 89 £-£££££ 41 54 166-172 184

Alto Adige (NE Italy) A.k.a. ITALIAN TYROL and SUD TIROL. DOC for a range of exciting, mainly white, wines, often from Germanic grape varieties by lederhosened German dialect-speaking producers. The few reds — made from the LAGREIN and VERNATSCH — are light and fruity 86 87 88 89 £-£££ 21 407 428

Alvarinho (Portugal) White grape at its best in VINHO VERDE blends and in the DO Alvarinho de Monção

Amabile (Italy) Semi-sweet

Amador County (California) Region noted for quality ZINFANDEL

Amaro (Italy) Bitter

Amarone (VENETO) Also 'bitter', used particularly to describe RECIOTOS 427

Amontillado (JEREZ) Literally 'like MONTILLA '. In Britain, medium-sweet sherry; in Spain, dry, nutty wine ££-£££££ Amontillado del Duque (OD)

Amoroso (JEREZ) Sweet sherry style devised for the British ££-££££ Sandemans Amoroso (OD)

Amtliche Prüfüngsnummer (Germany) Official identification number relating to quality. Appears on all QBA/QMP wines

Anbaugebiet (Germany) Term for eleven large wine regions (eg RHEINGAU). QBA and QMP wines must name their ANBAUGEBIET

Ancenis (Coteaux d') (LOIRE) Light reds and deep pinks from the CABERNET FRANC and GAMAY, and MUSCADET-style whites 88 89 90 ££ J.Guidon (YAP)

Anjou (LOIRE) Many dry and DEMI-SEC whites, mostly from the CHENIN BLANC. Usually awful rosé but good light claretty CABERNET reds 85 86 88 89 90 £-££££ 155 208 377

Annata (Italy) Vintage

Año (Spain) Year: preceded by a figure — eg 5 — indicates the wine's age at the time of bottling. Banned by the EC since 1986

AOC (France) See APPELLATION CONTROLEE

AP (Germany) Abbreviation for AMTLICHE PRUFUNGSNUMMER

Appellation Contrôlée (AC/AOC) (France) Designation for 'top quality' wine: guarantees origin, grape varieties and method of production — but not necessarily quality of winemaking

Apremont (E France) Floral, slightly PETILLANT white from skiing country **86 87 88** ££ Les Rocailles P.Boniface (THP UC)

Apulia (Italy) See PUGLIA

Arbois (E France) Light red PINOT NOIRS and dry whites from the JURA, most notably VIN JAUNE £££ -£££££ Ch d'Arlay (JS)

Ardèche (Coteaux de l') (RHONE) Light country reds, mainly from the SYRAH, and CHARDONNAY made by Burgundians who cannot get enough at home... **85 86 88 89** £-££ Louis Latour Chardonnay de l'Ardeche 1989 (SEL)

Argentina The great white hope of the 1990s? 174 263

Asciutto (Italy) Dry

Asenovgrad (BULGARIA) Demarcated northern wine region. Reds from CABERNET SAUVIGNON, MERLOT and MAVRUD **83 85** ££ Asenovgrad Mavrud 85 (MWW)

Assemblage (France) The art of blending wine from different grape varieties in a CUVEE. Associated with BORDEAUX and CHAMPAGNE

Asti (PIEDMONT) Town famous for sparkling SPUMANTE, lighter MOSCATO D'ASTI and red BARBERA D'ASTI 175

Astringent Makes the mouth pucker up. Mostly associated with young red wine. See TANNIN

Aszu (HUNGARY) The sweet 'syrup' made from 'nobly rotten' grapes (see BOTRYTIS) used to sweeten TOKAY **79** 81 83 ££-£££££ Hungarian State Cellars (THP ADN)

Aubance (Coteaux de l') (LOIRE) Light wines (often semi-sweet) grown on the banks of a Loire tributary **88 89** ££

Aude (Vin de Pays de l') (SW France) Prolific *département* producing much ordinary red, white and rosé. Contains a couple of VDQS reds and rosés **88 89 90** £

Ausbruch (AUSTRIA) Term for wines sweeter than German BEERENAUSLESEN but less sweet than TROCKENBEERENAUSLESEN

Auslese (Germany) Sweet wine from selected, ripe grapes usually affected by BOTRYTIS. Third rung on the QMP ladder 200

Austria Home of tangy, dry white GRÜNER VELTLINER, usually drunk within a year of the harvest; of light, fresh PINOT NOIRS and other, sweet Germanic-style whites, including good value dessert styles **81 83 85 87** 88 ££-£££££ Lenz Moser TBA Willi Opitz (T&W)

Auxerrois (LUXEMBOURG) Local name for the PINOT GRIS — and the fresh, clean wine it makes here ££ Alsace Auxerrois Moenchreben Rorschwihr Rolly Gassmann 1987 (THP, BI)

Auxey-Duresses (BURGUNDY) Best known for buttery rich whites but produces greater quantities of raspberryish reds. A slow developer **83 85 87 88 89 90** £££-££££ J P Diconne (DBY)

Avelsbach (MOSEL-SAAR-RUWER) RUWER village producing delicate, light-bodied wines **83 85 86 87 88 89 90** £££

Avize (CHAMPAGNE) Fine white grape village

Ay (CHAMPAGNE) Ancient regional capital, growing mainly black grapes **79 82 83 85 88 89** £££££-£££££ 19

Ayl (MOSEL-SAAR-RUWER) Distinguished SAAR village producing steely wines **85 86 87 88 89 90** ££ -£££ Ayler Kupp Riesling Kabinett 88Winzerverein Ayl, Ayler KuppRiesling Spätlese Bischofhinches Kanrikt (ADN)

Azienda (Italy) Estate

Bacchus White grape, a MULLER-THURGAU x RIESLING cross, making light, flowery wine. Grown in Germany and also England 182

Bad Durkheim (RHEINPFALZ) Chief Rheinpfalz town and source of some of the region's finest whites. Small production of reds **83 85 88 89 90** ££-£££££ Durkheimer Schenkenbohl Huxelrebe Beerenauslese 89 Kloster Limbourg (OD)

Bad Kreuznach (NAHE) Chief and finest wine town of the region, giving its name to the entire lower Nahe **83 85 88 89 90** ££-£££££ Kreuznacher Bruckes Riesling Auslese 89 Schloss Plettenberg (MWW)

Badacsony (HUNGARY) Wine region particularly renowned for good, full-flavoured whites

Baden (Germany) Southernmost ANBAUGEBIET, largely represented by the huge ZBW cooperative. Wines are among the ripest, fullest and driest in

Germany. Rarely classy, but can stand up well to food   83 85 86 88 89   ££-
£££££ Boetzinger Lasenberg 88 (WSC)

Baga (Portugal) One of the country's best, spicily fruity grape varieties — used
in BAIRRADA

Bairrada (Portugal) DO wine region south of Oporto, producing dull whites
and good value reds, often from the BAGA   75 78 80 83 85   £-£££ 443 444

Balance Harmony of fruitiness, ACIDITY, alcohol and TANNIN. Balance can
develop with age but should also be evident in youth

Balaton (HUNGARY) Wine region producing fair quality reds and whites

Ban de vendange (France) Officially sanctioned harvest date

Bandol (PROVENCE) AOC red and rosé. MOURVEDRE reds are particularly good
and spicy. They repay keeping   83 85 86 87 88 89   £££ Mas de la Rouvière 85
(YAP)

Banyuls (PROVENCE) France's answer to port. Fortified, GRENACHE-based VIN
DOUX NATUREL   85 86 88   ££-£££ Robert Doutres (OD)

Barbaresco (PIEDMONT) DOCG red from the NEBBIOLO grape, with spicy fruit,
depth and complexity. Approachable earlier (three to five years) than
neighbouring BAROLO   78 82 85 86 88 89   ££-£££££ BARBARESCO GAJA 1986 (OD
V&C)

Barbera (PIEDMONT) Grape making fruity, spicy, characterful wine (eg
B. d'Alba and B.d'Asti), usually with robust acidity. Now grown in
California   82 83 85 86 88 89   ££-££££ 415

Bardolino (VENETO) Light and unusually approachable for a traditional DOC
Italian red, refreshing with a hint of bitter cherries. Best drunk young   86
87 88 89 90   £-£££ Bardolino Classico Superiore la Canne Boscaini (WCE)

Barolo (PIEDMONT) Noblest of DOCG reds, made from NEBBIOLO. Old fashioned
versions are undrinkably dry and tannic when young, but from a good
producer and year, can last and develop extraordinary complexity. Modern
versions are drinkable earlier, but still last.   71 78 80 82 85 88 89   ££-£££££
422 423 429 433

Barossa Valley (Australia) Established wine region north-east of Adelaide,
famous for traditional SHIRAZ, 'ports' and RIESLINGS which age to oily
richness. CHARDONNAY and CABERNET are now taking over   85 86 87 88   ££-
££££ 107 165 180 344

Barrique French barrel, particularly in BORDEAUX, holding 225 litres. Term used
in Italy to denote barrel ageing

Barsac (BORDEAUX) AC neighbour of SAUTERNES, with similar, though not quite
so rich, SAUVIGNON/SEMILLON dessert wines   75 76 83 86 88 89 90   £££-£££££
Chateau Climens 86 (DBY)

Basilicata (Italy) Southern wine region chiefly known for AGLIANICO DEL
VULTURE and some improving VINI DA TAVOLA   83 85   £-£££ Aglianico del
Vulture 85 D'Angelo(WCE)

Bastardo Red grape used widely in port and previously in MADEIRA where
there are a few wonderful bottles left. Shakespeare refers to a wine called
'Brown Bastard'

Bâtard-Montrachet (BURGUNDY) Biscuity-rich white GRAND CRU of CHASSAGNE
and PULIGNY MONTRACHET, very fine. Very expensive
78 79 81 82 83 85 86 87 88 89 90 £££££ Domaine Leflaive 88 (ADN L&W)

Baux-en-Provence (Coteaux des) (S France) Inexpensive, fruity reds, whites
and rosés of improving quality   85 86 88 89   £-££££ Terres Blanches Rosé 89
(WCE) Domaine de Trevallon (YAP)

Beaujolais (BURGUNDY) Light, fruity red from the GAMAY, good chilled and for
early drinking; B.-Villages is better and one of the ten CRUS better still,
taking on pronounced Burgundian characteristics with age. See B.-VILLAGES,
MORGON, CHENAS, BROUILLY, COTE DE BROUILLY, JULIENAS, MOULIN A VENT,
FLEURIE, REGNIE, ST AMOUR, CHIROUBLES   83 85 87 88 89   ££-££££ 378 382-385

Beaujolais Blanc (BURGUNDY) From the CHARDONNAY, rarely seen under this
name. Commonly sold as ST VERAN   84 85 86 87 88 90   ££-£££ 49

Beaujolais-Villages (BURGUNDY) From the north of the region, fuller flavoured
and more alcoholic than plain BEAUJOLAIS though not necessarily from one of
the named 'CRU' villages   85 86 87 88 89   ££-£££ Chateau Bluizard (TO)

Beaumes de Venise (RHONE) Sweet, grapy, fortified VIN DOUX NATUREL from the Muscat and spicy reds which are just beginning to make their appearance in the UK   (White) 85 86 87 88   Dom de Coyeux 88 (TH M&S)   (Red) 85 86 88 89   Sainsbury's Beaumes de Venise (JS)

Beaune (Burgundy) Reliable commune for soft, raspberry and rose-petal Pinot Noir. The walled city is the site of the famous Hospices charity auction. Also (very rare) whites   78 80 82 83 85 88 89   £££-££££   390

Beerenauslese (Australia, Austria, Germany) Sweet, luscious wines from selected ripe grapes (*beeren*), hopefully affected by Botrytis   ££££-£££££ 466 468 470

Bellet (Provence) Tiny AC behind Nice, producing good red, white and rosé from local grapes including the Rolle, the Braquet and the Folle Noir. (Excessively) pricy and rarely seen in the UK   83 85 87 88   £££-££££   Ch de Crémat 87 (YAP)

Bentonite Clay used as a clarifying agent which attracts and absorbs impurities. Popular as a non animal-derived Fining material

Bereich (Germany) Vineyard area, subdivision of an Anbaugebiet. On its own indicates simple QbA wine, eg Niersteiner — finer wines are followed by the name of a Grosslage subsection and then, better, an individual vineyard

Bergerac (Bordeaux/SW) Lighter, often good value alternative to everyday claret or dry white Bordeaux. Fine sweet Monbazillac is produced here too   85 86 87 88 89 90   £-£££   40 238 243 267

Bernkastel (Mosel-Saar-Ruwer) Town and vineyard area on the Mittelmosel making some of the finest Riesling (including the famous Bernkasteler Doktor) and (sadly) a lake of poor quality cheap wine   76 79 83 85 86 88 89 90   ££-£££££   Bernkasteler Kurfustlay Kabinett, Franz Reh (G)

Bianco di Custoza (Veneto) Widely exported DOC, a reliable, crisp, light white from a blend of grapes. A better alternative to most basic Soave   88 89 90   £-££   Bianco di Custoza, Fraterni Portalupi 88 (WCE)

Bingen Village giving its name to a Rheinhessen Bereich which includes a number of well-known grosslagen   76 83 85 88 89   £-£££   Binger Scharlachberg Dry Riesling Kabinett 86 Villa Sachsen (TO)

Biscuity Flavour of biscuits (eg Digestive or Rich Tea) often associated with the Chardonnay grape, particularly in Champagne and top-class mature Burgundy, or with the yeast which fermented the wine

Black Muscat Grown chiefly as a table grape, also produces very mediocre wine — apart from at the Quady winery in California   Quady Elysium Black Muscat 89 (MWW GHS UC)

Blanc de Noirs White (or pink) wine made from black grapes   ££££-£££££   5

Blanc de Blancs White wine, usually sparkling, made solely from white grapes. In Champagne, denotes 100 per cent Chardonnay   12 16

Blanquette de Limoux (Midi) Methode Champenoise sparkler, at its best appley, crisp and clean. Takes on a yeasty, earthy flavour with age   ££-£££   Eric de Cairolle (OD)

Blauburgunder (Austria) The Pinot Noir, making light, sharp reds

Blauer Portugieser Red grape used in Germany and particularly Austria for light, pale wine

Blaye (Côtes de/Premières Côtes de) (Bordeaux) Reasonable Blayais whites and sturdy AC reds. Premières Côtes are better   81 82 83 85 86 88 89   £-£££   Chateau Bertinerie (OD)

Bodega (Spain) Winery or wine cellar; producer

Body Usually used as 'full-bodied', meaning a wine with mouth-filling flavours and probably a fairly high alcohol content

Bommes (Bordeaux) Sauternes Commune and village containing several Premiers Crus   75 76 79 80 81 83 86 88 89   ££££-£££££   Ch Lafaurie-Peyraguey 77 (SAF HUN)

Bonnezeaux (Loire) Delicious, sweet whites produced from the Chenin Blanc. They last for ever   75 76 83 85 88 89 90   ££-£££££   Bonnezeaux, Chateau du Fesles 89 J Boivin (NI)

Bordeaux (France) Largest quality wine region in France, producing reds from Cabernet Sauvignon, Cabernet Franc, Petit Verdot, and Merlot, and dry and sweet whites from (principally) blends of Semillon and Sauvignon. See THE WINES section for numerous examples

Botrytis *Botrytis cinerea*, a fungoid infection that attacks and shrivels grapes, evaporating their water and concentrating their sweetness. Vital to SAUTERNES and the finer German and Austrian sweet wines

Bottle-fermented Commonly found on the labels of US sparkling wines to indicate the METHODE CHAMPENOISE, gaining wider currency. Beware though, it can indicate inferior 'transfer method' wines

Bouquet Overall smell, often made up of several separate aromas

Bourg (Côtes de) (BORDEAUX) Inexpensive, fast-maturing, everyday AC reds with solid fruit; lesser whites 81 82 83 85 86 88 89 90 £-£££ Roc de Combes (WDW)

Bourgueil (LOIRE) Red AC in the TOURAINE area, producing crisp, grassy 100 per cent CABERNET FRANC wines 83 85 86 88 89 90 ££-£££ Pierre Jacques Druet (ADN M&V)

Bouzeron (BURGUNDY) Village in the COTE CHALONNAISE, principally known for ALIGOTE 85 86 87 88 89 ££-£££ Aubert de Villaine 87 (ADN)

Bouzy Rouge (CHAMPAGNE) Sideline of a black grape village: an often thin-bodied, rare and overpriced red wine 85 88 ££££-£££££ Georges Vesselle 86 (Jeroboams 071 225 2232)

Braquet (MIDI) Grape variety used in BELLET

Brauneberg (MOSEL-SAAR-RUWER) Village best known in UK for the Juffer vineyard Brauneberger Juffer Riesling Auslese 89 Fritz Haag (L&W)

Bricco Manzoni (PIEDMONT) Non-DOC red blend of NEBBIOLO and BARBERA grapes, round and fruity. Drinkable young 79 82 83 85 86 88 89 £££-£££££ Roche dei Manzoni 85 (ADN BD)

British Wine 'Made' wine from diluted grape concentrate bought in from a number of countries. Avoid it. ENGLISH wine is the real stuff — produced from grapes grown in England

Brouilly (BURGUNDY) Largest of the BEAUJOLAIS CRUS producing pure, fruity GAMAY 83 85 87 88 89 ££-££££ Brouilly E Loron 1989 (U CUM THP HUN CPL)

Brunello di Montalcino Prestigious DOCG red from a SANGIOVESE clone, needs at least five years to develop complex and intense fruit and flavour. 77 81 82 83 85 88 89 £££-£££££ 430

Brut Dry, particularly of CHAMPAGNE and sparkling wines. *Brut nature/sauvage/ zéro* are even drier

Bual MADEIRA grape producing a soft, nutty wine, good with cheese 496

Bucelas (Portugal) DO area near Lisbon, best known for intensely coloured yet delicate, aromatic white wines. Rare in Britain

Bugey (E France) SAVOIE district producing a variety of wines, including white ROUSSETTE DE BUGEY from the grape of that name

Bulgaria Country losing way after apparently conquering, one by one, the 'noble' grapes thanks to massive state-aided technology and advice from California. Now, source of decreasingly good value CABERNET SAUVIGNON and MERLOT, making (slow) progress with SAUVIGNON and CHARDONNAY. MAVRUD is the traditional red variety 81 83 84 85 86 87 £-££ 258

Burgenland (AUSTRIA) Wine region bordering HUNGARY, climatically ideal source of fine, sweet AUSLESEN and BEERENAUSLESEN ££-£££ Bouvier Trockenbeerenauslese 83 Alexander Unger (JS)

Burgundy (FRANCE) Home to PINOT NOIR and CHARDONNAY; wines ranging from banal to sublime, but never cheap 86 87 £££-£££££ See THE WINES section for numerous examples

Buttery The rich, fat smell often found in good CHARDONNAY. Sometimes found in wine which has been left on its LEES

Buzbag (TURKEY) Rich, dry red wine which, sadly, is rarely well made and often oxidised (SEL)

Buzet (Côtes de) (BORDEAUX) AC region adjoining BORDEAUX, producing light claretty reds, and whites from SAUVIGNON 81 82 83 85 86 88 89 £-££ 218

Cabernet d'Anjou/de Saumur (LOIRE) Light, fresh, grassy, blackcurranty rosés, typical of their grape, the CABERNET FRANC 83 85 86 87 88 89 90 £-£££££ 208

Cabernet Franc Red grape, the CABERNET SAUVIGNON's younger brother. Produces simpler, blackcurranty wines, particularly in the LOIRE and Italy, but plays a more sophisticated role in BORDEAUX, especially in ST EMILION 208

Cabernet Sauvignon The great red grape of BORDEAUX, where it is blended with MERLOT and other grape varieties. The most successful red VARIETAL, grown in every reasonably warm winemaking country. See THE WINES section for numerous examples.

Cadillac (BORDEAUX) Known for sweet whites (not quite as sweet or fine as SAUTERNES) for drinking young and well-chilled £-£££

Cahors (SW France) 'Rustic' BORDEAUX-like reds produced mainly from the local TANNAT and the Cot (MALBEC), full-flavoured and still quite full-bodied, though have lightened recently **82 83 85 86 88 89** £-£££ 233 235 236

Cairanne Named CÔTES DU RHÔNE village for powerful, sound reds **78 79 82 83 85 88 89** £££ Côtes du Rhône Villages Cairanne 87 N Thompson (LAY)

Calabria (Italy) The 'toe' of the boot, making little-seen Gaglioppo reds and Greco whites ££ Librandi (under the 'Ciro' brand) (V&C,WGA)

Campania (Italy) Region surrounding Naples, best known for TAURASI, LACRYMA CHRISTI and GRECO DI TUFO

Canada Surprising friends and foes alike, the winemakers of British Columbia and, more specifically Ontario, are producing very good CHARDONNAY and RIESLING 97

Cannonau Heady, robust DOC red from SARDINIA **82 83 84 85 86** 88 £-££ Cannonau del Parteolla, Dolcanova (WCE)

Canon Fronsac Small AC bordering on POMEROL for sound attractive reds from some good-value PETIT CHÂTEAUX **78 79 81 82 83** 85 86 88 89 ££-£££ Chateau Canon de Brem (M&V)

Cantenac (BORDEAUX) Haut Medoc Commune containing a number of top CHÂTEAUX including Palmer 78 79 81 82 83 85 86 88 89 90 ££-£££££

Cantina (Sociale) (Italy) Winery cooperative

Capsule On a wine bottle, the lead or plastic sheath covering the cork

Carbonic Maceration See MACERATION CARBONIQUE

Carcavelos (Portugal) Sweet, usually disappointing fortified wines from a region close to Lisbon. Rare in Britain

Carignan Prolific red grape making usually dull, coarse wine for blending, and classier fare in CORBIÈRES and FITOU £-££

Cariñena (Spain) Important DO of Aragon for rustic reds, high in alcohol. Also some whites 75 79 82 83 85 88 £-££ Don Mendo, Monte Ducay

Carmignano (TUSCANY) Exciting alternative to CHIANTI, in the same style but with the addition of CABERNET grapes **75 79 82 83 85 88** £££-££££ 425

Carneros (California) Small, cool, high-quality region shared between the NAPA and SONOMA VALLEYS, and producing top-class CHARDONNAY and PINOTNOIR **85 86 87 88** £££-££££ 112 391

Casa vinicola (Italy) Firm buying and vinifying grapes

Casa (Italy, Spain, Portugal) Firm (company)

Cassis (PROVENCE) Rare, spicy white made from UGNI BLANC, CLAIRETTE and MARSANNE Clos Ste Magdeleine 86 (Francois Sack) (YAP)

Cat's pee Describes the tangy smell often found in typical — and frequently delicious — MÜLLER-THURGAU and SAUVIGNON

Cava (Spain) Sparkling wine produced by the MÉTHODE CHAMPENOIS traditionally 'earthy' but now much improved ££-£££ Conde de Caralt (MOR)

Cave (France) Cellar

Cave Cooperative (France) Cooperative winery

Cépage (France) Grape variety

Cerasuolo (ABRUZZI) A pink wine from the grape, greatly benefiting from newer, cool fermentation techniques £££ Valentini 85 (WCE)

Cérons (BORDEAUX) Bordering on SAUTERNES with similar, less fine, but cheaper wines ££ The Society's Cérons (WSO)

Chablis (BURGUNDY) Often overpriced and overrated white, but a fine example still has that steely, European finesse that New World CHARDONNAYS have trouble capturing 78 79 81 85 86 87 88 89 90 ££-£££££ 74 75

Chai (France) Cellar/winery

Chalonnais/Côte Chalonnaise (BURGUNDY) Increasingly sought-after source of lesser-known, less complex BURGUNDIES — GIVRY, MONTAGNY, RULLY and MERCUREY. Potentially (rather than actually) good value **84 85 86 87 88** 89 90 £- ££££ Montagny 1er Cru, Cave de Buxy (TO)

Chambolle-Musigny (BURGUNDY) One of the finest red wine communes, producing rich, fragrant, deeply flavoured wines. Le Musigny is the GRAND CRU 78 80 83 85 86 88 89 90 £££-£££££ Machard de Gramont (D)

Champagne (France) In the north-east of France, source of the finest and greatest (and jealously guarded) sparkling wines, from the PINOT NOIR, PINOT MEUNIER and CHARDONNAY grapes ££££-£££££ 13 16 19 23-25

Chaptalisation The legal (in some regions) addition of sugar during fermentation to boost a wine's alcohol content

Chardonnay The great white grape of BURGUNDY, CHAMPAGNE and now the New World. Versatile, classy and as capable of fresh simple charm in Bulgaria as of buttery, hazelnutty richness in MEURSAULT. See THE WINES section for numerous examples

Charmat The inventor of the CUVE CLOSE method of producing cheaper sparkling wines

Charta (Germany) Syndicate of RHEINGAU producers using an arch as a symbol to indicate their new dry (TROCKEN) styles

Chassagne-Montrachet (BURGUNDY) COTE DE BEAUNE COMMUNE making grassy, biscuity, fresh yet rich whites and mid-weight, wild fruit reds. Pricy but recommended 78 79 81 83 85 86 88 89 ££££-£££££ 123

Chasselas Widely grown, prolific white grape making light, often dull fruity wine principally in Switzerland, eastern France and Germany

Château (usually BORDEAUX) Literally 'castle'; practically, vineyard or wine estate

Châteauneuf-du-Pape (RHONE) Traditionally, the best reds (rich and spicy) and whites (rich and floral) from the southern Rhône valley 78 79 80 81 83 85 86 88 89 £££-£££££ 363 372 373

Château-Chalon (E France) Speciality JURA AC for a VIN JAUNE of good keeping quality

Château-Grillet (RHONE) Tiny, pricy property, region and APPELLATION producing great VIOGNIER white 86 87 88 £££££ Châteâu-Grillet 1987 (YAP)

Chef de culture (France) Vineyard manager

Chénas (BURGUNDY) One of the ten BEAUJOLAIS CRUS, the least well-known but worth seeking out 83 85 88 89 90 £££ Jean-Georges 89 (AF)

Chêne (France) Oak, as in 'FUTS DE CHENE' — oak barrels

Chenin Blanc The white grape of the LOIRE, neutral and with high acidity; can produce anything from bone dry to very sweet, long-lived wines with a characteristic honeyed taste. Also grown with success in S Africa, USA and Australia. See VOUVRAY, QUARTS DE CHAUMES, BONNEZEAUX, SAUMUR 4 144 146 156 163 164

Cheverny (LOIRE) Light, floral VDQS whites from the SAUVIGNON and CHENINBLANC 86 87 88 89 £-££

Chianti (CLASSICO, PUTTO) (TUSCANY) Famous red DOCG, round and extrovert, but of variable quality. The cockerel or cherub insignia of the Classico or Putto growers should indicate a finer wine 79 81 82 83 85 88 ££-££££ 401 403 405 409 411 416

Chiaretto (LOMBARDY) Recommendable light red and rosé wines from around Lake Garda £-££ Portalupi 88 (WCE)

Chile Rising (if often old-fashioned) source of CABERNET SAUVIGNON, SAUVIGNON/SEMILLON whites and some experimental CHARDONNAY 81 82 83 84 85 86 88 £-££££ 81 83 87 299

Chinon (LOIRE) CABERNET FRANC-based reds, rosés and whites, light and grassy when young. From a hot summer, reds can age for up to ten years 83 85 86 88 89 ££-£££ 274

Chiroubles (BURGUNDY) One of the ten BEAUJOLAIS CRUS, drinks best when young and full of almost *nouveau*-style fruit 83 85 87 88 89 £££ 385

Chorey-lès-Beaune (BURGUNDY) Modest, warm reds once sold as COTE DE BEAUNE VILLAGES, now beginning to be appreciated 78 80 83 85 86 88 89 90 £££ Tollot-Beaut 88 (L&W)

Chusclan (RHONE) Named village of COTES DU RHONE with perhaps the best rosé of the area ££ Chusclan Rosé 89, Les Vignerons de Chusclan (BD)

Cinsaut/Cinsault Prolific hot climate fruity red grape with high acidity, often blended with GRENACHE. One of the thirteen permitted varieties of

CHATEAUNEUF-DU-PAPE and also in the blend of Château Musar in the Lebanon

Cissac (BORDEAUX) HAUT-MEDOC village close to ST ESTEPHE, producing similar though lesser wines 78 79 81 82 83 85 86 88 89 £££-££££ Chateau Cissac 1985

Clairette de Die (RHONE) Pleasant, if dull, sparkling wine. The Cuvée Tradition made with MUSCAT is far better; grapy and fresh — like a top-class French ASTI SPUMANTE £££ Archard Vincent (YAP)

Clairette Dull workhorse white grape of southern France

Clare Valley (Australia) Well-established region producing high quality Rieslings which age well. (Look for Tim Knappstein, Lindemans Watervale) 369

Clarete (Spain) Term for light red wine, frowned on by the EC

Classico (Italy) May only be used on a central, historic area of a DOC, eg CHIANTI CLASSICO, VALPOLICELLA CLASSICO 402 409 411 416

Climat (BURGUNDY) An individual vineyard

Clos (France) Literally, a walled vineyard — and often a finer wine

Colares (Portugal) DO region near Lisbon for heavy, tannic red wines. The vines are grown in deep sand. Surprisingly hard to find in the UK —— even from specialists ££-£££ Chitas Garrafeira 57 (SEL)

Colheita (Portugal) Harvest or vintage

Colle/colli (Italy) Hill/hills

Colli Berici (VENETO) DOC for red and white — promising CABERNETS

Colle Orientali del Friuli (Friuli-Venezia Giulia) Excellent clean, fresh, lively whites from near the Yugoslav border 86 87 88 89 £££ Pinot Grigio, Collio 1990 (WCE)

Colombard White grape grown in SW France principally for distillation into Armagnac, but sometimes blended with UGNI BLANC to make a crisp dry wine. Also planted in Australia and USA, where it is known as 'French Colombard' £ VdP des Cotes de Gascogne 89 (Grassa) widely available

Commandaria (Cyprus) Traditional, rich, dessert wine with concentrated raisiny fruit £-££ Commandaria St John (WOC)

Commune (France) Small demarcated plot of land named after its principal town or village. Equivalent to an English parish

Condrieu (RHONE) Fabulous, pricy white from the VIOGNIER grape — old-fashioned, full, rich, aromatic wine 84 85 86 87 88 89 £££££ 77

Consejo Regulador (Spain) Spain's administrative body for the enforcement of the DO laws

Consorzio (Italy) Syndicate of producers, often using their own seal of quality

Coonawarra (Australia) Important, southerly and cool climate wine area of South Australia, famed for excellent RIESLINGS, minty CABERNET SAUVIGNON and, more recently, CHARDONNAY (Red) 82 84 85 86 87 88 90 (White) 84 86 87 88 90 ££-£££££ 106 178 293 295 296 301

Corbières Highly successful everyday drinking red, of variable quality but at its best full, fruity country wine 85 86 88 89 £-££ 28 31 219 231

Corked Unpleasant, musty smell, caused by fungus attacking cork

Cornas (RHONE) Dark red from the SYRAH grape, hugely tannic when young but worth tucking away 76 78 79 82 83 85 88 89 90 ££££ Jean Lionnet 1988 (OD)

Corsica (France) Mediterranean island making robust reds, whites and rosés, often high in alcohol

Cosecha (Spain) Harvest or vintage

Costières du Gard (SW France) Good, fruity country reds, lesser-seen whites and rosés Ch St Vincent Costières du Gard 85 (WCE)

Cot The red grape of CAHORS and the LOIRE, also the MALBEC of BORDEAUX £-££ Touraine Cépage Cot 85, Marc Michaud (UC)

Côte de Beaune (Villages) A geographical distinction; with Villages on a label, indicates red wines from one or more of the villages in the Côte de Beaune. Confusingly, wine labelled simply 'Côte de Beaune' comes from a small area around Beaune itself. These (red and white) wines are very rare 85 88 89 90 £££-££££

Côte de Brouilly (BURGUNDY) One of the ten BEAUJOLAIS CRUS; distinct from BROUILLY and often finer. Floral and ripely fruity; will keep for a year or two 83 85 87 88 89 £££ Ch Thivin (ADN) Duboeuf 88/9 (LNR)

Côte de Nuits (BURGUNDY) Northern, and principally 'red' end of the CÔTE D'OR 85 88 89 90 Cote de Nuits Villages, 'Tasteviné' 1988 Charles Gruber (ROD)

Côte des Blancs (CHAMPAGNE) Principal CHARDONNAY-growing area Le Mesnil Blanc de Blancs NV (FWC RAE BI)

Côte d'Or (BURGUNDY) Geographical designation for the central, finest slopes running down the region, encompassing the CÔTE DE NUITS and CÔTE DE BEAUNE

Côte Rôtie (RHONE) Massive, powerful SYRAH reds from the northern Rhône, very fine, need at least six (better ten) years 76 78 79 82 83 85 88 89 90 £££££-£££££ 375

Coteaux Champenois (CHAMPAGNE) APPELLATION for the still wine of the area, thin and light 79 82 83 85 88 89 £££££ A.Bonnet (CDV)

Côtes de Provence Improving, good value fruity rosés and whites, and ripe spicy reds 85 86 87 88 89 £-£££ Dom de St Baillou 85 Dom Cuvee de Roudai 86 (BI)

Côtes du Rhône (Villages) Large APPELLATION for warm, fruity, spicy reds both medium and full-bodied, and full spicy reds. Villages, particularly if named, are finer and very good value 83 85 86 87 88 89 £-£££ 340 343 345 348 350 352 355 358

Cotesti (ROMANIA) Easterly vineyards growing some French varieties

Côte(s), Coteaux (France) Hillsides, slopes — prefixed to, e.g. Beaune indicates finer wine

Cotnari (ROMANIA) Traditional white dessert wine, of good repute

Coulure Vine disorder caused by adverse climatic conditions, causing grapes to shrivel and fall

Cream sherry Popular style produced by sweetening an OLOROSO £££-£££ Adnams Southwold Cream (ADN)

Crémant (France) In CHAMPAGNE, lightly sparkling. Elsewhere, e.g. Crémant de Bourgogne, de Loire and d'Alsace, MÉTHODE CHAMPENOISE fizz 20

Criado y Embotellado (por) (Spain) Grown and bottled (by)

Crianza (Spain) Literally 'keeping' — 'con crianza' means aged in wood

Crisp Fresh, with good acidity

Crozes-Hermitage (RHONE) A few nutty white wines — better known for pleasing SYRAH reds in a light style, which drink young but will keep. Hermitage's kid brother 78 79 82 83 85 88 89 90 ££-££££ 346

Cru artisan Antiquated classification for sub-CRU BOURGEOIS wines

Cru bourgeois (BORDEAUX) Wines beneath the CRUS CLASSÉS, satisfying certain requirements, which can be good value for money and, in certain cases, better in quality than supposedly classier classed growths

Cru classé (BORDEAUX) The best wines of the MEDOC are *crus classés*, divided into five categories from first (top) to fifth growth (or *cru*) in 1855. The GRAVES, ST EMILION and SAUTERNES have their own classifications

Cru grand bourgeois (exceptionnel) An estate-bottled HAUT MEDOC cru bourgeois, which is aged in oak barrels. *Exceptionnel* wines must come from the area encompassing the *crus classés* . Future vintages will not bear this designation, as it has fallen foul of the EC

Crusted (port) Affordable alternative to vintage port, a blend of different years bottled young and allowed to throw a deposit The Wine Society's Crusted Port

Curico (CHILE) Up-and-coming wine region 88 299

Cuve close The third best way of making sparkling wine, where the wine undergoes secondary fermentation in a tank and is then bottled. Also called the CHARMAT or TANK method

Cuvée Most frequently a blend, put together in a process called ASSEMBLAGE

Cuvée de Prestige What the producer considers a finer blend, or cuvée

Dão (Portugal) DO reds and whites, fairly full. 75 80 83 85 £-££ Asda Dão

Dealul Mare (ROMANIA) Carpathian region once known for whites, now producing reds from 'noble' varieties

Dégorgée (dégorgement) The removal of the deposit of inert yeasts from CHAMPAGNE after maturation. See RD

Deidesheim (RHEINPFALZ) Distinguished wine town producing quality, flavoursome RIESLING 83 85 86 88 89 90 £-££££ Deinhard Deidesheim Heritage (BU)

Demi-sec (France) Medium dry

Deutscher Tafelwein (Germany) Table wine, guaranteed German as opposed to Germanic-style EC TAFELWEIN

Deutches Weinsiegel (Germany) Seals of various colours awarded for merit to German wines, usually present as neck labels

Diabetiker Wein (Germany) Indicates a very dry wine with most of the sugar fermented out (as in a Diät lager), thus suitable for diabetics

DLG (Deutsche Landwirtschaft Gesellschaft) Body awarding medals for excellence to German wines

DO Denominaci/on/ão d'Origen (Spain, Portugal) Demarcated quality area, guaranteeing origin, grape varieties and production standards

DOC(G) Denominazione di Origine Controllata (é Garantita) (Italy) Quality control designation based on grape variety and/or origin. 'Garantita' is supposed to imply a higher quality level but it is not a reliable guide. All BAROLO is DOCG, as is the dull ALBANA DI ROMAGNA

Dolcetto (d'Alba, di Ovada) (PIEDMONT) Red grape making anything from soft, everyday wine to more robust, long-keeping DOCs 83 85 86 88 £££ 413

Dôle (SWITZERLAND) Light reds from the PINOT NOIR and/or GAMAY

Domaine (France) Wine estate, can encompass a number of vineyards

Dosage The addition of sweetening syrup to CHAMPAGNE, which is dry in its natural state

Douro (Portugal) The great port region and river, producing much demarcated and occasionally good table wines 79 **80 82** 83 85 ££ 484-488 490 493-495 497

Doux (France) Sweet

Dumb As in dumb nose, meaning without smell

Duras (Côtes de) (BORDEAUX) Inexpensive whites from the SAUVIGNON, often better value than basic Bordeaux Blanc **87 88** 89 £-££ 47

Durbach (BADEN) Top vineyard area of this ANBAUGEBIET

Edelfäule (Germany) BOTRYTIS CINEREA, or 'noble rot'

Edelzwicker (ALSACE) Generic name for white wine from a blend of grape varieties, increasingly rare

Eger (HUNGARY) Official wine district best known for 'Bulls' Blood'

Einzellage (Germany) Single vineyard; most precise and often the last part of a wine name, finer by definition than a GROSSLAGE

Eiswein (Germany) The finest QMP wine, made from BOTRYTIS-affected grapes naturally frozen on the vine. Concentrated, delicious, rare but often underpriced. Can only now be made from grapes of BEERENAUSLESE or TROCKENBEERENAUSLESE quality

Eitelsbach (MOSEL-SAAR-RUWER) One of the top two Ruwer wine towns; site of the famed Karthauserhofberg vineyard

Elaborado y Anejado Por (Spain) 'Made and aged for'

Elba (Italy) Island off the Tuscan coast making full, dry reds and whites

Elbling Inferior Germanic white grape

Elever/éléveur To mature or 'nurture' wine, especially in the cellars of the BURGUNDY NEGOCIANTS, who act as *éléveurs*

Eltville (RHEINGAU) Town housing the Rheingau state cellars and the German Wine Academy, producing good RIESLING with backbone 83 85 88 89 90 ££-££££ Eltviller Sonnenberg Riesling Kabinett 1988 (ADN)

Emerald Riesling (California) Bottom of the range white hybrid grape, at best fresh, fruity but undistinguished

Emilia-Romagna (Italy) Region surrounding Bologna best known for LAMBRUSCO

En primeur New wine, usually BORDEAUX — specialist merchants buy and offer wine 'en primeur' before it has been released; customers rely on their merchant's judgement to make a good buy

English wine Produced from grapes grown in England, as opposed to BRITISH WINE, which is made from imported concentrate ££-££££ 15 39 64 137 149 161 162 181 182 185 188 189 196 197

Enoteca (Italy) Literally, wine library or, nowadays, wine shop

Entre-Deux-Mers (BORDEAUX) Up-and-coming source of much basic Bordeaux Blanc, principally dry SAUVIGNON **86 87 88** 89 £-££ 44,48

Epernay (CHAMPAGNE) Centre of Champagne production, where many famous houses are based, such as Mercier, Moët & Chandon, Perrier Jouët and Pol Roger

Erbach (RHEINGAU) Town noted for fine, full RIESLING, notably from the Marcobrunn vineyard **85 86 88 89 90 ££-£££££** Schloss Reinhartshausen (ADN)

Erden (MOSEL-SAAR-RUWER) Northerly village producing full, crisp, dry RIESLING. In the Bernkastel BEREICH, includes the famous Treppchen vineyard **83 85 86 88 89 £££-£££££** Erdener Pralert Riesling Auslese 1979, Dr Loosen (ADN)

Erzeugerabfüllung (Germany) Bottled by the grower/estate

Espum/oso/ante (Spain/Portugal) Sparkling

Esters Chemical components in wine responsible for a variety of odours, many fruity

Estufa The vats in which MADEIRA is heated, speeding maturity and imparting its familiar 'cooked' flavour

Eszencia (HUNGARY) Essence of TOKAY, once prized for miraculous properties. Now virtually unobtainable, though supplies may improve as Hungary's winemakers benefit from privatisation and foreign investment **57 68 £££££** State Cellars (ADN)

Etna (Italy) From the Sicilian volcanic slopes, hot-climate, soft fruity DOC reds, whites and rosés. Can be flabby

Fattoria (Italy) Estate, particularly in Tuscany

Fat Has a silky texture which fills the mouth. More fleshy than meaty

Faugères (MIDI) Good, full-bodied AC reds, some whites and rosés, a cut above the surrounding COTEAUX DU LANGUEDOC **81 82 83 85 86 88 89 £-££** L'Estagnon 87 (TH)

Fendant (SWITZERLAND) The CHASSELAS grape and its white wines, so called in the VALAIS area

Fermentazione naturale (Italy) 'Naturally sparkling', but in fact indicates the CUVE CLOSE method

Fining The clarifying of young wine before bottling to remove impurities, using a number of agents including ISINGLASS and BENTONITE

Finish What you can still taste after swallowing

Fino (Spain) Dry, delicate sherry, the finest to aficionados. Drink chilled and drink up once opened **££-££££** 477

Fitou (MIDI) Reliable southern AC, making reds from the CARIGNAN grape. Formerly dark and stubborn, the wines have become more refined, with a woody warmth **81 82 83 85 86 88 89 £-££** Domaine du Grand Bosc (TH WR)

Fixin (BURGUNDY) Northerly village of the COTE DE NUITS, producing lean, tough, uncommercial reds which can mature splendidly **78 80 82 83 85 88 89 £££-££££** Dom Pierre Gelin 86 (OD)

Flabby Lacking balancing acidity

Flagey-Echezeaux (BURGUNDY) Prestigious red COTE DE NUITS COMMUNE. Echezeaux and Grands Echezeaux are the two best GRANDS CRUS **78 80 82 83 85 87 88 89 £££££** Grands Echezeaux, Dom de la Romanée- Conti 82 (ADN L&W)

Fleurie (BURGUNDY) One of the ten BEAUJOLAIS CRUS, fresh and fragrant as its name suggests. Much admired but most expensive Cru **83 85 87 88 89 £££**

Flor Yeast which grows naturally on the surface of some maturing sherries, making them potential FINOS

Flora Grape, a cross between SEMILLON and GEWURZTRAMINER best known in Brown Brothers Orange Muscat and Flora

Folle Blanche Widely planted workhouse white grape, high in acidity. Known as the GROS PLANT in MUSCADET. Some success in California

Folle Noir (MIDI) Grape used to make BELLET

Forst (RHEINPFALZ) Wine town producing great, concentrated RIESLING. Famous for the Jesuitengarten vineyard **75 76 79 83 85 86 88 89 ££-£££££** Forster Jesuitengarten Riessling Kabinett 88 Dr Burklin-Wolf

Franciacorta (LOMBARDY) DOC for good, light, French-influenced reds and a noted sparkler, Franciacorta Pinot **83 85 86 88 89 £-£££**

Franken (Germany) ANBAUGEBIET making characterful, sometimes earthy, dry whites, traditionally presented in the squat, flagon-shaped 'bocksbeutel' on which the Mateus bottle was modelled **83 85 86 87 88 89 90 ££-£££££** Weingut Hans (BWC)

Frascati (Italy) Cliched dry or semi-dry white from LATIUM, at best soft and clean, more usually dull. Drink within twelve months of vintage £-££££ Colle Gaio Villa Catone (WGA)

Friuli-Venezia Giulia (Italy) Northerly region containing a number of DOCs and notably successful with MERLOT, PINOT BIANCO and GRIGIO 82 83 85 86 87 88 89 ££-££££ 406 417 420

Frizzante (Italy) Semi-sparkling

Fronsac/Canon Fronsac (BORDEAUX) Below ST EMILION, producing comparable but tougher, often robust reds. Canon Fronsac is better and often good value 81 82 83 85 86 88 89 90 £££-££££ Ch la Rivière 85 (HUN) Ch La Rose Cheuvrol 85 (UC)

Frontignan (Muscat de) (PROVENCE) Rich, sweet, grapey fortified wine from the Bandol area in Provence. More forceful (and cheaper) than BEAUMES DE VENISE. Also a synonym for Muscat a Petits Grains ££-£££ Château de la Peyrade (JS HFW)

Frontonnais (Côtes du) (SW France) Up-and-coming, inexpensive red (and some rosé), full and fruitily characterful 85 86 88 89 ££ 229 251

Fruska Gora (YUGOSLAVIA) Hilly wine region best known for white wines, improving success with French grape varieties

Fume Blanc Name invented by Robert Mondavi for the SAUVIGNON grape, derived from POUILLY BLANC FUME Adler Fells Fumé Blanc 89 (OD)

Fürmint Eastern European white grape, used for TOKAY in HUNGARY

Füts de Chêne (France) Oak barrels, as in 'élévé en' ('matured in')

Gaillac (SW France) Light, fresh, good-value reds and whites, the result of an invasion of the GAMAY and SAUVIGNON grapes. PERLE is lightly sparkling 85 86 88 89 ££ 228 380

Galestro (TUSCANY) A light, grapey white ££ Antinori 88 (TH)

Gamay The BEAUJOLAIS grape, making wine with youthful, fresh, cherry/plummy fruit. Also successful in the LOIRE and GAILLAC 377 378 380 381 382-385

Gamay Beaujolais A misnamed variety of PINOT NOIR grown in California

Gamey Smell or taste reminiscent of hung game

Gard (Vin de pays du) (MIDI) Huge VIN DE TABLE producing area with one fair VDQS, COSTIERES DU GARD 85 86 88 89 £-££ Costières du Gard, Domaine St Cyrgues (OD)

Garganega (Italy) Uninspiring white grape used chiefly for SOAVE

Garrafeira (Portugal) Indicates a producer's 'reserve' wine, selected and given extra ageing 78 80 82 83 85 ££

Gascogne (Côtes de) (SW France) Source of Armagnac and good value fresh and floral whites. Source of our White Wine of the Year in 1989, made by Grassa 87 88 89 £ 33 34 214

Gattinara (PIEDMONT) Red DOC from the NEBBIOLO, varying in quality but at least full-flavoured and dry 78 80 82 85 88 89 ££-££££ Riserva Nervi (L&W)

Gavi (TUSCANY) Full, dry white from the CORTESE grape. Compared to white BURGUNDY (often for no good reason). Gavi and Gavi di Gavi tend to be creamily pleasant and overpriced 86 87 88 90 ££-££££ Banfi (AB)

Geelong (Australia) Vine growing area of VICTORIA, cool climate, well suited to CHARDONNAY and PINOT NOIR. Look for Bannockburn, Idyll and Hickinbotham

Geisenheim (RHEINGAU) Town and the home of the German Wine Institute, the most famous wine school in the world 83 85 88 89 90 ££-£££££ Geisenheimer Klauserweg Riesling Kabinett, Geisenheim Institute (OD)

Generoso (Spain) Fortified or dessert wine

Gevrey Chambertin (BURGUNDY) Best known red COTE DE NUITS COMMUNE, much exploited but still capable of superb, plummy rich wine from the best vineyards. The GRAND CRU is Le Chambertin 78 80 82 83 85 88 89 90 ££££-£££££ 399

Gewürztraminer White grape making dry, full, fleshy, spicy wine, best in ALSACE but also grown in Australasia, Italy, USA and E Europe 165-172

Gigondas (RHONE) Côtes du Rhône COMMUNE producing reliable, full-bodied, spicy/peppery, blackcurranty reds, best with food 78 79 82 83 85 86 88 89 ££-£££ Jaboulet 86 (OD) Domaine Les Goubert Cuvee Florence 1988

Giropalette Machines which, in the METHODE CHAMPENOISE, automatically perform the task of REMUAGE

Gisborne (New Zealand) North Island vine growing area since 1920s. Cool, wettish climate, mainly used for whites 85 86 87 89 ££-££££

Givry (BURGUNDY) COTE CHALONNAISE commune, making typical and affordable, if sometimes unexciting, PINOT NOIRS and creamy whites 83 85 88 89 £££ Baron Thenard 85 (LAY)

Graach (MOSEL-SAAR-RUWER) MITTELMOSEL village producing fine wines. Best known for Himmelreich vineyard 83 85 86 88 89 90 ££ -£££££ Graacher Himmelreich Riesling Kabinett, Zentralkellerei (TO)

Gran reserva (Spain) A quality wine aged for a designated number of years in wood and only produced in the best vintages

Grand cru (France) The finest vineyards. Official designation in BORDEAUX, BURGUNDY and ALSACE. Vague in Bordeaux and Alsace, but in Burgundy denotes single vineyard with its own AC, eg Montrachet

Grandes marques Syndicate of the major CHAMPAGNE houses

Grave del Friuli (Friuli-Venezia Giulia) DOC for young-drinking reds and whites. CABERNET and MERLOT increasingly successful 85 86 87 88 ££ 417

Graves (BORDEAUX) Large, southern region producing vast quantities of white, from good to indifferent. Reds have a better reputation for quality (Red) 78 79 81 82 83 85 86 88 89 90 (White) 83 85 86 87 88 89 90 ££-£££££ 58 259 270

Greco di Tufo (Italy) From Campania, best-known white from the ancient GRECO grape; dry, characterful southern wine Mastroberardino 87 (SAS)

Grenache Red grape of the RHONE (the GARNACHA in Spain) making spicy, peppery, full-bodied wine

Grignolino (PIEDMONT) Red grape and its modest, but refreshing, wine, eg the DOC Grignolino d'Asti 85 86 87 88 ££-£££

Gros Plant (du Pays Nantais) (LOIRE) Light, sharp white VDQS wine from the same region as MUSCADET, named after the grape elsewhere known as the FOLLE BLANCHE 87 88 89 £-££

Groslot/Grolleau Workhorse grape of the Loire, particularly ANJOU, used for white, rose and base wines for sparkling SAUMUR

Grosslage (Germany) Wine district, the third subdivision after ANBAUGEBIET (eg RHEINGAU) and BEREICH (eg NIERSTEIN). For example, Michelsberg is a GROSSLAGE of the Bereich PIESPORT

Grüner Veltliner White grape of AUSTRIA and Eastern Europe, producing light, fresh, aromatic wine 87 88 89 90 ££-£££ Lenz Moser (W)

Gumpoldskirchen (AUSTRIA) Town near Vienna famous for full, rather heady characterful wines 83 85 86 87 88 ££

Gutedel German name for the CHASSELAS grape

Halbtrocken (Germany) Semi-dry. Rising style intended to accompany food 183, 186

Hallgarten (RHEINGAU) Important town near Hattenheim producing quite robust wines (for Germany) Hallgartener Schonhell Riesling Green Gold QbA 81, Schloss Volrads (EP)

Haro (Spain) Town at the heart of the RIOJA region, home of many BODEGAS, eg CVNE, La Rioja Alta

Hattenheim (RHEINGAU) One of the greatest Johannisberg villages, producing some of the best German RIESLINGS 76 79 83 85 88 89 ££-££££ Von Simmenn

Haut-Médoc (BORDEAUX) Large APPELLATION which includes nearly all of the well-known CRUS CLASSES. Basic Haut-Médoc should be better than plain MÉDOC 78 81 82 83 85 86 88 89 90 ££-£££££ 304 310

Haut Poitou (LOIRE) Often boring VDQS red but reliable, good value SAUVIGNON and CHARDONNAY whites 85 86 87 88 89 ££ Gamay du Haut Poitou 88 (L&W), 2

Hautes Côtes de Beaune (BURGUNDY) Sound, soft, strawberry PINOT NOIR from a group of villages 83 85 88 89 90 ££-£££££ 387

Hautes Côtes de Nuits (BURGUNDY) Slightly tougher than HAUTES COTES DE BEAUNE, particularly when young 83 85 88 89 ££-££££ 393

Hawkes Bay (New Zealand) Major North Island vineyard area 85 86 87 88 89 90 ££-££££ 140

Hérault (Vin de pays de l') (France) Largest vine growing *département*, producing some 20 per cent of France's wine, nearly all VIN DE PAYS or

VDQS, of which COTEAUX DU LANGUEDOC is best known. Also home of the extraordinary Mas de Daumas Gassac where no expense is spared to produce easily the best of France's 'country wines' **86 87 88 89 £-££** 157

Hermitage (RHONE) Top-class, long-lived northern Rhône wines; superb, complex reds and sumptuous, nutty whites. Also Australian name for the SYRAH grape and, confusingly, the South African term for CINSAULT **76 78 79 82** 83 85 88 89 90 **££££-£££££** Chave 86 (OD YAP ADN) Paul Jaboulet Hermitage la Chapelle 1988 (OD)

Hessische Bergstrasse (Germany) Smallest ANBAUGEBIET, wines rarely seen in the UK

Hochfeinste (Germany) 'Very finest'

Hochgewächs QbA Recent official designation for RIESLINGS which are as ripe as a QMP but can still only call themselves QBA. This from a nation dedicated to simplifying what are acknowledged to be the most complicated labels in the world

Hochheim (RHEINGAU) Village whose fine RIESLINGS gave the English the word 'Hock' 192

Hock English name for Rhine wines, derived from HOCHHEIM in the RHEINGAU 194

Hospices de Beaune (BURGUNDY) Charity hospital, wines from whose vineyards are sold at an annual charity auction on the third Sunday in November, the prices setting the tone for the COTE D'OR year. Beware that although price lists often merely indicate 'Hospices de Beaune' as a producer, all of the wines bought at the auction are matured and bottled by local merchants, some of whom are more scrupulous than others

Huelva (Spain) DO of the Estremadura region, producing rather heavy whites and fortified wines

Hungary Country best known for its legendary TOKAY, and Bulls Blood. The source of much 'party wine', particularly OLASZ RIZLING

Hunter Valley (Australia) Famous wine region of New South Wales, producing many reds (often from SHIRAZ) and full, fleshy whites from SEMILLON and CHARDONNAY (Red) **82 84 85 86** 87 88 90 (White) **84 85 86** 87 88 90 **££-£££££** 93 179 271 361

Huxelrebe Minor white grape, often grown in England

Hybrid Cross-bred grape, usually *Vitis vinifera* (European) x *Vitis labrusca* (N American)

Hydrogen sulphide Naturally occurring gas given off by especially young red wine, resulting in smell of bad eggs. Often caused by insufficient racking

Imbottigliato nell'origine (Italy) Estate bottled

Imperiale Large bottle containing six litres of wine

Inferno (Italy) LOMBARDY DOC, chiefly red from NEBBIOLO, which needs at least five years ageing

Institut National des Appellations d'Origine (INAO) French administrative body which designates and polices quality areas

Irancy (BURGUNDY) Light reds and rosés made near CHABLIS from a blend of grapes. Little known **83 85 88** 89 90 **£££** Bourgogne Irancy 1987 Leon Bienvenue (HFW)

Irouléguy (SW France) Pyrenees/Basque area producing white, rosé and slightly better red

Isinglass FINING agent derived from the sturgeon fish

Israel Once the source of appalling wine, but the new-style VARIETAL wines are improving 319

Italian Riesling Not the great RHINE RIESLING, but a lesser version, going under many names, and widely grown in Northern and Eastern Europe

Jardin de la France (Vin de pays du) Marketing device to describe VINS DE PAYS from the LOIRE 134

Jasnières (LOIRE) Rare, sweet CHENIN BLANC wines from TOURAINE **83 85 86 87** 88 89 **£££** Caves aux Tuffieres 83/85 (YAP)

Jeunes Vignes Term occasionally seen in BURGUNDY, denotes wine from vines too young for their classified destiny, eg CHABLIS

Jerez (de la Frontera) (Spain) Centre of the SHERRY trade, gives its name to entire DO sherry-producing area 477-483

Jeroboam Large bottle containing three litres, usually containing CHAMPAGNE

Jesuitengarten (RHEINGAU) One of Germany's top vineyards

Johannisberg (RHEINGAU) Village making superb RIESLING, which has lent its name to a BEREICH covering all of the Rheingau   75 76 79 83 85 88 89 £-££££ Johannisberger Erttebringer Riesling Kabinett 1989 R Muller (TAN)

Johannisberg Riesling Californian name for the RHINE RIESLING

Jug wine American term for quaffable VIN ORDINAIRE

Juliénas (BURGUNDY) One of the ten BEAUJOLAIS CRUS producing classic, vigorous wine which often benefits from a few years in bottle   85 87 88 89 90 ££-£££ 382 384

Jumilla (Spain) Improving DO region, traditionally known for heavy, high alcohol wines but increasingly making lighter ones   82 83 84 85 86 87 88 £-££ Taja (WSO) Sainsbury's (JS)

Jura (E France) Region containing ARBOIS and SAVOIE, best known for specialities such as VIN GRIS, VIN JAUNE and VIN DE PAILLE   Ch d'Arlay (HAR) Ch Chalon (GNW)

Jurançon (SW France) Dry, spicy white, some rosé and very good sweet wines 86 87 88 89 ££-££££ 114 461

Kabinett First step in German quality ladder, for wines which fulfil a certain sweetness rating. Semi-dry wines

Kaiserstuhl (BADEN) Finest BADEN BEREICH with top villages producing rich, spicy RIESLING from volcanic slopes

Kallstadt (RHEINPFALZ) Village containing the best known and finest vineyard of Annaberg, making luscious, full RIESLING

Kalterersee (Italy) Germanic name for the LAGO DI CALDARO in the SUD TIROL/ ALTO ADIGE

Keller/kellerei/kellerabfüllung (German) Cellar/producer/estate-bottled

Keppoch/Padthaway (Australia)   Vineyard area north of COONAWARRA   84 85 86 87 88 90 ££-£££££ 104

Kerner White grape, a RIESLING cross, grown in Germany and now England

Kiedrich (RHEINGAU) Top village high in the hills with some renowned vineyards   75 76 79 83 85 88 89 90 £-£££££ Kiedricher Sandgrub Riesling Spätlese 83, Dr Weil (TO)

Kir White wine with a dash of cassis syrup, good for disguising a disappointing buy. With sparkling wine (properly CHAMPAGNE), a 'Kir Royale'

Klusserath (MOSEL-SAAR-RUWER) Small village best known in UK for Sonnenuhr and Konigsberg vineyards   76 79 83 85 88 89 90 £-£££££

Krajina Yugoslavian region noted for its PINOT NOIR   Pinot Noir Krajina 1986 (JEH)

Krems (AUSTRIA) Town and WACHAU vineyard area producing Austria's most stylish Rieslings from terraced vineyards

Kreuznach (NAHE) Northern BEREICH, with fine vineyards around the town of Bad Kreuznach

La Mancha (Spain) Over a million acres of vineyard on the central plain. Mostly VIN ORDINAIRE, but with some startling exceptions, for example, Castillo de Alhambra, the Guide's Wine of the Year in 1989   82 83 85 86 87 88 89 £

Labrusca *Vitis labrusca*, the North American species of vine, making wine which is always referred to as 'foxy'. All VINIFERA vine stocks are grafted on to PHYLLOXERA-proof labrusca roots, though the vine itself is banned in Europe

Lacryma Christi (Campania) Literally, 'tears of Christ'; melancholy name for some amiable, light, rather rustic reds and whites. Those from Vesuvio are DOC 86 87 88 89 90 ££ Lacryma Christi del Vesuvio Bianco 86 Mastroberardino (L&W)

Lago di Caldaro (TRENTINO-ALTO ADIGE) Also known as the KALTERERSEE, making cool, light reds with slightly unripe, though pleasant fruit 85 86 87 88 £-££

Lagrein Red grape grown in the TRENTINO-ALTO ADIGE region making dry, light, fruity DOC reds and rosés 407

Lake County (California) Vineyard district salvaged by improved irrigation techniques and now capable of some fine wines 84 85 86 87 88 89 ££-£££ Fetzer Cabernet Sauvignon 86 (TO)

Lalande de Pomerol (BORDEAUX) Bordering on POMEROL with similar, but less
fine wines. Some good value PETITS-CHATEAUX 81 83 85 86 88 89 90 *££-££££*
307

Lambrusco (EMILIA-ROMAGNA) Famous, rather sweet red fizzy wine, and now
some white versions produced for the Anglo-Saxon palate. Variable quality
but the best are the dry, Italian-style versions, ideal for picnics 87 88 *£-££*

Landwein (Germany) A relatively recent quality designation — the equivalent
of a French VIN DE PAYS from one of eleven named regions (ANBAUGEBIET).
Often dry

Langhe (PIEDMONT) A range of hills

Languedoc (Coteaux du) (MIDI) Big VDQS, a popular source of everyday reds
from RHONE and southern grapes 84 85 86 87 *£-£££££*

Laski Riesling/Rizling YUGOSLAV name for poor quality white grape, unrelated
to the RHINE RIESLING. Aka WELSCH, OLASZ and Italico

Late-bottled vintage (port) (LBV) Bottled either four or six years after a
specific vintage; the time in wood softens them up to be ready to drink
younger 485

Late Harvest Made from grapes which are picked after the main vintage,
giving a higher sugar level *££-£££££* 472

Latium/Lazio (Italy) The vineyard area surrounding Rome. Avoid most of its
Frascati although there are some exciting Bordeaux-style reds 87 88 89 90
£-££ B.Violo Frascati 87 (EP)

Laudun (RHONE) Named village of COTES DU RHONE, with some atypical fresh,
light wines and attractive rosés

Layon, Coteaux du (LOIRE) Whites from the CHENIN BLANC grape, slow to
develop and long lived. Lots of lean dry wine but the sweet BONNEZEAUX
and QUARTS DE CHAUME are superior 75 76 83 85 88 89 90 *££-£££££* Phillippe
LeBlanc 1989 (TAN)

Lazio SEE LATIUM

Lean Lacking body

Lebanon Chiefly represented in the UK by the remarkable Chateau Musar,
made in BORDEAUX style but from CABERNET SAUVIGNON, CINSAULT and SYRAH
61 64 67 70 72 78 79 80 81 82 *££-£££££* 288

Lees Or *lies*, the sediment of dead yeasts let fall as a white wine develops. See
SUR LIE

Length How long taste lingers in the mouth

Léognan (BORDEAUX) GRAVES COMMUNE containing many of the finest white
CHATEAUX 64 70 71 79 83 85 86 88 89 *££-£££££*

Leon (Spain) North-western region producing acceptable dry, fruity reds and
whites *££* Palacio de Leon (HUN)

Liebfraumilch (Germany) The most seditious exploitation of the German QbA
system — a good example is perfectly pleasant but the vast majority,
though cheap, is money down the drain. Responsible for the ruination of
the German wine market in the UK 88 89 90 *£-££*

Lie(s) See LEES/SUR LIE

Liqueur de Tirage (CHAMPAGNE) The yeast and sugar added to base wine to
induce secondary fermentation (bubbles) in bottle

Liqueur d'Expedition (CHAMPAGNE) The sweetening syrup used for DOSAGE

Liquoreux (France) Rich and sweet

Liquoroso (Italy) Rich and sweet

Lirac (RHONE) Confident, peppery, TAVEL-like rosés, though its deep, red-fruit
reds are becoming increasingly popular 78 82 83 85 88 89 *££* Lirac 'Les
Queyrades' 85, Dom A.Majan (ADN AB)

Listrac (BORDEAUX) Look out for Châteaux Fourcas-Hosten Fourcas-Dupré 78
79 81 82 83 85 86 88 89 *££-££££*

Livermore (Valley) (California) A warm climate vineyard area with fertile soil
producing full, rounded whites, including increasingly fine CHARDONNAY
Wente Brothers Zinfandel 86 (AB)

Loir (Coteaux du) Clean vigorous whites from a LOIRE tributary; JASNIERES is
little seen but worth looking out for 83 85 86 87 88 89 *£££* Jasnières 'Clos St
Jacques' 86 Dom Joel Gigou (ADN)

Loire (France) An extraordinary variety of wines emanate from this area — dry whites such as MUSCADET and the classier SAVENNIERES, SANCERRE and POUILLY FUME; grassy, summery reds; buckets of rosé, some good, mostly dreadful; glorious sweet whites and very acceptable sparkling wines. Refer to sub-categories for recommended wines

Lombardy (Italy) Milan's vineyard, known mostly for sparkling wine but also for some increasingly interesting reds. See LUGANA 20 408 434

Loupiac (BORDEAUX) Bordering on SAUTERNES, with similar, but less fine wines 83 85 86 88 89 90 ££-£££ 464

Luberon (Côtes du) (RHONE) Reds, like light COTES DU RHONE, pink and sparkling wines; the whites CHARDONNAY-influenced. A new APPELLATION and still good value 85 86 87 88 89 £-£££ 337

Ludon (BORDEAUX) HAUT-MEDOC VILLAGE and COMMUNE 78 79 81 83 85 86 88 89 £££-£££££ Ch La Lagune 85 (HUN)

Lugana (LOMBARDY) grown on the shores of Lake Garda, smooth, pungent white wine, a match for food. Lombardy's best wine 87 88 89 ££ Lugana ca dei Frati, Dal Cero (WCE)

Lugny (BURGUNDY) See MACON

Lussac-St-Emilion A satellite of ST EMILION 78 79 81 82 83 85 86 88 89 £££ Ch du Tabuteau (WSO)

Lutomer (YUGOSLAVIA) Wine producing area known mostly for its LUTOMER RIESLING, but now doing good things with CHARDONNAY . £ Lutomer Laski Rizling (AB)

Luxembourg Source of pleasant, fresh white wines from ALSACE-like grape varieties ££-£££ Cuvee de l'Ecusson NV, Bernard Massard (EP)

Lyonnais (Coteaux du) (RHONE) Just to the south of BEAUJOLAIS, making some very acceptable good value wines from the same grapes 85 86 88 89 £-££

Macau HAUT-MEDOC COMMUNE possessing some useful CRUS BOURDEOIS 82 83 85 86 88 89 £££-££££ 310

Macération carbonique Technique in which uncrushed grapes burst and ferment under pressure of a blanket of carbon dioxide gas, producing fresh, fruity wine. Used in BEAUJOLAIS, South of France and becoming increasingly popular in the New World

Mâcon/Mâconnais (BURGUNDY) Avoid unidentified 'rouge' or 'blanc' on restaurant wine lists. Mâcons with the suffix VILLAGES, SUPERIEUR or PRISSE, VIRE, LUGNY or CLESSE are better and can afford some pleasant, good value CHARDONNAY 85 86 87 88 89 90 ££-££££ 50 72 92

Madeira Atlantic island producing famed fortified wines, usually identified by style: BUAL, SERCIAL, VERDELHO or MALMSEY £££-£££££ 491 492 496

Maderisation Deliberate procedure in MADEIRA, produced by the warming of wine in ESTUFAS. Otherwise undesired effect, commonly produced by high temperatures during storage, resulting in a dull, flat flavour tinged with a sherry taste and colour

Madiran (SW France) Heavy, robust country reds, tannic when young but age extremely well 82 85 86 88 89 ££

Maître de chai (France) Cellar master

Malaga (Spain) Andalusian DO producing dessert wines in varying degrees of sweetness, immensely popular in the 19th century £££ Solera Scholtz 1885 (MOR)

Malbec Red grape that plays a cameo role in BORDEAUX but stars in CAHORS, where it is known as the COT or AUXERROIS

Malmsey Traditional, rich MADEIRA — the sweetest style, but with a dry finish £££-££££ 491

Malolactic fermentation Secondary effect of fermentation in which 'hard' malic acid is converted into the softer lactic acid

Malvasia MUSCATTY white grape vinified dry in Italy, but far more successfully as good, sweet traditional MADEIRA

Malvoisie (LOIRE) Local name for the PINOT GRIS 87 88 89 ££ J Guindon (YAP)

Manzanilla Dry, tangy SHERRY — a FINO-style wine widely (though possibly mistakenly) thought to take a salty tang from the coastal BODEGAS of SANLUCAR DE BARRAMEDA ££-£££ 479 481

Maranges (Burgundy) Brand new hillside appellation promising potentially affordable Côte d'Or wines

Marc Residue of pips, stalks and skins after grapes are pressed — often distilled into a woody unsubtle brandy of the same name, eg Marc de Bourgogne

Marches (Italy) Central region on the Adriatic coast best known for ROSSO CONERO and good, dry, fruity VERDICCHIO whites (Red) 85 86 87 88 (White) 86 87 88 89 ££-££££

Marcillac (SW France) Full-flavoured country reds principally from the Fer grape — may also contain CABERNET and GAMAY . Domaine du Cros 1989 (ADN)

Margaret River (Australia) Recently developed cool vineyard area on Western Australia coast, gaining notice for CABERNET SAUVIGNON and CHARDONNAY. Also, Australia's only ZINFANDEL from Cape Mentelle (best known wineries are Moss Wood, Cape Mentelle, Leeuwin, Vasse Felix and Chateau Xanadu) 85 86 87 88 £££-££££ 323

Margaux (BORDEAUX) COMMUNE that boasts a concentration of CRUS CLASSÉS; the most famous being the first growth Château Margaux 78 82 83 84 85 86 88 89 ££-£££££ 298 330

Marlborough (New Zealand) Newest but increasingly important wine area, with cool climate making excellent white wines 86 87 88 89 ££-££££ 11 150 281 313

Marmandais (Côtes du) (SW France) Uses the BORDEAUX grapes plus GAMAY, SYRAH and others to make a variety of pleasant, inexpensive wines

Marsala Dark, rich, fortified wine from SICILY crucial to a number of recipes, such as zabaglione ££-£££££ Vecchio Samperi de Bartoli (WCE)

Marsannay (BURGUNDY) Sought-after, delicate pale red and rosé from the PINOT NOIR 85 87 88 89 90 £££-££££ Philippe Charlopin 86 (ADN)

Marsanne Along with Roussanne, grape responsible for most whites of the northern RHONE. Also planted successfully in the Goulburn Valley in VICTORIA by Chateau Tahbilk and Mitchelton and in California by Randall Graham 85 86 88 78 79 53 157

Master of Wine (MW) One of a small number (under 200) who have passed a gruelling set of trade exams

Mavrodaphne Greek red grape and its wine, full-bodied, dark and strong, needs ageing ££

Mavrud (BULGARIA) Traditional red grape and characterful wine

Médoc (BORDEAUX) As a generic term, implies sound, everyday claret to be drunk young. As an area, that region of Bordeaux south of the Gironde and north of the town of Bordeaux 85 86 88 89 £-££ 252 253 256

Melon de Bourgogne White grape producing a dry, not very exciting wine but can be good in the LOIRE. Also known as MUSCADET (Loire), WEISSBURGUNDER (Germany) and PINOT BLANC (California) 131 132 135 136 141 142 471

Mendocino (California) Northern, coastal wine county successfully exploiting cool microclimates to make 'European-style' wines 83 84 85 86 87 88 90 ££-££££ 12

Ménétou-Salon (LOIRE) Bordering on SANCERRE making similar, less pricy SAUVIGNON and some PINOT NOIR red 87 88 89 ££-£££ Jean-Max Roger (HFW)

Mercaptans See HYDROGEN SULPHIDE

Mercurey (BURGUNDY) Good value wine from the Côte CHALONNAISE — tough, full reds worth waiting for, and nutty, buttery whites 85 86 87 88 89 90 £££ Michel Juillot 87 (Domaine Direct)

Merlot Red grape making soft, honeyed, even toffeed wine with plummy fruit. Used to balance the TANNIC CABERNET SAUVIGNON throughout the MEDOC but the main grape of POMEROL and ST EMILION. Also successful in VENETO, HUNGARY and Australia 247 249 279 294 301 317 324 417

Merlot di Pramaggiore (VENETO) Excellent, plummy red wine from the BORDEAUX grape

Méthode Champenoise As a term, now restricted by law to wines from CHAMPAGNE but in effect used by all quality sparkling wines; labour-intensive method where bubbles are produced by secondary fermentation in bottle

Methuselah Same as an IMPERIALE, usually applied to CHAMPAGNE

Meursault (BURGUNDY) Superb white Burgundy; the CHARDONNAY showing off its nutty, buttery richness in mellow, full-bodied dry wine 84 85 86 87 88 89 £££-£££££ 121 122 124

Midi (France) Vast and vastly improved region of southern France, including CORBIERES, ROUSSILLON, LANGUEDOC, MINERVOIS and the VIN DE PAYS departments of GARD, AUDE and HERAULT 62 82 86 202 209-213 216 218 219 222-227 230 231 237 241 246 247 249 254 306 364 453 500

Millesime (France) Year or vintage

Minervois (SW France) Suppertime reds, satisfyingly firm and fruity 85 86 87 88 89 £-££ 223

Mis en Bouteille au Château/Domaine (France) Bottled at the estate

Mittelhaardt (RHEINPFALZ) Central and best BEREICH 86 87 88 89 90 ££ Sainsbury's Auslese

Mittelmosel (MOSEL-SAAR-RUWER) Middle and best section of the Mosel, including the BERNKASTEL BEREICH 85 86 87 88 89 90 £-£££ 200 225 228

Mittelrhein (Germany) Small, northern section of the RHINE. Good RIESLINGS little seen in the UK 83 85 86 88 89 90 ££-£££

Moelleux (France) Sweet 471 472

Monbazillac (SW France) BERGERAC AOC, using the grapes of sweet BORDEAUX to make improving inexpensive alternatives to SAUTERNES 83 85 86 88 89 90 ££-£££ Ch Monbazillac 86 (HUN)

Monica (di Cagliari/Sardegna) (Italy) Red grape and wine of SARDINIA producing dry and fortified spicy wine £ Monica di Sardegna 86 Cantina Sociale di Dolianova (WCE)

Monopole (France) Literally, exclusive — in BURGUNDY denotes single ownership of an entire vineyard

Montagne St Emilion (BORDEAUX) A satellite of ST EMILION 83 85 86 88 89 90 ££-£££

Montagny (BURGUNDY) Tiny Côte CHALONNAISE COMMUNE producing good, lean CHARDONNAY, a match for many POUILLY FUISSES 86 87 88 89 90 £££ Ch de Davenay, Montagny 1er Cru (JS WWI VW)

Montalcino (TUSCANY) Village near Siena known for BRUNELLO DI MONTALCINO 419

Montepulciano (Italy) Red grape making red wines in central Italy; also see VINO NOBILE DI MONTEPULCIANO and ABRUZZI 387

Monthélie (Burgundy) Often overlooked COTE DE BEAUNE village producing potentially stylish reds and whites 85 86 88 89 90 £££ -££££ Domaine Monthelie Donhairet (M&V)

Montilla (-Moriles) (Spain) DO region producing SHERRY-type wines in SOLERA systems, often so high in alcohol that fortification is unnecessary £-££ Dos Reinos Dry Montilla (OD)

Montlouis (LOIRE) Neighbour of VOUVRAY making similar wines 85 88 89 90 ££-££££ 163

Montravel (Cotes de) (SW France) Dry and sweet whites from, and comparable to, BERGERAC ££-£££

Mor (HUNGARY) Hungarian town making clean, aromatic white wine — Mori Ejerzo

Morey St Denis (BURGUNDY) COTES DE NUIT village which produces deeply fruity, richly smooth reds, especially the GRAND CRU Clos de la Roche 82 83 85 86 88 89 £££-£££££ Clos Sorbets 85 J Truchot Martin (HUN)

Morgon (BURGUNDY) One of the ten BEAUJOLAIS CRUS, worth maturing, when it can take on a delightful chocolate/cherry character 85 86 87 88 89 90 ££-£££ 383

Morio Muskat White grape grown in Germany making full, fragrant wine 87 88 89 90 £-££

Mornington Peninsula (VICTORIA) Some of Australia's newest and most southerly vineyards which are producing minty CABERNET, tasty, slightly thin PINOT and fruity CHARDONNAY 84 85 86 87 88 90 £££ 95

Moscatel de Setúbal (Portugal) Delicious, honeyed fortified dessert wine from a peninsula south of Lisbon. Ages indefinitely £££-£££££ 457

Moscato The MUSCAT grape in Italy, at its best in fruity, low strength Spumante wines (eg Moscato d'Asti) or in sumptuous dessert wines ££-££££ 175 499

Moselblumchen Generic light, floral TAFELWEIN from the MOSEL-SAAR-RUWER, equivalent to the Rhine's LIEBFRAUMILCH

Mosel/Moselle River and loose term for MOSEL-SAAR-RUWER wines, equivalent to the 'HOCK' of the Rhine **85 86 87 88 89** £-£££££ 187 191 198 467

Mosel-Saar-Ruwer (MSR) (Germany) Major ANBAUGEBIET capable of superb RIESLINGS, differing noticeably in each of the three regions 187 191 198 467

Moulin-à-Vent (BURGUNDY) One of the ten BEAUJOLAIS CRUS, big and rich at its best and, like MORGON, benefits from a few years ageing **85 88 89** ££-£££ Moulin-a-Vent 1989, Jean-Georges (AF)

Moulis (BORDEAUX) Red wine village of the HAUT-MEDOC; like LISTRAC, some good value lesser growths **82 83** 85 86 88 89 90 ££-££££ Ch Maucaillou 86 (JS)

Mourvèdre RHONE grape usually found in blends. Increasingly popular

Mousseux (France) Sparkling. *Vin mousseux* tends to be cheap and unremarkable

Mousse The bubbles in CHAMPAGNE and sparkling wines

Mudgee (Australia) High altitude, isolated region undergoing a revival; previously known for robust, often clumsy wines. (Botobolar and Montrose are probably the best known producers) 366

Müller-Thurgau Workhouse white grape, a RIESLING/SYLVANER cross, making much unremarkable wine in Germany. Very successful in England 188

Murfatlar (ROMANIA) Major vineyard and research area having increasing success with the CHARDONNAY Murfatlar Gewürztraminer 1983 (Touchstone Wines, tel: 0562 74678)

Murray River Valley (Australia) Vineyard area between VICTORIA and NEW SOUTH WALES producing much wine which ends up in boxes

Murrumbidgee (Australia) Area formerly known for bulk dessert wines, now improving irrigation and vinification techniques to make good table wines and some stunning BOTRYTIS-affected sweet wines (look out for de Bortoli)

Muscadet (LOIRE) Large area at the mouth of the Loire making dry, appley white wine from the Melon de Bourgogne. Clean and refreshing when good but varies in quality. SUR LIE is best. May be barrel-fermented. **88 89 90** £-££££ 187 191 198 467

Muscat à Petits Grains A.k.a. FRONTIGNAN, the grape responsible for MUSCAT DE BEAUMES DE VENISE, ASTI SPUMANTE, Muscat of Samos, Rutherglen Muscats and Alsace Muscats 453 456 458 459 460

Muscat of Alexandria Grape responsible for MOSCATEL DE SETUBAL, Moscatel de Valencia and some sweet South Australian offerings. Also known as Lexia and not of as high quality as MUSCAT A PETITS GRAINS 454 455 457

Muscat Ottonel Muscat variety grown in Middle and Eastern Europe Murfatlar Muscat Ottonel 1979 (HUN)

Must Unfermented grape juice

MW See MASTER OF WINE

Nackenheim (RHEINHESSEN) Village in the NIERSTEIN BEREICH, producing good wines but better known for its debased GROSSLAGE, Gutes Domtal

Nahe (Germany) ANBAUGEBIET producing increasingly popular wines which combine a delicacy of flavour with full body **87** 88 89 £-£££ 190 470

Naoussa (Greece) Rich, dry red wines from the Xynomavro grape ££-£££ Ch Pegasus, Marlovitis (GWC)

Napa Valley (California) Established, top-quality vineyard area. 'Napa' is the American-Indian word for 'plenty' (Red) **84 85** 86 87 88 90 (White) **85 86 87** 88 90 ££-££££ 75 205 314 317 326 328 334 336 462

Navarra (Spain) Northern DO, traditionally for rosés and heavy reds but now producing some good value, exciting wines to rival RIOJA **81 82** 85 86 87 88 £-£££ 442 450

Nebbiolo Great red grape of Italy, producing wines which are slow to mature, then richly complex and fruity, epitomised by BAROLO 422 423 429 433

Négociant (-Éléveur) A BURGUNDY merchant who buys, matures and bottles wine

Négociant-manipulant (NM) Buyer and blender of wines for CHAMPAGNE, identifiable by NM number mandatory on label

Neusiedlersee (AUSTRIA) Burgenland region on the Hungarian border, best known for its fine, sweet, BOTRYTISED wines

New South Wales (Australia) Major wine-producing state including the HUNTER VALLEY, MUDGEE and MURRUMBIDGEE regions 93 179 271 361 366

New Zealand New, super-star nation, especially successful with Sauvignon

Blanc 3 98 117 118 120 148 150 281 313 465

Nierstein (RHEINHESSEN) Village and, with PIESPORT, BEREICH best known in the UK. Some very fine wines, obscured by the notoriety of Gütes Domtal 83 85 88 89 90 £-£££ 177

Noble rot Popular term for BOTRYTIS CINEREA

Nose Smell

Nouveau New wine, most popularly used of BEAUJOLAIS

Nuits St Georges (BURGUNDY) COMMUNE producing the most claret-like of red Burgundies, properly tough and lean when young but glorious in age 82 83 85 88 89 £££-£££££ 125

NV Non-vintage, meaning a blend of wines from different years

Oaky Flavour imparted by oak casks. 'Woody' is usually less complimentary

Ockfen (MOSEL-SAAR-RUWER) Village producing the best wines of the Saar-Ruwer BEREICH, especially from the Bockstein vineyard ££-£££££ Max Grunhauser Herrenberg Riesling (LV)

Oechsle (Germany) Sweetness scale used to indicate the amount of sugar in grapes or wine

Oenology The study of the science of wine

Oidium Insidious fungal infection of grapes, causing them to turn grey and shrivel

Olasz Rizling (HUNGARY) Term for the inferior WALSCHRIESLING

Oloroso (JEREZ) Style of full-bodied SHERRY, dry or semi-sweet ££-£££ 482

Oltrepó Pavese (Italy) Red and white LOMBARDY DOC for a range of wines from varying grape varieties ££ 482

Opol (YUGOSLAVIA) Source of dry, light, slightly spicy rosé

Oppenheim (RHEINHESSEN) Village in NIERSTEIN BEREICH best known, though often unfairly, for Krottenbrunnen vineyard. Elsewhere produces soft wines with concentrated flavour 76 83 85 86 88 89 ££-££££ Oppenheimer Krottenbrunnen Spätlese, 1988 R. Muller (TAN L&W)

Orange Muscat Yet another member of the MUSCAT family, best known for dessert wines in California and VICTORIA Quady Essencia (FWC)

Oregon (USA) Fashionable wine-producing state best known in the UK for its skill with the PINOT NOIR 83 85 86 87 88 ££-£££££

Oriahovitza (BULGARIA) Major source of reliable CABERNET SAUVIGNON and MERLOT 81 84 85 87 £-££ Reserve Cabernet Sauvignon 83 (MWW TH)

Orvieto (Italy) White Umbrian DOC responsible for a quantity of dull wine. Orvieto CLASSICO is better 86 88 89 90 ££-££££ Antinori 'Campo Grande' Orvieto Classico 90 (TH WR)

Oxidation The effect (usually detrimental) of oxygen on wine

Pacherenc-du-Vic-Bilh (SW France) Dry or fairly sweet white wine, a speciality of MADIRAN growers. Very rarely seen, worth trying ££-£££ Pacherenc du Vic Bilh Bouscasse Vendage Tardive, Alain Brumont (H&H)

Padthaway See KEPPOCH/PADTHAWAY

Pais CHILEAN red grape and its wine

Palate The taste of a wine

Palatinate (Germany) Region (ANBAUGEBIET) now known as the RHEINPFALZ

Pale Cream (Spain) A slightly sweetened FINO sherry ££ Duke of Wellington Pale Cream (SEL)

Palette (PROVENCE) AC rosé, a cut above the average. Also some fresh white 82 83 85 86 88 89 ££-£££££ Ch Simone 84 Rouge, 85 Rosé (LV YAP)

Palo Cortado (Spain) A rare SHERRY-style wine pitched between an AMONTILLADO and an OLOROSO ££-££££ Del Carrascal Palo\ Cortado, Valdespino (BI)

Palomino White grape responsible for all fine SHERRIES

Pasado/Pasada (Spain) Term applied to old or fine FINO and AMONTILLADO sherries £££-££££ 481

Passe-Tout-Grains (BURGUNDY) Wine made of two-thirds GAMAY, one third PINOT NOIR 83 85 86 87 88 89 ££-££££ Henri Jayer (THP) Rion 87 (M&V)

Passito (Italy) Sweet, raisiny wine, usually made from sun-dried grapes ££££-£££££ Caluso Passito 1985 (OD)

Pauillac (BORDEAUX) The home of Châteaux Lafite, Latour and Mouton — the epitome of full-flavoured, blackcurranty Bordeaux, very classy (and expensive) wine 78 79 81 82 83 85 86 88 89 90 £££-£££££ 316 318 335

Pécharmant (SW France) In the BERGERAC area, producing light, Bordeaux-like reds. Worth trying 83 85 86 88 89 Ch de Tiregand 86 (JS)

Pedro Ximenez (PX) White grape dried in the sun for sweet, curranty wine, added to produce the mellower SHERRY styles. Also produces one very unusual wine at de Bortoli's in Australia £££-£££££

Pelure d'Oignon 'Onion skin'; distinctive, orangey tint of some rosé

Peñafiel (Portugal) District producing some good VINHOS VERDES 86 88 89 Paço de Teixero 88 (WCE)

Penedés Largest DOC of Catalonia, with improving table wines following the example of the Torres BODEGA. More importantly the centre of the CAVA industry 82 83 85 86 87 ££-£££££ 305 446

Perlé/Perlant (France) Lightly sparkling

Perlwein (Germany) Sparkling wine

Pernand-Vergelesses (BURGUNDY) COMMUNE producing rather clumsy, jammy reds but fine whites, some of the best buys on the COTE D'OR 82 83 85 88 89 £££-££££ Dom Chanson 1er Cru 'Les Vergelesses' (TAN)

Pessac-Léognan (BORDEAUX) GRAVES COMMUNE recently given its own APPELLATION and containing all the better Graves CHATEAUX. 85 86 88 89 90 £££-£££££ 113 292

Pétillant (FRANCE) Lightly sparkling 500

Petit Chablis (BURGUNDY) Less fine than plain CHABLIS 85 86 87 88 89 ££-£££ Dom Gallois (FWC)

Petit château (BORDEAUX) Minor property, beneath CRU BOURGEOIS

Petite Sirah Red grape, a.k.a. Durif in the MIDI and grown in California. Has nothing to do with the SYRAH

Petrolly A not unpleasant overtone often found in mature RIESLING

Pfalz (Germany) See RHEINPFALZ

Phylloxera Dastardly louse that wiped out Europe's vines in the 19th century. Foiled by the practice of grafting VINIFERA vines onto American roots. Isolated pockets of pre-PHYLLOXERA vines still exist, eg in Chile and Portugal

Piave (VENETO) Area covering a number of DOCs, including reds made from a Bordeaux-like mix of grapes 82 83 85 86 87 88 89

Piedmont (Italy) North-western region producing many fine and popular wines, including BAROLO, BARBARESCO, OLTREPO PAVESE, ASTI SPUMANTE and DOLCETTO D'ALBA 35 175 415 418 420 422 423 429 430 433 473 499

Piemonte See PIEDMONT

Piesport (MOSEL-SAAR-RUWER) With its GROSSLAGE Michelsberg, infamous for dull wine. Try one of its single vineyards — Gunterslay or Goldtröppchen — for something eminently more drinkable 85 86 87 88 89 90 £-£££

Pineau d'Aunis Red grape grown in the LOIRE valley for red and rosé

Pineau de la Loire The CHENIN BLANC grape

Pineau des Charentes (SW France) White grape juice fortified with cognac — best chilled as an aperitif or with cheese ££-£££ (OD)

Pinot Blanc Not as classy or complex as its PINOT NOIR or CHARDONNAY relations, but fresh and adaptable. Widely grown, at its best in ALSACE (Pinot d'Alsace) and in Italy (as Pinot Bianco). In California, a synonym for MELON DE BOURGOGNE 41 66

Pinot Chardonnay Misleading name for the PINOT BLANC

Pinot Gris White grape of uncertain origins, making full, rather heady, spicy wine. Best in ALSACE (also known as TOKAY D'ALSACE) and Italy (as Pinot Grigio) Pinot Gris Reserve Spéciale 85, Schlumberger (L&W) 54

Pinot Meunier Dark pink-skinned grape that plays an unsung but major role in CHAMPAGNE, where it is the most widely planted variety. In England, it is grown as the Wrotham Pinot or Dusty Miller; Bests in VICTORIA produce a VARIETAL wine from it

Pinot Noir Noble red grape with the unique distinction of being responsible for some of the world's greatest red (BURGUNDY) and sparkling white (CHAMPAGNE) wine. Also grown, with varying degrees of success, in the New World 386 399

Pinotage Red grape, a PINOT NOIR-CINSAULT cross used in South Africa and New Zealand Montana Cabernet Sauvignon/Pinotage (OD)

Pomerol (BORDEAUX) With ST EMILION, the Bordeaux for lovers of the MERLOT grape, which predominates in its rich, soft, plummy wines. Château Pétrus is the big name **78 81 82** 83 85 86 88 89 90 *£££-£££££* Chateau Gaillard (M&S)

Pommard (BURGUNDY) COMMUNE blessed with a higher proportion of old vines, making slow to mature, then solid and complex reds **83 85** 88 89 *£££-£££££* Pommard Clos du Pavillon 86, Bouchard Père et Fils (AB)

Port (Portugal) Fortified, usually red wine made in the upper Douro valley. Comes in several styles; see TAWNY, RUBY, LBV, VINTAGE, CRUSTED and WHITE

Pouilly Fuissé (BURGUNDY)Fine white beloved by the Americans, with consequent vastly inflated prices. Other Mâconnais wines are affordable and often its equal, unless you can stretch to the finest examples 85 86 87 88 89 90 *££-£££££* 73

Pouilly Fumé (LOIRE) Distinguished, elegant SAUVIGNON BLANC with classic gooseberry fruit and 'flinty' overtones 86 87 88 89 *££-£££££* 153

Pourriture noble (France) BOTRYTIS CINEREA or NOBLE ROT

Prädikat (Germany) Short for QUALITATSWEIN MIT PRADIKAT (QMP), the higher quality level for German wines

Precipitation The creation of a harmless deposit, usually of tartrate crystals, in white wine

Premier Cru Principally a BURGUNDY ranking, indicates wines second only to a GRAND CRU

Primeur (France) New wine, eg BEAUJOLAIS Primeur

Propriétaire (-Récoltant) (France) Vineyard owner-manager

Prosecco (VENETO) Dry and sweet sparkling wines, less boisterous than ASTI SPUMANTE and often less fizzy *£-£££* Sainsbury's Prosecco (JS)

Provence (France) Southern region producing a quantity of honest, country wine with a number of minor ACs. Rosé de Provence should be dry and fruity with a hint of peppery spice 364

Puisseguin St Emilion (BORDEAUX) Satellite of ST EMILION 82 83 85 86 88 89 *££-£££££* Ch la Croix de Mouchet 88 (BI) Ch Durand Laplagne 85 (ADN TAN)

Puligny-Montrachet Aristocratic white COTE D'OR COMMUNE that shares the Montrachet vineyard with CHASSAGNE 78 79 81 83 85 86 88 89 *£££££-£££££* Louis Carrillon 88 (M&V)

Putto (Italy) As in CHIANTI PUTTO, wine from a consortium of growers who use the cherub ('putto') as their symbol

Puttonyos (HUNGARY) The measure of sweetness (from 1 to 6) of TOKAY

PX See PEDRO XIMENEZ

QbA (Germany) *Qualitätswein bestimmter Anbaugebiet*: basic quality German wine meeting certain standards from one of the eleven ANBAUGEBIET, eg RHEINHESSEN

QmP (Germany) *Qualitätswein mit Prädikat*: QBA wine with 'special qualities' subject to rigorous testing. The QMP blanket designation is broken into five sweetness rungs, from KABINETT to TROCKENBEERENAUSLESEN plus EISWEIN

Qualitätswein (Germany) Loose 'quality' definition to cover QBA and QMP wines, whose labels will carry more informative identification of their exact status

Quarts de Chaume (LOIRE) Luscious but light sweet wines, uncloying, ageing beautifully, from the COTEAUX DU LAYON 76 83 85 88 89 90 *£££-£££££* Chateau de l'Echarderie 89/90 (YAP)

Quincy (LOIRE) Dry SAUVIGNON, lesser-known and often good value alternative to SANCERRE or POUILLY FUME 86 87 88 89 *££-£££* Denis Jaumier 90 (YAP)

Quinta (Portugal) Vineyard or estate, particularly in port where 'single quinta' wines are much prized 493

Racking The drawing off of wine from its LEES into a clean cask or vat

Rainwater (MADEIRA) Light, dry style of Madeira popular in the US

Rancio Term for the peculiar yet prized oxidised flavour of certain fortified wines, particularly in France and Spain

Rasteau (RHONE) Southern village producing sound, spicy reds with rich berry fruit, and some dessert wine **83 85 86** 88 89 90 *££-£££* 349

RD (CHAMPAGNE) Récemment DEGORGEE — a term invented by Bollinger to describe their delicious vintage Champagne, which has been allowed a longer than usual period on its LEES. Other producers make their own versions but may not call them 'RD' *£££££*

Recioto (Italy) Sweet or dry alcoholic wine made from semi-dried, ripe grapes

Récoltant-manipulant (RM) (CHAMPAGNE) Individual winegrower and blender, identified by mandatory RM number on label

Récolte (France) Vintage, literally 'harvest'

Refosco (FRIULI-VENEZIA GIULIA) Red grape and its DOC wine, dry and full-bodied, benefits from ageing

Régisseur In BORDEAUX, the manager of a CHATEAU and its wine production

Régnié (BURGUNDY) Recently created the tenth BEAUJOLAIS CRU 85 86 87 88 89 ££-£££ Régnié Domaine de Ruyére 1988 Paul Collonge (ROG)

Reichensteiner Hybrid white grape popular in England Nutbourne Manor 89 (CPL)

Reims (CHAMPAGNE) Capital town of the area, base of many GRANDES MARQUES, eg Krug, Roederer

Remuage (CHAMPAGNE) Part of the METHODE CHAMPENOISE, the gradual turning and tilting of bottles so that the yeast deposit collects in the neck ready for DEGORGEMENT

Reserva (Spain) Indicates the wine has been aged for a number of years specific to the DO

Réserve (France) Legally meaningless, as in 'Réserve Personelle', but implying a wine selected and given more age

Residual sugar Tasting term for wines which have retained sugar not converted to alcohol by yeasts during fermentation

Retsina (Greece) Distinctive dry white wine characterised by a piney, resinated flavour

Reuilly (LOIRE) White AC for dry SAUVIGNONS, good value alternatives to Sancerre. Some spicy PINOT rosé 86 87 88 89 ££-£££ Gérard Cordier 90 (YAP)

Rheingau (Germany) Produces the finest German RIESLINGS of the eleven ANBAUGEBIETE, some extremely expensive 83 85 88 89 £-£££££ 192

Rheinhessen (Germany) Largest of the eleven ANBAUGEBIET, producing fine wines but better known for LIEBFRAUMILCH and NIERSTEINER 83 85 88 89 90 £-£££££ 177 183 476

Rheinpfalz (Gemany) Formerly known as the Palatinate, southerly ANBAUGEBIET noted for riper, spicier RIESLING 83 85 88 89 90 £-£££££ 186 199 200 468

Rhine Riesling/Rheinriesling Widely used name for the noble RIESLING grape

Rhône (France) Rich, round, warm, spicy reds from the GRENACHE and SYRAH, mostly underappreciated and hence undervalued. Some highly prized (and rightly so) rich, peachy, nutty wines 83 85 86 88 89 90 £-£££££ 76 77 207 337 342 346 359 363 368 372 373 375

Ribatejo (Portugal) DO area north of Lisbon making much white wine and good, full-bodied reds, especially GARRAFEIRAS 82 83 85 £-£££

Ribera del Duero (Spain) Northern DO region bordering Portugal, source of VINHO VERDE-type whites and newer stylish reds 82 83 85 86 89 ££-£££££ Pesquera (C&B)

Riesling The noble grape producing Germany's finest offerings, ranging from light, floral everyday wines to the delights of the BOTRYTIS-affected sweet wines, which still retain their freshness after several years. Also performs well in ALSACE, California and the BAROSSA/EDEN VALLEY (Australia) See THE WINES section for numerous examples

Riesling Italico See ITALIAN RIESLING

Rioja Alavesa (Spain) Minor subregion of the RIOJA area, with some fine reds 81 82 85 86 87 ££-£££££ 63 74 434 Contino Reserva 85 (ADN)

Rioja Alta (Spain) The best subregion of the RIOJA area 81 82 84 85 86 87 89 ££-£££££ 436 445 447 449 452

Rioja Baja (Spain) Largest subregion of the RIOJA area, producing less fine wines, most of which are blended with wine from the Alta and Alavesa regions 81 82 85 86 87 89

Ripasso (Italy) VALPOLICELLA which, having finished its fermentation, is pumped into fermenting vessels recently vacated by RECIOTO and AMARONE, causing a slight refermentation. This increases the alcohol and body of the wine

Riquewihr (ALSACE) Town and COMMUNE noted for RIESLING Riesling d'Alsace 86 Marcel Deiss (WC BD)

Riserva (Italy) DOC wines aged for a specified number of years

Rivaner The MULLER-THURGAU grape with reference to its RIESLING/SYLVANER parents

Rivesaltes (MIDI) Fortified dessert wine of both colours, the white made from Muscat lighter and more lemony than that of BEAUMES DE VENISE, the red made from GRENACHE almost like liquid Christmas pudding ££-£££ Muscat de Rivesaltes Dom Bresson (ADN) 459

Rolle (MIDI) Variety used to make BELLET

Romania Traditionally making sweet reds and whites, but trying to develop drier styles from classic European varieties £-£££ Sainsbury's Romanian Pinot Noir (JS)

Rosato (Italy) Rosé

Rose d'Anjou (LOIRE) Widely exported, usually dull pink from the CABERNET FRANC. Semi-sweet but getting better

Rosé des Riceys (CHAMPAGNE) Rare and delicious AC still rosé from the PINOT NOIR £££ Bonnet 85 (CDV)

Rosso Conero (Italy) Big DOC red from the MARCHES, from the MONTEPULCIANO and SANGIOVESE grapes with a hint of bitter, herby flavour. Needs five years Umani Ronchi 89 (W)

Roussillon (Côtes du) (MIDI) Sturdy red wines, soft amber-coloured whites and some rosé. Pleasant country wines, but not always worthy of their AC. Côtes du Roussillon Villages is better 86 87 88 89 £-££ 82 225

Rubesco di Torgiano (UMBRIA) Popular red DOC 82 83 85 88 ££-£££££ Torgiano Riserva Monticchio 79 Lungarotti (ADN,WSO)

Ruby Cabernet (California) A cross between CABERNET SAUVIGNON and CARIGNAN producing big, fruity wines which tend to lack subtlety

Ruby (port) Cheapest, basic port; young, blended, sweetly fruity wine 489

Rudesheim (RHEINGAU) Tourist town producing, at their best, rich and powerful RIESLINGS

Rueda (Spain) DO for clean dry whites and a traditional, FLOR growing sherry-type wine 82 84 85 86 £-£££ Marques de Griñon 89 (HAS)

Rufina (TUSCANY) Subregion of the CHIANTI DOC 81 83 85 86 88 ££-£££££ 405

Ruländer German name for the PINOT GRIS grape

Rully (BURGUNDY) COTE CHALONNAISE COMMUNE, the 'poor man's Volnay'. Much white is destined for Crémant de Bourgogne £££-££££ Rully Jaffelin 1988 (OD)

Ruppertsberg (RHEINPFALZ) Top-ranking village with a number of excellent vineyards making vigorous, fruity RIESLING 83 85 88 89 90 Ruppertsberger Geisbohl Riesling Kabinett 85 Burklin-Wolf (L&W)

Russia See USSR

Russian River Valley (California) Cool vineyard area north of SONOMA and west of NAPA

Rust (AUSTRIA) Wine centre of BURGENLAND, famous for Ruster AUSBRUCH, sweet white wine

Rutherglen (Australia) VICTORIA wine area on the MURRAY RIVER noted for rich, MUSCATTY dessert and port-style wines, and for incredibly tough reds £££-£££££ 458 460

Saar (Germany) Tributary of the MOSEL river 83 85 88 89 90 ££-££££

Sablet (RHONE) A named COTES DU RHONE village

Sacramento Valley (California) Another name for the CARNEROS region

St Amour (BURGUNDY) One of the ten BEAUJOLAIS CRUS, tends to be light and delicately fruity 83 85 86 87 88 89 ££-£££ Portenin (ADN)

St Aubin (BURGUNDY) Underrated COTE D'OR VILLAGE for reds and rich, flinty, nutty whites, affordable alternatives to MEURSAULT 81 83 85 86 87 88 89 £££ Roux Pére et Fils 89 (OD)

St Bris (Sauvignon de) (BURGUNDY) Burgundy's only VDQS, an affordable alternative to SANCERRE from the CHABLIS region 86 87 88 89 ££ Sauvignon De St Bris Domaine Du Relais De Poste 89 Luc Sorin (TH WR)

St Chinian (SW France) AC in the COTEAUX DU LANGUEDOC producing mid-weight, good-value wines ££ 210

St Emilion (BORDEAUX) COMMUNE for soft, MERLOT-dominated claret. Its lesser satellite neighbours — LUSSAC, PUISSEGUIN, etc — often prefix the name with theirs 78 79 81 82 83 85 86 88 89 ££-£££££ 290 333

St Estèphe (BORDEAUX) Northern MEDOC COMMUNE, often a shade more rustic than its neighbours, tough when young but very long-lived 78 **79** 81 82 83 85 86 88 89 ££-£££££ Ch Cos d'Estournel 85 (J&B)

St Georges St Emilion (BORDEAUX) Satellite of ST EMILION 78 **79** 81 82 83 85 86 88 89 ££-£££ Ch Macquin-St-George 85 (MWW)

St Joseph (RHONE) Vigorous, fruity reds from the northern Rhône, with the spice of the SYRAH. Generally good value 78 **82 83** 85 88 89 £££-£££££ 368

St Julien (BORDEAUX) Aristocratic MEDOC COMMUNE producing classic rich wines, full of cedar and deep, ripe fruit 78 **79 81 82 83** 85 86 88 89 £££-£££££ 312 332

St Nicolas de Bourgueil (LOIRE) Lightly fruity CABERNET FRANC, needs a warm year to ripen its raspberry fruit 83 85 **86** 87 88 89 ££ J Taluau (HFW)

St Péray (RHONE) AC for full-bodied, still white and METHODE CHAMPENOISE sparkling wine £££

St Pourçain (Central France) The local wine of Vichy, AC for red, white and rose

St Romain (BURGUNDY) High in the hills of the HAUTES COTES DE BEAUNE, a village producing undervalued fine whites and rustic reds 83 85 86 87 88 89 £££ 96

St-Véran (BURGUNDY) Affordable alternative to POUILLY FUISSE, delicious young. Head and shoulders above its MACONNAIS neighbours 83 85 86 88 89 £££-££££ 65 70 71

Sainte Croix-du-Mont (BORDEAUX) Neighbour of SAUTERNES, with comparable though less fine wines 83 85 86 88 89 ££-£££ Château Destours Ste-Croix-Du-Mont 86 (SUM MWW)

Sakar (Mountain) (BULGARIA) Source of much of the best CABERNET SAUVIGNON 81 84 85 ££ Sakar Mountain Cabernet, Vinimpex (MWW)

Samos (Greece) Aegean island producing sweet, fragrant, golden MUSCAT once called 'the wine of the Gods' ££-£££ 456

San Luis Obispo Californian region gaining a reputation for Chardonnay and Pinot Noir 111

Sancerre (LOIRE) Much exploited AC, but at its best the epitome of elegant, steely dry SAUVIGNON. Quaffable pale reds and rosés from the PINOT NOIR 87 88 89 ££-£££££ 152

Sangiovese The red grape of CHIANTI, used elsewhere but not to such great effect 401 403 405 409 411 416

Sanlúcar de Barrameda (Spain) Town neighbouring JEREZ, centre of production for MANZANILLA sherry

Santa Barbara Increasingly succesful southern-Californian cool-climate region for Pinot Noir and Chardonnay 116

Santenay (BURGUNDY) Pretty white CHARDONNAYS and good, though occasion-ally rather clumsy, reds from the southern tip of the COTE D'OR 82 83 85 86 £££-£££££ Vincent Girardin (HVW)

Sardinia (Italy) Good, hearty, powerful reds, robust whites and a number of interesting DOC fortified wines 129

Saumur (LOIRE) White and rosé METHODE CHAMPENOISE sparklers which are reliably clean and appley, fresh fruity whites plus reds and pinks made from CABERNET FRANC ££-£££££ 128 261

Saumur Champigny (LOIRE) Crisp, refreshing CABERNET FRANC red; like BEAUJOLAIS, serve slightly chilled 85 86 88 89 90 ££-£££ Clos Rougeard 86 (HFW)

Sauternes (BORDEAUX) Nobly rich, honeyed dessert wines, SAUVIGNON and SEMILLON blends, properly BOTRYTIS-affected. Worth splashing out on 83 86 88 89 £££-£££££ 463 469 474 475

Sauvignon (Sauvignon Blanc) White grape making gooseberry-fruity wine with a steely backbone, classically elegant in fine LOIRE but equally successful in the New World, particularly New Zealand ££-£££££ 56 57 58 78 91

Savagnin Jura variety used for VIN JAUNE and blended with CHARDONNAY for ARBOIS. Also, confusingly, the Swiss name for the GEWURZTRAMINER

Savennières (LOIRE) Fine, rarely seen, vigorous and characterful whites, very long-lived. Coulée de Serrant and La Roche aux Moines are the top names

82 83 84 85 86 88 89 £££-££££ La Roche Aux Moines 86 (LV)

Savigny-lès-Beaune (BURGUNDY) Rarely seen whites and delicious plummy/ raspberry reds, at their best can compare with neighbouring BEAUNE **82 83 85** 86 87 88 89 £££-£££££ Vincent Girardin (HVW)

Savoie (E France) Mountainous region best known for crisp, floral whites such as APREMONT, Seyssel and Crépy

Scharzhofberg (MOSEL-SAAR-RUWER) Top-class Saar vineyard, producing quintessential RIESLING £££-£££££ Scharzhofberger Riesling Auslese Cask 14 1987 Egon Muller (L&W)

Schaumwein (Germany) Low-priced sparkling wine

Scheurebe White grape, RIESLING /SYLVANER cross, grown in Germany and in England, where it imparts a grapefruity tang 476

Schloss (Germany) Literally 'castle', often (as in CHATEAU) designating a vineyard or estate

Schlossbockelheim (NAHE) Village giving its name to a large Nahe BEREICH, producing elegant, balanced Riesling. Best vineyard: Kupfergrube ££-£££ Schlossbockelheimer Kupfergrube Riesling QbA 83/85 (Staatliche Weinbaudomanen) (RAE)

Schluck (AUSTRIA) Generic term for a light, blended white wine from the WACHAU

Sciacarella (CORSICA) Corsican red grape variety, making smooth, aromatic, RHONE-style wine 85 86 Domaine Peraldi, Clos du Cardinale (BD,WC)

Second label (BORDEAUX) Wines produced principally by Bordeaux CHATEAUX which, because of the youth of the vines or a lessening of quality in a particular year, are sold under a 'second' name 301 309

Sec/secco/seco (France/Italy/Spain) Dry

Sekt (Germany) Not dry, but sparkling wine. Only the prefix 'DEUTSCHER' guarantees German origin

Sélection de Grains Nobles (ALSACE) Equivalent to German BEERENAUSLESEN: rich, sweet BOTRYTISED wine from selected grapes £££££ 173

Sémillon White grape blended with SAUVIGNON in BORDEAUX to give fullness in both dry and sweet wines, notably SAUTERNES and vinified separately in the Australia to produce savoury, peachy-buttery wine

Sercial Grape used for MADEIRA, making the driest and some say the finest wines

Servir frais (France) Serve chilled

Setúbal See MOSCATEL DE SETUBAL

Sèvre-et-Maine (Muscadet de) (LOIRE) Demarcated area producing a cut above plain Muscadet. (Actually, it is worth noting that this 'higher quality' region produces the vast majority of each Muscadet harvest) ££ 135

Seyval blanc Hybrid grape, a cross between French and American vines, successful in eastern US and England Thames Valley Vineyard 88 (HFW)

Shiraz The SYRAH grape in Australia

Sicily (Italy) Best known for MARSALA, but produces a variety of unusual fortified wines, also much sturdy 'southern' table wine

Sin crianza (Spain) Not aged in wood

Skin contact The longer the skins are left in with the juice after the grapes have been crushed, the greater the TANNINS and the deeper the colour

Soave (VENETO) Irredeemably dull white wine; the best one can hope for is that it is fresh and clean. Soave CLASSICO is better, single vineyard versions are best. Sweet RECIOTO di Soave is delicious 86 87 88 89 £-£££££ 55 69

Solera SHERRY-ageing system, a series of butts containing wine of ascending age, the older wine being continually 'refreshed' by the younger

Somlo (HUNGARY) Ancient wine district, now source of top-class whites. See FURMINT

Sonoma Valley (California) Region containing some of the state's top wineries, subdivided into the Sonoma, Alexander and RUSSIAN RIVER Valleys and Dry Creek

Spanna (Italy) In PIEDMONT, the NEBBIOLO grape, main ingredient of BAROLO Spanna del Piemonte 87 A Vallana (GHW)

Spätburgunder The PINOT NOIR in Germany Spätburgunder 86 Lingenfelder (WCE)

Spätlese (Germany) Second step in the QmP scale, late-harvested grapes making wine a notch drier than AUSLESE 198 199

Spritz Slight sparkle or fizz. Also PETILLANCE

Spritzig (Germany) Lightly sparkling

Spumante (Italy) Sparkling

Stalky or stemmy Flavour of the stem rather than of the juice

Steely Refers to young wine with evident acidity. A compliment when paid to CHABLIS and dry SAUVIGNONS

Steen Grape grown widely in South Africa, thought to be the CHENIN BLANC of the LOIRE

Structure All the component flavours fit well together. A young wine with structure should age well

Suhindol (BULGARIA) Source of good reds, particularly CABERNET SAUVIGNON **84 85** £-££

Sulfites (America) American term now featuring as a labelling requirement alerting those suffering from an (extremely rare) allergy to the presence of sulphur compounds

Supérieur (BORDEAUX) Technically meaningless in terms of discernible quality, but denotes wine with 1-2 per cent more alcohol

Superiore (Italy) As in France, indicates a degree or two more alcohol but not necessarily finer wine

Sur lie 'On its LEES', most commonly seen of MUSCADET, one of the few wines that benefits from ageing with its own dead YEASTS 131 135

Süssreserve (Germany) Unfermented grape juice used to bolster sweetness and fruitiness in German and ENGLISH wines, in a process known as back-blending

Swan River (W Australia) Well-established but not generally too exciting vineyard area. (Best known wines come from Houghton and Evans and Tate)

Switzerland Produces, in general, enjoyable but expensive light, floral wines for drinking when young Chicla Trevelin 1987 (TAN)

Sylvaner/Silvaner White grape, originally from Austria but adopted by other European areas, particularly ALSACE, as a prolific yielder of young, crisp, quaffable wine Boetzinger Lasenberg 88 E B R Zimmerlin (WSC)

Syrah The red RHONE grape, an exotic mix of ripe fruit and spicy, smokey, gamey, leathery flavours. Skilfully adopted by Australia where it is called SHIRAZ or HERMITAGE. See THE WINES section for numerous examples

Tafelwein (Germany) Table wine. Only the prefix 'DEUSTCHER' guarantees German origin

Tannat Rustic French grape variety used in CAHORS

Tannin Astringent component of red wine which comes from the skins, pips and stalks and helps the wine to age

Tarry Red wines from hot countries often have an aroma and flavour reminiscent of tar. The SYRAH grape in particular exhibits this characteristic

Tartrates Harmless white crystals that are often deposited by white wines in the bottle

Tasmania (Australia) Up-and-coming area with great potential which is producing more than adequate CHARDONNAY, PINOT NOIR and CABERNET SAUVIGNON. (Look out for Heemskerk, Moorilla, Piper's Brook) 110

Tastevin The silver BURGUNDY tasting cup. Much adopted as an insignia by vinous brotherhoods (confréries) and much used as ashtrays by wine buffs. The Chevaliers de Tastevin organise an annual tasting of Burgundies; successful wines may bear an ugly *Tastevinage* label

Taurasi (CAMPANIA) Big red from the AGLIANICO grape, needs years to soften. Develops a characteristic cherryish taste 83 85 88 ££-£££ Antonio Masteroberadino 85 (V&C)

Tavel (RHONE) Spicy, peppery, characterful dry rosé, usually (wrongly) said to age well 88 89 90 ££ 207

Tawny (port) Either ruby port that has been barrel-matured to mellow and fade or a cheap blend of RUBY and WHITE PORT. Examples with an indication of their age (eg 10-year-old) are the real thing 486 487 494

Tempranillo (Spain) The red grape of RIOJA, whose sturdy fruit is a match for the vanilla/oak flavours of barrel-ageing 436 442 445 447 449 451 452

Tenuta (Italy) Estate or vineyard

Terlano/Terlaner (TRENTINO-ALTO-Adige) Northern Italian village/its wines, usually fresh and crisp and carrying the name of their grape variety **87 88 89** £-££££ Cabernet Riserva 85 Lageder (WCE)

Teroldego (TRENTINO-ALTO-ADIGE) Dry reds, quite full-bodied with lean, slightly bitter berry flavours **85 86 87 88** £-££ Teroldego Rotaliano Gaierhof 88 (W V&C)

Tête de Cuvée (France) A producer's finest wine, or the one he is proudest of

Thouarsais (Vin de) (LOIRE) VDQS for a soft, light red from the CABERNET FRANC and whites from the CHENIN BLANC ££ Vin de Thouarsais Rouge 1989, M Gigon (YAP)

Tinta Negra Mole Versatile and widely used MADEIRA grape, said to be a distant cousin of the PINOT NOIR

Tocai White grape and its wines of northern Italy, of Venetian origin **87 88 89** £-££££ Friulano 87 Schiopetto (WCE)

Tokay (HUNGARY) Legendary dessert wine made only from NOBLE ROT-affected grapes **76 79 81** £££-£££££ Tokaji Aszu 5 putts (OD)

Tokay d'Alsace See PINOT GRIS

Toro (Spain) Region on the Portuguese border lying on the DOURO producing up-and-coming wines £-££ Sainsbury's Toro 87 (JS)

Toscana See TUSCANY

Touraine (LOIRE) Area encompassing the ACs CHINON, VOUVRAY and BOURGUEIL, also an increasing source of quaffable VARIETAL wines — SAUVIGNON, GAMAY DE TOURAINE etc 41 56 138 139 274

Touriga (Nacional) Red port grape, also seen in the New World

Traminer Alternative name for the GEWÜRZTRAMINER grape, particularly in Italy and Australia

Trebbiano Much appreciated and widely planted white grape in Italy, though less vaunted in France where it is called the UGNI BLANC Trebbiano d'Abruzzo 1989 (WCE)

Trentino-Alto Adige (Italy) Northern wine region variously known as the Italian Tyrol or Süd Tirol. Cool, fresh VARIETAL wines, non-Italian in style and often with Germanic labels 86 87 88 89 £-££££ 21 407 428

Tricastin (Coteaux du) (RHONE) Southern Rhône APPELLATION, emerging as a source of good value, soft, peppery/blackcurrant reds

Trittenheim (MOSEL-SAAR-RUWER) Village whose vineyards are said to have been the first in Germany planted with RIESLING, making soft, honeyed wine 76 79 83 85 86 88 89 ££-££££ 187

Trocken (Germany) Dry

Trockenbeerenauslese (Germany) Fifth rung of the QMP ladder, wine from selected dried grapes, with concentrated sugar and usually BOTRYTIS-affected. Only made in the best years, rare and expensive 476

Trollinger The German name for the Black Hamburg grape, used in Wurttemburg to make light red wines

Tunisia Best known for dessert MUSCAT wines

Turkey Producer of big, red, often oxidised table wine which is rarely seen in the UK

Tursan (Vin de) (SW France) MADIRAN VDQS whose big, country reds are most likely to be seen in the UK

Tuscany (Italy) Major wine region, the famous home of CHIANTI and some of the more intractable reds, BRUNELLO DI MONTALCINO and VINO NOBILE DI MONTEPULCIANO 401 403 405 409 411 416 419 424 425 426 431 432

Ugni Blanc Undistinguished white grape of southern France — comes into its own as the TREBBIANO in Italy, particularly in TUSCANY

Ull de Llebre (Spain) Literally 'hare's eye' — a pink wine from the TEMPRANILLO in Catalonia

Ullage Space between surface of wine and top of cask or, in bottle, cork. The wider the gap, the greater the danger of OXIDATION

Umbria (Italy) Central wine region, best known for white ORVIETO 86 87 88 89 ££-££££ Orvieto Classico Campo Grande 88 Antinori (widely available)

USSR A vast wine producer, exporting very little to the UK except heavy Crimean reds and sweet red and white 'Champanski'; horrible or amusing depending on your point of view

Utiel-Requeña (LOIRE) DO of VALENCIA, producing heavy reds widely used for blending and some of Spain's best rosé

Vacanzay (LOIRE) Near CHEVERNY, making comparable whites, light, clean and rather sharp

Vacqueyras (RHONE) COTES DU RHONE VILLAGE and COMMUNE producing fine, full-bodied, peppery reds 85 86 87 88 89 ££-£££ Paul Jaboulet 89 (OD)

Valais (SWITZERLAND) Vineyard area on the upper RHONE, making good FENDANT (CHASSELAS) and some reds Fendant Pierrafeu 87

Valdepeñas (Spain) LA MANCHA DO striving to refine its rather hefty, alcoholic reds and whites 78 81 82 83 84 86 87 88 £-££ 437

Valencia (Spain) Produces quite alcoholic red wines and also MOSCATEL DE VALENCIA. Can your fridge afford not to have a bottle? 454 455

Valle d'Aosta (Italy) Small wine-producing area between PIEDMONT and the French/Swiss border

Valpolicella (VENETO) Light red very similar in composition to BARDOLINO; should be nuttily pleasant but more often, in UK, is rather dull. It really is worth paying more for a bottle of AMARONE or RECIOTO 78 79 81 83 85 86 88 £-£££££ 402 409 410 412 427

Valréas (RHONE) Peppery and inexpensive red AOC 83 85 86 88 89 ££

Valtellina (LOMBARDY) Red DOC from the NEBBIOLO grape, of variable quality but improves with age

Varietal A wine made from and named after a single grape variety, eg California CHARDONNAY, GAMAY DE TOURAINE

Vaucluse (RHONE) COTES DU RHONE region producing much rosé and good reds from certain villages, eg VACQUEYRAS

VDQS (France) Vin Délimité de Qualité Supérieur; official designation for wines better than VIN DE PAYS but not fine enough for an AC. Source of much good value everyday drinking

Vecchio (Italy) Old

Vegetal Often used of SAUVIGNON BLANC and CABERNET FRANC, like 'grassy'. Frequently complimentary - though rarely in California or Australia.

Velho/velhas (Portugal) Old, as of red wine

Veltliner See GRÜNER VELTLINER

Vendange (France) Harvest or vintage

Vendange Tardive (France) Particularly in ALSACE, wine from late harvested grapes, usually fairly sweet 472

Vendemmia (Italy) Harvest or vintage

Vendimia (Spain) Harvest or vintage

Venegazzú (VENETO) Remarkably good VINO DA TAVOLA from the CABERNET SAUVIGNON, almost claret-like. Needs five years Venegazzú della Casa 1984 Conte Loredan (VW TAN UBC)

Veneto (Italy) North-eastern wine region, the home of SOAVE, VALPOLICELLA and BARDOLINO 55 400 402 404 410 412 427

Ventoux (Côtes du) (RHONE) Improving source of everyday, country reds 86 87 88 89 £-££ Côtes du Ventoux, Jaboulet Ainé 1989 (OD)

Verdelho White grape used for MADEIRA and WHITE PORT 89 492

Verdicchio (Italy) White grape seen as a number of DOCs in its own right; in UMBRIA, a major component of ORVIETO 86 87 88 89 £-££ Verdicchio Ca'Sal di Serra 88 Umani Ronchi (VW TAN FUL)

Verduzzo (FRIULI-VENEZIA GIULIA) White grape making a dry and a fine AMABILE style wine in the COLLI ORIENTALI

Vermentino (LIGURIA) The dry white wine of the Adriatic. Best drunk in situ with seafood

Vernaccia White grape making the Tuscan DOC Vernaccia di San Gimignano and Sardinian Vernaccia di Oristano, at best with a distinctive, characterful flavour 87 88 89 ££-££££ Vernaccia di San Gimignano 'Terre di Tufo' 89, Teruzzi e Puthod (WCE)

Victoria (Australia) Huge variety of wines from the liqueur MUSCATS of RUTHERGLEN to the peppery SHIRAZES of Bendigo and the elegant CHARDONNAYS of the YARRA VALLEY. See these, plus MURRAY RIVER, MORNINGTON PENINSULA, GOULBURN VALLEY, GEELONG and PYRENEES 63 109 151

297 309 327 365 367 379

VIDE (Italy) A marketing syndicate formed by enterprising producers for their finer estate wines

Vieilles Vignes (France) Wine from a producer's oldest, best vines 137

Vigneto (Italy) Vineyard

Vignoble (France) Vineyard; vineyard area

Villages (France) The suffix *'villages'* after e.g. Côtes du Rhône or Mâcon generally indicates a slightly superior wine (in the way that Classico does in Italy)

Vin de Corse Corsican wine

Vin de garde (France)Wine to keep

Vin de paille (Jura) Speciality of the region; rich and sweet golden wine from grapes laid out and dried on straw mats

Vin de pays (France) Lowest/broadest geographical designation, simple country wines with certain regional characteristics

Vin de table (France) Table wine from no particular area

Vin doux naturel (France) Fortified dessert wines, best known as the sweet, liquorous MUSCATS of the south, eg BEAUMES DE VENISE

Vin gris (France) Chiefly from ALSACE and the JURA, pale rosé from red grapes pressed before, not after, fermentation

Vin jaune (JURA) A speciality of ARBOIS, golden yellow, slightly oxidised wine, like a dry SHERRY

Vin santo (Italy) Powerful white dessert wine from grapes dried on the vine and after picking, especially in TUSCANY. Takes its name from a similar style from the Greek island of Santorini 80 81 82 84 £££££ Capezzana 84 Avignonesi 80 (WCE)

Vinho Verde (Portugal) Young, literally 'green' wine, confusingly, red or pale white often tinged with green. At best delicious, refreshing, slightly fizzy 89 90 £-££ 160

Vinifera Properly *Vitis vinifera*, the species name for all European vines

Vino de pasto (Italy) Table wine

Vino da tavola (Italy) Table wine, but the DOC quality designation net is so riddled with holes that many superb wines slip through with merely this modest APPELLATION

Vino Nobile di Montepulciano (TUSCANY) CHIANTI in long trousers; truly noble, made from the same grapes, ages superbly to produce a traditional full red 80 82 83 85 86 88 89 £££-££££ Vino Nobile Fattoria del Cerro 85 (WE MM EBA WGA)

Vino novello (Italy) New wine from this year's harvest, equivalent to French NOUVEAU

Vintage (port) Only produced in 'declared' years, the best quality, aged in wood then in bottle for many years. Must be decanted 490 493 495

Vintage Champagne Awine from a single, good 'declared' year 17 24

Vintage character (port) Inexpensive alternative to vintage, a blend of more than one year's wines. Pleasant enough £££-££££ 484 488

Viognier The white grape of the finest RHONE wines (eg Condrieu) making richly nutty, peaches-and-cream wine 76

Viticulteur (-Propriétaire) (France) Vine grower/vineyard owner

Viura (Spain) White grape of the RIOJA region

Vivarais (Côtes du) (PROVENCE) Light southern reds, a great deal of fruity rosé and occasional fragrant, light whites

Volnay (BURGUNDY) Village producing reds of such delicacy and complexity that tasters wax lyrical 78 80 82 83 85 86 87 88 89 ££££-£££££ 396

Vosne Romanée (BURGUNDY) Buy only the finest when you can afford it from the village which numbers Romanée-Conti among its many grand names 78 80 82 83 85 86 87 88 89 ££££ 395 397

Vougeot (BURGUNDY) COTE DE NUITS COMMUNE comprising the famous GRAND CRU Clos de Vougeot and a great number of growers of varying skill 78 80 82 83 85 87 88 89 £££££-£££££ Clos Vougeot Grand Cru 82 Chateau Latour (HV OBC)

Vouvray (LOIRE) White wines from the CHENIN BLANC, from clean, dry whites and refreshing sparklers to astonishingly long-lived, sweet wines with massive acidity 69 71 75 76 83 85 88 89 90 ££-£££££ 41 144 156 411

Wachau (AUSTRIA) Major wine region, producing some superlative RIESLING from steep, terraced vineyards

Wachenheim (RHEINPFALZ) Full, rich, unctuous RIESLING in all but the best years from this superior MITTELHAARDT village **75 76 79 83 85** 86 88 89 ££-£££££ Wachenheimer Gerumpel Riesling Eiswein 85, Burklin Wolf (ADN)

Walschriesling/Welschriesling The ITALIAN RIESLING or OLASZ RIZLING, unrelated to RHINE RIESLING, but widely cultivated in Central Europe

Washington State US region to watch for its RIESLING and MERLOT 324

Wehlen (MOSEL-SAAR-RUWER) MITTELMOSEL village making fresh, sweet, honeyed wines; look for the Sonnenuhr vineyard **75 76 79 83 85 86** 88 89 ££-£££££

Weingut (Germany) Wine estate

Weinkellerei (Germany) Cellar or winery

Weissburgunder The PINOT BLANC in Germany and Austria 41 66

White port (Portugal) Made from white grapes, an increasingly popular dry or semi-dry aperitif , though it's hard to say why. Apitiv (OD)

Wiltingen (MOSEL-SAAR-RUWER) Distinguished Saar village, making elegant, slaty wines. Well-known for the Scharzhofberg vineyard **75 76 79 83 85** 86 88 89 ££-£££ Wiltinger Schwarzberg Riesling Kabinett 88 Zentralkellerei (L&W)

Winkel (RHEINGAU) Village with an established reputation for complex, delicious wine, housing the famous Schloss Vollrads estate **75 76 79 83 85** 86 88 89 ££-£££££ Winkeler HasensprungRiesling Kabinett 1985 Von Brentano (L&W)

Wintrich (MOSEL-SAAR-RUWER) MITTELMOSEL village neighbouring PIESPORT, most often seen in UK coupled with Kurfurstlay GROSSLAGE

Winzerverein/Winzergenossenschaft (Germany) Cooperative

Wurttemburg (Germany) ANBAUGEBIET surrounding the Neckar region, producing more red than any other. Little seen in the UK

Yarra Valley (Australia) Revived historic wine district of VICTORIA, repopulated by small, adventurous, 'boutique' wineries using mostly noble varieties **82 84 86** 88 ££££-£££££ 109 308 327

Yeasts Naturally present in the 'bloom' on grapes, their function is to convert sugar to alcohol, or, in the case of sparkling wines, to create carbon dioxide. Some wines, eg CHAMPAGNE and MUSCADET — benefit from being aged in contact with their yeasts — or 'SUR LIE'

Yonne (BURGUNDY) Wine department, home of CHABLIS 74 75

Yugoslavia Established suppliers of mostly very average wines, white and fast-improving red, almost all made in giant cooperatives

Zell (MOSEL-SAAR-RUWER) BEREICH of lower Mosel and village, making pleasant, flowery RIESLING. Famous for the Schwarze Katz (black cat) GROSSLAGE **76 79 83 85 86** 88 89 90 ££ - ££££

Zentralkellerei (Germany) Massive, central cellars for groups of cooperatives in six of the ANBAUGEBIET — the MOSEL-SAAR-RUWER is Europe's largest

Zinfandel (California) Versatile red grape producing everything from dark, jammy, leathery reds to pale pink, spicy 'blush' wines. Also grown by Cape Mentelle in MARGARET RIVER, Australia ££-£££££ 201 341 362 374

WINE WITH FOOD

The first rule is...there are no rules. But we hope that we have provided suggestions, ideas and, above all, starting points for further experimentation in our recommendations for food and wine pairings throughout the *Guide's* pages. Below, we describe the food styles each letter refers to and, having consulted wine writers, chefs and 'foodies' alike, recommend not only the obvious perfect matchings but some unexpected successes too — just like those happy marriages that everybody said would never work. We also outline some of the more notorious pitfalls; though here, again, we would not wish to preach; one man's disastrous combination can be, like a peanut butter and jelly sandwich, another's all-time treat.

a Smoked fish

b Smoked meat

There are some wines which go equally well with smoked meats and fish — oaky whites and sherries, particularly finos, for example.With fish, a common mistake is to choose a light, lemony wine, thinking that it, like a wedge of lemon, will complement the dish. Head instead for a wine to match the smoky taste and oily texture — an oaky fat Chardonnay can fit the bill. Some of these also go well with smoked meats, but you might find a light red or a warm, spicy rosé equally appropriate.

c Light starters

All the starters designed to clean and brace one's palate — dressed salads, anything with vinaigrette or citrus fruit — will render any wine unpalatable. For other dishes, one good idea is to try and make your pre-prandial glass of fizz or sherry last through to the main course and wine; otherwise, keep the strength of flavours in food and wine running in parallel — the subtle flavours of, for example, a vegetable terrine are easily overpowered.

d Egg dishes

The slightest trace of 'egginess' in a fatter, fuller-bodied white wine will be horribly enhanced if drunk with eggs themselves. They need something absolutely clean and crisp, like a good Sauvignon, a Muscadet or even an English wine. Though it sounds unappealing, light reds are good with eggs too — a lightweight Burgundy or a northern Italian, perhaps.

e White meat without sauce

By which we mean simply roast or grilled chicken, pork or veal, for which there is enormous choice. For duck or goose, choose a fatter, weightier white, a spicier red or, for duck without a fruity sauce, provide the missing ingredient with the ripest, fruitiest wine you can find.

f   Fish without sauce

The fishiness of plainly cooked fish is one determining factor — again, match the degree of flavour in fish and wine. Delicate fish need something like a light Chardonnay or a good Soave — nothing with overpowering acidity— while for oily types like sardines you need the oral equivalent of a finger bowl — Muscadet or Vinho Verde.

g   White meat or fish in a creamy sauce

Poached salmon in a cream sauce is so nice that it deserves to win — pick a softish wine like an unoaked Chardonnay or a good Italian white. Something less refined like a chicken can be given a worthier opponent with firmer acidity; a fresh, gooseberryish Sauvignon or a dry Vouvray .

h   Shellfish

Steely whites like Sancerre and Chablis are the classic choice for oysters (things are usually the classic choice for a good reason); richer shellfish can take on more benevolent styles. Anything with garlic, butter or aioli (or indeed all three) will fight to the death with most wines— take them by surprise with a fino sherry or retsina.

i   White meat or fish in a Provençale-type sauce

For these stronger, tangier sauces try a white wine with strong acidity and freshness. Alternatively, a well-structured, 'definite' red with strong fruit and some tannin would create a happy marriage.

j   Red meat

Plain roast lamb or beef deserves something elegantly spiffing. For cheaper cuts, particularly when casseroled, more rustic reds can be brought into play. Recipes from a particular region, say of France and Italy, usually (rather obviously) go well with that region's wines.

k   Game

Lighter game needs a fruity, not too woody red — a Merlot-based Bordeaux or a cru Beaujolais. Stronger meat — hung game and venison — needs stronger wine; big Italian and Portuguese reds, Rhônes, Zinfandels and Shirazes.

l   Spicy food

Gewürztraminer is the grape for Chinese food, but demi-sec Loire-styles can be good - a sweeter Chenin Blanc, or a really ripe Sauvignon. For curries, we'd recommend something ice-cold, flavourless and sparkling — lager.

m   Cheese

An exciting area, this, for vinous and fromagical research. At the end of your meal, you will (possibly) have several half-empty bottles and several different cheeses. We have enjoyed matching English wines with English cheeses, creamy French cheeses with red Burgundies and extremely smelly offerings with Sauternes, but you are limited only by your imagination.

n   Pudding

If it's stodgy and floury, you could drink Sauternes or some of the stickier Germans, but if you want a real treat, try a Madeira or a Rutherglen Muscat. If it's creamy, you have more of a problem. Try sweet wines made from Chenin Blanc or Sémillon, or a good quality sparkling wine or Champagne.

o   Fresh fruit and fruit puddings

Fresh fruit deserves a fresh fruity wine such as a Muscat (but not the Australian fortified ones) or German Riesling of Spätlese quality. With fruit puddings, try slightly sweeter Rieslings from Germany or the New World.

p   Chocolate

Chocolate *and* wine? Isn't that just a bit too hedonistic? Hardly any combinations seem to work. Brown Brothers Orange Muscat and Flora stands up well (just think of chocolate oranges), as do the fortified Muscats, but any wine of a subtle nature will suffer.

q   Non-food wines

Just as you don't have to drink wine with every meal, you don't have to eat with every bottle you uncork. How about a warming little Crozes-Hermitage on a cold winter's evening, or a big, beefy Californian Chardonnay (but hold the oak) while staying up to watch the Superbowl? Sounds good. There are also the more traditional non-food wines like German semi-sweeties — and then there is Champagne, which you can drink on any day with a 'd' in.

r   Party wines

I suppose these fit into three categories, the wines which you serve at parties, the wines you take to parties and the wines you bring back from parties. If you have the sort of parties where people actually notice what they're drinking, I feel sorry for you. There are many wines in this book which are not only fun but great value for money; see our list on p.52.

s   Special occasions

You've won the pools, the cat has had kittens, Auntie Gladys has left you her set of porcelain thimbles or you've just caught a repeat of the third episode of *Twin Peaks* . Who cares what you drink, it's all going to taste good.

THE WINES

Sparkling Wine

Readers of last year's Guide will recall our warnings about imminent price rises which would push Champagne off a great many recession-hit tables. Well, the cost of a bottle of 'Big Name' fizz *did* shoot up into the stratosphere, and most of us very sensibly stopped buying it. Gravity and market forces are already beginning to react and we'd predict that prices next year will be lower than they are today. In the meantime, seek out the examples we have recommended, because they really do represent value for money - or try some of the brilliant alternative sparklers, many of which taste better than some Champagne - irrespective of their price.

1   **DRYADES SPARKLING BLANC DE BLANCS,** South West (F)

£4.89	☛ VW	⦿ o, r

Fresh, clean and full of the flavours of melons and grapes.

2   **DIANE DE POITIERS SPARKLING CHARDONNAY, LA CAVE DU HAUT POITOU,** Loire (F)

£6.80	☛ THP ADN RAV HEM HOT	⦿ c, o, q

Characterful Chardonnay which smells 'of celery and appley fruit salad' and tastes light, clean, and full of lemony fruit.

3   **LINDAUER, MONTANA** (NZ)

£7.10	☛ TH WR TO NZC VW CWW U TMW POR OD SWB JFR HVW H EVI CPW BNK BH WRB FWC A TP AF BWS DBY PTR MC BTH ADN W JCK
	⦿ c, o, q, r

Joint Sparkling Wine of the Year

Great, affordable New Zealand sparkling wine, with 'an enticing smell of soft summer garden flowers.' Brilliant for weddings.

4   **CHEVALIER DE MONCONTOUR VOUVRAY MOUSSEUX** 1987 Loire (F)

£7.20	☛ TO JN	⦿ c, o

Light, fresh, slightly sweet appley-peachy wine, balanced by a lemony tang and good, yeasty-biscuity richness.

5   **CUVEE NAPA BLANC DE NOIR, DOMAINE MUMM,** Napa Valley (Cal)

£7.99	☛ OD	⦿ q, r, s

Joint Sparkling Wine of the Year

Unashamedly, unblushingly, Californian (in Champagne, no one makes wine this pale a pink), this is quintessential raspberryish Pinot Noir. Satisfyingly rich, and great value. Why can't Mumm make wine of this quality and price - in France?

6   **TALTARNI BRUT TACHE,** Pyrenees (Aus)

£8.20	☛ OD TAN CDV H&H BEN AUC RD DAL CIW WOC
	⦿ c, o, q

Literally 'stained' - taché - pale pink, this is serious Australian fizz made in a cool region by the son of the former winemaker of Château Lafite. Rich, very plummy fruit, impeccably rounded out by nutty yeast.

7   **MAISON DEUTZ SPARKLING,** Napa Valley (Cal)

£9.99	☛ OD HAR SEL	⦿ c, n, o

Made by Deutz Champagne (see wine No 11), this has good, clean flavour and 'stylish, softly sweet fruit'.

8 SEPPELT'S GREAT WESTERN SHOW SPARKLING SHIRAZ 1985 (Aus)

| £9.99 | ☛ OD AUC | 🍴 b, j, k, l, r |

Called 'Sparkling Burgundy' in Australia, it's brilliant for barbecues. It has a bit of liquorice, a hint of flowers, and bags of ripe Shiraz fruit.

9 BRUT SAUVAGE CUVEE JACQUES ROUSSELL, P-B TERRIER-RABIDE, Coteaux de St Bernard (Sw)

| £9.99 | ☛ FWC | 🍴 a, r, m, l, e, g |

A wine 'with real bite' was Robert Yapp's dogged comment on this unusual wine, made from a blend of the red German Rotweiler and the French (Alsacien) Mordu de Dalmatie grape varieties.

10 SALINGER METHODE CHAMPENOISE, SEPPELT 1988/9 (Aus)

| £10.99 | ☛ OD AUC AMW | 🍴 n, o, q, s |

Joint Sparkling Wine of the Year

A brilliantly made, impeccably packaged pair of wines from Australia's top fizz-makers. The 1988 is richer, fuller-bodied and more emphatically Aussie in style, while the 1989 is distinctly European, with gently foaming bubbles and fresh, delicate grapefruit and banana flavours.

11 DEUTZ MARLBOROUGH CUVEE (NZ)

| £10.99 | ☛ VW TO ADN NZC TMW OD SK H CPW AB AF FWC HAS BWS |
| | 🍴 c, n, o, q |

This New Zealand South Island venture by Deutz Champagne has soft bubbles and smells of bananas, pears, lychees and fresh grapes, with just enough yeasty character to remind you of Champagne.

12 SCHARFFENBERGER BLANC DE BLANCS 1987 Mendocino (Cal)

| £12.46 | ☛ CWW MAW | 🍴 c, o, q |

The US subsidiary of Lanson/Pommery Champagne produces this nutty wine, with the tang of limes, gooseberries and pineapples.

13 HAMM CHAMPAGNE BRUT RESERVE PREMIER CRU (F)

| £12.95 | ☛ BU | 🍴 a, c, q |

Very bubbly, soft, young Champagne, with plenty of fresh appley, flowery, herby flavours and a delicious creamy, honeyed finish.

14 DEHOURS CHAMPAGNE (F)

| £12.99 | ☛ TO OD SC BNK CWI DBY | 🍴 a, c, q |

Toasty and smoky, this wine has the characteristic Champagne smell of newly baked bread. Loads of good, soft, ripe fruit flavour.

15 CARR TAYLOR VINTAGE BRUT 1985 East Sussex (UK)

| £14.50 | ☛ GEW | 🍴 a, c, o, q, s |

'Multifaceted' English méthode champenoise, with a blend of spicy kiwi fruit and pineapples and just enough creaminess.

16 ST MICHAEL CHAMPAGNE BLANC DE BLANCS, UNION CHAMPAGNE AVIZE (F)

| £14.99 | ☛ M&S | 🍴 c, q |

Good, strongly flavoured, ripe fizz with a fine thread of bubbles. 'Rich, creamy, with fresh, appley acidity'.

17 VICTORIA WINE VINTAGE CHAMPAGNE, MARNE ET CHAMPAGNE 1983 (F)

| £14.99 | ☛ VW | 🍴 a, c, q, s |

If only all own-label - and Grande Marque - Champagnes tasted this classy. Yeasty, nutty maturing fizz with a rich, long-lasting flavour.

18 IRON HORSE BRUT 1987 Sonoma (Cal)

| £15.50 | ☛ VW ADN | 🍴 n, o, q |

This is soft and fruity, with flavours of 'bananas and custard' or, alternatively, 'gooseberries and custard'.

(Arg) = Argentina; (Au) = Austria; (Aus) = Australia; (Bul) = Bulgaria; (Cal) = California; (Can) = Canada; (Ch) = Chile; (F) = France; (G) = Germany; (Gr) = Greece; (Is) = Israel; (It) = Italy; (Leb) = Lebanon; (NZ) = New Zealand; (P) = Portugal; (SA) = South Africa; (Sp) = Spain; (Sw) = Switzerland; (UK) = United Kingdom; (US) = United States excluding California

19 DEVAUX CHAMPAGNE CUVEE ROSEE (F)

£16.95	☛ FSW WRW MWW MTL NRW ROD WAC	
		101 s, q

Rosé Champagne can be over-sweetened, insipid stuff. But this is how it ought to taste: packed with Pinot ('plum 'n' raspberry') fruit and with real yeasty Champagne style.

20 CA' DEL BOSCO CREMANT, Lombardy (It)

£18.30	☛ V&C WCE OD	101 n, o, q

A very attractive wine full of flavours of vanilla and nuts, with a pungent, creamy aroma and a full, melony fruitiness.

21 FERRARI BRUT PERLE 1985 Trentino-Alto Adige (It)

£18.99	☛ HAR MM	101 a, c, q

In common with all Ferraris, this is 'powerful' with an 'interesting smoky character'. Our tasters were also impressed by its creamy, appley flavour.

22 VEUVE CLICQUOT DEMI-SEC CHAMPAGNE (F)

£20.50	☛ TH WR HOP VW BLW WRW WCE VLW U TMW JFR JEH	
FSW BH MM BBR HAR MTL CPL WOC SEL B&B DBY BTH GHL MAW		
		101 n, o, q

This is a gorgeously well balanced example of a style of Champagne that's rarely made nowadays. The sweetness is gently honeyed and perfectly counterpointed by fresh pineappley fruit. Hedonistic delight.

23 HEIDSIECK DRY MONOPOLE ROSE CHAMPAGNE 1985 (F)

£21.00	☛ OD JFR	101 c, q

Fresh, complex and biscuity with clean, concentrated fruit and 'excellent potential'. True quality vintage rosé.

24 LANSON VINTAGE CHAMPAGNE 1979 (F)

£22.00	☛ G	101 s, q, c

'The business!' This has the distinctive, rich taste of a mature vintage champagne - full, yet delicate, 'peaches and cream', with a pungent yeasty nose. 'Intense, creamy, honeyed, elegant, fat and ripe'.

25 BILLECART BRUT CHAMPAGNE 1985 (F)

£26.00	☛ OD DBY	101 c, q

A 'classy mouthful', with 'A light, elegant smell of bread and fruit'. 'Creamy, full and round - crisp, fresh finish'.

Richer dry whites

The wine world is heading in two directions at once - with half the drinkers embracing the flavour of new oak barrels as though it were an aphrodisiac (which, we suspect could be the case), while the others complain endlessly about not wanting to drink wine that tastes of a forestful of trees. Well, it takes all sorts - of wines and of wine drinkers - so we have separated the overtly oaky wines from the rest. The examples in this section should taste of little or no wood at all.

26 SAINSBURY VIN DE PAYS DE GERS, South West (F)

£2.75	☛ JS	101 c, d, f, r

A fresh wine with plenty of soft, clean lemony fruit. Great value.

27 LA CAUME DE PEYRE, VIN DE PAYS DES COTES DE GASCOGNE, South West (F)

£2.75	☛ SAF	101 c, e, f, r

Good, intensely fruity wine, nicely balanced with fresh acidity and a satisfying lasting finish.

28 SAINSBURY CORBIERES BLANC, Midi (F)

| £2.80 | ☞ JS | ⏁ c, e, g, r |

From a region once only known for its reds, this is lovely, dry and peachy, with a soft floral perfume.

29 CUVEE JEAN-PAUL BLANC SEC VIN DE TABLE, PAUL BOUTINOT (F)

| £2.89 | ☞ HEM CVR CAC ABB CGW HVW BGC P POR SAS WES WRK |
| CNL ASH BOO RTW DAL BRO SAN CWM AMW GNW BWS NRW |
| HOL DBY | ⏁ c, d, f |

Wines with names like Cuvée Jean Paul ought to be dross. But this one is astonishingly stylish with 'a good concentration of ripe fruit'.

30 ST MICHAEL DOMAINE DE PRADELLES, CO-OP BASTIDE DE LEVIS 1990 (F)

| £2.99 | ☞ M&S | ⏁ c, e, f, r |

A fat, grapey wine with just a touch of honey to round it off.

31 CORBIERES BLANC, CAVES DE MONT TAUCH, Midi (F)

| £3.19 | ☞ U AB EE GHS ABB AF CIW GNW | ⏁ e, i, l |

A fragrant wine with a tang of aniseed spice and freshly picked herbs. Packed with the flavour of summmer holidays.

32 DOM. DE LABALLE, VIN DE PAYS DES TERROIRS LANDAIS 1990 South West (F)

| £3.19 | ☞ THP | ⏁ c, f, i |

Fresh, lively wine with zesty fruit and a crisp finish. Very well made.

33 DOMAINE DU TARIQUET, VIN DE PAYS DES COTES DE GASCOGNE 1990 South West (F)

| £3.29 | ☞ TH WR TO OD CGW SWB VLW SOL CIW BWS BTH |
| | ⏁ c, e |

Intensely grapey and appley, with a smooth, rich finish.

34 DOMAINE DE BIAU, VIN DE PAYS DES COTES DE GASCOGNE, HUGH RYMAN 1990 South West (F)

| £3.39 | ☞ VW HUN | ⏁ c ,f |

Made by Hugh Ryman, the English-born producer of our White Wine of the Year, this is a well balanced wine with an almost Sauvignon-like, ripe gooseberry flavour.

35 SAINSBURY CORTESE DELL' ALTO MONFERRATO, Piedmont (It)

| £3.45 | ☞ JS | ⏁ c, e |

A well-made, quite aromatic and very characterful wine with light, creamy, greengage and gooseberry fruit.

36 COLDRIDGE ESTATE AUSTRALIAN WHITE 1989 Victoria (Aus)

| £3.59 | ☞ M&S BKW | ⏁ e, f |

A good-value Aussie with concentrated ripe fruit and spice flavours.

37 CHATEAU LES HAUTS DE TREYTIN, BORDEAUX BLANC, MANDREAU 1990 (F)

| £3.69 | ☞ TH WR | ⏁ e, g, i |

Rich, tropical fruit- flavoured wine with well-balanced acidity.

38 TOLLANA DRY WHITE 1988 S E Australia (Aus)

| £3.69 | ☞ TH WR WAW JEH EVI H&H MOR ABB AF WOC ECK GNW |
| RWW DBY | ⏁ g, h, i |

Great barbie-fare, with bags of ripe tropical fruit flavour.

39 TESCO ST EDMUND ENGLISH WINE, HIGHWAYMAN'S VINEYARD (UK)

| £3.69 | ☞ TO | ⏁ c, d |

A perfect patriotic tipple: light, fresh and nettley, with the flavour of honey and apple.

40 CHATEAU HAUT BERNASSE, BERGERAC BLANC, BLAIS 1990 South West (F)

| £3.75 | ☞ HEM | ⏁ c, e |

Appley, honeyed and toffeeish wine from an up-and-coming region.

☞ For an explanation of the stockist abbreviations, see page 16
⏁ For an explanation of food style codes, see page 66

41 TESCO ALSACE PINOT BLANC, KUEN 1989 (F)

£3.79	🖝 TO	🍽 e, g, i, l

A rival to the 1991 Guide's White Wine of the Year, this is soft and creamily fruity with just a touch of grassiness.

42 CEPAGE TERRET, VIN DE PAYS DE L'HERAULT, DELTA DOMAINES 1989 Midi (F)

£3.80	🖝 TO EE HHC	🍽 c, g, i

This southern white smells distinctly of grapefruit and lemon, and tastes deliciously of ripe apples.

43 MAUZAC, DOMAINE DE LA BATTEUSE, B DELMAS 1989 South West (F)

£3.90	🖝 VR VER CVR	🍽 e, g

Mauzac is one of France's most traditional grape varieties. This example is creamy, nutty and earthy, with plenty of fresh, spritzy fruit.

44 CHATEAU CANET, ENTRE DEUX MERS 1990 Bordeaux (F)

£3.99	🖝 SAF	🍽 c, e

A surprisingly classy wine with lingering mango and pear flavours.

45 CHARDONNAY, LES DUCS ST MARTIN, VAL D'ORBIEU 1990 Midi (F)

£3.99	🖝 TH WR	🍽 c, f, g

A light, appley, simple wine, with the scent of melons more usually associated with Californian Chardonnay.

46 CHARDONNAY, DOMAINE DES FLINES, VIN DE PAYS DE LA LOIRE 1990 (F)

£3.99	🖝 TH WR WES K&B BGC POR DAL NRW CVR HAS SAN	
		🍽 c, e, f, g

A clean, easy wine with a fresh hint of flowers and honey and a flavour of melons, herbs and guavas.

47 DOMAINE PETITOT, COTES DE DURAS 1990 South West (F)

£4.24	🖝 BU PD	🍽 c, e, f

Zippy, fruity wine with 'soft seaside flavours'.

48 CHATEAU HAUT REDON, ENTRE DEUX MERS, HUGH RYMAN 1990 Bordeaux (F)

£4.49	🖝 TH WR FUL MWW	🍽 c, e, f

White Wine of the Year

Englishman Hugh Ryman's Australian training has really paid off with this fresh young wine which shows the peachy flavours the Semillon can achieve in Bordeaux when it is well handled. A brilliantly accessible fruit salad of a dry white wine.

49 ST MICHAEL BEAUJOLAIS BLANC, CHAINTRE CO-OP 1988 (F)

£4.49	🖝 M&S	🍽 e, g

A refreshingly fruity, floral wine, with a hint of mashed banana.

50 TESCO MACON VILLAGES, CAVE DE VIRE 1990 Burgundy (F)

£4.59	🖝 TO G	🍽 f, i

A racy, appley, herby wine with an unusual crisp, zingy fruit flavour.

51 BLANC DES CEPAGES DE FRANCE, CHATEAU PECH-CELEYRAN 1990 Midi (F)

£4.60	🖝 ADN	🍽 e, i, l

Attractive spicy flavours and a lingering, fruity finish

52 BOURGOGNE ALIGOTE, JAFFELIN 1989 Burgundy (F)

£4.79	🖝 OD	🍽 e, i

Not the mean, lean Aligoté, good only for blending with cassis. This is a classy wine with good weight of pear fruit and balancing acidity.

53 MITCHELTON MARSANNE (UNWOODED) 1990 Goulburn Valley (Aus)

£4.89	🖝 OD A	🍽 g, q

A wonderful example of the Marsanne grape. Perfumed, buttery aromas with intense, sweet, ripe fruit. A long creamy vanilla finish.

54 ALSACE TOKAY PINOT GRIS, CAVE VINICOLE DE TURCKHEIM 1990 (F)

£4.95	🖝 GNW WR OD HVW TW WRK WNS POR WES WCE CGW VW	
ECK TH NRW ASH BOO CVR CWM AMW HEM HAS FWC BGC HOL		
DBY		🍽 e, g, i

A round, appley wine with a long, slightly tangy finish.

55 SOAVE CLASSICO MONTELEONE, BOSCAINI 1989 Veneto (It)

| £4.95 | ☛ VW RWC SAN | ᵀᴼ¹ e, f, g, h |

Admittedly most Soaves are only suitable for use on red wine stains, but this is attractively nutty, with fresh flavours of lemon and apples.

56 SIMON WHITLAM SAUVIGNON/SEMILLON 1989 Hunter Valley (Aus)

| £4.99 | ☛ OD | ᵀᴼ¹ a, e, g, h |

A successful Australian shot at the classic white Bordeaux blend. Full-flavoured, well balanced and flinty, with pleasant vanilla oakiness.

57 TESCO ORGANIC WHITE, CHATEAU VIEUX GABIRAN 1990 Bordeaux (F)

| £4.99 | ☛ TO | ᵀᴼ¹ e, f |

Organic white Bordeaux is a rarity. This example has rich tropical fruit with well balanced acidity. Fresh and richly textured.

58 CHATEAU COUCHEROY BLANC, GRAVES, ANDRÉ LURTON 1989 Bordeaux (F)

| £4.99 | ☛ JN WR TH CAC | ᵀᴼ¹ e, i |

Made by Jacques Lurton, superstar producer of a growing list of great dry whites in Bordeaux and now Australia, this is very fresh and grapey with lots of good acidity and a really long finish.

59 HOUGHTON SUPREME WHITE 1990 Swan Valley (Aus)

| £5.15 | ☛ OD AUC NRW GNW | ᵀᴼ¹ c, e, f |

In Australia they call this 'Burgundy'; we just call it delicious--soft, honeyed and rich.

60 PICPOUL DE PINET, DOMAINE GAUJOL 1989 Miidi (F)

| £5.20 | ☛ HFW | ᵀᴼ¹ e, g |

Made from a quirky indigenous French grape variety, this is at once floral, biscuity and rich. Very distinctive and memorable.

61 CHATEAU SAINT GALIER BORDEAUX BLANC 1990 (F)

| £5.29 | ☛ TH WR | ᵀᴼ¹ f, g, i |

A crisp, appley-grapefruity wine with a lovely long, tangy finish.

62 CHAI BAUMIERES CHARDONNAY, VIN DE PAYS D'OC, DOMAINE DE LA BAUME 1990 Miidi (F)

| £5.35 | ☛ WCE BOO WOC | ᵀᴼ¹ e, f, g |

When the Australians aren't making world beating wines at home, they're making them in southern France. Produced by a subsidiary of Hardy's, this is fresh and lively, with soft, luscious melon flavour.

63 SUNNYCLIFF ESTATES CHARDONNAY 1989 Victoria (Aus)

| £5.48 | ☛ TAN HOT | ᵀᴼ¹ e, g, i |

'Rich, elegant, smoky ripe bananas and zingy citric fruit.'

64 WOOTTON SCHONBURGER 1990 (UK)

| £5.50 | ☛ GEW H | ᵀᴼ¹ d, e, l |

Young, fresh and just off-dry, with a pronounced spicy flavour.

65 TESCO ST VERAN LES MONTS, CO-OP DE PRISSE 1988 Burgundy (F)

| £5.50 | ☛ TO | ᵀᴼ¹ c, e, f |

A clean, ripe, well-balanced wine with 'a good, long, appley finish'.

66 ALSACE PINOT BLANC BENNWIHR, MARCEL DEISS 1989 (F)

| £5.75 | ☛ SEB LEA | ᵀᴼ¹ e, g, i |

An unusually fruity version of this grape, packed with all sorts of ultra-ripe, exotic fruit flavours.

67 ASDA CHABLIS, GUY MOTHE 1989 Burgundy (F)

| £6.69 | ☛ A | ᵀᴼ¹ e, g, i |

Lovely, creamy wine from an excellent grower. The sweetly ripe nutty flavours are beautifully combined with savoury spice.

(Arg) = Argentina; (Au) = Austria; (Aus) = Australia; (Bul) = Bulgaria; (Cal) = California; (Can) = Canada; (Ch) = Chile; (F) = France; (G) = Germany; (Gr) = Greece; (Is) = Israel; (It) = Italy; (Leb) = Lebanon; (NZ) = New Zealand; (P) = Portugal; (SA) = South Africa; (Sp) = Spain; (Sw) = Switzerland; (UK) = United Kingdom; (US) = United States excluding California

68 BREGANZE DI BREGANZE, MACULAN 1990 Veneto (It)

£6.99	🖝 CPW WCE	🍴 c, g

This distinctive white is at once fresh, fruity, nutty and creamy with a fresh 'pear drops' and pineapple character.

69 SOAVE CLASSICO VIGNETO CALVARINO, PIEROPAN 1989 Veneto (It)

£7.15	🖝 WCE L&W EE GON BEN SAS HFW SAN BWS	
		🍴 e, f, g, l

It was Pieropan who first demonstrated the potential of single vineyard Soave. A creamy, spicy wine with apple, pear and citrus fruit flavours.

70 ST VERAN TERRES NOIRES, DOMAINE DEUX ROCHES 1989 Burgundy (F)

£7.20	🖝 H&H EBA HFW HHC BWS	🍴 e, f, g, h

A more affordable alternative to Pouilly Fuisse. Fat, buttery, very well balanced and carefully made. Slightly nutty with a richness of ripe fruit and a lingering creamy finish.

71 ST VERAN LES GRANDES BRUYERES, ROGER LUQUET 1989 Burgundy (F)

£7.20	🖝 L&W RD LHV	🍴 e, f, g

A bigger, fatter, concentrated wine which smells and tastes yeasty, buttery, aromatic and smoky with a crisp, spicy lemon finish.

72 MACON AZE, DOMAINE D'AZENAY 1989 Burgundy (F)

£7.50	🖝 U BRO FWC BTH BWS	🍴 c, e, g

An 'excellent varietal nose' - of soft apples and fresh, light fruit salad. Clean, warm and well-balanced, with plenty of ripe buttery fruit.

73 POUILLY FUISSE, LUC JAVELOT 1988 Burgundy (F)

£7.75	🖝 SAF	🍴 c, g

This wine smells deliciously of apples and has an attractive concentrated peachy, creamy flavour.

74 CHABLIS, BERNARD LEGLAND 1989 Burgundy (F)

£7.98	🖝 BI	🍴 e, f, g, h

Very typical Chablis. Fresh, young and tasty, with a slight earthiness.

75 CHABLIS ST MARTIN, DOMAINE LAROCHE 1990 Burgundy (F)

£8.99	🖝 AB	🍴 c, e, f, g, h

A fragrant, floral wine with bags of tropical fruit. Drink right now.

76 DOMAINE FONT DE MICHELLE, CHATEAUNEUF DU PAPE BLANC, GONNET 1990 Rhône (F)

£11.99	🖝 WR TH	🍴 e, f, g, l

A rich sweetly ripe wine with lots of lovely honeyed fruit and spice. A characterful alternative to ubiquitous Chardonnay.

77 CONDRIEU, COTEAUX DE CHERY, A PERRET 1989 Rhône (F)

£14.70	🖝 ADN J&B	🍴 e, f, g, l

A creamy, biscuity wine with honey, and fresh Spring flowers; very typical of the curious Viognier grape.

Oaked whites

Oak lovers, this is your playground — from Meursault to Rioja, via white Bordeaux, Australia and California. But never fear. We are no slavish followers of fashion and we don't normally enjoy nibbling away at planks. If the wines we recommend in this section all smell and taste oaky, they all have more than enough fruit to balance that woodiness.

78 CHATEAU LES COMBES, BORDEAUX BLANC, ESCHENAUER 1990 (F)

£3.15	🖝 SAF	🍴 a, b, i, r

Great, modern white Bordeaux with a clean burst of fresh gooseberry fruit, and just enough oak to add complexity.

79 COTES DE ST MONT, PLAIMONT 1990 South West (F)

£3.50	☛ AB ADN FUL SV TAN L&W BH SWB JFR GI HHC CAC FWC NI HOT NIC BWS	⏷ a, c, e, r

From one of France's most go-ahead co-operatives, a brilliant peachy wine with toasty oak and a beautiful long finish.

80 KILLAWARRA CHARDONNAY 1990 South Australia (Aus)

£3.75	☛ OD	⏷ a, b, r

A reliable, inexpensive and very typical Aussie Chardonnay with lots of sweet oaky flavour.

81 VILLARD CHARDONNAY 1990 Maipo (Ch)

£3.99	☛ TO	⏷ a, b, e, i

An instant success from Thierry Viallard, a Frenchman who learned his winemaking in Australia. Lemony, nutty and sweetly oaky.

82 COTES DE ROUSSILLON JEAN BESOMBES, LES VIGNERONS DE RIVESALTES 1988 Midi (F)

£4.69	☛ OD	⏷ e, g, i

'Sweet, tropical fruit and peaches with lovely hints of coconut and oak'.

83 CALITERRA CHARDONNAY 1990 Maipo Valley (Ch)

£4.75	☛ OD WAW WRW PIM BNK VW GHL NRW MWW LWL BOO WRB BBR A AHC CVR HEM HOL WOC LEF WNS DBY	⏷ a, e, i

A Chilean-Californian co-production, this is round and buttery with floral, marmaladey fruit.

84 OXFORD LANDING CHARDONNAY, YALUMBA 1990 South Australia (Aus)

£4.85	☛ A AUC MWW CAC JFR VLW SUP BLW PIM CPL HPD SAC MG CVR FWC GNW HOL PTR BWS JEH WOC	⏷ c, e, f, i, q

Wonderfully commercial Chardonnay with almost too much flavour.

85 CASTILLO FUENTE MAYOR BLANCO, AGE 1988 (Sp)

£4.99	☛ U	⏷ a, i, l

An appealing wine with complex flavours of nuts, buttery oak and rich, spicy fruit.

86 CHARDONNAY, VIN DE PAYS D'OC, HUGH RYMAN 1990 Midi (F)

£4.99	☛ VW JS FUL SV MWW CAC CVR	⏷ c, e, f, q

A light, fresh, delicious Chardonnay, full of tropical fruit flavours.

87 ORLANDO RF CHARDONNAY 1989 S E Australia (Aus)

£5.25	☛ LES HV OD U AB FSW JEH SK HYN BH TMW BGC WRB AUC DBY RHW BUD GDS CVR AF HEM MC PTR UBC LEF WOC WCE JCK HW POR RD CGW D GHL BI	⏷ e, f, i

Full, rich and buttery, this has style and surprising complexity.

88 MONTES CHARDONNAY, DISCOVER WINE LTDA 1990 Curico Valley (Ch)

£5.39	☛ HW CPL LWL ABB MC VIL	⏷ e, f, i, n

A crisp, citrusy, aromatic wine from Chile's top producer.

89 MOONDAH BROOK VERDELHO 1990 (Aus)

£5.49	☛ OD AUC AMW NI	⏷ a, e, i, o

An unusual Australian wine, made from a native Portugese grape variety. It's full, fresh and limey with buttery new oak.

90 LINDEMANS BIN 65 CHARDONNAY 1989 S E Australia (Aus)

£5.50	☛ AB JFR TW BEN POR WNS PD BU AUC ROD WSO CWM HHC BWS BWI GNW NI	⏷ e, g, i, m, q

Full and fat, with lots of buttery oak - this is what Aussie Chardonnay is all about.

☛ For an explanation of the stockist abbreviations, see page 16

⏷ For an explanation of food style codes, see page 66

91 CHEVALIER ST VINCENT BORDEAUX BLANC, UNION ST VINCENT 1989 (F)

£5.89	☞ OD JS	❍ a, e, i, m

Oaked white Bordeaux is set to become the white wine style of the 1990s - especially when we all grow tired of Chardonnay. This one combines peachy-appley Semillon flavours with lovely savoury oak.

92 MACON CHARDONNAY, J TALMARD 1988 Burgundy (F)

£6.15	☞ TAN JFR SHJ WAC	❍ e, g, i, q

Made in the village of Chardonnay from the grape of the same name, this is ripe, fruity, clean, fresh and fragrant.

93 BROKENBACK VINEYARD CHARDONNAY, ROTHBURY 1990 Hunter Valley (Aus)

£6.49	☞ WOC GRT SHJ CVR L&W JFR JEH VLW SK SEB RHW PIM	
WCE AUC L&W BI MWW D PEY RHV SEL		❍ c, e, g, q

Made by Len Evans, the Welshman who arguably introduced fine wine drinking to Australia, this is rich, peachy and oaky..

94 DOMAINE DE RIBONNET CHARDONNAY 1989 South West (F)

£6.95	☞ H&H OD FW RHV	❍ e, q

Proof that Southern France can master the Chardonnay too. Soft, elegant wine with a warm, nutty, bready smell.

95 SCHINUS MOLLE CHARDONNAY 1990 Mornington Peninsula (Aus)

£6.99	☞ HFW OD BH WCE AUC BOO HHC AMW LEF WFP	
		❍ e, i, q

This has the scent of soft, fresh apples and a creamy, crisp fruit flavour. 'Rich, full, classy and really delicious'. (Jane Hunt).

96 SAINT ROMAIN (TASTEVINE), BERNARD FEVRE 1986 Burgundy (F)

£7.45	☞ PWA	❍ e, o, q

From a little-known Burgundy village: 'Exotic pineapple', 'herbs, parsley', 'highly perfumed tropical fruit', 'rich, honeyed apricots'.

97 CHATEAU DES CHARMES CHARDONNAY 1988 Ontario (Can)

£7.89	☞ BU	❍ c, e, q

Ontario Chardonnay to worry the Californians. Clean tropical fruit and flowers - lychees and gooseberries. Soft, delicious.

98 WITTERS VINEYARD CHARDONNAY, COLLARD BROTHERS 1990 Henderson (NZ)

£7.98	☞ BI	❍ e, c, q

Classy wine from a small estate near Auckland. Fruit salad with hints of pineapple, banana and lemon. 'Elegant with a hint of spice'.

99 CUVEE DES JACOBINS BOURGOGNE CHARDONNAY, JADOT 1989 Burgundy (F)

£7.99	☞ TH WR	❍ a, e, i

For Burgundy lovers, this is a good 'French style' with plenty of oak.

100 CHARDONNAY CHAMPS PERRIERES, H LECLERC 1989 Burgundy (F)

£8.08	☞ TAN	❍ a, b, e, g, i

A very lemony, almost Sauvignon-like wine for the future.

101 HUGO CHARDONNAY 1988 Southern Vales (Aus)

£8.30	☞ HFW C CPW BH DX HPD AMW	❍ c, e, q

Aussie Chardonnays don't have to be heavyweights. This blend of pineappley, melony flavours gets complexity from its subtle oak.

102 MARQUES DE MURRIETA RIOJA BLANCO RESERVA 1985 Rioja (Sp)

£8.75	☞ VW RAE LEA ADN TRE BEN BH EVI SEB POR SAS TAN THP	
ECK W GHL GNW HAS DLM RHV UBC PTR MC HEM FWC WR BWS BTH		
WOC SEL DBY U WA WRW MM BI MOR TP		❍ a, b, e, m

Very powerfully oaky Rioja with a slight saltiness, rather like a lightweight sherry with a complex nutty finish. 'A special wine'.

103 KING VALLEY CHARDONNAY FAMILY RESERVE, BROWN BROTHERS 1987 N E Victoria (Aus)

£8.79	☞ HUN JFR CPW SWB AUC ROD HPD SAC BND GNW WOC SJH	
DBY ABY ECK		❍ e, q

A very creamy toffeeish wine with a full, silky, clean, fruity flavour.

104 PENFOLDS PADTHAWAY CHARDONNAY 1990 (Aus)

| £8.85 | ☛ OD HVW EVI CWW DBY | 🍴 e, i, q |

'Tropical, fragrant, juicy, cool(ish) climate wine - very fresh'.

105 HEGGIES CHARDONNAY, HILL-SMITH 1988 Adelaide Hills (Aus)

| £8.99 | ☛ AUC TW HW RD HPD WRB FDL LWL | 🍴 q, s |

From a vineyard high in the hills above the Barossa valley, this is a little leaner, with lovely, fresh pineappley - peachy fruit.

106 WYNNS COONAWARRA ESTATE CHARDONNAY 1989 (Aus)

| £9.25 | ☛ TH WR OD HVW THP RHV SK VW AUC HPD BOS HEM FWC |
| DBY | | 🍴 e, i, q, s |

If you like oaky Aussie whites, you'll love this. It smells of sawn oak and tropical fruit. Buttery and very rich.

107 KRONDORF SHOW RESERVE CHARDONNAY 1989 Barossa Valley (Aus)

| £9.45 | ☛ D OD THP BH BU AUC FWC GRT MC BWS DBY |
| | | 🍴 a, b, e, i, q |

A wonderfully delicious aroma of melons and rich pineapple syrup.

108 EILEEN HARDY CHARDONNAY, HARDY'S 1988 South Australia (Aus)

| £9.79 | ☛ OD AUC CVR DBY | 🍴 a, f, i |

Named after the founder's wife, this has lots of oak and tropical fruit.

109 ST HUBERTS CHARDONNAY 1988 Yarra Valley (Aus)

| £10.50 | ☛ AUC RD | 🍴 a, e, g, q |

A very classy New World Chardonnay, from the Yarra Valley: melons, pea-pods, exotic ripe mangoes and lychees - with heavily toasted oak.

110 PIPERS BROOK CHARDONNAY 1988 Tasmania (Aus)

| £10.99 | ☛ WR AUC | 🍴 e, g, o, q |

From Tasmania's - and one of Australia's - top producers , this is mouth-fillingly tropical, with lemon, lime, pineapple and melon flavours and some sweet coconut.

111 EDNA VALLEY CHARDONNAY 1989 San Luis Obispo (Cal)

| £11.25 | ☛ JEH BEN POR WCE WR LEA BI GHS HEM FWC HOL |
| PTR | | 🍴 c, e, f, i |

A lively Californian superstar, with honeyed, buttery richness.

112 SAINTSBURY RESERVE CHARDONNAY 1988 Carneros (Cal)

| £11.75 | ☛ ADN BI | 🍴 a, e, i, q |

A lovely, elegant wine with clean full, oaky vanilla flavours and thick vanilla. It is still very youthful and will improve.

113 CHATEAU LA LOUVIERE, PESSAC-LEOGNAN 1989 Bordeaux (F)

| £11.75 | ☛ OD HUN | 🍴 c, e, q |

A fresh and elegant wine, full flavoured with a touch of subtle vanilla oak. Lovely and long.

114 DOMAINE CAUHAPE, JURANCON SEC (OAKED) 1988 South West (F)

| £11.90 | ☛ EE BWS NI WCE FWC | 🍴 a, e, i |

Distinctive new oaky and pleasant tingly sherbet fruitiness. A powerful, superbly long wine.

115 VITA NOVA CHARDONNAY 1989 Santa Barbara (Cal)

| £11.99 | ☛ M&V OD GON | 🍴 a, f, i |

From Southern Californa, this has gentle, smoky, spicy oak and soft, rich peachy fruit. Well made, juicy wine.

116 CLOS DU BOIS CHARDONNAY, CALCAIRE VINEYARD 1988 Sonoma (Cal)

| £12.60 | ☛ THP BH | 🍴 e, q, s |

'Warm aromas of honey and hazelnut oak; supple rich fruity wine'.

(Arg) = Argentina; (Au) = Austria; (Aus) = Australia; (Bul) = Bulgaria; (Cal) = California; (Can) = Canada; (Ch) = Chile; (F) = France; (G) = Germany; (Gr) = Greece; (Is) = Israel; (It) = Italy; (Leb) = Lebanon; (NZ) = New Zealand; (P) = Portugal; (SA) = South Africa; (Sp) = Spain; (Sw) = Switzerland; (UK) = United Kingdom; (US) = United States excluding California

117 ELSTON CHARDONNAY, TE MATA 1989 (NZ)

£12.90	NZC SWB L&W JFR H BH BEN HPD RTW GHS BWS AMW NI	
GNW SEL		🍴 a, b, e, i

New Zealand's top Chardonnay? Smoky and oaky with lovely buttery, nutty fruit. A classic ripe wine.

118 VIDAL RESERVE CHARDONNAY 1989 Hawkes Bay (NZ)

£13.50	☛ CGW LEA P JEH H BH WRB NI	🍴 a, e, m

Rich oaky vanilla flavours combined with lovely flavours of apples, peaches, lychees and tropical fruits.

119 LES PIERRES CHARDONNAY, SONOMA CUTRER 1987 Sonoma (Cal)

£14.50	☛ AV JEH BEN SK LEA ADN GON TBW AHC HAR GNW UBC	
DBY		🍴 a, b, i, q, s

The most - justifiably - hyped Chardonnay in California. Big, oaky with bags of fruit, liquorice and asparagus. Well worth keeping.

120 KUMEU RIVER CHARDONNAY 1989 (NZ)

£16.99	☛ U	🍴 a, b, e

A subtle, yet stunning wine with toasty oak and tropical fruit flavours. A gold medal winner at the 1991 International Wine Challenge.

121 MEURSAULT BLAGNY, DOMAINE MATROT 1987 Burgundy (F)

£17.16	☛ C&B	🍴 e, q, m

Big, rich, mouthfilling wine with lovely buttery spice. Complex, long and nutty with tasty, peachy flavours. Ready now but will keep.

122 MEURSAULT, COCHE DURY 1988 Burgundy (F)

£18.75	☛ D L&W	🍴 a, e, f, q

A very hearty, typically Burgundian wine, a complex blend of smoky woodchips, nuts, and ripe fruit flavours.

123 CHASSAGNE MONTRACHET PREMIER CRU CHAUMEES, PIERRE MOREY 1987 Burgundy (F)

£19.45	☛ D MC	🍴 c, e, f, q

Rich, fine stylish wine with lovely parsley and butter flavours.

124 MEURSAULT PREMIER CRU LES CRAS, OLIVIER LEFLAIVE 1988 Burgundy (F)

£22.68	☛ C&B SEL	🍴 e, f, c, q, s

Very ripe-tasting wine with the richness of melted butter.

125 NUITS ST GEORGES BLANC, CLOS DE L'ARLOT 1988 Burgundy (F)

£23.50	☛ L&W HR ADN	🍴 e, i, q, s

White wines from Nuits St Georges are a real rarity. This has flavours of lemons, coconuts, limes, biscuits, nuts, toffee and ice cream.

126 CHASSAGNE MONTRACHET LES MORGEOTS, CHARTRON ET TREBUCHET 1988 Burgundy (F)

£23.99	☛ OD	🍴 a, e, q, s

Woodchips, honey and toffee, with a balancing touch of tangy citrus fruits. Classic modern white Burgundy.

Dry Loire-style whites

When everybody finally grows bored of the flavour of the Chardonnay, we suspect that one of the directions in which they may turn is towards the traditional tastes of the Loire — in the form of the appley Chenin Blanc, the gooseberryish Sauvignon, and the yeastily dry wines of Muscadet. If and when they do — quite probably via some of the brilliant Loire-style Sauvignons now being made in New Zealand — you could have got there first, simply by discovering a few of the wines on the following pages for yourself.

127 DONATIEN BLANC DE BLANC, DONATIEN BAHUAUD 1990 Loire (F)

£2.79	☛ TH WR	❑ d, e, g, r

From a reliable Muscadet producer, this is a well made wine with a zingy Sauvignon nose and appealing clean fruity flavours.

128 TESCO SAUMUR BLANC, CAVES DES VIGNERONS DE SAUMUR 1989 Loire (F)

£3.15	☛ TO	❑ c, e, f, h, r

Good, zippy, grapey wine with an appealing earthy quality.

129 NURAGUS DI CAGLIARI, CANTINA SOCIALE DI DOLIANOVA 1990 Sardinia (It)

£3.69	☛ V&C TO L&W	❑ c, f, g

A light, delicate, fruity wine with lovely zingy acidity.

130 ST MICHAEL SAUVIGNON DE TOURAINE, GUY SAGET 1990 Loire (F)

£3.79	☛ M&S	❑ c, e, f, i

Intensely tangy-lemony Sauvignon. Great value.

131 SAINSBURY MUSCADET SUR LIE (ORGANIC), DOMAINE COURSAY 1990 Loire (F)

£3.90	☛ JS	❑ a, c, f, r

Sainsbury deserve full credit for finding a genuine example of organic Muscadet at this price. Yeasty, flavoursome and rich.

132 CHATEAU DE LA BOTINERE, MUSCADET DE SEVRE ET MAINE, JEAN BEAUQUIN 1990 Loire (F)

£4.09	☛ SAF	❑ c, d, f, i, l

Slightly creamy cooked apple and peach flavour. An unusually spicy Muscadet with good acidity and a lovely crisp finish.

133 DOMAINE DU COLOMBET SAUVIGNON, COTES DE DURAS 1990 South West (F)

£4.19	☛ TH WR	❑ c, g, r

From up-and-coming Duras, this is a fresh, tangy object lesson to the Bordeaux Sauvignons it beat at the International Wine Challenge.

134 DOMAINE DU BREUIL, VIN DE PAYS DU JARDIN DE LA FRANCE, MARC MORGAT 1990 Loire (F)

£4.20	☛ CVR LEA	❑ c, f

Freshly herbaceous wine with excellent, crisp, lean, cherry fruit.

135 DOMAINE DE LA HAUT FEVRIE, MUSCADET DE SEVRE ET MAINE SUR LIE 1989 Loire (F)

£4.45	☛ HFW	❑ c, d, q

Clean 'bubble gum' flavour; a fresh and fruity wine.

136 DOMAINE DE LA CHAMBANDERIE, MUSCADET, BRUNO CORMERAIS 1990 Loire (F)

£4.59	☛ BGC	❑ c, e, f

Dry, full-bodied wine with soft apple and pear fruit. Very well made.

137 BOZE DOWN DRY 1989 Oxfordshire (UK)

£4.75	☛ GEW CWI	❑ d, e, f

OK, it's not from the Loire, but it was described by an experienced taster as having a classic Sauvignon nose. Plenty of fresh flavours of peaches and mint, most refreshing.

138 DOMAINE DES CORBILLIERES, SAUVIGNON DE TOURAINE 1989 Loire (F)

£4.80	☛ BWI JN PD	❑ c, d, f, g

Disappointed by Sancerre? Overpowered by New Zealand Sauvignon? This is your kind of wine; biting, gooseberryish Sauvignon.

139 DOMAINE DU PRE BARON, SAUVIGNON DE TOURAINE 1989 Loire (F)

£4.90	☛ CDV SAS CGW VW OLS	❑ c, d, g

The canny person's alternative to Pouilly Fumé or Sancerre. A full-bodied grassy wine at a very affordable price.

☛ For an explanation of the stockist abbreviations, see page 16
❑ For an explanation of food style codes, see page 66

140 COOKS HAWKES BAY SAUVIGNON BLANC 1989 Hawkes Bay (NZ)

£4.95	☛ NZC JS HOP G WES RHW POR SUP JFR HW H BH ASH	
W TH BAB NRW D WRB WOC GRT MC DBY A JCK B&B AF BUD		
		❍ c, d, e, f, i

A simple, refreshing wine with a smell of apples and gooseberries. Concentrated, lemony and zesty.

141 ST MICHAEL MUSCADET SUR LIE, SAUVION 1990 Loire (F)

£4.99	☛ M&S	❍ d, f, i

A sharp, zingy wine with green apple fruit and a refreshing finish.

142 MOULIN DE LA GRAVELLE, MUSCADET, CHEREAU-CARRE 1988 Loire (F)

£5.19	☛ FUL	❍ c, d, e, f

Pleasant, soft fruit and a nutty flavour are the keynotes of this wine.

143 DOMAINE DU RELAIS DE POSTE, SAUVIGNON DE ST BRIS, LUC SORIN 1989 Burgundy (F)

£5.49	☛ TH WR OD FUL WOC	❍ a, d, g

Herbaceous and smoky with delicate green, grassy, fruity flavours.

144 DOMAINE DES AUBUISIERES, VOUVRAY SEC 1990 Loire (F)

£5.89	☛ OD GON OLS	❍ c, g, q

Stylish dry Chenin Blanc, with a fruit cocktail of flowers combined with subtle oak. Gentle honeyed character with real finesse.

145 SAUVIGNON DE ST BRIS, DOMAINE FELIX 1990 Burgundy (F)

£5.89	☛ BGC POR NRW BOO BRO GNW GRT HAS DBY	
		❍ c, d, f, g

A 'squeaky clean', modern wine with good, crisp tropical flavours.

146 CHATEAU DE MONTFORT-VOUVRAY, CORDIER 1988 Loire (F)

£6.49	☛ THP	❍ e, g

Maturing, earthy melon fruitiness and honey 'n' almond sweetness.

147 KLEIN CONSTANTIA SAUVIGNON BLANC 1988 (SA)

£6.5♥	☛ AV LEA TRE H DAL CVR FWC	❍ d, g, h, q

From one of South Africa's oldest vineyards, this is full of asparagus, vanilla, apple and gooseberry flavours. A big classy mouthful.

148 SELAKS SAUVIGNON BLANC 1990 (NZ)

£6.60	☛ RAE ADN THP OD SK WSO CVR AMW MAW SAN DBY BWS	
		❍ e, f, g, h, q

The winery where Cloudy Bay winemaker Kevin Judd cut his New Zealand teeth is still making wine that gives his 1990 a run for its money. Quite classy, tropical fruit-and-gooseberry Kiwi wine.

149 BARKHAM MANOR 1988 East Sussex (UK)

£6.75	☛ C&B GEW	❍ d, e, f

Intense gooseberry aromas. Crisp and spicy fruit with beautiful balancing acidity and a great finish. English winemaking at its best!

150 STONELEIGH SAUVIGNON BLANC 1989 Marlborough (NZ)

£6.75	☛ TH UBC JCK HOP WR NZC CWW WA TMW TAN POR SUP	
PTR ECK BBR AF BLW WOC B&B VIL DBY AHC MG H BH MM BAB CDB		
HHC RTW HW		❍ e, f, g, h, q

This, Cooks' top vineyard, is next door to Cloudy Bay; the similarity in gooseberryish style is no coincidence. 'Serious', mouthfilling wine.

151 SCHINUS MOLLE SAUVIGNON BLANC 1990 Victoria (Aus)

£6.99	☛ HFW OD BH AUC AMW WFP BWS	
		❍ c, d, g, h

Grapefruity, nettley and great 'knock-out asparagus and gooseberry intensity'. A lovely, easy drinking, fruity mouthful.

152 SANCERRE, DOMAINE DES GROSSES PIERRES 1990 Loire (F)

£7.99	☛ BU	❍ e, g, h, q, s

Fresh, crisp and youthful wine with lovely lime flavours and an explosive, passionfruit and peardrop character.

153 POUILLY FUME LES CHANTALOUETTES 1989 Loire (F)

£8.25	☛ WRK JS NRW DBY	101 a, g, h, q, s

Pouilly Fumé should have the steely backbone for which the Upper Loire has become famous - as well as some good Sauvignon fruit. This has both. As mouthwatering as a freshly picked Cox's apple.

154 SHAW AND SMITH SAUVIGNON BLANC 1990 South Australia (Aus)

£8.40	☛ M&V L&W THP EE WCE AUC HOP ADN BI EBA FWC HOL	
		101 e, g, h, q, s

Made by Australia's only Master of Wine. Lively, fresh gooseberryish wine with fresh zingy asparagus. Very stylish.

Medium-dry whites

A very unfashionable part of the wine spectrum, this. But there are good, well-balanced examples which warrant tasting. Ah but, we hear you say, I don't like sweet wines. Fair enough; all we'd ask is for all of you anti-sweetness wine drinkers who enjoy chocolate, puddings and sugar in your coffee to stop and wonder whether your insistence on wine being dry does not have just a little more to do with prejudice than taste buds. The following wines should be seductive enough to woo the driest of palates.

155 GATEWAY ANJOU BLANC, REMY PANNIER, Loire (F)

£2.89	☛ G	101 c, e, f, r

Clean, fruity wine with just enough sweetness.

156 GATEWAY VOUVRAY, GUSTAVE RABIER, Loire (F)

£3.75	☛ G	101 e, g, r

A honeyed, floral wine with creamy, smooth and very ripe, soft fruit .

157 DOMAINE DU BOSC MARSANNE, VIN DE PAYS DE L'HERAULT, DELTA DOMAINES 1990 Midi (F)

£4.25	☛ DX ADN WSO	101 c, e, f

The Marsanne grape gives this wine a clean, crisp, ripe fruity flavour with a hint of marshmallow.

158 GROS MANSENG CUVEE TARDIVE, LA MOTTE 1989 South West (F)

£4.39	☛ OD	101 e, g, n

Honeyed, lemony, buttery and grapefruity - from a little-known variety.

159 ST MICHAEL CHATEAU DE POCE, CHAINIER 1990 (F)

£4.49	☛ M&S	101 c, e, f

A crisp, clean fresh appley wine. Very easy to drink.

160 VINHO VERDE, SOLAR DAS BOUCAS 1989 Minho (P)

£4.65	☛ JS HEM	101 d, e, f

Single-estate wine with flavours of fresh floral fruit, freshly baked bread and perfumed joss sticks.

161 VINTAGE SELECTION MEDIUM DRY, WICKHAM VINEYARDS 1990 Hants (UK)

£4.99	☛ GEW	101 l, n, o

An aromatic, fragrant wine with mouthwatering 'opal fruit' flavours .

162 SWEET LEE, THAMES VALLEY VINEYARD 1989 Berkshire (UK)

£5.49	☛ GEW BI	101 c, n, o, q

A crisp, light, lychee-ish wine, very easy to drink. Pity about the name.

(Arg) = Argentina; (Au) = Austria; (Aus) = Australia; (Bul) = Bulgaria; (Cal) = California; (Can) = Canada; (Ch) = Chile; (F) = France; (G) = Germany; (Gr) = Greece; (Is) = Israel; (It) = Italy; (Leb) = Lebanon; (NZ) = New Zealand; (P) = Portugal; (SA) = South Africa; (Sp) = Spain; (Sw) = Switzerland; (UK) = United Kingdom; (US) = United States excluding California

163 MONTLOUIS DEMI-SEC VIELLES VIGNES, DOMAINE DES LIARDS, BERGER FRERES 1989 Loire (F)

£7.10	☞ ADN BWS	ΙΟΙ e, u, q

Lovely, rich appley wine with fresh, tangy acidity and a touch of honeyed apricots. Will last very well.

164 CUVEE PIERRE DEMI SEC, DOMAINE BALLAND CHAPUIS 1990 Loire (F)

£12.99	☞ OD	ΙΟΙ n, o, q

A real curiosity: late-picked Sancerre. It's rich, unctuous and full of apricotty flavours. Powerful, intense and tremendously long.

Aromatic whites

Misunderstood for much the same reason as sweeter wines are misunderstood, aromatic wines in general, and the Gewürztraminer in particular, rarely feature on most wine drinkers' top-tens. Admitting that you actually enjoy that perfumed, let-it-all-hang-out style is rather like stating that you are having an affair with the most brazen and promiscuous flirt in town. Far better to stick to the more 'serious', acceptable flavours of the Chardonnay or Cabernet.

165 BAROSSA VALLEY ESTATES GEWURZTRAMINER 1987 Barossa Valley (Aus)

£3.49	☞ OD	ΙΟΙ a, l, m

A wine with perhaps less of the floral spiciness that one tends to expect from this variety but with plenty of honey and lemon fruit and a finish like 'luscious rich tea biscuits'.

166 ASDA ALSACE GEWURZTRAMINER, CAVES VINICOLE EGUISHEIM 1989 (F)

£4.59	☞ A	ΙΟΙ g, l, m

Good-value Gewürz: flowery, grapey and spicy flavour. 'Complex, long and impresssive'.

167 SAINSBURY ALSACE GEWURZTRAMINER (F)

£4.60	☞ JS	ΙΟΙ a, l, m

Rich and oily wine with flavours of exotic lychees and ripe grapefruits.

168 ALSACE GEWURZTRAMINER KAEFFERKOPF, CAVE VINICOLE DE KIENTZHEIM KAYSERBERG 1989 (F)

£6.75	☞ HW SV	ΙΟΙ l, m, q

A zesty, ripe and aromatic wine with a slight prickle, a hint of ginger and just a touch of sweetness.

169 ALSACE GEWURZTRAMINER ST HUBERT, KUEHN 1989 (F)

£8.30	☞ EVI SUM RWW	ΙΟΙ a, l, m, q

Classic Alsace - delicately perfumed, with rich citrus fruit flavours and a clean, rounded finish.

170 ALSACE GEWURZTRAMINER GRAND CRU GOLDERT, ZIND HUMBRECHT 1987 (F)

£11.75	☞ TH WR ABY	ΙΟΙ l, m

Aromatic spicy wine with flavours of vanilla and soft lemony fruit.

171 ALSACE TOKAY PINOT GRIS CLOS JEBSAL, ZIND HUMBRECHT 1988 (F)

£14.80	☞ WR LV	ΙΟΙ a, l, q

Another delicious wine from Zind Humbrecht. It's packed with lemons and lychees and spicy marmalade. 'A fat mouthful of fruit'.

172 ALSACE GEWURZTRAMINER HERRENWEG VENDAGE TARDIVE, ZIND HUMBRECHT 1986 (F)

£18.99	☞ WR TH ABY	ΙΟΙ i, l, m

Extraordinary wine with a deep greeny-yellow colour, aromas of pine cone and lemon, with beautiful, round and tart, yet spicy fruit flavours. A super wine with elegance and length.

173 ALSACE TOKAY PINOT GRIS SELECTION DE GRAINS NOBLES, CAVE VINICOLE DE TURCKHEIM 1989 (F)

£21.00	☛ WRK BOO CRV ECK DBY	❍ k, i, l, s

This will be very good. It's packed with barley sugar and spice, needs time, but will be a very classy wine.

Grapey whites

Every time a wine writer describes a wine as smelling or tasting of strawberries, peaches or pepper, some wine drinker somewhere is almost sure to send in a letter pointing out that quality wines are not made from these fruits, and that the only growing thing they ought to taste of is grapes. In fact, of course, very few wines do taste grapey but, for the substantial number of people who wish they did, we've chosen a delicious set that is packed with the flavour of the vineyard.

174 CAFAYATE TORRONTES, ETCHART 1990 Mendoza (Arg)

£3.95	☛ SV VW FWC BWS	❍ o, q, r

Wonderfully curious stuff. It smells as though it's going to be sweet Muscat but tastes quite dry. Refreshing, appley-grapey. For parties.

175 MOSCATO D'ASTI, MICHELE CHIARLO 1990 Piedmont (It)

£4.95	☛ EE TO W FWC NI	
		❍ o, q, r

Grapey and mouthfilling, a perfect summer holiday wine. Unashamedly enjoyable.

176 PIGGOTT HILL LATE HARVEST MUSCAT, QUALCO 1989 Barossa Valley (Aus)

£4.95	☛ BI	❍ n, o, p, q

A lovely, easy-going wine with clean lemon-and-lime flavours.

Dry Germanic Whites

The newest or, as the Germans and Alsatians would claim, one of the oldest styles of all, dry Riesling and Riesling-like wines are rapidly taking over from their sweeter equivalents, both in Germany where, unbelievably, two thirds of some estates' wines are now bone dry, and in England where producers have sensibly given up trying to mimic Liebfraumilch. The only problem with this style is that for 'dry' one often has to read 'raw' and 'unripe'.

177 NIERSTEINER SPIEGELBERG KABINETT, P J STEFFENS 1989 Rheinhessen (G)

£3.15	☛ G	❍ n, o, q

Richly fruity wine with a lovely round, ripe, oily texture and pineappley freshness.

178 SEAVIEW RHINE RIESLING 1988 Coonawarra (Aus)

£3.69	☛ OD ECK DBY	❍ c, o, q

Light oily Riesling - pleasantly toasty with a slight spritz. Great value.

179 ROSEMOUNT RIESLING 1990 Hunter Valley (Aus)

£4.25	☛ OD	❍ c, o, q

Packed with rich summer fruit and a touch of wood. Very drinkable.

☛ For an explanation of the stockist abbreviations, see page 16
❍ For an explanation of food style codes, see page 66

180 HILL SMITH OLD TRIANGLE RIESLING 1990 Barossa Valley (Aus)

£4.29	☞ A W FSW TAN JFR TW AUC BFI CNL WAC WFP DBY
	◎ c, o, q

A very reliable wine with fat, ripe, tropical fruit.

181 LAMBERHURST SEYVAL BLANC 1988 Kent (UK)

£4.50	☞ GEW HW CWW MTL MOR HOT WAC
	◎ c, e, q

Under fire from the EC (because it is a hybrid rather than a proper *vinifera* grape), in England, the Seyval Blanc can produce truly tasty, greengagey wine that's full of the flavour of the English hedgerow.

182 CODDINGTON BACCHUS 1989 Gloucs (UK)

£4.99	☞ GEW	◎ c, e, q

Aromatic and grapey. Beautifully balanced wine with a lovely light sweet finish.

183 BINGER SCHARLACHBERG KABINETT HALBTROCKEN, VILLA SACHSEN 1988 Rheinhessen (G)

£4.99	☞ TO	◎ c, f, q

Deliciously off-dry wine, with a ripe elderflower nose. Good, rich fruit balanced by soft acidity. Full-bodied and long. Ready now.

184 ALSACE RIESLING RESERVE PARTICULIERE, SELTZ 1988 (F)

£5.11	☞ WAW PTR BWS DBY	◎ c, e, f, q

Lovely fruity wine with body and acidity. Lovely now, but with a good future ahead of it.

185 MAGDALEN RIVANER, PULHAM VINEYARDS 1990 East Anglia (UK)

£5.25	☞ JFR ADN FDL	◎ c, l, q

Fascinating pungent, spicy wine with rosewater and grapefruit flavours.

186 FREINSHEIMER GOLDBERG KABINETT HALBTROCKEN, LINGENFELDER 1986 Rheinpfalz (G)

£5.49	☞ OD	◎ c, q

From a new superstar winemaker, this is a developed, complex, grapey-spicey wine with great balance, and good ageing potential.

187 TRITTENHEIMER APOTHEKE RIESLING KABINETT, F W GYMNASIUM 1989 Mosel-Saar-Ruwer (G)

£5.50	☞ TO ADN TAN THP	◎ c, o, q

A 'petrolly' wine with lovely maturing Riesling character and fresh green apple acidity.

188 STAPLE ST JAMES MULLER THURGAU 1989 Kent (UK)

£5.50	☞ GEW	◎ c, d, q

A well-made round and fruity wine with good acidity.

189 GLYNDWR WHITE TABLE WINE 1989 Cowbridge (UK)

£5.80	☞ GEW	◎ c, e, q

A wine to go with your Welsh Rarebit? Fresh peachy/appley wine with lovely length.

190 MUNSTERER PITTERSBERG RIESLING KABINETT, STAATLICHE WEIN-BAUDOMANEN SCHLOSS BOCKELHEIM 1988 Nahe (G)

£6.25	☞ VW PEY	◎ e, o, q

Lovely, complex wine with grapey, melony, buttery and nutty flavours.

191 WEHLENER SONNENUHR RIESLING KABINETT, WEINGUT DR LOOSEN 1989 Mosel-Saar-Ruwer (G)

£6.75	☞ DAL PEY NI BWS	◎ c, e, f, q

Gentle, limey wine from a producer who uses less sulphur than most of his colleagues.

192 DEINHARD HOCHHEIM HERITAGE SELECTION 1988 Rheingau (G)

£6.99	☞ WR CUM HW POR TH MTL ECK DBY
	◎ c, q

A fat, maturing classic wine with fresh lemon sherbet flavours.

193 RIESLING SCHOENENBURG GRAND CRU DE RIQUEWIHR, DOPFF AU MOULIN 1988 Alsace (F)

£9.50	☛ FWC JEH AHC	○ c, o, q

This smells extraordinarily of wild rose and tastes like an exotic fruit salad with cream.

Medium Germanic Whites

The most abused wine style of them all, the one most people start with and grow out of, off-dry wines are too often made carelessly by producers who would rather be turning out drier or sweeter stuff.

194 TESCO HOCK, RIETBURG (G)

£2.39	☛ TO	○ c, l, q

Surprisingly classy wine at this price. Maturing, spicy, appley, long.

195 JOHANNISBERGER KLAUS RIESLING, SCHLOSS SCHONBORN 1988 Rheingau (G)

£4.59	☛ TO	○ c, e, l

This ripe Riesling is wonderfully spicy, with the tangy freshness of a lemon jelly cube.

196 THREE CHOIRS MEDIUM DRY ENGLISH TABLE WINE 1989 Gloucs (UK)

£4.85	☛ CWS GEW TP WNS WA WR NRW RTW WSO GMV FWC BWS BTH NI SHJ	○ c, e, f, q

Delicate floral wine which smells of violets.

197 ASTLEY SEVERN VALE 1989 Worcestershire (UK)

£4.90	☛ TAN WA GEW	○ c, d, e, f, q

Lovely, bright, appley wine. Very refreshing, with a good long finish.

198 SERRIGER HEILIGENBORN RIESLING SPATLESE, STAATLICHE WEINBAUDOMANEN 1983 Mosel-Saar-Ruwer (G)

£5.95	☛ VW	○ c, e, f, q

Fresh limey Riesling with tangy fresh acidity to balance its sweetness.

199 UNGSTEINER HERRENBERG RIESLING SPATLESE, FUHRMANN EYNUEL 1989 Rheinpfalz (G)

£5.99	☛ OD	○ c, e, o, q

A rich honeyed wine with a distinctive redcurranty flavour.

200 MUSSBACHER ESELSHAUT RIESLANER AUSLESE, MULLER CATTOIR 1989 Rheinpfalz (G)

£9.99	☛ OD	○ c, o, q

A gloriously individualistic wine made from a grape of which even German wine buffs are unaware. This Riesling/Sylvaner cross ought to taste like a Müller-Thürgau which has the same parentage. Instead, it's packed with exotic cherry and tropical fruit.

Rosés

Decent rosé, dry or off-dry, can and should be delicious stuff. Here are several good examples of a style which only seems to interest people if it's called 'blush' or 'white'.

(Arg) = Argentina; (Au) = Austria; (Aus) = Australia; (Bul) = Bulgaria; (Cal) = California; (Can) = Canada; (Ch) = Chile; (F) = France; (G) = Germany; (Gr) = Greece; (Is) = Israel; (It) = Italy; (Leb) = Lebanon; (NZ) = New Zealand; (P) = Portugal; (SA) = South Africa; (Sp) = Spain; (Sw) = Switzerland; (UK) = United Kingdom; (US) = United States excluding California

201 SAINSBURY WHITE ZINFANDEL (Cal)

| £3.45 | 🖝 JS | ⏐○⏐ o, q, r |

'White' (coral pink) Zin with lightly fizzy grapefruit/raspberry flavour.

202 CO-OP PROVENCE ROSE, GILARDI, Midi (F)

| £3.49 | 🖝 CWS | ⏐○⏐ b, c, e, f, l, r |

A dry and peppery rosé with herby peppery flavours. Good with food.

203 CHATEAU BAUDUC, BORDEAUX CLAIRET, DAVID THOMAS 1990 (F)

| £4.25 | 🖝 HUN THP H SUM CVR | ⏐○⏐ c, e, q |

Remember David Thomas's name. He not only has a hotel close to Bordeaux, but also produces this deliciously dry blackcurranty rosé which puts most other pink wines firmly in the shade.

204 CHATEAU LE RAZ, BERGERAC ROSE 1990 South West (F)

| £4.39 | 🖝 GNW DBY POR WRK NRW BOO | ⏐○⏐ c, o, q |

A very lively cherryish wine that's perfect for Summer drinking.

205 CHRISTIAN BROTHERS WHITE ZINFANDEL 1989 Napa Valley (Cal)

| £4.66 | 🖝 SC AMW ECK | ⏐○⏐ b, o, q |

An appley, raisiny rosé with an attractive, soft sweet finish.

206 CHATEAU BEL AIR BORDEAUX CLAIRET (CABERNET SAUVIGNON) 1990 (F)

| £4.75 | 🖝 WSO GHS | ⏐○⏐ c, q |

A raspberryish and cherryish wine with the freshness of peardrops and just a bit of Cabernet blackcurrant.

207 DOMAINE DE LA MORDOREE, TAVEL ROSE 1990 Rhône (F)

| £6.95 | 🖝 LEA | ⏐○⏐ o, q |

An intensely pink wine which smells of perfumed fruit and tastes of ripe raspberries.

208 DOMAINE DE BABLUT, CABERNET D'ANJOU DEMI-SEC 1961 Loire (F)

| £19.25 | 🖝 ADN | ⏐○⏐ o, q, s |

Yes, the vintage is right - and so is the price. This is an extraordinary wine from a great vintage. Long and rich, with flavours of cherries, blackcurrants, honey and sweet spice. Serve it to your most anti-demi-sec, anti-rosé friends. On second thoughts, keep it for yourself.

Country reds

A curious category, but a useful one nonetheless. In theory, it ought to denote 'rustic' wines of the kind that we have all drunk and enjoyed on holiday but can never manage to find when we get home. In practice, just as country cottages are getting smarter, so too are the country wines.

209 VAL DU MONT CABERNET SAUVIGNON, VIN DE PAYS D'OC, SKALLI 1988 Midi (F)

| £2.69 | 🖝 TH WR | ⏐○⏐ e, j, m, r |

A plummy-tasting wine with a tinge of liquorice. A great buy.

210 ASDA ST CHINIAN, VIGNERONS DE LA MEDITERRANEE, Midi (F)

| £2.75 | 🖝 A | ⏐○⏐ e, i, j, m |

A clean, juicy, cherryish, plummy wine with voluptuous flavour.

211 ST MICHAEL FRENCH COUNTRY RED, VIGNERONS CATALANS (F)

| £2.79 | 🖝 M&S | ⏐○⏐ e, i, j, r |

A fresh, jammy wine with lots of soft, ripe Summer fruit flavours.

212 SAINSBURY ST CHINIAN, CHATEAU SALVANHIAC, MAISON JEAN JEAN 1990 Midi (F)

| £2.99 | 🖝 JS | ⏐○⏐ i, j, r |

This is emphatically fruity, Southern wine, with flavours of plums and raspberries.

213 VIN DE PAYS DU GARD, ALBARIC, Midi (F)

£3.09	🠔 VR ORG RAV	🍴 b, e, i, j, r

A very light, fresh wine which tastes of cooked strawberries and tropical fruit.

214 VIN DE PAYS DES COTES DE GASCOGNE ROUGE, MICHEL DE L'ENCLOS, South West (F)

£3.25	🠔 U	🍴 b, i, j, m

A gorgeous cocktail of berry fruit, pepper and cedar.

215 ST MICHAEL CHATEAU DE BEAULIEU ROUGE, TOUSSET 1989 (F)

£3.29	🠔 M&S	🍴 e, j, m

This has a delicious flavour of currants, summer pudding and spice.

216 FAUGERES DOMAINE DU COUDOGNO, TERROIRS D'OCCITANIE 1989 Midi (F)

£3.39	🠔 FUL	🍴 b, i, j

A tasty wine with a really (fresh pipe) tobaccoish character. Distinctive and delicious.

217 CAHORS FLEURET D'OLT, LES CAVES D'OLT 1989 South West (F)

£3.49	🠔 VW	🍴 i, j

An exotic cocktail of coffee and liquorice spice. Long, soft and very easy.

218 DOMAINE DE LA CROIX, BUZET 1988 Midi (F)

£3.59	🠔 TO	🍴 b, e, i, j

If you like damsons and plums, you're bound to enjoy chewing your way into this full bodied, classy Southern red wine.

219 CHATEAU HELENE ROUGE, CORBIERES, MARIE-HELENE GAU 1987 Midi (F)

£3.65	🠔 WAW OLS RWW	🍴 e, i, j, q

This beautifully well-made wine has a rich concentration of flavours, with what one taster called ' a hint of sea salt'.

220 CHRISTIAN BROTHERS CLASSIC RED, Napa Valley (Cal)

£3.69	🠔 SC M&S MRL BKW CWM ECK MC	
		🍴 e, i, j, q, r

'Classic', in Californian terms, clearly means fruity, and easy to drink.

221 BERGERIE DE L'ARBOUS ROUGE 1989 (F)

£3.75	🠔 JS	🍴 b, i, j, q, r

A well-balanced marriage of fruit, vanilla and peppery oak. Worth keeping.

222 CHATEAU DE MANDOURELLE, CORBIERES 1988 Midi (F)

£3.75	🠔 D MC BTH	🍴 b, i, j, m

A spicy, earthy, fruity wine with bags of Southern French character.

223 DOMAINE ST EULALIE, MINERVOIS 1988 Midi (F)

£3.85	🠔 D JFR WR TH ADN	🍴 e, j, q

A simple, light, curranty, tastily fruity wine.

224 DOMAINE BUNAN, VIN DE PAYS DU MONT CHAUME 1989 Midi (F)

£3.89	🠔 A	🍴 e, i, j

A pungent, youthful wine with interesting flavours of plum, blackberry and toasty oak.

225 CLOS DE LISA, COTES DU ROUSSILON, J BAISSAS ET FILS 1989

£3.99	🠔 CGW	🍴 e, i, j

A very concentrated blend of strawberry and herby flavours. Fresh and long.

226 DOMAINE DU BOSQUET CANET, LISTEL 1987 Midi (F)

£3.99	🠔 AB CUM HUN MM BFI BOO GI MTL CPL GHS GRT DLM	
		🍴 e, i, m, q

A brambley, blackberryish wine with bags of ripe Southern herbs.

🠔 For an explanation of the stockist abbreviations, see page 16

🍴 For an explanation of the food style codes, see page 66

227 CUVEE DE L'ARJOLLE ROUGE, VIN DE PAYS DES COTES DE THONGUE, TEISSERENC 1989 Midi (F)

| £4.09 | ☞ SV TAN WSO FWC | ⏺ e, j, q |

A very deeply coloured wine, packed with freshly picked berries.

228 CHATEAU CLEMENT TERMES, GAILLAC ROUGE 1988 South West (F)

| £4.30 | ☞ TH WRK WR BWS DBY | ⏺ b, e, i, j, m |

A subtly spicy wine with sweet plummy flavour to spare.

229 CHATEAU DE FLOTIS, COTES DE FRONTONNAIS 1988 South West (F)

| £4.30 | ☞ HFW CWI NI | ⏺ c, i, j |

A purple-black wine which combines ripe fruit and rich creamy toffee

230 MAS DE GOURGONNIER TRADITION, COTEAUX D'AIX EN PROVENCE LES BAUX 1989 Midi (F)

| £4.75 | ☞ HFW CWI BH ORG LEF WFP | ⏺ b, i, j, m |

Glorious and mouthwatering Southern French wine, packed with pepper, sweet berry, and cinnamon spice. Long, rich and delicious.

231 CHATEAU DE LASTOURS CUVEE SIMONE DESCAMPS, CORBIERES 1989 Midi (F)

| £4.75 | ☞ HVW POR WRK P WES WR TH BOO CVR OLS |
| AMW GNW GRT SAN | ⏺ e, i, j, q |

Made at a winery largely run by - and home to - mentally handicapped people, this classy, richly flavoured wine has achieved superstar status since its success at the 1989 International Wine Challenge.

232 DOMAINE MONBOUCHE, COTES DE BERGERAC 1988 South West (F)

| £4.85 | ☞ HFW CDV | ⏺ b, e, i, j |

An unusual wine which is at once blackcurranty and peppery.

233 CHATEAU BOVILA, CAHORS 1986 South West (F)

| £5.50 | ☞ HFW | ⏺ b, i, j |

Cahors used to be impenetrable stuff; this one is tannic but it's also full of the taste of ripe Victoria plums. Worth keeping.

234 CHATEAU DE CROUSEILLES, MADIRAN 1987 South West (F)

| £5.99 | ☞ U | ⏺ b, e, i, j |

Madiran is another South Western appellation which is escaping from obscurity with soft, rich, cherry-and-mulberryish wines like this.

235 DOMAINE LES HAUTES DE CHAMBERTS, CAHORS 1986 South West (F)

| £6.25 | ☞ TO EE HEM | ⏺ e, i, j, m |

A very approachable Cahors with lovely creamy, raspberry style and just a trace of mint.

236 PRIEURE DE CENAC, CAHORS, RIGAL 1986 South West (F)

| £6.30 | ☞ TH WR WCE | ⏺ e, i, j |

Even without its First Growth look-alike label, this liquoricey, raspberryish wine demands to be taken seriously.

Cabernet and claret-style wines

There are so many comparable alternatives to Bordeaux nowadays, produced in so many different corners of the winemaking world, that an adventurous wine drinker could probably drink a different Merlot or Cabernet every day for the rest of his or her life. We suspect that the experience would become a little boring after a while, but if one were to start with the wines on the following pages, there would be little reason to wander much further afield.

237 TESCO FRENCH MERLOT, SICA DES COTEAUX LIMOUSINS, Midi (F)

| £2.59 | ☞ TO | ⏺ e, i, j, k |

Very good value, soft, cherryish, easy-going wine to serve to people who still believe in Piat D'Or.

238 SAINSBURY BERGERAC ROUGE, South West (F)

£2.75	☛ JS	⦿ e, i, j, m

A well-made wine with plenty of ripe fruit and the tannic backbone of traditional claret.

239 DOMAINE DES CABANNES, COTES DU FRONTONNAIS 1989 South West (F)

£2.85	☛ SAF	⦿ e, i, j, q

A fat, curranty wine with lively spices galore. Very quaffable, inexpensive wine.

240 CO-OP CLARET, ESCHENAUER, Bordeaux (F)

£2.87	☛ CWS G	⦿ l, j, r

Very typical, traditional Bordeaux for people who don't want the juicy fruit flavours of Australia. Tannic, but rich and well balanced.

241 CABERNET SAUVIGNON, VIN DE PAYS D'OC, LUCIEN COSTE 1990 Midi (F)

£2.94	☛ COV AHC	⦿ c, e, i, j

A herby, blackcurranty Southern winner with a lovely smooth finish.

242 DOMAINE BEAULIEU SAINT SAUVEUR, MARMANDAIS, UNIVITIS 1988 South West (F)

£2.95	☛ TO	⦿ c, e, i, m

This is full of light, wild raspberry and blackcurrant fruit. Perfect for Summer drinking.

243 CO-OP BERGERAC ROUGE, CAVE DE SIGOULES, South West (F)

£2.99	☛ CWS	⦿ e, i, j, r

A lovely mouthful of juicy fruit flavours. There's tannin too, though, making this a surprisingly rich wine for the price.

244 CAMPO DEI FIORI CABERNET SAUVIGNON 1988 (Ch)

£2.99	☛ OD	⦿ d, e, j, q, r

Eucalyptus and piercing blackcurrant are the keynotes here. Very attractive, easy to drink wine with real Cabernet flavour.

245 VIN DE PAYS DE LA DORDOGNE CEPAGE CABERNET, CAVE DE SIGOULES 1990 South West (F)

£2.99	☛ AB JS	⦿ e, i, j, m

This is bursting with young, mouthfilling fruit. It finishes well with delicious cassis, fruit and could even develop.

246 SAFEWAY VIN DE PAYS D'OC CEPAGE MERLOT, DOMAINE ANTHEA 1990 Midi

£3.25	☛ SAF	⦿ b, e, i, j

Cherries and plums are the main flavours here - with the rich toffee taste characteristic of the Merlot.

247 DOMAINE DE MONTMARIN MERLOT, VIN DE PAYS DES COTES DE THONGUE 1989 Midi (F)

£3.29	☛ TH WR SK	⦿ l, j, m, r

A fresh young wine with fat, spicy flavours, balanced by some lovely minty green acidity.

248 COTES DU MARMANDAIS, COCUMENT 1989 South West (F)

£3.45	☛ CDB SAF	⦿ b, e, i, j

Gutsy, dark, spicy wine with a delicious long finish. Very affordable stuff.

249 DOMAINE DES CAUNETTES MERLOT, VIN DE PAYS DE L'AUDE, ROUQUET 1990 Midi (F)

£3.49	☛ TH WR	⦿ b, i, j, m

Mint, pepper and ripe fruit flavours blend to give this wine a really immediate appeal.

(Arg) = Argentina; (Au) = Austria; (Aus) = Australia; (Bul) = Bulgaria; (Cal) = California; (Can) = Canada; (Ch) = Chile; (F) = France; (G) = Germany; (Gr) = Greece; (Is) = Israel; (It) = Italy; (Leb) = Lebanon; (NZ) = New Zealand; (P) = Portugal; (SA) = South Africa; (Sp) = Spain; (Sw) = Switzerland; (UK) = United Kingdom; (US) = United States excluding California

250 CHATEAU TOUTIGEAC BORDEAUX ROUGE 1989 (F)

£3.55	☛ TO	⟲ e, i, j, q

Well made and very pleasing wine: plummy, berryish and lightly oaky.

251 CHATEAU BELLEVUE LA FORET, FRONTONNAIS 1989 South West (F)

£3.75	☛ JS OD JN	⟲ e, i, j

The wines of Fronton are among the most reliable, inexpensive Southern French reds. This one is juicy, young and full of berry fruit.

252 COOP MEDOC, CVBG, Bordeaux (F)

£3.89	☛ CWS	⟲ i, j, k

Lovers of old-fashioned House Claret will recognise this style: fruity, but quite tannic - Bordeaux the way the British like it.

253 GATEWAY MEDOC, CHAIS BEAUCAIROIS, Bordeaux (F)

£3.95	☛ G	⟲ e, i, j

Pure, concentrated cherry and blackcurrant Cabernet style.

254 SAINSBURY SELECTION CABERNET SAUVIGNON, Midi (F)

£3.95	☛ JS	⟲ b, e, j, l

One taster described this as 'distinguished'; another praised its 'intriguing spiciness'; a third identified the 'smell and taste of cinnamon'.

255 SAFEWAY OAK-AGED CLARET, CALVET 1987 Bordeaux (F)

£3.99	☛ SAF	⟲ i, j, q

A mature wine, full of ripe, figgy, almost raisiny, fruit.

256 TESCO MEDOC, DIPROVIN ET DIE, Bordeaux (F)

£3.99	☛ TO	⟲ c, e, i, j

An attractively rich, candied fruity, herby wine with really stylish flavours.

257 CHATEAU GUIBON BORDEAUX ROUGE, LURTON 1988 (F)

£3.99	☛ TH WR	⟲ e, j, m, q

Lovely, quite old fashioned Bordeaux with flavours of mature, dried sultana fruit, hints of vanilla and beeswax. Ripe, soft and characterful.

258 SVISCHTOV CABERNET SAUVIGNON CONTROLIRAN, BULGARIAN VINTNERS 1985 Svischtov (Bul)

£3.99	☛ POR PMS EVI BH WR CWW NRW TH D RAV AHC CVR ECK VIL NI WOC PTR DBY	⟲ e, i, j, m

An exception to the rule of increasingly dull Bulgarian wines, this has a concentrated cooked fruit flavour which lasts and lasts.

259 CHATEAU BRONDELLE, GRAVES 1988 Bordeaux (F)

£4.09	☛ SAF	⟲ e, i, j, m

A very attractive wine with Ribena-like blackcurrant flavours and rich cloves and cinnamon spice.

260 TESCO AUSTRALIAN CABERNET/SHIRAZ, HARDY'S South Australia (Aus)

£4.09	☛ TO	⟲ b, j, k, r

This is perfect barbecue wine, full of cassis, mint and spices.

261 DOMAINE DES SALAISES, SAUMUR 1989 Loire (F)

£4.12	☛ ADN SAF	⟲ b, i, j

A wine from the Loire, to prove that the Cabernet Franc can compete with its more illustrious cousin. Blackcurrant and ripe green pepper.

262 CHATEAU GOELANE BORDEAUX ROUGE 1988 Bordeaux (F)

£4.19	☛ TO	⟲ b, i, j, m

This wine is packed with blackcurrant and berry fruit flavour.

263 TRAPICHE CABERNET SAUVIGNON RESERVE OAK CASK 1986 (Arg)

£4.25	☛ GI CIW PTR	⟲ e, i, j, q

Argentinian wines are about to take off in Britain. This oaky, blackcurranty version is from that country's biggest producer.

264 BERRI ESTATES AUSTRALIAN CABERNET SHIRAZ 1987 (Aus)

£4.35	☛ G TW AUC FUL W GHS WRB A DBY	⟲ b, i, j, l

Lovely, purely Aussie blend of Cabernet cassis and Shiraz spice.

265 CHATEAU LEON BORDEAUX ROUGE 1987 (F)

£4.49	☛ TO	🍴 c, e, j, m

A very intriguing wine which offers a great slug of soft, plummy fruit made more complex by sweet vanilla.

266 CHATEAU LA CROIX SIMON BORDEAUX ROUGE 1989 (F)

£4.50	☛ OD VER HPD	🍴 e, i, j, m

A youthful and classy wine. Slightly minty with sweet fruit and enough tannins to make it worth keeping for 3-4 years.

267 CHATEAU LE RAZ, BERGERAC ROUGE 1989 South West (F)

£4.50	☛ GRT POR WRK NRW ASH BOO GNW	
		🍴 e, i, j, m

A very well-made alternative to Bordeaux, with cool blackberry and mint nose. Penetrating fruit flavours with a long, succulent finish.

268 CHATEAU DE PARENCHERE BORDEAUX ROUGE, J GAZANIOL 1988 (F)

£4.55	☛ A JN	🍴 e, i, q

A super-ripe combination of currants and raspberries. Beautifully balanced, long and full flavoured. Pretty good value too.

269 PIERRE CHAUMONT CHATEAU GRIMONT, PIERRE YUNG 1987 Bordeaux (F)

£4.59	☛ LES	🍴 e, i, j

A robust wine, tannic and fruity, with Cabernet Franc grassiness.

270 CHATEAU LUGAUD, GRAVES, DIDIER MAY 1988 Bordeaux (F)

£4.65	☛ WAW OLS	🍴 i, j, q

An intriguing, complex cocktail of cassis, coffee, nutmeg, figs and juicy fruit. Irresistible!

271 WYNDHAM ESTATE CABERNET SAUVIGNON 1988 Hunter Valley (Aus)

£4.75	☛ JS	🍴 c, e, i, q

A Hunter Valley winner with lots of young, ripe, plummy fruit and a good, long fruity finish. A very attractive, approachable wine.

272 CHATEAU BARRAIL CHEVROL, FRONSAC 1988 Bordeaux (F)

£4.75	☛ U	🍴 i, j, m

A great winter warmer of a wine with ripe, Christmas cake, and slightly sweet prune/plum flavours, plus a gutsy tannic finish.

273 ST MICHAEL MEDOC, CORDIER 1989 Bordeaux (F)

£4.79	☛ M&S	🍴 j, k, m

A well made wine with character. Concentrated, tarry fruit and soft tannins with 'some classic notes' and a pure blackcurrant finish. Keep for about three years.

274 DOMAINE DU COLOMBIER, CHINON 1990 Loire (F)

£4.85	☛ JS	🍴 i, j, k

Lovely ripe Loire Cabernet from a warm year. Earthy, blackcurranty and raspberryish with a really long, pastilley flavour.

275 TESCO BOURGUEIL, DOMAINE HUBERT 1989 Loire (F)

£4.89	☛ TO	🍴 c, e, i, j, q

A soft, well balanced and fruity wine - approachable, but with real style.

276 CHATEAU MENDOCE, BOURG 1986 Bordeaux (F)

£4.99	☛ D MC	🍴 e, j, m, q

A rich, mouthfilling blend of blackberry and apple fruit. Excellently balanced and very long.

277 CHATEAU BERTINERIE BARRAILH BORDEAUX ROUGE 1989 (F)

£4.99	☛ OD	🍴 b, e, j, q

A classy, approachable wine which brings together flavours of oak, sesame seeds, mint and olives.

☛ For an explanation of the stockist abbreviations, see page 16
🍴 For an explanation of food style codes, see page 66

278 FOUNDATION 1725 ROUGE, BARTON ET GUESTIER 1989 Bordeaux (F)

£4.99	☞ OD	ΙΟΙ c, e, i, j

Youthful wine, full of fresh, juicy fruit, sweet tannin and lots of potential.

279 GLEN ELLEN MERLOT 1987 Sonoma (Cal)

£4.99	☞ OD FUL PD BU DBY	ΙΟΙ i, j, k, m

From one of California's most successful wineries, this soft, sweet, warm, toffee n' plum Merlot, is laced with musky tobacco and leather.

280 ORLANDO RF CABERNET SAUVIGNON 1988 South Australia (Aus)

£4.99	☞ AB UBC TO OD WRB RAE TAN FSW JEH SK HYN BH SEB TMW
	BGC BU AUC D LES BI MC MTL DBY CAC WCE AHC HEM POR CVR WOC
	PTR SUP JS HW RHW AF TMW BU JCK	ΙΟΙ e, j, q

The Rowland Flat ('RF') of this wine's name is the Barossa Valley headquarters of Orlando, one of the biggest producers in Australia. As for this Cabernet, it's full of soft, mature and very ripe fruit.

281 MONTANA CABERNET SAUVIGNON 1988 Marlborough (NZ)

£5.15	☞ OD TO TH VW ADN ROD NZC WAW VLW TP TMW TAN
	PIM POR SWB SC WOC HYN HVW TAN BTH DBY JFR EVI HPD BWS GNW
	ECK AB RAV LES SEL WR CPW DLM JCK CIW SHJ H TBW BH
		ΙΟΙ b, d, e, i, j

New Zealand's answer to Bordeaux tastes a little like a red wine from the Loire, with mouthwateringly crunchy blackcurrant fruit.

282 CHATEAU COUCHEROY BORDEAUX ROUGE 1988 (F)

£5.25	☞ TH GNW JN WR CAC	ΙΟΙ b, i, j

From the ever-reliable producers of Chateau La Louvière, this is a spicily earthy claret which should develop well.

283 SEAVIEW LIMITED RELEASE CABERNET SAUVIGNON 1988 South Australia (Aus)

£5.49	☞ OD NI	ΙΟΙ l, j, k, m, q, s

The label says Seaview, but a small Australian bird (a Kookaburra?) told us that this brilliant blackcurranty, oaky, spicy mouthful was made by its sister winery, Wynns in Coonawarra, from first class McLaren Vale grapes. Just the kind of wine California rarely achieves.

284 SIRIUS ROUGE, PETER SICHEL 1988 Bordeaux (F)

£5.79	☞ TH WR L&W HYN JFR WES CNL WAC DBY
		ΙΟΙ i, j, m

Peter Sichel makes the wine at Châteaux Palmer and d'Angludet. This lovely big claret is his shot at an alternative to Mouton Cadet. It's full of redcurranty, earthy, 'cigar-box', flavours which make it a far better . buy than that better known wine.

285 CUVEE CLEMENT ADER CABERNET MERLOT, DOMAINE DE RIBONNET 1989 South West (F)

£5.95	☞ H&H OD	ΙΟΙ j, k, m

Remember the name of this domaine - you'll see it on the labels of all sorts of really good value south-western wine. This example is big, richly oaky and berryish. It could be worth keeping for 2-3 years, too.

286 SEPPELT GOLD LABEL CABERNET SAUVIGNON 1986 S E Australia (Aus)

£5.99	☞ AUC LV BNK DAL ABB AF MAW
		ΙΟΙ e, i, j, k

Full bodied, ripe and fruity, peppery and softly tannic, this wine will be even more delicious in a couple of years.

287 RAIMAT CABERNET SAUVIGNON 1985 Lérida (Sp)

£6.79	☞ TH WR TO VW HVW MOR FWC BOD DBY PTR
		ΙΟΙ e, i, j, q

Five years ago, the exciting name in Spain was Torres. Today, it's Raimat, the subsidiary of the giant Codorniú sparkling wine bodega. This wine is stuffed with ultra-ripe blackberry and loganberry fruit, and has just enough vanilla flavour to proclaim its nationality.

288 CHATEAU MUSAR 1982 Bekaa Valley (Leb)

£6.79	☞ CVR AV ADN CWI JS FUL VW CGW CWW G WRW WES UTP THP TAN POR LV K&B CAC PTR MM WE AHC BND A CNL UBC HOL NI LV ECK HAS MWW WOC DBY SAC H WR HW BH PD CPW TH DLM BTH VER CUM MC AB SAN LEF BU	℀ b, j, m

There can be very few people who have yet to try Serge Hochar's Lebanese wines, but if you don't know them, the 1982 is a perfect way to start. The blend of grapes brings together the Rhône and Bordeaux styles, but the lovely spicy, tobaccoey, herby style is Hochar's own. Worth keeping for 4-5 years.

289 LES CHARMES GODARD, COTES DE FRANCS 1988 Bordeaux (F)

£6.79	☞ C&B THP SK BI	℀ b, i, j

A classic 'pencil-shavingy' Bordeaux with great depth of warm fruit and enough tannin to ensure longevity.

290 CHATEAU ROCHER FIGEAC, ST EMILION, DE LUZE 1985 Bordeaux (F)

£6.99	☞ HOP	℀ e, i, j, m

Typical St Emilion, with all the plummy, toffeeish richness that makes the Merlot such an international success. Rich, intense and long.

291 CHATEAU DE FRANCS, COTES DE FRANCS, HEBRARD DE BOUARD 1988 Bordeaux (F)

£6.99	☞ WE	℀ i, j, k

An emphatically 'serious' wine, with bags of tannin, the charred, chocolatey aroma of new oak and some gorgeously complex and concentrated almondy flavours. Worth keeping 3-4 years.

292 'L' DE LOUVIERE, PESSAC LEOGNAN, ANDRE LURTON 1988 Bordeaux (F)

£7.25	☞ OD JN	℀ b, d, k, l

The 'second wine' of Chateau La Louvière, this has such seductively delicate, smoky flavours that, despite it's undoubted ageing potential, it is tempting to drink it all right away.

293 JAMIESONS RUN RED, MILDARA 1987 Coonawarra (Aus)

£7.29	☞ TO HVW H AUC VW PD BU SAC ADN NI GRT MC	
		℀ b, c, e, j, q

Jamiesons Run features in a poem of the Australian bard, Banjo Patterson (of 'Waltzing Mathilda' fame). A superstar trophy winner in Australia, this wine is at once ripely fruity and spicily cedary. It's lighter than some of its compatriots too, and very easy to drink.

294 PALMER VINEYARDS MERLOT 1988 Long Island N.Y. (US)

£7.35	☞ AHC	℀ i, j, k, q

Produced almost within sight of the Empire State Building, this is a great example of the Merlot at its silky best. A gently woody wine with ripe interesting fruit and subdued tannin some hyped Californians would *kill* to achieve.

295 WYNNS CABERNET SAUVIGNON 1985 Coonawarra (Aus)

£7.35	☞ TH WR OD TAN HVW RHV AUC VW BOS NIC DBY	
		℀ l, j, m, q

Typical Coonawarra Cabernet with ripe blackcurrant and mint flavours. Rich, deeply fruity wine with a finish that lasts and lasts.

296 HUNGERFORD HILL CABERNET SAUVIGNON 1988 Coonawarra (Aus)

£7.50	☞ C&B BH	℀ e, i, j, q

A richly warm, approachable Australian wine, with soft fruit and equally mellow tannin. Ready for drinking right now.

(Arg) = Argentina; (Au) = Austria; (Aus) = Australia; (Bul) = Bulgaria; (Cal) = California; (Can) = Canada; (Ch) = Chile; (F) = France; (G) = Germany; (Gr) = Greece; (Is) = Israel; (It) = Italy; (Leb) = Lebanon; (NZ) = New Zealand; (P) = Portugal; (SA) = South Africa; (Sp) = Spain; (Sw) = Switzerland; (UK) = United Kingdom; (US) = United States excluding California

297 TALTARNI CABERNET SAUVIGNON 1985 Pyrenees (Aus)

£7.50	☞ BH BEN CDV H&H AUC RD SAF WOC	
		¶O↑ b, e, i, j, m

Good Aussie style. Ripe mulberry and plum fruit with hints of spice and smoke and a rich, long finish. Quite minty too.

298 TESCO MARGAUX, YVON MAU Bordeaux (F)

£7.75	☞ TO	¶O↑ b, i, j, m

A well structured wine with Cabernet blackcurrant fruit and typical Bordeaux-style tannin. Keep for a couple of years.

299 MONTES ALPHA CABERNET SAUVIGNON, DISCOVER WINE LTDA 1987 Curico Valley (Ch)

£7.95	☞ SV TGB TO HW CPL HPD LWL ABB D AMW MC	
		¶O↑ e, i, j, q

The top wine from one of Chile's few genuinely international-standard winemakers. It has truly intense blackcurrant flavour and some very attractive, gentle oak. Other South American producers take note!

300 BAUDIN, CAPEL VALE 1987 Western Australia (Aus)

£7.99	☞ OD	¶O↑ e, i, j, k

Packed with ripe, rich fruit, this wine has a real depth of flavour with super acidity and tannins. 'A touch of class'.

301 HOLLICK CABERNET MERLOT 1988 Coonawarra (Aus)

£7.99	☞ HFW BH AUC BOO BWS	¶O↑ d, e, i, j

At their best, Coonawarra wines are recognisable for not being quite as 'big' in style as some other Australian reds. This lovely light, cedary, plummy red is impeccably well balanced and built to last.

302 CHATEAU RAMAGE LA BATISSE, HAUT MEDOC 1988 Bordeaux (F)

£8.15	☞ GNW HVW WES P WRK TH WR BOO HOL BWS	
		¶O↑ i, j, k, m

From a chateau which recently rethought its winemaking, this is a very deep, rich, long-flavoured wine with intense, sweet, exotic style.

303 ROSEMOUNT SHOW RESERVE CABERNET SAUVIGNON 1987 Coonawarra (Aus)

£8.29	☞ TH WR TO THP VLW HYN CUM AUC EBA BOO BND AHC MG	
	CIW HOT HOL BTH PTR DBY	¶O↑ e, i, j, q

Yet another star from Rosemount Estate. A quality wine, full of soft fruit and mellow tannins, ready for drinking now.

304 CHATEAU SOCIANDO MALLET, HAUT-MEDOC 1987 Bordeaux (F)

£8.50	☞ RAE THP WCE RD WR HOP WOC	
		¶O↑ e, i, j, m

Derided by 'experts' because of the harvest rain which diluted its flavour, 1987 produced many wines which, like this creamy soft, oaky example are good to drink while waiting for the 1986s to 'come round'.

305 JEAN LEON CABERNET SAUVIGNON 1983 Penedés (Sp)

£8.50	☞ LEA LV THP TW VLW WSO BOO AHC RWC EBA BAB UB DBY	
		¶O↑ b, i, j, k, q

A lovely, classy, rich, oaky, spicy wine with great blackcurranty intensity. Made by a Californian whose Bordeaux-style example has been followed by a growing number of Spaniards.

306 DOMAINE RICHEAUME CABERNET SAUVIGNON 1988 Midi (F)

£8.50	☞ VER RHV WOC	¶O↑ e, i, j, m

A very flavoursome organic wine with far more depth of blackcurranty fruit than many a Bordeaux.

307 CHATEAU GRAND ORMEAU, LALANDE DE POMEROL 1987 Bordeaux (F)

£8.70	☞ C&B SWB	¶O↑ b, i, j, k

Lalande de Pomerol is an appellation to watch out for - if you like juicy, plummy Merlot-based Bordeaux at an affordable price. This is cedary, smoky and very well balanced. It should last for a year or three, too.

308 COLDSTREAM HILLS CABERNET SAUVIGNON 1988 Yarra Valley (Aus)

£8.99	☛ TH WR HW AUC GI CVR PEY	⑩ e, i, j, k, s

Made by Australia's top wine writer, James Halliday, this is a very classy Bordeaux-style wine from the cool Yarra Valley where he also makes top quality Pinot Noir and Chardonnay. This blackcurranty, cherryish wine is very drinkable now, but it's built to last.

309 BLUE PYRENEES 1984 Victoria (Aus)

£9.44	☛ TAN	⑩ b, i, j, m

A stylish label and a very stylish wine. Plenty of the typical, blackcurranty-minty fruit of Central Victoria and a lovely, long, spicy/savoury finish.

310 BARON VILLENEUVE DE CANTERMERLE, HAUT-MEDOC, CHATEAU CANTEMERLE 1986 Bordeaux (F)

£9.50	☛ U THP EVI EE WRU SPR M&S SAC GI LWL OLS HOT DLM	
DBY BTH		⑩ e, i, j, q

Classic cedary, blackcurranty claret at an affordable price. This, the second label of Château Cantemerle, is almost like a Margaux in style, with plenty of silkiness and a lovely, elegant, ripe finish. Worth leaving for 3-4 years.

311 SIMI CABERNET SAUVIGNON 1984 Sonoma (Cal)

£9.50	☛ L&W JFR TAN BH	⑩ i, j, m

Less hyped than several far less impressive Californian wineries, Zelma Long's Simi winery has proved very adept at producing Cabernets and Chardonnays which need to be kept. This one has all the elements of a lovely wine right now, but its luscious blend of fruit, herbs and tannin will certainly repay keeping.

312 LES FIEFS DE LAGRANGE, ST JULIEN, CHATEAU LAGRANGE 1988 Bordeaux (F)

£10.25	☛ WR JFR TH HOT	⑩ i, j, m

A very big, creamy, concentrated Bordeaux from the Japanese-owned (and very comprehensively restored) Château Lagrange. This rich, sweet, ripe, coffeeish wine was made under the watchful eye of Michel Delon of Château Léoville-Lascases. It needs 3-4 years patience.

313 CLOUDY BAY CABERNET MERLOT 1989 Marlborough (NZ)

£10.29	☛ ADN CVR HEM RAE GHS M&V ROD FUL WCE VE SUP JFR HW	
HVW H BEN CNL BOO WTL EBA HOL HPD HW PEY FWC DBY WR BWS MC		
NI SAN		⑩ e, i, j, k, q

You've tried the white (or you know a man who has), now sample the red. Kevin Judd's oaky, blackcurrant pastilley, Bordeaux-style wine is one of the best to come out of New Zealand; it proves that the South Island is not too cool to make this style of wine too. Full flavoured, fruity and very classy.

314 NEWTON CABERNET SAUVIGNON 1986 Napa Valley (Cal)

£10.29	☛ LAY OD CWI VW WCE BH	⑩ e, i, j, k

This Chinese-style winery adds complexity to its wines by using Bordeaux varieties like the Petit Verdot and Cabernet Franc. This example has lovely concentrated raspberry and damson fruit.

315 MOUNTADAM CABERNET SAUVIGNON 1987 High Eden Ridge (Aus)

£10.75	☛ HFW OD THP BH AUC CWI BOO AMW	
		⑩ i, j, k, q, s

Adam Wynn who made this wine is the son of the founder of Wynns winery in Coonawarra. It's superlative stuff, smelling of truffles and tasting of rich currants and mint. 'As big as a house!'

☛ For an explanation of the stockist abbreviations, see page 16

⑩ For an explanation of food style codes, see page 66

316 TOURELLES DE LONGUEVILLE, PAUILLAC, CHATEAU PICHON-LONGUEVILLE-BARON 1988 Bordeaux (F)

£10.99	☛ TH WR RAE OD	🍽 e, i, j

Another second wine from a recently rejuvenated property, this super-ripe, voluptuous stunner was made by Jean-Michel Cazes of Château Lynch Bages. It's still quite tannic but is clearly up to the quality of many far more illustrious 'first wines'.

317 CLOS DU VAL MERLOT 1987 Napa Valley (Cal)

£11.35	☛ BEN BH RD UBC	🍽 b, i, k, q

Clos du Val have long been Californian Merlot specialists. This rich, spicily oaky wine has complex juicy-minty flavours to spare. Delicious now, but with future potential.

318 CHATEAU HAUT BAGES AVEROUS, PAUILLAC, CHATEAU LYNCH-BAGES 1985 Bordeaux (F)

£11.49	☛ VW NIC BWS	🍽 e, i, j, m

A typical blackcurrant pastilley Pauillac from Jean Michel Cazes' Lynch Bages. This is the 'second wine' of the extraordinarily successful 1985 Chateau Lynch Bages; rich cedary wine, packed with ripe fruit.

319 YARDEN CABERNET SAUVIGNON, GOLAN HEIGHTS WINERY 1985 Galilee (Is)

£12.75	☛ POR HEM WRB ECK	🍽 e, i, j

Yarden, Israel's only world class winery, produces one of the very few drinkable kosher dry wines in the cool hills beneath Mount Hermon. It's full of soft, fat blackberry and plum fruit and should last well.

320 CHATEAU LEOVILLE BARTON, ST JULIEN 1987 Bordeaux (F)

£12.75	☛ JS TAN HUN JEH JN GON BI BBR CAC HOT RWW LHV	
		🍽 i, j, k

Anthony Barton owns one of the few chateaux to have remained in the same hands since before The Revolution. His wines are almost invariably among the best made and most fairly priced of the vintage. This is a lingering, blackcurranty, oaky classic.

321 RENAISSANCE CABERNET SAUVIGNON 1984 North Yuba (Cal)

£13.75	☛ ADN GON LEA BH WOC	🍽 i, j, k, q

A blockbuster in every sense, with loads of intense, ripe Cabernet fruit, rich oak and powerful tannin. The long finish shows its potential.

322 SWANSON CABERNET SAUVIGNON 1987 Napa Valley (Cal)

£14.10	☛ AV WSC	🍽 e, i, j, k

From a young winery with off-beat, go-ahead, ideas (such as annually swapping winemakers with Yalumba in Australia), this is rich, smoky, plummy wine with a deliciously long, blackcurranty fresh finish. It really ought to be kept for about 5 years to be enjoyed at its best.

323 VASSE FELIX CABERNET SAUVIGNON 1988 Margaret River (Aus)

£14.99	☛ BH AUC SAC AF HOL UBC PTR BTH	
		🍽 e, j, k

A Western Australian classic, with flavours of mint, ripe bilberries and red, inky fruit. Warm, nicely balanced, with a long, attractive finish.

324 CHINOOK MERLOT 1987 Washington State (US)

£15.00	☛ LV RD	🍽 e, j, k, q

The irrigated vineyards of Washington State have proved to be an ideal place for the Merlot, a grape that can make dull wine elsewhere. This is a succulent blend of violets, woodsmoke and ripe plummy fruit. Very soft and lingering finish.

325 CARMENET CABERNET SAUVIGNON 1986 Sonoma (Cal)

£15.00	☛ BH SEB LEA FWC DBY	🍽 i, j, m

'Smells like real Bordeaux' was one comment on this wine when it was tasted blind. Only the oakiness gives away its New World origins; the ripe, sweet fruit and soft tannin are deliciously and classily European.

326 ZD CABERNET SAUVIGNON 1986 Napa Valley (Cal)

£15.25	☛ H	℮ e, i, j, q

A very youthful wine, with a flavour that put tasters in mind of smoky tar, currants and black cherries. Very tasty now but ideally needs time.

327 YARRA YERING CABERNET 1987 Yarra Valley (Aus)

£15.50	☛ VW TAN THP FW HW BEN BU WTL BOS GHS ECK GNW	
BAT DBY BTH SEL		℮ i, j, q, s

Dr Bailey Carrodus' gorgeous Aussie classic, with heady Ribena aromas. Deliciously ripe, fruit-cakey wine, which is traditionally known as 'Dry Red No. 1'.

328 BERINGER PRIVATE RESERVE CABERNET SAUVIGNON 1986 Napa Valley (Cal)

£15.50	☛ VW GON	℮ i, j, k, q

The rich, minty and cassis fruit flavours of this maturing New World Classic are balanced by a fairly hefty amount of tannin. Gutsy wine, with 'bags of quality'.

329 WOLF BLASS BLACK LABEL CABERNET SAUVIGNON 1986 South Australia (Aus)

£16.50	☛ OD AB AUC BH CWW GNW ABY	℮ i, j, k, s

Wolfgang Blass has revolutionised Australia's wines since he arrived from Germany. This is typical Blass: mature cherry and plum, with plenty of toffeeish softness. Extremely attractive now, it will stay like this for 2 or more years.

330 PAVILLON ROUGE DE CHATEAU MARGAUX 1988 Bordeaux (F)

£17.50	☛ TO OD	℮ i, j, k, q, s

Although still very young, this wine has great elegance combining rich fruit and lovely oak. An outstanding bottle which really is a chip off the sublime Château Margaux.

331 PENFOLDS BIN 707 CABERNET SAUVIGNON 1987 South Australia (Aus)

£18.90	☛ OD ADN AUC HVW EVI GON HEM CWW GNW WOC ECK NI	
MAW BAT MC BI EE JFR GHL DBY HAR PFY PWY WE HOL		
		℮ j, k, q, s

A massively dense wine, with intense flavours of ripe currants, mint and spice. Ready for drinking today, it'll be even better if you lock it away for a decade or so.

332 CHATEAU TALBOT, ST JULIEN 1982 Bordeaux (F)

£22.50	☛ PWY THP JFR BLW WA EE WE GHL D BI WTL HAR BWI PEY WRU	
MC WOC HOL BTH DBY LHV		℮ j, k, s

Intense and ripe, and from a very fine year, this is classic, high quality claret style with mature, concentrated fruit, a soft, velvety texture and great complexity.

333 CHATEAU PAVIE, ST EMILION 1985 Bordeaux (F)

£25.00	☛ U BLW WRK RD BWI FAR HAS	℮ j, k, m, q, s

1985 was a great year for the Merlot grape in Bordeaux, and no regions made better wines than Pomerol and St Emilion. Jean Pierre Valette of Chateau Pavie is a winemaker whose wines almost always display complex, rich, honey, plum and cassis flavours.

334 ROBERT MONDAVI CABERNET SAUVIGNON RESERVE 1977 Napa Valley (Cal)

£25.00	☛ ADN GON	℮ i, j, k, s

Californian wines are worth keeping - or at least this one has proved to be. Cedary, figgy, mature and classy from a vintage most Bordelais would rather forget.

(Arg) = Argentina; (Au) = Austria; (Aus) = Australia; (Bul) = Bulgaria; (Cal) = California; (Can) = Canada; (Ch) = Chile; (F) = France; (G) = Germany; (Gr) = Greece; (Is) = Israel; (It) = Italy; (Leb) = Lebanon; (NZ) = New Zealand; (P) = Portugal; (SA) = South Africa; (Sp) = Spain; (Sw) = Switzerland; (UK) = United Kingdom; (US) = United States excluding California

335 LES FORTS DE LATOUR, PAUILLAC, CHATEAU LATOUR 1982 Bordeaux (F)

£25.99	☛ HV TO HUN RTW MAW	⦿ j, q, s

A brilliant 'second wine' that is a match for many Cru Classés. Bags of intense, smoky blackcurrant and toasted oak flavours. Very rich, substantial, balanced. Soft and delicious now but will continue to develop well.

336 OPUS ONE, 1987 Napa Valley (Cal)

£46.50	☛ VW TAN L&W CPW JN BH TP BEN HYN MTL D BI MM HHC	
	HAR CVR NI ECK HOT MC RTW PTR SEL MC BTH	
		⦿ j, k, q, s

Hyped to the skies, the Mondavi-Rothschild co-production proved to be a real star when it was tasted blind against the first growths. It's packed full of sweet ripe fruit - blackberries, redcurrants and blackcurrants and mint. Attractive spicy wood - vanilla, nutmeg and cinnamon. Structure and power and great potential.

Rhônes and spicy reds

After working your way through the 'claret-types' in the preceding section, you probably need a mouthful of something different, something with a bit more of a punch to it. Well, you've come to the right place; these wines, most of which come from the Rhône or are made elsewhere from the Rhône varieties, all share a single characteristic: spice. Try the Guide's Australian Wine of the Year - and you may never want to drink Cabernet again.

337 COTES DE LUBERON, CELLIER DE MARRENON 1990 Rhône (F)

£2.59	☛ SAF LHV	⦿ b, i, k, l, r

Leathery, grassy and spicy ripe fruit, with bags of rich, full flavour.

338 TESCO SYRAH, C MUSSELL, Midi (F)

£3.15	☛ TO	⦿ j, k, l, m, r

An earthy wine with tasty marzipan and raspberry fruit. Well matured with syrah spice and lovely length. Excellent value.

339 VIN DE PAYS DES COLLINES RHODANIENNES SYRAH, CAVE TAIN L'HERMITAGE, Rhône (F)

£3.39	☛ VW GHS	⦿ j, k, l, r

Soft, jammy, fresh fruit with a good, meaty finish. Slightly sweet with a hint of pepper. Really easy drinking.

340 SAFEWAY CHATEAU JOANNY, COTES DU RHONE, P DUPOND 1989 (F)

£3.45	☛ SAF	⦿ l, j, k, m

Full of fruit, mingling interesting chocolate and raspberry flavours.

341 SAINSBURY CALIFORNIA ZINFANDEL Monterey County (Cal)

£3.50	☛ JS	⦿ i, j, m, v

Easy drinking, warm, spicy wine with subtle liquorice and berry fruit and pleasant tannic grip.

342 LES SABLES SYRAH, VIN DE PAYS DES COLLINES RHODANIENNES, DE VALLOUIT 1989 Rhône (F)

£3.79	☛ BU	⦿ j, k, l, m

Elegant, light and fruity wine with typical Syrah fruit. Finesse and style.

343 DOMAINE LA BERAUDE COTES DU RHONE, NICK THOMPSON 1989 (F)

£3.99	☛ AB	⦿ j, k, l, m

Fresh, bright with vibrant, raspberry fruit. Well structured and nicely balanced. Proof that ex-British Steel Industry executives can become first class wine makers.

344 PENFOLDS BIN 2 SHIRAZ/MATARO 1989 Barossa Valley (Aus)

£3.99	☞ OD HVW THP JEH EVI FUL WR TH TBW SAF CWW WOC ECK NI MAW DBY	⏐Ⓞ⏐ j, k, l, m, q

In California this Syrah/Mourvedre (Mataro) blend would be treated as a Rhône style innovation. Down under, it's almost as traditional as a beer belly. Big, spicy, minty wine packed with ripe fruit.

345 CHATEAU SAINT JEAN COTE DU RHONE, MEFFRE 1989 (F)

£4.19	☞ TH WR	⏐Ⓞ⏐ i, j, k, m

The young, tart fruit aromas of this wine precede flavours that are simple, lush, full and ripe . 'Zippy' and fresh.

346 CROZES HERMITAGE, LUIS MOUSSET Rhône (F)

£4.29	☞ CWS BU	⏐Ⓞ⏐ j, k, m

'Pepper and spice and wow it's nice' was one taster's enthusiastic note.

347 SEAVIEW CABERNET/SHIRAZ 1989 South Australia (Aus)

£4.40	☞ OD EVI AUC CPL SAF ECK DBY	⏐Ⓞ⏐ i, j, k, m

A lovely soft, blackcurrant wine with a hint of menthol too.

348 DOMAINE DE LA RENJARDE, COTES DU RHONE VILLAGES 1989 (F)

£4.41	☞ TP	⏐Ⓞ⏐ j, k, m

Raspberry fruit balanced by crisp acidity and tannin. Serious Rhône.

349 RASTEAU COTES DU RHONE VILLAGES, CAVE DES VIGNERONS DE RASTEAU 1989 (F)

£4.59	☞ OD WRK WNS POR BGC CGW NRW CVR BRO PD AMW DBY BWS SA GNW	⏐Ⓞ⏐ b, i, j, m

This smells of herbs and raspberries and has what one taster called an 'earthy Beaujolais' style with soft, sweet, jammy fruit.

350 CHATEAU DU GRAND MOULAS, COTES DU RHONE 1989 (F)

£4.79	☞ TAN FUL L&W CVR	⏐Ⓞ⏐ j, k, l, m

Always a Rhône star, this has a marvellously deep and fruity 'cinnamon spice' nose, a lovely velvety texture with ripe, bramble fruit, finely balanced acidity and a great finish. Still needs a little time.

351 DIEMERSDAL SHIRAZ 1986 Paarl (SA)

£4.89	☞ AB EVI HYN WNS WRW JCK HPD GHL WRB DBY BTH	
		⏐Ⓞ⏐ l, j, k, m

Lovely stylish wine with herbs, spices and sweet fruit.

352 COTES DU RHONE, GUIGAL 1988 (F)

£4.99	☞ OD ADN SHJ HVW H RHV JN CT GON WSO LWL BFI MG BWS BWI	⏐Ⓞ⏐ j, k, m

The Rhône's top négociant takes this 'basic' appellation seriously. This example has lots of complexity with a violety, soft, ripe nose, lush, ripe fruit, some well-integrated tannins and a juicy finish.

353 PENFOLDS BIN 28 KALIMNA SHIRAZ 1987/1988 South Australia (Aus)

£4.99	☞ OD SK WA AUC WR CPL D TH CWW GNW MC	
		⏐Ⓞ⏐ j, k, l, q

Red Wine of the Year

Two extraordinary examples from Australia's most consistently successful red wine makers. The 1987 is a little readier to drink than the 1988 but both won silver medals at the International Wine Challenge. Typically Aussie reds, with robust, smoky, leathery flavours, bags of ripe blackcurrant and mulberry and a sprinkling of cloves and aniseed.

354 BALGOWNIE SHIRAZ CABERNET 1987 Central Victoria (Aus)

£4.99	☞ WR AUC	⏐Ⓞ⏐ l, j, k, m

A classy wine, with rich, ripe berry flavours, and a good tannic backbone.

☞ For an explanation of the stockist abbreviations, see page 16
⏐Ⓞ⏐ For an explanation of food style codes, see page 66

355 DOMAINE ST APOLLINAIRE (ORGANIC), COTES DU RHONE 1989 (F)

| £4.99 | ☛ JS ORG VR CWI CVR | ❍ j, k, m, q |

Perfumed, spicy violets and fresh berries. Refreshing - and organic!

356 DAVID WYNN SHIRAZ 1990 High Eden Ridge (Aus)

| £5.19 | ☛ OD THP BH WCE CWI HFW HPD BOO AMW LEF | |
| | | ❍ j, k, l, m |

Lots of interesting spice and eucalyptus aromas. Delicate and ripe fruit with some caramel, leather and blackcurrants.

357 FETZER ZINFANDEL 1987 Mendocino (Cal)

| £5.25 | ☛ TO PIM K&B WR TH CVR WOC | ❍ j, k, m |

From one of California's longest-established Zinfandel specialists, this is spicy, plummy, 'inky' and very typical.

358 DOMAINE LA SOUMADE RASTEAU, COTES DU RHONE VILLAGES, ROMERO ANDRE 1988 (F)

| £5.45 | ☛ FUL THP CPW CAC WOC BAT | ❍ j, k, m |

'Freshly ground black pepper'. Good young Rhône with lots of spice.

359 CROZES HERMITAGE, DELAS FRERES 1989 Rhône (F)

| £5.45 | ☛ AB HW FV SV BOO OLS CWM BUD GRT VIL BAT DBY | |
| | | ❍ j, k, m |

This needs more time but already has typical Rhône characteristics. Lots of spices and herbs and lovely fruit cake flavours.

360 COTES DU RHONE SEGURET, CHATEAU LA COURANCONNE 1985 (F)

| £5.50 | ☛ BI HVW SAS UBC | ❍ j, k, q, s |

Despite the lowly Appellation, this is a full-blown, rich Rhône with some tannin and great potential. Classy pipe tobacco and peppery fruit with good weight and acidity.

361 CASSEGRAIN POKOLBIN SHIRAZ 1986 Hunter Valley (Aus)

| £5.79 | ☛ WR | ❍ i, j, k, m |

Well- structured Hunter Valley wine with light, fruity flavours and a pleasantly bitter-sweet finish.

362 VIKING ZINFANDEL, OLSON VINEYARD 1987 Mendocino (Cal)

| £5.99 | ☛ ORG | ❍ j, k |

Strangely, organic wines like this are still something of a novelty in health-conscious California. Plummy, spicy Zinfandel with character.

363 TESCO CHATEAUNEUF DU PAPE LES ARNEVELS, QUIOT 1988 Rhône (F)

| £6.49 | ☛ TO | ❍ j, k, m |

Rich, aromatic nose with hints of tobacco. A well made wine with soft, pleasant fruit and developed woody flavours.

364 CHATEAU REAL MARTIN, PROVENCE 1986 Midi (F)

| £6.52 | ☛ TP | ❍ j, k |

Wonderfully soft and spicy with gentle peppery overtones. A mature wine with good depth of fruit.

365 CHATEAU TAHBILK SHIRAZ 1987 Goulburn Valley (Aus)

| £6.75 | ☛ G THP SK K&B AUC WR BOS DBY | |
| | | ❍ j, k, m, q |

Subtle aromas of cherry and spice give way to lush, sweet red fruit and soft, sweet, minty flavours. One of Australia's true classics.

366 ST GILBERT BOTOBOLAR VINEYARD, GIL WAHLQUIST 1987 Mudgee (Aus)

| £6.99 | ☛ VR CWI HPD | ❍ j, k, l, m |

Quite a tough wine but with interesting, sweet berry and chocolate fruit. Big, leathery, chewy *and* organic.

367 TALTARNI SHIRAZ 1988 Pyrenees (Aus)

| £7.20 | ☛ OD BH CDV AUC RD AF WOC BTH | |
| | | ❍ j, k, m |

'Huge wine: deep, deep fruit'. Plenty of fruit and backbone, a very rich texture with chocolate, spice, tar and wood flavours.

368 SAINT JOSEPH, ST DESIRAT 1988 Rhône (F)

£7.34	☛ CVR BU	❏ j, k, m

This needs more time but is already showing lots of warm, peppery fruit with a firm, tannic 'grip'. Unusual, rich, 'caramel nose'.

369 MITCHELL PEPPERTREE VINEYARD SHIRAZ 1988 Clare Valley (Aus)

£7.40	☛ ADN AUC SUM	❏ j, k, m, q, s

Gorgeous nose of strawberries, raspberries and plums with hints of cheese. Soft, rounded, ripe fruit with a lovely refreshing finish.

370 WOLF BLASS PRESIDENTS SELECTION SHIRAZ 1987 South Australia (Aus)

£8.49	☛ OD AUC	❏ j, k, q

Another success from the ebullient Mr Blass. This is packed with fruit, vanilla and cedar wood. Concentrated, ripe and full flavoured.

371 HENSCHKE MOUNT EDELSTONE SHIRAZ 1987 Adelaide Hills (Aus)

£8.50	☛ L&W WCE AUC	❏ j, k, q

Very rich, smokey, blackcurranty wine. Very intense and with bags of fascinating oriental spice flavours. Classy and worth keeping.

372 CHATEAUNEUF DU PAPE DOMAINE FONT DE MICHELLE, GONNET 1988 Rhône (F)

£8.99	☛ TH WR AMW	❏ i, j, k, m

A typical spicy Rhône with strong cherry flavours and interesting complexity.

373 DOMAINE DU VIEUX TELEGRAPHE, CHATEAUNEUF DU PAPE, BRUNIER 1987 Rhône (F)

£9.50	☛ TAN L&W EVI K&B H HW ADN RD GHS CIW SHJ HOT J&B	
DBY		❏ j, k, m

Chunky wine with an interesting pruney character. The soft fruit flavour invites you to drink this wine now.

374 RIDGE GEYSERVILLE ZINFANDEL 1988 Santa Clara (Cal)

£10.25	☛ CPW BH JN LEA GON HHC HEM RWW PT DBY	
		❏ j, k, m

The First Growth of California 'Zins'. Really spicy, sweet American oak with pepper, coffee and delicious hints of sour cream. Beautifully sweet and long. Fascinating wine. Needs food.

375 COTE ROTIE SEIGNEUR DE MOUGIRON, DELAS FRERES 1988 Rhône (F)

£13.50	☛ AB BOO OLS GRT	❏ j, k, q, s

A wonderful balance of concentrated juicy, ripe fruit and strong acidity and tannin. Plenty of style and class. A great long finish.

376 ROUGE HOMME SHIRAZ CABERNET 1976 Coonawarra (Aus)

£15.50	☛ AV WAW AUC	❏ j, k, q, s

Lovely, sweet, Australian wine with bags of spice and tobacco and leather and far from being on its last legs.

Beaujolais and other Gamays

As people throughout the world turn to healthier foods and wines, another category should come into its own - the lighter reds. Some of these are so tangy, fruity and lightweight that you might almost imagine them to be white. Beaujolais prices have shot up recently, but fortunately we have found a number of very affordable alternatives.

(Arg) = Argentina; (Au) = Austria; (Aus) = Australia; (Bul) = Bulgaria; (Cal) = California; (Can) = Canada; (Ch) = Chile; (F) = France; (G) = Germany; (Gr) = Greece; (Is) = Israel; (It) = Italy; (Leb) = Lebanon; (NZ) = New Zealand; (P) = Portugal; (SA) = South Africa; (Sp) = Spain; (Sw) = Switzerland; (UK) = United Kingdom; (US) = United States excluding California

377 ANJOU GAMAY, PIERRE-YVES TIJOU 1990 Loire (F)

£3.60	☛ ASH NRW	℃ c, e,

Intensely fruity wine, concentrated and rich with flavours of raspberry, ending in a firm, peppery finish. Great value alternative to Beaujolais.

378 SAINSBURY BEAUJOLAIS Beaujolais (F)

£3.85	☛ JS	℃ c, d, e, i, j, r

'A nice, typical, quaffing Beaujolais' thought one taster. Smooth, fruity and well-made.

379 MITCHELTON CAB MAC 1990 Goulburn Valley (Aus)

£4.19	☛ OD	℃ c, e, i

Australia's answer to Beaujolais. Good, pleasing and strawberryish with aromas of 'rhubarb and custard' and aniseed. Rich, full, and luscious.

380 GAILLAC, CEPAGE GAMAY, DOMAINES JEAN CROS 1990 South West (F)

£4.60	☛ C&B JFR CPL ADN WSO BFI AF GNW UBC BTH	
		℃ c, e, i, q

Rich fruit with a smell of lemon, bananas and custard.

381 DOMAINE DE LA CHAMOISE, GAMAY DE TOURAINE, HENRY MARIONNET 1990 Loire (F)

£4.99	☛ BI RAE H&H	℃ e, i, j, q

A really good quaffer, full of rich, sweet, peppery fruit and flavours of cherry and plum.

382 JULIENAS LES ENVAUX, ANDRE PELLETIER 1990 Beaujolais (F)

£5.58	☛ HHC	℃ c, d, i, j

Rich, ripe, plummy fruit. An easy style with good ripeness and some warm spice. 'Big, sweet, juicy, cooked strawberries.'

383 ST MICHAEL MORGON, DUBOEUF 1989 Beaujolais (F)

£5.99	☛ M&S	℃ e, i, m

A Morgon worth keeping, with rich, clean, fruity flavours.

384 JULIENAS, DOMAINE JOUBERT 1990 Beaujolais (F)

£6.75	☛ ADN	℃ c, e, i, m

A real mouthful of cherry and raspberry fruit. Gorgeously refreshing.

385 CHIROUBLES, A MEZIAT 1989 Beaujolais (F)

£6.99	☛ OD	℃ c, e, i, k, q, s

Light, fresh and fruity. Lovely wild strawberry nose and a hint of nettles. Good, ripe, lipsmacking fruit - some tannic length. Excellent.

Burgundy and other Pinot Noirs

Still thought of as 'big and velvety' — presumably by people whose formative experiences have been of Burgundies which had shared their vats and barrels with a few gallons of deliciously dusky brew from North Africa — these, and their New World cousins should more realistically be described as middle-to-feather-weights.

386 TESCO RED BURGUNDY, MOILLARD (F)

£4.89	☛ TO	℃ d, e, j, m

Felt by most tasters to need further ageing as it is still slightly unripe but it has very appealing raspberry fruit. Should develop into a very appealing raspberryish wine.

387 HAUTES COTES DE BEAUNE LES PERRIERES, CAVES DES HAUTES COTES 1988 Burgundy (F)

£6.35	☛ JS	℃ j, k, m

From the 'high slopes' of the Cote d'Or in a great year, this has exciting juicy raspberry fruit with softish tannin grip and good use of oak.

388 TANNERS RED BURGUNDY, DOMAINE PARENT 1987 (F)

£6.42	☛ TAN	⦿ e, j, k, m

Full-bodied Pinot Noir. Well balanced, quite full, with lots of character.

389 AVERYS FINE RED BURGUNDY 1985 (F)

£7.90	☛ AV	⦿ c, e, j, m

Mature wine which blends grassy, fruit flavours with warm vanilla oak.

390 SAFEWAY BEAUNE, LABOURE-ROI 1988 Burgundy (F)

£7.99	☛ SAF	⦿ e, j, k, m

A wine with a stylish, rich fruit nose, and creamy, soft spicy flavours. Loads of Pinot character and excellent value.

391 SAINTSBURY PINOT NOIR 1988 Carneros (Cal)

£9.25	☛ ADN RAE BH BI WSO HHC	⦿ e, i, j, k, m

New oak gives away this wine's origins, but there is some wonderful, complex berry fruit there, revealing winemaker Dick Ward's appreciation of Burgundy. Very classy wine that needs at least five years.

392 SANFORD PINOT NOIR 1986 Santa Barbara (Cal)

£10.49	☛ VW JEH POR BEN WCE BH CAC NI GNW WOC UBC DBY	
		⦿ d, e, j, q

Full of raspberry and cherry fruit, this has bags of soft, sweet Pinot and a whiff of sweet charcoal and flowers.

393 HAUTES COTES DE NUITS, ALAIN VERDET 1986 Burgundy (F)

£10.50	☛ HFW ORG BH VER	⦿ d, e, i, j, m

This organic wine has lots of sweet jammy Pinot fruit, dried fig and morello cherry flavours. Still quite young but with classic Pinot character.

394 CALERA SELLECK PINOT NOIR 1987 San Benito (Cal)

£18.25	☛ LEA HEM BH NI	⦿ j, k, q, s

Is Calera the best producer of Pinot Noir in the States? Is Selleck its best vineyard? This is certainly a great wine with masses of ripe raspberry and cherry fruit, some perfume and a generous helping of vanilla. Lovely, mouthfilling richness and texture. Exciting stuff.

395 VOSNE-ROMANEE LES MALCONSORTS, MOILLARD 1988 Burgundy (F)

£19.90	☛ VW BH	⦿ j, k, m

Generously oaked, this has ripe berry fruit with hints of spice, liquorice and hung game. Still young, it has good potential.

396 VOLNAY TAILLEPIEDS, DOMAINE DE MONTILLE 1987 Burgundy (F)

£21.90	☛ C&B H&H HHC	⦿ e, j, k, m, q

From one of the finest small estates in Burgundy (and a winemaker who is also a lawyer). Rich and silky fruit with savoury overtones; Very ripe and opulent sweet cherry fruit. Lovely, well balanced and most attractive.

397 VOSNE ROMANEE LES BEAUX MONTS, DANIEL RION 1988 Burgundy (F)

£23.50	☛ OD M&V	⦿ d, e, j, m

Excellent, ripe ,young wine with solid rich fruit and attractive balancing acidity. Good use of oak. A very fine modern Pinot Noir.

398 CLOS DE LA ROCHE, JAFFELIN 1988 Burgundy (F)

£29.99	☛ OD	⦿ e, j, k, q, s

Gorgeous nose - soft, juicy raspberry and strawberry fruit, slightly smoky and spicy with good perfume and some oaky warm vanilla.

☛ For an explanation of the stockist abbreviations, see page 16
⦿ For an explanation of food style codes, see page 66

399 LE CHAMBERTIN, ARMAND ROUSSEAU 1987 Burgundy (F)

£38.90	☞ C&B GON WR CRT	◯ j, k, m, q, s

Vibrant and complex, this has 'star quality' written all over it. A rich tarry nose with smoky fruit and plenty of nutmeg. Rich velvety multi-dimensional summer fruit flavours, with a lingering smoky finish.

Italian reds

A gloriously mixed bag here, but one in which every example bears at least some resemblance to its neighbours. These Italian reds come in all shapes and sizes, and are made from a range of (often unfamiliar) grape varieties, but they all have at least a measure of the herby-spicy character that makes them such a delicious accompaniment to food.

400 SAINSBURY ROSSO DI VERONA, Veneto (It)

£2.59	☞ JS	◯ c, d, e, j, r

Youthful and crisp with attractive, light, cherry fruit and a good clean finish. 'Fresh and zippy.'

401 SAINSBURY CHIANTI, Tuscany (It)

£3.09	☞ JS	◯ c, e, j, m, r

A good, spicily refreshing Chianti with grassy, berry fruit.

402 VALPOLICELLA CLASSICO MARANO, BOSCAINI 1988 Veneto (It)

£3.65	☞ SAF	◯ e, i, j, k

A firm wine with good cherry ripe fruit, a characteristic bitter twist, some tannin and a great finish. A great exception to the rule of awful 'Valpol'.

403 TESCO CHIANTI CLASSICO, CANTINE CO-OP DI GREVEPESA 1988 Tuscany (It)

£3.79	☞ TO	◯ j, k, m, r

Stylish plummy wine with magnificent fruit concentration.

404 VIGNETI CASTERNA VALPOLICELLA CLASSICO, FRATELLI PASQUA 1987 Veneto (It)

£3.99	☞ MC BLW	◯ e, i, j, k

A succulent wine with good length, silky texture and ripe cherry fruit.

405 CHIANTI RUFINA, SELVAPIANA 1988 Tuscany (It)

£4.99	☞ WCE L&W V&C TO VLW HFW	◯ j, k, m

There is a delicious hint of bonfires to this, with plenty of subtle, smoky, juicy fruit. Very smooth and attractive.

406 REFOSCO GRAVE DEL FRIULI, COLLAVINI 1988 Friuli-Venezia-Giulia (It)

£5.20	☞ V&C BOO	◯ c, e, j, m

Fresh, ripe characterfully fruity wine with excellent length.

407 LAGREIN DUNKEL, VITICOLTORI ALTO ADIGE 1986 Trentino-Alto Adige (It)

£5.45	☞ V&C	◯ c, d, e, j

Made from indigenous grapes from the north east of Italy, this is at once herby and creamy with the flavour of fresh fruit salad.

408 BONARDA OLTREPO PAVESE, FUGAZZA 1987 Lombardy (It)

£5.65	☞ OD V&C WOC CE WRK RAV	◯ e, j, k

Long, savoury wine with big fruity flavours and a firm backbone.

409 CHIANTI CLASSICO LAMOLE, CASTELLI DEL GREVEPESA 1986 Tuscany (It)

£5.95	☞ A BU	◯ e, i, j, k

There's lots of soft fruit in this lovely, rounded, mature wine. Very attractive for drinking now.

410 CAPITEL VALPOLICELLA DEI NICALO, TEDESCHI 1986 Veneto (It)

£5.99	☞ WE WGA L&W BOO	◯ j, k, m

Great morello cherry-flavoured wine. Very classy and well made .

411 CHIANTI CLASSICO, SAN LEONINO 1988 Tuscany (It)

| £6.20 | ☞ ROD | ○ e, i, j, k, q |

Lovely scented, creamy, berryish wine with soft, spicy, herby fruit and subtle tannin. Ripe, lush and lasting.

412 CAMPO FIORIN VALPOLICELLA, MASI 1986 Veneto (It)

| £6.99 | ☞ CPW SEL V&C AB TMW TW MM MAW DBY WFP |
| | ○ j, k, m |

From one of the region's most reliable producers . Rich cherry fruit with a pleasant bitter twist on the finish. Very tannic; best kept for a few years.

413 DOLCETTO D'ALBA, CONTERNO 1988 Piedmont (It)

| £6.99 | ☞ OD HAS | ○ j, m, q |

Beautiful wine with delicate, fresh cherry and raspberry flavours that last right to the long finish. Ripe and quaffable.

414 BARBAROSSA, FATTORIA PARADISO 1986 Emilia-Romagna (It)

| £7.35 | ☞ V&C BH HEM | ○ e, i, j, m |

Terrific, full, ripe and juicy. Sweet damson fruit with crisp acidity, gentle tannin and a satisfying, long finish.

415 BARBERA D'ALBA PIAN ROMUALDO, PRUNOTTO 1988 Piedmont (It)

| £7.35 | ☞ SV LEA DBY | ○ c, j |

Fresh and slightly almondy, with refreshing bitter-sweet fruit and excellent depth of flavour.

416 CHIANTI CLASSICO, ISOLE E OLENA 1988 Tuscany (It)

| £7.65 | ☞ WCE V&C HOP LEA GON CWI H&H HVW RTW GI EBA HHC |
| HOT HAS | ○ e, i, j |

From a great young, innovative producer, this has lots of character with a mint and rhubarb nose, and rich mouth filling fruit.

417 COLLIO MERLOT, COLLAVINI 1985 Friuli-Venezia-Giulia (It)

| £7.99 | ☞ VW JCK | ○ l, j, k, q |

Deep, meaty and damsony, with ripe fruit and a touch of tannin.

418 PAIS, COLLE MANORA 1989 Piedmont (It)

| £8.95 | ☞ LEA | ○ j, m, q |

Sweet, spicy wine with a lovely redcurrant and strawberry finish.

419 ROSSO DI MONTALCINO, POGGIO ANTICO 1989 Tuscany (It)

| £8.99 | ☞ LEA SV DBY | ○ l, j, k |

Far more fun than supposedly classier Brunello di Montalcino, this is rich and elegant with ripe currant fruit. Stylish, peppery, with an attractive green edge of spice.

420 'SASTER' CABERNET SAUVIGNON, FRIULVINI 1988 Friuli-Venezia-Giulia (It)

| £10.50 | ☞ ROD LEA | ○ e, i, j |

Italian-style mellow Cabernet with attractive oaky, smoky nose, soft, blackberry fruit, gentle acidity and a long silky finish.

421 VIGNASERRA, VOERZIO 1988 Piedmont (It)

| £10.99 | ☞ OD | ○ e, i, j, q |

From a young superstar Barolo producer, this is full and quite tannic with bags of black cherry fruit, chocolate and cloves. A fabulous, really interesting wine.

422 BAROLO, MICHELE CHIARLO 1982 Piedmont (It)

| £12.15 | ☞ TO | ○ j, k |

A Barolo for traditionalists, rich, raisiny and minty with good oak and a firm dry finish.

(Arg) = Argentina; (Au) = Austria; (Aus) = Australia; (Bul) = Bulgaria; (Cal) = California; (Can) = Canada; (Ch) = Chile; (F) = France; (G) = Germany; (Gr) = Greece; (Is) = Israel; (It) = Italy; (Leb) = Lebanon; (NZ) = New Zealand; (P) = Portugal; (SA) = South Africa; (Sp) = Spain; (Sw) = Switzerland; (UK) = United Kingdom; (US) = United States excluding California

423 BAROLO VIGNA DEL GRIS, FANTINO CONTERNO 1985 Piedmont (It)

£12.95	☛ WCE	⏯ i, j, k

One for those who like their wines to be a little more approachable.
Round and full with mellow, velvety fruit, liquorice and fruit cake
flavours, but there's plenty of tannin in the background, so it will keep.

424 COLTASSALA, CASTELLO DI VOLPAIA 1986 Tuscany (It)

£12.99	☛ EE ADN WCE V&C RD GHS HEM	
		⏯ j, k m

From one of the best estates in Chianti, fresh and smoky with subtle
leather and oak. Lovely fruit cake richness.

425 CARMIGNANO RISERVA, VILLA DI CAPEZZANA 1985 Tuscany (It)

£13.50	☛ WCE TAN LEA CPL BWS	⏯ e, i, j

Attractive, mature and herby wine with appealing flavours of damsons and almonds, developing into lovely creamy and leathery tones.
Softly fruity but sufficient tannin to make it worth keeping.

426 CEPPARELLO, ISOLE E OLENA 1988 Tuscany (It)

£13.99	☛ WCE V&C CWI GON RD NRW HEM	⏯ j, k

Wonderful wild cherry nose with great weight of fruit. Complex, intense
and with good tannic 'grip', this young wine has great potential.

427 AMARONE CLASSICO DELLA VALPOLICELLA FIERAMONTE, ALLEGRINI 1983
Veneto (It)

£14.25	☛ WCE V&C BH HFW DAL BWS	⏯ j, k q

Full, warm, spicy, juicy damson fruit with a great bitter- almonds finish.
The Italians call this Vino da Meditazione. We know what they mean.

428 GRANATO TEROLDEGO, FORADORI 1988 Trentino-Alto Adige (It)

£14.50	☛ H&H	⏯ e, j, m

A rare chance to taste what the Teroldego grape can do when handled
with love, skill and respect. Great concentration of fresh fruit pastille
flavours. Deliciously juicy with spicy oak and fresh, tangy acidity.

429 BAROLO, 'CIABO MENTIN GINESTRA', CLERICO DOMENICO 1986 Piedmont (It)

£16.50	☛ BI	⏯ j, k

Modern single vineyard Barolo with the flavour of sweet damson jam.
Hints of coffee and bitter chocolate. Substantial length.

430 BRUNELLO DEL MONTALCINO, POGGIO ANTICO 1985 Piedmont (It)

£16.99	☛ OD SV LEA HAR HEM WSC GNW	
		⏯ j, k, q

Friendly and fruity. Soft, rich, bitter cherry and toffee fruit with a touch
of tannin. Lovely supple texture, but with a characteristic firm finish.

431 CABREO IL BORGO, RUFFINO 1986 Tuscany (It)

£17.90	☛ V&C BLW RD	⏯ j, k, q

Loads of everything. Chunky, ripe Sangiovese flavour with bilberries
and oak. Quality wine with positive character and a long, violetty finish.

432 LE PERGOLE TORTE, MONTE VERTINE 1986 Tuscany (It)

£19.20	☛ W RD V&C	⏯ i, j, k

Up-front flavours with a nice balance of rich, lively, sappy fruit and
bitter- chocolate. Beautifully balanced, with good acidity, firm tannins,
and a long exciting finish. Built to last.

433 BAROLO RISERVA, GIACOMO CONTERNO 1982 Piedmont (It)

£19.50	☛ OD V&C	⏯ j, k, s

Rich and intense with massive flavours of bittersweet cherries and
bitter chocolate, plums, coffee and mint.

434 MAURIZIO ZANELLA, CA' DEL BOSCO 1988 Lombardy (It)

£27.50	☛ WCE V&C OD LEA	⏯ i, j, k, q, s

Just the kind of classy modern Cabernet so many Californians (mistakenly) think they are making. Lovely toasty oak with great length and

complexity of mouthfilling blackcurrant and berry fruit and tannin. A brilliant wine with finesse and elegance. Needs at least a decade .

Iberian reds

Every year, we do our best to find new wines to recommend in the Guide. Usually, we achieve this with little difficulty, but Spain and Portugal remain the exceptions to the rule; sadly, the people making the good wines are a pretty unchanging bunch. Roll on the Iberian revolution.

435 DON DARIAS RED, BODEGAS VITORIANAS (Sp)

£2.79	☛ TO A WR TH SAF	ΙΟΙ e, j, m, v

If you like oaky Spanish wine, this is for you. It's spicy, blackcurrantly and delicious. Wonderfully reliable stuff.

436 SAINSBURY RIOJA 1986 Rioja (Sp)

£3.60	☛ JS	ΙΟΙ e, i, j, m, v

A wine which is full of the strawberry fruit of the Rioja Tempranillo grape. Sweet, rich and tangily fresh.

437 SEÑORIO DE LOS LLANOS RESERVA 1982 Valdepeñas (Sp)

£3.90 ☛	TO BEN JEH SEB WNS BOO HAR MOR UBC DBY
	ΙΟΙ j, m, v

If only Spain could produce more wine like this - it's precisely what Rioja fans are crying out to buy: soft, mellow with flavours of toffee and cherries for a very affordable price.

438 MARIUS RESERVA, BODEGAS PIQUERAS 1983 Almansa (Sp)

£4.59	☛ C&B EVI TAN WA WRW WE RWC HEM SEL	ΙΟΙ i, j, m

Tannic Spanish wines are rare, but this one has enough ripe plummy, berryish fruit to make it a delicious prospect for a couple of years' time.

439 QUINTA DA BACALHOA, JOAO PIRE S 1988 Palmela (P)

£4.95	☛ JS	ΙΟΙ i, j, m

A French-style, Portuguese wine made from Bordeaux varieties by an Australian, primarily for the British. Warm, earthy redcurrants with an attractive tannic edge of new wood.

440 TINTO VELHO REGUENGOS DE MONSARAZ, JOSE DE SOUSA ROSADO FERNANDES 1986 Alentejo (P)

£4.99	☛ TO EVI HVW SEB WCE BOO HEM HAS PTR
	ΙΟΙ i, j

Mellow, fruity wine with strong tannin and rich bitter-sweet finish.

441 QUINTA DE CAMARATE, J M DE FONSECA 1984 (P)

£5.39	☛ ADN WCE THP	ΙΟΙ e, j, m

J.M. de Fonseca is one of Portugal's most go-ahead producers. This Cabernet-based wine is rich and mature with lots of blackcurranty fruit.

442 TEMPRANILLO, BODEGAS OCHOA 1987 Navarra (Sp)

£5.50	☛ WR CWW BH EE EVI HVW JEH K&B POR PIM TP WNS WAW
WCE HAR BND SOL DAL CVR GNW LHV NRW CIW PIM GRT UBC BAT	
B&B SEL	ΙΟΙ c, j, m, q

A very soft, beautifully balanced example of the grape from which all good Rioja is primarily made. It's full of the flavours of cherries, plums, chocolate and oak, with just a hint of cigar box spice.

☛ For an explanation of the stockist abbreviations, see page 16
ΙΟΙ For an explanation of food style codes, see page 66

443 GARRAFEIRA PT81, J M DE FONSECA 1981 Azeitão (P)

£5.55	☛ TO	◯ j, q

Very intense, mellow, mature fruit with some good tannin.

444 BAIRRADA, LUIS PATO 1988 Bairrada (P)

£5.65	☛ EE CDV	◯ j, m

A meaty wine, and a good example of the spicy tannic Baga grape.

445 NAVAJAS RIOJA CRIANZA TINTO 1985 (Sp)

£5.79	☛ CWI BOO MOR HPD SAF MC	◯ e, i, j

A Spanish wine with evident but discreet oak and some really attractive floral-raspberry-spicy flavours. Would keep.

446 GRAN SANGREDETORO RESERVA, TORRES 1986 Penedés (Sp)

£5.79	☛ VW CGW ROD GON EVI FSW HVW HW JEH K&B SWB MFW	
	OD POR SAS TW CNL HAR G PTR	◯ j, m

A big wine with lovely flavour and length. There's 'bags of soft, nettley, cherryish, spicy fruit' with typical Spanish oaky richness.

447 EL COTO RIOJA RESERVA 1985 (Sp)

£5.79	☛ AB	◯ e, i, j, q

Gentle, stylish Rioja from one of the region's best producers. Spicy, soft and beautifully well balanced.

448 GARRAFEIRA TE, J M DE FONSECA 1985 Azeitão (P)

£6.40	☛ BOO	◯ i, j, m

Another J.M de Fonseca success, a Garrafeira - special reserve - that's packed with rich fruit and smoky tannins. Wonderfully Portuguese.

449 CAMPO VIEJO RIOJA GRAN RESERVA 1980 (Sp)

£7.95	☛ AB HW WSC WOC CWW GON PIM SAS WNS WRW MOR MTL	
	HPD CAC BKW GRT AMW DLM DBY GNW	◯ i, j, s

Classic maturing Rioja with raspberry fruit and spice. Savoury and long.

450 NAVARRA ANIVERSARO 125, CHIVITE 1981 Navarra (Sp)

£8.50	☛ TAN RTW RD BTH	◯ j, q, s

A rich, oaky, warmly fruity wine from the best producer in Navarra. Proof that the border between Rioja and Navarra is often best ignored.

451 MARQUES DE MURRIETA RIOJA TINTO RESERVA 1985 (Sp)

£9.50	☛ WR RAE LEA ADN BEN BH EVI JEH L&W SEB TAN TP VLW	
	WCE WRW MM BI MOR GHL HEM THV BWS FWC PTR ECK MC WOC	
	SEL	◯ j, k, q, s

From a potential Rioja First Growth, this is a beautifully fragrant wine with ripe, rich flavours of plum and strawberry that last 'for eons'.

452 RIOJA RESERVA 904, LA RIOJA ALTA 1978 (Sp)

£13.50	☛ LEA GON ADN TRE BEN CUM JEH L&W LV SAS THP BOO	
	AHC MOR RD HEM PEY FWC BWS DBY PTR SEL HHC ECK B&B MM	
		◯ j, q, s

A chewy, mouthfilling wine with lovely oaky-vanilla flavours. Good, mature Riojas of this quality are all too rare. Grab it while you can.

Muscats

One of the least appreciated and most wonderful of all grape varieties, the Muscat produces wines that are absolutely packed with the flavour of grapes and raisins. Dry or sweet, fortified or unfortified, these are probably the most drinkable examples of the kinds of wine our ancestors would have drunk and enjoyed.

453 MUSCAT DE ST JOHN DE MINERVOIS Midi (F)

£2.65	☛ JS	◯ n, o

A more westerly approach to Beaumes de Venise with a slightly

454 SAINSBURY MOSCATEL DA VALENCIA (Sp)

£2.85	JS	1Ol n, o, p

Rich and raisiny with luscious oranges with a superb long finish.

455 CASTILLO DE LIRIA MOSCATEL, VICENTE GANDIA Valencia (Sp)

£3.30	W FUL G TAN BOO	1Ol n, o

Sweet Muscat and lemon fruit with zest and a lovely long finish.

456 SAMOS MUSCAT Samos (Gr)

£4.50	OD TAN U WCE RAV DLM	1Ol n, o

Delightful orange marmalade aromas. Up-front muscat fruit creating
a super, rich wine with a clean zingy finish.

457 MOSCATEL DE SETUBAL, ADEGA COOPERATIVA DE PALMELA 1981 (P)

£6.10	FSW SOL	1Ol n, o, q

This ultra-traditional Muscat smells almost like sherry but tastes more
like Madeira with a rich, orangey concentration of sweetness.

458 YALUMBA MUSEUM SHOW RESERVE MUSCAT Rutherglen (Aus)

£6.50	AUC BH BEN HEM CVR WOC NI	1Ol n, o, p, q

Deep burnt caramel and toffee flavours packed full with delicious fruit
and spice. 'Very sweet but with a liquid Christmas pudding richness
of flavour which prevents it from cloying'.

459 DOMAINE CAZES RIVESALTES VIEUX 1978 Midi (F)

£12.00	LV FWC	1Ol n, q

'A Christmas treat'; 'packed with currants, sultanas and raisins - and
dollops of (Old English) marmalade and dark treacle'. 'Brilliant'.

460 CAMPBELLS OLD RUTHERGLEN LIQUEUR MUSCAT (Aus)

£13.50	SEL LV DAL NI RAE CPW SK GON ABB HAR AF AMW DBY
	1Ol n, o, p, q

Amazingly powerful, rich raisiny wine with a good long finish.

Botrytis and all that rot

More decadent stuff. Like perfume and *The Archers* on Sunday morning,
great botrytis-affected wines are among the world's indulgences. Try these
and cock a snook at the health fascists who'd rather you sucked a lemon.

461 JURANCON MOELLEUX CUVEE THIBAULT, DOMAINE BELLEGARDE 1989 South
West (F)

£4.99	OD	1Ol m, n, o

An unusual example of a nobly-rotten wine from an often forgotten
corner of South-West France. Fresh honeyed aromas with a lovely
syrup pudding richness.

462 JOSEPH PHELPS LATE HARVEST RIESLING 1988 Napa Valley (Cal)

£5.99	VW	1Ol n, o, q

Hedonism, California-style. Slightly petrolly, honeyed Riesling with
initial dry crisp fruit. Subtle and very likeable.

463 CHATEAU FILHOT, SAUTERNES 1985 Bordeaux (F)

£5.99	A	1Ol m, n, o, q

A truly classy Sauternes with a superbly concentrated nutty nose. Ripe
tropical fruits and good soft length.

(Arg) = Argentina; (Au) = Austria; (Aus) = Australia; (Bul) = Bulgaria; (Cal) = California; (Can) = Canada;
(Ch) = Chile; (F) = France; (G) = Germany; (Gr) = Greece; (Is) = Israel; (It) = Italy; (Leb) = Lebanon;
(NZ) = New Zealand; (P) = Portugal; (SA) = South Africa; (Sp) = Spain; (Sw) = Switzerland; (UK) =
United Kingdom; (US) = United States excluding California

464 CHATEAU LOUPIAC GAUDIET, LOUPIAC 1988 South West (F)

£6.10	☛ JEH W LWL PD BU ABY	℟ n, o

An alternative to Sauternes with a very comparable style. Very ripe, creamy and deliciously rich. Almost too appealing to keep for long.

465 REDWOOD VALLEY ESTATE LATE HARVEST RIESLING 1989 Nelson (NZ)

£6.25	☛ VW LEA WCE HW HVW H FSW BH RD GI HEM MG CAC AF	
FNZ SHJ		℟ n, o, q

From Nelson on New Zealand's South Island, this is powerful with bags of intense honeyed pineapple and apricot fruit. Superb length.

466 THE HARDY COLLECTION PADTHAWAY RHINE RIESLING BEERENAUSLESE 1987 (Aus)

£6.29	☛ OD AUC CVR CIW	℟ m, n, o

Ultra-late harvest wine from one of Australia's coolest regions. Fragrant apples, vanilla and caramel raisins. Juicy, upfront, rich and balanced.

467 LEIWENER LAURENTISLAY RIESLING AUSLESE, MARIENHOF 1983 Mosel-Saar-Ruwer (G)

£6.45	☛ G	℟ n, o

A youthful rich, oily bodied, elegant and classy Riesling, with gentle flavours of lemon, spice and apple.

468 HERXHEIMER HIMMELREICH HUXELREBE BEERENAUSLESE, WERNER PFLEGER 1988 Rheinpfalz (G)

£7.25	☛ A	℟ m, n, o

A text book example of a wine with bags of apricotty noble rot. Other exotic flavours include spicy mango, raisins and marmalade.

469 CHATEAU BASTOR LAMONTAGNE, SAUTERNES 1988 Bordeaux (F)

£9.90	☛ OD ROD VER EBA ROD SAF AMW WOC UBC	
		℟ m, n, o, q, s

Luscious young Sauternes from a great vintage. Rich, yet clean and elegant, with a modest note of lemony/orangey acidity and a long finish. A wine to keep.

470 BURGLAYER SCHLOSSBERG RIESLING BEERENAUALESE, B A SCHAFER 1989 Nahe (G)

£10.99	☛ OD	℟ n, o, q

Beautiful intensely flavoured Riesling with an apple crumble aroma. Elegant and enjoyable now, but well worth waiting for.

471 VOUVRAY MOELLEUX LE MARIGNY, DOMAINE DES AUBUISIERES 1990 Loire (F)

£10.99	☛ OD LV GON ADN OLS	℟ n, o

Good, sweet Vouvray is a rare treat. This is packed with honey, spice and ripe apple and is beautifully balanced. Raisin fruit and syrup. Massive, direct sweetness. Will easily outlast both Kinnock and Major.

472 JURANCON MOELLEUX VENDANGE TARDIVE, DOMAINE CAUHAPE 1988 South West (F)

£11.99	☛ EE BWS WCE GHS M&V BH RD PEY CIW FWC GNW NI	
		℟ n, o, q

Another opportunity to taste the honeyed, apricotty intensity of Manseng grapes which have been affected by noble rot.

473 CALUSO PASSITO, VITTORIO BORATTO 1985 Piedmont (It)

£13.50	☛ OD V&C	℟ n, o

An extraordinary sweet, concentrated, complex wine with a powerful plummy-treacley finish.

474 CHATEAU GUIRAUD, SAUTERNES 1988 Bordeaux (F)

£14.50	☛ OD HUN	℟ m, n, o, q, s

Very young green/gold rich, pineapply-lemony wine with superb balance of acidity. Lovely concentration and lots of intense botrytis flavour.

475 CHATEAU RIEUSSEC, SAUTERNES 1983 Bordeaux (F)

£28.50	☞ D OD HUN PWY FSW TVW GI WTL GHS BWI OLS FAR
SHJ UBC BWS FWC	⦿ m, n, o, q, s

Sheer class. Intense gold coloured wine with full flowery aromas.
Rich, luscious flavours of apricot, peaches and cream, mango, coconut
and vanilla and just a hint of pepper. Complex and exotic, already far
too drinkable but really should be kept for a few more years.

476 LAUBENHEIMER EDELMAN SCHEUREBE TROCKENBEERENAUSLESE, KUEHLING-GILLOT 1989 Rheinhessen (G)

£34.50	☞ WSC	⦿ m, n, o, q, s

Tremendous concentration of luscious pineapple fruit with excellent
balancing acidity. 'Liquid honey and lemons' with a hint of pink
grapefruit at the end. A very elegant wine, ready to drink now but it's
the sort of wine which will last for decades.

Sherry

Forget every glass of warm dry sherry you have ever been offered by vicars
and university dons; obliterate from your mind the ancient half-full bottle
of cream sherry which constituted Aunt Mildred's idea of hospitality. No,
the sherries which feature on the next few pages are among the greatest
wines in the world. Their flavour, dry or sweet, is unique.

477 SAFEWAY BLASQUEZ FINO CARTA BLANCA Jerez (Sp)

£2.55	☞ SAF	⦿ a, c, q

A young and delicious sherry with a fragrant, floral, fruity aroma.
Drink well chilled.

478 SODAP MEDIUM DRY (Cyp)

£3.69	☞ CWS LES	⦿ o, q

Cyprus 'sherry' is rarely even worth trifling with, this is an exception.
Golden, nutty, nicely balanced. A sweet, fruity wine.

479 LA GITANA MANZANILLA, HIDALGO Jerez (Sp)

£5.49	☞ ADN CWI BEN JEH JN MFW WSO GHS WE HHC W HPD HEM
PEY CWM AF SEL NI SHJ SAN	⦿ c, q

Hidalgo is an acknowledged master of Manzanilla. La Gitana - 'the
gypsy' - is deep and good; delicate, with a hint of sweetness.

480 DOS CORTADOS, WILLIAMS AND HUMBERT Jerez (Sp)

£8.99	☞ HAS EVI JEH K&B THP MM GNW SEL DLM
	⦿ a, c, q

Long-lasting, honeyed, caramely but essentially dry; old Oloroso the
way the Spaniards like it. Try it with *tapas* or just sip it through a long,
relaxed evening.

481 MANZANILLA PASADA DE SANLUCAR ALMACENISTA, LUSTAU Jerez (Sp)

£10.75	☞ A W BEN BLW JEH SWB TMW TP CNL MM MTL BKW HEM
SEL DBY	⦿ m, q

Almacenista sherries, like single-vineyard wines often have more
character than blended wines made in greater quantity. This is dry,
spicy and full bodied with a rich, nutty smell of toffee and caramel and
a fresh creamy, lemony flavour.

☞ For an explanation of the stockist abbreviations, see page 16
⦿ For an explanation of food style codes, see page 66

482 ROYAL CORREGIDOR RICH RARE OLD OLOROSO, SANDEMAN Jerez (Sp)

£10.99	☞ OD ROD JEH POR TMW HAR SEL BWS	
		◯ m, n, o, q, s

Not for the faint-of-heart, this is a flavour packed roller-coaster of a wine with an intense, sweet, burnt-toffee and chocolate nose and long-lasting lucious, vibrant walnut and raisin fruit flavours.

483 APOSTOLES, OLOROSO ABOCADO, GONZALEZ BYASS Jerez (Sp)

£15.49	☞ JEH RAE GON HYN OD THP TMW MM TBW WE RWC MOR	
MTL GHL AF WOC JFR SEL DBY		◯ m, q, s

Rich, intensely complex wine with great depth and a fascinating dry but off-dry flavour. Intense, burnt caramel with a long lasting finish.

Port and other fortified wines

We live in a world in which a taste for alcohol and sweetness are increasingly treated as though it were a perversion. In this kind of climate, what hope do sweet, fortified wines have? Vintage port is unthreatened (people invest in it) and other, classier Tawny, Single Quinta and good Late Bottled benefit from the fact that Vintage buyers tend to be attracted to other higher quality ports. But there are all sorts of great, indulgent fortified wines that are daily becoming less fashionable. Grab a few while you can.

484 SAINSBURY VINTAGE CHARACTER PORT Douro (P)

£5.89	☞ JS	◯ m, q

A firm, intense, spicy, fruity port. Very rich, yet elegant. Good value.

485 TESCO LATE BOTTLED VINTAGE PORT, SMITH WOODHOUSE 1985 Douro (P)

£6.85	☞ TO	◯ m, q

Lush, plummy and velvety round wine with sweet, good 'firm fruit'.

486 ASDA 10 YEAR OLD TAWNY PORT, CHARLES COVERLEY Douro (P)

£7.99	☞ A	◯ m, q

Ripe and easy port with lots of depth. Smoky, rich and nutty. Try it chilled as an aperitif - the way the makers drink it in the Douro.

487 TAYLOR'S FIRST ESTATE PORT LUGAR DAS LAGES Douro (P)

£8.15	☞ GHL MTL TO CPL VW ADN AB BEN BH CUM EVI HW	
JFR SWB SUP U WA MM D W SEL DBY BTH HOL		◯ m, q

Deep and rich with plum and fig overtones and a hint of pepper.

488 GOULD CAMPBELL VINTAGE CHARACTER PORT Douro (P)

£9.00	☞ VW LV	◯ m, q

Almondy port with hints of butterscotch and a bittersweet edge.

489 STARBOARD BATCH 88 RUBY, QUADY Central Valley (Cal)

£10.15	☞ LV HPD SWB WRW SK MAW	◯ m, q

Made by Andrew Quady, the Californian fortified wine enthusiast, this alternative to port is rich, raisiny, bold and unabashed.

490 HUCHESON COLHEITA 1975 Douro (P)

£11.99	☞ OD	◯ m, q

Colheita ports - tawnies of a specific year - are still something of a novelty in Britain, though they have always been popular in Portugal. This one is warm and complex with caramel/toffee flavours and plenty of tasty, sweet fruit.

491 MALMSEY 10 YEAR OLD, HENRIQUES & HENRIQUES (P)

£13.00	☞ WRK ASH	◯ m, n, q

Classic Madeira with intense flavours of caramel and burnt fruit. Nutty and stylish.

492 VERDELHO 10 YEAR OLD, COSSART GORDON (P)

£15.99	☛ EVI BH CVR HEM	🍽 m, n, q

Aperitif Madeira with subtle citrus and raisin flavours. Fresh, delicate and very drinkable.

493 WARRE'S QUINTA DA CAVADINHA 1982 Douro (P)

£16.50	☛ GON CPW EVI HYN OD WCE DAL CPL SUM CVR CWM AMW WOC GNW	🍽 m, q

A 'single quinta' port with real vintage quality, full, rich, spicy and soft. Really well balanced with lovely, aromatic fruit.

494 SANDEMAN IMPERIAL 20 YEAR OLD TAWNY PORT Douro (P)

£17.50	☛ OD TO LEA EVI WSO TH WR HAR	🍽 m, q, s

Raisiny, deeply fruity wine with creamy, rich, smoky flavours.

495 FONSECA-GUIMARAENS 1976 Douro (P)

£18.50	☛ ROD EVI FV H HW JEH K&B LV WCE MM MTL BAB HEM WOC	🍽 m, q, s

A powerfully intense wine with hints of mint and chocolate. Firm, luscious and classy.

496 DUO CENTENARY BUAL, COSSART GORDON (P)

£19.50	☛ AV ADN WCE THP EVI HHC MAW J&B PTR	🍽 m, q, s

Intense, nutty wine with a tangy richness and lovely, smoky wood.

497 DUQUE DE BRAGANZA 20 YEAR OLD TAWNY PORT, FERREIRA Douro (P)

£21.79	☛ CWS LEA OD	🍽 m, q, s

Vibrant with the flavours of raisins, fruit cake and vanilla, plus a slight smokiness. Put on your slippers and stoke up the fire.

Low- and non-alcohol wines

Not a lot to say about these. They are the best of an uninspiring bunch devised, like caffeine-free coffee and sugar-free sweeteners, to serve the needs of people who are looking for a compromise.

498 ST MICHAEL LIEBLING PEACH, KLOSTERHOF (G)

£1.19	☛ M&S	🍽 c, o, q, r

Guess what this smells and tastes of? A low-alcohol wine which scores because it is not trying to be anything other than a fruity mouthful.

499 MOSCATO FIZZ, VITICOLTORI DELL'ACQUESE, Piedmont (It)

£2.50	☛ SPR ADN RTW	🍽 c, o, q, r

If you are allergic to grapes, avoid this glorious, easy, quintessentially grapey wine from the producers of the Guide's Red Wine of the Year in 1991. If not lay it in by the dozen to serve at parties, as an aperitif and with dessert.

500 PETILLANT DE LISTEL Midi (F)

£2.65	☛ AB TO OD ROD FUL CUM EVI PIM SUP THP HUN RAV BFI BOO GI GHL MTL CPL A GHS BTH SAF PD BU GRT VIL	🍽 o, q

Smells like muscat and tastes of fresh apples with a rich finish.

(Arg) = Argentina; (Au) = Austria; (Aus) = Australia; (Bul) = Bulgaria; (Cal) = California; (Can) = Canada; (Ch) = Chile; (F) = France; (G) = Germany; (Gr) = Greece; (Is) = Israel; (It) = Italy; (Leb) = Lebanon; (NZ) = New Zealand; (P) = Portugal; (SA) = South Africa; (Sp) = Spain; (Sw) = Switzerland; (UK) = United Kingdom; (US) = United States excluding California

THE STOCKISTS

ABB | Abbey Cellars

The Abbey, Preston Road, Yeovil, Somerset BA21 3AR (0935 76228). Small but perfectly formed merchant - what better way to start this section? **Opening hours**: 11.30am - 6 pm Tue-Fri; 10am - 3pm Sat. **Delivery**: free locally. **Tastings**: wines always open in the shop, plus more formal events.

'With prices for Champagne rising so fast, why not try one of the many alternatives from elsewhere?' Just one of the many things that caught our eye in Andrew Mangles' concise but extremely sensible list. If you're ever near the exquisitely named Preston Plucknett, this is the place to find a range of ready-to-drink wines to suit all pockets and palates, including the Western Australian wines of Plantagenet and Rhônes from Pascal.

29	£2.99	CUVEE JEAN-PAUL BLANC SEC VIN DE TABLE, PAUL BOUTINOT (F)
31	£2.99	CORBIERES BLANC, CAVES DE MONT TAUCH, Midi (F)
38	£3.65	TOLLANA DRY WHITE 1988 S E Australia (Aus)
88	£5.15	MONTES CHARDONNAY, 1990 Curico Valley (Ch)
286	£5.85	SEPPELT GOLD LABEL CABERNET SAUVIGNON 1986 S E Australia (Aus)
299	£7.65	MONTES ALPHA CABERNET SAUVIGNON, 1987 Curico Valley (Ch)
460	£9.30	CAMPBELLS OLD RUTHERGLEN LIQUEUR MUSCAT (Aus)

WA | William Addison

67 High Street, Newport, Shropshire TF10 7AU (0952 810627). **Opening hours**: 9am - 5pm Mon-Sat.. **Delivery**: free within 30 miles. **Tastings**: occasional in-store.

A solid, rather than an innovative selection of wines, strong on the more traditional areas, but then Newport was never known as a place for radical thought. However, there's nothing wrong with Georges Duboeuf Beaujolais, nor Antonin Rodet Burgundy. When the wines do stray to the New World, there are the familiar but reliable names of Robert Mondavi, Penfolds and Brown Bros. Cockburn 1935 is not what you call a 'new' port...

102	£8.65	MARQUES DE MURRIETA RIOJA BLANCO RESERVA 1985 Rioja (Sp)
150	£5.95	STONELEIGH SAUVIGNON BLANC 1989 Marlborough (NZ)
196	£4.89	THREE CHOIRS MEDIUM DRY ENGLISH TABLE WINE 1989 Gloucs (UK)
197	£4.59	ASTLEY SEVERN VALE 1989 Worcestershire (UK)
332	£23.70	CHATEAU TALBOT, ST JULIEN 1982 Bordeaux (F)
353	£5.65	PENFOLDS BIN 28 KALIMNA SHIRAZ 1988 S Australia (Aus)
438	£4.19	MARIUS RESERVA, BODEGAS PIQUERAS 1983 Almansa (Sp)
487	£7.85	TAYLOR'S FIRST ESTATE PORT LUGAR DAS LAGES, Douro (P)

AHC | Ad Hoc Wines

363 Clapham Rd, London SW9 9BT(071 274 7433). Bulgarian capitalism in action: dynamic south London wine warehouse owned by Bulgarian Vintners. **Opening Hours**: Mon-Fri 9am - 7.30; Sat10am - 7.30pm; Sun11am - 3pm. **Delivery**: free locally; nationally at cost. **Tastings**: Monthly in-store, tutored tastings and theme dinners.

'1991 looks interesting but 1992 will be spectacular!' What can Benjamin Hulbert mean? Does he think he can improve on the likes of Mas de Daumas Gassac, 1947 Moulin Touchais and 1966 Giscours, not to mention the largest selection of Bulgarians in town? Will he be adding to his range of over 75 Italian wines? Has he found some port more ancient than the Martinez 1955? Watch this space...

83	£4.35	**CALITERRA CHARDONNAY** 1990 Maipo Valley (Ch)
119	£12.60	**LES PIERRES CHARDONNAY, SONOMA CUTRER** 1987 Sonoma (Cal)
150	£5.76	**STONELEIGH SAUVIGNON BLANC** 1989 Marlborough (NZ)
193	£9.99	**RIESLING SCHOENENBURG GRAND CRU, DOPFF AU MOULIN** 1988 Alsace (F)
258	£4.07	**SVISCHTOV CABERNET SAUVIGNON CONTROLIRAN,** 1985 Svischtov (Bul)
280	£4.34	**ORLANDO RF CABERNET SAUVIGNON** 1988 S Australia (Aus)
288	£5.60	**CHATEAU MUSAR** 1982 Bekaa Valley (Leb)
294	£7.35	**PALMER VINEYARDS MERLOT** 1988 Long Island N.Y. (US)
303	£7.89	**ROSEMOUNT SHOW RESERVE CABERNET SAUVIGNON** 1987 Coonawarra (Aus)
305	£7.64	**JEAN LEON CABERNET SAUVIGNON** 1983 Penedés (Sp)
452	£12.50	**RIOJA RESERVA 904, LA RIOJA ALTA** 1978 (Sp)

ADN | Adnams

Joint Wine Merchant of the Year

The Crown, High Street, Southwold, Suffolk IP18 6DP (0502 724222), & 109 Unthank Rd, Norwich NR2 2PE (0603 613998). Independent, wine-by-mail merchant, wine warehouse and kitchen utensil store. **Opening Hours** : Southwold: Mon - Sat 10am-6pm; Norwich: Mon - Sat. 9am-9pm. **Delivery:** Free nationally. **Tastings:** Regular tutored tastings and theme dinners galore. **Discounts:** Shop case prices are £3 less than mail order; 5% discount for orders of 12 cases and over.

In an increasingly bland world, wine drinkers should be grateful to the wilfully eccentric Simon Loftus and Alastair Marshall, the bearded bear-like general manager he appointed to run Adnams' day to day business. Together, these two men (Loftus still exercises buying control 'on a close and continuing' basis in the time he is not busily devising customers' tastings, writing for Country Life, finishing his next book, sponsoring the Aldeburgh Festival, fighting to save nature reserves and overseeing Adnams' Swan and Crown hostelries in Southwold) continue to strike out for new vinous ground. This year, following the 1990 initiative of introducing an Organic Wine Declaration, the firm has gone one step further by devoting major chunks of its list to describing the greenest of its growers.

Unlike some greenies, however, Adnams continues to put the quality of its wines before their environmental acceptability - and does so with such skill that its 'success rate' in the International Wine Challenge was un-equalled. But it was only partly this success which won Adnams our top award for the first time. Our judges simply thought that this company deserves the highest possible praise for just about everything it does.

And, if all that were not enough, there's the kitchenware shops, and a wine list which ought to be a model for up-market wine merchants everywhere. We know of none other that has given its erudite readers as much pleasure and, on occasion, amusement. Some, it is indeed reported, have yet to progress beyond page one of the 1991 list, so busy are they trying to devise a bilingual tongue-twister to better Loftus's own offering:

> *Le ver vert va vers le verre vert.*
> *The green grub goes to the green glass.*

2	£6.70	**DIANE DE POITIERS SPARKLING CHARDONNAY, HAUT POITOU,** Loire (F)		
3	£5.05	**LINDAUER, MONTANA** (NZ)		
11	£11.10	**DEUTZ MARLBOROUGH CUVEE** (NZ)		
18	£14.80	**IRON HORSE BRUT** 1987 Sonoma (Cal)		
51	£4.60	**BLANC DES CEPAGES DE FRANCE, CHATEAU PECH-CELEYRAN** 1990 Midi (F)		
77	£14.70	**CONDRIEU, COTEAUX DE CHERY, A PERRET** 1989 Rhône (F)		
79	£3.20	**COTES DE ST MONT, PLAIMONT** 1990 S W (F)		
102	£8.45	**MARQUES DE MURRIETA RIOJA BLANCO RESERVA** 1985 Rioja (Sp)		
112	£11.50	**SAINTSBURY RESERVE CHARDONNAY** 1988 Carneros (Cal)		
119	£14.10	**LES PIERRES CHARDONNAY, SONOMA CUTRER** 1987 Sonoma (Cal)		
125	£24.25	**NUITS ST GEORGES BLANC, CLOS DE L'ARLOT** 1988 Burgundy (F)		
148	£6.50	**SELAKS SAUVIGNON BLANC** 1990 (NZ)		
154	£8.10	**SHAW AND SMITH SAUVIGNON BLANC** 1990 S Australia (Aus)		
157	£4.40	**DOMAINE DU BOSC MARSANNE, VIN DE PAYS DE L'HERAULT, DELTA DOMAINES** 1990 Midi (F)		
163	£7.10	**MONTLOUIS DEMI-SEC VIELLES VIGNES, DOMAINE DES LIARDS, BERGER FRERES** 1989 Loire (F)		
185	£4.85	**MAGDALEN RIVANER, PULHAM VINEYARDS** 1990 East Anglia (UK)		
187	£5.55	**TRITTENHEIMER APOTHEKE KABINETT, F W GYMNASIUM** 1989 M-S-R (G)		
208	£19.25	**DOMAINE DE BABLUT, CABERNET D'ANJOU DEMI-SEC** 1961 Loire (F)		
223	£3.70	**DOMAINE ST EULALIE, MINERVOIS** 1988 Midi (F)		
261	£4.15	**DOMAINE DES SALAISES, SAUMUR** 1989 Loire (F)		
281	£5.05	**MONTANA CABERNET SAUVIGNON** 1988 Marlborough (NZ)		
288	£6.45	**CHATEAU MUSAR** 1982 Bekaa Valley (Leb)		
293	£7.55	**JAMIESONS RUN RED, MILDARA** 1987 Coonawarra (Aus)		
313	£11.00	**CLOUDY BAY CABERNET MERLOT** 1989 Marlborough (NZ)		
321	£17.50	**RENAISSANCE CABERNET SAUVIGNON** 1984 North Yuba (Cal)		
331	£18.65	**PENFOLDS BIN 707 CABERNET SAUVIGNON** 1987 S Australia (Aus)		
334	£27.80	**ROBERT MONDAVI CABERNET SAUVIGNON RESERVE** 1977 Napa Valley (Cal)		
352	£5.80	**COTES DU RHONE, GUIGAL** 1988 (F)		
369	£6.95	**MITCHELL PEPPERTREE VINEYARD SHIRAZ** 1988 Clare Valley (Aus)		
373	£8.15	**DOM. DU VIEUX TELEGRAPHE, CHATEAUNEUF DU PAPE** 1987 Rhône (F)		
380	£4.35	**GAILLAC, CEPAGE GAMAY, DOMAINES JEAN CROS** 1990 S W (F)		
384	£6.75	**JULIENAS, DOMAINE JOUBERT** 1990 Beaujolais (F)		
391	£9.00	**SAINTSBURY PINOT NOIR** 1988 Carneros (Cal)		
424	£11.50	**COLTASSALA, CASTELLO DI VOLPAIA** 1986 Tuscany (It)		
441	£5.15	**QUINTA DE CAMARATE, J M DE FONSECA** 1984 (P)		
451	£9.30	**MARQUIS DE MURRIETA RIOJA TINTO RESERVA** 1985 (Sp)		
452	£14.00	**RIOJA RESERVA 904, LA RIOJA ALTA** 1978 (Sp)		
471	£11.05	**VOUVRAY MOELLEUX LE MARIGNY, DOM. DES AUBUISIERES** 1990 Loire (F)		
479	£4.70	**LA GITANA MANZANILLA, HIDALGO,** Jerez (Sp)		
487	£4.95	**TAYLOR'S FIRST ESTATE PORT LUGAR DAS LAGES,** Douro (P)		
496	£19.95	**DUO CENTENARY BUAL, COSSART GORDON** (P)		
499	£2.65	**MOSCATO FIZZ, VITICOLTORI DELL'ACQUESE,** Piedmont (It)		

DAL | David Alexander

69 Queen St, Maidenhead, Berks SL6 1LT (0628 30295). Independent merchant with sense of humour - 'minimum purchase one bottle'. **Opening Hours:** Mon10am-7pm; Tue-Thu10am-8.30 pm; Fri, Sat 10am-9pm; Sun 12-2pm . **Delivery:** free within 20 miles of the M4, nationally at cost. **Tastings:** occasionally in-store plus tutored events. **Discounts:** 5% on mixed cases

David Alexander knows its customers. It is one of the few wine merchants in the country which helpfully explains what buying *en primeur* actually means ('that's buying wine by the case before it is shipped from Bordeaux...') as well as defining such terms as VSOP in its GRAPEVINE newsletter. Those who are entirely new to wine will find the list a commendably easy way into the subject - via, for example, the 'No. 1 and 2 Rhône Experience' cases and the tutored tastings which are held every six weeks - but they will have no reason to look elsewhere for further education. Not when there are wines like Tollot-Beaut's Aloxe Corton 1986 and Cheval Blanc 1962 on offer to drink when the stocks of Cuvée Jean Paul run low.

6	£7.50	**TALTARNI BRUT TACHE,** Pyrenees (Aus)	
29	£2.89	**CUVEE JEAN-PAUL BLANC SEC VIN DE TABLE, PAUL BOUTINOT** (F)	
46	£4.29	**CHARDONNAY, DOMAINE DES FLINES, VIN DE PAYS DE LA LOIRE** 1990 (F)	
147	£6.39	**KLEIN COSTANTIA SAUVIGNON BLANC** 1988 (SA)	
191	£7.39	**WEHLENER SONNENUHR RIESLING KABINETT, WEINGUT DR LOOSEN** M-S-R (G)	
286	£5.70	**SEPPELT GOLD LABEL CABERNET SAUVIGNON** 1986 S E Australia (Aus)	
427	£12.29	**AMARONE CLASSICO DELLA VALPOLICELLA FIERAMONTE, ALLEGRINI** 1983 Veneto (It)	
442	£5.75	**TEMPRANILLO, BODEGAS OCHOA** 1987 Navarra (Sp)	
460	£13.50	**CAMPBELLS OLD RUTHERGLEN LIQUEUR MUSCAT** (Aus)	
493	£16.50	**WARRE'S QUINTA DA CAVADINHA** 1982 Douro (P)	

AMW	Amey's Wines

83 Melford Road, Sudbury, Suffolk CO10 6JT (0787 77144).**Opening Hours**:Tue-Sat 10-7. **Delivery**: Free within 20 miles. **Tastings**: occasionally in-store, to outside groups on request. Discounts: 5% on (mixed) cases.

With a list that is frill-free but stylishly printed in an ink which must have been described as 'Burgundy' Ameys offers a range that gets better the more closely it is examined. Two pages of Champagnes and other sparkling wines take in basic French, good value Australians and 1983 La Grande Dame from Veuve Cliquot, but avoid the sillier excesses of Champagne pricing. This is clearly part of the Ameys philosophy, as even the red Burgundy list which includes a number of good, single-estate wines seems unwilling to stray too far beyond £10. An Antonin Guyon Aloxe Corton Premier Cru 1985, for example is the priciest in the section and costs just £16.50. Given this keenness on value for money, it is hardly surprising that the New World selection is the longest in the list, taking in a number of producers whose wines are rarely seen elsewhere.

Quality is clearly as important as price and we were pleased to see that, Amey's 'Eastern Europe - White Wines' section omitted the dull attempts at Bulgarian Chardonnay offered elsewhere, and limited itself to Retsina.

10	£10.99	**SALINGER METHODE CHAMPENOISE, SEPPELT** 1989 (Aus)	
29	£2.99	**CUVEE JEAN-PAUL BLANC SEC VIN DE TABLE, PAUL BOUTINOT** (F)	
54	£5.29	**ALSACE TOKAY PINOT GRIS, CAVE VINICOLE DE TURCKHEIM** 1990 (F)	
89	£5.29	**MOONDAH BROOK VERDELHO** 1990 (Aus)	
95	£7.29	**SCHINUS MOLLE CHARDONNAY** 1990 Mornington Peninsula (Aus)	
101	£8.29	**HUGO CHARDONNAY** 1988 Southern Vales (Aus)	
117	£12.19	**ELSTON CHARDONNAY, TE MATA** 1989 (NZ)	
148	£6.49	**SELAKS SAUVIGNON BLANC** 1990 (NZ)	
151	£7.29	**SCHINUS MOLLE SAUVIGNON BLANC** 1990 Victoria (Aus)	
205	£4.99	**CHRISTIAN BROTHERS WHITE ZINFANDEL** 1989 Napa Valley (Cal)	
231	£5.19	**CHATEAU DE LASTOURS CUVEE SIMONE DESCAMPS, CORBIERES** 1989 Midi (F)	
299	£7.99	**MONTES ALPHA CABERNET SAUVIGNON,** 1987 Curico Valley (Ch)	

315	£11.39	**MOUNTADAM CABERNET SAUVIGNON** 1987 High Eden Ridge (Aus)
349	£4.89	**RASTEAU COTES DU RHONE VILLAGES, VIGNERONS DE RASTEAU** 1989 (F)
356	£5.69	**DAVID WYNN SHIRAZ** 1990 High Eden Ridge (Aus)
372	£8.99	**CHATEAUNEUF DU PAPE DOMAINE FONT DE MICHELLE, GONNET** 1988 Rhône (F)
449	£8.29	**CAMPO VIEJO RIOJA GRAN RESERVA** 1980 (Sp)
460	£12.50	**CAMPBELLS OLD RUTHERGLEN LIQUEUR MUSCAT** (Aus)
469	£11.99	**CHATEAU BASTOR LAMONTAGNE, SAUTERNES** 1988 Bordeaux (F)
493	£16.50	**WARRE'S QUINTA DA CAVADINHA** 1982 Douro (P)

LAV | Les Amis du Vin See The Winery

JAR | John Armit Wines

190 Kensington Park Road, London W11 2ES (071 727 6846). **Opening Times**: Mon-Fri 8:30am-6pm. **Delivery**:   free nationally for 3+ cases. **Tastings**: bottles regularly opened for sampling, tutored tastings.

John Armit's name though unfamiliar to most people outside the wine trade should be well known to long-standing customers of Corney & Barrow, the firm he used to run and whose list he eloquently used to write. Now, with his own company, Armit has produced a list which looks like a catalogue for an art exhibition (the photographs in it are stunning) and reads like a company report from an unusually forthright chairman: 'It is possible to buy good commercial sherry at any off licence or supermarket so there is absolutely no point in our listing and selling them'; '1984 Bordeaux: We do not have an albatross, more like a sparrow around our necks, because we bought a little of the best wines to repay past favours, but we sold most of them below cost. We have little left and the wines are now ready to drink.' Throughout the list, the selection is clearly dictated by Armit's own enthusiasm - which explains a range which takes in a raft of Bordeaux, Olivier Leflaive Burgundies ('He is a delightful companion, and has a passionate interest in music. Indeed, he has his own band and recently made a record, so he is not a typical Burgundian'), Pesquera (the Spanish superstar partly 'discovered' by Armit) and Ponzi Oregon Pinot Noirs and Chardonnays. Armit customers can also enjoy occasional tastings and dinners within spitting distance of the glitterati at the fabled Groucho Club, of which Mr A was a founder.

AK | Arriba Kettle & Co

Buckle Street, Honeybourne, Evesham, Worcs WR11 5QB (0386 833 024). **Opening Hours**: by appointment. **Delivery**:free nationally. **Tastings**: regularly in-store, plus tutored events. **Discounts**: £2 collection discount per case.

As the number of would-be Spanish specialist grows, Barry Kettle bows to the inevitable by increasing his range of non non-Hispanic wines to take in the Loire, Bordeaux and New Zealand. Stated bluntly, there are too few really exciting Spanish bodegas for anyone to produce a list that is both long and impressive. Mr Kettle's selection is commendable, however and wines from producers like Montecillo and Chivite should keep at least some of his customers' attention from straying across the frontier or equator.

| A | Asda Stores Ltd |

Head Office: Asda House, Southbank, Great Wilson St, Leeds LS11 5AD (0532 435435). Increasingly up-market national supermarket chain with 204 licenced branches. **Opening Hours:** Generally Mon-Fri 9am - 8pm;Thurs 9am-9pm ; Sat 8.30am-8pm. **Tastings:**regularly in-store, tutored events.

Last year we commended the efforts Philip Clive of Asda's wine department was making to compete with Tesco, Waitrose and Sainsbury. In 1991, those efforts really began to pay off, earning the chain press comments which had previously been the preserve of those other, more established vinous supermarkets. Today, the title of the company's glossy list 'A collection of quality wines from around the world' really does ring true. The quality which is most striking is the buyers' readiness to introduce high quality wines such as Louis Carillon and Guy Mothe single-estate Burgundies as well as own-label bottles from regions with which Asda customers might previously have been unfamiliar - and to label them in ways that allow them to appear on all but the sniffiest dinner tables.

Following in its competitors' footsteps too, Asda has found a number of organic wines - including two green clarets. A few years ago, unkind observers might have termed Asda's wine range as being at the rent-a-wreck end of the business; today, the chain is very decidedly an Avis, trying for all its worth to be taken seriously.

3	£4.79	LINDAUER, MONTANA (NZ)
53	£4.99	MITCHELTON MARSANNE (UNWOODED) 1990 Goulburn Valley (Aus)
67	£6.69	ASDA CHABLIS, GUY MOTHE 1989 Burgundy (F)
83	£4.75	CALITERRA CHARDONNAY 1990 Maipo Valley (Ch)
84	£4.59	OXFORD LANDING CHARDONNAY, YALUMBA 1990 S Australia (Aus)
140	£5.25	COOKS HAWKES BAY SAUVIGNON BLANC 1989 Hawkes Bay (NZ)
166	£4.59	ASDA ALSACE GEWURZTRAMINER, CAVES VINICOLE EGUISHEIM 1989 (F)
180	£3.99	HILL SMITH OLD TRIANGLE RIESLING 1990 Barossa Valley (Aus)
210	£2.75	ASDA ST CHINIAN, VIGNERONS DE LA MEDITERRANEE, Midi (F)
224	£3.89	DOMAINE BUNAN, VIN DE PAYS DU MONT CHAUME 1989 Midi (F)
264	£4.50	BERRI ESTATES AUSTRALIAN CABERNET SHIRAZ 1987 (Aus)
268	£4.49	CHATEAU DE PARENCHERE BORDEAUX ROUGE, J GAZANIOL 1988 (F)
288	£6.25	CHATEAU MUSAR 1982 Bekaa Valley (Leb)
409	£5.95	CHIANTI CLASSICO LAMOLE, CASTELLI DEL GREVEPESA 1986 Tuscany (It)
435	£2.59	DON DARIAS RED, BODEGAS VITORIANAS (Sp)
463	£5.99	CHATEAU FILHOT, SAUTERNES 1985 Bordeaux (F)
468	£7.25	HERXHEIMER HIMMELREICH HUXELREBE BEERENAUSLESE, WERNER PFLEGER 1988 Rheinpfalz (G)
481	£10.49	MANZANILLA PASADA DE SANLUCAR ALMACENISTA, LUSTAU, Jerez (Sp)
486	£7.99	ASDA 10 YEAR OLD TAWNY PORT, CHARLES COVERLEY, Douro (P)
500	£1.99	PETILLANT DE LISTEL, Midi (F)

| AUC | Australian Wine Centre |

Down Under, S Australia House, 50 The Strand, London WC2N 5LW (071 925 0751). Specialist merchant and wine club buried in a cellar. **Opening Hours:** Mon-Fri 10-7, Sat 10-4. **Delivery:** free nationally. **Tastings:** regularly in-store, tutored events. **Discounts:** 5% collection discount.

Sales of Australian wines shot up by 80% in the first quarter of 1991 - and showed no signs of slowing down, despite the recession and renewed attempts at competition by the Californians. So, Margaret Francis and Craig Smith are in the happy position of offering a product everyone wants to buy.

To their credit though, they have not simply chosen to stock a long list of Aussie wines, they have looked for quality, and have taken the trouble to import interesting wines even when the quantities available are uncommercially small (watch out for the few cases of the extraordinary Rockford Sparkling Shiraz which are due to arrive sometime soon).

A new development this year was the launch of the New Zealand Wine Club, a mail order operation run from the same address, and offering a range of Kiwi wines which will hopefully eventually be as comprehensive as the Centre's list from Australia.

In the meantime, just look at the selection of Aussie recommended wines we were able to find on the Strand shop's shelves.

6	£7.99	**TALTARNI BRUT TACHE,** Pyrenees (Aus)
8	£5.49	**SEPPELT'S GREAT WESTERN SHOW SPARKLING SHIRAZ** 1985 (Aus)
10	£12.99	**SALINGER METHODE CHAMPENOISE, SEPPELT** 1989 (Aus)
59	£5.29	**HOUGHTON SUPREME WHITE** 1990 Swan Valley (Aus)
84	£4.69	**OXFORD LANDING CHARDONNAY, YALUMBA** 1990 S Australia (Aus)
87	£4.99	**ORLANDO RF CHARDONNAY** 1989 S E Australia (Aus)
89	£5.99	**MOONDAH BROOK VERDELHO** 1990 (Aus)
90	£5.99	**LINDEMANS BIN 65 CHARDONNAY** 1989 S E Australia (Aus)
93	£6.59	**BROKENBACK VINEYARD CHARDONNAY, ROTHBURY** 1990 Hunter Valley (Aus)
95	£8.49	**SCHINUS MOLLE CHARDONNAY** 1990 Mornington Peninsula (Aus)
103	£9.99	**KING VALLEY CHARDONNAY FAMILY RESERVE, BROWN BROS** 1987 N E Victoria (Aus)
105	£8.99	**HEGGIES CHARDONNAY, HILL-SMITH** 1988 Adelaide Hills (Aus)
106	£9.99	**WYNNS COONAWARRA ESTATE CHARDONNAY** 1989 (Aus)
107	£9.99	**KRONDORF SHOW RESERVE CHARDONNAY** 1989 Barossa Valley (Aus)
108	£10.49	**EILEEN HARDY CHARDONNAY, HARDY'S** 1988 S Australia (Aus)
109	£7.99	**ST HUBERTS CHARDONNAY** 1988 Yarra Valley (Aus)
110	£12.99	**PIPERS BROOK CHARDONNAY** 1988 Tasmania (Aus)
151	£8.49	**SCHINUS MOLLE SAUVIGNON BLANC** 1990 Victoria (Aus)
154	£8.49	**SHAW AND SMITH SAUVIGNON BLANC** 1990 S Australia (Aus)
180	£4.99	**HILL SMITH OLD TRIANGLE RIESLING** 1990 Barossa Valley (Aus)
264	£4.99	**BERRI ESTATES AUSTRALIAN CABERNET SHIRAZ** 1987 (Aus)
280	£4.99	**ORLANDO RF CABERNET SAUVIGNON** 1988 S Australia (Aus)
286	£5.99	**SEPPELT GOLD LABEL CABERNET SAUVIGNON** 1986 S E Australia (Aus)
293	£6.99	**JAMIESONS RUN RED, MILDARA** 1987 Coonawarra (Aus)
295	£8.99	**WYNNS CABERNET SAUVIGNON** 1985 Coonawarra (Aus)
297	£7.69	**TALTARNI CABERNET SAUVIGNON** 1985 Pyrenees (Aus)
301	£7.99	**HOLLICK CABERNET MERLOT** 1988 Coonawarra (Aus)
303	£8.49	**ROSEMOUNT SHOW RESERVE CABERNET SAUVIGNON** 1987 Coonawarra (Aus)
308	£8.49	**COLDSTREAM HILLS CABERNET SAUVIGNON** 1988 Yarra Valley (Aus)
315	£11.99	**MOUNTADAM CABERNET SAUVIGNON** 1987 High Eden Ridge (Aus)
323	£15.99	**VASSE FELIX CABERNET SAUVIGNON** 1988 Margaret River (Aus)
329	£16.99	**WOLF BLASS BLACK LABEL CABERNET SAUVIGNON** 1986 S Australia (Aus)
331	£18.99	**PENFOLDS BIN 707 CABERNET SAUVIGNON** 1987 S Australia (Aus)
347	£4.99	**SEAVIEW CABERNET SHIRAZ** 1989 S Australia (Aus)
353	£5.99	**PENFOLDS BIN 28 KALIMNA SHIRAZ** 1988 S Australia (Aus)
354	£5.99	**BALGOWNIE SHIRAZ CABERNET** 1987 Central Victoria (Aus)
365	£6.99	**CHATEAU TAHBILK SHIRAZ** 1987 Goulburn Valley (Aus)
367	£7.69	**TALTARNI SHIRAZ** 1988 Pyrenees (Aus)
369	£7.99	**MITCHELL PEPPERTREE VINEYARD SHIRAZ** 1988 Clare Valley (Aus)
370	£7.99	**WOLF BLASS PRESIDENTS SELECTION SHIRAZ** 1987 S Australia (Aus)
371	£8.49	**HENSCHKE MOUNT EDELSTONE SHIRAZ** 1987 Adelaide Hills (Aus)
376	£16.99	**ROUGE HOMME SHIRAZ CABERNET** 1976 Coonawarra (Aus)
458	£7.49	**YALUMBA MUSEUM SHOW RESERVE MUSCAT,** Rutherglen (Aus)

466   £6.49   THE HARDY COLLECTION PADTHAWAY RHINE RIESLING BEERENAUSLESE
                1987 (Aus)

AV   Averys of Bristol

7 Park Street, Bristol BS1 5NG (0272 214141). Traditional merchant and a Bristol institution.
Opening Hours: Mon-Fri 9am-6pm; Sat 9am-5pm . **Delivery:** free locally, free nationally for 2+
cases. **Tastings:** regularly in-store plus tutored events. **Discounts:** negotiable.

Over the last year Averys seems to have become decidedly more sprightly -
and even more avant-garde than ever (it was Averys, remember who
introduced the concept of New World wines to Britain). California is a
particular passion - promoted, through a glossy colourful leaflet which
described several wineries in some considerable detail and talks at length
about Averys' links with California, without ever quite troubling to mention that one of these, Swanson in the Napa Valley, belongs to the US
millionaire whose purchase of Averys helped to facilitate the firm's recent
activities in both the New and Old Worlds. The Swanson wines are both
good, and good value - which is more than we could say for the Mondavi
White Zinfandel (a medium-sweet rosé by any other name) on *special offer*
by the case for just under £6 a bottle. Take our advice and pay Averys
another £2.75 a bottle for a case of 1990 Duhart Milon in bond.

119   £14.00   LES PIERRES CHARDONNAY, SONOMA CUTRER 1987 Sonoma (Cal)
147   £6.50   KLEIN CONSTANTIA SAUVIGNON BLANC 1988 (SA)
288   £8.15   CHATEAU MUSAR 1982 Bekaa Valley (Leb)
322   £14.10   SWANSON CABERNET SAUVIGNON 1987 Napa Valley (Cal)
376   £17.10   ROUGE HOMME SHIRAZ CABERNET 1976 Coonawarra (Aus)
389   £7.90   AVERYS FINE RED BURGUNDY 1985 (F)
496   £19.40   DUO CENTENARY BUAL, COSSART GORDON (P)

BH   B H Wines

Boustead Hill House, Boustead Hill, Burgh-by-Sands, Carlisle, Cumbria CA5 6AA (0228 76 711) Also
in Newcastle-upon-Tyne through Mark Savage (091 2723019). Independent merchant committed
to wine education. **Opening Hours:** phone first to check. **Delivery:** free locally, nationally at cost.
Tastings: regularly in-store plus tutored events.

To say that this is the best wine merchant in Carlisle understates its quality,
its role in running Newcastle University's vinous evening classes - and the
quirkily individual way in which it chooses its wines. Burgundy, for
instance, is represented by no less than three Beaunes, and not a single other
red wine commune. Priorato is given more space than on the lists of some
so-called Spanish specialists, and the Australian list includes McWilliams
Hunter Valley Semillons from 1979 and 1980. Credit is due too to Linda and
Richard Neville for the quality of their wine selections - and the way they
invite prospective visitors to their monthly tastings: 'Typical cost of an
evening £5. You do not need to know anything about wine'.

3   £6.49   LINDAUER, MONTANA (NZ)
22   £20.25   VEUVE CLICQUOT DEMI-SEC CHAMPAGNE (F)
79   £4.24   COTES DE ST MONT, PLAIMONT 1990 S W (F)
87   £4.94   ORLANDO RF CHARDONNAY 1989 S E Australia (Aus)
95   £6.50   SCHINUS MOLLE CHARDONNAY 1990 Mornington Peninsula (Aus)

101	£7.33	**HUGO CHARDONNAY** 1988 Southern Vales (Aus)
102	£7.67	**MARQUES DE MURRIETA RIOJA BLANCO RESERVA** 1985 Rioja (Sp)
107	£8.99	**KRONDORF SHOW RESERVE CHARDONNAY** 1989 Barossa Valley (Aus)
116	£11.99	**CLOS DU BOIS CHARDONNAY, CALCAIRE VINEYARD** 1988 Sonoma (Cal)
117	£11.50	**ELSTON CHARDONNAY, TE MATA** 1989 (NZ)
118	£12.59	**VIDAL RESERVE CHARDONNAY** 1989 Hawkes Bay (NZ)
140	£5.12	**COOKS HAWKES BAY SAUVIGNON BLANC** 1989 Hawkes Bay (NZ)
150	£6.06	**STONELEIGH SAUVIGNON BLANC** 1989 Marlborough (NZ)
151	£6.50	**SCHINUS MOLLE SAUVIGNON BLANC** 1990 Victoria (Aus)
230	£4.94	**MAS DE GOURGONNIER TRADITION, COTEAUX D'AIX EN PROVENCE LES BAUX** 1989 Midi (F)
258	£4.44	**SVISCHTOV CABERNET SAUVIGNON CONTROLIRAN,** 1985 Svischtov (Bul)
280	£4.94	**ORLANDO RF CABERNET SAUVIGNON** 1988 S Australia (Aus)
281	£4.69	**MONTANA CABERNET SAUVIGNON** 1988 Marlborough (NZ)
288	£6.80	**CHATEAU MUSAR** 1982 Bekaa Valley (Leb)
296	£7.99	**HUNGERFORD HILL CABERNET SAUVIGNON** 1988 Coonawarra (Aus)
297	£6.71	**TALTARNI CABERNET SAUVIGNON** 1985 Pyrenees (Aus)
301	£7.80	**HOLLICK CABERNET MERLOT** 1988 Coonawarra (Aus)
311	£9.50	**SIMI CABERNET SAUVIGNON** 1984 Sonoma (Cal)
314	£9.35	**NEWTON CABERNET SAUVIGNON** 1986 Napa Valley (Cal)
315	£10.00	**MOUNTADAM CABERNET SAUVIGNON** 1987 High Eden Ridge (Aus)
317	£10.06	**CLOS DU VAL MERLOT** 1987 Napa Valley (Cal)
321	£16.00	**RENAISSANCE CABERNET SAUVIGNON** 1984 North Yuba (Cal)
323	£14.00	**VASSE FELIX CABERNET SAUVIGNON** 1988 Margaret River (Aus)
325	£13.52	**CARMENET CABERNET SAUVIGNON** 1986 Sonoma (Cal)
329	£15.00	**WOLF BLASS BLACK LABEL CABERNET SAUVIGNON** 1986 S Australia (Aus)
336	£40.00	**OPUS ONE, ROBERT MONDAVI** 1987 Napa Valley (Cal)
356	£4.77	**DAVID WYNN SHIRAZ** 1990 High Eden Ridge (Aus)
367	£7.00	**TALTARNI SHIRAZ** 1988 Pyrenees (Aus)
374	£9.23	**RIDGE GEYSERVILLE ZINFANDEL** 1988 Santa Clara (Cal)
391	£9.37	**SAINTSBURY PINOT NOIR** 1988 Carneros (Cal)
392	£9.30	**SANFORD PINOT NOIR** 1986 Santa Barbara (Cal)
393	£14.12	**HAUTES COTES DE NUITS, ALAIN VERDET** 1986 Burgundy (F)
394	£15.00	**CALERA SELLECK PINOT NOIR** 1987 San Benito (Cal)
395	£17.54	**VOSNE-ROMANEE LES MALCONSORTS, MOILLARD** 1988 Burgundy (F)
414	£7.97	**BARBAROSSA, FATTORIA PARADISO** 1986 Emilia-Romagna (It)
427	£15.65	**AMARONE CLASSICO DELLA VALPOLICELLA FIERAMONTE, ALLEGRINI** 1983 1989 Veneto (It)
442	£5.14	**TEMPRANILLO, BODEGAS OCHOA** 1987 Navarra (Sp)
451	£8.50	**MARQUIS DE MURRIETA RIOJA TINTO RESERVA** 1985 (Sp)
458	£5.91	**YALUMBA MUSEUM SHOW RESERVE MUSCAT,** Rutherglen (Aus)
465	£5.46	**REDWOOD VALLEY ESTATE LATE HARVEST RIESLING** 1989 Nelson (NZ)
472	£10.50	**JURANCON MOELLEUX VENDANGE TARDIVE, DOMAINE CAUHAPE** 1988 S.W.(F)
487	£7.81	**TAYLOR'S FIRST ESTATE PORT LUGAR DAS LAGES,** Douro (P)
492	£14.50	**VERDELHO 10 YEAR OLD, COSSART GORDON** (P)

NB	Nigel Baring & Co Ltd

325 Kennington Road, London SE11 4QE (071 587 0331). Independent merchant. **Opening Hours:** Mon-Fri 9:30am-5:30pm. **Delivery:** free within 8 miles, nationally at cost. **Tastings:** bottles regularly opened for sampling, plus tutored events. **Discounts:** negotiable.

En primeur specialist *par excellence* Nigel Baring has had an interesting 1991, keeping his head while others have been in evident danger of losing theirs. Mr Baring knows all about the vicissitudes of the market, having famously crashed in the 1970s when, to his credit, he ensured that all of his customers received the wine they had bought. Today, his list outlining a set of reasons for buying *en primeur* points out in bold type that 'the supply of all wines under our control is personally guaranteed by Nigel Baring', subtly reminding potential City-conscious customers of his family link to a financial institution with which they are familiar.

BWS | The Barnes Wine Shop

51 Barnes High St, London SW13 9LN (081 878 8643). Modern independent retailer with enthusiastic staff and customers. **Opening Hours:** 9.30am-8.30pm Mon-Sat; 12-2pm Sun. **Delivery:** free locally or for two cases or more in London, nationally at cost.. **Tastings:** bottles always open plus regular tutored events.

When independent wine merchants complain that they find it hard to compete with the likes of Oddbins and Thresher, they should pay a visit to Francis Murray's shop, an establishment which, by all accounts, does rather better business than the Goughs-turned-Oddbins further up the road. Murray's success is all too easily explained: a reliable and eclectic list of wines selected (and characteristically described) by James Rogers, a pleasantly designed shop, helpfully knowledgeable staff - and an established position in the local community demonstrated by the popular annual Barnes Wine Festival which is run by Murray and Rogers in aid of charity. If you want to buy inexpensive Burgundy, Marechal Foch from Inniskillin in Canada or classy old Bordeaux and the glasses from which to drink it, this is the place for you.

3	£6.95	LINDAUER, MONTANA (NZ)	
11	£10.99	DEUTZ MARLBOROUGH CUVEE (NZ)	
29	£3.12	CUVEE JEAN-PAUL BLANC SEC VIN DE TABLE, PAUL BOUTINOT (F)	
33	£3.29	DOMAINE DU TARIQUET, COTES DE GASCOGNE 1990 South West (F)	
69	£7.95	SOAVE CLASSICO VIGNETO CALVARINO, PIEROPAN 1989 Veneto (It)	
70	£10.45	ST VERAN TERRES NOIRES, DOMAINE DEUX ROCHES 1989 Burgundy (F)	
72	£8.45	MACON AZE, DOMAINE D'AZENAY 1989 Burgundy (F)	
79	£4.39	COTES DE ST MONT, PLAIMONT 1990 S W (F)	
84	£5.45	OXFORD LANDING CHARDONNAY, YALUMBA 1990 S Australia (Aus)	
90	£5.49	LINDEMANS BIN 65 CHARDONNAY 1989 S E Australia (Aus)	
101	£7.95	HUGO CHARDONNAY 1988 Southern Vales (Aus)	
102	£9.45	MARQUES DE MURRIETA RIOJA BLANCO RESERVA 1985 Rioja (Sp)	
107	£9.45	KRONDORF SHOW RESERVE CHARDONNAY 1989 Barossa Valley (Aus	
114	£9.95	DOMAINE CAUHAPE, JURANCON SEC (OAKED) 1988 S W (F)	
117	£12.95	ELSTON CHARDONNAY, TE MATA 1989 (NZ)	
148	£8.45	SELAKS SAUVIGNON BLANC 1990 (NZ)	
151	£7.95	SCHINUS MOLLE SAUVIGNON BLANC 1990 Victoria (Aus)	
154	£7.95	SHAW AND SMITH SAUVIGNON BLANC 1990 S Australia (Aus)	
163	£7.95	MONTLOUIS DEMI-SEC VIELLES VIGNES, DOMAINE DES LIARDS, BERGER FRERES 1989 Loire (F)	
174	£4.95	CAFAYATE TORRONTES, ETCHART 1990 Mendoza (Arg)	
175	£5.29	MOSCATO D'ASTI, MICHELE CHIARLO 1990 Piedmont (It)	
184	£12.45	ALSACE RIESLING RESERVE PARTICULIERE, SELTZ 1988 (F)	
191	£5.95	WEHLENER SONNENUHR RIESLING KABINETT, WEINGUT DR LOOSEN 1989 M-S-R (G)	
196	£4.95	THREE CHOIRS MEDIUM DRY ENGLISH TABLE WINE 1989 Gloucs (Eng)	
228	£4.95	CHATEAU CLEMENT TERMES, GAILLAC ROUGE 1988 S W (F)	
281	£6.95	MONTANA CABERNET SAUVIGNON 1988 Marlborough (NZ)	

301	£8.75	**HOLLICK CABERNET MERLOT** 1988 Coonawarra (Aus)
302	£10.95	**CHATEAU RAMAGE LA BATISSE, HAUT MEDOC** 1988 Bordeaux (F)
313	£10.95	**CLOUDY BAY CABERNET MERLOT** 1989 Marlborough (NZ)
318	£11.95	**CHATEAU HAUT BAGES AVEROUS, PAUILLAC, CHATEAU LYNCH-BAGES** 1985 Bordeaux (F)
349	£6.45	**RASTEAU COTES DU RHONE VILLAGES, VIGNERONS DE RASTEAU** 1989 (F)
352	£12.95	**COTES DU RHONE, GUIGAL** 1988 (F)
425	£8.45	**CARMIGNANO RISERVA, VILLA DI CAPEZZANA** 1985 Tuscany (It)
427	£14.95	**AMARONE CLASSICO DELLA VALPOLICELLA FIERAMONTE, ALLEGRINI** 1983 Veneto (It)
451	£9.45	**MARQUIS DE MURRIETA RIOJA TINTO RESERVA** 1985 (Sp)
452	£13.95	**RIOJA RESERVA 904, LA RIOJA ALTA** 1978 (Sp)
459	£7.95	**DOMAINE CAZES RIVESALTES VIEUX** 1978 Midi (F)
472	£13.95	**JURANCON MOELLEUX VENDANGE TARDIVE, DOM CAUHAPE** 1988 S W (F)
475	£14.95	**CHATEAU RIEUSSEC, SAUTERNES** 1983 Bordeaux (F)
482	£11.95	**ROYAL CORREGIDOR RICH RARE OLD OLOROSO, SANDEMAN,** Jerez (Sp)

| AB | Augustus Barnett Ltd |

Head Office: 3, The Maltings, Wetmore Road, Burton on Trent, Staffordshire DE14 1SE. Brewery-owned (Bass), 600 shop-strong High Street chain. **Opening Hours:** Mon-Sat10am-10pm; Sun12-2pm. **Delivery:** free locally, nationally at cost. **Tastings:** regularly at selected stores. **Discounts:** 5% on full cases, special offers on part cases.

Sometimes we wonder whether there isn't a curse associated with words of praise in the Guide. Like several other buyers we have applauded, Peter Carr, the man who began to drag Augustus Barnett into quality wine retailing, has now left for pastures new. But Carr's efforts seem to have paid off and despite the enduringly off-putting appearance of the shops, the shelves are increasingly interestingly stocked and the list is as comprehensive as that of many so-called specialists. Barnett's next job is to justify its - in our experience - questionable claim that 'staff and management...can now give sound advice based on in-depth product knowledge'.

11	£10.99	**DEUTZ MARLBOROUGH CUVEE** (NZ)
31	£2.99	**CORBIERES BLANC, CAVES DE MONT TAUCH,** Midi (F)
75	£8.99	**CHABLIS ST MARTIN, DOMAINE LAROCHE** 1990 Burgundy (F)
79	£3.49	**COTES DE ST MONT, PLAIMONT** 1990 S W (F)
87	£5.19	**ORLANDO RF CHARDONNAY** 1989 S E Australia (Aus)
90	£5.29	**LINDEMANS BIN 65 CHARDONNAY** 1989 S E Australia (Aus)
226	£3.79	**DOMAINE DU BOSQUET CANET, LISTEL** 1987 Midi (F)
245	£5.19	**VIN DE PAYS DE LA DORDOGNE CEPAGE CABERNET, CAVE DE SIGOULES** 1990 S W (F)
280	£5.19	**ORLANDO RF CABERNET SAUVIGNON** 1988 S Australia (Aus)
281	£5.29	**MONTANA CABERNET SAUVIGNON** 1988 Marlborough (NZ)
288	£6.49	**CHATEAU MUSAR** 1982 Bekaa Valley (Leb)
329	£17.49	**WOLF BLASS BLACK LABEL CABERNET SAUVIGNON** 1986 S Australia (Aus)
343	£3.99	**DOMAINE LA BERAUDE COTES DU RHONE, NICK THOMPSON** 1989 (F)
351	£4.79	**DIEMERSDAL SHIRAZ** 1986 Paarl (SA)
359	£5.19	**CROZES HERMITAGE, DELAS FRERES** 1989 Rhône (F)
375	£12.99	**COTE ROTIE SEIGNEUR DE MOUGIRON, DELAS FRERES** 1988 Rhône (F)
412	£6.19	**CAMPO FIORIN VALPOLICELLA, MASI** 1986 Veneto (It)
447	£5.19	**EL COTO RIOJA RESERVA** 1985 (Sp)
449	£7.29	**CAMPO VIEJO RIOJA GRAN RESERVA** 1980 (Sp)
487	£5.19	**TAYLOR'S FIRST ESTATE PORT LUGAR DAS LAGES,** Douro (P)
500	£2.79	**PETILLANT DE LISTEL,** Midi (F)

BAT   The Battersea Wine Company

2A Battersea Rise, London SW11 1ED (071-924 3631). Promising new, independent merchant. **Opening Hours:** Mon-Fri12-9pm; Sat 10.30am-9pm; Sun 1-2pm & 7pm-10pm. **Delivery:** free locally, nationally at cost.. **Tastings:** regularly in-store. **Discounts:** variable (5%-10%) on whole cases.

Michael Gould, manager of this merchant last year has left, giving way to Rory MacNally whose experience was in Belfast, a town where we suspect that reformed yuppie wine drinkers are rather less plentiful than they are on the south bank of the Thames. The photocopied list is worth lingering over, as it reveals some very careful, and often adventurous, buying . There are no less than seven white Rhônes, nine different single-estate Beaujolais and a California selection which includes such rarely- seen producers as Shafer and Villa Mount Eden. And all at affordable prices.

327	£15.25	YARRA YERING CABERNET SAUVIGNON 1987 Yarra Valley (Aus)
358	£5.55	DOMAINE LA SOUMADE RASTEAU, COTES DU RHONE VILLAGES, ROMERO ANDRE 1988 (F)
359	£5.45	CROZES HERMITAGE, DELAS FRERES 1989 Rhône (F)
442	£5.99	TEMPRANILLO, BODEGAS OCHOA 1987 Navarra (Sp)

BFI   Bedford Fine Wines

Faulkners Farm, The Marsh, Carlton, Bedford, MK43 7JU (0234 721153). Independent merchant. **Opening Hours**: phone for details. **Delivery**: free locally. **Tastings**: regularly in-store, plus tutored events.

Burgundy fans should take careful note of Brian Chadwick's address; he shares their weakness sufficiently to offer Burgundy en primeur from such serious estates as Jean Grivot, Mongeard-Mugneret, Réné Engel and Domaine Anne et François Gros. Mr Chadwick's Bordeaux are interesting too - from 1982 Chateau de la Rivière at £9.75 to Palmer 1970 - at £81.50. Other regions are more patchily covered, but trouble has been taken to offer interesting wines. The 'Open House Tastings' are to be recommended too - as occasions presumably when there could be said to be Much Wining in the Marsh.

180	£3.95	HILL SMITH OLD TRIANGLE RIESLING 1990 Barossa Valley (Aus)
226	£4.64	DOMAINE DU BOSQUET CANET, LISTEL 1987 Midi (F)
352	£5.60	COTES DU RHONE, GUIGAL 1988 (F)
380	£4.10	GAILLAC, CEPAGE GAMAY, DOMAINES JEAN CROS 1990 S W (F)
500	£2.65	PETILLANT DE LISTEL, Midi (F)

BEN   Bennetts

Centre of England, Wine-Merchant of the Year

High St, Chipping Campden, Glos GL55 6AG (0386 840392). Blossoming independent merchant. **Opening Hours:** Mon-Sat.9am-1pm & 2pm-5.30pm. **Delivery:** free locally, nationally at cost. **Tastings:** regularly in-store plus tutored events. **Discounts:** 5% on mixed cases.

'Future plans are to take life at a more leisurely pace and to make some money! (Neither of these seem any closer than when we started six years ago).' Looking at Charles Bennett's list, it is easy to see why he has been so busy; Bennetts is the kind of wine merchant that has been built up, bit by bit, with evident care. There is little fat here - indeed the Champagne list has been trimmed of 'some well known names that no longer represent value for money' - but there are tremendous wines to be found at every turn, from the extensive range of Bordeaux to the four vintages each of Yarra Yering Cabernet, and Olivier Leflaive Meursaults and three of Chateau Musar. There are almost no unrecommendable wines.

Bennetts has rapidly become one of the very best wine merchants in the country, a firm which finally succeeded in wresting our Centre of England Award away from Tanners.

6	£8.35	**TALTARNI BRUT TACHE,** Pyrenees (Aus)
69	£6.95	**SOAVE CLASSICO VIGNETO CALVARINO, PIEROPAN** 1989 Veneto (It)
90	£5.99	**LINDEMANS BIN 65 CHARDONNAY** 1989 S E Australia (Aus)
102	£9.35	**MARQUES DE MURRIETA RIOJA BLANCO RESERVA** 1985 Rioja (Sp)
111	£12.85	**EDNA VALLEY CHARDONNAY** 1989 San Luis Obispo (Cal)
117	£13.40	**ELSTON CHARDONNAY, TE MATA** 1989 (NZ)
119	£14.75	**LES PIERRES CHARDONNAY, SONOMA CUTRER** 1987 Sonoma (Cal)
297	£8.25	**TALTARNI CABERNET SAUVIGNON** 1985 Pyrenees (Aus)
313	£11.65	**CLOUDY BAY CABERNET MERLOT** 1989 Marlborough (NZ)
317	£11.35	**CLOS DU VAL MERLOT** 1987 Napa Valley (Cal)
327	£16.10	**YARRA YERING CABERNET SAUVIGNON** 1987 Yarra Valley (Aus)
336	£47.75	**OPUS ONE, ROBERT MONDAVI** 1987 Napa Valley (Cal)
392	£11.80	**SANFORD PINOT NOIR** 1986 Santa Barbara (Cal)
437	£4.35	**SENORIO DE LOS LLANOS RESERVA** 1982 Valdepeñas (Sp)
451	£10.20	**MARQUIS DE MURRIETA RIOJA TINTO RESERVA** 1985 (Sp)
452	£14.95	**RIOJA RESERVA 904, LA RIOJA ALTA** 1978 (Sp)
458	£7.30	**YALUMBA MUSEUM SHOW RESERVE MUSCAT,** Rutherglen (Aus)
479	£6.00	**LA GITANA MANZANILLA, HIDALGO,** Jerez (Sp)
481	£11.20	**MANZANILLA PASADA DE SANLUCAR ALMACENISTA, LUSTAU,** Jerez (Sp)
487	£5.49	**TAYLOR'S FIRST ESTATE PORT LUGAR DAS LAGES,** Douro (P)

BSN | Benson Fine Wines

96 Ramsden Road, London SW12 8QZ (081 673 4439). Independent merchant. **Opening Hours:** phone first. **Delivery**: free locally, nationally at cost.

Our first reaction on picking up Clare Benson's list was to check that it wasn't 10 years out of date. Gruaud Larose 1934 for £55; Cos d'Estournel 1934 for £60; 1908 La Romanée from Jules Regnier for £60... Wines of this maturity and at these prices make us wonder why none of the people who've been filling their cellars with overpriced young claret haven't been emptying Ms Benson's cellars by the truckful. Happily for the rest of us, Benson Fine Wines remains a secret treasure. Just imagine a merchant in New York stating 'We specialise in Fine and Rare only. Usually pre-1961'. The range extends beyond wine though. We were just as tempted by a 1920 Jerez 'Specially for the infirm' (£35), a 19th century Blue Curacao in 'old blown, long-neck Fockink bottles' and the 'Utility marked British Make U.M. Co., LDN, incorporating English corkscrew, cap lifter, glass cutter, coin tester, bottle-stopped wrench and other unidentifiable uses...'

BKW | Berkeley Wines

Head Office: Cellar 5, China Lane, Warrington, Cheshire WA4 6RT (0925 444 555). **Opening Hours:** phone first. **Delivery:** free locally. **Tastings:** occasionally in-store. **Discounts:** 5% on (mixed) case.

The 'serious' face of the generally down-market Cellar Five chain.

36	£3.69	**COLDRIDGE ESTATE AUSTRALIAN WHITE** 1989 Victoria (Aus)
220	£3.69	**CHRISTIAN BROTHERS CLASSIC RED,** Napa Valley (Cal)
449	£7.69	**CAMPO VIEJO RIOJA GRAN RESERVA** 1980 (Sp)
481	£11.99	**MANZANILLA PASADA DE SANLUCAR ALMACENISTA, LUSTAU,** Jerez (Sp)

BBR | Berry Bros & Rudd

3 St James St, London SW1A 1EG (071 839 9033) & The Wine Shop Hamilton Close, Houndmills, Basingstoke, Hants RG21 2YB (0256 23566). Traditional family merchants since the 1690s. **Opening Hours:** Mon-Fri 9.30am-5pm. **Delivery:** free nationally. **Tastings:** regularly in-store plus tutored events. **Discounts:** 3% on two cases, 5% on five cases, 7.5% on ten cases.

Our list of recommended wines shows just how far the St James's traditionalists have come over the last few years. As the old ledgers have given way to computer, the London-bottled Bordeaux and emphatically un-modern Burgundy have been joined by wines such as the Snoqualmie Chardonnay from Washington State, Errazuriz Panquehue Cabernet Sauvignon from Chile and Ngatarawa Sauvignon from New Zealand. We sometimes wonder how disconcerting these new names and styles must be to some of Berry's more conservative customers. But maybe they're changing with the times, too. After all, even Berry Brothers' list concedes that rising Champagne prices have 'made some people look more seriously at sparkling alternatives.'

In the Old World, Berry's has acknowledged too that there is an alternative to those old-fashioned Burgundies. Indeed, the list is peppered with names like Drouhin and Amiot among the inevitable soupy Doudet-Naudins.

22	£20.95	**VEUVE CLICQUOT DEMI-SEC CHAMPAGNE** (F)
83	£5.95	**CALITERRA CHARDONNAY** 1990 Maipo Valley (Ch)
150	£8.25	**STONELEIGH SAUVIGNON BLANC** 1989 Marlborough (NZ)
320	£12.35	**CHATEAU LEOVILLE BARTON, ST JULIEN** 1987 Bordeaux (F)

BI | Bibendum

113 Regents Park Road, London NW1 8UR (071 586 9761). High-class by-the-case merchant .**Opening Hours:** Mon-Sat 10am-8pm. **Delivery:** free within London, nationally at cost. **Tastings:** regularly in-store plus tutored events.

Last year's London Wine Merchant of the Year has gone from strength to strength over the last twelve months, developing new skills, as a specialist which make it a formidable competitor for all sorts of companies who thought they had cornered their bits of the market. An Italian tasting, featuring a bus-load of growers, was as good as any held this year, and Burgundy fans are often to be found poring over the elegantly printed list. Even so, this year it was a remarkable selection of Rhônes which won Bibendum one of the Guide's Specialist of the Year awards.

One of the joys of Bibendum, though in its ability and desire to offer the unexpected- Champagne at £10 a bottle when everybody else was reducing prices to £15, and a first chance to taste wines made in Australia by Bordeaux superstar Andre Lurton. In short, the Bibendum tasting is one of the few which all the serious wine writers take the trouble to attend.

74	£7.98	CHABLIS, BERNARD LEGLAND 1989 Burgundy (F)
87	£5.25	ORLANDO RF CHARDONNAY 1989 S E Australia (Aus)
93	£6.75	BROKENBACK VINEYARD CHARDONNAY, ROTHBURY 1990 Hunter Valley (Aus)
98	£7.98	WITTERS VINEYARD CHARDONNAY, COLLARD BROTHERS 1990 Henderson (NZ)
102	£9.95	MARQUES DE MURRIETA RIOJA BLANCO RESERVA 1985 Rioja (Sp)
111	£11.75	EDNA VALLEY CHARDONNAY 1989 San Luis Obispo (Cal)
112	£11.95	SAINTSBURY RESERVE CHARDONNAY 1988 Carneros (Cal)
154	£7.95	SHAW AND SMITH SAUVIGNON BLANC 1990 S Australia (Aus)
162	£5.95	SWEET LEE, THAMES VALLEY VINEYARD 1989 Berkshire (UK)
176	£4.95	PIGGOTT HILL LATE HARVEST MUSCAT, QUALCO 1989 Barossa Valley (Aus)
280	£5.25	ORLANDO RF CABERNET SAUVIGNON 1988 S Australia (Aus)
289	£6.95	LES CHARMES GODARD, COTES DE FRANCS 1988 Bordeaux (F)
320	£11.95	CHATEAU LEOVILLE BARTON, ST JULIEN 1987 Bordeaux (F)
332	£20.50	CHATEAU TALBOT, ST JULIEN 1982 Bordeaux (F)
336	£44.95	OPUS ONE, ROBERT MONDAVI 1987 Napa Valley (Cal)
360	£5.75	COTES DU RHONE SEGURET, CHATEAU LA COURANCONNE 1985 (F)
381	£4.98	DOMAINE DE LA CHAMOISE, GAMAY DE TOURAINE, MARIONNET 1990 Loire (F)
391	£8.95	SAINTSBURY PINOT NOIR 1988 Carneros (Cal)
429	£16.50	BAROLO, 'CIABO MENTIN GINESTRA', CLERICO DOMENICO 1986 Piedmont (It)
451	£9.95	MARQUIS DE MURRIETA RIOJA TINTO RESERVA 1985 (Sp)

BIN | Bin 89 Wine Warehouse

89 Trippet Lane, Sheffield S1 4EL (0742 755889). Independent one-man operation. **Opening Hours:** Tue-Fri 11am-6pm; Sat 10am-1pm. **Delivery:** free within South Yorkshire, nationally at cost. **Tastings:** occasionally. **Discounts:** negotiable on large orders.

Imagine a wine bar where you could buy a case of the stuff you are enjoying drinking - or a wine warehouse with a comfortable place to sit and sip. Jonathan Park's Bin 89 Wine bar/Wine Warehouse is both - or at least that's what it is on Saturdays when the warehouse is open for customers to collect their purchases. For the rest of the week, it's more of a sampling bar where customers can work their way through a weekly selection of 15 of Mr Parks' frequently changing, 350-line list. It is almost impossible to predict precisely which wines you may find, but there's every chance that they will be a varied bunch, given his predilection for offering such oddities as Texan Chardonnay alongside some tasty single estate Burgundies.

BND | Bin Ends

83-85 Badsley Moor Lane, Rotherham S65 2PH (0709 367771). Independent merchant selling by the bottle or case. **Opening Hours:** Mon-Fri 10am-5.30pm; Sat 9.30am-12.30pm. **Delivery:** free locally, nationally at cost. **Tastings:** regularly in-store plus tutored events. **Discounts:** 5% on unbroken cases, 7.5 % on 3 or more cases.

Patrick Toone, whose notepaper is adorned by his own serious-looking portrait, describes Bin Ends as a very small firm. He is too modest. The list is long and full of quite exciting wines, ranging from 1947 Barolo to 1989 Villa Montes from Chile. The Australian list is good though California remains strangely unexplored. The comment with a note 'we are now listing a few wines from the Ernest & Julio Gallo range' says it all.

| 103 | £9.95 | KING VALLEY CHARDONNAY FAMILY RESERVE, BROWN BROS 1987 Milawa (Aus) |
| 288 | £6.75 | CHATEAU MUSAR 1982 Bekaa Valley (Leb) |

| 303 | £7.30 | **ROSEMOUNT SHOW RESERVE CABERNET SAUVIGNON** 1987 Coonawarra (Aus) |
| 442 | £6.25 | **TEMPRANILLO, BODEGAS OCHOA** 1987 Navarra (Sp) |

BLW | Blayneys

Head Office: Riverside Rd, Sunderland SR5 3JW (091 548 4488). 185-branch chain in Tyne and Wear and the Birmingham area. **Opening Hours:** Mon-Sat 10am-10pm; Sun 12-2pm & 7pm-9.30pm. **Delivery:** free locally (certain branches), nationally at cost. **Tastings:** occasionally in-store plus tutored events. **Discounts:** 5% on 1-4 cases, 7.5% on 5+ cases.

Mr Bill Ridley, the proprietor of the 185-strong chain, has firm ideas about the future progress of Blayneys. As a regional grocer/wine merchant operation, he would like not only to come out ahead of the competition, but to be on par with the better-known chains further South.

As an integral part of these efforts, Mr Ridley is concentrating on improving staff training on all levels by strongly encouraging staff to gain WSET qualifications, and sending all managerial staff on 'Customer Feeling Courses'. We hope these prove to be more than a grope in the dark. Nonetheless, we feel that Mr Ridley would do well to be somewhat more adventurous with his choice of wines. The wines listed *are* solid and reliable. Perhaps next year we can see some less well-known names.

22	£18.65	**VEUVE CLICQUOT DEMI-SEC CHAMPAGNE** (F)
84	£4.55	**OXFORD LANDING CHARDONNAY, YALUMBA** 1990 S Australia (Aus)
150	£6.29	**STONELEIGH SAUVIGNON BLANC** 1989 Marlborough (NZ)
332	£16.50	**CHATEAU TALBOT, ST JULIEN** 1982 Bordeaux (F)
333	£22.75	**CHATEAU PAVIE, ST EMILION** 1985 Bordeaux (F)
404	£3.99	**VIGNETI CASTERNA VALPOLICELLA CLASSICO, PASQUA** 1987 Veneto (It)
431	£17.50	**CABREO IL BORGO, RUFFINO** 1986 Tuscany (It)
481	£10.45	**MANZANILLA PASADA DE SANLUCAR ALMACENISTA, LUSTAU,** Jerez (Sp)

BOO | Booths (of Stockport)

62 Heaton Moor Road, Stockport, Cheshire SK4 4NZ (061 432 3309). Independent family merchant. **Opening Times:** Mon, Tue, Thur, Fri 9am-7pm; Wed 9am-1pm; Sat 8:30am-5:30pm. **Delivery:** free locally. **Tastings:** regularly in-store plus tutored tastings. **Discounts:** 5% on mixed case, 8% on unbroken case.

'We now specialise in wines to the same extent as food, ie. Auslese to Zinfandel and artichokes to zucchini.' Booth's is the kind of shop everyone wishes they had around the corner. From Zimbabwean Nyala ('medium-dry wine with flavour from a hot country') to Jensen Calera Pinot Noir and Chateau La Gurgue the range is dazzling and very eclectic. The list is similarly successful in getting away with its combination of inexpensive presentation, curious descriptions - 'Ferret i Mateu 1975-no wood, stored in large glass keg for 12 years. Needs aerating!' - and quotable by misquotes, one of which particularly appealed to the Guide's editor: 'I was convinced forty years ago - and the conviction remains to this day - that in wine tasting and wine talk there is an enormous amount of Humbug.'

29	£2.85	**CUVEE JEAN-PAUL BLANC SEC VIN DE TABLE, PAUL BOUTINOT** (F)
54	£5.10	**ALSACE TOKAY PINOT GRIS, CAVE VINICOLE DE TURCKHEIM** 1990 (F)
62	£5.40	**CHAI BAUMIERES CHARDONNAY, VIN DE PAYS D'OC, DOMAINE DE LA BAUME** 1990 Midi (F)

83	£4.75	**CALITERRA CHARDONNAY** 1990 Maipo Valley (Ch)
95	£7.20	**SCHINUS MOLLE CHARDONNAY** 1990 Mornington Peninsula (Aus)
145	£5.80	**SAUVIGNON DE ST BRIS, DOMAINE FELIX** 1990 Burgundy (F)
173	£22.00	**ALSACE TOKAY PINOT GRIS SELECTION DE GRAINS NOBLES, CAVE VINICOLE DE TURCKHEIM** 1989 (F)
204	£4.30	**CHATEAU LE RAZ, BERGERAC ROSE** 1990 S W (F)
226	£3.80	**DOMAINE DU BOSQUET CANET, LISTEL** 1987 Midi (F)
231	£5.00	**CHATEAU DE LASTOURS CUVEE SIMONE DESCAMPS, CORBIERES** 1989 Midi (F)
267	£4.30	**CHATEAU LE RAZ, BERGERAC ROUGE** 1989 S W (F)
301	£8.20	**HOLLICK CABERNET MERLOT** 1988 Coonawarra (Aus)
302	£9.40	**CHATEAU RAMAGE LA BATISSE, HAUT MEDOC** 1988 Bordeaux (F)
303	£11.40	**ROSEMOUNT SHOW RESERVE CABERNET SAUVIGNON** 1987 Coonawarra (Aus)
305	£9.00	**JEAN LEON CABERNET SAUVIGNON** 1983 Penedés (Sp)
313	£10.20	**CLOUDY BAY CABERNET MERLOT** 1989 Marlborough (NZ)
315	£11.00	**MOUNTADAM CABERNET SAUVIGNON** 1987 High Eden Ridge (Aus)
356	£5.20	**DAVID WYNN SHIRAZ** 1990 High Eden Ridge (Aus)
359	£5.00	**CROZES HERMITAGE, DELAS FRERES** 1989 Rhône (F)
375	£15.00	**COTE ROTIE SEIGNEUR DE MOUGIRON, DELAS FRERES** 1988 Rhône (F)
406	£5.40	**REFOSCO GRAVE DEL FRIULI, COLLAVINI** 1988 Friuli-Venezia-Giulia (It)
410	£5.75	**CAPITEL VALPOLICELLA DEI NICALO, TEDESCHI** 1986 Veneto (It)
437	£4.00	**SENORIO DE LOS LLANOS RESERVA** 1982 Valdepeñas (Sp)
440	£5.40	**TINTO VELHO REGUENGOS DE MONSARAZ, JOSE DE SOUSA ROSADO FERNANDES** 1986 Alentejo (P)
445	£5.20	**NAVAJAS RIOJA CRIANZA TINTO** 1985 (Sp)
448	£6.40	**GARRAFEIRA TE, J M DE FONSECA** 1985 Azeitão (P)
452	£13.75	**RIOJA RESERVA 904, LA RIOJA ALTA** 1978 (Sp)
455	£3.80	**CASTILLO DE LIRIA MOSCATEL, VICENTE GANDIA,** Valencia (Sp)
500	£2.40	**PETILLANT DE LISTEL,** Midi (F)

BTH | E H Booth

Head Office: 4-6 Fishergate, Preston, Lancs PR1 3LJ (0772 51701). Classy supermarket chain with 21 shops in Lancashire, Cumbria and Cheshire. **Opening Hours:** 9am-5.30pm Mon-Fri; 9am-5pm Sat. **Delivery:** £5 per case for 1-4 cases, 5+ cases free nationally. **Tastings:** occasionally in-store plus tutored tastings.

Last years' joint Regional Wine Merchant of the Year, EH Booth has treated 1991 as a year for consolidation, moving from mail-order to exclusive over-the-counter sales, and in a possibly unfortunate choice of phrase 'beefing up' the range of Burgundies and Beaujolais.

Edwin Booth's efforts at being a specialist supermarket are paying off as the company's reputation spreads south. The broad range of the wines is such that this is still a company from whom more than one much larger supermarket chain could have much to learn.

3	£6.63	**LINDAUER, MONTANA** (NZ)
22	£18.38	**VEUVE CLICQUOT DEMI-SEC CHAMPAGNE** (F)
33	£4.59	**DOMAINE DU TARIQUET, COTES DE GASCOGNE** 1990 South West (F)
72	£6.49	**MACON AZE, DOMAINE D'AZENAY** 1989 Burgundy (F)
102	£8.67	**MARQUES DE MURRIETA RIOJA BLANCO RESERVA** 1985 Rioja (Sp)
196	£4.85	**THREE CHOIRS MEDIUM DRY ENGLISH TABLE WINE** 1989 Gloucs (Eng)
222	£3.25	**CHATEAU DE MANDOURELLE, CORBIERES** 1988 Midi (F)
281	£4.89	**MONTANA CABERNET SAUVIGNON** 1988 Marlborough (NZ)
288	£6.75	**CHATEAU MUSAR** 1982 Bekaa Valley (Leb)
303	£7.88	**ROSEMOUNT SHOW RESERVE CABERNET SAUVIGNON** 1987 Coonawarra (Aus)

310	£8.16	BARON VILLENEUVE DE CANTERMERLE, HAUT-MEDOC, CHATEAU CANTEMERLE 1986 Bordeaux (F)
323	£15.49	VASSE FELIX CABERNET SAUVIGNON 1988 Margaret River (Aus)
327	£15.28	YARRA YERING CABERNET 1987 Yarra Valley (Aus)
332	£21.45	CHATEAU TALBOT, ST JULIEN 1982 Bordeaux (F)
336	£40.82	OPUS ONE, ROBERT MONDAVI 1987 Napa Valley (Cal)
351	£4.08	DIEMERSDAL SHIRAZ 1986 Paarl (SA)
352	£5.29	COTES DU RHONE, GUIGAL 1988 (F)
367	£6.63	TALTARNI SHIRAZ 1988 Pyrenees (Aus)
380	£4.15	GAILLAC, CEPAGE GAMAY, DOMAINES JEAN CROS 1990 S W (F)
450	£7.92	NAVARRA ANIVERSARO 125, CHIVITE 1981 Navarra (Sp)
487	£7.41	TAYLOR'S FIRST ESTATE PORT LUGAR DAS LAGES, Douro (P)
500	£1.99	PETILLANT DE LISTEL, Midi (F)

BD | Bordeaux Direct

Head Office: New Aquitaine House, Paddock Rd, Reading, Berks RG4 0JY (0734 481711). Chain of six shops round the Reading area. **Opening Hours:** Mon-Wed 10.30am-7pm, Thu, Fri 10.30am-8pm ; Sat 9am-6pm. **Delivery:** free for orders over £50, £3.50 for orders under 50 cases. **Tastings:** regularly in-store plus tutored events.

The Sunday Times Wine Club (qv) by any other name (- well almost).

BGC | Borg Castel

Samlesbury Mill, Goosefoot Lane, Samlesbury Bottoms, Preston, Lancashire PR5 0RN (0254 852 128). Independent merchant. **Opening hours:** 10am-5pm Mon-Fri; first Sunday of every month, 12 noon-4pm. **Delivery:** free within 30 miles, nationally at cost. **Tastings:** regular in-store, plus tutored events. **Discounts:** negotiable.

Despite our usual allergy to wine lists decorated with baby Bacchi seated astride wine casks, our curiosity was sufficiently aroused for us to delve within its covers. What we found was a very serious range of wines with Burgundies from Vallet-Frères and a long list of Turckheim's Alsatians. There are some fairly priced Bordeaux too in the £6-£12 range including Chateau Labégorce Zédé 1983 for £10.42. Apart from South Africa, the New World remains largely undiscovered. Maybe the infant Bacchus is too young to stray that far away from Samlesbury Bottoms.

29	£2.98	CUVEE JEAN-PAUL BLANC SEC VIN DE TABLE, PAUL BOUTINOT (F)
46	£4.20	CHARDONNAY, DOMAINE DES FLINES, VIN DE PAYS DE LA LOIRE 1990 (F)
54	£5.29	ALSACE TOKAY PINOT GRIS, CAVE VINICOLE DE TURCKHEIM 1990 (F)
87	£5.91	ORLANDO RF CHARDONNAY 1989 S E Australia (Aus)
136	£4.59	DOMAINE DE LA CHAMBANDERIE, MUSCADET, BRUNO CORMERAIS 1990 Loire (F)
145	£6.05	SAUVIGNON DE ST BRIS, DOMAINE FELIX 1990 Burgundy (F)
280	£5.91	ORLANDO RF CABERNET SAUVIGNON 1988 S Australia (Aus)
349	£4.89	RASTEAU COTES DU RHONE VILLAGES, VIGNERONS DE RASTEAU 1989 (F)

B&B | Bottle & Basket

15 Highgate High St, London N6 5JT (081 341 7018). Independent merchant. **Opening Hours:** Mon-Fri 11am-3pm & 5pm-9pm; 11am-9pm Sat; 12-3pm & 7pm-9pm Sun. **Delivery:** free locally. **Tastings:** regularly in-store. **Discounts:** 5% for case collection.

Our comment last year about the use of a John Bull printing set to produce the Bottle & Basket list has clearly had an effect on Fernando Munoz. The list is now hand-written. It's almost as if he doesn't want his range to be taken seriously. Well, we've seen through this ruse and can recognise such goodies as the organic Ch Grand Canyon (really!) from Pauillac and Faiveley Nuit (sic) St Georges. The Spanish range is as good as ever but California-philes may leave unsatisfied unless their particular taste is for Gallo.

22	£19.75	**VEUVE CLICQUOT DEMI-SEC CHAMPAGNE** (F)	
140	£4.99	**COOKS HAWKES BAY SAUVIGNON BLANC** 1989 Hawkes Bay (NZ)	
150	£5.66	**STONELEIGH SAUVIGNON BLANC** 1989 Marlborough (NZ)	
442	£5.23	**TEMPRANILLO, BODEGAS OCHOA** 1987 Navarra (Sp)	
452	£13.78	**RIOJA RESERVA 904, LA RIOJA ALTA** 1978 (Sp)	

BNK The Bottleneck

7 Charlotte Street, Broadstairs, Kent CT10 1LR (0843 60195). **Delivery**: free within 25 miles. **Tastings**: regularly in-store, plus tutored events. **Discounts**: 5% 1 case, 6% 2 cases, 7.5% 3 cases 10% 5+ cases.

What is it about hand-written lists! We have no way of knowing who is responsible for the calligraphy of this glow-in-the-dark list, nor whether the same person was responsible for its minefield selections. Lynch-Bages 83 should be delicious as is Durup Chablis. We are less excited by Le Piat d'Or Blanc, and Nobility British Sherry. Mind you, there are some Mondavis for those who can resist the temptation of (you've guessed it) the Gallos.

3	£6.99	**LINDAUER, MONTANA** (NZ)	
14	£12.99	**DEHOURS CHAMPAGNE** (F)	
83	£4.99	**CALITERRA CHARDONNAY** 1990 Maipo Valley (Ch)	
286	£7.99	**SEPPELT GOLD LABEL CABERNET SAUVIGNON** 1986 S E Australia (Aus)	

BOS Bottles of Brock Street

24 Brock Street, Bath, Avon BA1 2LN (0225 482 886). **Opening Hours:** Mon-Thu 11am-8pm; Fri,Sat 11am-8pm. The retail arm of wholesalers Godwin & Godwin. **Delivery**: free within 50 miles. **Tastings**: regularly in-store plus tutored events.

Sparkling Hungarian wine (Frater Julianus 88 at around a fiver)? Yeringberg Chardonnay? Or just the same old Charmes Chambertin from Domaine Dujac? Whatever you fancy, Bottles seem to have something to fit the bill. Ten years of wholesaling experience, plus 'popular demand and interest' gave Kent and Ralph Godwin the confidence to open the shop in November 1990 and already they stock several top clarets (four vintages of Latour), Vega Sicilia and probably the widest range of Hungarian wine in Bath.

84	£4.95	**OXFORD LANDING CHARDONNAY, YALUMBA** 1990 S Australia (Aus)	
106	£9.50	**WYNNS COONAWARRA ESTATE CHARDONNAY** 1989 (Aus)	
295	£7.85	**WYNNS CABERNET SAUVIGNON** 1985 Coonawarra (Aus)	
327	£15.95	**YARRA YERING CABERNET SAUVIGNON** 1987 Yarra Valley (Aus)	
357	£5.99	**FETZER ZINFANDEL** 1987 Mendocino (Cal)	
365	£7.50	**CHATEAU TAHBILK SHIRAZ** 1987 Goulburn Valley (Aus)	
373	£11.95	**DOMAINE DU VIEUX TELEGRAPHE, CHATEAUNEUF DU PAPE,** 1987 Rhône (F)	

BU | Bottoms Up

Head Office: Astra House, Edinburgh Way, Harlow, Essex CM20 2EA (0279 451145). An expanding chain, now with 78 branches. **Opening Hours:** Mon-Fri 10am-10pm; 12-2pm & 7pm-9pm Sun. **Delivery:** free locally. **Tastings:** regularly in-store.

The arrival at the Guide's office of a Bottoms Up wine list free of misprints and full of good wines caused the same glee as the news that they now have a wine buyer. This once quirkily interesting chain began life as a reincarnation of the original Augustus Barnett, the chain which turned a generation of Britons on to wine in the late 1960's. Over the last five or six years, however, it has slumbered, serving more as a place to buy trail mix and beer rather than good wine. But Oddbins had better beware. Debbie Worton has already begun some adventurous buying across the board. What is needed now is for staff training to be given the same attention.

13	£12.95	HAMM CHAMPAGNE BRUT RESERVE PREMIER CRU (F)
47	£4.24	DOMAINE PETITOT, COTES DE DURAS 1990 S W (F)
87	£5.25	ORLANDO RF CHARDONNAY 1989 S E Australia (Aus)
90	£4.99	LINDEMANS BIN 65 CHARDONNAY 1989 S E Australia (Aus)
97	£7.89	CHATEAU DES CHARMES CHARDONNAY 1988 Ontario (Can)
107	£9.35	KRONDORF SHOW RESERVE CHARDONNAY 1989 Barossa Valley (Aus)
152	£7.99	SANCERRE, DOMAINE DES GROSSES PIERRES 1990 Loire (F)
279	£4.85	GLEN ELLEN MERLOT 1987 Sonoma (Cal)
280	£5.19	ORLANDO RF CABERNET SAUVIGNON 1988 S Australia (Aus)
288	£7.25	CHATEAU MUSAR 1982 Bekaa Valley (Leb)
293	£7.29	JAMIESONS RUN RED, MILDARA 1987 Coonawarra (Aus)
327	£15.95	YARRA YERING CABERNET SAUVIGNON 1987 Yarra Valley (Aus)
333	£23.99	CHATEAU PAVIE, ST EMILION 1985 Bordeaux (F)
342	£3.79	LES SABLES SYRAH, VIN DE PAYS DES COLLINES RHODANIENNES, DE VALLOUIT 1989 Rhône (F)
346	£4.99	CO-OP CROZES HERMITAGE, LUIS MOUSSET, Rhône (F)
368	£8.25	SAINT JOSEPH, ST DESIRAT 1988 Rhône (F)
409	£6.89	CHIANTI CLASSICO LAMOLE, CASTELLI DEL GREVEPESA 1986 Tuscany (It)
464	£5.99	CHATEAU LOUPIAC GAUDIET, LOUPIAC 1988 S W (F)
500	£1.99	PETILLANT DE LISTEL, Midi (F)

BRO | The Broad Street Wine Co.

The Hollaway, Market Place, Warwick CV34 4SJ (0926 493951). Small, by-the-case only merchant with a good bin-end list. **Opening Hours:** Mon-Fri 9am-6pm; 9am-1pm Sat. **Delivery:** nationally at cost. **Tastings:** regularly in-store. **Discounts:** at discretion of management.

'I just get switched on by good wines' is Russell Hobbs' own response to our saying that his was a list to get steamed up about. References to kettles inevitably put us in mind of pots - or in this case the pot-stills used to produce some of Broad Street's extraordinary list of brandies and Calvados. But the wines - of which quantities are often admittedly quite limited - are well chosen too. We also appreciated Mr Hobbs' comments: '1986 Chateau Xanadu Chardonnay 52 bottles £13.75 - The Montrachet of Oz? Money back if you find any better at this price; 1988 Cloudy Bay Chardonnay 38 bottles £975, We found this in the back cellar. First come first served'. Give our regards to Broad Street any time...

29	£2.96	CUVEE JEAN-PAUL BLANC SEC VIN DE TABLE, PAUL BOUTINOT (F)

72	£6.98	**MACON AZE, DOMAINE D'AZENAY** 1989 Burgundy (F)
145	£5.73	**SAUVIGNON DE ST BRIS, DOMAINE FELIX** 1990 Burgundy (F)
349	£4.69	**RASTEAU COTES DU RHONE VILLAGES, VIGNERONS DE RASTEAU** 1989 (F)

BUD Budgens

Head Office: PO Box 9, Stonefield Way, Ruislip, Middx HA4 0JR (081 422 3422). Regional supermarket chain with 95 stores in the South-East, Norfolk and the Midlands. **Opening Hours:** Mon-Fri 8.30am-8.30pm; 8.30am-6pm Sat. **Tastings:** occasionally in-store.

Sarah King, the buyer who began to revolutionise this chain's list has been spirited away to Safeway, but her place has been ably filled by another name which should be familiar to Guide readers: Julian Twaites, who became available following the sale of his Drinksmart business to the German Aldi supermarket giant. Twaites freely acknowledges that the major hurdle he faces lies in persuading his employers to believe in the potential of the wine department, and to allow him to increase the range from 150 to somewhere closer to the 500 of his competitors. So far, he has doubled the Fine Wine section (from 12-24) and is trying to get it into a larger number of shops. Julian Twaites is a keen and skilled buyer; he and Budgens need our encouragement if they are to escape the mire of Acute Piat d'Ordom.

87	£5.15	**ORLANDO RF CHARDONNAY** 1989 S E Australia (Aus)
140	£5.29	**COOKS HAWKES BAY SAUVIGNON BLANC** 1989 Hawkes Bay (NZ)
359	£4.95	**CROZES HERMITAGE, DELAS FRERES** 1989 Rhône (F)

BWI Bute Wines

Mount Stuart, Rothesay, Isle of Bute, PA20 9LR (0700 502730) Fax (0700 505313) Friendly, recently founded independent specialist combining an aristocratic range of Bordeaux and Burgundy with New World wines which display an atractively common touch. **Opening Hours:** Mon-Fri 9-5, 24-hr answerphone. **Delivery:** free on the Isle of Bute, and elsewhere free of charge for orders of over 5 cases. Otherwise nationally at cost. **Tastings:** regularly and to outside clubs on request.

The inhabitants of the Isle of Bute are extraordinarily lucky: they not only have one of Britain's best Bordeaux and Burgundy cellars on their doorstep, but they also benefit from free delivery of any wine they may care to buy. Apart from recent vintages from these regions, Jennifer, Marchioness of Bute - a far more approachable merchant than many a non-aristocratic competitor - can also offer such rarities as 1987 Cloudy Bay Chardonnay, 1978 Jekel Cabernet Sauvignon and 1982 Sassicaia, as well as extensive lists of en primeur Bordeaux.

90	£6.28	**LINDEMANS BIN 65 CHARDONNAY** 1989 S E Australia (Aus)
125	£9.32	**NUITS ST GEORGES BLANC, CLOS DE L'ARLOT** 1988 Burgundy (F)
138	£4.80	**DOMAINE DES CORBILLIERES, SAUVIGNON DE TOURAINE** 1989 Loire (F)
332	£22.59	**CHATEAU TALBOT, ST JULIEN** 1982 Bordeaux (F)
333	£19.14	**CHATEAU PAVIE, ST EMILION** 1985 Bordeaux (F)
352	£5.91	**COTES DU RHONE, GUIGAL** 1988 (F)
475	£38.35	**CHATEAU RIEUSSEC, SAUTERNES** 1983 Bordeaux (F)

BUT | The Butlers Wine Cellar

247 Queens Park Road, Brighton Sussex BN2 2XJ (0273 698 724). **Opening Hours:** Tue-Fri 9am-5:30pm; Sat 9am-1pm. **Delivery**: free anywhere in the UK for orders of 3+ cases, otherwise at cost.

Geoffrey and Henry Butler run an astonishing shop, stocked with wines ranging from Livadia White Muscat 1931 from Russia (£75 'Ideal for that 60th birthday present') Herz-Konig Sekt- ('medium-dry, a good pick-me-up, £1.35, 37 quarter bottles) and 1943 Ch Cantemerle ('an interesting war-time vintage'). The day to day list is rather more down to earth, with a range of good French regional wines from £3-£5

ABY | Anthony Byrne Fine Wines

88 High St, Ramsey, Huntingdon, Cambs PE17 1BS (0487 814555). Burgundy- and Australia-loving traditional merchant. **Opening Hours:** Mon-Sat 9am-5.30pm. **Delivery:** free nationally for 2 cases plus; below 2 cases, £6.50. **Tastings:** bottles open every day plus tutored events.

Anthony Byrne's success has been built on a sensible principle of seeking out good producers and stocking and selling wide ranges of their wines, so Duboeuf Beaujolais, Cuvaison Californians and Delatite Australians share a list with the stunning Alsaces of Zind Humbrecht.

103	£8.35	KING VALLEY CHARDONNAY FAMILY RESERVE, BROWN BROS 1987 N E Victoria (Aus)	
170	£11.20	ALSACE GEWURZTRAMINER GRAND CRU GOLDERT, ZIND HUMBRECHT 1987 (F)	
172	£19.10	ALSACE GEWURZTRAMINER HERRENWEG VENDANGE TARDIVE, ZIND HUMBRECHT 1986 (F)	
329	£15.95	WOLF BLASS BLACK LABEL CABERNET SAUVIGNON 1986 S Australia (Aus)	
412	£6.03	CHIANTI CLASSICO, SAN LEONINO 1986 Veneto (It)	
464	£6.15	CHATEAU LOUPIAC GAUDIET, LOUPIAC 1988 S W (F)	

DBY | D Byrne & Co

Victoria Buildings, 12 King St, Clitheroe, Lancs (0200 23152).Part one of the Clitheroe phenomenon. **Opening Hours:** Mon-Wed 9am-6pm;Thu,Fri 9am-8pm; Sat 9am-6pm. **Delivery:** free locally. **Tastings:** occasionally, tutored events on request, plus a -week-long annual tasting.

Wine lovers who have never strayed into Clitheroe now have a pretty solid reason for doing so. From 1991, none of the D Byrne list of wines is available by mail order, as apparently this aspect of the business was detracting from the retail operation. There are merchants whose mail order lists are entirely dispensable but Byrne's was one of the most comprehensive in the country. But as Philip Byrne says 'many of our customers already travel over 100 miles to shop with us.' From Omar Khayyam Indian fizz to 15-year old Buichladdich malt whisky, they have every good reason to make the detour.

3	£6.59	LINDAUER, MONTANA (NZ)	
14	£12.59	DEHOURS CHAMPAGNE (F)	
22	£18.49	VEUVE CLICQUOT DEMI-SEC CHAMPAGNE (F)	
25	£22.99	BILLECART BRUT CHAMPAGNE 1985 (F)	
29	£2.79	CUVEE JEAN-PAUL BLANC SEC VIN DE TABLE, PAUL BOUTINOT (F)	
38	£3.19	TOLLANA DRY WHITE 1988 S E Australia (Aus)	
54	£4.69	ALSACE TOKAY PINOT GRIS, CAVE VINICOLE DE TURCKHEIM 1990 (F)	
83	£5.09	CALITERRA CHARDONNAY 1990 Maipo Valley (Ch)	

87	£5.39	ORLANDO RF CHARDONNAY 1989 S E Australia (Aus)
102	£8.75	MARQUES DE MURRIETA RIOJA BLANCO RESERVA 1985 Rioja (Sp)
103	£6.39	KING VALLEY CHARDONNAY FAMILY RESERVE, BROWN BROS 1987 N E Victoria (Aus)
104	£8.49	PENFOLDS PADTHAWAY CHARDONNAY 1990 (Aus)
106	£8.65	WYNNS COONAWARRA ESTATE CHARDONNAY 1989 (Aus)
107	£7.09	KRONDORF SHOW RESERVE CHARDONNAY 1989 Barossa Valley (Aus)
108	£7.09	EILEEN HARDY CHARDONNAY, HARDY'S 1988 S Australia (Aus)
119	£12.65	LES PIERRES CHARDONNAY, SONOMA CUTRER 1987 Sonoma (Cal)
140	£4.69	COOKS HAWKES BAY SAUVIGNON BLANC 1989 Hawkes Bay (NZ)
145	£5.39	SAUVIGNON DE ST BRIS, DOMAINE FELIX 1990 Burgundy (F)
148	£8.29	SELAKS SAUVIGNON BLANC 1990 (NZ)
150	£5.79	STONELEIGH SAUVIGNON BLANC 1989 Marlborough (NZ)
153	£8.09	POUILLY FUME LES CHANTALOUETTES 1989 Loire (F)
173	£16.35	ALSACE TOKAY PINOT GRIS SELECTION DE GRAINS NOBLES, CAVE VINICOLE DE TURCKHEIM 1989 (F)
178	£4.39	SEAVIEW RHINE RIESLING 1988 Coonawarra (Aus)
180	£3.79	HILL SMITH OLD TRIANGLE RIESLING 1990 Barossa Valley (Aus)
184	£10.35	ALSACE RIESLING RESERVE PARTICULIERE, SELTZ 1988 (F)
192	£6.14	DEINHARD HOCHHEIM HERITAGE SELECTION 1988 Rheingau (G)
204	£4.25	CHATEAU LE RAZ, BERGERAC ROSE 1990 S W (F)
228	£4.10	CHATEAU CLEMENT TERMES, GAILLAC ROUGE 1988 S W (F)
231	£4.69	CHATEAU DE LASTOURS CUVEE SIMONE DESCAMPS, CORBIERES 1989 Midi (F)
258	£3.89	SVISCHTOV CABERNET SAUVIGNON CONTROLIRAN 1985 Svischtov (Bul)
264	£4.65	BERRI ESTATES AUSTRALIAN CABERNET SHIRAZ 1987 (Aus)
267	£4.25	CHATEAU LE RAZ, BERGERAC ROUGE 1989 S W (F)
279	£5.09	GLEN ELLEN MERLOT 1987 Sonoma (Cal)
280	£5.39	ORLANDO RF CABERNET SAUVIGNON 1988 S Australia (Aus)
281	£4.99	MONTANA CABERNET SAUVIGNON 1988 Marlborough (NZ)
284	£5.29	SIRIUS ROUGE, PETER SICHEL 1988 Bordeaux (F)
287	£6.59	RAIMAT CABERNET SAUVIGNON 1985 Lerida (Sp)
288	£5.99	CHATEAU MUSAR 1982 Bekaa Valley (Leb)
295	£6.99	WYNNS CABERNET SAUVIGNON 1985 Coonawarra (Aus)
303	£7.09	ROSEMOUNT SHOW RESERVE CABERNET SAUVIGNON 1987 Coonawarra (Aus)
305	£12.35	JEAN LEON CABERNET SAUVIGNON 1983 Penedes (Sp)
310	£8.69	BARON VILLENEUVE DE CANTERMERLE, HAUT-MEDOC, CHATEAU CANTEMERLE 1986 Bordeaux (F)
313	£9.89	CLOUDY BAY CABERNET MERLOT 1989 Marlborough (NZ)
325	£14.89	CARMENET CABERNET SAUVIGNON 1986 Sonoma (Cal)
327	£13.45	YARRA YERING CABERNET 1987 Yarra Valley (Aus)
331	£19.49	PENFOLDS BIN 707 CABERNET SAUVIGNON 1987 S Australia (Aus)
332	£24.59	CHATEAU TALBOT, ST JULIEN 1982 Bordeaux (F)
344	£4.88	PENFOLDS BIN 2 SHIRAZ/MATARO 1989 Barossa Valley (Aus)
347	£4.59	CABERNET/SHIRAZ 1989 S Australia (Aus)
349	£4.39	RASTEAU COTES DU RHONE VILLAGES, VIGNERONS DE RASTEAU 1989 (F)
351	£4.59	DIEMERSDAL SHIRAZ 1986 Paarl (SA)
359	£5.39	CROZES HERMITAGE, DELAS FRERES 1989 Rhône (F)
365	£6.59	CHATEAU TAHBILK SHIRAZ 1988 Goulburn Valley (Aus)
373	£9.39	DOMAINE DU VIEUX TELEGRAPHE, CHATEAUNEUF DU PAPE 1987 Rhône (F)
374	£10.19	RIDGE GEYSERVILLE ZINFANDEL 1988 Santa Clara (Cal)
392	£10.59	SANFORD PINOT NOIR 1986 Santa Barbara (Cal)
412	£6.79	CHIANTI CLASSICO, SAN LEONINO 1986 Veneto (It)
415	£7.09	BARBERA D'ALBA PIAN ROMUALDO, PRUNOTTO 1988 Piedmont (It)
419	£8.25	ROSSO DI MONTALCINO, POGGIO ANTICO 1989 Tuscany (It)
437	£4.59	SENORIO DE LOS LLANOS RESERVA 1982 Valdepenas (Sp)
446	£5.19	GRAN SANGREDETORO RESERVA, TORRES 1986 Penedes (Sp)
449	£7.55	CAMPO VIEJO RIOJA GRAN RESERVA 1980 (Sp)

451	£8.75	MARQUES DE MURRIETA RESERVA 1985 (Sp)
452	£12.75	RIOJA RESERVA 904, LA RIOJA ALTA 1978 (Sp)
460	£9.49	CAMPBELLS OLD RUTHERGLEN LIQUEUR MUSCAT (Aus)
481	£10.79	MANZANILLA PASADA DE SANLUCAR ALMACENISTA, LUSTAU, Jerez (Sp)
483	£12.95	APOSTOLES, GONZALEZ BYASS, Jerez (Sp)
487	£6.99	TAYLOR'S FIRST ESTATE PORT LUGAR DAS LAGES, Douro (P)

CAC | Cachet Wines

Lysander Close, Clifton Moor, York YO3 8XB (0904 690090). Independent merchant selling by the case. **Opening Hours:** Mon-Fri 9am-6pm; Sat 10am-4pm . **Delivery:** free locally, nationally at cost. **Tastings:** occasionally in-store plus tutored events.

Visitors to the Great Yorkshire Show who manage to drag their attention away from prize heifers and the country clothing stands often seem to spend an inordinately long time perusing Cachet Wines' list. The emphasis is most definitely on France, with reasonably-priced Bordeaux , Burgundies, and regional wines, including the Corbieres of Château de Lastours. Among the New World wines appear one which is referred to in a curious note: 'Oxford Landing Chardonnay has been our best-selling Australian wine in the past year, despite not being on the list during that period.'

29	£2.75	CUVEE JEAN-PAUL BLANC SEC VIN DE TABLE, PAUL BOUTINOT (F)
58	£5.29	CHATEAU COUCHEROY BLANC, GRAVES, ANDRE LURTON 1989 Bordeaux (F)
79	£3.40	COTES DE ST MONT, PLAIMONT 1990 S W (F)
84	£4.69	OXFORD LANDING CHARDONNAY, YALUMBA 1990 S Australia (Aus)
86	£5.25	CHARDONNAY, VIN DE PAYS D'OC, HUGH RYMAN 1990 Midi (F)
280	£5.25	ORLANDO RF CABERNET SAUVIGNON 1988 S Australia (Aus)
288	£6.80	CHATEAU MUSAR 1982 Bekaa Valley (Leb)
392	£10.95	SANFORD PINOT NOIR 1986 Santa Barbara (Cal)
449	£8.25	CAMPO VIEJO RIOJA GRAN RESERVA 1980 (Sp)
465	£5.85	REDWOOD VALLEY ESTATE LATE HARVEST RIESLING 1989 Nelson (NZ)

CWI | A Case of Wine

Cwn Tawel, Horeb, Llandysul Dyfed SA44 4HY (0559 363342). Farmer with wholesale and retail wine business. **Delivery:** free within 50 miles and nationally at cost. **Tastings:** regularly in-store plus own tutored tastings. **Discounts:** 2.5% unmixed case.

Mike Dentten put us right following last year's *Guide* in which we described him as a Welsh, non-Rugby-playing farmer. In fact, he's an English ex-prop-forward who only farms 'as an unprofitable sideline.' We can, however, confirm that he has the best organic wine list in Wales, as well as a long range of well chosen Italian wines, an improved selection of Rhône wines, Georgian Zhiguihl beer and Ty Nant Welsh spring water.

14	£12.65	DEHOURS CHAMPAGNE (F)
137	£4.50	BOZE DOWN DRY 1989 Oxfordshire (UK)
229	£4.40	CHATEAU DE FLOTIS, COTES DE FRONTONNAIS 1988 S W (F)
230	£4.98	MAS DE GOURGONNIER TRADITION, COTEAUX D'AIX EN PROVENCE LES BAUX 1989 Midi (F)
288	£6.79	CHATEAU MUSAR 1982 Bekaa Valley (Leb)
315	£11.50	MOUNTADAM CABERNET SAUVIGNON 1987 High Eden Ridge (Aus)
355	£4.99	DOMAINE ST APOLLINAIRE (ORGANIC), COTES DU RHONE 1989 (F)

356	£5.45	**DAVID WYNN SHIRAZ** 1990 High Eden Ridge (Aus)
366	£6.99	**ST GILBERT BOTOBOLAR VINEYARD, GIL WAHLQUIST** 1987 Mudgee (Aus)
416	£7.65	**CHIANTI CLASSICO, ISOLE E OLENA** 1988 Tuscany (It)
426	£13.75	**CEPPARELLO, ISOLE E OLENA** 1988 Tuscany (It)
445	£5.99	**NAVAJAS RIOJA CRIANZA TINTO** 1985 (Sp)
479	£5.65	**LA GITANA MANZANILLA, HIDALGO,** Jerez (Sp)

CVR | The Celtic Vintner

Welsh Merchant of the Year

73 Derwen Fawr Rd, Sketty, Swansea, West Glamorgan SA2 8DR (0792 206661). Friendly, well-stocked independent merchant who can't stop winning prizes. **Opening Hours:** Mon-Fri 8am-6pm; weekends by arrangement. **Delivery**: free within South & West Wales, nationally at cost. **Tastings:** regularly in-store tastings.

Brian Johnson once again can celebrate winning our award for Welsh Wine Merchant of the Year. To those outside the Principality, the achievement may not seem as impressive as it is. Wales may not be full of wine merchants, but the Celtic Vintner list could stand comparison with those of any of the best companies in the rest of the UK. French country wines are well represented but so are Burgundies (from Domaine Parent), Bordeaux and Australians (from wineries including Moss Wood and Coldstream Hills). The Celtic Vintner is probably also the only place in Britain to sell a full range of Moroccan wines, introduced to help out a local restaurant.

29	£2.64	**CUVEE JEAN-PAUL BLANC SEC VIN DE TABLE, PAUL BOUTINOT** (F)
43	£3.82	**MAUZAC, DOMAINE DE LA BATTEUSE, B DELMAS** 1989 S W (F)
46	£3.88	**CHARDONNAY, DOMAINE DES FLINES, VIN DE PAYS DE LA LOIRE** 1990 (F)
54	£4.88	**ALSACE TOKAY PINOT GRIS, CAVE VINICOLE DE TURCKHEIM** 1990 (F)
83	£4.64	**CALITERRA CHARDONNAY** 1990 Maipo Valley (Ch)
84	£4.35	**OXFORD LANDING CHARDONNAY, YALUMBA** 1990 S Australia (Aus)
86	£4.99	**CHARDONNAY, VIN DE PAYS D'OC, HUGH RYMAN** 1990 Midi (F)
87	£5.17	**ORLANDO RF CHARDONNAY** 1989 S E Australia (Aus)
93	£5.82	**BROKENBACK VINEYARD CHARDONNAY, ROTHBURY** 1990 Hunter Valley (Aus)
108	£10.28	**EILEEN HARDY CHARDONNAY, HARDY'S** 1988 S Australia (Aus)
134	£4.11	**DOMAINE DU BREUIL, VIN DE PAYS DU JARDIN DE LA FRANCE, MARC MORGAT** 1990 Loire (F)
147	£5.88	**KLEIN COSTANTIA SAUVIGNON BLANC** 1988 (SA)
148	£6.17	**SELAKS SAUVIGNON BLANC** 1990 (NZ)
203	£4.11	**CHATEAU BAUDUC, BORDEAUX CLAIRET, DAVID THOMAS** 1990 (F)
231	£4.76	**CHATEAU DE LASTOURS CUVEE SIMONE DESCAMPS, CORBIERES** 1989 Midi (F)
258	£4.17	**SVISCHTOV CABERNET SAUVIGNON CONTROLIRAN,** 1985 Svischtov (Bul)
280	£5.17	**ORLANDO RF CABERNET SAUVIGNON** 1988 S Australia (Aus)
288	£6.58	**CHATEAU MUSAR** 1982 Bekaa Valley (Leb)
308	£7.34	**COLDSTREAM HILLS CABERNET SAUVIGNON** 1988 Yarra Valley (Aus)
313	£10.28	**CLOUDY BAY CABERNET MERLOT** 1989 Marlborough (NZ)
336	£41.13	**OPUS ONE, ROBERT MONDAVI** 1987 Napa Valley (Cal)
349	£4.52	**RASTEAU COTES DU RHONE VILLAGES, VIGNERONS DE RASTEAU** 1989 (F)
350	£4.52	**CHATEAU DU GRAND MOULAS, COTES DU RHONE** 1989 (F)
355	£5.17	**DOMAINE ST APOLLINAIRE (ORGANIC), COTES DU RHONE** 1989 (F)
357	£4.82	**FETZER ZINFANDEL** 1987 Mendocino (Cal)
368	£7.34	**SAINT JOSEPH, ST DESIRAT** 1988 Rhône (F)
442	£5.29	**TEMPRANILLO, BODEGAS OCHOA** 1987 Navarra (Sp)
458	£6.55	**YALUMBA MUSEUM SHOW RESERVE MUSCAT,** Rutherglen (Aus)

466	£6.58	**THE HARDY COLLECTION PADTHAWAY RHINE RIESLING BEERENAUSLESE** 1987 (Aus)
492	£15.99	**VERDELHO 10 YEAR OLD, COSSART GORDON** (P)
493	£15.28	**WARRE'S QUINTA DA CAVADINHA** 1982 Douro (P)

CDV   Champagne de Villages

9 Fore St, Ipswich, Suffolk IP4 1JW (0473 256922). Independent specialist merchant. **Opening Hours:** Mon-Sat 9am-5.30pm. **Delivery:** free locally, free nationally for orders over £250, otherwise £7 per case. **Tastings:** regularly in-store plus tutored events for outside organisations.

'As a small specialist company, we are constantly searching for individual and interesting wines from the Champagne region.' This is a search which has only been relatively succesful for Champagne de Villages, whose Burgundy list is rather longer than its Champagnes. Both parts of the list, however, include recommendable wines, as do the excursions into other regions and countries such as Portugal and New Zealand. Anyone fancying a vertical tasting of Pauillac might be interested in 8 vintages from 52 - 61. A serious wine merchant in every respect.

6	£9.25	**TALTARNI BRUT TACHE,** Pyrenees (Aus)
139	£5.95	**DOMAINE DU PRE BARON, SAUVIGNON DE TOURAINE** 1989 Loire (F)
232	£4.95	**DOMAINE MONBOUCHE, COTES DE BERGERAC** 1988 S W (F)
297	£7.50	**TALTARNI CABERNET SAUVIGNON** 1985 Pyrenees (Aus)
367	£6.95	**TALTARNI SHIRAZ** 1988 Pyrenees (Aus)
444	£5.95	**BAIRRADA, LUIS PATO** 1988 Bairrada (P)

CPL   Chaplin & Son

35 Rowlands Rd, Worthing, W Sussex BN11 3JJ (0903 35888). Independent merchant able to obtain most wines 'if they can be found'. **Opening Hours:** Mon-Sat 8:45am-5:30pm (closed for lunch). **Delivery**: nationally at cost. **Tastings:** regularly in-store plus tutored events. **Discounts:** 5%(mixed) case.

Debbie Lush (what a wonderful name for a wine merchant), in a previous existence, had much to do with the success of The Upper Crust, a former award winner in this *Guide*. Now at Chaplin's, she is 'launching a new concept to offer greater flexibility and choice to the customer with a more adventurous feel.'

We don't know what this means either, but we like the sound of it. Just as we like the sound of a list which includes inexpensive Chardonnay from Chablis, well-chosen Germans, and such 'culinary props' as 1988 Gros Plant Pays Nantais - a firm, bone-dry white that is ideal for poaching fish or any meat that needs marinating ... also very good with cassis, or as a spritzer-- in other words, don't drink it neat.

22	£20.39	**VEUVE CLICQUOT DEMI-SEC CHAMPAGNE** (F)
84	£4.95	**OXFORD LANDING CHARDONNAY, YALUMBA** 1990 S Australia (Aus)
88	£5.95	**MONTES CHARDONNAY,** 1990 Curico Valley (Ch)
226	£4.25	**DOMAINE DU BOSQUET CANET, LISTEL** 1987 Midi (F)
299	£8.50	**MONTES ALPHA CABERNET SAUVIGNON,** 1987 Curico Valley (Ch)
347	£4.57	**SEAVIEW CABERNET SHIRAZ** 1989 S Australia (Aus)
353	£5.25	**PENFOLDS BIN 28 KALIMNA SHIRAZ** 1988 S Australia (Aus)

380	£4.45	GAILLAC, CEPAGE GAMAY, DOMAINES JEAN CROS 1990 S W (F)
425	£13.85	CARMIGNANO RISERVA, VILLA DI CAPEZZANA 1985 Tuscany (It)
487	£7.99	TAYLOR'S FIRST ESTATE PORT LUGAR DAS LAGES, Douro (P)
493	£16.25	WARRE'S QUINTA DA CAVADINHA 1982 Douro (P)
500	£2.69	PETILLANT DE LISTEL, Midi (F)

CFW | Christchurch Fine Wine

1-3 Vine Lane, High Street, Christchurch, Dorset BH23 1AS (0202 473 255). Independent merchant. **Opening Hours**: Mon-Thur 10am-1pm; Fri 10am-7pm; Sat 10am-5pm. **Delivery**: free locally, nationally at cost. **Tastings**: regular in-store, plus special events and customers' club. **Discounts**: 5% per case.

If you're the sort of person who likes rummaging in jumble sales, you'll love this list, except there's no dross to obscure the good stuff: wines from Hospices de Beaune from the 1960's and '70's, Bordeaux such as Latour '48 and Cheval Blanc '64 and German Rieslings from 1971 and 1976. Stocks are generally, by definition, very limited, so a visit to Vine Lane at a weekend is likely to be worthwhile. At a less elevated level, Christchurch could be described as specialists in current-drinking wines from the Loire, Rhône, Alsace, and Savoie.

CHP | Chateau Pleck See Whittalls

CIW | City Wines

221 Queens Road, Norwich NR1 3AE (0603 660741). Independent merchant. **Opening Hours**: Mon, Tue 12-3pm,4pm-9pm;Wed-Sat 9am-9pm; Sun 12-2pm,7pm-9pm. **Delivery**: free locally, nationally at cost. **Tastings**: regularly in-store. **Discounts**:5% (mixed) case discount.

'After a traumatic period of financial foolishness which reached its peak in 1990', City Wines have rebuilt themselves, to the point at which they like to say that they can serve customers 'from Mr Special Brew to Mrs Puffa jacket' - both of whom, we presume, must live in Norwich. This is the third stage of City Wines' existence from up-market and comprehensive, down-market and cheap (in 1990) and back to a happier medium. Customers who suffer from sea-sickness may be interested to know City Wines offer French supermarket beer for £1.69 a litre -- though whether this would satisfy Mr Special Brew, we cannot say.

6	£9.49	TALTARNI BRUT TACHE, Pyrenees (Aus)
31	£3.49	CORBIERES BLANC, CAVES DE MONT TAUCH, Midi (F)
33	£5.99	DOMAINE DU TARIQUET, COTES DE GASCOGNE 1990 South West (F)
263	£5.49	TRAPICHE CABERNET SAUVIGNON RESERVE OAK CASK 1986 (Arg)
281	£5.49	MONTANA CABERNET SAUVIGNON 1988 Marlborough (NZ)
373	£9.99	DOMAINE DU VIEUX TELEGRAPHE, CHATEAUNEUF DU PAPE 1987 Rhône (F)
442	£5.79	TEMPRANILLO, BODEGAS OCHOA 1987 Navarra (Sp)
466	£6.15	THE HARDY COLLECTION PADTHAWAY RHINE RIESLING BEERENAUSLESE 1987 (Aus)
472	£7.99	JURANCON MOELLEUX VENDANGE TARDIVE, DOMAINE CAUHAPE 1988 South West (F)

CWW | Classic Wine Warehouses

Unit A2, Stadium Industrial Estate, Sealand Road, Chester, CH1 4LU (0244 390444). **Opening Hours:** Mon-Fri 8-6; Sat 9-5. **Delivery:** free nationally. **Tastings:** regularly in-store, plus special events. **Discounts:** Negotiable.

'Classic' in more than one sense. This is the company whose list of directors includes James Dean and John Lennon. Imagine that. The background was as an offshoot of Lennon's, a chain of off-licenses noted in the 1980's for a fairly adventurous range. For the moment at least, the use of the plural in the title merely leaves scope for the future, as there is just one shop-- in Chester. The range of wines is impressive, including some classic Drouhin Burgundies, and 'giant' bottles of Champagne in which Classic specialise, claiming to be the cheapest supplier in the country. A good set of Bordeaux comes from Nathaniel Johnston, whose fellow negociant, Dulong, produces a good blended red called Rebelle whose cause has yet to be taken up by Mr Dean. A word of warning; Classic uses a single list for retail and wholesale customers, so the price you pay will be 17.5% higher than that shown.

3	£7.20	LINDAUER, MONTANA (NZ)
12	£12.46	SCHARFFENBERGER BLANC DE BLANCS 1987 Mendocino (Cal)
104	£8.32	PENFOLDS PADTHAWAY CHARDONNAY 1990 (Aus)
150	£7.14	STONELEIGH SAUVIGNON BLANC 1989 Marlborough (NZ)
181	£4.70	LAMBERHURST SEYVAL BLANC 1988 Kent (UK)
258	£4.80	SVISCHTOV CABERNET SAUVIGNON CONTROLIRAN 1985 Svischtov (Bul)
288	£7.20	CHATEAU MUSAR 1982 Bekaa Valley (Leb)
329	£16.29	WOLF BLASS BLACK LABEL CABERNET SAUVIGNON 1986 S Australia (Aus)
331	£19.58	PENFOLDS BIN 707 CABERNET SAUVIGNON 1987 S Australia (Aus)
344	£4.85	PENFOLDS BIN 2 SHIRAZ/MATARO 1989 Barossa Valley (Aus)
353	£6.16	PENFOLDS BIN 28 KALIMNA SHIRAZ 1988 S Australia (Aus)
442	£8.00	TEMPRANILLO, BODEGAS OCHOA 1987 Navarra (Sp)
449	£8.16	CAMPO VIEJO RIOJA GRAN RESERVA 1980 (Sp)

CNL | Connollys

110 Edmund St, Birmingham, W Midlands B3 2ES (021 236 3837). Independent merchant whose wines are better than his poetry. **Opening Hours:** Mon-Fri 9am-5.30pm; Sat 9.30am-1pm. **Delivery:** free locally. **Tastings:** regularly in-store plus tutored events. **Discounts:** 5% mixed case.

Sadly, we we were only able to see an interim price list while preparing this year's Guide, and so are unable to bring you further examples of Chris Connolly's versification which proved so popular in previous years. We can, however, report on the diversification of a list which is steadily growing to take in a broad range of good Australians to join such other New World rarities as the Bodegas Weinert 1983 Cabernet Sauvignon from Argentina. Prices throughout are fair, including such potential delights as Corton Clos de Corton from Faiveley 1982 for £26.00

29	£2.82	CUVEE JEAN-PAUL BLANC SEC VIN DE TABLE, PAUL BOUTINOT (F)
180	£4.19	HILL SMITH OLD TRIANGLE RIESLING 1990 Barossa Valley (Aus)
284	£5.99	SIRIUS ROUGE, PETER SICHEL 1988 Bordeaux (F)
288	£6.87	CHATEAU MUSAR 1982 Bekaa Valley (Leb)
313	£10.69	CLOUDY BAY CABERNET MERLOT 1989 Marlborough (NZ)
446	£5.64	GRAN SANGREDETORO RESERVA, TORRES 1986 Penedés (Sp)
481	£9.45	MANZANILLA PASADA DE SANLUCAR ALMACENISTA, LUSTAU, Jerez (Sp)

CWS | The Co-op

Head Office: Fairhills Rd, Irlam, Manchester M30 8BD (061 834 1212). Well-known, but slightly confusing, supermarket chain. See Leo's. **Opening Hours:** variable. **Tastings:** occasionally in-store.

First things first: the labels. In previous editions of the Guide we have been pretty critical of the naff labels Britain's largest retailer has stuck on the bottles of some very well-chosen wine. This year the Co-op has proudly revealed a new set of labels which have been specially designed for them. These are certainly better than the old ones. But not much. Which seems a pity because the quality of the Co-op's wines continues to rise to the point at which the smart folk might be perfectly happy to have them on their dinner tables. Perhaps Co-op customers like naff labels. Other wine drinkers might consider the use of a decanter.

196	£4.29	THREE CHOIRS MEDIUM DRY ENGLISH TABLE WINE 1989 Gloucs (UK)
202	£3.49	CO-OP PROVENCE ROSE, GILARDI, Midi (F)
240	£2.89	CO-OP CLARET, ESCHENAUER, Bordeaux (F)
243	£2.99	CO-OP BERGERAC ROUGE, CAVE DE SIGOULES, S W (F)
252	£3.89	CO-OP MEDOC, CVBG, Bordeaux (F)
346	£4.29	CO-OP CROZES HERMITAGE, LUIS MOUSSET, Rhône (F)
497	£21.79	DUQUE DE BRAGANZA 20 YEAR OLD TAWNY PORT, FERREIRA, Douro (P)

C&B | Corney & Barrow

12 Helmet Row, London, EC1V 3QJ (071 251 4951). Established merchant with branches in London, Newmarket (Belvoir House, High Street, Suffolk CB8 8OH), and Edinburgh. **Opening Hours:** Mon-Fri 9am-7pm. **Delivery:** free within M25 for 2+ cases, free nationally for 3+ cases. **Tastings:** regularly in-store plus tutored events.

Of all the companies affected by de-Yuppiefication, Corney & Barrow ought to have been the most sorely affected. Its wine bars were, after all, among the places where a lot of new money was most conspicuously spent. But the wine merchant arm of C & B seems to have embraced the straitened times with something akin to enthusiasm by putting out leaflets headlined 'Devil Dancing in an Empty Pocket.' That publication is merely a supplement to a veritable volume which includes information on wine storage, ('look after your wines and your wines will look after you') and recommended red wines for chilling, plus an offer to help 'the corporate customer' - 'just as glamorously high profile and expensive wine can damage your reputation, so too can a cheap branded item.'

The company's list is broad-ranging and reliable, including Burgundies from Olivier and Domaine Leflaive, Bordeaux galore from Jean-Pierre Mouiex (of Petrus fame) and Californians from Simi and Stag's Leap.

121	£17.16	MEURSAULT BLAGNY, DOMAINE MATROT 1987 Burgundy (F)
124	£22.68	MEURSAULT PREMIER CRU LES CRAS, OLIVIER LEFLAIVE 1988 Burgundy (F)
149	£7.40	BARKHAM MANOR 1988 East Sussex (Eng)
289	£6.93	LES CHARMES GODARD, COTES DE FRANCS 1988 Bordeaux (F)
296	£7.05	HUNGERFORD HILL CABERNET SAUVIGNON 1988 Coonawarra (Aus)
307	£7.76	CHATEAU GRAND ORMEAU, LALANDE DE POMEROL 1987 Bordeaux (F)
380	£4.82	GAILLAC, CEPAGE GAMAY, DOMAINES JEAN CROS 1990 S W (F)
396	£21.15	VOLNAY TAILLEPIEDS, DOMAINE DE MONTILLE 1987 Burgundy (F)
399	£39.48	LE CHAMBERTIN, ARMAND ROUSSEAU 1987 Burgundy (F)
438	£5.17	MARIUS RESERVE, BODEGAS PIQUERAS 1983 Almansa (Sp)

CWM | Cornwall Wine Merchants

Chapel Rd, Tuckingmill, Camborne, Cornwall (0209 715765). Wholesaler selling to the public by the mixed case. **Opening Hours:** Mon-Fri 9am-5pm.**Delivery:** free locally, nationally at less than cost. **Tastings:** organised on request.

'We don't waste money on printing expensive lists-the customer would have to pay for it in the end.' Actually, the current offering, printed using a smarter home computer than last time, is a model of how such lists ought to look. The contents are pretty good, too, including William Fèvre Chablis and Delas Frères Rhônes and a more ambitious Bordeaux list than in the past. Nick Richards is also proud to be importing Hidalgo sherries directly, though on which part of the Cornish coast they land is not made clear.

29	£2.99	CUVEE JEAN-PAUL BLANC SEC DE TABLE, PAUL BOUTINOT (F)
54	£5.35	ALSACE TOKAY PINOT GRIS, CAVE VINICOLE DE TURCKHEIM 1990 (F)
90	£5.86	LINDEMANS BIN 65 CHARDONNAY 1989 S E Australia (Aus)
220	£4.05	CHRISTIAN BROTHERS CLASSIC RED, Napa Valley (Cal)
359	£5.60	CROZES HERMITAGE, DELAS FRERES 1989 Rhône (F)
479	£5.42	LA GITANA MANZANILLA, HIDALGO, Jerez (Sp)
493	£17.35	WARRE'S QUINTA DA CAVADINHA 1982 Douro (P)

CGW | The Cote Green Wine Company

45/47 Compstall Road, Marple Bridge, Stockport, Cheshire (061 462 0155). Independent family merchant. Wine club. **Delivery:** free within 25 miles, nationally at cost. **Tastings:** regularly in-store plus tutored events. **Discounts:** 7% on mixed cases.

When we asked The Cote Green Wine Co to specify in-house staff training, the reply was 'I frequently write articles for the local press; staff are encouraged to read these.'
Over the last year, the company has slightly changed its name (from Cote Green Wines), gone further into direct importation from France, and launched a free wine club which offers the Cote Green shop wines to members at discount prices.

29	£2.95	CUVEE JEAN-PAUL BLANC SEC VIN DE TABLE, PAUL BOUTINOT (F)
33	£3.49	DOMAINE DU TARIQUET, COTES DE GASCOGNE 1990 SW (F)
54	£4.64	ALSACE TOKAY PINOT GRIS, CAVE VINICOLE DE TURCKHEIM 1990 (F)
87	£5.82	ORLANDO RF CHARDONNAY 1989 S E Australia (Aus)
118	£12.99	VIDAL RESERVE CHARDONNAY 1989 Hawkes Bay (NZ)
139	£5.59	DOMAINE DU PRE BARON, SAUVIGNON DE TOURAINE 1989 Loire (F)
225	£3.99	CLOS DE LISA, COTES DU ROUSSILON, J BAISSAS ET FILS 1989 Midi (F)
288	£7.39	CHATEAU MUSAR 1982 Bekaa Valley (Leb)
349	£3.99	RASTEAU COTES DU RHONE VILLAGES, VIGNERONS DE RASTEAU 1989 (F)
446	£6.18	GRAN SANGREDETORO RESERVA, TORRES 1986 Penedés (Sp)

CUM | Cumbrian Cellar

1 St Andrews Square, Penrith, Cumbria CA11 7AN (0768 63664). Independent merchant with a taste for exotica. **Opening Hours:** Mon-Sat 9am-5.30pm. **Delivery:** free within Cumbria, nationally at cost. **Tastings:** occasionally in-store plus tutored events. **Discounts:** 5% on mixed case.

Last year, we praised The Cumbrian Cellar for its broad ranging selection.

This year, though more basically produced, it is even more impressive. If you want to buy a white from Peru, an organic wine from Somerset, a sparkling wine from Cyprus, or some excellent Hérault Vin de Pays, Penrith is your place.

192	£6.30	**DEINHARD HOCHHEIM HERITAGE SELECTION** 1988 Rheingau (G)
226	£4.60	**DOMAINE DU BOSQUET CANET, LISTEL** 1987 Midi (F)
288	£7.10	**CHATEAU MUSAR** 1982 Bekaa Valley (Leb)
303	£8.75	**ROSEMOUNT SHOW RESERVE CABERNET SAUVIGNON** 1987 Coonawarra (Aus)
452	£13.95	**RIOJA RESERVA 904, LA RIOJA ALTA** 1978 (Sp)
487	£7.75	**TAYLOR'S FIRST ESTATE PORT LUGAR DAS LAGES,** Douro (P)
500	£2.65	**PETILLANT DE LISTEL,** Midi (F)

D	Davisons

Regional Chain of the Year

Head Office: 7 Aberdeen Rd, Croydon, Surrey CR0 1EQ (081 681 3222). London and Home Counties chain with 78 branches, allied to the Master Cellar warehouse (q.v.). **Opening Hours:** Mon-Sat 10am-2pm & 5pm-10pm; 12-2pm & 7pm-9pm Sun. **Delivery** free locally. **Tastings:** regularly in certain stores. **Discounts:** a hefty 8.5 % off mixed cases.

Winner yet again of our Regional Chain Award, Davisons were also short-listed as Bordeaux specialists-as well they might be. In Michael Davies' own words 'we are probably the only company in the world to be continuing a policy of buying all our clarets "en primeur"- not for immediate resale, but to mature and sell in the years and decades to come.' Which explains how the company has 17 years' stock and ten vintages of Chateau Lynch-Bages as well as good supplies of 1983 and 1985 red Burgundy. Once decidedly old-fashioned and suburban-looking, Davisons has upgraded the appearance of both lists and shops. One of Davisons other strengths is their policy of employing couples who live above the shop and thus tend to remain with the company far longer than most of their High Street counterparts.

87	£5.25	**ORLANDO RF CHARDONNAY** 1989 S E Australia (Aus)
88	£5.25	**MONTES CHARDONNAY,** 1990 Curico Valley (Ch)
93	£7.25	**BROKENBACK VINEYARD CHARDONNAY, ROTHBURY** 1990 Hunter Valley (Aus)
107	£9.45	**KRONDORF SHOW RESERVE CHARDONNAY** 1989 Barossa Valley (Aus)
122	£19.12	**MEURSAULT, COCHE DURY** 1988 Burgundy (F)
123	£19.45	**CHASSAGNE MONTRACHET PREMIER CRU CHAUMEES, PIERRE MOREY** 1987 Burgundy (F)
140	£4.99	**COOKS HAWKES BAY SAUVIGNON BLANC** 1989 Hawkes Bay (NZ)
222	£3.75	**CHATEAU DE MANDOURELLE, CORBIERES** 1988 Midi (F)
223	£3.95	**DOMAINE ST EULALIE, MINERVOIS** 1988 Midi (F)
258	£2.99	**SVISCHTOV CABERNET SAUVIGNON CONTROLIRAN,**1985 Svischtov (Bul)
276	£4.99	**CHATEAU MENDOCE, BOURG** 1986 Bordeaux (F)
280	£5.25	**ORLANDO RF CABERNET SAUVIGNON** 1988 S Australia (Aus)
299	£7.95	**MONTES ALPHA CABERNET SAUVIGNON,** 1987 Curico Valley (Ch)
332	£27.25	**CHATEAU TALBOT, ST JULIEN** 1982 Bordeaux (F)
336	£46.25	**OPUS ONE, ROBERT MONDAVI** 1987 Napa Valley (Cal)
353	£5.49	**PENFOLDS BIN 28 KALIMNA SHIRAZ** 1988 S Australia (Aus)
475	£26.75	**CHATEAU RIEUSSEC, SAUTERNES** 1983 Bordeaux (F)
487	£8.59	**TAYLOR'S FIRST ESTATE PORT LUGAR DAS LAGES,** Douro (P)

DLM | Del Monico

23 South Street, St Austell, Cornwall PL25 5BH (0726 73593). Independent merchant, wine club. **Opening Hours**: Mon, Sat 9-7, Tue-Fri 9-6. **Delivery**:free within 30 miles, nationally at cost. **Tastings**: regularly in-store, and to customers club. **Discounts**: 5-10% depending on quantity.

'As always, we will attempt to locate single bottles for customers and are frequently succesful.' Pat and Tony Lawes are about to celebrate two years of running this St Austell shop. Over that time, they have built up a remarkable range of representative wines from all the classic regions, generally from reliable but not necessarily obvious producers. Theirs may also be one of the very rare shops to sell the medium-sweet, locally-produced Polmassick Gwynkemysky.

102	£8.95	MARQUES DE MURRIETA RIOJA BLANCO RESERVA 1985 Rioja (Sp)
226	£4.25	DOMAINE DU BOSQUET CANET, LISTEL 1987 Midi (F)
281	£5.65	MONTANA CABERNET SAUVIGNON 1988 Marlborough (NZ)
288	£6.65	CHATEAU MUSAR 1982 Bekaa Valley (Leb)
310	£9.95	BARON VILLENEUVE DE CANTERMERLE, HAUT-MEDOC 1986 Bordeaux (F)
456	£6.90	SAMOS MUSCAT, Samos (Gr)
449	£8.55	CAMPO VIEJO RIOJA GRAN RESERVA 1980 (Sp)
480	£8.55	DOS CORTADOS, WILLIAMS AND HUMBERT, Jerez (Sp)

ROD | Rodney Densem

Stapeley Bank, London Rd, Nantwich, Cheshire CW5 7JW (0270 623665). Independent merchant operating retail and wholesale. **Opening Hours:** Mon,Tue 10am-6pm; Wed 9am-1pm; 9am-6pm Thu-Sat. **Delivery:** free within 30 miles, nationally at cost. **Tastings:** regularly in-store plus tutored events. **Discounts:** 5% on mixed cases.

Rodney and Margie Densem are among the first of the new breed of Cheshire wine merchants. Now, as retailers and wholesalers - with a shop given to eye-catching window displays - their range includes fairly-priced Bordeaux, single-estate Burgundies and top-flight New World wines.

19	£16.90	DEVAUX CHAMPAGNE CUVEE ROSEE (F)
90	£5.50	LINDEMANS BIN 65 CHARDONNAY 1989 S E Australia (Aus)
103	£7.15	KING VALLEY CHARDONNAY FAMILY RESERVE, BROWN BROS 1987 N E Victoria (Aus)
281	£5.25	MONTANA CABERNET SAUVIGNON 1988 Marlborough (NZ)
313	£8.51	CLOUDY BAY CABERNET MERLOT 1989 Marlborough (NZ)
411	£6.20	CHIANTI CLASSICO, SAN LEONINO 1988 Tuscany (It)
420	£9.90	'SASTER' CABERNET SAUVIGNON, FRIULVINI 1988 Friuli-Venezia-Giulia (It)
446	£7.10	GRAN SANGREDETORO RESERVA, TORRES 1986 Penedés (Sp)
469	£10.95	CHATEAU BASTOR LAMONTAGNE, SAUTERNES 1988 Bordeaux (F)
482	£11.95	ROYAL CORREGIDOR RICH RARE OLD OLOROSO, SANDEMAN, Jerez (Sp)
495	£17.50	FONSECA-GUIMARAENS 1976 Douro (P)
500	£3.47	PETILLANT DE LISTEL, Midi (F)

DWS | Direct Wine Shipments

5/7 Corporation Square, Belfast , Co Antrim BT13 3AJ (0232 238700). Independent merchant, wine club. **Opening Hours:** Mon-Fri 9-5:30 and 'til 8 on Thurs, Sat 10-1. **Delivery:** Free locally, nationally at cost. **Tastings:** regularly in-store, plus dinners and theme events. **Discounts:** 5% on 6 or more bottles of the same wine.

Belfast is not an easy place to do business, and running a wine shop between the Falls Road and the Shankill Road is arguably the nearest most people come to finding themselves between the proverbial rock and a hard place. But the McAlindons persevered before removing themselves to Antrim Road and Corporation Square, both of which are a little calmer. Today they import wines from a wide range of producers, though the emphasis is on the traditional areas, with names such as Hugel, Olivier Leflaive, Burklin Wolf, Antinori, and Torres.

PD | Peter Dominic

Head Office: Astra House, River Way, Harlow, Essex CM20 2DT (0279 26801). High Street chain with over 600 branches. **Opening Hours:** Mon-Sat 9am-9pm; 12-2pm & 7pm-9pm Sun at most stores. **Delivery:** free within 20 miles, nationally at cost. **Tastings:** regularly in-store. **Discounts:** 5% on case price, special quotations on larger volumes.

Deaths: Hunter & Oliver, the Peter Dominic associated 'up-market' chain launched at great cost, but with neither skill nor forethought and laid to rest early in 1991. Mourners - if any there be - may place their wreaths at the doors of a number of unusually smart shops with new Peter Dominic signs. *Births:* To Peter Dominic, a wine buyer. At long last, we are delighted to report that the management of Peter Dominic has decided that its chain should employ a person with a good palate to select its wines. It would be churlish of us to suggest that the realisation came a little late, considering that almost all of Dominic's competitors have had one (or usually more) for a decade or so. Instead, we welcome Debbie Worton (ex-Majestic and Sainsbury) and applaud the efforts she has already made for both Peter Dominic and Bottoms Up (qv). And with any luck, we ain't seen nothing yet.

47	£4.25	**DOMAINE PETITOT, COTES DE DURAS** 1990 S W (F)	
90	£4.99	**LINDEMANS BIN 65 CHARDONNAY** 1989 S E Australia (Aus)	
138	£4.99	**DOMAINE DES CORBILLIERES, SAUVIGNON DE TOURAINE** 1989 Loire (F)	
279	£4.99	**GLEN ELLEN MERLOT** 1987 Sonoma (Cal)	
288	£7.29	**CHATEAU MUSAR** 1982 Bekaa Valley (Leb)	
293	£8.29	**JAMIESONS RUN RED, MILDARA** 1987 Coonawarra (Aus)	
333	£23.99	**CHATEAU PAVIE, ST EMILION** 1985 Bordeaux (F)	
349	£4.99	**RASTEAU COTES DU RHONE VILLAGES, VIGNERONS DE RASTEAU** 1989 (F)	
464	£6.79	**CHATEAU LOUPIAC GAUDIET, LOUPIAC** 1988 S W (F)	
500	£2.09	**PETILLANT DE LISTEL,** Midi (F)	

DX | Drinkx plc

406-408 Merton Road, London SW18 5AD (081-877 0444) & Arch 85, Goding St, London SE11 5EZ (071 582 4540). Young independent company ready to take on the world. **Opening Hours:** Mon-Sat 10am-8pm; 12-3pm Sun. **Delivery:** free locally, nationally at cost. **Tastings:** regularly in-store plus tutored events.

Very few British wine merchants actively looked forward to the difficult trading conditions of 1991. Giles Clarke, former boss of Majestic, greeted it with relish for the simple reason that whereas most members of the wine trade are in the business out of love, Clarke never quite ceases to be a hard-nosed dealer. Nothing pleases him more than the acquisition of a job lot of top-class Bordeaux at a rock-bottom price from a company that's been forced to sell. Unless, of course, it is the re-sale of that wine at a decent margin. The Drinkx shop has built up a loyal following in South London and its shelves are filled with some attractively chosen and priced wines. We suspect, however, that some of the greatest beneficiaries of the Drinkx service are the corporate clients who buy Perrier, some of those inexpensive Burgundies... and job lots of Bordeaux.

| 101 | £9.39 | HUGO CHARDONNAY 1988 Southern Vales (Aus) |
| 157 | £3.99 | DOMAINE DU BOSC MARSANNE, VIN DE PAYS DE L'HERAULT, DELTA DOMAINES 1990 Midi (F) |

| EE | Eaton Elliot |

15 London Rd, Alderley Edge, Cheshire SK9 7JT (0625 582354). Independent Merchant and mail-order firm. **Opening Hours**: Mon-Thu 10am-7pm, Fri 10am-8pm, Sat 10am-5pm. **Delivery:** free locally, nationally at cost. **Tastings:** regularly in-store, plus tutored events. **Discounts:** 5% on case orders.

In the '80s, this area of Cheshire had a number of specialist outlets such as Whynot Wine and Willoughby's of Wilmslow. Today, as Nick Elliot points out, only Eaton Elliot remain. The local populace have little to complain about, however, as the range offered is exemplary, especially in the classic regions of France and Italy. It is these which are beloved of Christopher Tatham, the senior Master of Wine, whose voice can be heard in the 'Golden Age of Wine - a philosophical note' included in the current list.

31	£2.95	CORBIERES BLANC, CAVES DE MONT TAUCH, Midi (F)
42	£3.95	CEPAGE TERRET, VIN DE PAYS DE L'HERAULT, DELTA DOMAINES 1989 Midi (F)
69	£7.20	SOAVE CLASSICO VIGNETO CALVARINO, PIEROPAN 1989 Veneto (It)
114	£10.90	DOMAINE CAUHAPE, JURANCON SEC (OAKED) 1988 S W (F)
154	£7.90	SHAW AND SMITH SAUVIGNON BLANC 1990 S Australia (Aus)
175	£5.50	MOSCATO D'ASTI, MICHELE CHIARLO 1990 Piedmont (It)
235	£5.75	DOMAINE LES HAUTES DE CHAMBERTS, CAHORS 1986 S W (F)
310	£9.20	BARON VILLENEUVE DE CANTERMERLE, HAUT-MEDOC, CHATEAU CANTEMERLE 1986 Bordeaux (F)
332	£22.95	CHATEAU TALBOT, ST JULIEN 1982 Bordeaux (F)
424	£14.45	COLTASSALA, CASTELLO DI VOLPAIA 1986 Tuscany (It)
442	£5.70	TEMPRANILLO, BODEGAS OCHOA 1987 Navarra (Sp)
444	£5.35	BAIRRADA, LUIS PATO 1988 Bairrada (P)
472	£13.50	JURANCON MOELLEUX VENDANGE TARDIVE, DOMAINE CAUHAPE 1988 SW (F)

| ECK | Eckington WInes |

2 Ravencar Road, Eckington, Sheffield S31 9GJ (0246 433 213). Independent merchant, wine club. **Opening Hours:** Phone for details. **Delivery:** free locally, nationally at cost.**Tastings:** Regularly in-store, tutored tastings for customer's club and to outside clubs on request. **Discounts:** negotiable.

Dr Andrew Loughran is clearly a real enthusiast, the kind of person from whom regular customers ought to be sure to receive very committed service. Indeed, this is precisely what he offers in his monthly/quarterly wine scheme whereby people undertake to buy one or more cases of wine at a fixed price and regular intervals, leaving the selection to Dr Loughran. Judging by the list, this scheme would be a pretty safe bet, though we'd be sorry to receive too many of the Eastern European bottles which Dr Loughran evidently thinks highly of.

38	£3.13	**TOLLANA DRY WHITE** 1988 S E Australia (Aus)	
54	£4.49	**ALSACE TOKAY PINOT GRIS, CAVE VINICOLE DE TURCKHEIM** 1990 (F)	
102	£8.50	**MARQUES DE MURRIETA RIOJA BLANCO RESERVA** 1985 Rioja (Sp)	
103	£8.90	**KING VALLEY CHARDONNAY FAMILY RESERVE, BROWN BROS** 1987 N E Victoria (Aus)	
150	£6.50	**STONELEIGH SAUVIGNON BLANC** 1989 Marlborough (NZ)	
173	£17.85	**ALSACE TOKAY PINOT GRIS SELECTION DE GRAINS NOBLES, CAVE VINICOLE DE TURCKHEIM** 1989 (F)	
178	£4.05	**SEAVIEW RHINE RIESLING** 1988 Coonawarra (Aus)	
192	£6.36	**DEINHARD HOCHHEIM HERITAGE SELECTION** 1988 Rheingau (G)	
205	£4.39	**CHRISTIAN BROTHERS WHITE ZINFANDEL** 1989 Napa Valley (Cal)	
220	£3.59	**CHRISTIAN BROTHERS CLASSIC RED**, Napa Valley (Cal)	
258	£2.85	**SVISCHTOV CABERNET SAUVIGNON CONTROLIRAN**, 1985 Svischtov (Bul)	
281	£4.65	**MONTANA CABERNET SAUVIGNON** 1988 Marlborough (NZ)	
288	£6.16	**CHATEAU MUSAR** 1982 Bekaa Valley (Leb)	
319	£10.99	**YARDEN CABERNET SAUVIGNON, GOLAN HEIGHTS WINERY** 1985 Galilee (Is)	
327	£15.75	**YARRA YERING CABERNET SAUVIGNON** 1987 Yarra Valley (Aus)	
331	£14.65	**PENFOLDS BIN 707 CABERNET SAUVIGNON** 1987 S Australia (Aus)	
336	£44.00	**OPUS ONE, ROBERT MONDAVI** 1987 Napa Valley (Cal)	
344	£3.95	**PENFOLDS BIN 2 SHIRAZ/MATARO** 1989 Barossa Valley (Aus)	
347	£4.05	**SEAVIEW CABERNET SHIRAZ** 1989 S Australia (Aus)	
451	£9.50	**MARQUIS DE MURRIETA RIOJA TINTO RESERVA** 1985 (Sp)	
452	£14.69	**RIOJA RESERVA 904, LA RIOJA ALTA** 1978 (Sp)	

EP | Eldridge Pope

Head Office: Weymouth Ave, Dorchester, Dorset, DT1 1QT (0305 251251). South of England chain with 13 shops including four Reynier Wine Libraries. **Opening Hours:** Mon-Sat 9am-6pm. **Delivery:** free locally for one case and nationally for two or more cases. **Tastings:** regularly in-store plus tutored events. **Discounts:** 5% on mixed cases.

A company with a reassuringly solid ring to it. Not for them, the fashionable flavours of Australia (only four wines), New Zealand (three wines) or South America (no wines). This is a place to buy a good selection of the more conservative wines available.

'Country wines' are something of a speciality, with regions like Faugères, Costières de Nîmes and Côtes de Vivarais all represented alongside Abymes from Savoie and Pacherenc de Vic Bilh.

But the real wealth of the range lies in the traditional areas. Burgundies come from Louis Latour, Armand Rousseau and Comte Georges de Vogüé while the clarets include Palmer 1953 in magnums and 9 vintages of Chateau Cissac (a property also responsible for 'The Chairman's Claret') As buyer Joe Naughalty MW says, 'We have old-fashioned principles - good service, good quality, value for money!' Mind you, they must have adventurous moments - otherwise they would not find many takers for its list of wines from Switzerland, Luxembourg, or for wines from the bizarrely-named Californian wineries Grgich Hills and Gundlach Bundschu.

EBA | Ben Ellis & Assocs

The Harvesters, Lawrence Lane, Buckland, Betchworth, Surrey RH3 7BE (073 784 2160). Independent mail-order firm selling by the case. **Delivery:** free locally, nationally at cost. **Tastings:** regularly in-store plus tutored events.

'We *never* buy on price alone and always seek the best ratio between quality and value for money'. A quietly confident young company with a recently-qualified M W, Mark Pardoe, as one of the Associates. The range isn't the largest we've seen but it includes every style of wine which you could want. We were particularly impressed by the partners' choice, which includes the Chardonnays of Shaw and Smith, Hamilton Russell and Tarrawarra, Jean Leon Cabernet Sauvignon and Isole e Olena Chianti Classico.

70	£7.69	ST VERAN TERRES NOIRES, DOMAINE DEUX ROCHES 1989 Burgundy (F)
154	£8.76	SHAW AND SMITH SAUVIGNON BLANC 1990 S Australia (Aus)
303	£7.89	ROSEMOUNT SHOW RESERVE CABERNET SAUVIGNON 1987 Coonawarra (Aus)
305	£8.32	JEAN LEON CABERNET SAUVIGNON 1983 Penedés (Sp)
313	£10.67	CLOUDY BAY CABERNET MERLOT 1989 Marlborough (NZ)
416	£7.78	CHIANTI CLASSICO, ISOLE E OLENA 1988 Tuscany (It)
469	£8.81	CHATEAU BASTOR LAMONTAGNE, SAUTERNES 1988 Bordeaux (F)

EVI | Evingtons

120 Evington Rd, Leicester, LE2 1HH (0533 542702). Independent merchant. **Opening Hours:** Mon-Sat 9.30am-6pm. **Delivery:** free locally, nationally at cost. **Tastings:** regularly in-store plus tutored events. **Discounts:** 5% mixed case, 1-3 cases; 10% mixed case, 4+ cases.

Since the closure of Drinksmart in Wigston, Evington's remains one of the few places that people in Leicester (Leicestonians?) can buy decent wine. Simon March's range isn't the largest in the world, but it's carefully chosen, and includes Millton Late-Harvest Riesling and six different Châteauneufs.

3	£7.20	LINDAUER, MONTANA (NZ)
38	£3.69	TOLLANA DRY WHITE 1988 S E Australia (Aus)
102	£8.75	MARQUES DE MURRIETA RIOJA BLANCO RESERVA 1985 Rioja (Sp)
104	£9.69	PENFOLDS PADTHAWAY CHARDONNAY 1990 (Aus)
169	£8.50	ALSACE GEWURZTRAMINER ST HUBERT, KUEHN 1989 (F)
258	£3.70	SVISCHTOV CABERNET SAUVIGNON CONTROLIRAN, 1985 Svischtov (Bul)
281	£5.35	MONTANA CABERNET SAUVIGNON 1988 Marlborough (NZ)
310	£9.50	BARON VILLENEUVE DE CANTERMERLE, HAUT-MEDOC, CHATEAU CANTEMERLE 1986 Bordeaux (F)
331	£19.80	PENFOLDS BIN 707 CABERNET SAUVIGNON 1987 S Australia (Aus)
344	£4.89	PENFOLDS BIN 2 SHIRAZ/MATARO 1989 Barossa Valley (Aus)
347	£4.99	SEAVIEW CABERNET SHIRAZ 1989 S Australia (Aus)
351	£4.99	DIEMERSDAL SHIRAZ 1986 Paarl (SA)
373	£9.95	DOMAINE DU VIEUX TELEGRAPHE, CHATEAUNEUF DU PAPE, 1987 Rhône (F)
438	£4.29	MARIUS RESERVA, BODEGAS PIQUERAS 1983 Almansa (Sp)
440	£5.55	TINTO VELHO REGUENGOS DE MONSARAZ, JOSE DE SOUSA ROSADO FERNANDES 1986 Alentejo (P)
442	£5.89	TEMPRANILLO, BODEGAS OCHOA 1987 Navarra (Sp)
446	£6.08	GRAN SANGREDETORO RESERVA, TORRES 1986 Penedés (Sp)
451	£9.85	MARQUIS DE MURRIETA RIOJA TINTO RESERVA 1985 (Sp)
480	£7.25	DOS CORTADOS, WILLIAMS AND HUMBERT, Jerez (Sp)
487	£8.45	TAYLOR'S FIRST ESTATE PORT LUGAR DAS LAGES, Douro (P)
492	£16.50	VERDELHO 10 YEAR OLD, COSSART GORDON (P)
493	£16.65	WARRE'S QUINTA DA CAVADINHA 1982 Douro (P)
494	£17.00	SANDEMAN IMPERIAL 20 YEAR OLD TAWNY PORT, Douro (P)
495	£18.95	FONSECA-GUIMARAENS 1976 Douro (P)
496	£18.40	DUO CENTENARY BUAL, COSSART GORDON (P)
500	£2.49	PETILLANT DE LISTEL, Midi (F)

PEY | Philip Eyres

Chalk Pit House, Coleshill, Amersham, Bucks HP7 0LW (0494 433823). Wholesale merchant selling by mail-order to the public. **Delivery**: free locally. **Tastings**: regular at various locations.

Or more correctly, Philip Eyres and Associates. The Associates include a former partner of solicitors Slaughter and May, the author of 'British Gastronomy' and an ex-wine buyer for Gerard Harris (qv). Eyres himself founded Henry Townsend & Co in the sixties. Following the sale of that company, he set up with his associates in Amersham.

There are regular customer offers for such things as 1989 Mosel and mixed cases of Cloudy Bay Sauvignon and Cabernet/Merlot, as well as en primeur claret. These supplement a list which is strongest on German estate wines, including Dr Loosen, Friedrich Wilhelm Gymnasium and Lingenfelder. But all areas are represented, usually by carefully chosen wines, and this is a company to watch. After all, how many other merchants have plans to offer German red wine *en primeur*?

93	£6.16	BROKENBACK VINEYARD CHARDONNAY, ROTHBURY EST. 1990 Hunter Valley (Aus)
190	£6.19	MUNSTERER PITTERSBERG RIESLING KABINETT, STAATLICHE WEINBAUDOMANEN SCHLOSS BOCKELHEIM 1988 Nahe (G)
191	£5.90	WEHLENER SONNENUHR RIESLING KABINETT, WEINGUT DR LOOSEN 1989 M-S-R (G)
308	£10.32	COLDSTREAM HILLS CABERNET SAUVIGNON 1988 Yarra Valley (Aus)
313	£10.24	CLOUDY BAY CABERNET MERLOT 1989 Marlborough (NZ)
332	£22.87	CHATEAU TALBOT, ST JULIEN 1982 Bordeaux (F)
452	£11.80	RIOJA RESERVA 904, LA RIOJA ALTA 1978 (Sp)
472	£7.11	JURANCON MOELLEUX VENDANGE TARDIVE, DOMAINE CAUHAPE 1988 SW (F)
479	£4.46	LA GITANA MANZANILLA, HIDALGO, Jerez (Sp)

FAR | Farr Vintners

Fine and Rare Merchant of the Year

19 Sussex Street, Pimlico, London, SW1V 4RR (071 828 1960). Very up-market supplier of ancient wine. **Opening Hours:** Mon-Fri 9:30-6. **Delivery:** nationally at cost. **Tastings:** tutored tastings and 'theme evenings'. **Discounts:** 5% on 10+ cases.

Last year Farr Vintners took offence at being called snooty, preferring instead to be termed 'specialists in and purveyors of en primeur and rare old wines'. Nonetheless, they do have wines from outside France, including everyday wines such as Cloudy Bay Sauvignon, Sassicaia, Grange and Dominus. But what this company is really about is the classics. Page 2 of their Summer 1991 list contains the wines of just four properties: Petrus, Lafite, Mouton and Latour. If you have a friend or relation who is keen on wine, there is a fair chance that you'll find a wine in stock from their birth year. Or if you just want to organise a vertical tasting of 22 vintages of Romanée-Conti, this is the place to call. Which is why Farr have been awarded our Fine and Rare Wine Merchant of the year prize for 1992.

| 333 | £15.37 | CHATEAU PAVIE, ST EMILION 1985 Bordeaux (F) |
| 475 | £23.70 | CHATEAU RIEUSSEC, SAUTERNES 1983 Bordeaux (F) |

AF	Alexr Findlater & Co. Ltd

Heveningham High House, Nr Halesworth, Suffolk IP19 0EA (0986 83 274) & 72 Goding Street, London SE11 5AW (071 587 0982). Australian specialist selling by the case. **Opening Hours:** Mon-Fri 9.30am-8pm; 9.30am-6pm Sat. **Delivery:** free locally. **Tastings:** regularly in-store.

Many companies have increased their stock of Australian wines in the last few years and now offer wines from various well-known Aussie wineries. Alexr Findlater has those familiar names, but he also has wines from lesser-known (and for us, more interesting) producers, which are well worth seeking out. Who else could provide a horizontal tasting of Shirazes from Evans & Tate, Mitchell, Tim Adams and Dalwhinnie?

3	£6.60	LINDAUER, MONTANA (NZ)
11	£10.40	DEUTZ MARLBOROUGH CUVEE (NZ)
31	£3.29	CORBIERES BLANC, CAVES DE MONT TAUCH, Midi (F)
38	£3.40	TOLLANA DRY WHITE 1988 S E Australia (Aus)
87	£4.79	ORLANDO RF CHARDONNAY 1989 S E Australia (Aus)
140	£4.90	COOKS HAWKES BAY SAUVIGNON BLANC 1989 Hawkes Bay (NZ)
150	£6.00	STONELEIGH SAUVIGNON BLANC 1989 Marlborough (NZ)
280	£4.66	ORLANDO RF CABERNET SAUVIGNON 1988 S Australia (Aus)
286	£6.19	SEPPELT GOLD LABEL CABERNET SAUVIGNON 1986 S E Australia (Aus)
323	£13.99	VASSE FELIX CABERNET SAUVIGNON 1988 Margaret River (Aus)
367	£7.28	TALTARNI SHIRAZ 1988 Pyrenees (Aus)
380	£4.73	GAILLAC, CEPAGE GAMAY, DOMAINES JEAN CROS 1990 S W (F)
460	£11.99	CAMPBELLS OLD RUTHERGLEN LIQUEUR MUSCAT (Aus)
465	£6.20	REDWOOD VALLEY ESTATE LATE HARVEST RIESLING 1989 Nelson (NZ)
479	£5.00	LA GITANA MANZANILLA, HIDALGO, Jerez (Sp)
483	£16.00	APOSTOLES, GONZALEZ BYASS, Jerez (Sp)

FDL	Findlater Mackie Todd & Co

Deer Park Road, Merton Abbey, London SW19 3TU (081 543 0956). Well-established, Royal warrant-holding mail order specialist. **Opening Hours:** Mon-Fri 9am-6pm. **Delivery:** free on UK mainland. **Tastings:** regularly in-store. **Discounts:** £3 per case for collection.

Now exclusively mail-order, following the closure of their Covent Garden shop, this is a traditional merchant whose selection offers plenty of good, ready-to-drink wines, if not at the keenest prices. The Dry Fly sherry and Duc house Champagne which featured on the 1948 Findlater Mackie Todd list are still part of their range. However there are concessions to modernity, with fair Italian and Spanish ranges, and a large proportion of their Australian selection coming from their namesake listed above. The Californian wines seems to be chosen in a more haphazard fashion, with Paul Masson rubbing shoulders with Ridge Zinfandel.

349	£5.41	RASTEAU COTES DU RHONE VILLAGES, VIGNERONS DE RASTEAU 1989 (F)
479	£5.95	LA GITANA MANZANILLA, HIDALGO, Jerez (Sp)

LEF	Le Fleming Wines

9 Longcroft Avenue, Harpenden, Herts AL5 2RB (0582 760125). Wholesale and mail-order one-woman wine merchant. **Opening Hours:** 24-hour answering service, deliveries by arrangement. **Delivery:** free locally. **Tastings:** on request.

'My forté is organising', says Cherry Jenkins. All those who worked with her at the 1991 International Wine Challenge will know this to be true (although she managed to leave her kettle behind). Most of the wines on her list have been chosen because of their taste, rather than prestige, although we're not sure how the name Gallo crept in. Each is described with great enthusiasm. So we have two Georges Duboeuf wines: the 87 Julienas is 'A feminine wine ... with a lovely fresh end', while the 88 Morgon is 'more masculine, with a good meaty middle and a robust end'. Discuss.

83	£4.83	CALITERRA CHARDONNAY 1990 Maipo Valley (Ch)
87	£4.92	ORLANDO RF CHARDONNAY 1989 S E Australia (Aus)
95	£6.03	SCHINUS MOLLE CHARDONNAY 1990 Mornington Peninsula (Aus)
230	£4.70	MAS DE GOURGONNIER TRADITION, COTEAUX D'AIX EN PROVENCE LES BAUX 1989 Midi (F)
288	£6.67	CHATEAU MUSAR 1982 Bekaa Valley (Leb)
356	£4.50	DAVID WYNN SHIRAZ 1990 High Eden Ridge (Aus)

JFR   John Frazier

252 Longmore Road, Shirley, Solihull, West Midlands B90 3ER (021 711 2710). Also branches at 169 Albert Road, Stechford; 4 Trinity Court, Stoke Road, Aston Fields, Bromsgrove; and New Inn Stores, Stratford Road, Wootton Wawen, Solihull. **Opening Hours:** 10am-10pm Mon-Sat, 12-2pm and 7pm-9pm Sun. **Delivery:** free locally. **Tastings:** wines regularly opened for sampling.

Here is a family-owned chain of four shops in the West Midlands of which we had heard next to nothing until we began to write this *Guide*. They have an exemplary list which, apart from the wines listed below, includes a range of Germans from Deinhard, Cornas from de Barjac and the Western Australian wines of Moss Wood. If there are any more good merchants hiding in Solihull, could someone please tell us about them?

3	£5.49	LINDAUER, MONTANA (NZ)
22	£22.70	VEUVE CLICQUOT DEMI-SEC CHAMPAGNE (F)
23	£22.25	HEIDSIECK DRY MONOPOLE ROSE CHAMPAGNE 1985 (F)
79	£3.19	COTES DE ST MONT, PLAIMONT 1990 S W (F)
84	£5.95	OXFORD LANDING CHARDONNAY, YALUMBA 1990 S Australia (Aus)
90	£5.49	LINDEMANS BIN 65 CHARDONNAY 1989 S E Australia (Aus)
92	£6.25	MACON CHARDONNAY, J TALMARD 1988 Burgundy (F)
93	£6.49	BROKENBACK VINEYARD CHARDONNAY, ROTHBURY EST 1990 Hunter Valley (Aus)
103	£9.35	KING VALLEY CHARDONNAY FAMILY RESERVE, BROWN BROS 1987 N E Victoria (Aus)
117	£12.99	ELSTON CHARDONNAY, TE MATA 1989 (NZ)
140	£5.69	COOKS HAWKES BAY SAUVIGNON BLANC 1989 Hawkes Bay (NZ)
180	£4.89	HILL SMITH OLD TRIANGLE RIESLING 1990 Barossa Valley (Aus)
185	£5.75	MAGDALEN RIVANER, PULHAM VINEYARDS 1990 East Anglia (UK)
223	£3.69	DOMAINE ST EULALIE, MINERVOIS 1988 Midi (F)
281	£5.49	MONTANA CABERNET SAUVIGNON 1988 Marlborough (NZ)
284	£6.25	SIRIUS ROUGE, PETER SICHEL 1988 Bordeaux (F)
311	£10.09	SIMI CABERNET SAUVIGNON 1984 Sonoma (Cal)
312	£10.75	LES FIEFS DE LAGRANGE, ST JULIEN, CHATEAU LAGRANGE 1988 Bordeaux (F)
313	£12.95	CLOUDY BAY CABERNET MERLOT 1989 Marlborough (NZ)
332	£25.65	CHATEAU TALBOT, ST JULIEN 1982 Bordeaux (F)
380	£4.99	GAILLAC, CEPAGE GAMAY, DOMAINES JEAN CROS 1990 S W (F)
483	£16.75	APOSTOLES, GONZALEZ BYASS, Jerez (Sp)
487	£8.65	TAYLOR'S FIRST ESTATE PORT LUGAR DAS LAGES, Douro (P)

FWC   Fulham Rd Wine Centre

899-901 Fulham Rd, London SW6 5HU (071 736 7009). Confident (and deservedly so) young merchant. **Opening Hours:** 10am-8pm Mon-Sat; 12-3pm Sun. **Delivery:** nationally at cost. **Tastings:** regularly in-store plus some of the best tutored events. **Discounts:** 5% off 12+ bottles.

Among the awards made in 1991 by the Wine Guild of the United Kingdom (one of which, we have immodestly to say, went to the editor of this Guide) was a highly deserved prize for the wine courses organised by James Rogers at the Fulham Road Wine Centre. The courses, which are based on tasting wine rather than revering it, provide an ideal introduction to the shop's extremely eclectic, well-chosen range. If you want keen, enthusiastic and knowledgeable staff to sell you inexpensive fizz, Argentinian Cabernet or 1967 Russian red (as well as a good selection of the classics), this is the place to come.

3	£7.45	LINDAUER, MONTANA (NZ)
9	£9.99	BRUT SAUVAGE CUVEE JACQUES ROUSSELL, P-B TERRIER-RABIDE, Coteaux de St Bernard (Sw)
11	£11.95	DEUTZ MARLBOROUGH CUVEE (NZ)
54	£5.45	ALSACE TOKAY PINOT GRIS, CAVE VINICOLE DE TURCKHEIM 1990 (F)
72	£9.95	MACON AZE, DOMAINE D'AZENAY 1989 Burgundy (F)
79	£4.45	COTES DE ST MONT, PLAIMONT 1990 S W (F)
84	£5.45	OXFORD LANDING CHARDONNAY, YALUMBA 1990 S Australia (Aus)
102	£9.25	MARQUES DE MURRIETA RIOJA BLANCO RESERVA 1985 Rioja (Sp)
106	£10.95	WYNNS COONAWARRA ESTATE CHARDONNAY 1989 (Aus)
107	£10.95	KRONDORF SHOW RESERVE CHARDONNAY 1989 Barossa Valley (Aus)
111	£13.95	EDNA VALLEY CHARDONNAY 1989 San Luis Obispo (Cal)
114	£9.95	DOMAINE CAUHAPE, JURANCON SEC (OAKED) 1988 S W (F)
147	£6.95	KLEIN COSTANTIA SAUVIGNON BLANC 1988 (SA)
154	£7.95	SHAW AND SMITH SAUVIGNON BLANC 1990 S Australia (Aus)
174	£4.95	CAFAYATE TORRONTES, ETCHART 1990 Mendoza (Arg)
175	£6.25	MOSCATO D'ASTI, MICHELE CHIARLO 1990 Piedmont (It)
196	£4.95	THREE CHOIRS MEDIUM DRY ENGLISH TABLE WINE 1989 Gloucs (UK)
227	£4.95	CUVEE DE L'ARJOLLE ROUGE, VIN DE PAYS DES COTES DE THONGUE, TEISSERENC 1989 Midi (F)
287	£7.95	RAIMAT CABERNET SAUVIGNON 1985 Lérida (Sp)
313	£10.95	CLOUDY BAY CABERNET MERLOT 1989 Marlborough (NZ)
325	£18.95	CARMENET CABERNET SAUVIGNON 1986 Sonoma (Cal)
451	£9.95	MARQUIS DE MURRIETA RIOJA TINTO RESERVA 1985 (Sp)
452	£14.95	RIOJA RESERVA 904, LA RIOJA ALTA 1978 (Sp)
459	£10.95	DOMAINE CAZES RIVESALTES VIEUX 1978 Midi (F)
472	£14.95	JURANCON MOELLEUX VENDANGE TARDIVE, DOMAINE CAUHAPE 1988 S W (F)
475	£27.50	CHATEAU RIEUSSEC, SAUTERNES 1983 Bordeaux (F)

FUL   Fuller's

Head Office: Griffin Brewery, Chiswick Lane South, Chiswick, London W4 2QB (081 994 3691). Regional High Street chain with 59 shops, mainly in the Thames Valley. **Opening Hours:** Mon-Sat 9am-9pm;12-2pm & 7pm-9pm Sun. **Delivery:** free locally; nationally, £3.00 case. **Tastings:** regularly in-store plus tutored events. **Discounts:** free bottle with every unmixed case. Other discounts negotiable.

Following its worthy Award as last year's Southern Wine Merchant of the Year, Fullers has worked hard to maintain the momentum established by Mark Dally in his desire for the shops to be taken seriously. Good new wines are being added to the range regularly and a (welcome) overhaul of the beer-'n-faggy looking shops is planned for 1992. Perhaps being a brewery-owned wine merchant isn't such a bad idea after all.

79	£3.65	COTES DE ST MONT, PLAIMONT 1990 S W (F)
86	£5.15	CHARDONNAY, VIN DE PAYS D'OC, HUGH RYMAN 1990 Midi (F)
142	£5.19	MOULIN DE LA GRAVELLE, MUSCADET, CHEREAU-CARRE 1988 Loire (F)
143	£4.99	DOMAINE DU RELAIS DE POSTE, SAUVIGNON DE ST BRIS, LUC SORIN 1989 Burgundy (F)
216	£3.39	FAUGERES DOMAINE DU COUDOGNO, TERROIRS D'OCCITANIE 1989 Midi (F)
264	£5.05	BERRI ESTATES AUSTRALIAN CABERNET SHIRAZ 1987 (Aus)
279	£5.19	GLEN ELLEN MERLOT 1987 Sonoma (Cal)
288	£6.69	CHATEAU MUSAR 1982 Bekaa Valley (Leb)
313	£10.49	CLOUDY BAY CABERNET MERLOT 1989 Marlborough (NZ)
344	£3.99	PENFOLDS BIN 2 SHIRAZ/MATARO 1989 Barossa Valley (Aus)
350	£4.19	CHATEAU DU GRAND MOULAS, COTES DU RHONE 1989 (F)
358	£5.19	DOMAINE LA SOUMADE RASTEAU, COTES DU RHONE VILLAGES, ROMERO ANDRE 1988 (F)
455	£3.15	CASTILLO DE LIRIA MOSCATEL, VICENTE GANDIA, Valencia (Sp)
500	£2.05	PETILLANT DE LISTEL, Midi (F)

G	Gateway

Head Office: Gateway House, Hawkfield Business Park, Whitchurch Lane, Bristol, Avon BS14 0TJ (0272 359359). National supermarket chain with over 700 stores. **Opening Hours:** vary. **Tastings:** occasionally in-store.

In the past few years, Gateway has done little to live up to its previous reputation as a supermarket where tinned beans and limp carrots vie for the attention of curler-festooned housewives amid a sea of cabbages, crisps, and convenience foods. Indeed, their image has improved vastly since the take-over by Isosceles almost two years ago, and as we've learned from their performance in the International Wine Challenge over the last two years, they know their business when it comes to wine. Wine buyer Angela Mount has proved to be quite canny in offering Gateway customers good value wines that are somewhat off the beaten track. And with the forthcoming conversion of some Gateway stores to the new, up-market Somerfield stores, there will be more scope for innovation in an expanded and more adventurous wine department. Worth steering a trolley towards.

24	£21.69	LANSON VINTAGE CHAMPAGNE 1979 (F)
50	£4.44	TESCO MACON VILLAGES, CAVE DE VIRE 1990 Burgundy (F)
140	£4.95	COOKS HAWKES BAY SAUVIGNON BLANC 1989 Hawkes Bay (NZ)
155	£2.89	GATEWAY ANJOU BLANC, REMY PANNIER, Loire (F)
156	£3.75	GATEWAY VOUVRAY, GUSTAVE RABIER, Loire (F)
177	£3.15	NIERSTEINER SPIEGELBERG KABINETT, P J STEFFENS 1989 Rheinhessen (G)
240	£2.85	COOP CLARET, ESCHENAUER, Bordeaux (F)
253	£3.95	GATEWAY MEDOC, CHAIS BEAUCAIROIS, Bordeaux (F)
264	£3.95	BERRI ESTATES AUSTRALIAN CABERNET SHIRAZ 1987 (Aus)
288	£6.25	CHATEAU MUSAR 1982 Bekaa Valley (Leb)
365	£6.25	CHATEAU TAHBILK SHIRAZ 1987 Goulburn Valley (Aus)
449	£7.55	CAMPO VIEJO RIOJA GRAN RESERVA 1980 (Sp)
455	£2.95	CASTILLO DE LIRIA MOSCATEL, VICENTE GANDIA, Valencia (Sp)
467	£6.45	LEIWENER LAURENTISLAY RIESLING AUSLESE, MARIENHOF 1983 M-S-R (G)

GON | Gauntleys of Nottingham

4 High St, Exchange Arcade, Nottingham NG1 2ET (0602 417973). Independent family merchant. **Opening Hours:** Mon-Sat 7.30am-5.30pm. **Delivery:** free locally, nationally at cost. **Tastings:** regularly in-store plus tutored events. **Discounts:** variable on case purchases.

Just three years after expanding the scope of the family-owned tobacco shop to include wine, John Gauntley has managed to earned a reputation as a reliable - and enthusiastic - merchant. At present, Gauntley's concentrate on the Rhône, the Loire Valley, Italy, and South Africa. But, as Mr Gauntley and a tasting associate have recently been in Burgundy and Alsace, we can no doubt look forward to having a few new stars from these areas on next year's list.

69	£6.05	SOAVE CLASSICO VIGNETO CALVARINO, PIEROPAN 1989 Veneto (It)
115	£10.10	VITA NOVA CHARDONNAY 1989 Santa Barbara (Cal)
119	£11.30	LES PIERRES CHARDONNAY, SONOMA CUTRER 1989 Sonoma (Cal)
144	£4.99	DOMAINE DES AUBULSIERES, VOUVRAY SEC 1990 Loire (F)
320	£12.90	CHATEAU LEOVILLE BARTON, ST JULIEN 1987 Bordeaux (F)
321	£11.90	RENAISSANCE CABERNET SAUVIGNON 1984 North Yuba (Cal)
328	£13.70	BERINGER PRIVATE RESERVE CABERNET SAUVIGNON 1986 Napa Valley (Cal)
331	£19.39	PENFOLDS BIN 707 CABERNET SAUVIGNON 1987 S Australia (Aus)
334	£22.00	ROBERT MONDAVI CABERNET SAUVIGNON RESERVE 1977 Napa Valley (Cal)
352	£4.67	COTES DU RHONE, GUIGAL 1988 (F)
374	£9.34	RIDGE GEYERSVILLE ZINFANDEL 1988 Santa Clara (Cal)
399	£38.60	LE CHAMBERTIN, ARMAND ROUSSEAU 1987 Burgundy (F)
416	£6.20	CHIANTI CLASSICO, ISOLE E OLENO 1988 Tuscany (It)
426	£10.88	CEPPARELLO, ISOLE E OLENA 1988 Tuscany (It)
446	£4.20	GRAN SANGREDETORO RESERVA, Torres 1986 Penedes (Sp)
449	£8.90	CAMPO VIEJO RIOJA GRAN RESERVA 1980 (Sp)
452	£11.00	RIOJA RESERVA 904, LA RIOJA RITA 1978 (Sp)
460	£12.80	CAMPBELLS OLD RUTHERGLEN LIQUEUR MUSCAT, (Aus)
471	£9.03	VOUVRAY MOELLEUX LE MARIGNY, DOMAINE DES AUBUISIERES 1990 Loire (F)
483	£13.65	APOSTOLES, GONZALES BYASS, Jerez (Sp)
493	£17.50	WARRE'S QUINTA DA CAVADINHA 1982 Douro (P)

GEL | Gelston Castle

Castle Douglas, Scotland DG7 1QE (0556 3012). Traditional mail-order merchant who sums up books such as this as 'only for the paid-up member of the Ruling Consumer Class who just wants to be told where to go and what to buy, full stop.' **Delivery:** free nationally, £2 per case collection discount. **Tastings:** regular tutored events.

The Gelston list is packed with vintage information, quotes from people ranging from Kermit Lynch to Brillat Savarin and plenty of Mr Scott's vino-philosophical opinions. 'Sauternes without botrytis is the body without the soul'. We couldn't agree more, but we're not sure which of the three vintages of Lamothe Guignard (89, 88 or 83) to take a punt on. The range of German wines range is broad and described with a love which can only convert people to the sadly neglected top wines of that country. And when you've finished with the 140 page list, there's 'Savoir-Boire', a handbook on how to get the best out of whatever you drink.

MG | Matthew Gloag Ltd

Bordeaux House, 33 Kinnoull Street, Perth PH1 5EU (0738 21101). Independent merchant since 1800. **Opening Hours:** Mon-Fri 9am-5pm. **Delivery:** free within Scotland, nationally at cost. **Tastings:** tutored events for customers club. **Discounts:** 5% discount for club members.

Two Scottish merchants in a row who don't come from Edinburgh? Shome mishtake shurely. Gloag's elegant, pocket sized list (like all decent pocket tomes, full of good sense and difficult to focus on) doesn't contain as large a range as other companies', but every page contains delicious wines. Our selection from pages 26 and 27 would include '75 Giscours,'70 Gruaud Larose and Albert Pic's '88 Chablis Montée de Tonnerre .

84	£4.95	OXFORD LANDING CHARDONNAY, YALUMBA 1990 S Australia (Aus)
150	£6.95	STONELEIGH SAUVIGNON BLANC 1989 Marlborough (NZ)
303	£9.45	ROSEMOUNT SHOW RESERVE CABERNET SAUVIGNON 1987 Coonawarra (Aus)
352	£5.65	COTES DU RHONE, GUIGAL 1988 (F)
465	£7.55	REDWOOD VALLEY ESTATE LATE HARVEST RIESLING 1989 Nelson (NZ)

G&G | Godwin & Godwin See Bottles of Brock Street

G&M | Gordon & MacPhail

58/60 South Street, Elgin, Moray IV30 1JY (0343 545111). Whisky distillers and bottlers *par excellence*. **Opening Hours:** Mon-Fri 9am-5.15pm, 9am-5pm Sat. **Delivery:** free locally.

We suppose you could go to Gordon & MacPhail for 1943 Lafaurie-Peyraguey or 1948 Fonseca. But if you're looking for something a little older, you'll have to resort to the whisky selection which offers their own distillations from as far back as 1937. Every whisky you could never pronounce is here, and we'd partlcarly like to recommend the Campbeltown malts from the Longrow and Springbank distilleries.

GI | Grape Ideas

3/5 Hythe Bridge St, Oxford, Oxon OX1 2EW (0865 791313) & Grape Ideas Fine Vintage Wine Warehouse, 2a Canfield Gardens, London NW1. Retail arm of wholesale operation. **Opening Hours:** Oxford 10am-7pm Mon-Sat; 11am-2pm Sun; London 10am-9pm Mon-Sat; 12-2pm Sun. **Delivery:** free locally, nationally at cost. **Tastings:** regularly in-store plus tutored events. **Discounts:** 5% off full unmixed cases, 2.5% off mixed cases.

Despite trying to drop its 'wine warehouse' image and be thought of as 'traditional wine merchants', Grape Ideas remains a place to buy good wines at a price at which buying a case is not a huge investment. It would be easy to make up a case of extremely good wine for around £60 but it is possible to leave with just one bottle of 82 Krug (for around the same price).

79	£3.15	COTES DE ST MONT, PLAIMONT 1990 S W (F)
226	£3.99	DOMAINE DU BOSQUET CANET, LISTEL 1987 Midi (F)
263	£4.25	TRAPICHE CABERNET SAUVIGNON RESERVE OAK CASK 1986 (Arg)
308	£8.99	COLDSTREAM HILLS CABERNET SAUVIGNON 1988 Yarra Valley (Aus)
310	£9.99	BARON VILLENEUVE DE CANTERMERLE, HAUT-MEDOC, CHATEAU CANTEMERLE 1986 Bordeaux (F)

416	£6.75	CHIANTI CLASSICO, ISOLE E OLENA 1988 Tuscany (It)
446	£5.45	GRAN SANGREDETORO RESERVA, TORRES 1986 Penedés (Sp)
449	£8.50	CAMPO VIEJO RIOJA GRAN RESERVA 1980 (Sp)
465	£5.99	REDWOOD VALLEY ESTATE LATE HARVEST RIESLING 1989 Nelson (NZ)
475	£29.90	CHATEAU RIEUSSEC, SAUTERNES 1983 Bordeaux (F)
500	£2.39	PETILLANT DE LISTEL, Midi (F)

GEW | Great English Wines

254 Kentwood Hill, Tilehurst, Reading RG3 6DP (0734 451958). English specialist. **Opening Hours:** Ring first to check: 24 hour answerphone. **Delivery:** free locally, nationally at cost. **Tastings:** regularly in-store plus tutored events. **Discounts:** 5-10% for case sales.

The former Great Western Wine now has a more befitting name. If you haven't tried English or Welsh wine before, this is the place for you. As well as the more familiar English names (and less familiar grape varieties), you can now buy Beenleigh Manor red, England's first commercial Cabernet-Merlot, Kingsley Pinot Noir and several *méthode champenoise* sparklers made from Chardonnay and the two Pinots. If you need further reasons for visiting the shop, they also stock Rock's Country Wines and Old Percy's Berkshire Cider.

15	£14.50	CARR TAYLOR VINTAGE BRUT 1985 East Sussex (UK)
64	£5.99	WOOTTON SCHONBURGER 1990 (UK)
137	£4.85	BOZE DOWN DRY 1989 Oxfordshire (UK)
149	£5.99	BARKHAM MANOR 1988 East Sussex (UK)
161	£4.99	VINTAGE SELECTION MEDIUM DRY, WICKHAM VINEYARDS 1990 Hants (UK)
162	£4.99	SWEET LEE, THAMES VALLEY VINEYARD 1989 Berkshire (UK)
181	£4.99	LAMBERHURST SEYVAL BLANC 1988 Kent (UK)
182	£4.99	CODDINGTON BACCHUS 1989 Gloucs (UK)
188	£5.50	STAPLE ST JAMES MULLER THURGAU 1989 Kent (UK)
189	£5.80	GLYNDWR WHITE TABLE WINE 1989 Cowbridge (UK)
196	£4.99	THREE CHOIRS MEDIUM DRY ENGLISH TABLE WINE 1989 Gloucs (UK)
197	£4.99	ASTLEY SEVERN VALE 1989 Worcestershire (UK)

GNW | Great Northern Wine Co

The Dark Arches, Leeds Canal Basin, Leeds, W Yorks LS1 4BR (0532 461200). Independent merchant. **Opening Hours:** 9am-6.30pm Mon-Fri; 9am-5.30pm Sun. **Delivery:** free locally, nationally at cost. **Tastings:** regularly in-store plus tutored events. **Discounts:** wholesale price for 12 bottles.

A list oozing confidence, packed with stylish wines from producers such as Jermann, Cune and Drouhin. Gavin Barlow has been busy cooking up many plans under those Dark Arches. September sees the start of their wine appreciation classes and a 'monthlywine plan' has been launched which offers customers a specially selected case of wine at a favourable price. If that were not enough, the editor of the Guide will be appearing Underneath the Arches as guest speaker at their Annual Wine Fair. On second thoughts...

29	£2.85	CUVEE JEAN-PAUL BLANC SEC VIN DE TABLE, PAUL BOUTINOT (F)
31	£3.49	CORBIERES BLANC, CAVES DE MONT TAUCH, Midi (F)
38	£3.35	TOLLANA DRY WHITE 1988 S E Australia (Aus)

54	£5.19	ALSACE TOKAY PINOT GRIS, CAVE VINICOLE DE TURCKHEIM 1990 (F)
59	£4.99	HOUGHTON SUPREME WHITE 1990 Swan Valley (Aus)
84	£4.65	OXFORD LANDING CHARDONNAY, YALUMBA 1990 S Australia (Aus)
90	£5.19	LINDEMANS BIN 65 CHARDONNAY 1989 S E Australia (Aus)
102	£8.59	MARQUES DE MURRIETA RIOJA BLANCO RESERVA 1985 Rioja (Sp)
103	£7.79	KING VALLEY CHARDONNAY FAMILY RESERVE, BROWN BROS 1987 N E Victoria (Aus)
117	£12.65	ELSTON CHARDONNAY, TE MATA 1989 (NZ)
119	£11.24	LES PIERRES CHARDONNAY, SONOMA CUTRER 1987 Sonoma (Cal)
145	£6.09	SAUVIGNON DE ST BRIS, DOMAINE FELIX 1990 Burgundy (F)
204	£4.35	CHATEAU LE RAZ, BERGERAC ROSE 1990 S W (F)
231	£4.99	CHATEAU DE LASTOURS CUVEE SIMONE DESCAMPS, CORBIERES 1989 Midi (F)
267	£4.35	CHATEAU LE RAZ, BERGERAC ROUGE 1989 S W (F)
281	£5.19	MONTANA CABERNET SAUVIGNON 1988 Marlborough (NZ)
282	£5.95	CHATEAU COUCHEROY BORDEAUX ROUGE 1988 (F)
302	£9.15	CHATEAU RAMAGE LA BATISSE, HAUT MEDOC 1988 Bordeaux (F)
327	£15.65	YARRA YERING CABERNET SAUVIGNON 1987 Yarra Valley (Aus)
329	£9.89	WOLF BLASS BLACK LABEL CABERNET SAUVIGNON 1986 S Australia (Aus)
331	£19.65	PENFOLDS BIN 707 CABERNET SAUVIGNON 1987 S Australia (Aus)
349	£4.78	RASTEAU COTES DU RHONE VILLAGES, VIGNERONS DE RASTEAU 1989 (F)
353	£5.45	PENFOLDS BIN 28 KALIMNA SHIRAZ 1988 S Australia (Aus)
380	£4.15	GAILLAC, CEPAGE GAMAY, DOMAINES JEAN CROS 1990 S W (F)
392	£11.20	SANFORD PINOT NOIR 1986 Santa Barbara (Cal)
430	£18.15	BRUNELLO DEL MONTALCINO, POGGIO ANTICO 1985 Piedmont (It)
442	£5.29	TEMPRANILLO, BODEGAS OCHOA 1987 Navarra (Sp)
449	£8.99	CAMPO VIEJO RIOJA GRAN RESERVA 1980 (Sp)
472	£7.35	JURANCON MOELLEUX VENDANGE TARDIVE, DOMAINE CAUHAPE 1988 S W(F)
480	£9.95	DOS CORTADOS, WILLIAMS AND HUMBERT, Jerez (Sp)
493	£17.98	WARRE'S QUINTA DA CAVADINHA 1982 Douro (P)

GRT | Great Western Wine Co

2-3 Mile End, London Rd, Bath BA1 6PT (0225 446009). Independent merchant selling by the case.
Opening Hours: 10am-7pm Mon-Sat. **Delivery:** locally, nationally at cost. **Tastings:** regularly in-store plus tutored events.

Although Philip Addis does deal with companies throughout the UK, the bulk of his custom consists of restaurants, hotels and private clients within a few miles of the spa. His range contains much to keep them singing in the bath, including Rhônes from Delas, Burgundies from Jaffelin and the delicious Pomerol from Clos du Clocher. But what happened to the names of those German producers?

93	£6.65	BROKENBACK VINEYARD CHARDONNAY, ROTHBURY EST. 1990 Hunter Val. (Aus)
107	£7.29	KRONDORF SHOW RESERVE CHARDONNAY 1989 Barossa Valley (Aus)
140	£5.59	COOKS HAWKES BAY SAUVIGNON BLANC 1989 Hawkes Bay (NZ)
145	£5.93	SAUVIGNON DE ST BRIS, DOMAINE FELIX 1990 Burgundy (F)
226	£4.25	DOMAINE DU BOSQUET CANET, LISTEL 1987 Midi (F)
231	£5.45	CHATEAU DE LASTOURS CUVEE SIMONE DESCAMPS, CORBIERES 1989 Midi (F)
267	£4.40	CHATEAU LE RAZ, BERGERAC ROUGE 1989 S W (F)
293	£6.99	JAMIESONS RUN RED, MILDARA 1987 Coonawarra (Aus)
359	£5.29	CROZES HERMITAGE, DELAS FRERES 1989 Rhône (F)
375	£13.35	COTE ROTIE SEIGNEUR DE MOUGIRON, DELAS FRERES 1988 Rhône (F)
442	£5.70	TEMPRANILLO, BODEGAS OCHOA 1987 Navarra (Sp)
449	£8.17	CAMPO VIEJO RIOJA GRAN RESERVA 1980 (Sp)
500	£2.41	PETILLANT DE LISTEL, Midi (F)

37a/b Warrender Park Rd, Edinburgh EH9 1HJ (031 229 5925). Independent merchant who seems to get almost everything right. **Opening Hours:** 9.30am-6.30pm Mon-Fri; 9.30am-6.30pm Sat. **Tastings:** large annual tasting. **Discounts:** 5% on unbroken cases.

Joint winners of the Scottish Merchant of the Year award for 1991 and again short-listed for this year's prize, the fact that a company like this does not automatically win a prize shows the quality of merchants north of the Border. There is a long list of Germans from which it would be easy to concoct a tasting of wines with silly names (Escherndorfer Lump Riesling Kabinett), plus five vintages of Château Musar (and the rare white). An interesting Californian Cabernet Sauvignon tasting could be arranged from the trio of Mondavi Reserve 1980, Ridge York Creek 1985 and Heitz Martha's Vineyard 1982. And more fun could be derived from nine different New Zealand Sauvignon Blancs. So hard luck, Michael Romer, if you move your shop to a different part of Britain, you'll probably receive an award next year.

3	£6.75	**LINDAUER, MONTANA** (NZ)
84	£4.59	**OXFORD LANDING CHARDONNAY, YALUMBA** 1990 S Australia (Aus)
87	£4.89	**ORLANDO RF CHARDONNAY** 1989 S E Australia (Aus)
102	£7.85	**MARQUES DE MURRIETA RIOJA BLANCO RESERVA** 1985 Rioja (Sp)
111	£11.50	**EDNA VALLEY CHARDONNAY** 1989 San Luis Obispo (Cal)
150	£5.99	**STONELEIGH SAUVIGNON BLANC** 1989 Marlborough (NZ)
184	£9.85	**ALSACE RIESLING RESERVE PARTICULIERE, SELTZ** 1988 (F)
258	£3.99	**SVISCHTOV CABERNET SAUVIGNON CONTROLIRAN,** 1985 Svischtov (Bul)
263	£4.99	**TRAPICHE CABERNET SAUVIGNON RESERVE OAK CASK** 1986 (Arg)
280	£4.89	**ORLANDO RF CABERNET SAUVIGNON** 1988 S Australia (Aus)
287	£6.25	**RAIMAT CABERNET SAUVIGNON** 1985 Lerida (Sp)
288	£6.65	**CHATEAU MUSAR** 1982 Bekaa Valley (Leb)
303	£7.75	**ROSEMOUNT SHOW RESERVE CABERNET SAUVIGNON** 1987 Coonawarra (Aus)
306	£8.99	**DOMAINE RICHEAUME CABERNET SAUVIGNON, HENNING HOESCH** 1988 Midi (F)
323	£13.75	**VASSE FELIX CABERNET SAUVIGNON** 1988 Margaret River (Aus)
336	£38.50	**OPUS ONE, ROBERT MONDAVI** 1987 Napa Valley (Cal)
374	£9.95	**RIDGE GEYSERVILLE ZINFANDEL** 1988 Santa Clara (Cal)
440	£5.45	**TINTO VELHO REGUENGOS DE MONSARAZ, JOSE DE SOUSA ROSADO FERNANDES** 1986 Alentejo (P)
446	£5.40	**GRAN SANGREDETORO RESERVA, TORRES** 1986 Penedes (Sp)
451	£8.70	**MARQUIS DE MURRIETA RIOJA TINTO RESERVA** 1985 (Sp)
452	£13.30	**RIOJA RESERVA 904, LA RIOJA ALTA** 1978 (Sp)
483	£14.99	**APOSTOLES, GONZALEZ BYASS,** Jerez (Sp)
496	£7.80	**DUO CENTENARY BUAL, COSSART GORDON** (P)

---

66 Notting Hill Gate, London W11 3HT (071 792 3834); 253 West End Lane, West Hampstead, London NW6 1XN (071 794 7808); 160 High Road, London N2 9AS (081 883 3588). Small independent chain. **Delivery:** free within 2 miles. **Tastings:** regularly in-store. **Discounts:** 5% on case sales.

The three shops in this mini-chain are still going strong. Apart from the usual wines that such shops stock, like 63 Fonseca, 83 Grange and 83 Hermitage La Chapelle, they have a range of nine rosés which they do not confine to a corner of their broadsheet list. Oh, and they've acquired 50 more beers in the last year, taking their total now to over 250. Stocks of individual wines are too limited for us to be able to include recommendations here.

PGR | Patrick Grubb Selections

Orchard Lea House, Steeple Aston, Oxford OX5 3RT. (0869 40229). Small-scale mail order specialist with penchant for Madeira. **Delivery:** free for orders of over £200; otherwise £8.

Patrick Grubb is about to celebrate his 40th year in the wine business, as a merchant and as an auctioneer for Sotheby's .

His own company has been going for three years now and has already built up a loyal following for a good range of Burgundies, some fairly prices Clarets and a set of mouth-watering Madeiras dating back to 1875 at a mere £1048.00 per case.

HLV | Halves

Brookside Cottage, Wyson Lane, Brimfield, Nr.Ludlow, Shropshire SY8 4NQ (058472 656). Less than pint-sized mail order specialist. **Delivery:** free nationally. **Discounts:** 4% on unbroken cases.

Tim Jackson's decision to launch a wine company selling exclusively by the half bottle was perfectly timed to coincide with a move towards cutting consumption and spending. His only difficulty lies in persuading a sufficient number of the right producers to package their wines in anything other than full-sized bottles. So far he has done very well with Alsace from Zind Humbrecht, Burgundy from Domaines Leflaive and Bordeaux from Lynch Bages and Potensac. But beware - half bottles don't come at half price - far from it in the case of the Leflaives. Of the Halves list, the wines we would most immediately go for would be the sherries from Hidalgo, one of the few producers who believe that the British should be allowed to drink their sherry from the same size bottles as the Jerezanos. A company which doesn't do things by magnums...

HAM | The Hampden Wine Co

The Hampden Wine Company, 8 Upper High Street, Thames, Oxon OX9 3ER (0844 213251) 9.30 am - 5.30 pm Monday - Friday. Wednesday 9.30 am - 1.00 pm. Saturday 9.00 am - 5.00 pm. Delivery free locally, nationally at cost. Tastings: Bottles for sampling on Saturdays, tutored tastings, theme dinners.

'It's very easy to exaggerate the public's interest in wine. One has to tread carefully between enthusing and creating interest and not being too off-puttingly serious'. Lance Foyster and Ian Hope-Morley run their business from a shop they share with Jordans Delicatessen - which explains why their food and wine hampers are some of the best in the country. We'd put one right at the top of our Christmas present list - particularly if you could persuade them to include a bottle of Sonoma Cutrer Les Pierres, Moss Wood Semillion, Dr Loosen Reisling or Chateau Fuissé. Throughout the list, wines of this quality abound, along with often highly evocative notes.

HFV | Harcourt Fine Wines

3 Harcourt Street, London W1LI 1DS (071 723 7202). English specialist merchant. **Opening Hours:** 11.30am-6.30pm Tues-Fri; 10am-3pm Sat. **Delivery:** free locally, nationally at cost. **Tastings:** regularly in-store plus organised events. **Discounts:** 5% on1-2 cases, up to 12% depending on quantity.

As we have said before in the Guide, English wine - even the finest English wine - is probably more difficult to sell in London than it might be in Paris, Rome or Berlin, which helps to explain why the English Wine Shop is now known as Harcourt Fine Wines, and why, from an exclusively home-produced set of wines, the emphasis has shifted to its present proportions of 67 Germans to 63 English (including no less than 8 reds!) Even so, Harcourt remain one of the few places where English men and women can obtain such first class English wines as Nutbourne Manor, Thames Valley Vineyard, Wootton and the wonderfully named Breaky Bottom.

HPD | Harpenden Wines

68 High St, Harpenden, Herts AL5 2SP (0582 765605) & The Watford Wine Co, 185 The Parade, Watford, Herts WD1 1NJ (0923 211254). Expanding independent merchant. **Opening Hours:** 10am -10pm Mon-Fri; 9am-10pm Sat; 12-3pm & 7pm-9pm Sun. **Delivery:** free locally, nationally at cost. **Tastings:** regularly in-store. **Discounts:** 5% mixed case, 7.5% unbroken case (not credit cards).

Now firmly established at the helm of two Hertfordshire merchants - Harpenden and the newer Watford Wine Company - Paul Beaton is eager to prove that there is more to this part of England than the frontier between North and South. The hand-written price list, which serves both companies, reveals some adventurous buying. Alongside the expected Brown Bros, Montana and Christian Brothers, there are Lilly Langtree's Guenoc winery in California, the brilliant Te Mata estate in New Zealand and the organic Botobolar from Mudgee in Australia, recommended below. Buying has been just as careful in France, though the list of wines is shorter, with just two red Burgundies picked to represent their region - a reason for by-passing the Watford by-pass.

84	£5.29	OXFORD LANDING CHARDONNAY, YALUMBA 1990 S Australia (Aus)
101	£9.79	HUGO CHARDONNAY 1988 Southern Vales (Aus)
103	£9.89	KING VALLEY CHARDONNAY FAMILY RESERVE, BROWN BROS 1987 N E Victoria (Aus)
105	£8.99	HEGGIES CHARDONNAY, HILL-SMITH 1988 Adelaide Hills (Aus)
106	£9.99	WYNNS COONAWARRA ESTATE CHARDONNAY 1989 (Aus)
117	£12.95	ELSTON CHARDONNAY, TE MATA 1989 (NZ)
266	£5.25	CHATEAU LA CROIX SIMON BORDEAUX ROUGE 1989 (F)
281	£5.75	MONTANA CABERNET SAUVIGNON 1988 Marlborough (NZ)
299	£8.59	MONTES ALPHA CABERNET SAUVIGNON, 1987 Curico Valley (Ch)
313	£10.59	CLOUDY BAY CABERNET MERLOT 1989 Marlborough (NZ)
351	£4.95	DIEMERSDAL SHIRAZ 1986 Paarl (SA)
356	£5.45	DAVID WYNN SHIRAZ 1990 High Eden Ridge (Aus)
366	£7.99	ST GILBERT BOTOBOLAR VINEYARD, GIL WAHLQUIST 1987 Mudgee (Aus)
445	£6.65	NAVAJAS RIOJA CRIANZA TINTO 1985 (Sp)
449	£8.25	CAMPO VIEJO RIOJA GRAN RESERVA 1980 (Sp)
479	£6.49	LA GITANA MANZANILLA, HIDALGO, Jerez (Sp)
489	£9.49	STARBOARD BATCH 88 RUBY, Central Valley (Cal)

GHS | Gerard Harris

2 Green End St, Aston Clinton, Aylesbury, Bucks HP22 5HP (0296 631041). Independent merchant.
Opening Hours: 9.30am-8.00pm Tues-Sat. **Delivery:** free within 20 miles, nationally at cost.
Tastings: regularly in-store plus tutored tastings and dinners. **Discounts:** 10% on case sales.

"The staff would be glad to discuss your requirements and advise you on the choice of wines. Please telephone for an appointment if this is likely to be a lengthy process.' We would begin dialing right now; the Gerard Harris list is so long and broad-ranging that it is impossible to imagine picking out a bottle or two without considerable humming and ha-ing. We would be tempted by the Château ChalonVin Jaune, the Mas de Daumas Gassac and the Pavie 1983. Or then again perhaps we would go for the Meerlust. After all, what better reason could one need for weekending at the Bell Inn at Aston Clinton, the country hotel to which the wine shop is attached.

31	£3.50	**CORBIERES BLANC, CAVES DE MONT TAUCH,** Midi (F)	
111	£12.40	**EDNA VALLEY CHARDONNAY** 1989 San Luis Obispo (Cal)	
117	£11.70	**ELSTON CHARDONNAY, TE MATA** 1989 (NZ)	
206	£4.75	**CHATEAU BEL AIR BORDEAUX CLAIRET (CABERNET SAUVIGNON)** 1990 (F)	
226	£4.05	**DOMAINE DU BOSQUET CANET, LISTEL** 1987 Midi (F)	
264	£5.20	**BERRI ESTATES AUSTRALIAN CABERNET SHIRAZ** 1987 (Aus)	
313	£10.65	**CLOUDY BAY CABERNET MERLOT** 1989 Marlborough (NZ)	
327	£14.90	**YARRA YERING CABERNET SAUVIGNON** 1987 Yarra Valley (Aus)	
339	£3.50	**VIN DE PAYS DES COLLINES RHODANIENNES SYRAH, CAVE TAIN L'HERMITAGE,** Rhône (F)	
373	£9.85	**DOMAINE DU VIEUX TELEGRAPHE, CHATEAUNEUF DU PAPE,** 1987 Rhône (F)	
424	£13.60	**COLTASSALA, CASTELLO DI VOLPAIA** 1986 Tuscany (It)	
472	£11.25	**JURANCON MOELLEUX VENDANGE TARDIVE, DOMAINE CAUHAPE** 1988 S W(F)	
475	£25.00	**CHATEAU RIEUSSEC, SAUTERNES** 1983 Bordeaux (F)	
479	£6.99	**LA GITANA MANZANILLA, HIDALGO,** Jerez (Sp)	
500	£2.50	**PETILLANT DE LISTEL,** Midi (F)	

ROG | Roger Harris

Loke Farm, Weston Longville, Norfolk NR9 5LG (0603 880171) Nothing (well almost nothing) but the best in Beaujolais. **Opening hours:** 9 am-5 pm Mon-Fri. **Delivery:** free nationally. Tutored tastings, **Discounts:** £2.00/£2.50 per case.

If you enjoyed A Year in Provence, you have to get hold of a copy of Roger Harris's list. The area described is rather further north but the flavour and smell of rural France leap at you from every page of a list which incidentally is the only one we know to recommend the best hotels and restaurants of its region. Harris, who clearly loves Beaujolais and probably knows more about it than anyone else in the world, steers a well-controlled course between the blasé and the folklorique. As Beaujolais prices have shot through the roof , the need for a guide like this is greater than ever and no one offers a better guarantee of your drinking really good, typical Beaujolais from a range of individual producers.

HAR | Harrods Ltd

Knightsbridge, London SW1X 7XL (071 730 1234). Undeniably singular store with deluxe wine department. **Opening Hours:** 9am-6pm (7pm Wed) Mon-Sat. **Delivery:** free locally, nationally at cost. **Tastings:** regularly in-store plus occasional special events. **Discounts:** unbroken cases for the price of 11 bottles of most wines.

The image of the Knightsbridge store has changed so much in recent years that it is encouraging to find that the wine department, at least, still maintains some of the style for which Harrods was once renowned. Of course style, like Harrods' wine, does not come cheap and wine prices reflect costs of what the company describes as a 'Luxurious shopping environment, informed helpful service and full delivery.' (Free in the smarter parts of the Capital). We'd recommend that Central Londoners take full advantage of this last facility phoning for a dozen quails eggs and a bottle of, say, Harrods own label English wine, Grange Hermitage, Solaia or any of the following...

7	£13.75	**MAISON DEUTZ SPARKLING,** Napa Valley (Cal)
21	£19.35	**FERRARI BRUT PERLE** 1985 Trentino-Alto Adige (It)
22	£24.50	**VEUVE CLICQUOT DEMI-SEC CHAMPAGNE** (F)
119	£16.25	**LES PIERRES CHARDONNAY, SONOMA CUTRER** 1987 Sonoma (Cal)
332	£28.00	**CHATEAU TALBOT, ST JULIEN** 1982 Bordeaux (F)
336	£55.00	**OPUS ONE, ROBERT MONDAVI** 1987 Napa Valley (Cal)
430	£22.50	**BRUNELLO DEL MONTALCINO, POGGIO ANTICO** 1985 Piedmont (It)
437	£4.65	**SENORIO DE LOS LLANOS RESERVA** 1982 Valdepeñas (Sp)
442	£6.50	**TEMPRANILLO, BODEGAS OCHOA** 1987 Navarra (Sp)
446	£6.75	**GRAN SANGREDETORO RESERVA, TORRES** 1986 Penedés (Sp)
460	£16.00	**CAMPBELLS OLD RUTHERGLEN LIQUEUR MUSCAT** (Aus)
482	£14.00	**ROYAL CORREGIDOR RICH RARE OLD OLOROSO, SANDEMAN,** Jerez (Sp)
494	£21.00	**SANDEMAN IMPERIAL 20 YEAR OLD TAWNY PORT,** Douro (P)

HV | Harveys of Bristol

Harvey House, 31 Denmark St, Bristol, Avon BS1 5DQ (0272 268882). Reassuringly solid traditional merchant with large fortified wine interests. **Opening Hours:** 9am-4.45pm Mon-Fri; 9am-1pm Sat. **Delivery:** free nationally for 2+ cases, otherwise a charge of £5.00. **Tastings:** regularly in-store plus tutored events.

This year's Harveys list has a foreword by Nick Brabner of the Gliffaes Country House Hotel which, it must be said, is no match for the name-dropping piece by the late Roald Dahl in 1989. Beyond the foreword, the list is a far more impressive piece of work than in the past. The Claret selection, always a mainstay, has been expanded and for once Harveys is among the avant garde in promoting modern dry white Bordeaux. The New World is better represented than in the past and includes such wines as Te Mata Coleraine from New Zealand and Calera Jensen Pinot Noir. Also commendable is the policy of grouping Bordeaux by price - 'Médoc up to £7.50 per bottle' - and clearly indicating the wine's state of readiness. Further changes are due at Harveys following the closure of its Pall Mall shop and the announcement that henceforth the wine range will be changed on a more frequent basis - watch this space.

87	£6.04	**ORLANDO RF CHARDONNAY** 1989 S E Australia (Aus)
335	£25.65	**LES FORTS DE LATOUR, PAUILLAC, CHATEAU LATOUR** 1982 Bordeaux (F)

RHV | Richard Harvey Wines

Home Farm, Morden, Wareham, Dorset BH20 7DW (092945 224). Independent merchant and mail-order firm. **Delivery**: Free locally, nationally at cost. **Tastings**: Occasional tutored tastings and events. **Discounts**: 2.5% on unmixed cases, 5% on 6+ unmixed cases.

Now firmly based in the Archeresque setting of Home Farm, Richard Harvey makes no bones about his philosophy 'We do not aim to have a complete selection from around the world merely for the sake of it and we don't have a retail shop to display our wines'. What Mr Harvey does have is a good range of French classics and an even better one of French regional ones of which he is particulary fond and of which we imagine such rural caterers as Jack Woolley and Nelson Gabriel would fully approve.

93	£6.50	**BROKENBACK VINEYARD CHARDONNAY, ROTHBURY** 1990 Hunter Valley (Aus)
94	£6.95	**DOMAINE DE RIBONNET CHARDONNAY** 1989 S W (F)
102	£8.78	**MARQUES DE MURRIETA RIOJA BLANCO RESERVA** 1985 Rioja (Sp)
106	£8.50	**WYNNS COONAWARRA ESTATE CHARDONNAY** 1989 (Aus)
295	£7.95	**WYNNS CABERNET SAUVIGNON** 1985 Coonawarra (Aus)
306	£8.95	**DOMAINE RICHEAUME CABERNET SAUVIGNON, HENNING HOESCH** 1988 Midi (F)
352	£4.95	**COTES DU RHONE, GUIGAL** 1988 (F)
451	£9.75	**MARQUIS DE MURRIETA RIOJA TINTO RESERVA** 1985 (Sp)

HFW | Haughton Fine Wines

Wine list of the Year and Northern Merchant of the Year

Chorley Green Lane, Chorley, Nantwich, Cheshire CW5 8JR (0270 74537). Friendly, hard-to-fault independent merchant with good organic selection. **Opening Hours:** 9.00am-5.30pm Mon-Fri; 9.00am-12.30pm Sat. **Delivery:** free nationally with single-case surcharge. **Tastings:** regular in-store plus tutored tastings and dinner events.

Bruce and Judy Kendrick's company seemed bound to win a prize this year as it was short listed for its wine list and as Northern Wine Merchant of the Year, the prize it won in 1990. In the event Haughton Fine Wines took both awards, proving that the combination of business-like expertise (Bruce came into wine via ICI) and unbridled enthusiasm can see off any competition. The list - more properly 'a year book' - does everything a wine merchant's tariff is supposed to and then some. It serves as a wine handbook which is more informative than many a pricey offering in Waterstones. As for its contents, the quality of these will come as no surprise to followers of this company who will recognise the range of established and pioneering producers, and growing number of 'green wine makers' whose presence in the list is made evident by the leaf coloured ink. All credit too to Mr Kendrick for revealing precisely how his list was produced: in his own office with a desk top computer and the same software that was used for this *Guide*. Would-be 'smart' merchants with scruffier lists, please take note.

60	£5.20	**PICPOUL DE PINET, DOMAINE GAUJOL** 1989 Midi (F)
69	£7.85	**SOAVE CLASSICO VIGNETO CALVARINO, PIEROPAN** 1989 Veneto (It)
70	£6.95	**ST VERAN TERRES NOIRES, DOMAINE DEUX ROCHES** 1989 Burgundy (F)
95	£6.55	**SCHINUS MOLLE CHARDONNAY, DROMANA ESTATE** 1990 Mornington Peninsula (Aus)
101	£8.22	**HUGO CHARDONNAY** 1988 Southern Vales (Aus)

135	£4.45	**DOMAINE DE LA HAUT FEVRIE, MUSCADET DE SEVRE ET MAINE SUR LIE** 1989 Loire (F)
151	£6.55	**SCHINUS MOLLE SAUVIGNON BLANC** 1990 Victoria (Aus)
229	£4.25	**CHATEAU DE FLOTIS, COTES DE FRONTONNAIS** 1988 S W (F)
230	£4.75	**MAS DE GOURGONNIER TRADITION, COTEAUX D'AIX EN PROVENCE LES BAUX** 1989 Midi (F)
232	£4.70	**DOMAINE MONBOUCHE, COTES DE BERGERAC** 1988 S W (F)
233	£5.50	**CHATEAU BOVILA, CAHORS** 1986 S W (F)
301	£8.07	**HOLLICK CABERNET MERLOT** 1988 Coonawarra (Aus)
315	£9.95	**MOUNTADAM CABERNET SAUVIGNON** 1987 High Eden Ridge (Aus)
356	£4.99	**DAVID WYNN SHIRAZ** 1990 High Eden Ridge (Aus)
393	£8.95	**HAUTES COTES DE NUITS, ALAIN VERDET** 1986 Burgundy (F)
405	£5.80	**CHIANTI RUFINA, SELVAPIANA** 1988 Tuscany (It)
427	£15.75	**AMARONE CLASSICO DELLA VALPOLICELLA FIERAMONTE, ALLEGRINI** 1983 Veneto (It)

	HHC	Haynes Hanson & Clarke

17 Lettice St, London, SW6 4EH (071 736 7878) and 36 Kensington Church Street, London W8 4BX. Independent merchant with heavy Burgundian bent. **Opening Hours:** 9.30am-7.00pm Mon-Sat. **Delivery:** free nationally for 5+ cases; less than 5 cases, at cost. **Tastings:** regular in-store plus tutored and organised events. **Discounts:** 10% on unmixed cases.

Anthony Hanson's name will ring louder bells with wine drinkers by the end of this year when the long-awaited revised edition of his book on Burgundy finally hits the shelves. In the meantime, fans of the region who want to Beaune up on the subject will inevitably find their way to the Haynes Hanson tastings at which an astonishing range of truly individual wines is always shown. This is one of the rare companies from whom Burgundy can be bought en primeur - though we were surprised to see that all the 1990s were produced by the widely-represented Olivier Leflaive. Like his fellow author, Jasper Morris, Anthony Hanson has also taken to some of the more subtle New World winemakers, so this is the place to come for Chardonnays from Matanzas Creek. You can, as we might wincingly say, place your trust in Hanson.

42	£4.09	**CEPAGE TERRET, VIN DE PAYS DE L'HERAULT, DELTA DOMAINES** 1989 Midi (F)
70	£6.92	**ST VERAN TERRES NOIRES, DOMAINE DEUX ROCHES** 1989 Burgundy (F)
79	£3.55	**COTES DE ST MONT, PLAIMONT** 1990 S W (F)
90	£6.14	**LINDEMANS BIN 65 CHARDONNAY** 1989 S E Australia (Aus)
95	£7.53	**SCHINUS MOLLE CHARDONNAY** 1990 Mornington Peninsula (Aus)
150	£6.39	**STONELEIGH SAUVIGNON BLANC** 1989 Marlborough (NZ)
336	£45.10	**OPUS ONE, ROBERT MONDAVI** 1987 Napa Valley (Cal)
374	£10.65	**RIDGE GEYSERVILLE ZINFANDEL** 1988 Santa Clara (Cal)
382	£5.58	**JULIENAS LES ENVAUX, ANDRE PELLETIER** 1990 Beaujolais (F)
391	£9.82	**SAINTSBURY PINOT NOIR** 1988 Carneros (Cal)
396	£25.10	**VOLNAY TAILLEPIEDS, DOMAINE DE MONTILLE** 1987 Burgundy (F)
416	£8.39	**CHIANTI CLASSICO, ISOLE E OLENA** 1988 Tuscany (It)
452	£12.50	**RIOJA RESERVA 904, LA RIOJA ALTA** 1978 (Sp)
479	£5.49	**LA GITANA MANZANILLA, HIDALGO**, Jerez (Sp)
496	£18.35	**DUO CENTENARY BUAL, COSSART GORDON** (P)

H&H | Hector & Honorez

7 East St, Kimbolton, Cambs PE18 0HJ (0480 861444). High-class independent merchant. **Delivery:** free within 30 miles, nationally at cost. **Tastings:** occasional tutored tastings and events. **Discounts:** 5% on unmixed case sales.

Hector Scicluna and Christian Honorez have one of the essential skills of a successful wine merchant: they're great head-hunters scouring vineyards of the world for growers in whom they truly believe. The Domaine de Ribonnet was a particularly good find for its varietal wines from the South West of France, as was Rainer Zeiroch , a revolutionary winemaker in Italy who single-handedly pleads the cause of the Teroldego grape. Wines from these producers and from an impressive team of Burgundians make this a firm to watch.

6	£10.00	TALTARNI BRUT TACHE, Pyrenees (Aus)
38	£3.95	TOLLANA DRY WHITE 1988 S E Australia (Aus)
70	£8.00	ST VERAN TERRES NOIRES, DOMAINE DEUX ROCHES 1989 Burgundy (F)
94	£7.95	DOMAINE DE RIBONNET CHARDONNAY 1989 S W (F)
285	£5.95	CUVEE CLEMENT ADER CABERNET MERLOT, DOMAINE DE RIBONNET 1989 S W (F)
297	£8.15	TALTARNI CABERNET SAUVIGNON 1985 Pyrenees (Aus)
381	£4.95	DOMAINE DE LA CHAMOISE, GAMAY DE TOURAINE, HENRY MARIONNET 1990 Loire (F)
396	£19.90	VOLNAY TAILLEPIEDS, DOMAINE DE MONTILLE 1987 Burgundy (F)
416	£8.60	CHIANTI CLASSICO, ISOLE E OLENA 1988 Tuscany (It)
428	£14.50	GRANATO TEROLDEGO, FORADORI 1988 Trentino-Alto Adige (It)

HW | Hedley Wright

The Country Wine Cellars, 10-11 Twyford Centre, London Rd, Bishops Stortford, Herts (0279 506512).Independent by-the-case merchant. **Opening Hours:** 10.00am-6.00pm Mon-Wed, Sat; 10.00am-8.00pm Thurs, Fri. **Delivery:** free within 15 miles, free nationally for 2 cases at mail order prices. **Tastings:** regular in-store plus tutored tastings and dinner events. **Discounts:** 5% for members of the Hedley Wright 'Bonus Club'.

David Sandys-Renton and Martin Wright are in the fortunate position of having been in the right place at the right time. Just as the rest of the wine trade has begun to become interested in Chile - and discovered how disappointing were so many of its wines - Hedley Wright was able to hold its head high with their exclusive agency for the only really international standard modern Chilean winery. Every time you see a bottle of Montes or Nogales wine it came to Britain via Hedley Wright. Outside South America, the list is a little more patchy: Torres accounts for the vast majority of Spanish wines for example, and the German selections are a little hit or miss. Burgundy and Bordeaux show more careful thought and the Rhône and Southern France are well worth a careful trawl.

87	£5.25	ORLANDO RF CHARDONNAY 1989 S E Australia (Aus)
88	£5.50	MONTES CHARDONNAY, 1990 Curico Valley (Ch)
105	£8.99	HEGGIES CHARDONNAY, HILL-SMITH 1988 Adelaide Hills (Aus)
140	£4.95	COOKS HAWKES BAY SAUVIGNON BLANC 1989 Hawkes Bay (NZ)
150	£7.05	STONELEIGH SAUVIGNON BLANC 1989 Marlborough (NZ)
168	£7.50	ALSACE GEWURZTRAMINER KAEFFERKOPF, CAVE VINICOLE DE KIENTZHEIM KAYSERBERG 1989 (F)
181	£4.15	LAMBERHURST SEYVAL BLANC 1988 Kent (UK)

192	£7.35	DEINHARD HOCHHEIM HERITAGE SELECTION 1988 Rheingau (G)
280	£5.25	ORLANDO RF CABERNET SAUVIGNON 1988 S Australia (Aus)
288	£7.45	CHATEAU MUSAR 1982 Bekaa Valley (Leb)
299	£7.95	MONTES ALPHA CABERNET SAUVIGNON, 1987 Curico Valley (Ch)
308	£11.80	COLDSTREAM HILLS CABERNET SAUVIGNON 1988 Yarra Valley (Aus)
313	£8.99	CLOUDY BAY CABERNET MERLOT 1989 Marlborough (NZ)
327	£16.50	YARRA YERING CABERNET SAUVIGNON 1987 Yarra Valley (Aus)
359	£6.00	CROZES HERMITAGE, DELAS FRERES 1989 Rhône (F)
373	£10.35	DOMAINE DU VIEUX TELEGRAPHE, CHATEAUNEUF DU PAPE, 1987 Rhône (F)
446	£5.90	GRAN SANGREDETORO RESERVA, TORRES 1986 Penedés (Sp)
449	£8.30	CAMPO VIEJO RIOJA GRAN RESERVA 1980 (Sp)
465	£6.65	REDWOOD VALLEY ESTATE LATE HARVEST RIESLING 1989 Nelson (NZ)
487	£7.95	TAYLOR'S FIRST ESTATE PORT LUGAR DAS LAGES, Douro (P)
495	£16.95	FONSECA-GUIMARAENS 1976 Douro (P)

HEM | The Hermitage

124 Fortis Green Road, London N10 3DU (081 365 2122). Stylish new independent merchant. **Opening Hours:** 10.30am-8.00pm Tues-Sat; 12.00-2.30pm Sun. **Delivery:** free locally, nationally at cost. **Tastings:** regular in-store ; outside events on request. **Discounts:** 5% on (mixed) case sales.

London has its own North/South divide. Customers of Bibendum near Primrose Hill are loathe to venture across the river to Winecellars in Wandsworth and vice versa - which may help to explain why Gill Reynolds' N10 shop has not received some of the recognition it has deserved among all the 'southern' wine writers and buffs. Even a brief glance at the list reveals the Hermitage to be well worth a detour. There are very few shops anywhere in London which cover the ground quite as comprehensively and well. This is quite simply a range from which it would require a peculiar skill and remarkably bad luck to choose anything other than a delicious bottle. N.B. The accessories are good too.

2	£7.25	DIANE DE POITIERS SPARKLING CHARDONNAY, HAUT POITOU, Loire (F)
29	£2.95	CUVEE JEAN-PAUL BLANC SEC VIN DE TABLE, PAUL BOUTINOT (F)
40	£3.75	CHATEAU HAUT BERNASSE, BERGERAC BLANC, BLAIS 1990 S W (F)
54	£4.99	ALSACE TOKAY PINOT GRIS, CAVE VINICOLE DE TURCKHEIM 1990 (F)
83	£4.95	CALITERRA CHARDONNAY 1990 Maipo Valley (Ch)
87	£5.50	ORLANDO RF CHARDONNAY 1989 S E Australia (Aus)
102	£8.75	MARQUES DE MURRIETA RIOJA BLANCO RESERVA 1985 Rioja (Sp)
106	£9.75	WYNNS COONAWARRA ESTATE CHARDONNAY 1989 (Aus)
111	£13.75	EDNA VALLEY CHARDONNAY 1989 San Luis Obispo (Cal)
160	£4.99	VINHO VERDE, SOLAR DAS BOUCAS 1989 Minho (P)
235	£6.99	DOMAINE LES HAUTES DE CHAMBERTS, CAHORS 1986 S W (F)
280	£5.50	ORLANDO RF CABERNET SAUVIGNON 1988 S Australia (Aus)
313	£10.95	CLOUDY BAY CABERNET MERLOT 1989 Marlborough (NZ)
319	£12.99	YARDEN CABERNET SAUVIGNON, GOLAN HEIGHTS WINERY 1985 Galilee (Is)
331	£19.50	PENFOLDS BIN 707 CABERNET SAUVIGNON 1987 S Australia (Aus)
374	£11.95	RIDGE GEYSERVILLE ZINFANDEL 1988 Santa Clara (Cal)
394	£18.95	CALERA SELLECK PINOT NOIR 1987 San Benito (Cal)
414	£7.65	BARBAROSSA, FATTORIA PARADISO 1986 Emilia-Romagna (It)
424	£14.99	COLTASSALA, CASTELLO DI VOLPAIA 1986 Tuscany (It)
426	£15.85	CEPPARELLO, ISOLE E OLENA 1988 Tuscany (It)
430	£16.99	BRUNELLO DEL MONTALCINO, POGGIO ANTICO 1985 Piedmont (It)
438	£4.45	MARIUS RESERVA, BODEGAS PIQUERAS 1983 Almansa (Sp)

440	£5.85	TINTO VELHO REGUENGOS DE MONSARAZ, JOSE DE SOUSA ROSADO FERNANDES 1986 Alentejo (P)
451	£9.65	MARQUIS DE MURRIETA RIOJA TINTO RESERVA 1985 (Sp)
452	£14.25	RIOJA RESERVA 904, LA RIOJA ALTA 1978 (Sp)
458	£7.50	YALUMBA MUSEUM SHOW RESERVE MUSCAT, Rutherglen (Aus)
465	£5.95	REDWOOD VALLEY ESTATE LATE HARVEST RIESLING 1989 Nelson (NZ)
479	£5.95	LA GITANA MANZANILLA, HIDALGO, Jerez (Sp)
481	£11.35	MANZANILLA PASADA DE SANLUCAR ALMACENISTA, LUSTAU, Jerez (Sp)
492	£16.75	VERDELHO 10 YEAR OLD, COSSART GORDON (P)
495	£18.95	FONSECA-GUIMARAENS 1976 Douro (P)

H&D | Hicks & Don Ltd

Blandford St Mary, Blandford Forum, Dorset DT11 9LS (0258 456040). Independent merchant selling by-the-case. **Opening Hours:** 9.00am-5.30pm Mon-Fri. **Delivery:** free nationally for orders over 3 cases. **Tastings:** organised/tutored events.

25th birthdays are often turning points and so it was for Robin Don and Ronnie Hicks, the two Masters of Wine, who had begun trading in 1966 when they pioneered the sale of *en primeur* claret. Now they have married a far older company - Hall and Woodhouse - which is looking forward to their 250th, so, from 1991 Messrs Hicks, Don and Angus Avery will run the new Hicks and Don company between them continuing to specialise, we suspect, in traditional wines from Europe including such delights as an impressive set of *en primeur* Germans.

HBV | High Breck Vintners

Bentworth House, Bentworth, Nr Alton, Hampshire GU34 5RB (0420 62218). Independent merchant with a number of regional agents in the south and East Anglia. **Opening Hours:** 9.30am-6pm Mon-Fri; 9.30am-12 Sat. **Delivery:** free locally, free nationally for 4+ cases; otherwise at cost. **Tastings:** regularly in-store, plus organised tutored tastings.

Since last year, there have been some changes. Howard Baveystock , the ex-Mothercare cot maker who bought his favourite wine merchant, has expanded - both the scope of his list where there has been explosion of good new Italian wines to join the admirable, fairly-priced French range to which we referred in the last Guide - and, dare we say it, of his girth. He now looks every inch of the traditional wine merchant, competing heavily with one of our favourites in the West Country.

HBR | The Hilbre Wine Co.Ltd.

Unit 20, Gibraltar Row, King Edward Street, Liverpool L3 7HJ (051 236 8800). **Opening hours:** 9am -5 pm Mon - Fri,. 9am - 12.30 pm Sat. **Delivery:** free locally, nationally at cost. **Tastings:** tutored, regularly. **Discounts:** negotiable.

It is far from easy to teach customers about wine without, on the one hand, alienating the buffs who read the wine magazines, or on the other, putting off the novice who is venturing beyond Liebfraumilch. Hilbre achieves this feat admirably in its list, introducing a broad Liverpudlian clientele to wines such as Guy Saget's Muscadet and Krug Grande Cuvée. The range is workaday rather than dazzling, but the wines are generally good.

GHL | George Hill of Loughborough

The Wine Shop, 59 Wards End, Loughborough, Leics LE11 3HB (0509 212717). Independent merchant. **Opening Hours:** 9am-6pm Mon-Sat. **Delivery:** free locally, nationally at cost. **Tastings:** tutored tastings plus organised events. **Discounts:** very good – 8-10% on case sales.

'With the wide and extensive range offered by the chain stores, we now have to be more informed and helpful as this must be our main and principal offering'. Well done, Andrew Hill, for acknowledging the chains as competitors to be matched rather than enemies to be feared or despised. Would that more merchants took as positive a view. Mr Hill's attitude is made more explicable by the quality and the range of a list which very few of the multiples could begin to match. From good dry German reds to a Bruisyard St Peter English white and Château Rausan Segla, the wines are representative of their style and reasonably priced.

22	£21.04	VEUVE CLICQUOT DEMI-SEC CHAMPAGNE (F)
83	£4.55	CALITERRA CHARDONNAY 1990 Maipo Valley (Ch)
87	£5.38	ORLANDO RF CHARDONNAY 1989 S E Australia (Aus)
102	£8.20	MARQUES DE MURRIETA RIOJA BLANCO RESERVA 1985 Rioja (Sp)
332	£22.65	CHATEAU TALBOT, ST JULIEN 1982 Bordeaux (F)
351	£4.79	DIEMERSDAL SHIRAZ 1986 Paarl (SA)
451	£8.99	MARQUIS DE MURRIETA RIOJA TINTO RESERVA 1985 (Sp)
483	£15.93	APOSTOLES, GONZALEZ BYASS, Jerez (Sp)
487	£7.93	TAYLOR'S FIRST ESTATE PORT LUGAR DAS LAGES, Douro (P)
500	£2.34	PETILLANT DE LISTEL, Midi (F)

JEH | J E Hogg

61 Cumberland St, Edinburgh, EH3 6RA (031 556 4025). Traditional independent family merchant. **Opening Hours:** 9am-1pm & 2.30pm-6pm Mon, Tue, Thu, Fri; 9am-1pm Wed, Sat. **Delivery:** free locally. **Tastings:** Occasional in-store tastings, tutored tastings and organised events.

The J E Hogg list remains almost willfully utilitarian with (nicely) hand written headings and very basically word-processed. It is only when one begins to read those word-processed words that one discovers quite how remarkable a selection Jim Hogg offers. Five vintages of Côte Rôtie les Jumelles, all the top Penfolds reds, 11 different Barolos...we could go on but as we said last year this is a secret source of wine everyone wants to keep to themselves. And why should we be any different?

22	£18.00	VEUVE CLICQUOT DEMI-SEC CHAMPAGNE (F)
38	£3.32	TOLLANA DRY WHITE 1988 S E Australia (Aus)
84	£4.08	OXFORD LANDING CHARDONNAY, YALUMBA 1990 S Australia (Aus)
87	£4.36	ORLANDO RF CHARDONNAY 1989 S E Australia (Aus)
93	£5.41	BROKENBACK VINEYARD CHARDONNAY, ROTHBURY 1990 Hunter Valley (Aus)
111	£10.21	EDNA VALLEY CHARDONNAY 1989 San Luis Obispo (Cal)
118	£13.51	VIDAL RESERVE CHARDONNAY 1989 Hawkes Bay (NZ)
119	£12.11	LES PIERRES CHARDONNAY, SONOMA CUTRER 1987 Sonoma (Cal)
193	£8.95	RIESLING SCHOENENBURG GRAND CRU, DOPFF AU MOULIN 1988 Alsace (F)
280	£4.36	ORLANDO RF CABERNET SAUVIGNON 1988 S Australia (Aus)
320	£11.04	CHATEAU LEOVILLE BARTON, ST JULIEN 1987 Bordeaux (F)
344	£3.99	PENFOLDS BIN 2 SHIRAZ/MATARO 1989 Barossa Valley (Aus)
392	£9.87	SANFORD PINOT NOIR 1986 Santa Barbara (Cal)
437	£3.56	SENORIO DE LOS LLANOS RESERVA 1982 Valdepeñas (Sp)

442	£4.70	TEMPRANILLO, BODEGAS OCHOA 1987 Navarra (Sp)
446	£4.83	GRAN SANGREDETORO RESERVA, TORRES 1986 Penedés (Sp)
451	£7.88	MARQUIS DE MURRIETA RIOJA TINTO RESERVA 1985 (Sp)
452	£12.28	RIOJA RESERVA 904, LA RIOJA ALTA 1978 (Sp)
464	£6.10	CHATEAU LOUPIAC GAUDIET, LOUPIAC 1988 S W (F)
479	£5.72	LA GITANA MANZANILLA, HIDALGO, Jerez (Sp)
480	£8.24	DOS CORTADOS, WILLIAMS AND HUMBERT, Jerez (Sp)
481	£9.68	MANZANILLA PASADA DE SANLUCAR ALMACENISTA, LUSTAU, Jerez (Sp)
482	£10.53	ROYAL CORREGIDOR RICH RARE OLD OLOROSO, SANDEMAN, Jerez (Sp)
483	£14.40	APOSTOLES, GONZALEZ BYASS, Jerez (Sp)
495	£16.00	FONSECA-GUIMARAENS 1976 Douro (P)

RHW | Rodney Hogg Wines

52 High St, Higham Ferrers, Northants NN9 8BL (0933 317420). Independent merchant. **Opening Hours:** 9.30am-5.30pm Mon-Fri, but ring first to check. **Delivery:** free within 30 miles, nationally at cost, collection discount. **Tastings:** regularly in-store plus tutored tastings and organised events. **Discounts:** 5% for prompt payment.

Some wine merchants are better fitted to survive a recession than others, but companies such as Rodney Hogg deserve to be supported in lean times. Affordability has always been a key consideration for Hogg, a merchant whose list rarely strays into the heady stratosphere beyond £10. European wines still predominate, but the New World - in the shape of Australia - shows how good it is at providing value for money.

87	£5.50	ORLANDO RF CHARDONNAY 1989 S E Australia (Aus)
93	£6.50	BROKENBACK VINEYARD CHARDONNAY, ROTHBURY 1990 Hunter Valley (Aus)
140	£4.35	COOKS HAWKES BAY SAUVIGNON BLANC 1989 Hawkes Bay (NZ)
280	£5.50	ORLANDO RF CABERNET SAUVIGNON 1988 S Australia (Aus)

HOL | Holland Park Wine Co

12 Portland Rd, Holland Park, London W11 4LA (071 221 9614). Independent merchant. **Opening Hours:** 10am-9pm Mon-Fri; 10am-6pm Sat. **Delivery:** free within central London, nationally at cost. **Tastings:** regular in-store plus tutored events. **Discounts:** 5% case.

In the two years since taking over the Holland Park Wine Company from its Business Expansion Scheme founders, James Handford has steadily developed it into a merchant which can compete on very level terms with such illustrious London retailers as The Barnes Wine Shop and Fulham Road Wine Centre. With each list, his own personality seems to be given greater rein and now 'personal choice' wines abound alongside sensibly devised 'taste' and 'dinner party' sample cases at special introductory rates. The next project involves tutored tastings followed by traditional meals which, following Mr Handford's recent marriage to an Australian may well follow the Holland Park range in taking on a distinctly Antipodean tone.

29	£2.99	CUVEE JEAN-PAUL BLANC SEC VIN DE TABLE, PAUL BOUTINOT (F)
54	£5.49	ALSACE TOKAY PINOT GRIS, CAVE VINICOLE DE TURCKHEIM 1990 (F)
83	£4.69	CALITERRA CHARDONNAY 1990 Maipo Valley (Ch)
84	£5.45	OXFORD LANDING CHARDONNAY, YALUMBA 1990 S Australia (Aus)
111	£13.99	EDNA VALLEY CHARDONNAY 1989 San Luis Obispo (Cal)

154	£9.95	SHAW AND SMITH SAUVIGNON BLANC 1990 S Australia (Aus)
288	£7.25	CHATEAU MUSAR 1982 Bekaa Valley (Leb)
302	£7.95	CHATEAU RAMAGE LA BATISSE, HAUT MEDOC 1988 Bordeaux (F)
303	£8.49	ROSEMOUNT SHOW RESERVE CABERNET SAUVIGNON 1987 Coonawarra (Aus)
313	£13.95	CLOUDY BAY CABERNET MERLOT 1989 Marlborough (NZ)
323	£14.95	VASSE FELIX CABERNET SAUVIGNON 1988 Margaret River (Aus)
332	£24.95	CHATEAU TALBOT, ST JULIEN 1982 Bordeaux (F)
487	£8.95	TAYLOR'S FIRST ESTATE PORT LUGAR DAS LAGES, Douro (P)

HOP | Hopton Wines

Hopton Court, Cleobury Mortimer, Kidderminster, Worcs DY14 0HH (0299 270482) & Teme Street, Tenbury Wells. Expanding independent merchant selling by the case. **Opening Hours:** Hopton Court manned during office hours, Tenbury Wells shop open 9am-9pm Mon-Sat. **Delivery:** free within 50 miles, nationally at cost. **Tastings:** regularly in-store plus tutored events. **Discounts:** for quantity.

Hopton is the kind of company that is worth getting to know. Its list is full of all sorts of oddities including bottles of The Antipodean, a heavily hyped New Zealand red produced in only two vintages before its owners came to blows, the wonderfully named Old Luxters English wine, half a dozen Argentinians and South African wines unavailable elsewhere. This is a list to linger over and to be perused with interest by anyone curious to know what Ronald Reagan's favourite wine was said to be.

22	£19.94	VEUVE CLICQUOT DEMI-SEC CHAMPAGNE (F)
140	£5.39	COOKS HAWKES BAY SAUVIGNON BLANC 1989 Hawkes Bay (NZ)
150	£7.07	STONELEIGH SAUVIGNON BLANC 1989 Marlborough (NZ)
154	£9.54	SHAW AND SMITH SAUVIGNON BLANC 1990 S Australia (Aus)
290	£6.99	CHATEAU ROCHER FIGEAC, ST EMILION, DE LUZE 1985 Bordeaux (F)
304	£8.72	CHATEAU SOCIANDO MALLET, HAUT-MEDOC 1987 Bordeaux (F)
416	£8.58	CHIANTI CLASSICO, ISOLE E OLENA 1988 Tuscany (It)

HOT | House of Townend

Head Office: Red Duster House, York Street, Hull, North Humberside HU2 0QX (0482 26891) 13 link traditionalist chain in Yorkshire and Humberside. **Opening hours:** Depends on branches but generally 10.00 am - 10.00 pm Mon - Sat. 12.00pm - 2.00 pm and 7.00pm - 10.00 pm Sun. **Delivery:** Free within 60 miles, nationally at cost. **Tastings:** in store and tutored. **Discounts:** approx 10%

There is something different about Yorkshire. Not only is there muck and brass galore but also a unique pair of Tory MPs (one in York - Master of Wine, Conal Gregory - and the other - John Townend - in Hull) who share distinctly vinous interests. Mr Townend can claim a vital role in the formation of the modern British wine trade. He it was who created an organisation of Merchant Vintners which enabled small firms to purchase as a group and thus buy at prices normally only obtained by multiple chains. Many of the French wines in particular on the House of Townend list still benefit from that bulk buying, but the company buys elsewhere as well boasting for instance one of the longest lists of South African wines in the country preceded by the following thought-provoking comment: 'Reform is never cheap, somebody has always to pay the bill.... wages are now rising quite rapidly in South Africa and most people accept that this is necessary, but the price has to be paid.'

2	£6.65	DIANE DE POITIERS SPARKLING CHARDONNAY, HAUT POITOU, Loire (F)
63	£5.09	SUNNYCLIFF ESTATES CHARDONNAY 1989 Victoria (Aus)
79	£3.69	COTES DE ST MONT, PLAIMONT 1990 S W (F)
181	£6.94	LAMBERHURST SEYVAL BLANC 1988 Kent (UK)
310	£8.89	BARON VILLENEUVE DE CANTERMERLE, HAUT-MEDOC, CHATEAU CANTEMERLE 1986 Bordeaux (F)
320	£12.17	CHATEAU LEOVILLE BARTON, ST JULIEN 1987 Bordeaux (F)
336	£44.99	OPUS ONE, ROBERT MONDAVI 1987 Napa Valley (Cal)
373	£8.12	DOMAINE DU VIEUX TELEGRAPHE, CHATEAUNEUF DU PAPE, 1987 Rhône (F)

HUN | Hungerford Wine Co

Unit 3, Station Yard, Hungerford, Berks RG17 0DY (0488 683238) & 24 High St, Hungerford, Berks RG17 0NF (0488 683238). Flamboyant Bordeaux buffs with restaurant 'The Galloping Crayfish'. **Opening Hours:** 9am-5.30pm Mon-Fri. **Delivery:** free locally, nationally at cost. **Tastings:** regularly in-store plus tutored events at the restaurant. **Discounts:** 5% unbroken case.

Nick Davies's always noticeable firm was the object of particular attention this year as questions were asked internationally about the *en primeur* market, a sector which Davies has over the years more or less made his own. He acknowledged the queasy mood among buyers by undertaking to lodge a list of customers' purchases with a lawyer in the UK, thus endeavouring to whip up interest in the 1990 vintage. 'Barking Mad' sales were also held to encourage purchases of older vintages and one of the biggest ever Champagne offers was announced at just the time when the fizzy pinch was first beginning to be felt. Hungerford has always been a good place to buy Bordeaux in particular - both *en primeur* and in old vintages - though prospective purchasers should be warned that some customers have complained of unexpectedly high delivery charges and unacceptable delays...

34	£3.69	DOMAINE DE BIAU, COTES DE GASCOGNE, HUGH RYMAN 1990 S W (F)
103	£10.30	KING VALLEY CHARDONNAY FAMILY RESERVE, BROWN BROS 1987 N E Victoria (Aus)
113	£11.00	CHATEAU LA LOUVIERE, PESSAC-LEOGNAN 1989 Bordeaux (F)
203	£4.50	CHATEAU BAUDUC, BORDEAUX CLAIRET, DAVID THOMAS 1990 (F)
226	£4.45	DOMAINE DU BOSQUET CANET, LISTEL 1987 Midi (F)
320	£11.35	CHATEAU LEOVILLE BARTON, ST JULIEN 1987 Bordeaux (F)
335	£24.55	LES FORTS DE LATOUR, PAUILLAC, CHATEAU LATOUR 1982 Bordeaux (F)
474	£16.50	CHATEAU GUIRAUD, SAUTERNES 1988 Bordeaux (F)
475	£35.00	CHATEAU RIEUSSEC, SAUTERNES 1983 Bordeaux (F)
500	£2.65	PETILLANT DE LISTEL, Midi (F)

H | Hunters

93 Crown Road, St,Margarets, Twickenham, Middlesex (081 891 0670) **Opening hours**: Mon - Sat 10.00 am - 8.00 pm. **Delivery**: free locally, nationally at cost. **Tastings**: Bottles regularly opened, occasional tastings. **Discount**: 5% on case.

Wild boar wafers and apricot chutney do not feature on many wine merchants lists but then nor do New Zealand rosés, but all these are to be found in this small shop in a decidedly non-suburban backwater of Twickenham. New Zealand is the special subject here with an astonishing range including no less than a dozen different reds and nine Sauvignons and just as many Chardonnays. We would be tempted to stop right there and work our way through those but to do so would be to miss out on a list almost all of whose contents are recommendable.

3	£6.75	LINDAUER, MONTANA (NZ)
11	£9.95	DEUTZ MARLBOROUGH CUVEE (NZ)
64	£5.25	WOOTTON SCHONBURGER 1990 (UK)
117	£12.95	ELSTON CHARDONNAY, TE MATA 1989 (NZ)
118	£14.25	VIDAL RESERVE CHARDONNAY 1989 Hawkes Bay (NZ)
140	£4.95	COOKS HAWKES BAY SAUVIGNON BLANC 1989 Hawkes Bay (NZ)
147	£6.45	KLEIN COSTANTIA SAUVIGNON BLANC 1988 (SA)
150	£6.75	STONELEIGH SAUVIGNON BLANC 1989 Marlborough (NZ)
203	£3.95	CHATEAU BAUDUC, BORDEAUX CLAIRET, DAVID THOMAS 1990 (F)
281	£5.30	MONTANA CABERNET SAUVIGNON 1988 Marlborough (NZ)
288	£7.25	CHATEAU MUSAR 1982 Bekaa Valley (Leb)
293	£7.95	JAMIESONS RUN RED, MILDARA 1987 Coonawarra (Aus)
313	£9.95	CLOUDY BAY CABERNET MERLOT 1989 Marlborough (NZ)
326	£15.25	ZD CABERNET SAUVIGNON 1986 Napa Valley (Cal)
352	£5.25	COTES DU RHONE, GUIGAL 1988 (F)
373	£11.95	DOMAINE DU VIEUX TELEGRAPHE, CHATEAUNEUF DU PAPE, 1987 Rhône (F)
465	£6.25	REDWOOD VALLEY ESTATE LATE HARVEST RIESLING 1989 Nelson (NZ)
495	£17.95	FONSECA-GUIMARAENS 1976 Douro (P)

HYN Hynard Hughes

The Wine Warehouse, 4-6 Overton Road, Leicester LES 0JA (0533 769496) also at 6 Church Square, Market Harborough, Leicestershire (0858 466168) **Opening hours:** 9 am - 6pm Mon - Fri, 9 am - 1 pm Sat. **Delivery:** free locally, nationally at cost. **Tastings:** monthly in store. **Discounts:** 3% - 8% depending on quantity.

Some merchants have expensively-produced attractive lists; others favour the cheap-and-nasty. Hynard Hughes has opted for a compromise between the two: a glossy piece of work with really horrible pack-shots of Harveys Bristol Cream and LitreVin plonk. Those who are not too deterred by this, however, will find a long selection of wines from which it is remarkably easy to choose several cases of good bottles, including several real bargains unavailable elsewhere.

87	£5.49	ORLANDO RF CHARDONNAY 1989 S E Australia (Aus)
280	£5.49	ORLANDO RF CABERNET SAUVIGNON 1988 S Australia (Aus)
281	£5.29	MONTANA CABERNET SAUVIGNON 1988 Marlborough (NZ)
284	£5.75	SIRIUS ROUGE, PETER SICHEL 1988 Bordeaux (F)
303	£7.99	ROSEMOUNT SHOW RESERVE CABERNET SAUVIGNON 1987 Coonawarra (Aus)
336	£48.50	OPUS ONE, ROBERT MONDAVI 1987 Napa Valley (Cal)
351	£5.29	DIEMERSDAL SHIRAZ 1986 Paarl (SA)
483	£16.99	APOSTOLES, GONZALEZ BYASS, Jerez (Sp)
493	£19.95	WARRE'S QUINTA DA CAVADINHA 1982 Douro (P)

JOB Jeroboams

51 Elizabeth St, London SW1W 9PP (071 823 5623) & 24 Bute Street London SW7 3EX.(071 225 2232) Up-market deli. **Opening Hours:** 9am-7pm Mon-Fri; 9am-6pm Sat. **Delivery:** free locally **Tastings:** occasionally in-store. **Discounts:** 5% on case sales.

This well-known Elizabeth Street continental-style deli certainly knows its nuts from its biscuits--not to mention the wines. Jeroboams are agents for Georges Vesselle, whose Champage and Bouzy Rouge they stock and either of these would be a perfect match for a fair few of Jeroboam's cheeses. For those who find that extravagance on olive oil and tapenade has eaten a hole in their wallets, there is a good selection of country wines as well.

| SHJ | S H Jones |

27 High Street, Banbury, Oxon OX16 8EW (0295 251179). Old-fasioned independent merchant and mail-order firm. **Opening Hours**: Mon-Fri 9-5:30. **Delivery**: free locally, nationally at cost. **Tastings**: regular in-store, plus tutored tastings and special events. **Discounts**: 5% for case purchase, 7.5% for 10+ cases.

A combination of traditional design and modern sensibilities (recycled paper) make S H Jones' wine list seem at first glance like the kind of Edwardian booklet one picks up in church jumble sales. Within the covers, however, lies a thoroughly up-to-date publication, with unusually useful vintage charts and the best kind of merchant's note: 'So much red wine around the world is... great big voluptuous...mouthfilling, tannic...head-turning. Somehow tasting in Burgundy - and especially at the moment - is like returning to the beginning; the grape flavours can be so clean and pure. The North West States of the USA and, in time, New Zealand and South Africa will open our eyes to new horizons but for now, the vintages of 1985, 1988 and 1990 demand our attention'.

S H Jones's wines from the classic regions are as carefully chosen as the words on its list, and the range of half bottles is dazzling. To say that the New World - those 'New Horizons' - could do with slightly deeper attention is to cavil.

92	£6.40	MACON CHARDONNAY, J TALMARD 1988 Burgundy (F)
93	£6.55	BROKENBACK VINEYARD CHARDONNAY, ROTHBURY 1990 Hunter Valley (Aus)
103	£7.80	KING VALLEY CHARDONNAY FAMILY RESERVE, BROWN BROS 1987 N E Victoria (Aus)
196	£5.50	THREE CHOIRS MEDIUM DRY ENGLISH TABLE WINE 1989 Gloucs (UK)
281	£5.25	MONTANA CABERNET SAUVIGNON 1988 Marlborough (NZ)
352	£6.05	COTES DU RHONE, GUIGAL 1988 (F)
373	£8.65	DOMAINE DU VIEUX TELEGRAPHE, CHATEAUNEUF DU PAPE, 1987 Rhône (F)
465	£5.85	REDWOOD VALLEY ESTATE LATE HARVEST RIESLING 1989 Nelson (NZ)
475	£29.15	CHATEAU RIEUSSEC, SAUTERNES 1983 Bordeaux (F)
479	£4.70	LA GITANA MANZANILLA, HIDALGO, Jerez (Sp)

| J&B | Justerini & Brooks |

Bordeaux Merchant of the Year

61 St James St, London SW1A 1LZ (071 493 8721) & 39 George St, Edinburgh EH2 2HN (031 226 4202). Traditional merchant, a subsidiary of drinks giant IDV. **Opening Hours**: 9am- 5.30pm Mon-Fri (till 6pm in Edinburgh); 9.30am-1pm Sat (Edinburgh only). **Delivery**: free within 20 miles for over 2 cases. **Tastings**: occasional public tastings, plus tutored and organised events. **Discounts**: upto £3 per case depending on quantity.

The competition for Bordeaux Merchant of the Year was bound to be tough but Justerini was a popular winner with the judges who acknowledged the reliability with which this firm has always constantly handled this often tricky part of the trade. But Bordeaux is only part of the Justerini story. Over the last few years, Justerini has broadened its scope considerably, accepting the need to offer a greater number of lower priced wines. The 'wines at under £6.00' section of the list now begins with Justerini's Claret at £3.95 and gently makes its way via the Private Cuvée Méthode Traditionelle to Wynns Coonawarra Riesling. The major brewery chains have generally made such a botch of running wine companies in the past it is hard to believe that Justerini is in any way related to the Grand Metropolitan giant which until very recently, has overseen the floundering of Peter Dominic, Bottoms Up and the late, unlamented, Hunter & Oliver chains.

77	£16.66	CONDRIEU, COTEAUX DE CHERY, A PERRET 1989 Rhône (F)
373	£8.75	DOMAINE DU VIEUX TELEGRAPHE, CHATEAUNEUF DU PAPE, 1987 Rhône (F)
496	£17.60	DUO CENTENARY BUAL, COSSART GORDON (P)

JCK | J C Karn

7 Lansdowne Place, Cheltenham Glos CL5 2HU (0242 513265). Independent merchant specialising in wines from New Zealand and the Loire. **Opening Hours**: Mon-Fri 9am-6pm. **Delivery**: free within Gloucestershire. **Tastings**: regular in-store, plus tutored tastings and dinner events.

J C Karn were 'a little wounded' about not being included in last year's Guide. The oversight was not to be taken personally, as J C Karn's list contains a number of very good and carefully chosen wines. In addition to the New Zealand names that are now becoming industry-standard, you can also find Aotea wines and the excellent Ngatarawa range. Wines from the Loire are just as lovingly chosen, bought as they all are from good, small growers. Firms who specialise in both the Loire and New Zealand are rare, so anyone interested in setting up an in-depth Sauvignon tasting should leap on the next train to Cheltenham. Other styles and regions are well covered too in a range which runs to some 600 wines, but don't ask Richard Gooch to send you a list to prove the fact; he'll only explain quite reasonably that quantities of each wine are often too small for it to be possible to print one.

3	£7.29	LINDAUER, MONTANA (NZ)
87	£4.99	ORLANDO RF CHARDONNAY 1989 S E Australia (Aus)
140	£5.25	COOKS HAWKES BAY SAUVIGNON BLANC 1989 Hawkes Bay (NZ)
280	£4.99	ORLANDO RF CABERNET SAUVIGNON 1988 S Australia (Aus)
281	£5.35	MONTANA CABERNET SAUVIGNON 1988 Marlborough (NZ)
351	£4.59	DIEMERSDAL SHIRAZ 1986 Paarl (SA)
417	£8.99	COLLIO MERLOT, COLLAVINI 1985 Friuli-Venezia-Giulia (It)

K&B | King & Barnes

The Horsham Brewery, 18 Bishopric, Horsham, West Sussex RH12 1QP (0403 69344). Wine retailing arm of a country brewery. **Opening Hours:** 9am-6pm Mon-Sat. **Delivery:** free locally. **Tastings:** occasionally in-store (Saturdays), organised events, tutored tastings and dinners for 'Case and Cellar Club' members. **Discounts:** 5% on (mixed) cases.

Recession? What recession? As the rest of the world has been feeling the profound effects of negative cash flow, King & Barnes have been quietly maintaining its assault on the widely held (and often justified) prejudice against brewery-owned wine merchants. Wine buyer Simon Deakin's enthusiasm and hard work seem to have paid off, and plans for the future include improved staff training and further ventures into stocking wines from around the world, as customers grow more willing to brave new vinous territory.

46	£3.88	CHARDONNAY, DOMAINE DES FLINES, VIN DE PAYS DE LA LOIRE 1990 (F)
288	£6.35	CHATEAU MUSAR 1982 Bekaa Valley (Leb)
357	£4.95	FETZER ZINFANDEL 1987 Mendocino (Cal)
365	£6.52	CHATEAU TAHBILK SHIRAZ 1987 Goulburn Valley (Aus)
373	£9.65	DOMAINE DU VIEUX TELEGRAPHE, CHATEAUNEUF DU PAPE, 1987 Rhône (F)

L&W | Lay & Wheeler

6 Culver Street West, Colchester, Essex CO1 1JA (0206 764446) & The Wine Market, Gosbecks Road, Colchester, Essex . Essex's- and one of England's- finest. **Opening Hours**: 8am-8pm Mon-Sat (Wine Market); 8.30am-5.30pm Mon-Sat (Culver Street). **Delivery**: free locally and nationally for 2+ cases. **Tastings**: regular in-store plus organised events. **Discounts**: variable.

'Lay & Wheeler is rather like a top flight three-star restaurant - the kind whose staff instinctively know what you would most like to eat, and offer it almost without being asked'. The comment from a regular customer struck us as very appropriate. Everything about this company is discretely confident and professional; the list and the shop are as modern as any in the world, but the style is timeless. Mature claret (1970 Ducru-Beaucaillou) and the most *dans-le-vent* New World wines (1988 Frog's Leap Cabernet Sauvignon) are given equal effort - both in the list, and at the firm's legendary tastings and meals. It is worth noting too, in times of a precarious *en primeur* market, that of all the independent merchants in Britain, Lay & Wheeler is one of the most financially secure.

69	£7.56	SOAVE CLASSICO VIGNETO CALVARINO, PIEROPAN 1989 Veneto (It)
71	£6.84	ST VERAN LES GRANDES BRUYERES, ROGER LUQUET 1989 Burgundy (F)
79	£3.31	COTES DE ST MONT, PLAIMONT 1990 South West (F)
93	£6.51	BROKENBACK VINEYARD CHARDONNAY, ROTHBURY EST. 1990 Hunter Valley (Aus)
117	£11.84	ELSTON CHARDONNAY, TE MATA 1990 (NZ)
122	£18.22	MEURSAULT, COCHE DURY 1988 Burgundy (F)
125	£21.55	NUITS ST GEORGES BLANC, CLOS DE L'ARLOT 1988 Burgundy (F)
129	£3.77	NURAGUS DI CAGLIARI, CANTINA SOCIALE DI DOLIANOVA 1990 Sardinia (It)
154	£8.62	SHAW AND SMITH SAUVIGNON BLANC 1990 South Australia (Aus)
284	£5.71	SIRIUS ROUGE, PETER SICHEL 1988 Bordeaux (F)
311	£8.78	SIMI CABERNET SAUVIGNON 1984 Sonoma (Cal)
336	£36.82	OPUS ONE, ROBERT MONDAVI 1987 Napa Valley (Cal)
350	£4.79	CHATEAU DU GRAND MOULAS, COTES DU RHONE 1989 (F)
371	£8.21	HENSCHKE MOUNT EDELSTONE SHIRAZ 1987 Adelaide Hills (Aus)
373	£7.86	DOMAINE DU VIEUX TELEGRAPHE, CHATEAUNEUF DU PAPE, 1987 Rhône (F)
405	£5.71	CHIANTI RUFINA, SELVAPIANA 1988 Tuscany (It)
410	£6.53	CAPITEL VALPOLICELLA DEI NICALO, TEDESCHI 1986 Veneto (It)
451	£9.80	MARQUIS DE MURRIETA RIOJA TINTO RESERVA 1985 (Sp)
452	£14.12	RIOJA RESERVA 904, LA RIOJA ALTA 1978 (Sp)

LAY | Laytons See André Simon

| LEA | Lea & Sandeman |

301 Fulham Road, London SW10 9QH (071 376 4767). Independent merchant. **Opening Hours:** 9.30am-8.30pm Mon-Sat. **Delivery:** nationally at cost, free for orders over £100. **Tastings:** regularly in-store plus tutored tastings. **Discounts:** 5% on a case if collected.

'White South African'. The heading of a section of Lea & Sandeman's smart list caught our attention, prompting us to leaf through it in search of 'Red Chinese'. Our quest was in vain, but it took us past some very tempting French and Italian wines, ranging from the oak-aged Domaine de Joy 'Cuvée Speciale' and Pomino 'Il Benefizio', to Jean-Marie Ponsot's eccentric white Morey St Denis and Eleonora Limonci's pungent Italian Sauvignon Mimosa.

The list reveals there to be as many white South Africans - Klein Constantia, Hamilton Russell and Rustenberg - as red Australians - Rouge Homme, Houghton, Cape Mentelle - but with an Oddbins directly across the road, presumably, L&S saw no reason to compete. Besides, with no less than seven red New Zealand wines (including the delicious Vidal Private Bin Cabernet Merlot), they have clearly found a speciality market unexplored by almost anybody else.

66	£6.25	ALSACE PINOT BLANC BENNWIHR, MARCEL DEISS 1989 (F)
102	£9.50	MARQUES DE MURRIETA RIOJA BLANCO RESERVA 1985 Rioja (Sp)
111	£11.75	EDNA VALLEY CHARDONNAY 1989 San Luis Obispo (Cal)
118	£14.45	VIDAL RESERVE CHARDONNAY 1989 Hawkes Bay (NZ)
119	£14.95	LES PIERRES CHARDONNAY, SONOMA CUTRER 1987 Sonoma (Cal)
134	£4.25	DOMAINE DU BREUIL, VIN DE PAYS DU JARDIN DE LA FRANCE 1990 Loire (F)
147	£6.75	KLEIN CONSTANTIA SAUVIGNON BLANC 1988 (SA)
207	£6.95	DOMAINE DE LA MORDOREE, TAVEL ROSE 1990 Rhône (F)
305	£8.50	JEAN LEON CABERNET SAUVIGNON 1983 Penedés (Sp)
321	£15.95	RENAISSANCE CABERNET SAUVIGNON 1984 North Yuba (Cal)
325	£16.50	CARMENET CABERNET SAUVIGNON 1986 Sonoma (Cal)
374	£10.75	RIDGE GEYSERVILLE ZINFANDEL 1988 Santa Clara (Cal)
394	£17.75	CALERA SELLECK PINOT NOIR 1987 San Benito (Cal)
415	£7.95	BARBERA D'ALBA PIAN ROMUALDO, PRUNOTTO 1988 Piedmont (It)
416	£8.50	CHIANTI CLASSICO, ISOLE E OLENA 1988 Tuscany (It)
418	£8.95	PAIS, COLLE MANORA 1989 Piedmont (It)
419	£10.50	ROSSO DI MONTALCINO, POGGIO ANTICO 1989 Tuscany (It)
420	£10.95	'SASTER' CABERNET SAUVIGNON, FRIULVINI 1988 Friuli-Venezia-Giulia (It)
425	£13.95	CARMIGNANO RISERVA, VILLA DI CAPEZZANA 1985 Tuscany (It)
430	£18.95	BRUNELLO DEL MONTALCINO, POGGIO ANTICO 1985 Piedmont (It)
434	£39.00	MAURIZIO ZANELLA, CA' DEL BOSCO 1988 Lombardy (It)
451	£10.50	MARQUIS DE MURRIETA RIOJA TINTO RESERVA 1985 (Sp)
452	£15.75	RIOJA RESERVA 904, LA RIOJA ALTA 1978 (Sp)
465	£8.35	REDWOOD VALLEY ESTATE LATE HARVEST RIESLING 1989 Nelson (NZ)
483	£16.75	APOSTOLES, GONZALEZ BYASS, Jerez (Sp)
494	£17.95	SANDEMAN IMPERIAL 20 YEAR OLD TAWNY PORT, Douro (P)
497	£24.95	DUQUE DE BRAGANZA 20 YEAR OLD TAWNY PORT, FERREIRA, Douro (P)

| LES | Leo's |

Head office: 29 Dantzic Street, Manchester, M4 4BA (061 832 8152). 121-branch (relatively) up-market subsidiary of the Co-op; associated with 261 Stop and Shop outlets. **Delivery**: Free within 10 miles; nationally at cost. **Tastings**: in store. **Discounts**: 5% on unmixed cases; 2.5% on mixed.

Previous editions of the *Guide* have treated Leo's and the Co-op as one and the same. This year, though, we were finally convinced that the leonine division of Co-operative Retail Services Ltd - and its associated Stop and Shop stores - deserved to be considered on their own merits.

Like Spar, Leo's clearly wants to change its image, attract customers who might not otherwise shop there - and persuade the existing clientele to be more adventurous. As a fellow retailer wrily said, 'that's a far tougher cross than being Oddbins', so Christine Oliver, who herself acknowledges its 'somewhat "difficult" customer profile', deserves great credit for the steps which have already been taken. The range available throughout the stores, and most particularly in the 'superstores', has been expanded, and now includes organic Vin de Pays de l'Hérault, Cooks New Zealand Sauvignon and even that conservative wine buff's favourite, Château Cissac.

With the help of Arabella Woodrow's wine buying at the Co-op, the own-label - Carissa, Lohengrin and Pierre Chaumont - range is increasingly commendable too and offers like the 50p-off-3-bottles multi-purchase ought to encourage at least a little spirit of adventure. Staff training has been taken in hand and vinous perestroika is gradually taking effect throughout the chain. Leos are worth watching; they are ideally placed to deal a mortal blow to the producers of the awful 'British' Rougemont Castle and Concord, a death we'd love to applaud. In the meantime, bear in mind that this is the only company we know which offers the free loan of a punch bowl.

87	£4.85	**ORLANDO RF CHARDONNAY** 1989 S E Australia (Aus)	
269	£4.59	**PIERRE CHAUMONT CHATEAU GRIMONT, PIERRE YUNG** 1987 Bordeaux (F)	
280	£4.85	**ORLANDO RF CABERNET SAUVIGNON** 1988 South Australia (Aus)	
281	£4.99	**MONTANA CABERNET SAUVIGNON** 1988 Marlborough (NZ)	
478	£3.69	**SODAP MEDIUM DRY** (Cyp)	

LWL   London Wine Ltd

Chelsea Wharf, 15 Lots Road, London SW10 (071 351 6856). Independent by-the-case merchant. **Opening Hours:** 9am-9pm Mon-Fri; 10am-7pm Sat; 10.30am-5.30pm Sun. **Delivery:** free locally, nationally at cost. **Tastings:** regularly in-store. **Discounts:** 5% on sales over £1,000. That's right, £1,000.

A few years ago, Chelsea Wharf was a flagship of 1980s development, attracting all manner of be-Porsched residents and eager new businesses. It must have been galling for London Wine to see the yuppies who lived on its doorstep eagerly crossing the Thames to buy their wine in the brighter, more interestingly stocked Majestic. Today, however, much has changed; the yuppies are busily *bicycling* around in search of a cheaper place to live, and Majestic has (for the moment at least) foresworn its previous vinous ambitions.

London Wine's moment may have come. Its list, focused as ever on affordability, now puts its neighbour's in the shade. This is an ideal place to buy the Duboeuf range, Pascal Rhônes, Bordeaux from Nathaniel Johnston. London Wine also offers, though this is less well known - a good range of vintage ports and Classed Growth clarets.

83	£4.69	**CALITERRA CHARDONNAY** 1990 Maipo Valley (Ch)
88	£4.99	**MONTES CHARDONNAY, DISCOVER WINE LTDA** 1990 Curico Valley (Ch)
299	£6.99	**MONTES ALPHA CABERNET SAUVIGNON** 1987 Curico Valley (Ch)

310	£8.29	**BARON VILLENEUVE DE CANTERMERLE, HAUT-MEDOC** 1986 Bordeaux (F)
352	£4.99	**COTES DU RHONE, GUIGAL** 1988 (F)
464	£5.99	**CHATEAU LOUPIAC GAUDIET, LOUPIAC** 1988 South West (F)

LHV | Lorne House Vintners

Unit 5, Hewitts Industrial Estate, Cranleigh, Surrey, GU6 8LW (0483 271445). Doggedly Independent merchant. **Opening Hours:** 9am-5pm Mon-Thurs; 9am-7pm Fri; 9am-1pm Sat. **Delivery:** free locally. **Tastings:** regularly in-store plus tutored tastings. **Discounts:** 10% for members of the shipping club.

'If it goes on like this, soon us wine merchants will be as English winemakers, either the wealthy or the insane. And I am certainly not the former!' Dirk Collingwood's *cri de coeur* following the rise in wine duty expressed the dismay of almost every merchant in country, but unlike some of his competitors, he seems resolved to fight his way out of the recession, using methods which are far more inventive than insane. Who else is offering Mâcon Blanc *en primeur* for example? Well, it's not actually *en primeur*, but it is 'pre-shipment', and buying this way does save you 10% off the Lorne House list price.

From his standard list, it is easy to choose any number of good French and Italian wines from individual estates, as well as a slowly growing selection from the New World. The only fault we can find with it is a stream-of-consciousness writing style which can be quite hard to follow on occasion.

71	£6.25	**ST VERAN LES GRANDES BRUYERES, ROGER LUQUET** 1989 Burgundy (F)
320	£11.25	**CHATEAU LEOVILLE BARTON, ST JULIEN** 1987 Bordeaux (F)
332	£25.00	**CHATEAU TALBOT, ST JULIEN** 1982 Bordeaux (F)
337	£3.10	**COTES DE LUBERON, CELLIER DE MARRENON** 1990 Rhone (F)
442	£5.15	**TEMPRANILLO, BODEGAS OCHOA** 1987 Navarra (Sp)

MWW | Majestic Wine Warehouses

421 Kings Rd, London SW6 4RN (071 731 3131). National chain with nearly 50 warehouses, mostly in south & central England. **Opening Hours:** Mon - Sat 10am - 8pm Sun 10am - 6pm **Delivery:** free within five miles of a partcular warehouse, nationally at cost. **Tastings:** regularly in-store, occasional tutored tastings.

If ever there were a justification for producing this *Guide* annually, Majestic provides it. Last year, this chain was packed to the gunwalls with exciting wines; this time round, the list is a pathetic shadow of its former self. The 1991 *Guide* was, for example, able to recommend three Majestic New Zealand wines; the current list only offers one, the perfectly adequate Oak Vale. California is similarly represented by three basic-standard wineries; only one German wine breaks through the £4.99 barrier. This is not a range that is remotely comparable to that of its former competitors, Oddbins or Sainsbury.

To be fair to the new management team, which took over just as the 1991 *Guide* went to press, they inherited a company which, by all accounts, was in imminent risk of capsizing. The reduction in range and stock is hopefully a short-term measure, intended to keep the ship afloat during a recession which may well lead to the scuppering of some of Majestic's competitors. On the bright side, the staff about whom we have always been so complimentary are still working in the stores, and the selection on the shelves is not quite as dismal as the list. Even so, for the moment at least, we can only recommend Majestic very halfheartedly.

19	£15.99	DEVAUX CHAMPAGNE CUVEE ROSEE (F)
83	£4.59	CALITERRA CHARDONNAY 1990 Maipo Valley (Ch)
84	£4.75	OXFORD LANDING CHARDONNAY, YALUMBA 1990 South Australia (Aus)
86	£4.75	CHARDONNAY, VIN DE PAYS D'OC, HUGH RYMAN 1990 Midi (F)
93	£6.59	BROKENBACK VINEYARD CHARDONNAY, ROTHBURY EST. 1990 Hunter Valley (Aus)
288	£5.99	CHATEAU MUSAR 1982 Bekaa Valley (Leb)

M&S | Marks & Spencer

Head office: St Michael House, 57 Baker St, London W1A 1DN (071 935 4422). Up-market supermarket chain beloved by the thirtysomethings. **Opening Hours**: Many (most London) branches open until 8pm Mon-Fri, 9am-6pm Sat. **Delivery**: nationally at cost. **Tastings**: occasional. **Discounts**: 12 bottles for the price of 11.

In the WINE Magazine International Wine Challenge, well-liked wines are awarded Gold, Silver or Bronze medals - or Commendations. M&S entered a long list of wines and received a long list of Commendations... This clearly disappointed the chain's buyers who were hoping for a few more medals, but it came as no surprise to well-informed observers of the UK wine trade, nor we would suspect to many of M&S's customers. This is a company (it doesn't want to be thought of as a supermarket, but we can't think of a better definition) which *aims* to be commendable.

No one could ever accuse the M&S' wine buyers of taking risks. The German list currently consists of the following: Liebfraumilch, hock, Moselle (sic), Piesporter Michelsberg, Bereich Neirstein. Mouth-watering, nicht war? Australian fizz and Chilean Cabernet - great successes for Sainsbury - have yet to reach these shelves, and the majority of wines tend to come from familiar, tried-and-tested suppliers like Christian Bros, Cordier and Duboeuf. On the other hand, a clear and welcome effort has been made to offer bottles at the lower end of the price spectrum - particularly among French country wines. Unless you like the sip-sized mini-bottles or the peculiar-tasting 'Planters Punch' and 'Sangria' flavoured wines, Marks' best buys remain its Bordeaux Second Labels and its Champagne.

16	£14.99	ST MICHAEL CHAMPAGNE BLANC DE BLANCS, UNION CHAMPAGNE AVIZE (F)
30	£2.99	ST MICHAEL DOMAINE DE PRADELLES, CO-OP BASTIDE DE LEVIS 1990 (F)
36	£3.49	COLDRIDGE ESTATE AUSTRALIAN WHITE 1989 Victoria (Aus)
49	£4.49	ST MICHAEL BEAUJOLAIS BLANC, CHAINTRE CO-OP 1988 (F)
130	£3.79	ST MICHAEL SAUVIGNON DE TOURAINE, GUY SAGET 1990 Loire (F)
141	£4.99	ST MICHAEL MUSCADET SUR LIE, SAUVION 1990 Loire (F)
159	£4.49	ST MICHAEL CHATEAU DE POCE, CHAINIER 1990 (F)
211	£2.79	ST MICHAEL FRENCH COUNTRY RED, VIGNERONS CATALANS (F)
215	£3.29	ST MICHAEL CHATEAU DE BEAULIEU ROUGE, TOUSSET 1989 (F)
220	£3.79	CHRISTIAN BROTHERS CLASSIC RED, Napa Valley (Cal)
273	£4.79	ST MICHAEL MEDOC, CORDIER 1989 Bordeaux (F)
383	£5.99	ST MICHAEL MORGON, DUBOEUF 1989 Beaujolais (F)
498	£1.19	ST MICHAEL LIEBLING PEACH, KLOSTERHOF (G)

MC | The Master Cellar

5 Aberdeen Road, Croydon, Surrey CR01EQ (081 686 9989). Wine warehouse sibling of the Davisons chain, situated at the HQ of their parent, J T Davies. **Opening Hours:** 10am-8pm Tues-Fri; 10am-6pm Sat, Sun. **Delivery:** free locally, nationally at cost. **Tastings:** regularly in-store plus tutored and organised events. **Discounts:** 8.5% per case.

As recommendable as ever, this offshoot of Davisons (qv) remains a wonderful place in which to buy serious Bordeaux and Burgundy, as well as a good range of fairly priced daily-drinking wines.

3	£6.99	LINDAUER, MONTANA (NZ)
87	£5.25	ORLANDO RF CHARDONNAY 1989 S E Australia (Aus)
88	£5.25	MONTES CHARDONNAY, DISCOVER WINE LTDA 1990 Curico Valley (Ch)
102	£8.99	MARQUES DE MURRIETA RIOJA BLANCO RESERVA 1985 Rioja (Sp)
103	£10.20	KING VALLEY CHARDONNAY FAMILY RESERVE, BROWN BROS 1987 N E Victoria (Aus)
107	£9.45	KRONDORF SHOW RESERVE CHARDONNAY 1989 Barossa Valley (Aus)
123	£19.45	CHASSAGNE MONTRACHET PREMIER CRU CHAUMEES, PIERRE MOREY 1987 Burgundy (F)
140	£4.99	COOKS HAWKES BAY SAUVIGNON BLANC 1989 Hawkes Bay (NZ)
220	£3.99	CHRISTIAN BROTHERS CLASSIC RED, Napa Valley (Cal)
222	£3.75	CHATEAU DE MANDOURELLE, CORBIERES 1988 Midi (F)
276	£4.99	CHATEAU MENDOCE, BOURG 1986 Bordeaux (F)
280	£5.25	ORLANDO RF CABERNET SAUVIGNON 1988 South Australia (Aus)
288	£6.95	CHATEAU MUSAR 1982 Bekaa Valley (Leb)
293	£7.49	JAMIESONS RUN RED, MILDARA 1987 Coonawarra (Aus)
299	£7.95	MONTES ALPHA CABERNET SAUVIGNON, 1987 Curico Valley (Ch)
313	£11.15	CLOUDY BAY CABERNET MERLOT 1989 Marlborough (NZ)
332	£27.25	CHATEAU TALBOT, ST JULIEN 1982 Bordeaux (F)
336	£46.25	OPUS ONE, ROBERT MONDAVI 1987 Napa Valley (Cal)
353	£5.49	PENFOLDS BIN 28 KALIMNA SHIRAZ 1988 South Australia (Aus)
404	£5.40	VIGNETI CASTERNA VALPOLICELLA CLASSICO, FRATELLI PASQUA 1987 Veneto (It)
445	£6.50	NAVAJAS RIOJA CRIANZA TINTO 1985 (Sp)
451	£8.99	MARQUIS DE MURRIETA RIOJA TINTO RESERVA 1985 (Sp)

MYS | Mayor Sworder

21 Duke Street Hill, London SE2 2SW (071 407 5111). Independent specialist mail order merchant, offering wine by mail - and by-the-glass in Cuddeford's Wine Bar. **Delivery**: free within M25. **Tastings**: tutored and in Cuddefords. **Discounts**: negotiable for large orders.

Mayor Sworder's name is less well known to the wine world in general than, say, Adnams or Lay & Wheeler, but for real wine buffs this low-profile company is one of the country's best and most reliable.

One's first impression when perusing the elegant list is of a firm which really knows its producers and their wines. Indeed, regular customers can follow the progress of domaines from one generation to another almost as though they were watching a soap opera. Wines are well chosen throughout the list; new trends - towards Australia and halbtrocken (rather than trocken) Germans - are acknowledged, but in a decidedly measured way.

Perhaps the best way to convey the Mayor Sworder style is to quote managing director, Martin Everett's comments on 1989 Bordeaux: 'We only offered a few Cru Bourgeois...The crop was a large one, prices of the lesser appellations are unlikely to rise much in the short term and by biding our time, we think we will get the best deal...During all of this, normal trading has almost been forgotten...there is some very good value to be found amongst the older vintages. When the dust settles this will become more evident, but in the meantime we have been busy.'

MCL | McLeods

Bridge Street, Louth, Lincs LN11 0DR (0507 601094). Probably the only wine merchant selling 'Mariner' bottled gas and offering a dry-cleaning service, in the world. **Opening Hours:** 9.00am-8.30pm every day (normal licensing hours). **Delivery:** free locally. **Tastings:** wines occasionally open for sampling. **Discounts:** 5% for case orders, 10% for over 2 cases.

By the time this Guide appears, God and British roadbuilders willing, Stuart and Rose McLeod will be reaping the rewards of a by-pass which will deflect heavy traffic from Louth, leaving the town to the locals and tourists who have come to visit England's highest church.

For our part, we feel sorry for the people who will be hurtling down the A16; they may never get the chance to explore Mcleod's frequently inovative list of 200 wines (changed frequently 'to ensure variety'), 60 whiskies, snake soup, fortune cookies and dried octopus.

MM | Michael Menzel

297-299 Eccleshall Rd, Sheffield, South Yorks S11 8NX (0742 683557). Realistic but not unimaginative independent merchant. **Opening Hours:** 10am-9pm Mon-Sat; 12-2pm & 7pm-9pm Sun. **Delivery:** free within 50 miles, nationally at cost. **Tastings:** occasionally in-store. **Discounts:** 10% for 14 or more cases.

Barolo 'crushed by foot' , red wine from Champagne, Sparkling Red Burgundy, Red Blauer Portuguiser from Germany, Chilean Pisco and Sakura Sake... The Michael Menzel list is nothing if not individualistic - a feat made doubly impressive by the fact that the number of items on it is quite moderate. The quality of the wines is generally high, thanks to producers such as Hugel, Drouhin and Guigal . Lucky customers who rushed to the shop as soon as the current list appeared could also have fought over a single case of Guigal's Côte Rôtie La Landonne for a bargain price of £29.50 (plus VAT) per bottle.

21	£18.75	FERRARI BRUT PERLE 1985 Trentino-Alto Adige (It)
22	£18.98	VEUVE CLICQUOT DEMI-SEC CHAMPAGNE (F)
102	£8.95	MARQUES DE MURRIETA RIOJA BLANCO RESERVA 1985 Rioja (Sp)
150	£7.60	STONELEIGH SAUVIGNON BLANC 1989 Marlborough (NZ)
226	£4.25	DOMAINE DU BOSQUET CANET, LISTEL 1987 Midi (F)
288	£7.85	CHATEAU MUSAR 1982 Bekaa Valley (Leb)
336	£52.00	OPUS ONE, ROBERT MONDAVI 1987 Napa Valley (Cal)
412	£8.88	CAMPO FIORIN VALPOLICELLA, MASI 1986 Veneto (It)
451	£9.75	MARQUIS DE MURRIETA RIOJA TINTO RESERVA 1985 (Sp)
452	£15.00	RIOJA RESERVA 904, LA RIOJA ALTA 1978 (Sp)
480	£11.50	DOS CORTADOS, WILLIAMS AND HUMBERT, Jerez (Sp)
481	£11.75	MANZANILLA PASADA DE SANLUCAR ALMACENISTA, LUSTAU, Jerez (Sp)
483	£16.98	APOSTOLES, GONZALEZ BYASS, Jerez (Sp)
487	£8.60	TAYLOR'S FIRST ESTATE PORT LUGAR DAS LAGES, Douro (P)
495	£19.75	FONSECA-GUIMARAENS 1976 Douro (P)

MIL   Millevini

3 Middlewood Road, High Lane, Stockport, Cheshire (0663 64366). Mail order Italian specialist; no shop, though orders may be collected. **Delivery:** free within 20 miles, nationally at cost, 3% collection discount. **Tasting:** for outside clubs on request. **Discounts:** 4% on orders over 3 cases.

Last year, we reported that Richard Lever's company was beginning to reap the benefits of the growing interest in Italian wine. Unfortunately, he could have done without the interest of one sizeable customer which proved to be unable to pay for any of its purchases. The blow was severe enough to force Millevini to stop buying completely for three months, and to live on its stocks.

It is never easy being an independent merchant at the best of times; the beginning of the 1990s has been especially unkind to firms like Mr Lever's, which are too small to withstand the successive blows of interest rates, duty increases, business rates and bad debts.

Millevini deserves the support of Italian wine lovers and anyone else with even the slightest curiosity about good wines; bottles from Cornacchia, Valentini and Fenocchio are, Richard Lever claims, particularly good value because he imports them directly. We would also recommend wines from Tedeschi, Allegrini and Pieropan, and hopefully, though stocks were unconfirmed as we went to press, the wonderful Isole e Olena Ceparello.

MTL   Mitchells Wine Merchants

354 Meadowhead, Sheffield, S.Yorkshire S8 7UJ (0742 745587/740311). Expanding independent family merchant with 3 branches in Sheffield. **Opening Hours:** 8.30am-10pm Mon-Sat; 12 -3pm, 7pm-9pm Sun. **Delivery:** free within 10 miles, nationally at cost. **Tastings:** regularly in-store plus tutored tastings with more organised events planned. **Discounts:** 5% on unbroken cases, 2.5% on mixed cases.

John Mitchell and Dave Marriott , we suspect, get more *fun* out of selling booze of every kind than the vast majority of their peers. It is easy to imagine them sitting in their tasting room (complete with Union Jack tablecloth) sampling a range of beers (of every nationality, from Australia to Zimbabwe) whiskies (the Mitchells list offer 60 malts) and wines from their range of 600 - including, quite possibly the Majorcan wines of which they are probably the only stockists.

The reason we like Mitchells so much is the down-to-earth way in which they approach the subject. How many other companies' handwritten 'Vintage Choice' list begins with Georges Duboeuf Beaujolais and progresses to 'Belle Epoque + loads more' via La Tâche, Lafite 1979 and Muscadet 'Le Prestige'? Mitchells like to describe themselves as 'Sheffield's leading independent Wine Merchants for the last 25 Years'; we prefer to think of them as the ones with whom we'd most like to share a pint - or a glass of (very decent) wine.

19	£16.65	DEVAUX CHAMPAGNE CUVEE ROSEE (F)
22	£20.75	VEUVE CLICQUOT DEMI-SEC CHAMPAGNE (F)
181	£4.25	LAMBERHURST SEYVAL BLANC 1988 Kent (UK)
192	£6.95	DEINHARD HOCHHEIM HERITAGE SELECTION 1988 Rheingau (G)
226	£4.19	DOMAINE DU BOSQUET CANET, LISTEL 1987 Midi (F)
280	£5.25	ORLANDO RF CABERNET SAUVIGNON 1988 South Australia (Aus)
336	£47.55	OPUS ONE, ROBERT MONDAVI 1987 Napa Valley (Cal)

449	£5.29	**CAMPO VIEJO RIOJA GRAN RESERVA** 1980 (Sp)
481	£9.95	**MANZANILLA PASADA DE SANLUCAR ALMACENISTA, LUSTAU**, Jerez (Sp)
483	£15.99	**APOSTOLES, GONZALEZ BYASS**, Jerez (Sp)
487	£7.59	**TAYLOR'S FIRST ESTATE PORT LUGAR DAS LAGES**, Douro (P)
495	£16.69	**FONSECA-GUIMARAENS** 1976 Douro (P)
500	£2.09	**PETILLANT DE LISTEL**, Midi (F)

TMW The Moffat Wine Shop

8 Well Street, Moffat, DG10 9DP, South West-Scotland (0683 20554). Ambitiously-stocked local wine merchant to 200 Lowland Scots and keen wine drinkers from Carlisle. **Opening Hours**: 9-5, Monday-Saturday. **Delivery**: free locally, nationally at cost. **Tastings**: occasional. **Discounts**: 5% on case purchases.

Tony McIlwrick's wine business grew out of the cellar of the hotel he used to run in Moffat. Today, this family-run merchant ('we have no staff') is an exemplary blend of modern vinous curiosity and good old traditional small town service.

3	£7.45	**LINDAUER, MONTANA** (NZ)
11	£10.86	**DEUTZ MARLBOROUGH CUVEE** (NZ)
22	£17.25	**VEUVE CLICQUOT DEMI-SEC CHAMPAGNE** (F)
87	£4.95	**ORLANDO RF CHARDONNAY** 1989 S E Australia (Aus)
150	£6.59	**STONELEIGH SAUVIGNON BLANC** 1989 Marlborough (NZ)
280	£4.95	**ORLANDO RF CABERNET SAUVIGNON** 1988 South Australia (Aus)
281	£4.99	**MONTANA CABERNET SAUVIGNON** 1988 Marlborough (NZ)
412	£7.99	**CAMPO FIORIN VALPOLICELLA, MASI** 1986 Veneto (It)
481	£10.48	**MANZANILLA PASADA DE SANLUCAR ALMACENISTA, LUSTAU**, Jerez (Sp)
482	£9.18	**ROYAL CORREGIDOR RICH RARE OLD OLOROSO, SANDEMAN**, Jerez (Sp)
483	£13.75	**APOSTOLES, GONZALEZ BYASS**, Jerez (Sp)

MOR Moreno Wines

Spanish and Portuguese Specialist of the Year

2 Norfolk Place, London W2 1QN (071 723 6897) & 11 Marylands Road, London W9 2DU (071 286 0678). Independent Spanish specialist. **Opening Hours**: 9.30am-8pm Mon-Fri; 10am-8pm Sat. **Delivery**: free locally and nationally for orders over 5 cases. **Tastings**: monthly club meetings, in-store tastings. **Discounts**: on mixed cases (collected).

We are delighted to be able to give Manuel Moreno and his two associates, the colourfully-named Theo Sloot and Harold Heckle, the award for Spanish and Portuguese specialist of the year, particularly because we know how hard it can be to specialise in these particular countries. Australians, Frenchmen and Italians galore are endlessly available to lecture fascinatingly on their wines; Iberian winemakers are more reticent. Similarly, those other countries are forever coming up with exciting new wines; in Spain and Portugal you really have to go looking for them. But over the last year, through initiatives like their Wine Club and the regular tutored tastings, the Moreno team have done a great job in focusing attention on the developments which are beginning to happen. The shops, by the way, also contain a good range of non-Hispanic wines, including the South Americans for which Moreno is the UK importer.

38	£4.35	**TOLLANA DRY WHITE** 1988 S E Australia (Aus)
102	£7.95	**MARQUES DE MURRIETA RIOJA BLANCO RESERVA** 1985 Rioja (Sp)
181	£4.39	**LAMBERHURST SEYVAL BLANC** 1988 Kent (UK)
287	£7.79	**RAIMAT CABERNET SAUVIGNON** 1985 Lérida (Sp)
437	£3.99	**SENORIO DE LOS LLANOS RESERVA** 1982 Valdepeñas (Sp)
445	£5.39	**NAVAJAS RIOJA CRIANZA TINTO** 1985 (Sp)
449	£8.25	**CAMPO VIEJO RIOJA GRAN RESERVA** 1980 (Sp)
451	£8.85	**MARQUIS DE MURRIETA RIOJA TINTO RESERVA** 1985 (Sp)
452	£13.65	**RIOJA RESERVA 904, LA RIOJA ALTA** 1978 (Sp)
483	£16.95	**APOSTOLES, GONZALEZ BYASS**, Jerez (Sp)

M&V | Morris & Verdin

Burgundy Specialist of the Year

28 Churton St, London SW1V 2LP (071 630 8888). Serious- but not too serious- independent merchant. **Opening Hours:** 9.30am-5.30pm Mon-Fri; 10am-5pm Sat. **Delivery:** free locally, nationally at cost. **Tastings:** occasionally in-store. **Discounts:** negotiable.

This year, if the rumours we have heard are correct, Jasper Morris will take over the running of the Institute of Masters of Wine, the hyper-august body of which he has been a member since being the youngest candidate to pass its exams.

The Award his firm was given by the *Guide's* judges this year was for its Burgundy list, which scored particularly for its combination of quality and - a major achievement in this region - value for money. Unlike some apologists for Burgundy, Morris does not slavishly follow producers from one year to the next; where standards fall, he reacts swiftly, by de-listing them; where prices are exaggerated, he argues his corner and refuses to buy.

But Burgundy is not Morris's only interest; his is one of the best selections of top class New World Pinot Noirs and Chardonnays in the country and he is a reliable source of *en primeur* claret. If you can drag yourself away from the seductions of Burgundies from growers like Dominique Lafon and the indomitable Mademoiselle Monthélie Douharet.

115	£12	**VITA NOVA CHARDONNAY** 1989 Santa Barbara (Cal)
154	£8	**SHAW AND SMITH SAUVIGNON BLANC** 1990 South Australia (Aus)
313	£10.50	**CLOUDY BAY CABERNET MERLOT** 1989 Marlborough (NZ)
397	£25.50	**VOSNE ROMANEE LES BEAUX MONTS, DANIEL RION** 1988 Burgundy (F)
472	£12.40	**JURANCON MOELLEUX VENDANGE TARDIVE, DOMAINE CAUHAPE** 1988 South West (F)

NZC | New Zealand Wine Club

PO Box 110, London WC2N 52H (071 930 1309). Mail order, free-membership club for Kiwi-ophiles. Delivery: free for orders over £75. **Tastings:** regular tutored, plus the annual Great Australasian Wine Tasting.

Keep the month of May 1992 free. We don't yet know precisely which date you should block off in your diary, but we'd certainly hate to miss the Great Australasian Wine Tasting at which some 300 wines from both coasts of the Tasman will be available for tasting. While waiting for that event, you could slake some of your more immediate thirst and curiosity, by becoming a member of this new Club which, if it develops half as well as the Australian Wine Centre from which it was spawned, will provide a pretty comprehensive range of Kiwi wines.

3	£7.49	**LINDAUER, MONTANA** (NZ)
11	£10.99	**DEUTZ MARLBOROUGH CUVEE** (NZ)
117	£11.99	**ELSTON CHARDONNAY, TE MATA** 1989 (NZ)
140	£4.99	**COOKS HAWKES BAY SAUVIGNON BLANC** 1989 Hawkes Bay (NZ)
150	£5.99	**STONELEIGH SAUVIGNON BLANC** 1989 Marlborough (NZ)
281	£5.49	**MONTANA CABERNET SAUVIGNON** 1988 Marlborough (NZ)

LNR | Le Nez Rouge Wine Club

12 Brewery Road, London N7 9NH (071 609 4711) & The Birches Trading Estate, East Grinstead, Sussex RH19 1XZ. Mail-order club, now with retail outlets. **Opening Hours:** 9am-5.30pm Mon-Fri; 10am-2pm Sat. **Delivery:** free locally, nationally at cost. **Tastings:** in-store every Saturday, plus tutored events. **Discounts:** £2 per unbroken case, £1 per mixed case on wines collected.

'Wines that we used to drink before poverty struck, wines of the standard to which one had got used, to use a favourite expression of my second wife's lawyer during the divorce...' Joseph Berkmann is inimitable (however tempting it is to mimic his unmistakable Middle-European accented expletives), as are the wines offered by this, the retail arm of Berkmann Wine Cellars. If you love good Burgundy, you almost certainly already know the producers whose wines Le Nez Rouge sells; if you want an instant course in the subject, the list is a first class guide. And then you could move on to Bordeaux and, via the excellent Petersons and Morton Estate, Australasia.

JN | James Nicholson Wine Merchants

27a Killyleagh St, Crossgar, Co. Down, N Ireland (0396 830091). New outlet for established import & wholesale business. **Opening Hours:** 10am-7pm Mon-Thurs; 10am-8pm Fri; 10am-6pm Sat. **Delivery:** free nationally. **Tastings:** regularly in-store plus tutored tastings and organised events. **Discounts:** 10% (approx) per case.

Making a second appearance in the *Guide*, James Nicholson continues to offer a range of wines which ought to send at least a few English wine lovers scurrying across the water. If they get their timing right, they could also attend one of this keen merchants tastings or dinners which, if the prices of the 1991 events were typical (£12.50 for a tasting tutored by Gerard Uhlen of Joseph Drouhin) are among the wine world's best buys.

4	£7.50	**CHEVALIER DE MONCONTOUR VOUVRAY MOUSSEUX** 1987 Loire (F)
58	£5.40	**CHATEAU COUCHEROY BLANC, GRAVES, ANDRE LURTON** 1989 Bordeaux (F)
138	£4.80	**DOMAINE DES CORBILLIERES, SAUVIGNON DE TOURAINE** 1989 Loire (F)
251	£4.45	**CHATEAU BELLEVUE LA FORET, FRONTONNAIS** 1989 South West (F)
268	£4.65	**CHATEAU DE PARENCHERE BORDEAUX ROUGE, J GAZANIOL** 1988 (F)
282	£9.95	**CHATEAU COUCHEROY BORDEAUX ROUGE** 1988 (F)
292	£7.75	**'L' DE LOUVIERE, PESSAC LEOGNAN, ANDRE LURTON** 1988 Bordeaux (F)
320	£13.25	**CHATEAU LEOVILLE BARTON, ST JULIEN** 1987 Bordeaux (F)
336	£48.00	**OPUS ONE, ROBERT MONDAVI** 1987 Napa Valley (Cal)
352	£5.75	**COTES DU RHONE, GUIGAL** 1988 (F)

| 374 | £11.25 | **RIDGE GEYSERVILLE ZINFANDEL** 1988 Santa Clara (Cal) |
| 479 | £5.30 | **LA GITANA MANZANILLA, HIDALGO,** Jerez (Sp) |

N&P | Nickolls & Perks

37 High Street, Stourbridge, West Midlands, DY8 1TA (0384 440786). Brilliant Bordeaux specialists with a branch in nearby Lye. **Opening Hours:** 9am-10pm Mon-Sat. **Delivery**; free locally; **Tastings**: regularly in store and tutored. **Discounts:** 12.5%.

Pages 42 and 43 of the Nickolls & Perks list say a lot about this firm. Nearly three dozen 1989 en primeur Bordeaux - and the choice between 1904 and 1908 Cockburns, or 1922 Fonseca. This last wine, priced at £90, is a relative bargain in this company; this is no place for the bargain hunter or the penny-pincher but with Japanese buyers eager to buy, why should it be?. The list cover claims that if 'you wish to trace the world's finest wines, you should look no further.' We might feel tempted to stray a little to find a broader range of Burgundies (the now less-than-brilliant Pierre Ponnelle holds sway) and Californians, but the Bordeaux and ports would hold our attention very easily.

NIC | Nicolas

157 Great Portland St, London W1N 5FPB (071 436 9636). 5-branch West London chain. **Opening Hours:** 9am - 9pm Mon-Sat; 12 - 3pm & 7pm - 9pm Sun. **Delivery:** free locally, nationally at cost. **Tastings:** regularly in-store, tutored tastings. **Discounts:** 5% for up to 5 cases, 7.5% for 6+ cases.

'Gift wrapping *French style* has proved to be very popular'. Actually, the reference to Gallic style was unnecessary; since its purchase by Nicolas in 1989, the former Buckinghams shops have become very difficult to distinguish from the original item on the other side of the Channel. Cursory examination of the chain's newsletter similarly reveals it to be a (not always perfect) translation from the French. Profit margins are still pretty much *à la française*.

Given the traditional lack of interest in non Gallic wines in France, (and despite the price list's evident confusion over one or two nationalities) it is encouraging to see a number of New World wines appearing in the shops, including examples from Coldstream Hills and Ridge. And worth remembering that Nicolas' French cellars give the chain access to some wonderful old wines.

79	£3.95	**COTES DE ST MONT, PLAIMONT** 1990 South West (F)
295	£9.95	**WYNNS CABERNET SAUVIGNON** 1985 Coonawarra (Aus)
318	£17.50	**CHATEAU HAUT BAGES AVEROUS, PAUILLAC, CHATEAU LYNCH-BAGES** 1985 Bordeaux (F)

NRW | Noble Rot Wine Warehouse

18 Market Street, Bromsgrove, Worcs B61 8DA (0527) 575606. Majestic-style, innovative warehouse. breaking new ground. **Opening hours:** 10am-7pm Mon-Sat. **Delivery:** free for 3 or more cases within a 5 mile radius. **Tastings:** regular and tutored.

'We aim to play an active and enthusiastic part in promoting awareness and knowledge of wine in the north Worcestershire area where, historically, there has been little to satisfy growing consumer demands'.

Peter Weston and his daughter Julie Wyres have clearly learned from their experience at Wilsons, Peter Dominic and - clearly - Majestic. After the depressing experience of reading the current list from that once-brilliant chain, we were delighted to find much of its old style on offer in Bromsgrove. The range is broad, the producers reliable and the prices reasonable. What more could anyone ask?

19	£17.99	DEVAUX CHAMPAGNE CUVEE ROSEE (F)
29	£2.79	CUVEE JEAN-PAUL BLANC SEC VIN DE TABLE, PAUL BOUTINOT (F)
46	£3.99	CHARDONNAY, DOMAINE DES FLINES, VIN DE PAYS DE LA LOIRE 1990 (F)
54	£5.25	ALSACE TOKAY PINOT GRIS, CAVE VINICOLE DE TURCKHEIM 1990 (F)
59	£5.25	HOUGHTON SUPREME WHITE 1990 Swan Valley (Aus)
83	£4.35	CALITERRA CHARDONNAY 1990 Maipo Valley (Ch)
140	£5.39	COOKS HAWKES BAY SAUVIGNON BLANC 1989 Hawkes Bay (NZ)
145	£5.99	SAUVIGNON DE ST BRIS, DOMAINE FELIX 1990 Burgundy (F)
153	£8.99	POUILLY FUME LES CHANTALOUETTES 1989 Loire (F)
196	£4.85	THREE CHOIRS MEDIUM DRY ENGLISH TABLE WINE 1989 Gloucs (UK)
204	£4.39	CHATEAU LE RAZ, BERGERAC ROSE 1990 South West (F)
258	£3.99	SVISCHTOV CABERNET SAUVIGNON CONTROLIRAN 1985 Svischtov (Bul)
267	£4.39	CHATEAU LE RAZ, BERGERAC ROUGE 1989 South West (F)
349	£4.75	RASTEAU COTES DU RHONE VILLAGES,VIGNERONS DE RASTEAU 1989 (F)
377	£3.79	ANJOU GAMAY, PIERRE-YVES TIJOU 1990 Loire (F)
426	£15.75	CEPPARELLO, ISOLE E OLENA 1988 Tuscany (It)
442	£5.75	TEMPRANILLO, BODEGAS OCHOA 1987 Navarra (Sp)

N1	The Nobody Inn

Doddiscombsleigh, Nr Exeter, Devon. (0647 52394) .Restaurant, hotel, wine shopetc... **Opening hours**: 11am-11pm Mon-Sat; 12pm-3pm Sun. **Delivery**: free locally. **Tastings**: top class tutored events. **Discount**: 5% on mixed cases.

This is, quite simply, an astonishing list. Astonishingly long, well thought-out and written. Nick Borst Smith clearly enjoys putting it together almost as much as he must relish choosing its wines. The tasting notes are among the most characterful around - 'Ch. Smith Haut-Lafitte: A renovated property now producing excellent wines after years of rubbish...' 'Essling Sparkling: I will call this English Champagne until the Wine Standards Board catches up with me'. If only more of the wine trade could learn to be so forthright.

The range is so good that it is almost impossible to choose a single area of over-riding excellence, but the Loires ranging back to 1935 and the malt whiskies are particulary stunning.

79	£3.69	COTES DE ST MONT, PLAIMONT 1990 South West (F)
89	£5.22	MOONDAH BROOK VERDELHO 1990 (Aus)
90	£5.78	LINDEMANS BIN 65 CHARDONNAY 1989 S E Australia (Aus)
114	£8.04	DOMAINE CAUHAPE, JURANCON SEC (OAKED) 1988 South West (F)
117	£10.33	ELSTON CHARDONNAY, TE MATA 1989 (NZ)
118	£12.11	VIDAL RESERVE CHARDONNAY 1990 Hawkes Bay (NZ)
175	£5.75	MOSCATO D'ASTI, MICHELE CHIARLO 1990 Piedmont (It)
191	£7.98	WEHLENER SONNENUHR RIESLING KABINETT, WEINGUT DR LOOSEN 1989 M-S-R (G)
196	£4.50	THREE CHOIRS MEDIUM DRY ENGLISH TABLE WINE 1989 Gloucs (UK)
229	£6.46	CHATEAU DE FLOTIS, COTES DE FRONTONNAIS 1988 South West (F)

258	£4.29	**SVISCHTOV CABERNET SAUVIGNON CONTROLIRAN**, 1985 Svischtov (Bul)
283	£4.52	**SEAVIEW LIMITED RELEASE CABERNET SAUVIGNON** 1988 South Australia (Aus)
288	£6.65	**CHATEAU MUSAR** 1982 Bekaa Valley (Leb)
293	£6.94	**JAMIESONS RUN RED, MILDARA** 1987 Coonawarra (Aus)
313	£9.91	**CLOUDY BAY CABERNET MERLOT** 1989 Marlborough (NZ)
331	£17.99	**PENFOLDS BIN 707 CABERNET SAUVIGNON** 1987 South Australia (Aus)
336	£43.17	**OPUS ONE, ROBERT MONDAVI** 1987 Napa Valley (Cal)
344	£4.41	**PENFOLDS BIN 2 SHIRAZ/MATARO** 1989 Barossa Valley (Aus)
392	£11.63	**SANFORD PINOT NOIR** 1986 Santa Barbara (Cal)
394	£17.49	**CALERA SELLECK PINOT NOIR** 1987 San Benito (Cal)
458	£7.05	**YALUMBA MUSEUM SHOW RESERVE MUSCAT,** Rutherglen (Aus)
460	£13.36	**CAMPBELLS OLD RUTHERGLEN LIQUEUR MUSCAT** (Aus)
472	£9.62	**JURANCON MOELLEUX VENDANGE TARDIVE, DOMAINE CAUHAPE** 1988 SW (F)
479	£5.30	**LA GITANA MANZANILLA, HIDALGO,** Jerez (Sp)

RN | **Rex Norris**

50 Queens Rd, Haywards Heath, W Sussex RH16 1EE (0444 454756). Independent merchant with a constantly changing selection. **Opening Hours:** 9am-5.30pm Mon,Tues,Thurs; 9am-1pm Wed; 9am-7.30pm Fri; 9am-4.30pm Sat. **Delivery:** free within 5 miles. **Tastings:** wines regularly open for sampling plus occasional in-store tastings. **Discounts:** 10% on cases (7% if paying by credit card).

Still surviving, despite last year's fears of the Business Rate, Rex Norris continues to offer the citizenry of Haywards Heath and its environs an ever changing array of sensibly chosen wines. Don't ask for a list by the way; quantities are too small for one to exist.

OD | **Oddbins**

Joint Wine Merchant of the Year and German Specialist of the Year

Head Office, 31-33 Weir Rd, Durnsford Industrial Estate, Wimbledon, London SW19 8UG (081 879 1199). 144-branch heavyweight champion of the High Street. **Opening Hours:** Mon - Sat 9am - 9pm Sun 12 - 3pm 7pm - 9pm **Delivery:** free locally. **Tastings:** regularly in-store plus organised events. **Discounts:** 5% on cases and a '7 for the price of 6' offer on all Champagnes.

Well, Martina Navratilova won Wimbledon more times than Oddbins has received our top Award. So far. What can we say? Except that, this unpredictable, irreverent and infuriatingly gifted firm was equally shortlisted for Best Wine List, New World Specialist and German Specialist. Having watched the Oddbins buyers at work, and seen the bruised shins of producers and wholesalers who have tried to sell them anything ordinary or overpriced, we know what has given this chain its edge. And then of course, the keen interest of both shop staff and customers has helped too.

Oddbins was removed from the National High Street category by our judges - for the simple reason that they felt that the company's increasingly successful Oddbins Card (effectively a mail order club offering special batches of wine) took it into a category of its own.

What Oddbins does involves no magic - merely a different way of approaching their business. In 1991, Victoria Wine expanded its German range, following the rule book to the letter; it bought wines made from the right grape varieties, grown in big-name vineyards by top-rank producers. Oddbins opted instead for a team mostly made up of unknowns. So guess whose customers got the tastiest wines and the best bargains? Guess which company (we suspect) derived the greatest profit from the excercise? (And guess which company was voted our German Specialist of the Year?) It's a lesson that could be learned by every merchant in the country that has ever taken the lazy, easy way out by buying the first wine they are offered.

Today, after four previous wins, Oddbins is a worthy joint recipient of its award. Stated simply, its range, its spirit of innovation, its list(s), its staff and the ambience of its shops all make it a role model for almost all of Britain's other wine merchants

3	£6.99	LINDAUER, MONTANA (NZ)
5	£7.99	CUVEE NAPA BLANC DE NOIR, DOMAINE MUMM, Napa Valley (Cal)
6	£7.99	TALTARNI BRUT TACHE, Pyrenees (Aus)
7	£9.49	MAISON DEUTZ SPARKLING, Napa Valley (Cal)
8	£9.99	SEPPELT'S GREAT WESTERN SHOW SPARKLING SHIRAZ 1985 (Aus)
10	£9.99	SALINGER METHODE CHAMPENOISE, SEPPELT 1989 (Aus)
11	£10.99	DEUTZ MARLBOROUGH CUVEE (NZ)
14	£12.99	DEHOURS CHAMPAGNE (F)
20	£19.99	CA DEL BOSCO CREMANT, Lombardy (It)
23	£19.99	HEIDSIECK DRY MONOPOLE ROSE CHAMPAGNE 1985 (F)
25	£26.00	BILLECART BRUT CHAMPAGNE 1985 (F)
33	£3.19	DOMAINE DU TARIQUET, COTES DE GASCOGNE 1990 SW (F)
52	£4.79	BOURGOGNE ALIGOTE, JAFFELIN 1989 Burgundy (F)
53	£4.75	MITCHELTON MARSANNE (UNWOODED) 1990 Goulburn Valley (Aus)
54	£4.49	ALSACE TOKAY PINOT GRIS, CAVE VINICOLE DE TURCKHEIM 1990 (F)
56	£4.99	SIMON WHITLAM SAUVIGNON/SEMILLON 1989 Hunter Valley (Aus)
59	£4.99	HOUGHTON SUPREME WHITE 1990 Swan Valley (Aus)
80	£3.75	KILLAWARRA CHARDONNAY 1990 South Australia (Aus)
82	£4.69	COTES DE ROUSSILLON JEAN BESOMBES, LES VIGNERONS DE RIVESALTES 1988 Midi (F)
83	£4.39	CALITERRA CHARDONNAY 1990 Maipo Valley (Ch)
87	£4.69	ORLANDO RF CHARDONNAY 1989 S E Australia (Aus)
89	£4.99	MOONDAH BROOK VERDELHO 1990 (Aus)
91	£5.49	CHEVALIER ST VINCENT BORDEAUX BLANC, UNION ST VINCENT 1989 (F)
94	£5.99	DOMAINE DE RIBONNET CHARDONNAY 1989 South West (F)
95	£6.49	SCHINUS MOLLE CHARDONNAY 1990 Mornington Peninsula (Aus)
104	£7.99	PENFOLDS PADTHAWAY CHARDONNAY 1990 (Aus)
106	£7.99	WYNNS COONAWARRA ESTATE CHARDONNAY 1989 (Aus)
107	£7.99	KRONDORF SHOW RESERVE CHARDONNAY 1989 Barossa Valley (Aus)
108	£8.99	EILEEN HARDY CHARDONNAY, HARDY'S 1988 South Australia (Aus)
113	£12.49	CHATEAU LA LOUVIERE, PESSAC-LEOGNAN 1989 Bordeaux (F)
115	£12.99	VITA NOVA CHARDONNAY 1989 Santa Barbara (Cal)
126	£23.99	CHASSAGNE MONTRACHET LES MORGEOTS, CHARTRON ET TREBUCHET 1988 Burgundy (F)
143	£4.99	DOMAINE DU RELAIS DE POSTE, SAUVIGNON DE ST BRIS, LUC SORIN 1989 Burgundy (F)
144	£5.79	DOMAINE DES AUBUISIERES, VOUVRAY SEC 1990 Loire (F)
148	£6.49	SELAKS SAUVIGNON BLANC 1990 (NZ)
151	£6.99	SCHINUS MOLLE SAUVIGNON BLANC 1990 Victoria (Aus)
158	£4.39	GROS MANSENG CUVEE TARDIVE, LA MOTTE 1989 South West (F)
164	£12.99	CUVEE PIERRE DEMI SEC, DOMAINE BALLAND CHAPUIS 1990 Loire (F)
165	£3.49	BAROSSA VALLEY ESTATES GEWURZTRAMINER 1987 Barossa Valley (Aus)
178	£3.69	SEAVIEW RHINE RIESLING 1988 Coonawarra (Aus)
179	£4.25	ROSEMOUNT RIESLING 1990 Hunter Valley (Aus)

186	£5.49	FREINSHEIMER GOLDBERG KABINETT HALBTROCKEN, LINGENFELDER 1986 Rheinpfalz (G)
199	£5.99	UNGSTEINER HERRENBERG RIESLING SPATLESE, FUHRMANN EYNUEL 1989 Rheinpfalz (G)
200	£9.99	RUSSBACHER ESELSHAUT RIESLANER AUSLESE, MULLER CATTOIR 1989 Rheinpfalz (G)
244	£2.99	CAMPO DEI FIORI CABERNET SAUVIGNON 1988 (Ch)
251	£3.69	CHATEAU BELLEVUE LA FORET, FRONTONNAIS 1989 South West (F)
266	£3.99	CHATEAU LA CROIX SIMON BORDEAUX ROUGE 1989 (F)
277	£4.99	CHATEAU BERTINERIE BARRAILH BORDEAUX ROUGE 1989 (F)
278	£4.99	FOUNDATION 1725 ROUGE, BARTON ET GUESTIER 1989 Bordeaux (F)
279	£4.69	GLEN ELLEN MERLOT 1987 Sonoma (Cal)
280	£4.69	ORLANDO RF CABERNET SAUVIGNON 1988 South Australia (Aus)
281	£5.25	MONTANA CABERNET SAUVIGNON 1988 Marlborough (NZ)
283	£5.49	SEAVIEW LIMITED RELEASE CABERNET SAUVIGNON 1988 South Australia (Aus)
285	£5.99	CUVEE CLEMENT ADER CABERNET MERLOT, DOMAINE DE RIBONNET 1989 SW (F)
292	£6.99	'L' DE LOUVIERE, PESSAC LEOGNAN, ANDRE LURTON 1988 Bordeaux (F)
295	£6.25	WYNNS CABERNET SAUVIGNON 1985 Coonawarra (Aus)
300	£7.99	BAUDIN, CAPEL VALE 1987 Western Australia (Aus)
314	£9.99	NEWTON CABERNET SAUVIGNON 1986 Napa Valley (Cal)
315	£9.99	MOUNTADAM CABERNET SAUVIGNON 1987 High Eden Ridge (Aus)
316	£11.99	TOURELLES DE LONGUEVILLE, PAUILLAC, CHATEAU PICHON-LONGUEVILLE-BARON 1988 Bordeaux (F)
329	£14.99	WOLF BLASS BLACK LABEL CABERNET SAUVIGNON 1986 South Australia (Aus)
330	£14.99	PAVILLON ROUGE DE CHATEAU MARGAUX 1988 Bordeaux (F)
331	£14.99	PENFOLDS BIN 707 CABERNET SAUVIGNON 1987 South Australia (Aus)
344	£3.95	PENFOLDS BIN 2 SHIRAZ/MATARO 1989 Barossa Valley (Aus)
347	£4.19	SEAVIEW CABERNET SHIRAZ 1989 South Australia (Aus)
349	£4.29	RASTEAU COTES DU RHONE VILLAGES, VIGNERONS DE RASTEAU 1989 (F)
352	£4.99	COTES DU RHONE, GUIGAL 1988 (F)
353	£4.69	PENFOLDS BIN 28 KALIMNA SHIRAZ 1988 South Australia (Aus)
356	£4.99	DAVID WYNN SHIRAZ 1990 High Eden Ridge (Aus)
367	£6.99	TALTARNI SHIRAZ 1988 Pyrenees (Aus)
370	£8.99	WOLF BLASS PRESIDENTS SELECTION SHIRAZ 1987 South Australia (Aus)
379	£4.19	MITCHELTON CAB MAC 1990 Goulburn Valley (Aus)
385	£6.99	CHIROUBLES, A MEZIAT 1989 Beaujolais (F)
397	£21.99	VOSNE ROMANEE LES BEAUX MONTS, DANIEL RION 1988 Burgundy (F)
398	£29.99	CLOS DE LA ROCHE, JAFFELIN 1988 Burgundy (F)
408	£4.99	BONARDA OLTREPO PAVESE, FUGAZZA 1987 Lombardy (It)
413	£6.99	DOLCETTO D'ALBA, CONTERNO 1988 Piedmont (It)
421	£10.99	VIGNASERRA, VOERZIO 1988 Piedmont (It)
430	£15.99	BRUNELLO DEL MONTALCINO, POGGIO ANTICO 1985 Piedmont (It)
433	£18.99	BAROLO RISERVA, GIACOMO CONTERNO 1982 Piedmont (It)
434	£24.99	MAURIZIO ZANELLA, CA' DEL BOSCO 1988 Lombardy (It)
446	£5.89	GRAN SANGREDETORO RESERVA, TORRES 1986 Penedés (Sp)
456	£4.29	SAMOS MUSCAT, Samos (Gr)
461	£4.99	JURANCON MOELLEUX CUVEE THIBAULT, DOMAINE BELLEGARDE 1989 SW (F)
466	£5.99	THE HARDY COLLECTION PADTHAWAY RHINE RIESLING BEERENAUSLESE 1987 (Aus)
469	£9.98	CHATEAU BASTOR LAMONTAGNE, SAUTERNES 1988 Bordeaux (F)
470	£10.99	BURGLAYER SCHLOSSBERG RIESLING BEERENAUALESE, B A SCHAFER 1989 Nahe (G)
471	£10.99	VOUVRAY MOELLEUX LE MARIGNY, DOMAINE DES AUBUISIERES 1990 Loire (F)
473	£11.99	CALUSO PASSITO, VITTORIO BORATTO 1985 Piedmont (It)
474	£12.99	CHATEAU GUIRAUD, SAUTERNES 1988 Bordeaux (F)
475	£13.99	CHATEAU RIEUSSEC, SAUTERNES 1983 Bordeaux (F)

482	£14.49	ROYAL CORREGIDOR RICH RARE OLD OLOROSO, SANDEMAN, Jerez (Sp)
483	£14.49	APOSTOLES, GONZALEZ BYASS, Jerez (Sp)
490	£11.99	HUCHESON COLHEITA 1975 Douro (P)
493	£16.49	WARRE'S QUINTA DA CAVADINHA 1982 Douro (P)
494	£15.99	SANDEMAN IMPERIAL 20 YEAR OLD TAWNY PORT, Douro (P)
497	£18.95	DUQUE DE BRAGANZA 20 YEAR OLD TAWNY PORT, FERREIRA, Douro (P)
500	£1.89	PETILLANT DE LISTEL, Midi (F)

OLS | The Old St Wine Co

309 Old St, London EC1V 6LE (071 729 1768). Traditional City merchant. **Opening Hours:** 10am-7pm Mon-Fri; 11am-2pm Sat. **Delivery:** free within 18 miles, free nationally for orders over 4 cases. **Tastings:** regularly in-store, plus tutored events. **Discounts:** 5%per case, pay and carry.

Loire fans have two havens in London: the extraordinary RSJ restaurant on the South Bank, and the Old Street Wine Co. Both are run by people who are clearly passionate about the Chenin Blanc, Sauvignon Blanc and other assorted Loire varieties and by people who, in the case of Old Street, can and do tell you that 1984 was a great vintage for Muscadet.

Burgundies are somewhat more patchily dealt with, but the Bordeaux section is peppered with good value bottles.

139	£4.85	DOMAINE DU PRE BARON, SAUVIGNON DE TOURAINE 1989 Loire (F)
144	£6.95	DOMAINE DES AUBUISIERES, VOUVRAY SEC 1990 Loire (F)
219	£4.25	CHATEAU HELENE ROUGE, CORBIERES, MARIE-HELENE GAU 1987 Midi (F)
231	£4.98	CHATEAU DE LASTOURS CUVEE SIMONE DESCAMPS, CORBIERES 1989 Midi (F)
270	£4.95	CHATEAU LUGAUD, GRAVES, DIDIER MAY 1988 Bordeaux (F)
310	£8.50	BARON VILLENEUVE DE CANTERMERLE, HAUT-MEDOC, CHATEAU CANTEMERLE 1986 Bordeaux (F)
359	£5.95	CROZES HERMITAGE, DELAS FRERES 1989 Rhône (F)
375	£11.78	COTE ROTIE SEIGNEUR DE MOUGIRON, DELAS FRERES 1988 Rhône (F)
471	£10.75	VOUVRAY MOELLEUX LE MARIGNY, DOMAINE DES AUBUISIERES 1990 Loire (F)
475	£19.85	CHATEAU RIEUSSEC, SAUTERNES 1983 Bordeaux (F)

ORG | Organic Wine Co

PO Box 81, High Wycombe, Bucks, HP13 5QN (0494 446557). Independent merchant specialising in organic wine, but only if it tastes good. **Opening Hours:** 9am-5.30pm Mon-Fri; 9am-1pm Sat. **Delivery:** free within 15 miles, nationally at cost. **Tastings:** regular tastings at various locations; vineyard visits. **Discounts:** negotiable.

1991 has been a busy year for Tony Mason, the man with the mobile Organic Jazz Bar. He has been benefiting amply from the growing interest in Organic wine and in the shaking-out of some of his less quality-conscious competitors. Mr Mason has always chosen his Organic wines for their quality rather than their level of green-ness, and the success of the extremely varied range of wines he entered into the International Wine Challenge proves just how well healthily-made wines can fare in blind tastings.

213	£2.89	VIN DE PAYS DU GARD, ALBARIC, Midi (F)
230	£4.49	MAS DE GOURGONNIER TRADITION, COTEAUX D'AIX EN PROVENCE LES BAUX 1989 Midi (F)
355	£4.69	DOMAINE ST APOLLINAIRE (ORGANIC), COTES DU RHONE 1989 (F)

| 362 | £5.99 | VIKING ZINFANDEL, OLSON VINEYARD 1987 Mendocino (Cal) |
| 393 | £12.99 | HAUTES COTES DE NUITS, ALAIN VERDET 1986 Burgundy (F) |

PAL | Pallant Wines

Apuldram Manor Farm, Appledram Lane,Chichester,West Sussex PO20 7PE (0243 788475). Cow shed based by -the-bottle wine warehouse. **Delivery**: free locally, nationally at cost. **Opening hours**: 9.30 am-5pm Mon-Sat; 10.30 am-1 pm Sun. **Tastings**: Occasional in-store plus wine of the month.**Discount**; 50p-£1 per case.

Visitors to the D-Day Museum should turn their back on the Spitfire and head into the converted cow shed where they will find a small but growing range of wines including a number of commendable organics (a category which does not however apply to Entre-deux-Greens the "golfers Bordeaux". You have to pick and chose carefully from the list but we'd be happy with the 1985 Rouge Homme Cabernet Shiraz, the Jean Cros Gaillac Gamay, and Prosper Maufoux's sparkling red Burgundy. The difference in the spelling between the lane and the farm is a deliberate trick to annoy editors.

P | Parfrements

68 Cecily Rd, Cheylesmore Rd, West Midlands CV3 5LA (0203 503646). One-man wholesale/retail business. **Opening Hours:** n/a - orders taken by telephone. **Delivery:** nationally at cost. **Tastings:** tutored tastings and organised events. **Discounts:** various.

The phrase 'Direct selling via tutored tastings in the home' rings awful bells with anyone familiar with the rip-off nature of some of the German companies who seduce addresses from unsuspecting visitors to the Ideal Home and Bristol Wine Fairs. But Gerald Gregory proves that this can be a really good way to buy some really good wine. The range is broad - from the wonderfully named Hungarian Kisburgundi, 'Germanic, fruity rather than grapey' red, to serious Vallet Frères Burgundies and single-estate ports from the Quinta do Infantado. What Gregory calls his 'Non EEC' selection is growing too. Beware, though, of the fact that prices are quoted excluding VAT.

29	£3.11	CUVEE JEAN-PAUL BLANC SEC VIN DE TABLE, PAUL BOUTINOT (F)
118	£13.00	VIDAL RESERVE CHARDONNAY 1989 Hawkes Bay (NZ)
231	£5.70	CHATEAU DE LASTOURS CUVEE SIMONE DESCAMPS, CORBIERES 1989 Midi (F)
302	£8.03	CHATEAU RAMAGE LA BATISSE, HAUT MEDOC 1988 Bordeaux (F)

THP | Thos. Peatling

Head office: Westgate House, Bury St Edmunds, Suffolk IP33 1QS (0284 755948). East of England chain with 33 branches. **Opening Hours:** varied. **Delivery:** free locally and for orders over 5 cases. **Tastings:** regularly in-store plus tutored tastings and organised events. **Discounts:** 5% on cases.

Over the last few years the quaintly named Thos. Peatling (previously Peatling and Cawdron) seems to getting younger. The previously unenticing shops have been re-fitted, the list has broadened in scope and in 1991 displayed the hand of some very up-to-the-minute designers. It is the only one we know which includes an illustration of Bishop Odo blessing wine and of a Picasso model drinking it. As for the contents of the list these are, as ever, exemplary. If you want individual estate Burgundies, 1961 Lafite or good Israeli Gamla Cabernet, you're in luck. Look out too for the Warre's Fine Old Port a weirdly wonderful 1966 vintage wine left in barrel for a decade; it can be bought from Peatling's and no-one else.

2	£6.79	**DIANE DE POITIERS SPARKLING CHARDONNAY,** Loire (F)	
32	£3.19	**DOMAINE DE LABALLE, VIN DE PAYS DES TERROIRS LANDAIS** 1990 S W (F)	
102	£9.09	**MARQUES DE MURRIETA RIOJA BLANCO RESERVA** 1985 Rioja (Sp)	
106	£8.75	**WYNNS COONAWARRA ESTATE CHARDONNAY** 1989 (Aus)	
107	£10.29	**KRONDORF SHOW RESERVE CHARDONNAY** 1989 Barossa Valley (Aus)	
116	£13.29	**CLOS DU BOIS CHARDONNAY, CALCAIRE VINEYARD** 1988 Sonoma (Cal)	
146	£6.49	**CHATEAU DE MONTFORT-VOUVRAY, CORDIER** 1988 Loire (F)	
148	£6.79	**SELAKS SAUVIGNON BLANC** 1990 (NZ)	
154	£7.99	**SHAW AND SMITH SAUVIGNON BLANC** 1990 South Australia (Aus)	
187	£6.99	**TRITTENHEIMER APOTHEKE KABINETT, F W GYMNASIUM** 1989 M-S-R (G)	
203	£4.59	**CHATEAU BAUDUC, BORDEAUX CLAIRET, DAVID THOMAS** 1990 (F)	
288	£7.25	**CHATEAU MUSAR** 1982 Bekaa Valley (Leb)	
289	£6.79	**LES CHARMES GODARD, COTES DE FRANCS** 1988 Bordeaux (F)	
303	£8.19	**ROSEMOUNT SHOW RESERVE CABERNET SAUVIGNON** 1987 Coonawarra (Aus)	
304	£8.29	**CHATEAU SOCIANDO MALLET, HAUT-MEDOC** 1987 Bordeaux (F)	
305	£13.39	**JEAN LEON CABERNET SAUVIGNON** 1983 Penedés (Sp)	
310	£10.39	**BARON VILLENEUVE DE CANTERMERLE, HAUT-MEDOC** 1986 Bordeaux (F)	
315	£11.49	**MOUNTADAM CABERNET SAUVIGNON** 1987 High Eden Ridge (Aus)	
327	£15.19	**YARRA YERING CABERNET SAUVIGNON** 1987 Yarra Valley (Aus)	
332	£24.69	**CHATEAU TALBOT, ST JULIEN** 1982 Bordeaux (F)	
344	£4.29	**PENFOLDS BIN 2 SHIRAZ/MATARO** 1989 Barossa Valley (Aus)	
356	£5.29	**DAVID WYNN SHIRAZ** 1990 High Eden Ridge (Aus)	
358	£5.79	**DOMAINE LA SOUMADE RASTEAU, COTES DU RHONE VILLAGES, ROMERO ANDRE** 1988 (F)	
365	£7.09	**CHATEAU TAHBILK SHIRAZ** 1987 Goulburn Valley (Aus)	
441	£5.79	**QUINTA DE CAMARATE, J M DE FONSECA** 1984 (P)	
452	£14.45	**RIOJA RESERVA 904, LA RIOJA ALTA** 1978 (Sp)	
480	£10.39	**DOS CORTADOS, WILLIAMS AND HUMBERT,** Jerez (Sp)	
483	£15.49	**APOSTOLES, GONZALEZ BYASS,** Jerez (Sp)	
496	£20.59	**DUO CENTENARY BUAL, COSSART GORDON** (P)	
500	£2.25	**PETILLANT DE LISTEL,** Midi (F)	

PIM	**Pimlico Dozen**

46,Tichbrook St. London SW1 U2LX (071-834-3647). Small specialists close to the House, selling by the case. **Opening hours**: 9am-6pm Mon-Fri. **Delivery**: free locally, nationally at cost. **Tastings**: regularly in-store

Just the place for anyone wanting to make superior Buck's Fizz. Pimlico Dozen offers freshly-squeezed orange juice by the half gallon (by arrangement) and a range of fizz from the major Grands Marques and Herbert Beaufort, a Bouzy grower, as well as Parsons Creek fizz from California. Burgundies are good and include several from the small negociant house of Naigon Chauveau. There are some fairly-priced Bordeaux Crus Bourgeois and a good shot at Spain, but throughout, it is easy to find tempting titbits.

83	£4.40	**CALITERRA CHARDONNAY** 1990 Maipo Valley (Ch)
84	£4.65	**OXFORD LANDING CHARDONNAY, YALUMBA** 1990 South Australia (Aus)
93	£6.10	**BROKENBACK VINEYARD CHARDONNAY, ROTHBURY** 1990 Hunter Valley (Aus)
281	£5.20	**MONTANA CABERNET SAUVIGNON** 1988 Marlborough (NZ)
357	£5.25	**FETZER ZINFANDEL** 1987 Mendocino (Cal)
442	£5.35	**TEMPRANILLO, BODEGAS OCHOA** 1987 Navarra (Sp)
449	£8.20	**CAMPO VIEJO RIOJA GRAN RESERVA** 1980 (Sp)
500	£2.99	**PETILLANT DE LISTEL,** Midi (F)

CPW | Christopher Piper Wines

1 Silver St, Ottery St Mary, Devon EX11 1D. (0404 814139). Jolly independent merchant with passion for Burgundy and Beaujolais. **Opening Hours:** 8.30am-6.30pm Mon-Fri; 9.30am-5pm Sat. **Delivery:** Free locally for 3+ cases, nationally for 6+ cases. **Tastings:** regularly in-store plus tutored events on request. **Discounts:** 5% on (mixed) cases, trade price on orders over 3 cases.

The word primeur has two meanings for Christopher Piper: new Bordeaux and new Beaujolais about which Christopher Piper is peculiarly knowledgeable, as wine maker at Château Des Tours in Brouilly. This is not a merchant to whom you should express your snooty attitude towards the annual Nouveau jamboree. Piper is one of the best liked wine merchants in the country and his experience in France really has made him look like a jolly Beaujolais grower, but he has a serious understanding of Bordeaux which is clearly evident from the list. Canny wine buyers should contact him as soon as they read this, as following the purchase of David Baillie Vintners, he had an enticing set of bin ends on offer. They may not all have been sold.

3	£7.24	**LINDAUER, MONTANA** (NZ)
11	£11.20	**DEUTZ MARLBOROUGH CUVEE** (NZ)
68	£7.18	**BREGANZE DI BREGANZE, MACULAN** 1990 Veneto (It)
101	£7.87	**HUGO CHARDONNAY** 1988 Southern Vales (Aus)
103	£8.72	**KING VALLEY CHARDONNAY FAMILY RESERVE, BROWN BROTHERS** 1987 N E Victoria (Aus)
281	£5.11	**MONTANA CABERNET SAUVIGNON** 1988 Marlborough (NZ)
288	£6.90	**CHATEAU MUSAR** 1982 Bekaa Valley (Leb)
336	£44.20	**OPUS ONE, ROBERT MONDAVI** 1987 Napa Valley (Cal)
358	£5.73	**DOMAINE LA SOUMADE RASTEAU, COTES DU RHONE VILLAGES, ROMERO ANDRE** 1988 (F)
374	£9.76	**RIDGE GEYSERVILLE ZINFANDEL** 1988 Santa Clara (Cal)
412	£6.16	**CAMPO FIORIN VALPOLICELLA, MASI** 1986 Veneto (It)
460	£14.98	**CAMPBELLS OLD RUTHERGLEN LIQUEUR MUSCAT** (Aus)
493	£16.12	**WARRE'S QUINTA DA CAVADINHA** 1982 Douro (P)

TP | Terry Platt Wines

Ferndale Rd, Llandudno Junction, Gwynned LL31 9NT (0492 592971). Wholesale/retail merchant selling by the case. **Delivery:** free locally, nationally at cost. **Tastings:** occasionally in-store.

The Celtic Vintner may have been nominated Welsh Merchant of the Year but Terry Platt ran them a very close second. The selection is one of familiar classics (Châteaux Palmer and Climens, Louis Latour, Jaboulet), more modern 'names' (Mondavi, Brown Brothers, Hunters in New Zealand) and practically unknown wines which they have discovered themselves. Such as four wines from Platt's winery in Mudgee. Jeremy Platt doesn't think they are in any way related, '... but enquiries continue. It would be nice to have a slice of a vineyard.'

3	£5.28	**LINDAUER, MONTANA** (NZ)	
102	£7.95	**MARQUES DE MURRIETA RIOJA BLANCO RESERVA** 1985 Rioja (Sp)	
196	£5.42	**THREE CHOIRS MEDIUM DRY ENGLISH TABLE WINE** 1989 Gloucs (UK)	
281	£5.28	**MONTANA CABERNET SAUVIGNON** 1988 Marlborough (NZ)	
288	£6.64	**CHATEAU MUSAR** 1982 Bekaa Valley (Leb)	
336	£48.07	**OPUS ONE, ROBERT MONDAVI** 1987 Napa Valley (Cal)	
348	£4.41	**DOMAINE DE LA RENJARDE, COTES DU RHONE VILLAGES** 1989 (F)	
364	£6.52	**CHATEAU REAL MARTIN, PROVENCE** 1986 Midi (F)	
442	£5.45	**TEMPRANILLO, BODEGAS OCHOA** 1987 Navarra (Sp)	
451	£9.59	**MARQUIS DE MURRIETA RIOJA TINTO RESERVA** 1985 (Sp)	
481	£10.03	**MANZANILLA PASADA DE SANLUCAR ALMACENISTA, LUSTAU,** Jerez (Sp)	

POR | Portland Wine Company

16 North Parade, Sale Moor Manchester M33 3JS (061 962 8752). Independent merchant formerly known as Superbrew. **Opening Hours:** 10am-10pm Mon-Sat; 12-2pm & 7pm-9.30pm Sun. **Delivery:** free locally. **Tastings:** regular in-store plus tutored tastings. **Discounts:** 5% on (mixed) case sales.

The new Portland Wine Company list will probably arrive the day after this Guide goes to press. Geoff Dickinson was only able to send us a draft copy, which didn't contain all the wines which will eventually appear on the final version. So all we can say do is applaud his range, and tell you to seek out the Corbières from Château de Lastours (including the white), the Australian Chardonnays of Mountadam, Rothbury and Petaluma and one (or indeed all) of the 5 vintages of Château Musar.

3	£6.79	**LINDAUER, MONTANA** (NZ)	
29	£2.75	**CUVEE JEAN-PAUL BLANC SEC VIN DE TABLE, PAUL BOUTINOT** (F)	
46	£3.89	**CHARDONNAY, DOMAINE DES FLINES, VIN DE PAYS DE LA LOIRE** 1990 (F)	
54	£4.89	**ALSACE TOKAY PINOT GRIS, CAVE VINICOLE DE TURCKHEIM** 1990 (F)	
87	£4.79	**ORLANDO RF CHARDONNAY** 1989 S E Australia (Aus)	
90	£5.79	**LINDEMANS BIN 65 CHARDONNAY** 1989 S E Australia (Aus)	
102	£7.99	**MARQUES DE MURRIETA RIOJA BLANCO RESERVA** 1985 Rioja (Sp)	
111	£9.95	**EDNA VALLEY CHARDONNAY** 1989 San Luis Obispo (Cal)	
140	£4.79	**COOKS HAWKES BAY SAUVIGNON BLANC** 1989 Hawkes Bay (NZ)	
145	£5.79	**SAUVIGNON DE ST BRIS, DOMAINE FELIX** 1990 Burgundy (F)	
150	£5.79	**STONELEIGH SAUVIGNON BLANC** 1990 Marlborough (NZ)	
192	£6.95	**DEINHARD HOCHHEIM HERITAGE SELECTION** 1988 Rheingau (G)	
204	£4.19	**CHATEAU LE RAZ, BERGERAC ROSE** 1990 South West (F)	
231	£4.99	**CHATEAU DE LASTOURS CUVEE SIMONE DESCAMPS, CORBIERES** 1989 Midi (F)	
258	£4.49	**SVISCHTOV CABERNET SAUVIGNON CONTROLIRAN, BULGARIAN VINTNERS** 1985 Svischtov (Bul)	
267	£4.19	**CHATEAU LE RAZ, BERGERAC ROUGE** 1989 South West (F)	
280	£4.79	**ORLANDO RF CABERNET SAUVIGNON** 1988 South Australia (Aus)	
281	£4.95	**MONTANA CABERNET SAUVIGNON** 1988 Marlborough (NZ)	
288	£6.79	**CHATEAU MUSAR** 1982 Bekaa Valley (Leb)	
319	£12.49	**YARDEN CABERNET SAUVIGNON, GOLAN HEIGHTS WINERY** 1985 Galilee (Is)	
349	£4.59	**RASTEAU COTES DU RHONE VILLAGES, VIGNERONS DE RASTEAU** 1989 (F)	
392	£10.49	**SANFORD PINOT NOIR** 1986 Santa Barbara (Cal)	
442	£5.39	**TEMPRANILLO, BODEGAS OCHOA** 1987 Navarra (Sp)	

| 446 | £5.49 | GRAN SANGREDETORO RESERVA, TORRES 1986 Penedés (Sp) |
| 482 | £10.99 | ROYAL CORREGIDOR RICH RARE OLD OLOROSO, SANDEMAN, Jerez (Sp) |

PUG | Pugsons of Buxton

Cliff House, Terrace Road, Buxton SK17 6DR (0298 77696). One of England's best delicatessens. **Opening Hours**: 9am-5.30pm Mon, Tue, Thu-Sat. 9am-4.15pm Wed, 11am-5pm Sun. **Delivery:** free locally. **Discounts:** 5% on a (mixed) case.

A delightful shop to introduce to the *Guide*, providing the people of Buxton with not only wine, but freshly-baked French bread (made from imported dough), 16 different mustards and a lovingly selected cheese selection. In fact we get the feeling that the wines, despite including Pichon Lalande, Beaujolais from Gerard Brisson and Fonseca port, do rather take second place to cheeses in Peter Pugson's heart. So instead of recommending any specific wines. may we offer Bonchester ('a sort of creamy Scottish Camembert'), Petit Breton ('a lovely dairy cheese from Normandy which, when it grows up, wants to be Pont l'Eveque') and Mrs Kirkham's unpasteurised Farmhouse Lancashire ('creamy, crumbly, richly-buttered and deliciously deep in flavour with a joyous aftertaste').

RAE | Raeburn Fine Wine & Foods

23 Comely Bank Rd, Edinburgh, EH4 1DS (031 332 5166). Grocery store with an ace fine wine merchant attached. Or vice versa. **Opening Hours:** Mon - Sat 9am - 7pm. **Delivery:** free locally, nationally at cost. **Tastings:** tutored tastings and organised events. **Discounts:** 2.5% on a mixed case, 5% on unmixed cases.

What is there to say about Zubair Mohamed that hasn't been said before? You know that nothing on his unpretentious list is there for reasons other than quality. That he has one of the largest range of individual domaine Burgundies in Britain, all of which he imports himself. That his New World selection features the splendid wines of Balgownie in Central Victoria and the remarkable Bonny Doon. And that his range of half-bottles includes First Growth clarets and Sauternes. So we'll just leave you wishing that every grocer's shop in Britain could be as remarkable as Raeburn.

102	£8.25	MARQUES DE MURRIETA RIOJA BLANCO RESERVA 1985 Rioja (Sp)
148	£6.75	SELAKS SAUVIGNON BLANC 1990 (NZ)
280	£4.99	ORLANDO RF CABERNET SAUVIGNON 1988 South Australia (Aus)
304	£9.95	CHATEAU SOCIANDO MALLET, HAUT-MEDOC 1987 Bordeaux (F)
313	£10.50	CLOUDY BAY CABERNET MERLOT 1989 Marlborough (NZ)
316	£9.95	TOURELLES DE LONGUEVILLE, PAUILLAC, CHATEAU PICHON-LONGUEVILLE-BARON 1988 Bordeaux (F)
381	£4.99	DOMAINE DE LA CHAMOISE, GAMAY DE TOURAINE, MARIONNET 1990 Loire (F)
391	£9.30	SAINTSBURY PINOT NOIR 1988 Carneros (Cal)
451	£9.30	MARQUIS DE MURRIETA RIOJA TINTO RESERVA 1985 (Sp)
460	£13.35	CAMPBELLS OLD RUTHERGLEN LIQUEUR MUSCAT (Aus)
483	£12.99	APOSTOLES, GONZALEZ BYASS, Jerez (Sp)

RAV | Ravensbourne Wine Co

13 Bell House, 49 Greenwich High Rd London SE10 8JL (081 692 9655). Independent merchant selling by the case. **Opening Hours:** 9am-5pm Mon-Fri; 10am-2pm Sat. **Delivery:** free within Greater London, nationally at cost. **Tastings:** regular tutored events. **Discounts:** variable.

Thank you, Terry Short for setting us to rights. We wondered last year about the 'Arbours' to which he was a supplier. Apparently, the term is now used to describe an open marquee at outdoor events. There are several wines in the Ravensbourne range which would be appropriate for such a setting. The Beaujolais of Henry Fessy, including each of the ten *crus*, would be very refreshing, as would the any of the English wines from Biddenden or Sedlescombe. But the most fitting, we feel, would be the Seaview Brut. Just the thing to drink in a safe arbour...

2	£6.75	**DIANE DE POITIERS SPARKLING CHARDONNAY,** Loire (F)	
213	£3.45	**VIN DE PAYS DU GARD, ALBARIC,** Midi (F)	
258	£4.59	**SVISCHTOV CABERNET SAUVIGNON CONTROLIRAN, BULGARIAN VINTNERS** 1985 Svischtov (Bul)	
281	£5.20	**MONTANA CABERNET SAUVIGNON** 1988 Marlborough (NZ)	
408	£6.30	**BONARDA OLTREPO PAVESE, FUGAZZA** 1987 Lombardy (It)	
456	£4.09	**SAMOS MUSCAT,** Samos (Gr)	
500	£2.30	**PETILLANT DE LISTEL,** Midi (F)	

RD | Reid Wines

West of England Wine Merchant of the Year

The Mill, Marsh Lane, Hallatrow, Nr Bristol BS18 5EB (0761 52645) & Unit 2, Block 3, Vestry Trading Estate, Otford Road, Sevenoaks. Delightfully unique independent merchant. **Opening Hours:** telephone first if visiting Hallatrow; Sevenoaks 10am-6pm Mon-Fri; 10am-1pm Sat. **Delivery:** free within 25 miles, nationally at cost. **Tastings:** regularly in-store plus tutored events.

1956 Lafite: 'Appalling vintage, but very rare'. 1968 Latour: 'Revolting, when last tasted'. 1974 Smith Haut Lafite: 'Just a joke, you understand'. 1957 La Tâche: 'Pretty manky'. Yes folks, just some of the highlights from the 10th anniversary edition of Reid's wine list, which narrowly missed being voted our Wine List of the Year. The substance is just as entertaining as the style, and although the astonishing ranges from Champagne, Bordeaux, Burgundy and the Rhône all go back to, at latest, the thirties, it was the Australian section which caught our eyes. 5 different wineries from the up-and-coming Mornington Peninsula are represented and they also stock De Bortoli Botrytis Semillon and the brilliant, seldom-seen Craiglee Shiraz. And if you didn't think that Aussie wines aged well, try one of the Lindemans 'Classic Release' wines dating back to 1965.

All this plus a good range of French country wines, and Champagnes which are 'consistently cheaper than a much-applauded national chain, even taking account of the "free" one' (who can they mean?). Just some of the reasons why our judges voted them the West of England Wine Merchant of the Year for 1992.

6	£8.50	**TALTARNI BRUT TACHE,** Pyrenees (Aus)	
71	£7.65	**ST VERAN LES GRANDES BRUYERES, ROGER LUQUET** 1989 Burgundy (F)	
105	£9.22	**HEGGIES CHARDONNAY, HILL-SMITH** 1988 Adelaide Hills (Aus)	

109	£12.65	ST HUBERTS CHARDONNAY 1988 Yarra Valley (Aus)
297	£6.95	TALTARNI CABERNET SAUVIGNON 1985 Pyrenees (Aus)
304	£10.28	CHATEAU SOCIANDO MALLET, HAUT-MEDOC 1987 Bordeaux (F)
317	£11.89	CLOS DU VAL MERLOT 1987 Napa Valley (Cal)
324	£13.25	CHINOOK MERLOT 1987 Washington (US)
333	£20.60	CHATEAU PAVIE, ST EMILION 1985 Bordeaux (F)
367	£6.95	TALTARNI SHIRAZ 1988 Pyrenees (Aus)
373	£10.15	DOMAINE DU VIEUX TELEGRAPHE, CHATEAUNEUF DU PAPE 1987 Rhône (F)
424	£12.30	COLTASSALA, CASTELLO DI VOLPAIA 1986 Tuscany (It)
426	£16.75	CEPPARELLO, ISOLE E OLENA 1988 Tuscany (It)
431	£19.85	CABREO IL BORGO, RUFFINO 1986 Tuscany (It)
432	£20.85	LE PERGOLE TORTE, MONTE VERTINE 1986 Tuscany (It)
450	£8.65	NAVARRA ANIVERSARO 125, CHIVITE 1981 Navarra (Sp)
452	£15.00	RIOJA RESERVA 904, LA RIOJA ALTA 1978 (Sp)
465	£6.40	REDWOOD VALLEY ESTATE LATE HARVEST RIESLING 1989 Nelson (NZ)
472	£11.25	JURANCON MOELLEUX VENDANGE TARDIVE, DOMAINE CAUHAPE 1988 S W (F)

RES   La Réserve

56 Walton St, London SW3 1RB (071 589 2020). **Opening Hours:** 9.30am-8pm Mon-Fri; 9.30am-6pm Sat. **Delivery:** free locally, nationally at cost. **Tastings:** regular programme of tastings held at the Ski Club of Great Britain. **Discounts:** 5% on case.

Part of the Mark Reynier organisation. See Le Sac à Vin.

REW   La Reserva

Unit 6, Spring Grove Mills, Manchester Road, Linthwaite, Huddersfield HD7 5QG (0484 846732). Independent Hispanophile specialist. **Opening hours:** 9am-5.30pm Mon-Fri, 9am-5.30pm Sat. **Delivery:** free locally, nationally at cost. **Tastings:** in-store every Saturday and occasional tutored events.

Saturday is a great day to be in Linthwaite if you have even the faintest curiosity about Spanish wines. Keith Gomersall is running the nearest thing to a full time Spanish masterclass outside London, and it is on Saturday that bottles are open for tasting. Really assiduous students could study their way through over two dozen different bodegas' Riojas before exploring wines from every corner of the rest of Spain. And if after all that you still can't find one you like, Mr Gomersall will probably forgive you for buying a bottle from Australia or New Zealand.

RWW   Richmond Wine Warehouse

138 Lower Mortlake Road, Richmond, Surrey TW9 2JZ (081 948 4196). Independent, family-run warehouse selling by the (mixed) case. **Opening Hours:** 10am-7pm Mon-Sat. **Delivery:** free locally, nationally at cost. **Tastings:** in-store every Saturday.

Looking at the Bordeaux range at Richmond Wine Warehouse, you get the impression that if they like a property, they'll stick with it. So you'll find 5 vintages of Léoville Barton, 6 of Grand Puy Ducasse and 7 of Kirwan. Burgundies are chosen in the same way (not with perhaps as much discretion), with several wines coming from Ligeret, Mommessin and Chanson. And all the ports come from the house of De Souza. Still, the range attracts a band of 'very loyal' customers, and you know where to come now to set up a vertical tasting.

38	£3.50	**TOLLANA DRY WHITE** 1988 S E Australia (Aus)
169	£7.80	**ALSACE GEWURZTRAMINER ST HUBERT, KUEHN** 1989 (F)
219	£3.79	**CHATEAU HELENE ROUGE, CORBIERES, MARIE-HELENE GAU** 1987 Midi (F)
320	£10.99	**CHATEAU LEOVILLE BARTON, ST JULIEN** 1987 Bordeaux (F)
374	£10.20	**RIDGE GEYSERVILLE ZINFANDEL** 1988 Santa Clara (Cal)

RWC   The Rioja Wine Company

Argoed House, Llanfwrog, Ruthin Clwyd, N. Wales LL15 1LG (08242 3407). By the case Italian and Spanish specialists, and dessert campaigner.**Delivery**:free locally. **Tastings**: occasionally in-store, tutored and theme dinners.**Discounts**; for collection.

Despite its name this small company has as much expertise in the field of Italian and Portugese wines as it does in Spain. In all three countries the list includes classic representative producers and wines at very fair prices. Readers with a sweet tooth should also seek out the selection of dessert wines, as this is one of the rare companies to take Marsala seriously.

55	£5.15	**SOAVE CLASSICO MONTELEONE, BOSCAINI** 1989 Veneto (It)
305	£7.55	**JEAN LEON CABERNET SAUVIGNON** 1983 Penedés (Sp)
438	£4.57	**MARIUS RESERVA, BODEGAS PIQUERAS** 1983 Almansa (Sp)
483	£15.53	**APOSTOLES, GONZALEZ BYASS,** Jerez (Sp)

HR   Howard Ripley

35, Eversley Crescent, London N21 1EL (081 360 8904). Arch Burgundophile. **Delivery**: free locally and nationally for 5+ cases. **Opening hours**: Mon-Fri 9am-5pm.

Former dentist Howard Ripley has a first class reason for offering Château Kirwan 1983 at a bargain £11.50: 'I am withdrawing completely from the Bordeaux scene to specialise in Burgundy'. This will come as something of a surprise to some people who are under the impression that that was exactly what he has been doing since 1982.There are 14 pages of closely typed text all devoted to the Burgundian gods and demi-gods for which he is such an ardent enthusiast, the astonishing thing about this list is not so much its length and the quality of its growers as the fact that here and there, there are some real bargains.

125	£25.85	**NUITS ST GEORGES BLANC, CLOS DE L'ARLOT** 1988 Burgundy (F)

WRB   Wm Robbs

48 Fore St, Hexham, Northumberland NE46 (0434 602151) & Robbs at Tynedale, Hexham, Northumberland (0434 607788). Supermarket with enthusiastic wine department which has its own wine club **Opening Hours:** 9am-5pm Mon-Thu; 9am-7pm Fri; 9am-5.30pm Sat. **Delivery:** free locally. **Tastings:** regular in-store tastings. **Discounts:** 5-15% depending on quantity.

It must be difficult for supermarket chains with two branches to compete with larger organisations, but Robbs in Hexham is doing very nicely, thank you. Despite the bias of the list below, they do stock wines from the Northern Hemisphere, including the ranges of Duboeuf and Torres, as well as Demi-Sec Champagnes from Mercier and Veuve Clicquot.

3	£7.49	LINDAUER, MONTANA (NZ)	
83	£6.15	CALITERRA CHARDONNAY 1990 Maipo Valley (Ch)	
87	£5.89	ORLANDO RF CHARDONNAY 1989 S E Australia (Aus)	
105	£8.85	HEGGIES CHARDONNAY, HILL-SMITH 1988 Adelaide Hills (Aus)	
118	£14.29	VIDAL RESERVE CHARDONNAY 1989 Hawkes Bay (NZ)	
140	£5.75	COOKS HAWKES BAY SAUVIGNON BLANC 1989 Hawkes Bay (NZ)	
264	£4.55	BERRI ESTATES AUSTRALIAN CABERNET SHIRAZ 1987 (Aus)	
280	£5.89	ORLANDO RF CABERNET SAUVIGNON 1988 South Australia (Aus)	
319	£12.89	YARDEN CABERNET SAUVIGNON, GOLAN HEIGHTS WINERY 1985 Galilee (Is)	
351	£5.15	DIEMERSDAL SHIRAZ 1986 Paarl (SA)	

CAR   C A Rookes

Unit 7, Western Road Industrial Estate, Western Road, Stratford upon Avon CV37 0AH (0789 297777). Honest independent merchant which looks after its customers. **Opening Hours:** 9am-6pm Mon-Fri, 9am-2pm Sat. **Delivery:** free locally, nationally at cost. **Tastings:** regularly in-store, plus tutored events. **Discounts:** negotiable.

'C A Rookes intend to develop further the policy of discovery and support of the small independent producers, thus ensuring a continued supply of interesting wines from producers who do not wish their traditions to be lost on the shelves of the supermarket'. We applaud John Freeland's sentiments and found much to commend in the firm's lists and monthly newsletters. The range includes Moillard Burgundies, Valdespino sherries and ports dating back to 1924. Customers are invited to buy several wines ex-cellars from producers, enabling them to obtain a substantial discount (£18 on a case of Charles Ellner Champagne). And we also like the wry sense of humour that pervades the operation. 'Cavas de Weinert Argentinian Cabernet Sauvignon. We wonder whether they are trying to win our hearts by giving us such good quality wine, or are they still after the Falklands?' If the author would like to apply for a position writing for this *Guide*...

RTW   The Rose Tree Wine Co.

15 Suffolk Parade, Cheltenham, Glos GL50 2AE (0242 583732). Independent merchant. **Opening Hours:** 9am-7pm Mon-Fri; 9am-6pm Sat. **Delivery:** free locally, nationally at cost. **Tastings:** regularly in-store plus tutored events. **Discounts:** 5% on (mixed) cases.

Rose Tree may not have as wide a range as some other merchants, but most areas and pockets are catered for with well-chosen examples, as the list below shows. Burgundy is well-represented by names such as Bouchard Père et Fils and Bruno Clair, and they have a good range of Champagne and other sparkling wines. They ran an *en primeur* campaign for the first time in 1990 which proved very successful with their 'strong loyal following'. But the spring water they stock is Tudor Rose from an undefined area of the Cotswolds. Does this mean they have no confidence in the local spa water?

29	£3.20	CUVEE JEAN-PAUL BLANC SEC VIN DE TABLE, PAUL BOUTINOT (F)	
117	£13.00	ELSTON CHARDONNAY, TE MATA 1989 (NZ)	

150	£7.62	**STONELEIGH SAUVIGNON BLANC** 1989 Marlborough (NZ)
335	£30.00	**LES FORTS DE LATOUR, PAUILLAC, CHATEAU LATOUR** 1982 Bordeaux (F)
336	£52.68	**OPUS ONE, ROBERT MONDAVI** 1987 Napa Valley (Cal)
416	£8.30	**CHIANTI CLASSICO, ISOLE E OLENA** 1988 Tuscany (It)
450	£8.80	**NAVARRA ANIVERSARO 125, CHIVITE** 1981 Navarra (Sp)
499	£3.00	**MOSCATO FIZZ, VITICOLTORI DELL'ACQUESE,** Piedmont (It)

WRU William Rush

Tecklewood, Uplands Close, Gerrards Cross SL9 7JH (0753 882659). Small independent mail-order merchant. **Delivery:** free locally, nationally at cost. **Tastings:** regular events throughout the year. **Discounts:** 5% on (mixed) cases.

David Rush has assembled an entertaining little list full of advice on particular areas and on wine in general. If you want to learn Winespeak (essential info on how to fend off boring people at tastings), learn about the grapes of the Loire, or be told to ignore Late Bottled Vintage port ('best used in the kitchen'), then this is the list for you. The range of wines is small, but if you're not satisfied with Burgundies from Faiveley and Girardin, or Poniatowski Vouvray, the company will be able to find most wines you could want. And we're sure that the name given to founder William Rush, 'the old bastard', does not apply to the present head of the firm.

| 310 | £8.25 | **BARON VILLENEUVE DE CANTERMERLE, HAUT-MEDOC, CHATEAU CANTEMERLE** 1986 Bordeaux (F) |
| 332 | £27.00 | **CHATEAU TALBOT, ST JULIEN** 1982 Bordeaux (F) |

R&I Russell & McIver Ltd

The Rectory, St Mary-at-Hill, London EC3R 8EE (071 283 3575). City merchants offering more than first meets the eye. **Opening Hours:** 9am-5.30pm Mon-Fri. **Delivery:** free within London, nationally at cost. **Tastings:** regularly in-store plus tutored events. **Discounts:** negotiable.

Not many wine merchants can boast a former Lord Mayor of London as managing director. But then not many merchants have as deep roots in The City as Russell & McIver. The company was founded in the London Coal Exchange in 1865 and still maintains links with many City institutions, both civic and corporate, as well as with several Oxbridge colleges. As you would expect from such a company, the wines are mostly from the more traditional areas. But the buying is carefully done and besides the classed growths and grands crus, there are plenty of clarets and burgundies in the £5-£8 range. There are a few New World wines, such as Jekel Cabernet Sauvignon and Redwood Valley Sauvignon Blanc. However the majority of the selection is chosen to appeal to their important customers who appreciate 'courtesy on the telephone, prompt reply to letters and speedy delivery'.

SAC Le Sac à Vin

Head Office (of Mark Reynier Fine Wines Ltd): 13 Grant Road, London SW11 2NV (071 978 5601), Le Sac à Vin, 203, Munster Road, SW6 (071 381 6930), Le Picoleur, 47 Kendal Street WC2 2BU (071 402 6920), Clapham Cellars 13 Grant Road, Clapham Junction, SW11 (071 978 5601), Heath Street Wine Company, 29 Heath Street, London NW3 (071 435 6845), La

Réserve, 56 Walton Street, London SW3 1RB (071 589 2020). Quintet of differently named and subtlely different up-market shops. **Delivery**: free locally, nationally at cost. **Opening hours**: 7am-8pm Mon-Fri, 10am-6pm Sat. **Discounts**: 5% per case. **Tastings**: tutored events and occasionally in-store.

Confused? So were we, when we came to try to make some sense of this multi-named mini chain, so we are grateful to David Penny, Manager of Le Sac à Vin, for clarifying the picture. The group grew out of the La Reserve chain, quintessential 'smart' wine merchants. Today each branch, though coming beneath the same owner-Mark Reynier-runs semi-independently adding the managers own choice of wines to the list which applies to all 5 shops. On that list are to be found a good range of inexpensive French country wines, serious Bordeaux and champagnes, some rare Italians and in the case of the La Réserve shop a great range of seductive older bottles.

84	£4.95	OXFORD LANDING CHARDONNAY, YALUMBA 1990 South Australia (Aus)
103	£8.30	KING VALLEY CHARDONNAY FAMILY RESERVE, BROWN BROTHERS 1987 N E Victoria (Aus)
288	£6.50	CHATEAU MUSAR 1982 Bekaa Valley (Leb)
293	£7.95	JAMIESONS RUN RED, MILDARA 1987 Coonawarra (Aus)
310	£9.50	BARON VILLENEUVE DE CANTERMERLE, HAUT-MEDOC, CHATEAU CANTEMERLE 1986 Bordeaux (F)
323	£15.95	VASSE FELIX CABERNET SAUVIGNON 1988 Margaret River (Aus)

SAF   Safeway

Head Office: Argyll House, 6 Millington Rd, Hayes, Middx UB3 4HY (081 848 8744). Increasingly green and upmarket national chain with 312 stores. **Opening Hours**: 8am-8pm Mon-Thu; 8am-9pm Fri; 8am-7pm Sat. **Tastings**: occasionally in-store.

If we had a Making-an-Effort award this year the contest would be between Asda, Safeway and Gateway. Safeway was a surprising latecomer to the world of wine, but since its takeover by Argyll, it has embraced the subject with all the enthusiasm of a new convert to a religion. Among the efforts that have been made most noticeably the determined introduction of the range of 10 organic wines and the sponsorship of the annual organic wine fair at Ryton Gardens, where in 1991 Wine Magazine helped to co-ordinate the first organic Wine Challenge. The range remains patchy but is improving fast and the arrival of Nick Wakefield from Morrisons and Sarah King from Budgens is already bearing fruit.

27	£2.75	LA CAUME DE PEYRE, VIN DE PAYS DES COTES DE GASCOGNE, South West (F)
44	£3.99	CHATEAU CANET, ENTRE DEUX MERS 1990 Bordeaux (F)
73	£7.75	POUILLY FUISSE, LUC JAVELOT 1988 Burgundy (F)
78	£3.15	CHATEAU LES COMBES, BORDEAUX BLANC, ESCHENAUER 1990 (F)
132	£4.09	CHATEAU DE LA BOTINERE, MUSCADET DE SEVRE ET MAINE, JEAN BEAUQUIN 1990 Loire (F)
239	£2.85	DOMAINE DES CABANNES, COTES DU FRONTONNAIS 1989 South West (F)
246	£3.25	SAFEWAY VIN DE PAYS D'OC CEPAGE MERLOT, DOMAINE ANTHEA 1990 Midi (F)
248	£2.79	COTES DU MARMANDAIS, COCUMENT 1989 South West (F)
255	£3.99	SAFEWAY OAK-AGED CLARET, CALVET 1987 Bordeaux (F)
259	£4.09	CHATEAU BRONDELLE, GRAVES 1988 Bordeaux (F)
261	£4.09	DOMAINE DES SALAISES, SAUMUR 1989 Loire (F)
297	£7.49	TALTARNI CABERNET SAUVIGNON 1985 Pyrenees (Aus)
337	£2.59	SAFEWAY COTES DE LUBERON, CELLIER DE MARRENON 1990 Rhône (F)

340	£3.45	SAFEWAY CHATEAU JOANNY, COTES DU RHONE, P DUPOND 1989 (F)
344	£3.99	PENFOLDS BIN 2 SHIRAZ/MATARO 1989 Barossa Valley (Aus)
347	£3.99	SEAVIEW CABERNET SHIRAZ 1989 South Australia (Aus)
390	£7.99	SAFEWAY BEAUNE, LABOURE-ROI 1988 Burgundy (F)
402	£3.65	VALPOLICELLA CLASSICO MARANO, BOSCAINI 1988 Veneto (It)
435	£2.65	DON DARIAS RED, BODEGAS VITORIANAS (Sp)
445	£3.65	NAVAJAS RIOJA CRIANZA TINTO 1985 (Sp)
469	£5.04	CHATEAU BASTOR LAMONTAGNE, SAUTERNES 1988 Bordeaux (F)
477	£2.55	SAFEWAY BLASQUEZ FINO CARTA BLANC, Jerez (Sp)
500	£2.05	PETILLANT DE LISTEL, Midi (F)

JS	J Sainsbury plc

Head Office: Stamford House, Stamford St, London SE1 9LL (071 921 6000). The 300-branch supermarket most others would like to be. **Opening Hours:** 8.30am-8pm Mon-Thu; 8.30am-9pm Fri; 8.30am-6pm Sat.

The fact that Sainsbury did not quite manage to achieve a hat-trick with a third consecutive Supermarket of the Year Award, is not to the superstore's discredit. The battle with Tesco was long and very closely fought. We doubt whether their buying teams would like to admit it but the two companies sometimes seem like a pair of Formula One racing cars which are so well matched that neither can maintain the lead....The only criticism of Sainsbury voiced by any of the judges was that the chain had been less innovative over the last year. We would not quite agree, applauding unusual wines listed below, such as the Cortese Dell'Alto Monferrato from Piedmont and the Solar Das Boucas single estate Vinho Verde. However, we concede that this has, indeed, been a year when new people have been settling into the wine department, following the promotion of Allan Cheesman, the man who more or less created Sainsbury's vinous reputation.

Other kinds of wine retailer can be as sniffy as they like about what they still call 'the grocers', but we would set the following set of wines up against a comparable team from any merchant in the land.

26	£2.75	SAINSBURY'S VIN DE PAYS DE GERS, South West (F)
28	£2.80	SAINSBURY'S CORBIERES BLANC, Midi (F)
35	£3.45	SAINSBURY'S CORTESE DELL' ALTO MONFERRATO, Piedmont (It)
86	£4.95	CHARDONNAY, VIN DE PAYS D'OC, HUGH RYMAN 1990 Midi (F)
91	£6.35	CHEVALIER ST VINCENT BORDEAUX BLANC, UNION ST VINCENT 1989 (F)
131	£3.90	SAINSBURY'S MUSCADET SUR LIE (ORGANIC), DOMAINE COURSAY 1990 Loire (F)
140	£4.95	COOKS HAWKES BAY SAUVIGNON BLANC 1989 Hawkes Bay (NZ)
153	£6.95	POUILLY FUME LES CHANTALOUETTES 1989 Loire (F)
160	£4.25	VINHO VERDE, SOLAR DAS BOUCAS 1989 Minho (P)
167	£4.60	SAINSBURY'S ALSACE GEWURZTRAMINER (F)
201	£3.45	SAINSBURY'S WHITE ZINFANDEL (Cal)
212	£2.99	SAINSBURY'S ST CHINIAN, CHATEAU SALVANHIAC 1990 Midi (F)
221	£3.75	BERGERIE DE L'ARBOUS ROUGE 1989 (F)
238	£2.75	SAINSBURY'S BERGERAC ROUGE, South West (F)
245	£2.75	VIN DE PAYS DE LA DORDOGNE CEPAGE CABERNET, CAVE DE SIGOULES 1990 South West (F)
251	£3.55	CHATEAU BELLEVUE LA FORET, FRONTONNAIS 1989 South West (F)
254	£3.95	SAINSBURY'S SELECTION CABERNET SAUVIGNON, Midi (F)
271	£4.45	WYNDHAM ESTATE CABERNET SAUVIGNON 1988 Hunter Valley (Aus)
274	£4.85	DOMAINE DU COLOMBIER, CHINON 1990 Loire (F)

280	£4.85	ORLANDO RF CABERNET SAUVIGNON 1988 South Australia (Aus)
288	£6.45	CHATEAU MUSAR 1982 Bekaa Valley (Leb)
320	£12.15	CHATEAU LEOVILLE BARTON, ST JULIEN 1987 Bordeaux (F)
341	£3.50	SAINSBURY'S CALIFORNIA ZINFANDEL, Monterey County (Cal)
355	£4.95	DOMAINE ST APOLLINAIRE (ORGANIC), COTES DU RHONE 1989 (F)
378	£3.85	SAINSBURY'S BEAUJOLAIS, Beaujolais (F)
387	£6.35	HAUTES COTES DE BEAUNE LES PERRIERES, CAVES DES HAUTES COTES 1988 Burgundy (F)
400	£2.59	SAINSBURY'S ROSSO DI VERONA, Veneto (It)
401	£3.09	SAINSBURY'S CHIANTI, Tuscany (It)
436	£3.60	SAINSBURY'S RIOJA 1986 Rioja (Sp)
439	£4.95	QUINTA DA BACALHOA, JOAO PIRES 1988 Palmela (P)
453	£2.65	MUSCAT DE ST JOHN DE MINERVOIS, Midi (F)
454	£2.85	SAINSBURY'S MOSCATEL DA VALENCIA (Sp)
484	£5.89	SAINSBURY'S VINTAGE CHARACTER PORT, Douro (P)

SB Sainsbury Brothers

On The High Pavement, 3 Edgar Buildings, George Street, Bath BA1 2EG (0225 460481), G M Vintners, 3 Alphinbrook Rd, Marsh Barton,Exeter (0392 218186), G M Vintners, 7 Wellington Terrace, Truro, Cornwall TR1 3JA (0872 79680). Three outlet independent chain. **Opening hours:** 10am-6pm Mon-Fri, 10am-5.30pm Sat. **Delivery:**free locally. **Tastings:**regularly and tutored.

Sainsbury Brothers 'the wine merchants of Bath since 1802' share an address, a telephone number and a wine list with G M Vintners which however has two extra branches. Sainsbury Brothers first sprang to adventurous wine drinkers' notice in the mid 1980's, when they were one of the only sources for the Australian Penfolds wines which are now so readily available. Those wines still feature on a list which in peculiar alphabetical order (Alsace, Australia, Bordeaux), attempts to cover the world, so the result is hit and miss. But Beaucastel, Gaja, and Loron all feature, as does the entire Barbadillo range. But beware of high prices, to which VAT must be added.

SC Sandgate Cellars

132 Sandgate High Street, Sandgate, Folkestone, Kent CT20 3BZ (0303 49686). Small, but ambitious independent merchant. **Opening Hours:** 5pm-7pm Mon, Thur, Fri; 10am-5-pm Sat and by appointment.. **Delivery:** free locally. **Tastings:** regularly in store. **Discount:** 5% off case purchases.

The opening hours reveal all: Christine and Tony Murless are teachers who are trying hard to build a part-time business into a fully-fledged wine merchant. This is an ambition we applaud, especially in difficult times and in a town whose primary relationship to wine is as the port through which holidaymakers return with it by the carload. Even so, the Murlesses are going to have to pay a bit more attention to the basics if they are to succeed: producers' names *must* appear alongside the name of every wine on the list. Whose, for instance, was the Irancy we were interested to see listed?

14	£13.02	DEHOURS CHAMPAGNE (F)
205	£4.66	CHRISTIAN BROTHERS WHITE ZINFANDEL 1989 Napa Valley (Cal)
220	£3.78	CHRISTIAN BROTHERS CLASSIC RED, Napa Valley (Cal)
281	£4.89	MONTANA CABERNET SAUVIGNON 1988 Marlborough (NZ)

SAN | Sandiway Wine Co.

2 School Way, Sandiway, Cheshire CW8 2NH (0606 882101). Down-to-earth independent merchant. **Opening Hours:** 9am-10pm (with lunch and tea breaks) Mon, Tue, Thu-Sat; 9am-1pm Wed; 11am-2pm & 7pm-10pm Sun. **Delivery:** free locally. **Tastings:** occasionally in-store plus tutored events. **Discounts:** 5% on (mixed) cases.

'It's a very odd shop. I don't quite know how we got it to look this way or to be like this. We sell Heinz soups, Happy Shopper coffee and Mars Bars alongside Bonne Mares 1955, Scavino Barolo and Moss Wood Estate wines. Some days I come down in the morning and absolutely hate it, but most days I think it's so funny it's brilliant... I suspect that many of our best customers might even leave us if we were to smarten our act up significantly'. Graham Wharmby describes his oddball shop perfectly, only omitting to mention that, unlike Raeburn Fine Wines, the Edinburgh merchant it resembles, Sandiway Wine Co really is a village shop with a range broad and good enough to attract wine lovers from Manchester. Italian wines are a particular passion, but look out too for 'deals' - Selaks Sauvignon bought from a cash-strapped fellow merchant and 'Cuvée Ford Fiesta', surplus special labelling of the excellent Cuvée Jean Paul.

29	£2.76	CUVEE JEAN-PAUL BLANC SEC VIN DE TABLE, PAUL BOUTINOT (F)
46	£3.99	CHARDONNAY, DOMAINE DES FLINES, VIN DE PAYS DE LA LOIRE 1990 (F)
55	£4.73	SOAVE CLASSICO MONTELEONE, BOSCAINI 1989 Veneto (It)
69	£6.99	SOAVE CLASSICO VIGNETO CALVARINO, PIEROPAN 1989 Veneto (It)
148	£6.30	SELAKS SAUVIGNON BLANC 1990 (NZ)
231	£5.07	CHATEAU DE LASTOURS CUVEE SIMONE DESCAMPS, CORBIERES 1989 Midi (F)
288	£7.29	CHATEAU MUSAR 1982 Bekaa Valley (Leb)
313	£10.95	CLOUDY BAY CABERNET MERLOT 1989 Marlborough (NZ)

SPS | Sapsford Wines

33 Musley Lane, Ware, Herts, SG12 7EW (0920) 467040. Passionate Loire specialists. **Opening Hours:** 'all hours'. **Delivery:** free locally; **Tastings:** tutored and dinners. **Discounts:** negotiable.

Loires galore. Barry and Mary Sapsford offer Domaine Octavie, as an alternative to *red* Sancerre, a demi-sec Cheverny made from the rare Romorantin, and just about every other Loire style you might ever wish to find. There are fewer Italians, Burgundies and Bordeaux, but the ones listed are all recommendable.

SWB | Satchells of Burnham

North Street, Burnham Market, Norfolk DE31 8HG. (0328 738272). Helpful small independent. **Opening Hours:** 10am-6pm Mon-Sat. **Delivery:** free locally. **Tastings:** sampling in-store. **Discounts:** 5% on a case.

Maxwell Graham-Wood's philosophy is easily stated: to keep 'return business'. He deserves to succeed in this because the wines he offers are as varied and carefully chosen as the list below indicates. He has clearly sidestepped obvious wines to seek out better (and better-value) bottles. But Graham-Wood is not proud; if there's a wine you'd like that is not on his list, he'll happily try to find it for you.

3	£7.99	LINDAUER, MONTANA (NZ)
33	£3.49	DOMAINE DU TARIQUET, COTES DE GASCOGNE 1990 South West (F)
79	£4.22	COTES DE ST MONT, PLAIMONT 1990 South West (F)
103	£7.09	KING VALLEY CHARDONNAY FAMILY RESERVE, BROWN BROTHERS 1987 N E Victoria (Aus)
117	£11.99	ELSTON CHARDONNAY, TE MATA 1989 (NZ)
281	£5.09	MONTANA CABERNET SAUVIGNON 1988 Marlborough (NZ)
307	£9.75	CHATEAU GRAND ORMEAU, LALANDE DE POMEROL 1987 Bordeaux (F)
446	£6.05	GRAN SANGREDETORO RESERVA, TORRES 1986 Penedés (Sp)
481	£10.23	MANZANILLA PASADA DE SANLUCAR ALMACENISTA, LUSTAU, Jerez (Sp)
487	£7.65	TAYLOR'S FIRST ESTATE PORT LUGAR DAS LAGES, Douro (P)
489	£10.90	STARBOARD BATCH 88 RUBY, Central Valley (Cal)

ASH | Ashley Scott

PO Box 28. The Highway, Hawarden, Deeside, Clwyd CH5 3RY. (0244 520655). Small-scale, mail order generalist. **Delivery**: free locally. **Tastings**: tutored. **Discount**: 5% on unsplit cases.

Michael and Jean Scott say that they are 'willing to visit customers at any time to discuss their requirements'. We'd welcome a visit from them, if they brought a selection from their list - provided it were a selection we had made for ourselves. We'd take the Vallet Frères Burgundies and Cooks New Zealand wines, for example, but we'd leave the Chansons and Thorins and the Clos Pegase Californians. But there's plenty to choose from and prices are remarkably fair.

29	£2.85	CUVEE JEAN-PAUL BLANC SEC VIN DE TABLE, PAUL BOUTINOT (F)
54	£5.26	ALSACE TOKAY PINOT GRIS, CAVE VINICOLE DE TURCKHEIM 1990 (F)
140	£5.35	COOKS HAWKES BAY SAUVIGNON BLANC 1989 Hawkes Bay (NZ)
267	£4.45	CHATEAU LE RAZ, BERGERAC ROUGE 1989 South West (F)
377	£3.45	ANJOU GAMAY, PIERRE-YVES TIJOU 1990 Loire (F)
491	£11.75	MALMSEY 10 YEAR OLD, HENRIQUES & HENRIQUES (P)

SEB | Sebastopol Wines

Sebastopol Barn, London Rd, Blewbury, Oxon OX11 9HB. (0235 850471). Independent merchant offering good value for money. **Opening Hours:** 10.30am-5.30pm Mon-Sat. **Delivery:** free locally, nationally at cost, £1 collection discount. **Tastings:** regularly in-store plus tutored events. **Discounts:** 5% on unsplit cases.

'We welcome the enthusiasm of new wine drinkers'. Lots of merchants make this kind of claim, but we believe Barbara Affleck because her seven-year-old business is clearly founded on her own enthusiasm for the subject. The list, once exclusively European, is now resolutely international, but never for the sake of it. We applaud the comment beneath the California heading: 'Sadly we were unable to find a value-for-money Chardonnay for this list. However, the quality of the red wines is excellent.'

66	£5.40	ALSACE PINOT BLANC BENNWIHR, MARCEL DEISS 1989 (F)
93	£7.29	BROKENBACK VINEYARD CHARDONNAY, ROTHBURY 1990 Hunter Valley (Aus)
102	£8.78	MARQUES DE MURRIETA RIOJA BLANCO RESERVA 1985 Rioja (Sp)
280	£5.95	ORLANDO RF CABERNET SAUVIGNON 1988 South Australia (Aus)
325	£16.24	CARMENET CABERNET SAUVIGNON 1986 Sonoma (Cal)

437	£3.96	SENORIO DE LOS LLANOS RESERVA 1982 Valdepeñas (Sp)
440	£5.65	TINTO VELHO REGUENGOS DE MONSARAZ, JOSE DE SOUSA ROSADO FERNANDES 1986 Alentejo (P)
451	£9.75	MARQUIS DE MURRIETA RIOJA TINTO RESERVA 1985 (Sp)

SK   Seckford Wines

2 Betts Ave, Martlesham Heath, Ipswich, Suffolk IP5 7RH (0473 626072). Independent merchant with particularly good range of fine old wine. **Opening Hours:** 10am-6pm Mon-Fri. **Delivery:** free locally, nationally at cost. **Tastings:** regularly in-store plus tutored events.

Seckford's Fine Wine Warehouse now provides a good reason for wine lovers to travel to Ipswich (possibly by plane, if the company's 'where-to-find us' map is to be believed), where they will find 20-40 wines stored under vacuum and available for tasting. The range, as ever, is impressive throughout, from country wines at less than £3 to Muscats from the Massandra Collection at several times that price. The New World, thanks to wines such as Moss Wood Pinot Noir and Cape Mentelle Chardonnay, could now almost be described as a speciality area.

11	£10.99	DEUTZ MARLBOROUGH CUVEE (NZ)
87	£4.99	ORLANDO RF CHARDONNAY 1989 S E Australia (Aus)
93	£6.59	BROKENBACK VINEYARD CHARDONNAY, ROTHBURY 1990 Hunter Valley (Aus)
106	£10.99	WYNNS COONAWARRA ESTATE CHARDONNAY 1989 (Aus)
119	£14.65	LES PIERRES CHARDONNAY, SONOMA CUTRER 1987 Sonoma (Cal)
148	£6.95	SELAKS SAUVIGNON BLANC 1990 (NZ)
247	£3.29	DOMAINE DE MONTMARIN MERLOT, VIN DE PAYS DES COTES DE THONGUE 1989 Midi (F)
280	£4.99	ORLANDO RF CABERNET SAUVIGNON 1988 South Australia (Aus)
289	£6.35	LES CHARMES GODARD, COTES DE FRANCS 1988 Bordeaux (F)
353	£5.49	PENFOLDS BIN 28 KALIMNA SHIRAZ 1988 South Australia (Aus)
365	£6.75	CHATEAU TAHBILK SHIRAZ 1987 Goulburn Valley (Aus)
460	£13.95	CAMPBELLS OLD RUTHERGLEN LIQUEUR MUSCAT (Aus)
489	£9.95	STARBOARD BATCH 88 RUBY, QUADY, Central Valley (Cal)

SEL   Selfridges

400 Oxford St, London W1A 1AB (071 629 1234). Department store with very active wine section. **Opening Hours:** 9.30am-6pm Mon-Wed, Fri, Sat; 9.30am-8pm Thu. **Delivery:** free within M25 ring. **Tastings:** regularly in-store plus tutored events. **Discounts:** 12 bottles for price of 11 on most wines.

'We sell over 500 table wines (though to be honest, I lost count after that)'. This London department store is often overlooked by wine buyers heading towards less impressive merchants with duller ranges. Selfridges' range is long and good enough to be termed truly comprehensive and the staff are admirably knowledgeable too. Prices aren't the lowest in town, but they are less exaggerated than at some stores we could name...

7	£11.79	MAISON DEUTZ SPARKLING, Napa Valley (Cal)
22	£21.99	VEUVE CLICQUOT DEMI-SEC CHAMPAGNE (F)
93	£7.39	BROKENBACK VINEYARD CHARDONNAY, ROTHBURY 1990 Hunter Valley (Aus)
102	£8.99	MARQUES DE MURRIETA RIOJA BLANCO RESERVA 1985 Rioja (Sp)
117	£13.29	ELSTON CHARDONNAY, TE MATA 1989 (NZ)

124	£22.00	MEURSAULT PREMIER CRU LES CRAS, OLIVIER LEFLAIVE 1988 Burgundy (F)
281	£5.69	MONTANA CABERNET SAUVIGNON 1988 Marlborough (NZ)
327	£11.95	YARRA YERING CABERNET SAUVIGNON 1987 Yarra Valley (Aus)
336	£50.00	OPUS ONE, ROBERT MONDAVI 1987 Napa Valley (Cal)
412	£4.79	CAMPO FIORIN VALPOLICELLA, MASI 1986 Veneto (It)
438	£4.25	MARIUS RESERVA, BODEGAS PIQUERAS 1983 Almansa (Sp)
442	£5.89	TEMPRANILLO, BODEGAS OCHOA 1987 Navarra (Sp)
451	£9.99	MARQUIS DE MURRIETA RIOJA TINTO RESERVA 1985 (Sp)
452	£12.75	RIOJA RESERVA 904, LA RIOJA ALTA 1978 (Sp)
460	£14.75	CAMPBELLS OLD RUTHERGLEN LIQUEUR MUSCAT (Aus)
479	£6.39	LA GITANA MANZANILLA, HIDALGO, Jerez (Sp)
480	£7.29	DOS CORTADOS, WILLIAMS AND HUMBERT, Jerez (Sp)
481	£9.75	MANZANILLA PASADA DE SANLUCAR ALMACENISTA, LUSTAU, Jerez (Sp)
482	£11.85	ROYAL CORREGIDOR RICH RARE OLD OLOROSO, SANDEMAN, Jerez (Sp)
483	£17.49	APOSTOLES, GONZALEZ BYASS, Jerez (Sp)
487	£7.79	TAYLOR'S FIRST ESTATE PORT LUGAR DAS LAGES, Douro (P)

SHV | Sherborne Vintners

The Old Vicarage, Leigh, Sherborne, Dorset DT9 6HL (0935 872222). Two-man-band with good Iberian selection. **Opening Hours:** 9.00am-7.00pm Mon-Sat. **Delivery:** free within 20 miles, nationally at cost. **Tastings:** wines occasionally open for tasting, organised customers' club events. **Discounts:** available on 6+ cases.

Last year, we reported that Ian Sinnott ran this company single-handedly. Now he has been joined by David Olive a 'clinical psychologist with a lifelong interest in wine', who presumably will provide insight into why some customers make straight for 'The Spanish List' while others are drawn towards the expanding range from France, Australia and New Zealand. Whatever their motives, both groups' desires should be amply satisfied.

SAS | Sherston Wine Co (St Albans)

97 Victoria St, St Albans, Herts AL1 3TJ (0727 58841). Enthusiastic independent merchant. **Opening Hours:** Tues - Thurs 11.30am - 7pm, Fri 11.30am - 8pm, Sat 9.30am - 6pm. **Delivery:** free locally, nationally at cost. **Tastings:** regularly in-store and tutored tastings plus organised events. **Discounts:** 5% on (mixed) cases, 7.5% for Sherston Wine Club members.

Ernest Jacoby's 'taste-before-you-buy' Saturday morning sessions have become a weekly fixture for a growing number of St Albanites. Spain and Italy are especially well represented, but the French range is good (Schlumberger Alsace, Tollot-Beaut Burgundies) as is the brief New World list. Look out for good one-off offers of mature Bordeaux and Burgundy.

29	£2.99	CUVEE JEAN-PAUL BLANC SEC VIN DE TABLE, PAUL BOUTINOT (F)
69	£7.99	SOAVE CLASSICO VIGNETO CALVARINO, PIEROPAN 1989 Veneto (It)
102	£9.25	MARQUES DE MURRIETA RIOJA BLANCO RESERVA 1985 Rioja (Sp)
139	£5.39	DOMAINE DU PRE BARON, SAUVIGNON DE TOURAINE 1989 Loire (F)
360	£5.99	COTES DU RHONE SEGURET, CHATEAU LA COURANCONNE 1985 (F)
446	£6.35	GRAN SANGREDETORO RESERVA, TORRES 1986 Penedés (Sp)
449	£8.49	CAMPO VIEJO RIOJA GRAN RESERVA 1980 (Sp)
452	£15.25	RIOJA RESERVA 904, LA RIOJA ALTA 1978 (Sp)

Head Office: 20 Midland Road, London NW1 2AD (071 388 5088). Branches at:14 Davies St, London W1Y 1LJ ; 50 Elizabeth Street, London SW1 & 21 Motcomb Street, London SW1. Small up-market traditional chain acting as the retail arm of Laytons. **Opening Hours**: 9.30am - 7pm Mon-Fri; 9.30am-1pm Sat. **Delivery**: free locally, nationally at cost. **Tastings**: regularly in-store plus tutored events.

This year, Graham Chidgey's two companies, Laytons and André Simon, have at last officially become one, allowing the latter firm to sell the Laytons range over the counter. The Chidgey style is very apparent: 'If you shop regularly with us then you will obtain the best attention as we shall begin to know your tastes'. Go to André Simon for its Burgundies especially, but also for the New World selection and red Russians from the 1960s.

Rectory Cottage, Luton, Beds LU2 8LU (046 276 214). Sensible independent merchant. **Opening Hours**: 8.30am-9pm Mon-Fri (and by appointment at weekends). **Delivery**: free within 50 miles, nationally at cost. **Tastings**: regularly in-store plus tutored events. **Discounts**: on unbroken cases.

With a clientele ranging from unknowledgeable but interested blue-collar Vauxhall workers to pin-striped (though, often just as unknowledgeable) buyers for company boardrooms, Master of Wine Derek Smedley's small business has built up an enviable reputation for offering value for money across the board. There are lots of French country wines, Petits Châteaux Bordeaux and good wines from the southern hemisphere. Mr Smedley would be most specially pleased, though, if you asked for a bottle of the delicious Warden Vineyard English wine. He made it.

79	£3.64	COTES DE ST MONT, PLAIMONT 1990 South West (F)
86	£5.04	CHARDONNAY, VIN DE PAYS D'OC, HUGH RYMAN 1990 Midi (F)
168	£5.08	ALSACE GEWURZTRAMINER KAEFFERKOPF, CAVE VINICOLE DE KIENTZHEIM KAYSERBERG 1989 (F)
174	£4.16	CAFAYATE TORRONTES, ETCHART 1990 Mendoza (Arg)
227	£4.24	CUVEE DE L'ARJOLLE ROUGE, VIN DE PAYS DES COTES DE THONGUE, TEISSERENC 1989 Midi (F)
299	£6.74	MONTES ALPHA CABERNET SAUVIGNON, DISCOVER WINE LT DA 1987 Curico Valley (Ch)
359	£5.50	CROZES HERMITAGE, DELAS FRERES 1989 Rhône (F)
415	£6.76	BARBERA D'ALBA PIAN ROMUALDO, PRUNOTTO 1988 Piedmont (It)
419	£7.66	ROSSO DI MONTALCINO, POGGIO ANTICO 1989 Tuscany (It)
430	£13.50	BRUNELLO DEL MONTALCINO, POGGIO ANTICO 1985 Piedmont (It)

24-25 Scala St, London W1P 1LU (071 637 4767) & also in at 56 Lamb's Conduit St, London WC1 (071 405 3106), Ancient and modern city stalwart. **Opening Hours**: 9.30am-6.30pm Mon-Fri; 10am-1pm Sat. **Delivery**: free in Central London, nationally at cost. **Tastings**: regularly in-store, tutored events. **Discounts**: 5% mixed case.

Once thought of as specialists in Spanish and German wines, this Royal Warranted firm has gradually bowed to reality ('It is a sad fact that the wines of Germany are currently greatly overlooked by the majority of wine drinkers') by increasing its French regional range, and particularly its Burgundies. All are worth seeking out, as are the J M da Fonseca Portuguese wines for which it is the UK agent.

11	£10.99	DEUTZ MARLBOROUGH CUVEE (NZ)
46	£4.45	CHARDONNAY, DOMAINE DES FLINES, VIN DE PAYS DE LA LOIRE 1990 (F)
54	£5.95	ALSACE TOKAY PINOT GRIS, CAVE VINICOLE DE TURCKHEIM 1990 (F)
102	£9.25	MARQUES DE MURRIETA RIOJA BLANCO RESERVA 1985 Rioja (Sp)
145	£6.85	SAUVIGNON DE ST BRIS, DOMAINE FELIX 1990 Burgundy (F)
288	£7.95	CHATEAU MUSAR 1982 Bekaa Valley (Leb)
333	£23.00	CHATEAU PAVIE, ST EMILION 1985 Bordeaux (F)
413	£5.95	DOLCETTO D'ALBA, CONTERNO 1988 Piedmont (It)
416	£8.25	CHIANTI CLASSICO, ISOLE E OLENA 1988 Tuscany (It)
440	£4.95	TINTO VELHO REGUENGOS DE MONSARAZ, JOSE DE SOUSA ROSADO FERNANDES 1986 Alentejo (P)
480	£8.65	DOS CORTADOS, WILLIAMS AND HUMBERT, Jerez (Sp)

SOL La Solitude

The Cellar, 4 The Street, Wittersham, Kent TN30 7ED. (0797) 270696. Keen young independent. **Delivery**: free locally, nationally at cost. **Tastings**: in-store and theme dinners. **Discounts**: 5-8%.

Malcolm Smith and Alexandra Jarvis have succeded in breathing fresh life into a business which they took over in 1990. France is clearly the principal area of interest, with a plenitude of good wines from familiar and unfamiliar names. The Italian selection is worth consideration too, but we'd like the Californians to extend beyond a pair of Gallos.

33	£3.38	DOMAINE DU TARIQUET, COTES DE GASCOGNE 1990 South West (F)
442	£5.40	TEMPRANILLO, BODEGAS OCHOA 1987 Navarra (Sp)
457	£5.38	MOSCATEL DE SETUBAL, ADEGA COOPERATIVA DE PALMELA 1981 (P)

SPR Spar (UK) Ltd

Head Office: 32-40 Headstone Drive, Harrow, Middx HA3 5QT (081 863 5511). 2,000-branch national chain of independent grocers and supermarkets. **Opening Hours**: '8 till late'. **Tastings**: occasional in-store. **Discounts**: depends on the individual retailer.

Like the Co-op, Spar is handicapped by the fact that it is a huge chain formed out of 2,000 independent links. Wine buyer Philippa Carr has an unenviable job trying to persuade Spar managers to take wine seriously, but she is beginning to score victories, and truly recommendable bottles are finding their way into at least a few of the shops. Watch this space.

310	£9.39	BARON VILLENEUVE DE CANTERMERLE, HAUT-MEDOC, CHATEAU CANTEMERLE 1986 Bordeaux (F)
499	£2.09	MOSCATO FIZZ, VITICOLTORI DELL'ACQUESE, Piedmont (It)

FSW Frank E Stainton

3 Berrys Yard, Finkle St, Kendal, Cumbria LA9 4AB (0539 731886). Invigorated independent merchant. **Opening Hours**: 8.30am-6pm Mon-Sat. **Delivery**: free within 30 miles, nationally at cost.

Tastings: wines regularly open for sampling, tutored and organised events. **Discounts**: 5% for cash payment on a (mixed) case.

'We trade according to our market, which differs a great deal from London. Our wine list may not be the most innovative, but it is very functional.' We take Chris Leather's point, but fear he is too modest. Albania may not feature on his list, but he's got a far more innovative and fairly priced range of Antipodeans and Australians than a great many firms in the Capital. And his 'classics' (Drouhin, Deinhard, Schlumberger...) beat many of theirs too.

19	£16.95	**DEVAUX CHAMPAGNE CUVEE ROSEE** (F)		
22	£21.00	**VEUVE CLICQUOT DEMI-SEC CHAMPAGNE** (F)		
87	£5.30	**ORLANDO RF CHARDONNAY** 1989 S E Australia (Aus)		
180	£4.15	**HILL SMITH OLD TRIANGLE RIESLING** 1990 Barossa Valley (Aus)		
280	£5.30	**ORLANDO RF CABERNET SAUVIGNON** 1988 South Australia (Aus)		
446	£5.90	**GRAN SANGREDETORO RESERVA, TORRES** 1986 Penedés (Sp)		
457	£6.95	**MOSCATEL DE SETUBAL, ADEGA COOPERATIVA DE PALMELA** 1981 (P)		
465	£6.15	**REDWOOD VALLEY ESTATE LATE HARVEST RIESLING** 1989 Nelson (NZ)		
475	£17.00	**CHATEAU RIEUSSEC, SAUTERNES** 1983 Bordeaux (F)		

SUM | Summerlee Wines

Summerlee Wine Centre, 64 High St, Earls Barton, Northants NN6 0JG (0604 810488). Quality conscious merchant majoring on Germany. **Opening Hours**: 9am-1pm Mon; 9am-1pm & 2pm-5.30pm Tues-Fri. **Delivery**: free in Oxford, Cambridge and London, nationally at cost. **Tastings**: occasional in-store plus organised events.

Freddy Price remains one of our favourite German specialists, largely because he has refused to be taken in by the nonsense of over-priced, mouth-strippingly acidic dry whites, and has instead concentrated on finding good examples of German regional styles which taste ripe, whatever their level of sweetness. But Summerlee should not be pigeon-holed. Its non-Germanic list is long and enticing, with wines from Ngatarawa in New Zealand, Delas in the Rhône and Nathaniel Johnston in Bordeaux. And we can confirm that throughout the selection, the prices are decidedly 'right'.

169	£8.07	**ALSACE GEWURZTRAMINER ST HUBERT, KUEHN** 1989 (F)
203	£4.25	**CHATEAU BAUDUC, BORDEAUX CLAIRET, DAVID THOMAS** 1990 (F)
369	£7.64	**MITCHELL PEPPERTREE VINEYARD SHIRAZ** 1988 Clare Valley (Aus)
493	£15.56	**WARRE'S QUINTA DA CAVADINHA** 1982 Douro (P)

WC | The Sunday Times Wine Club

New Aquitaine House, Paddock Rd, Reading, Berks RG4 0JY (0734 481711). Mail-order only wine-club. **Delivery**: free nationally for orders over £50. **Tastings**: tutored and organised events.

Criticising the Sunday Times Wine Club can be a little like questioning the Royal Family's relationship with the Inland Revenue. Tony Laithwaite is very likeable and the Club, which runs an enjoyable annual Wine Fair, seems to have tens of thousands of loyal fans. Presumably few of them mind the very high prices they are asked to pay for what are often pretty basic wines. Infuriatingly, too, the Club's most innovative efforts have rarely borne close examination. The Australian 'Flying Winemakers' have, with a few exceptions (such as Nick Butler's efforts in Navarra), produced wines in Europe and South America which would get scant applause Down Under, and the Czechoslovakian range is of greatest interest to those building museum collections of the way Eastern Europe used to be. Customers seeking a bit of - but not too much - variety should try Bordeaux Direct, the sister company which sells most (75%) of the same wines by mail and through its shops. We wonder how many wines from either range are frequently drunk by Wine Club President Hugh Johnson for his own pleasure.

SUP | Supergrape

81 Replingham Road, London, SW18 5LU (081) 874 5963. Ambitious, expanding South London generalist. **Delivery**: free (very) locally, nationally at cost. **Tastings**: in-store and for members of the Wine Club. **Discount**: 5% per case.

Mike Hall's recently acquired business has become an instant hit in SW18, where local residents are as likely to want Lambrusco Light as Opus One. Supergrape offers both, along with serious Morgon (from Jacky Janodet), less serious Moulin à Vent 1982 (from Patriarche) and Château Palmer (1980 and 1982). Wine Club members meet four times a year and receive greater discounts.

84	£4.95	**OXFORD LANDING CHARDONNAY, YALUMBA** 1990 South Australia (Aus)	
140	£5.50	**COOKS HAWKES BAY SAUVIGNON BLANC** 1989 Hawkes Bay (NZ)	
150	£6.75	**STONELEIGH SAUVIGNON BLANC** 1989 Marlborough (NZ)	
280	£5.95	**ORLANDO RF CABERNET SAUVIGNON** 1988 South Australia (Aus)	
313	£11.25	**CLOUDY BAY CABERNET MERLOT** 1989 Marlborough (NZ)	
487	£8.20	**TAYLOR'S FIRST ESTATE PORT LUGAR DAS LAGES,** Douro (P)	
500	£3.30	**PETILLANT DE LISTEL,** Midi (F)	

SWIG

See The Fulham Road Wine Centre for details.

James Rogers of Fulham Road Wine Centre and Barnes Wine Shop fame, has launched the 'Serious Wine Imbibers Group' as an alternative wine club, offering good wines by mail and excellent vinous advice. The venture is still in its infancy, but if it is half as good as Rogers' previous ventures (which included the Cullens Wine Club), it will be well worth following.

T&W | T&W Wines

51 King Street, Thetford, Norfolk IP24 2AU (0842 765646). Independent California-mad merchant running vinous old folks' home. **Opening Hours:** 9.30-5.30 Mon-Fri; 9.30am-2.30pm Sat. **Delivery:** free within 15 miles and nationally for 4+ cases. **Tastings:** regularly in-store.

Do not ask Trevor Hughes to recommend wines in which to invest; 'We do not like wine to be traded as a commodity - we like to sell to people who drink wine'. We like Mr Hughes attitude as much as we like his extraordinary list of wines. The Fine and Rare range includes 1952 Krug in magnums, Château Gilette 1934 and 1929 Barolet Collection Beaune, a set of wines which could interestingly be compared with more current vintages from the T&W list. Other companies offer good Bordeaux and Burgundy; T&W's secret lies in innovatively offering brilliant modern wines from producers like Flora Springs and Kent Rasmussen in California, Bava in Italy and Opitz in Austria. The east of England is positively burgeoning with classy wine merchants, but it was T&W who were closest to taking the award for that region away from Adnams.

TBW | Talbot Wines

6 Shakespeare Drive, Shirley, Solihull. West Midlands. (021) 744 5775. Retail arm of wholesalers, C.C.M. Wines. **Delivery**: free locally, nationally at cost. **Tastings**: occasionally in-store. **Discount**:5% on case sales.

Nick & Tim Underwood's company, C.C.M. Wines, is one of the best-respected wholesalers in the Midlands. As well it might be with a range that starts with 'Lambrusco -All Colours' and goes on to take in Mme Joly's rare Coulée de Serrant 1984, Château Fuissé 1988, and Vieux Château Certan 1982. Older bottles include Domigny 1943 Champagne.

119	£11.99	LES PIERRES CHARDONNAY, SONOMA CUTRER 1987 Sonoma (Cal)
281	£4.89	MONTANA CABERNET SAUVIGNON 1988 Marlborough (NZ)
344	£4.41	PENFOLDS BIN 2 SHIRAZ/MATARO 1989 Barossa Valley (Aus)
353	£5.38	PENFOLDS BIN 28 KALIMNA SHIRAZ 1988 South Australia (Aus)
483	£15.40	APOSTOLES, GONZALEZ BYASS , Jerez (Sp) 1988 (F)

TAN | Tanners

Head office and main shop: 26 Wyle Cop, Shrewsbury, Shropshire SY1 1XD (0743 232400). Model country wine merchant with 6 branches around the Welsh borders. **Opening Hours**: 9am - 5.30pm Mon-Sat. **Delivery**: free locally for orders over 1 case and nationally for orders over £75. **Tastings**: occasionally in-store plus regular tutored events. **Discounts**: available on quantities over 6 cases or for cash payment and collection.

Richard Tanner and Richard Haydon, his deputy, have created the kind of wine company others envy. While others bleat about how difficult it is to compete with supermarkets and high street chains, this two-time winner of our Centre of England Award has made sure that its shops have something special to offer: a combination of good wines and really first class service. Tanners customers can drink wines from just about everywhere, but whatever their choice, we would expect it to have been selected with care.

6	£8.81	TALTARNI BRUT TACHE, Pyrenees (Aus)
63	£5.48	SUNNYCLIFF ESTATES CHARDONNAY 1989 Victoria (Aus)
79	£3.69	COTES DE ST MONT, PLAIMONT 1990 South West (F)
92	£5.85	MACON CHARDONNAY, J TALMARD 1988 Burgundy (F)
100	£8.08	CHARDONNAY CHAMPS PERRIERES, H LECLERC 1989 Burgundy (F)
102	£9.18	MARQUES DE MURRIETA RIOJA BLANCO RESERVA 1985 Rioja (Sp)
150	£7.16	STONELEIGH SAUVIGNON BLANC 1989 Marlborough (NZ)
180	£4.78	HILL SMITH OLD TRIANGLE RIESLING 1990 Barossa Valley (Aus)
187	£7.31	TRITTENHEIMER APOTHEKE KABINETT, F W GYMNASIUM 1989 M-S-R (G)
197	£5.16	ASTLEY SEVERN VALE 1989 Worcestershire (UK)
227	£4.09	CUVEE DE L'ARJOLLE ROUGE, VIN DE PAYS DES COTES DE THONGUE, TEISSERENC 1989 Midi (F)
280	£6.03	ORLANDO RF CABERNET SAUVIGNON 1988 South Australia (Aus)

281	£5.42	MONTANA CABERNET SAUVIGNON 1988 Marlborough (NZ)
288	£7.26	CHATEAU MUSAR 1982 Bekaa Valley (Leb)
295	£8.26	WYNNS CABERNET SAUVIGNON 1985 Coonawarra (Aus)
309	£9.44	BLUE PYRENEES 1984 Victoria (Aus)
311	£9.02	SIMI CABERNET SAUVIGNON 1984 Sonoma (Cal)
320	£12.76	CHATEAU LEOVILLE BARTON, ST JULIEN 1987 Bordeaux (F)
327	£15.67	YARRA YERING CABERNET SAUVIGNON 1987 Yarra Valley (Aus)
336	£47.24	OPUS ONE, ROBERT MONDAVI 1987 Napa Valley (Cal)
350	£4.68	CHATEAU DU GRAND MOULAS, COTES DU RHONE 1989 (F)
373	£8.89	DOMAINE DU VIEUX TELEGRAPHE, CHATEAUNEUF DU PAPE 1987 Rhône (F)
388	£6.42	TANNERS RED BURGUNDY, DOMAINE PARENT 1987 (F)
425	£14.01	CARMIGNANO RISERVA, VILLA DI CAPEZZANA 1985 Tuscany (It)
438	£4.28	MARIUS RESERVA, BODEGAS PIQUERAS 1983 Almansa (Sp)
450	£7.50	NAVARRA ANIVERSARO 125, CHIVITE 1981 Navarra (Sp)
451	£9.69	MARQUIS DE MURRIETA RIOJA TINTO RESERVA 1985 (Sp)
455	£3.51	CASTILLO DE LIRIA MOSCATEL, VICENTE GANDIA, Valencia (Sp)
456	£6.42	SAMOS MUSCAT, Samos (Gr)

TO | **Tesco**

Supermarket Wine Merchant of the Year

Head Office: Tesco House, Delamere Rd, Cheshunt, Herts EN8 9SL (0992 32222). Vigorously vinous nationwide supermarket chain. **Opening Hours:** varied. **Tastings:** occasionally in-store.

After two years of being runners-up to Sainsbury, Tesco has once again taken the Award of Supermarket Wine Merchant of the Year. In voting for Tesco, the judges complimented the chain for its consistent spirit of innovation and, in particular for the steadfast way it has sought out unusual and interesting wines from Italy and Germany, two countries which are far too often considered in a far more shallow way. The judges also commented favourably on the initiative taken by Tesco to indicate on labels the relative strength of all of their wines. But it was Tesco's range which won it the prize. As one judge said, if they take advantage of even a fraction of this list, Tesco customers are among the best served wine drinkers in the world.

3	£6.99	LINDAUER, MONTANA (NZ)
4	£6.89	CHEVALIER DE MONCONTOUR VOUVRAY MOUSSEUX 1987 Loire (F)
11	£11.39	DEUTZ MARLBOROUGH CUVEE (NZ)
14	£13.45	DEHOURS CHAMPAGNE (F)
33	£2.75	DOMAINE DU TARIQUET, COTES DE GASCOGNE 1990 South West (F)
39	£3.69	TESCO ST EDMUND ENGLISH WINE, HIGHWAYMAN'S VINEYARD (UK)
41	£3.79	TESCO ALSACE PINOT BLANC, KUEN 1989 (F)
42	£3.05	CEPAGE TERRET, VIN DE PAYS DE L'HERAULT, DELTA DOMAINES 1989 Midi (F)
50	£4.69	TESCO MACON VILLAGES, CAVE DE VIRE 1990 Burgundy (F)
57	£4.99	TESCO ORGANIC WHITE, CHATEAU VIEUX GABIRAN 1990 Bordeaux (F)
65	£5.50	TESCO ST VERAN LES MONTS, CO-OP DE PRISSE 1988 Burgundy (F)
81	£3.99	VILLARD CHARDONNAY 1990 Maipo (Ch)
128	£3.15	TESCO SAUMUR BLANC, CAVES DES VIGNERONS DE SAUMUR 1989 Loire (F)
129	£3.19	NURAGUS DI CAGLIARI, CANTINA SOCIALE DI DOLIANOVA 1990 Sardinia (It)
175	£4.69	MOSCATO D'ASTI, MICHELE CHIARLO 1990 Piedmont (It)
183	£4.99	BINGER SCHARLACHBERG KABINETT HALBTROCKEN, VILLA SACHSEN 1988 Rheinhessen (G)
187	£4.89	TRITTENHEIMER APOTHEKE KABINETT, F W GYMNASIUM 1989 M-S-R (G)

194	£2.39	**TESCO HOCK, RIETBURG** (G)
195	£4.59	**JOHANNISBERGER KLAUS RIESLING, SCHLOSS SCHONBORN** 1988 Rheingau (G)
218	£3.59	**DOMAINE DE LA CROIX, BUZET** 1988 Midi (F)
235	£6.25	**DOMAINE LES HAUTES DE CHAMBERTS, CAHORS** 1986 South West (F)
237	£2.59	**TESCO FRENCH MERLOT, SICA DES COTEAUX LIMOUSINS,** Midi (F)
242	£2.95	**DOMAINE BEAULIEU SAINT SAUVEUR, MARMANDAIS** 1988 South West (F)
250	£3.55	**CHATEAU TOUTIGEAC BORDEAUX ROUGE** 1989 (F)
256	£3.99	**TESCO MEDOC, DIPROVIN ET DIE,** Bordeaux (F)
260	£4.09	**TESCO AUSTRALIAN CABERNET/SHIRAZ, HARDY'S,** South Australia (Aus)
262	£4.19	**CHATEAU GOELANE BORDEAUX ROUGE** 1988 Bordeaux (F)
265	£4.49	**CHATEAU LEON BORDEAUX ROUGE** 1987 (F)
275	£4.89	**TESCO BOURGUEIL, DOMAINE HUBERT** 1989 Loire (F)
280	£4.59	**ORLANDO RF CABERNET SAUVIGNON** 1988 South Australia (Aus)
281	£5.05	**MONTANA CABERNET SAUVIGNON** 1988 Marlborough (NZ)
287	£6.35	**RAIMAT CABERNET SAUVIGNON** 1985 Lérida (Sp)
293	£6.85	**JAMIESONS RUN RED, MILDARA** 1987 Coonawarra (Aus)
298	£7.75	**TESCO MARGAUX, YVON MAU,** Bordeaux (F)
299	£7.99	**MONTES ALPHA CABERNET SAUVIGNON** 1987 Curico Valley (Ch)
303	£7.25	**ROSEMOUNT SHOW RESERVE CABERNET SAUVIGNON** 1987 Coonawarra (Aus)
330	£19.49	**PAVILLON ROUGE DE CHATEAU MARGAUX** 1988 Bordeaux (F)
335	£26.65	**LES FORTS DE LATOUR, PAUILLAC, CHATEAU LATOUR** 1982 Bordeaux (F)
338	£3.15	**TESCO SYRAH, C MUSSELL,** Midi (F)
357	£4.85	**FETZER ZINFANDEL** 1987 Mendocino (Cal)
363	£6.49	**TESCO CHATEAUNEUF DU PAPE LES ARNEVELS, QUIOT** 1988 Rhône (F)
386	£4.89	**TESCO RED BURGUNDY, MOILLARD** (F)
403	£3.79	**TESCO CHIANTI CLASSICO, CANTINE CO-OP DI GREVEPESA** 1988 Tuscany (It)
405	£4.99	**CHIANTI RUFINA, SELVAPIANA** 1988 Tuscany (It)
422	£12.15	**BAROLO, MICHELE CHIARLO** 1982 Piedmont (It)
435	£2.59	**DON DARIAS RED, BODEGAS VITORIANAS** (Sp)
437	£3.65	**SENORIO DE LOS LLANOS RESERVA** 1982 Valdepeñas (Sp)
440	£4.49	**TINTO VELHO REGUENGOS DE MONSARAZ, JOSE DE SOUSA ROSADO FERNANDES** 1986 Alentejo (P)
443	£5.55	**GARRAFEIRA PT81, J M DE FONSECA** 1981 Azeitão (P)
485	£6.85	**TESCO LATE BOTTLED VINTAGE PORT, SMITH WOODHOUSE** 1985 Douro (P)
487	£4.69	**TAYLOR'S FIRST ESTATE PORT LUGAR DAS LAGES,** Douro (P)
494	£18.59	**SANDEMAN IMPERIAL 20 YEAR OLD TAWNY PORT,** Douro (P)
500	£2.05	**PETILLANT DE LISTEL,** Midi (F)

TW	Thames Wine Sellers

6 Marmion Road, London SW11 5PA (071 228 4921). **Delivery**: free in London for 2+ cases. **Tastings**: bottles regularly opened for sampling, plus tutored events. **Discounts**: on large quantities.

A slim list, both in size and content, but one which could teach many merchants a thing or two. The design is so simple (five sheets of Conqueror paper, lots of space and a decent typeface) that the production costs are probably as low as for any list we've seen, but it is strikingly effective. The wines themselves are also eminently sensible. Burgundy is the most widely-stocked area, with wines from Armand Rousseau, Louis Latour and the La Chablisienne cooperative, and the Spanish selection is small, but includes the likes of Vega Sicilia and Pesquera. And if you don't trust yourself to pick wines off the list, you can always join the 'Private Vine Club', where for a cool £1,100 a year, Julian Kirk will help you lay down a cellar to be proud of.

54	£5.25	**ALSACE TOKAY PINOT GRIS, CAVE VINICOLE DE TURCKHEIM** 1990 (F)
90	£5.85	**LINDEMANS BIN 65 CHARDONNAY** 1989 S E Australia (Aus)
105	£8.75	**HEGGIES CHARDONNAY, HILL-SMITH** 1988 Adelaide Hills (Aus)
180	£4.20	**HILL SMITH OLD TRIANGLE RIESLING** 1990 Barossa Valley (Aus)
264	£4.30	**BERRI ESTATES AUSTRALIAN CABERNET SHIRAZ** 1987 (Aus)
305	£9.30	**JEAN LEON CABERNET SAUVIGNON** 1983 Penedés (Sp)
412	£7.95	**CAMPO FIORIN VALPOLICELLA, MASI** 1986 Veneto (It)
446	£5.50	**GRAN SANGREDETORO RESERVA, TORRES** 1986 Penedés (Sp)

TH | **Thresher Wine Shops**

Joint Winner: National High Street Chain of the Year

Head Office: Sefton House, 42 Church Rd, Welwyn Garden City, Herts AL8 6PJ (0707 328244). Rapidly improving High Street chain with 462 branches nationwide. **Opening Hours**: 10am-10.30pm Mon-Sat, 12-2pm and 7pm-9pm Sun (with some regional variations). **Delivery**: free locally. **Tastings**: occasionally in-store. **Discounts**: vary with the amount spent, plus selected promotions.

'Commitment' was the keynote of the judges' comments about Threshers, the chain which has so dramatically leapt from the dull, brewery-owned mire of five years ago to join the serious wine world. This year, apart from the wine buyers' loyalty to the impressive selection of Alsace introduced in 1990, there were two other, similarly impressive initiatives. 'The Beautiful South' consisted of 42 wines from various regions of Southern France, and was cleverly linked to a cassette in which the wines were discussed and described by Charles Metcalfe of WINE Magazine and Granada Television's This Morning. 'The Case for Bordeaux' was, if anything, more innovative still, consisting as it did of a set of 12 modern white wines from a region few people associate with anything other than red wine. It is efforts like these and the quality of Thresher's range that won it this Award for the first time.

N.B. The 445 Drinks Stores from Threshers may stock some of the wines listed below, but the above description and the award apply only to Thresher Wine Shops.

3	£6.99	**LINDAUER, MONTANA** (NZ)
22	£20.59	**VEUVE CLICQUOT DEMI-SEC CHAMPAGNE** (F)
33	£3.15	**DOMAINE DU TARIQUET, COTES DE GASCOGNE** 1990 South West (F)
37	£3.69	**CHATEAU LES HAUTS DE TREYTIN, BORDEAUX BLANC, MANDREAU** 1990 (F)
38	£3.29	**TOLLANA DRY WHITE** 1988 S E Australia (Aus)
45	£3.99	**CHARDONNAY, LES DUCS ST MARTIN, VAL D'ORBIEU** 1990 Midi (F)
46	£3.99	**CHARDONNAY, DOMAINE DES FLINES, VIN DE PAYS DE LA LOIRE** 1990 (F)
48	£4.49	**CHATEAU HAUT REDON, ENTRE DEUX MERS, HUGH RYMAN** 1990 Bordeaux (F)
54	£4.59	**ALSACE TOKAY PINOT GRIS, CAVE VINICOLE DE TURCKHEIM** 1990 (F)
58	£4.75	**CHATEAU COUCHEROY BLANC, GRAVES, ANDRE LURTON** 1989 Bordeaux (F)
61	£5.29	**CHATEAU SAINT GALIER BORDEAUX BLANC** 1990 (F)
76	£11.99	**DOMAINE FONT DE MICHELLE, CHATEAUNEUF DU PAPE BLANC** 1990 Rhône (F)
99	£7.99	**CUVEE DES JACOBINS BOURGOGNE CHARDONNAY, JADOT** 1989 Burgundy (F)
106	£8.85	**WYNNS COONAWARRA ESTATE CHARDONNAY** 1989 (Aus)
127	£2.79	**DONATIEN BLANC DE BLANC, DONATIEN BAHUAUD** 1990 Loire (F)
133	£4.19	**DOMAINE DU COLOMBET SAUVIGNON, COTES DE DURAS** 1990 South West (F)
140	£4.99	**COOKS HAWKES BAY SAUVIGNON BLANC** 1989 Hawkes Bay (NZ)
143	£5.99	**DOMAINE DU RELAIS DE POSTE, SAUVIGNON DE ST BRIS** 1989 Burgundy (F)
150	£5.99	**STONELEIGH SAUVIGNON BLANC** 1989 Marlborough (NZ)

170	£11.75	ALSACE GEWURZTRAMINER GRAND CRU GOLDERT, ZIND HUMBRECHT 1987 (F)
172	£18.99	ALSACE GEWURZTRAMINER HERRENWEG VENDANGE TARDIVE, ZIND HUMBRECHT 1986 (F)
192	£7.59	DEINHARD HOCHHEIM HERITAGE SELECTION 1988 Rheingau (G)
209	£2.69	VAL DU MONT CABERNET SAUVIGNON, VIN DE PAYS D'OC 1988 Midi (F)
223	£3.69	DOMAINE ST EULALIE, MINERVOIS 1988 Midi (F)
231	£4.49	CHATEAU DE LASTOURS CUVEE SIMONE DESCAMPS, CORBIERES 1989 Midi (F)
236	£6.49	PRIEURE DE CENAC, CAHORS, RIGAL 1986 South West (F)
247	£3.29	DOMAINE DE MONTMARIN MERLOT, COTES DE THONGUE 1989 Midi (F)
249	£3.49	DOMAINE DES CAUNETTES MERLOT, VIN DE PAYS DE L'AUDE 1990 Midi (F)
257	£3.99	CHATEAU GUIBON BORDEAUX ROUGE, LURTON 1988 (F)
258	£4.59	SVISCHTOV CABERNET SAUVIGNON CONTROLIRAN 1985 Svischtov (Bul)
281	£5.29	MONTANA CABERNET SAUVIGNON 1988 Marlborough (NZ)
282	£5.25	CHATEAU COUCHEROY BORDEAUX ROUGE 1988 (F)
284	£5.79	SIRIUS ROUGE, PETER SICHEL 1988 Bordeaux (F)
287	£6.79	RAIMAT CABERNET SAUVIGNON 1985 Lérida (Sp)
288	£7.29	CHATEAU MUSAR 1982 Bekaa Valley (Leb)
295	£6.99	WYNNS CABERNET SAUVIGNON 1985 Coonawarra (Aus)
303	£7.99	ROSEMOUNT SHOW RESERVE CABERNET SAUVIGNON 1987 Coonawarra (Aus)
308	£9.99	COLDSTREAM HILLS CABERNET SAUVIGNON 1988 Yarra Valley (Aus)
312	£9.99	LES FIEFS DE LAGRANGE, ST JULIEN, CHATEAU LAGRANGE 1988 Bordeaux (F)
316	£11.29	TOURELLES DE LONGUEVILLE, PAUILLAC, CHATEAU PICHON-LONGUEVILLE-BARON 1988 Bordeaux (F)
344	£3.99	PENFOLDS BIN 2 SHIRAZ/MATARO 1989 Barossa Valley (Aus)
345	£4.19	CHATEAU SAINT JEAN COTE DU RHONE, MEFFRE 1989 (F)
353	£4.99	PENFOLDS BIN 28 KALIMNA SHIRAZ 1988 South Australia (Aus)
357	£5.49	FETZER ZINFANDEL 1987 Mendocino (Cal)
372	£8.99	CHATEAUNEUF DU PAPE DOMAINE FONT DE MICHELLE 1988 Rhône (F)
435	£2.99	DON DARIAS RED, BODEGAS VITORIANAS (Sp)
494	£17.99	SANDEMAN IMPERIAL 20 YEAR OLD TAWNY PORT, Douro (P)

TRE | Tremaynes

40A Bell Street, Henley, Oxon. RG9 2BG. (0491) 575061. Riverside Independent. **Delivery**: Free locally, nationally at cost. **Tastings**: regularly in-store and tutored. **Discount**: up to 10%.

Tremaynes likes to be thought of as specialists in port, whisky and South African and fine old wine. We'd hate to disagree, but we were pretty impressed by Mr Bonner-Davies skills in buying wines of various of styles and nationalities, as the following list shows.

22	£21.00	VEUVE CLICQUOT DEMI-SEC CHAMPAGNE (F)
102	£8.80	MARQUES DE MURRIETA RIOJA BLANCO RESERVA 1985 Rioja (Sp)
147	£6.80	KLEIN CONSTANTIA SAUVIGNON BLANC 1988 (SA)
437	£4.40	SENORIO DE LOS LLANOS RESERVA 1982 Valdepeñas (Sp)

UBC | The Ubiquitous Chip

Scottish Wine Merchant of the Year

12 Ashton Lane, Glasgow, G12 9U2 (041 334 5007). Excellent Independent merchant and restaurant. **Opening Hours**: 12-10pm Mon-Fri; 10am-10pm Sat. **Delivery**: free locally for 2+ cases, nationally at cost. **Tastings**: regular tutored events. **Discounts**: 5% off (mixed) cases.

It can take a very long time to order a wine in Rod Clydesdale's restaurant - or to buy a bottle in its associated shop. Not because the service is slow, but because it is extremely difficult to make a choice from a list only a page or two shorter than the Bible. Rolly Gassmann, Gaston Huët, Jean Cros, Jermann, Pieropan, Jean Leon, Vasse Felix... Just name a classy modern winemaker and you're almost sure to find not just one but probably several examples of his wine. And then there are the whiskies, including what seems to be a roll call of dead distilleries. We cannot believe that anyone has a much better range of wines and whiskies; The Ubiquitous Chip is a very worthy winner of this year's award.

87	£5.10	**ORLANDO RF CHARDONNAY** 1989 S E Australia (Aus)
102	£9.50	**MARQUES DE MURRIETA RIOJA BLANCO RESERVA** 1985 Rioja (Sp)
119	£14.35	**LES PIERRES CHARDONNAY, SONOMA CUTRER** 1987 Sonoma (Cal)
150	£6.40	**STONELEIGH SAUVIGNON BLANC** 1989 Marlborough (NZ)
280	£4.99	**ORLANDO RF CABERNET SAUVIGNON** 1988 South Australia (Aus)
305	£7.35	**JEAN LEON CABERNET SAUVIGNON** 1983 Penedés (Sp)
317	£9.98	**CLOS DU VAL MERLOT** 1987 Napa Valley (Cal)
323	£13.75	**VASSE FELIX CABERNET SAUVIGNON** 1988 Margaret River (Aus)
360	£4.90	**COTES DU RHONE SEGURET, CHATEAU LA COURANCONNE** 1985 (F)
380	£4.15	**GAILLAC, CEPAGE GAMAY, DOMAINES JEAN CROS** 1990 South West (F)
392	£12.65	**SANFORD PINOT NOIR** 1986 Santa Barbara (Cal)
437	£4.90	**SENORIO DE LOS LLANOS RESERVA** 1982 Valdepeñas (Sp)
442	£5.10	**TEMPRANILLO, BODEGAS OCHOA** 1987 Navarra (Sp)
469	£14.25	**CHATEAU BASTOR LAMONTAGNE, SAUTERNES** 1988 Bordeaux (F)
475	£17.90	**CHATEAU RIEUSSEC, SAUTERNES** 1983 Bordeaux (F)

U	**Unwins**

Head Office: Birchwood House, Victoria Rd, Dartford, Kent DA1 5AJ (0322 72711). Unassuming 305-branch chain in the South of England. **Opening Hours:** 10am-10pm Mon - Sat; 12-2pm & 7pm-9.30pm Sun. **Delivery:** free locally, nationally at cost. **Tastings:** regularly in-store plus tutored events. **Discounts:**10% off mixed cases for table wines and 5% for sparkling wines.

There's something very strange about the Unwins range: it's lop-sided. So, New Zealand is represented by an interesting set of wines while Australia (Berri Estates, Orlando, Rosemount) and California (Gallo, Wente, Almaden) are almost wholly predictable. The Portuguese offerings are more exciting than the Italians; there are brilliant classed growth Bordeaux (bought *en primeur* and well cellared) - and a Bichot label on every Burgundy. If you took Unwins' highly trained staff and gave them Victoria Wine's range, now then you'd be talking.

3	£7.35	**LINDAUER, MONTANA** (NZ)
22	£20.59	**VEUVE CLICQUOT DEMI-SEC CHAMPAGNE** (F)
31	£3.19	**CORBIERES BLANC, CAVES DE MONT TAUCH,** Midi (F)
72	£7.85	**MACON AZE, DOMAINE D'AZENAY** 1989 Burgundy (F)
85	£4.99	**CASTILLO FUENTE MAYOR BLANCO, AGE** 1988 (Sp)
87	£5.25	**ORLANDO RF CHARDONNAY** 1989 S E Australia (Aus)
102	£9.25	**MARQUES DE MURRIETA RIOJA BLANCO RESERVA** 1985 Rioja (Sp)
120	£16.99	**KUMEU RIVER CHARDONNAY** 1989 (NZ)
214	£3.25	**VIN DE PAYS DES COTES DE GASCOGNE ROUGE, MICHEL DE L'ENCLOS,** S W(F)
234	£5.99	**CHATEAU DE CROUSEILLES, MADIRAN** 1987 South West (F)
272	£4.75	**CHATEAU BARRAIL CHEVROL, FRONSAC** 1988 Bordeaux (F)
288	£7.59	**CHATEAU MUSAR** 1982 Bekaa Valley (Leb)

310	£10.35	BARON VILLENEUVE DE CANTERMERLE, HAUT-MEDOC 1986 Bordeaux (F)
333	£31.75	CHATEAU PAVIE, ST EMILION 1985 Bordeaux (F)
456	£4.49	SAMOS MUSCAT, Samos (Gr)
487	£5.25	TAYLOR'S FIRST ESTATE PORT LUGAR DAS LAGES, Douro (P)

V&C | Valvona & Crolla Ltd

19 Elm Row, Edinburgh, EH7 4AA (031 556 6066). Italian specialists. **Opening Hours:** 8.30am-6pm Mon-Sat. **Delivery:** free locally, nationally at cost. **Tastings:** regular in-store plus tutored events. **Discounts:** 5% on (mixed) cases.

Of all Edinburgh's plethora of quality wine merchants, Valvona & Crolla, winner of last year's Specialist Award, remains quite unique. If it's Italian and worth drinking, they will probably be able to sell it to you - as well as the appropriate foods to enjoy with it. The only problem facing every would-be comprehensive retailer - lack of space - will soon be solved when the shop expands to twice its present size. So by the time you get to visit, there should be ample room to display all 13 listed vintages of Gaja's Barbaresco.

20	£17.39	CA DEL BOSCO CREMANT, Lombardy (It)
129	£3.89	NURAGUS DI CAGLIARI, CANTINA SOCIALE DI DOLIANOVA 1990 Sardinia (It)
405	£4.99	CHIANTI RUFINA, SELVAPIANA 1988 Tuscany (It)
406	£5.15	REFOSCO GRAVE DEL FRIULI, COLLAVINI 1988 Friuli-Venezia-Giulia (It)
407	£5.45	LAGREIN DUNKEL, VITICOLTORI ALTO ADIGE 1986 Trentino-Alto Adige (It)
408	£5.25	BONARDA OLTREPO PAVESE, FUGAZZA 1987 Lombardy (It)
412	£6.65	CAMPO FIORIN VALPOLICELLA, MASI 1986 Veneto (It)
414	£6.89	BARBAROSSA, FATTORIA PARADISO 1986 Emilia-Romagna (It)
416	£7.65	CHIANTI CLASSICO, ISOLE E OLENA 1988 Tuscany (It)
424	£12.99	COLTASSALA, CASTELLO DI VOLPAIA 1986 Tuscany (It)
426	£14.65	CEPPARELLO, ISOLE E OLENA 1988 Tuscany (It)
427	£13.70	AMARONE CLASSICO DELLA VALPOLICELLA FIERAMONTE, ALLEGRINI 1983 Veneto (It)
431	£16.49	CABREO IL BORGO, RUFFINO 1986 Tuscany (It)
432	£17.49	LE PERGOLE TORTE, MONTE VERTINE 1986 Tuscany (It)
433	£20.00	BAROLO RISERVA, GIACOMO CONTERNO 1982 Piedmont (It)
434	£27.50	MAURIZIO ZANELLA, CA' DEL BOSCO 1988 Lombardy (It)
473	£15.29	CALUSO PASSITO , VITTORIO BORATTO 1985 Piedmont (It)

HVW | Helen Verdcourt

Spring Cottage, Kimbers Lane, Maidenhead, Berks SL6 2QP (0628 25577). Very independent merchant. **Opening Hours:** telephone first to check. **Delivery:** free within 40 miles, nationally at cost. **Tastings:** regular tastings, tutored events. **Discounts:** reductions for unmixed cases, 5% discount on orders over 12 cases.

Whirlwind Helen Verdcourt is not only a lecturer in wine appreciation and an organiser of her *two* wine clubs' guest speakers and tours. She is also one of the most reliable independent merchants in the area. Though her list of wines is briefer than many of other merchants in the *Guide*, her disproportionally long list of medal winners in the International Wine Challenge confirm her skills as a buyer.

| 3 | £6.70 | LINDAUER, MONTANA (NZ) |
| 29 | £2.75 | CUVEE JEAN-PAUL BLANC SEC VIN DE TABLE, PAUL BOUTINOT (F) |

54	£4.55	ALSACE TOKAY PINOT GRIS, CAVE VINICOLE DE TURCKHEIM 1990 (F)
104	£8.85	PENFOLDS PADTHAWAY CHARDONNAY 1990 (Aus)
106	£9.25	WYNNS COONAWARRA ESTATE CHARDONNAY 1989 (Aus)
231	£4.60	CHATEAU DE LASTOURS CUVEE SIMONE DESCAMPS, CORBIERES 1989 Midi (F)
281	£4.95	MONTANA CABERNET SAUVIGNON 1988 Marlborough (NZ)
287	£6.40	RAIMAT CABERNET SAUVIGNON 1985 Lérida (Sp)
293	£7.00	JAMIESONS RUN RED, MILDARA 1987 Coonawarra (Aus)
295	£7.35	WYNNS CABERNET SAUVIGNON 1989 Coonawarra (Aus)
302	£7.30	CHATEAU RAMAGE LA BATISSE, HAUT MEDOC 1988 Bordeaux (F)
313	£9.95	CLOUDY BAY CABERNET MERLOT 1989 Marlborough (NZ)
331	£17.95	PENFOLDS BIN 707 CABERNET SAUVIGNON 1987 South Australia (Aus)
344	£4.30	PENFOLDS BIN 2 SHIRAZ/MATARO 1989 Barossa Valley (Aus)
352	£5.35	COTES DU RHONE, GUIGAL 1988 (F)
360	£4.70	COTES DU RHONE SEGURET, CHATEAU LA COURANCONNE 1985 (F)
416	£7.15	CHIANTI CLASSICO, ISOLE E OLENA 1988 Tuscany (It)
440	£5.10	TINTO VELHO REGUENGOS DE MONSARAZ, JOSE DE SOUSA ROSADO FERNANDES 1986 Alentejo (P)
442	£5.50	TEMPRANILLO, BODEGAS OCHOA 1987 Navarra (Sp)
446	£5.55	GRAN SANGREDETORO RESERVA, TORRES 1986 Penedés (Sp)
465	£5.65	REDWOOD VALLEY ESTATE LATE HARVEST RIESLING 1989 Nelson (NZ)

VW | Victoria Wine

Head Office: Brook House, Chertsey Rd, Woking, Surrey GU21 5BE (0483 715066). Vastly improved High Street chain with 845 branches nationwide. **Opening Hours:** varied - often 'till late. **Delivery:** nationally at cost. **Tastings:** occasionally in-store. Discounts: 5% on 12 bottles or more.

Thresher and Wine Rack pipped Victoria Wine to the post this year. But only just. All of the judges acknowledged the huge efforts which the chain's new 'wine team' have made to improve the range, to redesign the shops and introduce an atmosphere that will attract people who are interested in wine. The route taken has been to divide the shops into four 'families'. Basic corner shops are designated 'Family Four' while the smartest outlets in the country are 'Family One'. By this apparently arcane method, the chain has tried to ensure that each shop's customers are offered the wines they are most likely to want to buy. The system seems to be beginning to work, particularly with the help of some very smart lists, but one bug-bear remains: staff training and product knowledge. Good wines need the support of good shop managers and assistants.

1	£4.89	DRYADES SPARKLING BLANC DE BLANCS, South West (F)
3	£6.99	LINDAUER, MONTANA (NZ)
11	£11.45	DEUTZ MARLBOROUGH CUVEE (NZ)
17	£14.99	VICTORIA WINE VINTAGE CHAMPAGNE, MARNE ET CHAMPAGNE 1983 (F)
18	£15.99	IRON HORSE BRUT 1987 Sonoma (Cal)
22	£21.69	VEUVE CLICQUOT DEMI-SEC CHAMPAGNE (F)
34	£3.15	DOMAINE DE BIAU, COTES DE GASCOGNE, HUGH RYMAN 1990 South West (F)
54	£4.69	ALSACE TOKAY PINOT GRIS, CAVE VINICOLE DE TURCKHEIM 1990 (F)
55	£4.75	SOAVE CLASSICO MONTELEONE, BOSCAINI 1989 Veneto (It)
83	£4.35	CALITERRA CHARDONNAY 1990 Maipo Valley (Ch)
86	£4.79	CHARDONNAY, VIN DE PAYS D'OC, HUGH RYMAN 1990 Midi (F)
102	£8.49	MARQUES DE MURRIETA RIOJA BLANCO RESERVA 1985 Rioja (Sp)
106	£9.69	WYNNS COONAWARRA ESTATE CHARDONNAY 1989 (Aus)
139	£3.99	DOMAINE DU PRE BARON, SAUVIGNON DE TOURAINE 1989 Loire (F)
174	£3.69	CAFAYATE TORRONTES, ETCHART 1990 Mendoza (Arg)

190	£6.30	MUNSTERER PITTERSBERG RIESLING KABINETT, STAATLICHE WEINBAUDOMANEN SCHLOSS BOCKELHEIM 1988 Nahe (G)
198	£5.95	SERRIGER HEILIGENBORN RIESLING SPATLESE, STAATLICHE WEINBAUDOMANEN 1983 Mosel-Saar-Ruwer (G)
217	£3.49	CAHORS FLEURET D'OLT, LES CAVES D'OLT 1989 South West (F)
281	£5.39	MONTANA CABERNET SAUVIGNON 1988 Marlborough (NZ)
287	£7.19	RAIMAT CABERNET SAUVIGNON 1985 Lérida (Sp)
288	£6.99	CHATEAU MUSAR 1982 Bekaa Valley (Leb)
293	£7.49	JAMIESONS RUN RED, MILDARA 1987 Coonawarra (Aus)
295	£8.99	WYNNS CABERNET SAUVIGNON 1985 Coonawarra (Aus)
314	£10.99	NEWTON CABERNET SAUVIGNON 1986 Napa Valley (Cal)
318	£11.49	CHATEAU HAUT BAGES AVEROUS, PAUILLAC 1985 Bordeaux (F)
327	£15.15	YARRA YERING CABERNET SAUVIGNON 1987 Yarra Valley (Aus)
328	£16.49	BERINGER PRIVATE RESERVE CABERNET SAUVIGNON 1986 Napa Valley (Cal)
336	£45.00	OPUS ONE, ROBERT MONDAVI 1987 Napa Valley (Cal)
339	£3.35	VIN DE PAYS DES COLLINES RHODANIENNES SYRAH, CAVE TAIN L'HERMITAGE, Rhône (F)
392	£11.49	SANFORD PINOT NOIR 1986 Santa Barbara (Cal)
395	£22.79	VOSNE-ROMANEE LES MALCONSORTS, MOILLARD 1988 Burgundy (F)
417	£7.29	COLLIO MERLOT, COLLAVINI 1985 Friuli-Venezia-Giulia (It)
446	£6.15	GRAN SANGREDETORO RESERVA, TORRES 1986 Penedés (Sp)
462	£5.99	JOSEPH PHELPS LATE HARVEST RIESLING 1988 Napa Valley (Cal)
465	£6.39	REDWOOD VALLEY ESTATE LATE HARVEST RIESLING 1989 Nelson (NZ)
487	£4.99	TAYLOR'S FIRST ESTATE PORT LUGAR DAS LAGES, Douro (P)
488	£6.99	GOULD CAMPBELL VINTAGE CHARACTER PORT, Douro (P)

LV | La Vigneronne

Southern Wine Merchant of the Year

105 Old Brompton Rd, London SW7 3LE (071 589 6113). Independent merchant famous for fine and old wines. **Opening Hours:** 10am-9pm Mon-Sat; 12-2pm Sun. **Delivery:** free locally, nationally at cost. **Tastings:** occasionally in-store plus tutored events and dinners. **Discounts:** 5% on (mixed) case, collected from shop.

We suspect that when news of this prize is made public, there will be a large number of wine lovers around the world who will want to toast Liz and Mike Berry's success. This is not so much a wine merchant as an institution, as a working vinous library to which anyone seeking reference bottles almost always has to make their way. The range is as eclectic as it is comprehensive, including as it does, Red Meursault 1989, Bonnes Mares 1961, Klevener de Heiligenstein 1989 (an Alsace made from a grape almost extinct in that region), Torres Gran Sangre de Toro 1961... We could go on. But it wasn't just the range and the friendliness of the shop which impressed our judges. It was also the quality of the tastings organised by La Vigneronne for their customers, at which some of the greatest winemakers in the world have shared their wine and knowledge.

117	£14.50	ELSTON CHARDONNAY, TE MATA 1989 (NZ)
171	£14.95	ALSACE TOKAY PINOT GRIS CLOS JEBSAL, ZIND HUMBRECHT 1988 (F)
286	£8.35	SEPPELT GOLD LABEL CABERNET SAUVIGNON 1986 S E Australia (Aus)
288	£8.25	CHATEAU MUSAR 1982 Bekaa Valley (Leb)
305	£11.85	JEAN LEON CABERNET SAUVIGNON 1983 Penedés (Sp)
324	£16.75	CHINOOK MERLOT 1987 Washington (US)

452	£15.50	RIOJA RESERVA 904, LA RIOJA ALTA 1978 (Sp)
459	£12.95	DOMAINE CAZES RIVESALTES VIEUX 1978 Midi (F)
460	£16.95	CAMPBELLS OLD RUTHERGLEN LIQUEUR MUSCAT (Aus)
471	£13.95	VOUVRAY MOELLEUX LE MARIGNY, DOMAINE DES AUBUISIERES 1990 Loire (F)
488	£9.95	GOULD CAMPBELL VINTAGE CHARACTER PORT, Douro (P)
489	£10.95	STARBOARD BATCH 88 RUBY, QUADY, Central Valley (Cal)
495	£21.95	FONSECA-GUIMARAENS 1976 Douro (P)

VIL   Village Wines

Arch 6, Mill Row, High Street, Bexley, Kent DA5 1LA (0322 59772) **Opening hours**: Mon - Fri 10am - 6pm, Sat 10am - 5pm. **Delivery**: free within 15 miles, nationally at cost. **Tastings**: regularly in store, tutored tastings, theme dinners. **Discount**: on orders over £200.

John Blanchard may stock some of the Germany's best red wines (they're 'a very popular choice, especially with the ladies'). He may have a range of classed growth Bordeaux and top quality Alsace, including wines from Zind Humbrecht. And he may have a good range of Eastern Europeans, among them some rare Romanian wines. But we think that his real love is motor bikes. After all, he was a member of the British motor cycle Grand Prix team back in the sixties. In which case, why doesn't he stock Hook Norton beer or Triomphe d'Alsace?

88	£5.99	MONTES CHARDONNAY, DISCOVER WINE LTDA 1990 Curico Valley (Ch)
150	£5.99	STONELEIGH SAUVIGNON BLANC 1989 Marlborough (NZ)
258	£3.99	SVISCHTOV CABERNET SAUVIGNON CONTROLIRAN, BULGARIAN VINTNERS 1985 Svischtov (Bul)
359	£4.85	CROZES HERMITAGE, DELAS FRERES 1989 Rhône (F)
500	£2.25	PETILLANT DE LISTEL, Midi (F)

VLW   Villeneuve Wines

27 Northgate, Peebles, Scotland EH45 8RX (0721 22500) Broad ranging Scottish specialist. **Opening hours**: Mon-Wed 10am-6pm, Fri 10am-8pm, Sat 9am-10pm. **Delivery**: free within 30 miles, nationally at cost. **Tastings**: regularly in store, tutored events. **Discount**: 5% on (mixed) case

Small is beautiful in Peebles. Kenneth Vannan packs a huge range of wines into his tiny shop, very skilfully allowing browsers to work their way from Berberana's Rioja's to Borgogno's Barolo's (6 vintages) and Bollinger (2 vintages of RD). The house style is to stock several wines and/or several vintages from each producer. This, and the wide selection of half bottles, makes Villeneuve a perfect place to find wines for a blind tasting.

22	£20.95	VEUVE CLICQUOT DEMI-SEC CHAMPAGNE (F)
33	£3.19	DOMAINE DU TARIQUET, COTES DE GASCOGNE 1990 South West (F)
84	£4.49	OXFORD LANDING CHARDONNAY, YALUMBA 1990 South Australia (Aus)
86	£4.69	CHARDONNAY, VIN DE PAYS D'OC, HUGH RYMAN 1990 Midi (F)
93	£5.99	BROKENBACK VINEYARD CHARDONNAY, ROTHBURY 1990 Hunter Valley (Aus)
281	£4.99	MONTANA CABERNET SAUVIGNON 1988 Marlborough (NZ)
303	£7.99	ROSEMOUNT SHOW RESERVE CABERNET SAUVIGNON 1987 Coonawarra (Aus)
305	£11.95	JEAN LEON CABERNET SAUVIGNON 1983 Penedés (Sp)
405	£3.89	CHIANTI RUFINA, SELVAPIANA 1988 Tuscany (It)
451	£9.35	MARQUIS DE MURRIETA RIOJA TINTO RESERVA 1985 (Sp)

VER | Vinceremos Ltd.

Unit 10, Ashley Industrial Estate, Wakefield Road, Ossett WF5 9JD (0924 276 393). Organic specialist operating as a co-operative. **Opening Hours:** 9.15am-5pm Mon-Fri; 10am-4pm Sat. **Delivery:** free within 25 miles and free nationally for 5+ cases. **Tastings:** regular tutored events. **Discounts:** 5% for 5+cases,10% 10+ cases.

Some wine companies have taken pride in offering South African wines over the last 20 years; Vinceremos, we suspect, is just as committed in its support of the Nicaraguan Flor de Caña rum which features on its list, just beyond the Cuban rum, Armenian Brandy, Zimbabwean wine and Russian Zhiguli beer. And substantially beyond a really impressive range of (mostly) organic wines. The greatest range is from France, where the organic lobby really does seem to have made its mark, but there are good 'green' wines from Germany, Spain, Hungary, England and New Zealand, in the shape of the excellent Millton range. Oh yes, Vinceremos also offer a potential beverage to drink with curry. Veena Red and White are Indian wines 'enhanced with spices for an authentic Indian flavour'.

43	£3.99	MAUZAC, DOMAINE DE LA BATTEUSE, B DELMAS 1989 South West (F)
266	£3.99	CHATEAU LA CROIX SIMON BORDEAUX ROUGE 1989 (F)
288	£6.95	CHATEAU MUSAR 1982 Bekaa Valley (Leb)
306	£7.85	DOMAINE RICHEAUME CABERNET SAUVIGNON 1988 Midi(F)
393	£7.99	HAUTES COTES DE NUITS, ALAIN VERDET 1986 Burgundy (F)
469	£9.90	CHATEAU BASTOR LAMONTAGNE, SAUTERNES 1988 Bordeaux (F)

VR | Vintage Roots

Sheeplands Farm, Wargrave Road, Wargrave, Berkshire RF10 8DT (0734 401222). **Opening Hours:** Telephone first to check. **Delivery:** free within 30 miles and nationally for 5+ cases. **Tastings:** tutored events organised for outside clubs on request. **Discounts:** dependent upon quantity.

'We are having a change of image this year - smarter and more modern - which hopefully will start to convey that we are also a serious wine merchant who are proud of their range of wines to stand up in their own right. Not just under an organic banner or only for those sulphur-allergic vegans who only drink wine on a full moon'. Messrs Pigott, Greet and Palmer win plentiful brownie points for flying the organic flag in a way that is both serious (in quality terms) and light-hearted. Throughout the range which goes from Champagne to New Zealand Chenin the wines really do seem to have been chosen for their quality and - a crucial point this - value for money has been taken into account. Affordably and drinkably green.

43	£3.90	MAUZAC, DOMAINE DE LA BATTEUSE, B DELMAS 1989 South West (F)
213	£2.95	VIN DE PAYS DU GARD, ALBARIC, Midi (F)
355	£4.80	DOMAINE ST APOLLINAIRE (ORGANIC), COTES DU RHONE 1989 (F)
366	£6.15	ST GILBERT BOTOBOLAR VINEYARD, GIL WAHLQUIST 1987 Mudgee (Aus)

ALV | A L Vose

Town House, Main Street, Grange-over-Sands, Cumbria LA11 6DY (05395 33328) Whacky merchant who has cornered the Brazilian market. **Opening hours**: Mon-Sat 9 am-6 pm. **Delivery**: free locally, nationally at cost 'but free if it fits in with our delivery round'. **Tastings**: regularly in store. **Discounts**: 10% per case.

A list which is nothing if not ambitious and eye-catching and which defies you to ignore it. Printed in 'robin's egg blue' and hand-written with sketches (including bull-fighters, camels and giraffes), advice on what food to eat with what, and which grape varieties every wine is made from. Buried in the middle of it is a list of Brazilian wines, for which Alan Vose is the importer. These are more of curiosity value than vinous excellence, for which one has to trawl the list very carefully. We would, for example, be more pleased to find a Châteauneuf du Papes (sic) from Mont Redon than a Borolo (sic again) from Villadoria. Perhaps the best way of finding the goodies is to join 'Lacey's Club', where the members decide when and what to taste, and to which you are advised to wear warm clothing.

W   Waitrose Ltd

Head Office: Doncastle Rd, South Industrial Area, Bracknell, Berks RG12 4YA (0344 424680). Up-market but slightly reclusive supermarket chain with 95 branches in the South of England and Midlands. **Opening Hours**: 9am-6pm Mon, Tues; 9am-8pm Wed, Thu; 8.30am-9pm Fri; 8.30am-5.30pm Sat. **Discounts**: 5% on unbroken cases or orders over £100.

We were, we must admit, a little harsh on Waitrose last year but it did seem that their previous spirit of innovation had lost its spark. Over the last year, possibly following the arrival of Neil Somerfelt MW, the range does appear to have been given a newer lease of life, though there are still less revolutionary discoveries than we would - perhaps unfairly - like to find. Even so, the Waitrose buyers are a skilful bunch and poor wines are a rarity.

3	£7.35	LINDAUER, MONTANA (NZ)
22	£20.59	VEUVE CLICQUOT DEMI-SEC CHAMPAGNE (F)
102	£9.25	MARQUES DE MURRIETA RIOJA BLANCO RESERVA 1985 Rioja (Sp)
140	£4.95	COOKS HAWKES BAY SAUVIGNON BLANC 1989 Hawkes Bay (NZ)
175	£4.65	MOSCATO D'ASTI, MICHELE CHIARLO 1990 Piedmont (It)
180	£3.95	HILL SMITH OLD TRIANGLE RIESLING 1990 Barossa Valley (Aus)
264	£3.99	BERRI ESTATES AUSTRALIAN CABERNET SHIRAZ 1987 (Aus)
432	£19.75	LE PERGOLE TORTE, MONTE VERTINE 1986 Tuscany (It)
455	£2.99	CASTILLO DE LIRIA MOSCATEL, VICENTE GANDIA, Valencia (Sp)
464	£6.25	CHATEAU LOUPIAC GAUDIET, LOUPIAC 1988 South West (F)
479	£5.45	LA GITANA MANZANILLA, HIDALGO, Jerez (Sp)
487	£5.25	TAYLOR'S FIRST ESTATE PORT LUGAR DAS LAGES, Douro (P)

PWA   Peter Warburton Wines

17 Moorlands Drive, Wybunbury, Nantwich, Cheshire CW5 7PA. (0270 841714) Burgundophile specialist. **Opening hours**: Mon - Fri 9am - 5pm. **Delivery**: free locally

Peter Warburton is that most beleaguered of wine lovers, the Burgundy fan. Over the last two years he has built up a small list of individual domaine wines generally from good growers previously undiscovered in the UK. Only one of his range made its way into the Guide but the success of some of the others in the International Wine Challenge confirms his skill as a buyer. Fellow Burgundy lovers will be double delighted to discover that prices are moderate too - a remarkable achievement in this region.

96	£7.45	SAINT ROMAIN (TASTEVINE), BERNARD FEVRE 1986 Burgundy (F)

WAW | Waterloo Wine Co.

6 Vine Yard, Borough, London SE1 1QL (071 403 7967), 59-61 Lant St Borough, London SE1 1QL. Independent merchant. **Opening Hours:** 10am-6.30pm Mon-Fri; 10am-5.30pm Sat. **Delivery:** Free locally; nationally at cost. **Tastings:** regularly in-store and for groups by arrangement.

Customers of Tutton's Brasserie should have a word with the owner. We *know* that the House Wines could be better, because Paul Tutton who supplies the wine has shown his wine tasting skills very adequately in his buying for Waterloo Wine Company and as owner of the Waipara Springs winery in New Zealand. The Antipodean connection has ensured that Waterloo Wine customers are offered a range of first class Aussies and Kiwis including the hard-to-find Mount Hurtle wines. French Country Wines feature in profusion as does the Loire where some particularly interesting examples have been found.

38	£3.31	TOLLANA DRY WHITE 1988 S E Australia (Aus)
83	£4.27	CALITERRA CHARDONNAY 1990 Maipo Valley (Ch)
184	£5.11	ALSACE RIESLING RESERVE PARTICULIERE, SELTZ 1988 (F)
219	£3.16	CHATEAU HELENE ROUGE, CORBIERES, MARIE-HELENE GAU 1987 Midi (F)
270	£4.35	CHATEAU LUGAUD, GRAVES, DIDIER MAY 1988 Bordeaux (F)
281	£4.69	MONTANA CABERNET SAUVIGNON 1988 Marlborough (NZ)
376	£13.75	ROUGE HOMME SHIRAZ CABERNET 1976 Coonawarra (Aus)
442	£5.35	TEMPRANILLO, BODEGAS OCHOA 1987 Navarra (Sp)

WAC | Waters of Coventry

Collins Road, Heathcote, Warwick CV34 6TF (0926 888889). Retail arm of wholesale merchant. **Opening Hours:** 9.30am-5.30pm Mon-Fri; 9.30am-3pm Sat. **Delivery:** free within 25 miles and nationally for 5+ cases. **Tastings:** regularly in-store. **Discounts:** negotiable.

200 years after David Shakespeare Waters founded the company, Waters of Coventry have fled the city, finally admitting defeat to the town planners who have sought to make it both unworkable and uninhabitable. In theory the name ought to change to Waters of Warwick - WOW! but quite sensibly the old identity has been retained as has the style of a fairly priced list which covers the gamut from four sizes of Laski Rizling (including handy half bottles) to classy clarets, Jean Germain and Antonin Rodet Burgundies and Beaucastel Châteauneuf.

19	£15.95	DEVAUX CHAMPAGNE CUVEE ROSEE (F)
92	£6.10	MACON CHARDONNAY, J TALMARD 1988 Burgundy (F)
180	£4.11	HILL SMITH OLD TRIANGLE RIESLING 1990 Barossa Valley (Aus)
181	£4.48	LAMBERHURST SEYVAL BLANC 1988 Kent (UK)
284	£5.67	SIRIUS ROUGE, PETER SICHEL 1988 Bordeaux (F)

WES | Wessex Wines

197 St Andrews Rd, Bridport, Dorset DT6 3BT (0308 23400). Good-value independent merchant. **Opening Hours:** 8.30am-9.30pm Mon-Sat. **Delivery:** free within 20 miles with collection discount. **Tastings:** regularly in-store plus tutored events. **Discounts:** 5% on 9 bottles of the same wine.

'Because I work from home I can offer a very flexible service and it is not unknown for me to deliver 'emergency' cases of wine late at night or on a Sunday afternoon'. We are not certain quite what kind of emergency would drive us to order a bottle of Peter Herres German Sparkling wine flavoured with wild strawberries. However, we would be very happy to welcome anybody who showed up on our door-step bearing bottles from most of the rest of the list, including the rarely available St Felicien wines from Argentina and Inniskillin Marechal Foch from Canada. And we wouldn't be so rude as to slam the door in the face of Wessex's Zimbabweans either.

29	£2.85	CUVEE JEAN-PAUL BLANC SEC VIN DE TABLE, PAUL BOUTINOT (F)
46	£3.45	CHARDONNAY, DOMAINE DES FLINES, VIN DE PAYS DE LA LOIRE 1990 (F)
54	£5.07	ALSACE TOKAY PINOT GRIS, CAVE VINICOLE DE TURCKHEIM 1990 (F)
140	£4.70	COOKS HAWKES BAY SAUVIGNON BLANC 1989 Hawkes Bay (NZ)
231	£4.84	CHATEAU DE LASTOURS CUVEE SIMONE DESCAMPS, CORBIERES 1989 Midi (F)
284	£5.60	SIRIUS ROUGE, PETER SICHEL 1988 Bordeaux (F)
288	£5.59	CHATEAU MUSAR 1982 Bekaa Valley (Leb)
302	£7.09	CHATEAU RAMAGE LA BATISSE, HAUT MEDOC 1988 Bordeaux (F)

WOC | Whitesides of Clitheroe

Shawbridge St, Clitheroe, Lancs BB7 1NA (0200 22281) and 39, The Grove, Ilkley, West Yorkshire LS29 9NJ (0943 816015). The Clitheroe phenomenon part two (see D. Byrne) **Opening Hours:** 9.30am - 5.30pm Mon-Sat . **Delivery:** free within 50 locally, nationally at cost. **Tastings:** regularly in-store plus tutored events. **Discounts:** 5% on unbroken cases.

The award last year of the Northern Wine Merchant of the Year prize to Whiteside's neighbour D Byrne has, we suspect, fired Brian Hayward with the ambition to make it a winning pair for Clitheroe as soon as possible, and he is going the right way about it. The price list, previously a home spun masterpiece, is being smartened up and expanded, and a retail shop has been opened in Ilkley, making Whitesides a haven for New World-Mad Yorkshiremen, as well as Lancastrians. As long as the two shops do not engage in a new War of the Rosés...

6	£8.29	TALTARNI BRUT TACHE, Pyrenees (Aus)
22	£19.35	VEUVE CLICQUOT DEMI-SEC CHAMPAGNE (F)
38	£3.39	TOLLANA DRY WHITE 1988 S E Australia (Aus)
62	£5.49	CHAI BAUMIERES CHARDONNAY, VIN DE PAYS D'OC 1990 Midi (F)
83	£4.69	CALITERRA CHARDONNAY 1990 Maipo Valley (Ch)
84	£4.55	OXFORD LANDING CHARDONNAY, YALUMBA 1990 South Australia (Aus)
87	£5.19	ORLANDO RF CHARDONNAY 1989 S E Australia (Aus)
93	£6.09	BROKENBACK VINEYARD CHARDONNAY, ROTHBURY 1990 Hunter Valley (Aus)
102	£8.29	MARQUES DE MURRIETA RIOJA BLANCO RESERVA 1985 Rioja (Sp)
103	£8.75	KING VALLEY CHARDONNAY FAMILY RESERVE, BROWN BROTHERS 1987 N E Victoria (Aus)
140	£4.99	COOKS HAWKES BAY SAUVIGNON BLANC 1989 Hawkes Bay (NZ)
143	£5.95	DOMAINE DU RELAIS DE POSTE, SAUVIGNON DE ST BRIS 1989 Burgundy (F)
150	£5.95	STONELEIGH SAUVIGNON BLANC 1989 Marlborough (NZ)
258	£4.49	SVISCHTOV CABERNET SAUVIGNON CONTROLIRAN 1985 Svischtov (Bul)
280	£5.19	ORLANDO RF CABERNET SAUVIGNON 1988 South Australia (Aus)
281	£4.99	MONTANA CABERNET SAUVIGNON 1988 Marlborough (NZ)
288	£6.75	CHATEAU MUSAR 1982 Bekaa Valley (Leb)
297	£6.59	TALTARNI CABERNET SAUVIGNON 1985 Pyrenees (Aus)
304	£9.75	CHATEAU SOCIANDO MALLET, HAUT-MEDOC 1987 Bordeaux (F)
306	£9.19	DOMAINE RICHEAUME CABERNET SAUVIGNON 1988 Midi (F)

321	£15.75	**RENAISSANCE CABERNET SAUVIGNON** 1984 North Yuba (Cal)
331	£18.49	**PENFOLDS BIN 707 CABERNET SAUVIGNON** 1987 South Australia (Aus)
332	£28.99	**CHATEAU TALBOT, ST JULIEN** 1982 Bordeaux (F)
344	£4.35	**PENFOLDS BIN 2 SHIRAZ/MATARO** 1989 Barossa Valley (Aus)
357	£5.09	**FETZER ZINFANDEL** 1987 Mendocino (Cal)
358	£5.85	**DOMAINE LA SOUMADE RASTEAU, COTES DU RHONE VILLAGES** 1988 (F)
367	£6.15	**TALTARNI SHIRAZ** 1988 Pyrenees (Aus)
392	£10.55	**SANFORD PINOT NOIR** 1986 Santa Barbara (Cal)
408	£5.65	**BONARDA OLTREPO PAVESE, FUGAZZA** 1987 Lombardy (It)
449	£7.95	**CAMPO VIEJO RIOJA GRAN RESERVA** 1980 (Sp)
451	£9.20	**MARQUIS DE MURRIETA RIOJA TINTO RESERVA** 1985 (Sp)
458	£6.35	**YALUMBA MUSEUM SHOW RESERVE MUSCAT,** Rutherglen (Aus)
469	£11.95	**CHATEAU BASTOR LAMONTAGNE, SAUTERNES** 1988 Bordeaux (F)
483	£14.99	**APOSTOLES, GONZALEZ BYASS,** Jerez (Sp)
493	£15.85	**WARRE'S QUINTA DA CAVADINHA** 1982 Douro (P)
495	£17.55	**FONSECA-GUIMARAENS** 1976 Douro (P)

WTL | Whittalls Wines

Château Pleck, Darlaston Road, Walsall, West Midlands (0922 36161) By the case merchant with a memorable address. **Opening hours**: 9.15am - 5.30pm Mon - Fri. **Delivery**: free locally.

Confusingly, there are two companies operating from this address, Whittalls and Château Pleck, who between them offer a good solid range of wines in which very reliable producers such as Antonin Rodet and Guigal are well represented. But there are also some serious Bordeaux including, in a recent offer, 1978 Cos d'Estournel for £240 a dozen (well, £240 plus duty at £10.85 and 17.5% VAT).

313	£10.00	**CLOUDY BAY CABERNET MERLOT** 1989 Marlborough (NZ)
327	£14.99	**YARRA YERING CABERNET SAUVIGNON** 1987 Yarra Valley (Aus)
332	£19.00	**CHATEAU TALBOT, ST JULIEN** 1982 Bordeaux (F)
475	£29.61	**CHATEAU RIEUSSEC, SAUTERNES** 1983 Bordeaux (F

WDW | Windrush Wines

The Barracks, Cecily Hill, Cirencester, Glos GL7 2EF (0285 650466) & 3 Market Place, Cirencester (0285 657807). Independent pig-loving merchant. **Opening Hours**: 9am-6pm Mon-Sat. **Delivery**: free nationally for 2+ cases. **Tastings**: regularly in-store plus tutored events.

Last year we reported that Windrush was the place to go for advice on setting up a vineyard. Well it was then. The directors who launched that scheme have gone elsewhere, and Mark Savage MW is now in full control of the tiller of the company. Savage's own taste in wine is pretty 'European', preferring restrained rather than demonstrative flavours. This makes his speciality list of New World Wines all the more interesting - and explains his support for the Oregon and Washington State wines which are often so much more impressive than their Californian counterparts. Oh yes, and the brief Italian section is pretty good too.

WE   The Wine Emporium

7 Devon Place, Haymarket, Edinburgh EH12 5HG (031 346 1113). Independent wine warehouse selling by the case. **Opening Hours:** 10am-8pm Mon-Fri; 10am-7pm Sat. **Delivery:** free locally, nationally at cost. **Tastings:** regularly in-store plus tutored events. **Discounts:** negotiable.

Last year, we described this as Edinburgh's answer to Majestic. Anyone who has read this far through the Guide will realise that the Wine Emporium didn't need to make much effort this year to smash its southern opponent off the court in a single game. In fact, however, comparisons with Majestic are decreasingly appropriate, given the Wine Emporium's readiness to supply wine by the bottle. As for the range, it is a model of variety and value, matching big names like Louis Jadot and Brown Brothers with less familiar ones like Lapierre (Pouilly Fuissé) and Château Tahbilk (Shiraz), and covering the range from £2.99 to £20 and beyond.

288	£6.49	CHATEAU MUSAR 1982 Bekaa Valley (Leb)
291	£6.99	CHATEAU DE FRANCS, COTES DE FRANCS 1988 Bordeaux (F)
332	£17.89	CHATEAU TALBOT, ST JULIEN 1982 Bordeaux (F)
410	£5.45	CAPITEL VALPOLICELLA DEI NICALO, TEDESCHI 1986 Veneto (It)
438	£3.99	MARIUS RESERVA, BODEGAS PIQUERAS 1983 Almansa (Sp)
479	£5.99	LA GITANA MANZANILLA, HIDALGO, Jerez (Sp)
483	£15.00	APOSTOLES, GONZALEZ BYASS, Jerez (Sp)

WR   Wine Rack

Joint Winner: National High Street Wine Merchant of the Year

Head Office: Sefton House, 42 Church Road, Welwyn Garden City AL8 6PJ (0707 328244). Chain of 'up-market Thresher' shops. **Opening Hours:** typically 10am-10.30pm Mon-Sat. **Delivery:** free locally. **Tastings:** regularly in-store plus tutored events. **Discounts:** variable case discounts.

The winner of last year's regional chain award has this year grown sufficiently in size to be considered for the national prize. And our judges were happy to give it that prize, asking Wine Rack to share the award with its associated company, Threshers. The creation from scratch of a chain like Wine Rack is probably only possible for a company with the resources of a major brewery; unfortunately, most such firms have tended to prefer beer turnover to wine turnover and quantity to quality. The commitment of the Wine Rack team - from wine buyers and tough marketeers to shop managers - has impressed everyone who has spent any time in one of these shops. Here at last are non-Oddbins wine shops whose staff take an interest in the wines they stock and the way they taste. Wine Rack and Threshers did not boot Oddbins off its pedestal - that chain still won the overall prize - but the judges were unanimous in making Wine Rack the co-recipient of this highly deserved award.

3	£6.99	LINDAUER, MONTANA (NZ)
22	£20.59	VEUVE CLICQUOT DEMI-SEC CHAMPAGNE (F)
24	£44.95	LANSON VINTAGE CHAMPAGNE 1979 (F)
33	£3.15	DOMAINE DU TARIQUET, COTES DE GASCOGNE 1990 South West (F)
37	£3.69	CHATEAU LES HAUTS DE TREYTIN, BORDEAUX BLANC, MANDREAU 1990 (F)
38	£3.29	TOLLANA DRY WHITE 1988 S E Australia (Aus)
45	£3.99	CHARDONNAY, LES DUCS ST MARTIN, VAL D'ORBIEU 1990 Midi (F)
46	£3.99	CHARDONNAY, DOMAINE DES FLINES, VIN DE PAYS DE LA LOIRE 1990 (F)

48	£4.49	CHATEAU HAUT REDON, ENTRE DEUX MERS, HUGH RYMAN 1990 Bordeaux (F)
54	£4.59	ALSACE TOKAY PINOT GRIS, CAVE VINICOLE DE TURCKHEIM 1990 (F)
58	£4.75	CHATEAU COUCHEROY BLANC, GRAVES, ANDRE LURTON 1989 Bordeaux (F)
61	£5.29	CHATEAU SAINT GALIER BORDEAUX BLANC 1990 (F)
76	£11.99	DOMAINE FONT DE MICHELLE, CHATEAUNEUF DU PAPE BLANC 1990 Rhône (F)
99	£7.99	CUVEE DES JACOBINS BOURGOGNE CHARDONNAY, JADOT 1989 Burgundy (F)
102	£8.69	MARQUES DE MURRIETA RIOJA BLANCO RESERVA 1985 Rioja (Sp)
106	£8.85	WYNNS COONAWARRA ESTATE CHARDONNAY 1989 (Aus)
110	£8.99	PIPERS BROOK CHARDONNAY 1988 Tasmania (Aus)
111	£11.99	EDNA VALLEY CHARDONNAY 1989 San Luis Obispo (Cal)
127	£2.79	DONATIEN BLANC DE BLANC, DONATIEN BAHUAUD 1990 Loire (F)
133	£4.19	DOMAINE DU COLOMBET SAUVIGNON, COTES DE DURAS 1990 South West (F)
143	£5.99	DOMAINE DU RELAIS DE POSTE, SAUVIGNON DE ST BRIS 1989 Burgundy (F)
150	£5.99	STONELEIGH SAUVIGNON BLANC 1989 Marlborough (NZ)
170	£11.75	ALSACE GEWURZTRAMINER GRAND CRU GOLDERT, ZIND HUMBRECHT 1987 (F)
171	£14.65	ALSACE TOKAY PINOT GRIS CLOS JEBSAL, ZIND HUMBRECHT 1988 (F)
172	£18.99	ALSACE GEWURZTRAMINER HERRENWEG VENDANGE TARDIVE, ZIND HUMBRECHT 1986 (F)
192	£7.59	DEINHARD HOCHHEIM HERITAGE SELECTION 1988 Rheingau (G)
196	£4.85	THREE CHOIRS MEDIUM DRY ENGLISH TABLE WINE 1989 Gloucs (UK)
209	£2.69	VAL DU MONT CABERNET SAUVIGNON, VIN DE PAYS D'OC 1988 Midi (F)
223	£3.69	DOMAINE ST EULALIE, MINERVOIS 1988 Midi (F)
228	£3.99	CHATEAU CLEMENT TERMES, GAILLAC ROUGE 1988 South West (F)
231	£4.49	CHATEAU DE LASTOURS CUVEE SIMONE DESCAMPS, CORBIERES 1989 Midi (F)
236	£6.49	PRIEURE DE CENAC, CAHORS, RIGAL 1986 South West (F)
247	£3.29	DOMAINE DE MONTMARIN MERLOT, COTES DE THONGUE 1989 Midi (F)
249	£3.49	DOMAINE DES CAUNETTES MERLOT, VIN DE PAYS DE L'AUDE 1990 Midi (F)
257	£3.99	CHATEAU GUIBON BORDEAUX ROUGE, LURTON 1988 (F)
258	£4.59	SVISCHTOV CABERNET SAUVIGNON CONTROLIRAN 1985 Svischtov (Bul)
281	£5.29	MONTANA CABERNET SAUVIGNON 1988 Marlborough (NZ)
282	£5.25	CHATEAU COUCHEROY BORDEAUX ROUGE 1988 (F)
284	£5.79	SIRIUS ROUGE, PETER SICHEL 1988 Bordeaux (F)
287	£5.79	RAIMAT CABERNET SAUVIGNON 1985 Lérida (Sp)
288	£7.29	CHATEAU MUSAR 1982 Bekaa Valley (Leb)
295	£6.99	WYNNS CABERNET SAUVIGNON 1985 Coonawarra (Aus)
303	£7.99	ROSEMOUNT SHOW RESERVE CABERNET SAUVIGNON 1987 Coonawarra (Aus)
304	£6.99	CHATEAU SOCIANDO MALLET, HAUT-MEDOC 1987 Bordeaux (F)
308	£9.99	COLDSTREAM HILLS CABERNET SAUVIGNON 1988 Yarra Valley (Aus)
312	£9.99	LES FIEFS DE LAGRANGE, ST JULIEN, CHATEAU LAGRANGE 1988 Bordeaux (F)
313	£10.79	CLOUDY BAY CABERNET MERLOT 1989 Marlborough (NZ)
316	£11.29	TOURELLES DE LONGUEVILLE, PAUILLAC 1988 Bordeaux (F)
344	£3.99	PENFOLDS BIN 2 SHIRAZ/MATARO 1989 Barossa Valley (Aus)
345	£4.19	CHATEAU SAINT JEAN COTE DU RHONE, MEFFRE 1989 (F)
353	£4.99	PENFOLDS BIN 28 KALIMNA SHIRAZ 1988 South Australia (Aus)
354	£4.49	BALGOWNIE SHIRAZ CABERNET 1987 Central Victoria (Aus)
357	£5.49	FETZER ZINFANDEL 1987 Mendocino (Cal)
361	£5.79	CASSEGRAIN POKOLBIN SHIRAZ 1986 Hunter Valley (Aus)
365	£5.99	CHATEAU TAHBILK SHIRAZ 1987 Goulburn Valley (Aus)
372	£8.99	CHATEAUNEUF DU PAPE DOMAINE FONT DE MICHELLE 1988 Rhône (F)
399	£38.25	LE CHAMBERTIN, ARMAND ROUSSEAU 1987 Burgundy (F)
435	£2.99	DON DARIAS RED, BODEGAS VITORIANAS (Sp)
442	£5.95	TEMPRANILLO, BODEGAS OCHOA 1987 Navarra (Sp)
451	£9.65	MARQUIS DE MURRIETA RIOJA TINTO RESERVA 1985 (Sp)
494	£17.99	SANDEMAN IMPERIAL 20 YEAR OLD TAWNY PORT, Douro (P)

WSC | The Wine Schoppen

1 Abbeydale Road South, Sheffield, S7 2QL (0742 365684) Loyally dynamic German specialist trying to buck the trend. **Opening Hours**: 9.30 am-6 pm Mon-Fri. 9.30 am-5 pm Sat. **Delivery**: free within 15 miles. **Tastings**: Bottles always open, regular tutored tastings and theme dinners.

Anne and Eddie Coghlan are members of a small beleaguered band. They have continued to remain loyal to Germany while the producers of that country have all too often given up trying to make good wine, and while most British consumers equate German wine with hock and mosel at £1.99. The Coghlans have taken the trouble to seek out a very impressive list of single estate wines from all of the main regions. The range runs from unusual Pinot Noirs to luscious Beerenausleses, via a few of the better examples of dry Trockens and Halbtrockens. Such specialisation would be useless without accompanying efforts to educate people about this wilfully complicated country. The Coghlan's list and their regular tastings have arguably done as much to promote the cause of German wine in Britain as almost the entire annual effort funded by the German wine industry. However, The Wine Schoppen does stock wines from other countries, as the following list demonstrates...

322	£14.99	SWANSON CABERNET SAUVIGNON 1987 Napa Valley (Cal)
430	£17.88	BRUNELLO DEL MONTALCINO, POGGIO ANTICO 1985 Piedmont (It)
449	£8.69	CAMPO VIEJO RIOJA GRAN RESERVA 1980 (Sp)
476	£29.90	LAUBENHEIMER EDELMAN SCHEUREBE TROCKENBEERENAUSLESE, KUEHLING-GILLOT 1989 Rheinhessen (G)

WSO | The Wine Society

By the Case / Mail Order Merchant of the Year.

Gunnels Wood Rd, Stevenage, Herts SG1 2BG (0438 741177). Independent wine club, owned by its members and selling mail order, by-the-case. **Delivery**: free nationally . **Tastings**: regular club events. **Discounts**: £2 per case for 10 +cases; collection discount.

All too often overlooked when trendier - or apparently trendier - companies have leapt into the limelight, The Wine Society has quietly and steadfastly gone on doing its job supremely well. Perhaps the greatest compliment paid to it is the number of wine writers and other wine merchants who remain members, and who take advantage of its offers and use it when buying *en primeur*. Any comparison between The Society and its would be competitor The Sunday Times Wine Club in its current state is all too odious. The Wine Society genuinly belongs to its members (a virtually unique phenomenon) and offers carefully chosen wines at fair prices ranging from hardy perennials such as The Society's Full Red Decanter Wine to some of the most modern of Italian Vini da Tavola and rising stars from the New World. Our judges had no hesitation in making this year's award to the Society and we are certain that their choice will be applauded by its 70,000 or so members.

90	£5.75	LINDEMANS BIN 65 CHARDONNAY 1989 S E Australia (Aus)
148	£6.90	SELAKS SAUVIGNON BLANC 1990 (NZ)
157	£4.50	DOMAINE DU BOSC MARSANNE, VIN DE PAYS DE L'HERAULT 1990 Midi (F)
196	£4.65	THREE CHOIRS MEDIUM DRY ENGLISH TABLE WINE 1989 Gloucs (UK)
206	£4.75	CHATEAU BEL AIR BORDEAUX CLAIRET (CABERNET SAUVIGNON) 1990 (F)

227	£3.95	CUVEE DE L'ARJOLLE ROUGE, VIN DE PAYS DES COTES DE THONGUE, TEISSERENC 1989 Midi (F)
305	£8.90	JEAN LEON CABERNET SAUVIGNON 1983 Penedés (Sp)
352	£3.35	COTES DU RHONE, GUIGAL 1988 (F)
380	£4.60	GAILLAC, CEPAGE GAMAY, DOMAINES JEAN CROS 1990 South West (F)
391	£9.65	SAINTSBURY PINOT NOIR 1988 Carneros (Cal)
479	£5.25	LA GITANA MANZANILLA, HIDALGO, Jerez (Sp)
494	£17.50	SANDEMAN IMPERIAL 20 YEAR OLD TAWNY PORT, Douro (P)

WTR | The Wine Treasury

143 Ebury Street, London SW1W 9QN (071 730 6774) Restaurateur cum independent wine merchant with New World leanings. **Opening hours:** 9 am - 6 pm Mon - Fri. By appointment Sat. **Delivery:** 4+ cases free. **Tastings:** occasional. **Discounts:** negotiable. Credit cards: 'NO!'

'Our wines are appreciated by a bold, adventurous and discerning clientele - if your approach to wine is faint hearted and conservative, we can probably help'. Neville Blech's new business, which runs alongside his Mijanou restaurant in London, offers classy wines across the board, including some hard-to-find New World wineries such as Williams Selyem. But beware of the prices; it was Mr Blech who described the Cloverdale Ranch Cabernet Sauvignon '88 as 'cheap and cheerful' at £87.85 plus VAT per case. We *think* he was joking.

WCE | Winecellars

Italian Specialist Wine Merchant of the Year

153-155 Wandsworth High St, London SW18 (081 871 3979) & The Market, 213-215 Upper Street, London N1 (071 359 5386). Brilliant all-round merchant with heavy Italian bias. **Opening Hours:** 10.30am-8.30pm Mon-Fri; 10.30am-8pm Sat. **Delivery:** free within M25, nationally at cost. **Tastings:** wines always open plus regular tutored events and dinners. **Discounts:** variable case discounts, collection discounts.

This south London merchant was so good last year - it won the Guide Award as Independent Merchant of the Year - that it was hard to imagine how it could improve. But it has. The Italian list has gone from strength to strength, benefiting from the explosion of winemaking talent in that country, so it had little difficulty in carrying off this year's Award for Best Italian Specialist. But David Gleave MW has found time to build up the selection of Burgundies, and to introduce such exciting new world-class wines as the Shaw and Smith Sauvignon and Chardonnay from Australia. All in all, a brilliant place to buy wine and a brilliant place to browse and taste on a Saturday morning where, according to one regular, it can be one of the most sociable places in town.

20	£17.95	CA DEL BOSCO CREMANT, Lombardy (It)
22	£20.49	VEUVE CLICQUOT DEMI-SEC CHAMPAGNE (F)
54	£4.95	ALSACE TOKAY PINOT GRIS, CAVE VINICOLE DE TURCKHEIM 1990 (F)
62	£5.29	CHAI BAUMIERES CHARDONNAY, VIN DE PAYS D'OC 1990 Midi (F)
68	£6.89	BREGANZE DI BREGANZE, MACULAN 1989 Veneto (It)
69	£7.25	SOAVE CLASSICO VIGNETO CALVARINO, PIEROPAN 1989 Veneto (It)
87	£4.99	ORLANDO RF CHARDONNAY 1989 S E Australia (Aus)
93	£5.39	BROKENBACK VINEYARD CHARDONNAY, ROTHBURY 1990 Hunter Valley (Aus)

95	£6.95	SCHINUS MOLLE CHARDONNAY 1990 Mornington Peninsula (Aus)
111	£11.25	EDNA VALLEY CHARDONNAY 1989 San Luis Obispo (Cal)
114	£12.95	DOMAINE CAUHAPE, JURANCON SEC (OAKED) 1988 South West (F)
154	£7.95	SHAW AND SMITH SAUVIGNON BLANC 1990 South Australia (Aus)
236	£5.99	PRIEURE DE CENAC, CAHORS, RIGAL 1986 South West (F)
280	£4.99	ORLANDO RF CABERNET SAUVIGNON 1988 South Australia (Aus)
304	£7.95	CHATEAU SOCIANDO MALLET, HAUT-MEDOC 1987 Bordeaux (F)
313	£10.29	CLOUDY BAY CABERNET MERLOT 1989 Marlborough (NZ)
314	£10.65	NEWTON CABERNET SAUVIGNON 1986 Napa Valley (Cal)
356	£5.49	DAVID WYNN SHIRAZ 1990 High Eden Ridge (Aus)
371	£8.95	HENSCHKE MOUNT EDELSTONE SHIRAZ 1987 Adelaide Hills (Aus)
392	£11.25	SANFORD PINOT NOIR 1986 Santa Barbara (Cal)
405	£5.25	CHIANTI RUFINA, SELVAPIANA 1988 Tuscany (It)
408	£5.85	BONARDA OLTREPO PAVESE, FUGAZZA 1987 Lombardy (It)
416	£7.65	CHIANTI CLASSICO, ISOLE E OLENA 1988 Tuscany (It)
423	£12.95	BAROLO VIGNA DEL GRIS, FANTINO CONTERNO 1985 Piedmont (It)
424	£14.75	COLTASSALA, CASTELLO DI VOLPAIA 1986 Tuscany (It)
425	£11.95	CARMIGNANO RISERVA, VILLA DI CAPEZZANA 1985 Tuscany (It)
426	£13.75	CEPPARELLO, ISOLE E OLENA 1988 Tuscany (It)
427	£14.25	AMARONE DELLA VALPOLICELLA FIERAMONTE, ALLEGRINI 1983 Veneto (It)
434	£26.45	MAURIZIO ZANELLA, CA' DEL BOSCO 1988 Lombardy (It)
440	£4.95	TINTO VELHO REGUENGOS DE MONSARAZ 1986 Alentejo (P)
441	£4.99	QUINTA DE CAMARATE, J M DE FONSECA 1984 (P)
442	£5.95	TEMPRANILLO, BODEGAS OCHOA 1987 Navarra (Sp)
451	£8.99	MARQUIS DE MURRIETA RIOJA TINTO RESERVA 1985 (Sp)
456	£4.75	SAMOS MUSCAT, Samos (Gr)
465	£5.85	REDWOOD VALLEY ESTATE LATE HARVEST RIESLING 1989 Nelson (NZ)
472	£9.90	JURANCON MOELLEUX VENDANGE TARDIVE, DOMAINE CAUHAPE 1988 S W (F)
493	£16.89	WARRE'S QUINTA DA CAVADINHA 1982 Douro (P)
495	£15.95	FONSECA-GUIMARAENS 1976 Douro (P)
496	£19.95	DUO CENTENARY BUAL, COSSART GORDON (P)

WRK | Wineraks

21 Springfield Road, Aberdeen (0224 311460) and 1 Urquhart Road, Aberdeen AB2 1LU. 'Fine Wine, Port and Coffee Merchants throughout Scotland'. **Delivery**: free locally, nationally at cost..**Tastings**: regularly in-store plus tutored events. **Discounts**: 5% on a (mixed) case.

We are not quite sure whether two shops in Aberdeen constitutes being 'Fine Wine Merchants throughout Scotland', but perhaps there are other stores in this enterprising mini-chain of which we are unaware. Still, if you're after anything ranging from Peter Lehmann and Errazuriz Panquehue to Vallet Frères Clos de la Roche and Röederer Cristal, we know of no better place in Aberdeen to visit.

29	£2.99	CUVEE JEAN-PAUL BLANC SEC VIN DE TABLE, PAUL BOUTINOT (F)
54	£5.39	ALSACE TOKAY PINOT GRIS, CAVE VINICOLE DE TURCKHEIM 1990 (F)
153	£9.45	POUILLY FUME LES CHANTALOUETTES 1989 Loire (F)
173	£14.65	ALSACE TOKAY PINOT GRIS SELECTION DE GRAINS NOBLES, CAVE VINICOLE DE TURCKHEIM 1989 (F)
204	£4.59	CHATEAU LE RAZ, BERGERAC ROSE 1990 South West (F)
228	£4.65	CHATEAU CLEMENT TERMES, GAILLAC ROUGE 1988 South West (F)
231	£5.25	CHATEAU DE LASTOURS CUVEE SIMONE DESCAMPS, CORBIERES 1989 Midi (F)
267	£4.59	CHATEAU LE RAZ, BERGERAC ROUGE 1989 South West (F)
302	£8.15	CHATEAU RAMAGE LA BATISSE, HAUT MEDOC 1988 Bordeaux (F)

333	£33.50	CHATEAU PAVIE, ST EMILION 1985 Bordeaux (F)
349	£4.70	RASTEAU COTES DU RHONE VILLAGES, VIGNERONS DE RASTEAU 1989 (F)
408	£5.65	BONARDA OLTREPO PAVESE, FUGAZZA 1987 Lombardy (It)
491	£14.25	MALMSEY 10 YEAR OLD, HENRIQUES & HENRIQUES (P)

WIN   The Winery

4 Clifton Rd, London W9 1SS (071 286 6475). Pretty shop packed with wines from California-import supremo Geoffrey Roberts. **Opening Hours:** 10.30am-8.30pm Mon-Fri; 10am-6.30pm Sat. **Delivery.** free in London and nationally for 2+ cases, otherwise at cost. **Tastings:** occasionally in-store. **Discounts:** 5% mixed cases, 7.5% unbroken cases.

Now that Les Amis du Vin has decamped from Charlotte Street to Company Headquarters out in the suburbs, this charming little shop has become the visible face of the club, offering its wines - including the Geoffrey Roberts California range (Ridge, Heitz, Firestone et al) as well as some good Tuscans from Frescobaldi - over the counter to members and non-members alike. Among the most loyal fans of The Winery are the MCC members who pop in to buy a bottle on their way to Lords.

WFP   Wines from Paris

The Vaults, 4 Giles St, Leith, Edinburgh EH6 6DJ (031 554 2652). Independent merchant selling by the case. **Opening Hours:** 10am-6pm Mon-Sat. **Delivery:** free on Scottish mainland, nationally at cost. **Tastings:** wines always available for tasting plus regular tutored events. **Discounts:** available.

Judith Paris's list reveals the hand of many of Britain's top wholesalers, with Burgundies such as Daniel Rion and Comtes Lafon from Morris and Verdin (qv) and the Australian selections of Alexr Findlater and Haughton Fine Wines (qqv). The range throughout is of a uniformly high quality, but we couldn't find any wines as old as her 12th Century premises.

95	£6.99	SCHINUS MOLLE CHARDONNAY 1990 Mornington Peninsula (Aus)
151	£6.99	SCHINUS MOLLE SAUVIGNON BLANC 1990 Victoria (Aus)
180	£4.52	HILL SMITH OLD TRIANGLE RIESLING 1990 Barossa Valley (Aus)
230	£5.20	MAS DE GOURGONNIER TRADITION, COTEAUX D'AIX EN PROVENCE LES BAUX 1989 Midi (F)
412	£7.16	CHIANTI CLASSICO, SAN LEONINO 1986 Veneto (It)

WNS   Winos

63 George Street, Oldham, Lancs (061 652 9396). Independent wholesaler and retailer. **Delivery:** free locally, nationally at £3 per case. **Tastings:** occasionally in-store plus tutored events. **Discount:** 5% on (mixed) cases.

Oldham is not exactly a wine drinkers paradise, especially following the closure of the local branch of Willoughby's. Which makes Phil Garratt and Steve Whitehead's shop all the more welcome. What is also welcome is the refreshing enthusiasm which they bring to wine, an enthusiasm which shows that they know their range well. So if you arrive at Mumps station and are in search of Lindemans Pyrus, Freemark Abbey Cabernet Bosche or Château de Lastours Corbières - 'Drink a bottle of that and you'll sleep well' - you'll know where to come (they're behind the police station). But we hope that when their next list comes out, they'll have added producers for all those German wines.

54	£4.50	ALSACE TOKAY PINOT GRIS, CAVE VINICOLE DE TURCKHEIM 1990 (F)
83	£4.55	CALITERRA CHARDONNAY 1990 Maipo Valley (Ch)
90	£5.15	LINDEMANS BIN 65 CHARDONNAY 1989 S E Australia (Aus)
196	£4.95	THREE CHOIRS MEDIUM DRY ENGLISH TABLE WINE 1989 Gloucs (UK)
288	£6.25	CHATEAU MUSAR 1982 Bekaa Valley (Leb)
349	£3.75	RASTEAU COTES DU RHONE VILLAGES, VIGNERONS DE RASTEAU 1989 (F)
351	£4.65	DIEMERSDAL SHIRAZ 1986 Paarl (SA)
437	£3.65	SENORIO DE LOS LLANOS RESERVA 1982 Valdepeñas (Sp)
442	£5.65	TEMPRANILLO, BODEGAS OCHOA 1987 Navarra (Sp)
449	£7.95	CAMPO VIEJO RIOJA GRAN RESERVA 1980 (Sp)

MAW | M & A Winter

181 High Road Chigwell, Essex 1G7 6NU. (081 500 2074). Independent merchant combining daily drinking with the finest of the fine. **Delivery**: free locally.**Discounts**: 10% by the case.

Essex has made great strides to lose its 'grey' image in recent years and, as a county, it can claim the distinction of being the region in which Hugh Johnson chooses to live, write and garden.

We do not know whether the world's greatest wine writer does much of his shopping in Chigwell, but have no doubt that he would appreciate the chance to pick up treasures like Dominus, Mouton 1943 and, why not?, Lascases 1967 and Averys Corton 1969 (a snip at £15.) All these are from a current bin end list. Mr Winter's more recent vintages include the following:

12	£11.95	SCHARFFENBERGER BLANC DE BLANCS 1987 Mendocino (Cal)
22	£18.99	VEUVE CLICQUOT DEMI-SEC CHAMPAGNE (F)
148	£7.15	SELAKS SAUVIGNON BLANC 1990 (NZ)
286	£6.75	SEPPELT GOLD LABEL CABERNET SAUVIGNON 1986 S E Australia (Aus)
331	£18.95	PENFOLDS BIN 707 CABERNET SAUVIGNON 1987 South Australia (Aus)
335	£28.00	LES FORTS DE LATOUR, PAUILLAC, CHATEAU LATOUR 1982 Bordeaux (F)
344	£4.65	PENFOLDS BIN 2 SHIRAZ/MATARO 1989 Barossa Valley (Aus)
412	£8.15	CAMPO FIORIN VALPOLICELLA, MASI 1986 Veneto (It)
489	£10.44	STARBOARD BATCH 88 RUBY, Cantral Valley (Cal)
496	£17.35	DUO CENTENARY BUAL, COSSART GORDON (P)

WIZ | Wizard Wine Warehouses

Head Office: 6 Theobald Court, Borehamwood, Herts, WD6 4RN (081 207 4455). 12-outlet South London wine warehouse chain selling by the case and bottle. **Opening Hours:** 10am - 8pm every day. **Delivery:** free within 20 miles and nationally for orders over £100. **Tastings:** regularly in-store plus tutored events. **Discounts:** on unsplit cases and large quantities.

Throughout the latter part of 1990 and the beginning of 1991, the wine trade was almost constantly readying itself for the news that Tony Mason of Wizard would finally regain control of Majestic, the company from which he was ousted in the 1980s. Well, it hasn't happened yet, but that's not to say that it won't by the time the next *Guide* appears. In the meantime, Mr Mason will remain busy running a chain of (mostly) by-the-bottle warehouses which he fills with anything he can buy at the right price. In 1991, for example, Louis Latour Burgundies made their first apppearance here when that company reduced the price of its 1989s. The range is broad and provides yet another reminder of Majestic in the Good Old Days, but the selection process is only varyingly quality-conscious. Never forget that Mr Mason's reputation in the wine trade is of a merchant who is always ready to buy a hard-to-sell parcel of wine. If it's at the right price, of course.

WRW | The Wright Wine Co

The Old Smithy, Raikes Rd, Skipton, N Yorks BD23 1NP (0756 794175). Unpretentious and affable independent merchant operating from a picturesque 17th century smithy. **Opening Hours:** 9am-6pm Mon-Sat. **Delivery:** free within 35 miles, nationally at cost. **Tastings:** regularly in-store plus tutored events. **Discounts:** 5% on mixed case, wholesale prices for complete cases.

Bob Wright's long list remains as frippery-free and tightly-packed as ever; indeed it makes the print of the *Guide* seem positively huge. But it's worth putting on those reading glasses because, as Mr Wright immodestly says, it really is 'an Aladdin's Cave for the wine lover'. Some areas are particularly well handled - do you prefer your Alsace to be made by Muré, Hugel, Schlumberger or Dopff "Au Moulin"? - while others demand greater caution on the part of the buyer. We suspect for example that Mr Wright likes his Burgundies to taste 'old fashioned' (Doudet Naudin and Jaboulet Vercherre are both well-represented) which perhaps makes it all the more surprising that the northern Rhône gets such short shrift. But it takes all sorts, and we defy anyone not to find a reasonably-priced collection of wines here.

19	£18.90	DEVAUX CHAMPAGNE CUVEE ROSEE (F)
22	£21.00	VEUVE CLICQUOT DEMI-SEC CHAMPAGNE (F)
83	£5.15	CALITERRA CHARDONNAY 1990 Maipo Valley (Ch)
102	£8.90	MARQUES DE MURRIETA RIOJA BLANCO RESERVA 1985 Rioja (Sp)
288	£6.85	CHATEAU MUSAR 1982 Bekaa Valley (Leb)
351	£5.35	DIEMERSDAL SHIRAZ 1986 Paarl (SA)
438	£4.90	MARIUS RESERVA, BODEGAS PIQUERAS 1983 Almansa (Sp)
449	£8.30	CAMPO VIEJO RIOJA GRAN RESERVA 1980 (Sp)
451	£9.85	MARQUIS DE MURRIETA RIOJA TINTO RESERVA 1985 (Sp)
489	£10.15	STARBOARD BATCH 88 RUBY, Central Valley (Cal)

WWI | Woodhouse Wines See Hicks & Don

PWY | Peter Wylie Fine Wines

Plymtree Manor, Plymtree, Cullompton, Devon, EXE15 2LE (088 47 555). Independent merchant specialising in fine and ancient wines **Opening Hours:** 9am-6pm Mon-Fri; 9am-3pm Sat but ring first to check. **Delivery:** free locally, nationally at cost. **Discounts:** reductions for straight cases.

Last year, one of the wines which caught our attention on this list was the Brane Cantenac 1890. Well, Mr Wylie's either still got the same bottle - or been able to buy another from the Château. Our fickle interest has, however, turned to a younger wine: '1892 Vintage legible on cork, unable to identify wine, still some signs of life, not much flavour, re-tried May 1988, (the wine, presumably) had more time to breathe, marked im-

provement. £30'. If it's fine and old and you can drink it, Peter Wylie
either has a bottle - or knows a man who does. A treasure trove in almost
every conceivable vintage.

| 332 | £20.00 | **CHATEAU TALBOT, ST JULIEN** 1982 Bordeaux (F) |
| 475 | £27.00 | **CHATEAU RIEUSSEC, SAUTERNES** 1983 Bordeaux (F) |

| YAP | Yapp Bros |

The Old Brewery, Water St, Mere, Wilts BA12 6DY (0747 860423). Rhône and Loire specialist.
Opening Hours: 9am-5pm Mon-Fri; 9am-1pm Sat. **Delivery:** free locally, free nationally for 2 or
more cases. **Tastings:** reguarly in-store plus tutored events. **Discounts:** for quantity and collection.

'We no longer stock any New World wines - the ones you mentioned in
last year's *Guide* were a one-off purchase.' Having enjoyed the Australian Giaconda Chardonnay, we are sorry to see it disappear from Mere,
but do not blame Robin Yapp for deciding to stick to his last: Southern
France, the Rhône, Loire, Alsace and Champagne. At first glance, the
Yapp list - like its author - appears to be rather slimmer than it was a year
ago but, in the case of the booklet at least, this is an illusion; there are just
as many wines, descriptions and anecdotes as ever. After 22 years, this
remains a merchant for those who are almost as interested in the people
behind the wine, as in the stuff in the bottle. Robin Yapp quite evidently
falls in love with his growers, remaining faithful to them and, in some
cases, their offspring through thick and thin. Which helps to explain
why, if you want wines from such (thanks to R. Parker) illustrious names
as Grippat, Jasmin and Champet, you have little alternative but to make
your way to the Yapp's walled courtyard in Wiltshire where you could
sip a glass or two by the fountain. Or then again, you could always
simply place your order over the 'phone.

MERCHANTS' SERVICES
AND SPECIALITIES

The two charts on the following pages, introduced last year as a brand new feature to the Guide, have proved popular with those readers who requested an at-a-glance guide to the overall style of the merchants we recommend in later pages.

Should you have an acquired taste for, or perhaps have newly been introduced to, and enjoyed, the wines of a particular area, the chart on p.254 listing which of our merchants consider this to be their 'speciality' field will point the way towards the source of further examples. The chart summarising services offered to customers on p.242 has also, as we hoped, been a salutary lesson to those firms — particularly in the High Street — who, with a little more effort, could make marked improvements in some of these areas.

Though of course one would not expect, for example, a supermarket to be able to offer the individual service available at a specialist wine merchant, there are cases where the High Street shop that has trained its staff to be informed and helpful can be a far more attractive proposition than the intimidatingly snooty specialist where one doesn't dare ask a vital question — 'Should I drink it now, or wait?'— for fear of being thought ignorant.

Notes for merchants' services chart (p.242)

STYLE OF BUSINESS

It is sometimes difficult to tie merchants down and ask them to define their style of business coherently. Wine warehouses sell by the bottle, supermarkets run their own wine clubs and mail-order-only firms run in-store tastings. The information presented is the description given to us by each company, to which we would add the following interpretations.

National High Street: a large chain of off-licences covering a very substantial part of Britain — for example, Victoria Wine.

Regional High Street: a smaller chain confined to a particular region. In general, these should offer more of a specialist approach to selling wine. Awards in this category are always fiercely fought.

Wine club: either mail-order only, or a merchant with some sort of scheme (for which there may or may not be a fee) whereby members receive, for example, regular newsletters, priority on wine orders, discounts, invitations to tastings etc.

Wine warehouse: this once indicated a by-the-case-only operation, and though this still holds true for some, the term has become much looser, often being used simply to describe the general atmosphere of the shop.

BY-THE-BOTTLE

It can be infuriating, having trawled round a so-called wine warehouse dutifully making up a case, to discover that you could have just bought the bottle you needed for Sunday lunch after all. And the '12 or nothing' rule can be equally frustrating when you just fancy trying a bottle of something new. However, most by-the-case outlets allow that case to be mixed, which gives a lot more pleasure in the choosing and drinking than a dozen frantic stops at the late-night grocers that happens to lie on your way home from work.

CREDIT CARDS

Many small merchants would rather offer customers a discount for cheque or cash than accept credit cards, thus saving themselves the paperwork and the commission levied by the card companies. Worth enquiring.

ACCOUNT FACILITIES

Personal account facilities are available at the merchant's discretion. References are usually needed.

DELIVERY

L = free local delivery; N = free national delivery, though in many cases a premium is paid for this service; that is, the price of wines delivered 'free' may be rather high. Firms that acknowledge this — e.g. Adnams, The Wine Society — offer a 'collection discount'. More detailed information can usually be found in the firms' individual entries.

CELLARAGE

The firm has, or has access to, secure, temperature-controlled storage for customers' wines. Charges vary.

INVESTMENT ADVICE

Advice on wines to lay down for future drinking or profit will be freely available. Many firms in this category have their own cellar schemes whereby customers are informed and/or assisted to take advantage of special purchases.

EN PRIMEUR

The firm will regularly offer and advise on *en primeur* (in-the-barrel) purchases, making all the necessary arrangements.

PARTY PLANNING

The reverse of the 'investment' coin; the company will give sensible and economical advice on wine styles, quantities per person, etc. Particularly valuable if the company also offers 'sale or return'.

TASTINGS

'In-store' means that informal tastings of opened or promoted wines take place, often on an ad hoc basis, so luck will prevail. 'Ticketed/tutored' tastings imply a more organised event, though not necessarily charged. Fuller details may appear under companies' individual entries.

When contemplating a major purchase, any good specialist merchant should, except in the case of the most expensive wines, be more than happy to open a bottle for tasting. (It's worth noting that if Scottish merchants seem a little reluctant to offer wines for tasting, this is not confirmation of a hackneyed racial stereotype but an indication that the merchant is unwilling to break Scottish laws by allowing you to drink on the premises. Some canny firms have devised cunning ways of getting round this.)

PAGE NUMBER

A full entry for this merchant, including address, opening hours and the *Guide's* report, will be found on this page.

		Nat. High Street	Reg. High Street	Ind. Merchant	Wine Club	Supermarket
ABB	Abbey Cellars			•		
AHC	Ad Hoc Wines			•		
WA	William Addison (Newport) Ltd			•		
ADN	Adnams			•		
DAL	David Alexander			•		
AMW	Amey's Wines			•		
JAR	John Armit Wines			•		
LAV	Les Amis du Vin			•	•	
AK	Arriba Kettle & Co			•		
A	Asda Stores Limited					•
AUC	Australian Wine Centre			•		
AV	Averys of Bristol			•	•	
BH	B H Wines			•	•	
NB	Nigel Baring & Co Ltd			•		
BWS	The Barnes Wine Shop			•		
AB	Augustus Barnett Limited	•				
BAT	The Battersea Wine Company			•		
BFI	Bedford Fine Wines Ltd			•		
BEN	Bennetts			•		
BSN	Benson Fine Wines Ltd			•		
BKW	Berkeley Wines					
BBR	Berry Bros & Rudd			•		
BI	Bibendum Wine Ltd			•		
BIN	Bin 89 Wine Warehouse					
BND	Bin Ends			•		
BLW	Blayneys		•			
BTH	Booths (of Preston)					•
BOO	Booths (of Stockport)			•		
BD	Bordeaux Direct					
BGC	Borg Castel			•		
B&B	Bottle & Basket					
BKN	The Bottleneck			•		
BOS	Bottles			•		
BU	Bottoms Up	•		•		
BRO	The Broad Street Wine Co.			•		
BUD	Budgens					•
BWI	Bute Wines			•		
BUT	The Butlers Wine Cellar			•		
ABY	Anthony Byrne Fine Wines Ltd			•	•	

Wine W'House	By The Bottle	No. of Branches	Credit Cards	Own Charge Card	Account Facilities	Mail Order	Delivery	Coll. Discount	Cellerage	Invest. Advice	En Primeur	Free Glass Loan	Glass Loan	Ice	Party Planning	Gift Mailing	Books	In-Store Tastings	Tutored Tastings	Page No.
•		1	•		•		L				•	•		•	•				•	115
•	•	1	•		•		L					•	•			•			•	115
•	•	1	•		•	•	L		•	•	•	•		•	•	•			•	115
•	•	3	•		•			•	•	•	•	•		•		•	•	•	•	116
	•	1	•		•		L	•	•	•	•	•		•		•			•	117
	•	1	•		•		L					•	•						•	118
		1	•		•		N	•	•			•			•					119
	•	3	•		•			•	•		•	•		•		•			•	119
		1	•		•	•	N	•				•			•					119
	•	204	•									•		•	•				•	120
	•	1	•			•	N	•				•		•	•	•		•	•	120
	•	1	•		•	•				•		•	•					•		122
		1	•			•	L					•		•				•		122
		1	•		•	•	L		•	•	•	•						•		123
	•	1	•			•	L		•	•	•	•		•		•		•	•	124
	•	600	•		•		L					•		•	•	•		•	•	125
	•	1	•		•		L					•		•	•			•		125
		1	•			•	L		•	•	•	•						•	•	126
	•	1	•		•		L	•				•		•				•	•	126
	•	1	•		•		L					•								127
		1	•		•															127
	•	2	•		•		N	•	•	•		•		•			•	•	•	128
•		1	•		•	•	L					•			•			•	•	128
•		1	•			•	L					•		•				•		129
	•	1	•		•		L	•	•	•		•						•	•	129
	•	185	•		•		L					•	•		•	•		•	•	130
	•	21	•		•							•	•			•		•	•	131
	•	1	•		•							•	•		•			•	•	130
	•	6	•		•	•				•						•	•	•	•	132
	•	1	•				L	•				•		•	•	•		•	•	132
	•	1	•				L	•				•						•		132
	•	1	•		•		L					•			•	•		•	•	133
	•	1	•		•	•	L		•	•	•	•		•	•	•		•	•	133
	•	78	•		•							•	•		•	•		•	•	134
	•	1	•			•	L	•		•	•	•				•	•	•	•	134
	•	95	•		•													•		135
		1	•				L		•		•	•							•	135
	•	1	•		•	•	L			•		•			•			•	•	136
	•	1	•		•	•	L		•	•	•	•	•	•	•			•	•	136

		Nat. High Street	Reg. High Street	Ind. Merchant	Wine Club	Supermarket
DBY	D Byrne & Co			•		
CAC	Cachet Wines			•		
CWI	A Case of Wine			•		
CVR	The Celtic Vintner Ltd			•		
CDV	Champagne de Villages			•	•	
CPL	Chaplin & Son			•		
CHP	Chateau Pleck					
CFW	Christchurch Fine Wine Co			•	•	
CIW	City Wines			•		
CWW	Classic Wine Warehouses Ltd			•		
CNL	Connollys (Wine Merchants) Ltd			•		
C&B	Corney & Barrow Ltd			•		
CWM	Cornwall Wine Merchants Ltd			•		
CGW	The Cote Green Wines Ltd			•	•	
CWS	Co-op					•
CUM	Cumbrian Cellar			•		
D	Davisons Wine Merchants		•			
DLM	Del Monico Wines Ltd			•	•	
ROD	Rodney Densem Wines			•		
DIR	Direct Wine Shipments			•	•	
PD	Peter Dominic	•				
DX	Drinkx plc			•		
EE	Eaton Elliot Fine Wines			•		
ECK	Eckington Wines			•		
EP	Eldridge Pope & Co			•		
EBA	Ben Ellis & Assocs Ltd			•		
EVI	Evingtons			•		
PEY	Philip Eyres Wine Merchants			•		
FAR	Farr Vintners Ltd			•		
AF	Alex Findlater & Co			•		
LEF	Le Fleming Wines			•		
JFR	John Frazier			•		
FWC	Fulham Road Wine Centre			•		
FUL	Fuller Smith & Turner		•			
G	Gateway					•
GON	T.F. Gauntley Ltd			•		
GEL	Gelston Castle Fine Wines			•		
MG	Matthew Gloag & Son			•	•	
G&M	Gordon & Macphail			•		

Wine W'House	By The Bottle	No. of Branches	Credit Cards	Own Charge Card	Account Facilities	Mail Order	Delivery	Coll. Discount	Cellerage	Invest. Advice	En Primeur	Free Glass Loan	Glass Loan	Ice	Party Planning	Gift Mailing	Books	In-Store Tastings	Tutored Tastings	Page No.
·	•	1			•	•	L		•		•	•			•	•				136
•		1	•		•	•	L		•	•		•			•	•			•	138
		1			•	•	L	•	•	•		•			•	•		•	•	138
		1			•	•	L		•	•	•	•			•	•			•	139
	•	1	•		•	•	L		•		•	•			•	•		•	•	140
•	•	1			•	•			•	•	•	•		•	•	•			•	140
•		1			•	•	L		•	•		•			•	•			•	141
	•	1			•	•	L		•	•		•			•	•			•	141
	•	2			•		L		•			•			•	•			•	141
•		1	•		•		L		•			•	•		•	•			•	142
	•	1			•	•	L		•	•	•	•			•	•			•	142
	•	3	•		•		L		•	•	•	•			•	•			•	143
		1	•		•		L		•	•		•			•	•			•	144
	•	1					L			•		•			•	•			•	144
	•	2400	•		•														•	143
		1	•		•	•	L		•	•		•			•	•			•	144
•	•	80	•		•	•	L			•		•		•	•	•			•	145
		1	•		•	•	L		•	•		•			•	•			•	146
	•	1	•		•	•	L			•	•	•			•	•			•	146
	•	1	•		•	•	L		•	•		•			•	•			•	146
	•	607	•		•															147
•		1			•	•	N		•	•		•			•	•			•	147
	•	1			•	•	L		•	•		•			•	•			•	148
		1			•	•	L		•	•	•	•			•	•			•	148
•	•	13	•		•		L		•	•	•	•		•	•	•		•	•	149
		1			•	•	L		•	•	•	•			•	•		•	•	149
	•	1	•		•	•	L		•	•	•	•			•	•			•	150
		1			•	•	L			•	•	•			•	•			•	151
		1			•	•			•	•	•					•			•	151
•		1			•	•	L		•										•	152
·		1			•	•	L		•	•		•			•				•	152
•	•	4							•	•	•					•			•	153
	•	1					L		•	•		•			•	•			•	154
	•	61	•		•		L		•			•			•	•			•	154
	•	700	•				L		•			•			•	•			•	155
	•	1	•				L		•	•		•			•	•			•	156
		1																		156
	•	1	•		•	•	L		•	•	•	•			•	•	•		•	157
	•	1	•		•	•	L			•		•			•	•	•	•	•	157

		Nat. High Street	Reg. High Street	Ind. Merchant	Wine Club	Supermarket
GI	Grape Ideas			•		
GEW	Great English Wines					
GNW	Great Northern Wine Co			•		
GRT	Great Western Wine Co Ltd			•		
PTR	Peter Green			•		
TGB	The Grog Blossom			•		
PGR	Patrick Grubb Selections					
HLV	Halves Ltd			•		
HAM	Hampden Wine Co			•		
HFV	Harcourt Fine Wines			•		
HPD	Harpenden Wines			•		
GHS	Gerard Harris Fine Wines			•		
ROG	Roger Harris Wines			•		
HAR	Harrods Ltd					
RHV	Richard Harvey Wines			•		
HV	John Harvey & Sons			•		
HFW	Haughton Fine Wines			•		
HHC	Haynes Hanson & Clarke			•		
H&H	Hector & Honorez Wines Ltd			•		
HW	Hedley Wright Co Ltd			•		
HEM	The Hermitage			•		
H&D	Hicks & Don Woodhouse Wines			•		
HBV	High Breck Vintners			•		
HBR	Hilbre Wines Co Ltd			•		
GHL	George Hill of Loughborough			•		
JEH	J E Hogg			•		
RHW	Rodney Hogg Wines			•		
HOL	Holland Park Wine Co			•		
HOP	Hopton Wines			•		
HOT	House of Townend			•		
HUN	Hungerford Wine Co			•		
H	Hunters Food and Wine Ltd			•		
HYN	Hynard Hughes & Co Ltd			•		
JCK	JC Karn & Sons			•		
JOB	Jeroboams			•		
SHJ	SH Jones & Co Ltd			•		
J&B	Justerini & Brooks			•		
K&B	King & Barnes			•		
L&W	Lay & Wheeler			•		

Wine W'House	By The Bottle	No. of Branches	Credit Cards	Own Charge Card	Account Facilities	Mail Order	Delivery	Coll. Discount	Cellerage	Invest. Advice	En Primeur	Free Glass Loan	Glass Loan	Ice	Party Planning	Gift Mailing	Books	In-Store Tastings	Tutored Tastings	Page No.
	•	2	•			•	• L			•	•		•		•	•	•	•	•	157
	•	1	•		•	•	• L			•	•		•		•	•		•	•	158
•	•	1	•		•	•	• L			•	•	•			•	•	•	•	•	158
•	•	1	•	•		•	• L			•	•	•			•	•	•	•	•	159
	•	1				•	•					•			•				•	160
	•	3	•			•	L				•	•		•	•	•			•	160
	•	1				•				•	•							•	•	161
						•	N													161
	•	1	•		•	•	• L		•		•	•			•	•			•	161
	•	1	•		•	•	• L			•	•				•	•		•	•	162
	•	1	•		•	•	• L				•				•	•		•	•	162
	•	1	•	•	•	•	• L			•	•	•		•	•	•		•	•	163
	•	1	•		•	•	• L			•	•				•	•			•	163
	•	1	•	•	•	•	L			•	•				•	•		•	•	164
	•	1	•		•	•	• L	•		•	•	•		•	•	•			•	165
	•	1	•		•	•	• L			•	•	•			•	•		•	•	164
	•	1	•		•		L			•	•	•			•	•			•	165
	•	1	•		•		N		•		•	•		•	•	•			•	166
	•	1	•		•		L			•	•		•		•	•			•	167
•	•	1	•	•	•	•	• L	•		•	•	•		•	•	•	•		•	167
	•	1	•				L				•			•	•	•				168
	•	1	•		•	•	• L			•	•	•		•	•	•			•	169
•	•	1	•		•	•	• L	•			•				•	•			•	169
•	•	1	•		•	•	• L			•	•			•	•	•			•	169
	•	1	•		•	•	• L		•	•	•	•		•	•	•			•	170
	•	1	•		•	•	• L			•	•				•	•	•		•	170
	•	1	•		•	•	• L	•			•			•	•	•	•		•	171
	•	1	•		•	•	• L			•	•	•		•	•	•			•	171
	•	1			•	•				•	•	•		•	•	•	•		•	172
	•	14	•		•	•	L		•	•	•	•		•	•	•	•		•	172
	•	1	•		•	•	• L			•	•	•		•	•	•			•	173
	•	1	•		•	•	• L			•	•	•		•	•	•			•	173
•	•	2	•		•	•	L		•	•	•	•		•	•	•			•	174
	•	1	•		•	•	L			•	•	•			•	•			•	176
	•	2	•		•	•	L			•	•				•	•	•		•	174
	•	1	•	•	•	•	L		•	•	•	•		•	•	•			•	175
	•	2	•		•	•			•	•	•	•		•	•	•	•		•	175
	•	1	•		•		L				•		•		•	•	•		•	176
•	•	2	•		•	•	L			•	•	•		•	•	•			•	177

	Nat. High Street	Reg. High Street	Ind. Merchant	Wine Club	Supermarket
LEA	Lea & Sandeman Co Ltd			•		
LES	CRS Ltd – Leos					•
LWL	London Wine Ltd			•		
LHV	Lorne House Vintners			•	•	
MWW	Majestic Wine Warehouses					
M&S	Marks & Spencer	•				
MC	The Master Cellar					
MYS	Mayor Sworder & Co Ltd			•		
MCL	McLeod's					
MM	Michael Menzel Wines			•		
MIL	Millevini			•		
MTL	Mitchells Wine Merchants Ltd			•		
TMW	Moffat Wine Shop			•		
MOR	Moreno Wines			•		
M&V	Morris & Verdin			•		
NZC	New Zealand Wine Club				•	
LNR	Le Nez Rouge			•	•	
JN	James Nicholson			•		
N&P	Nickolls & Perks Ltd			•		
NIC	Nicolas			•		
NRW	Noble Rot Wine Warehouse Ltd			•		
NI	Nobody Inn			•		
OD	Oddbins	•				
OLS	The Old St Wine Co			•		
ORG	The Organic Wine Co					
PAL	Pallant Wines Ltd					
P	Parfrements			•		
THP	Thos Peatling			•		
PIM	Pimlico Dozen			•		
CPW	Christopher Piper Wines Ltd			•		
TP	Terry Platt Wine Merchant			•		
POR	Portland Wine Company			•		
PUG	Pugsons of Buxton			•		
RAE	Raeburn Fine Wine			•		
RAV	Ravensbourne Wine Co Ltd			•		
RD	Reid Wines			•		
REW	La Reserva Wines			•		
RWW	Richmond Wine Warehouse			•		
RWC	Rioja Wine Co Ltd			•		

Wine W'House	By The Bottle	No. of Branches	Credit Cards	Own Charge Card	Account Facilities	Mail Order	Delivery	Coll. Discount	Cellerage	Invest. Advice	En Primeur	Free Glass Loan	Glass Loan	Ice	Party Planning	Gift Mailing	Books	In-Store Tastings	Tutored Tastings	Page No.
	•	1	•		•	•	L	•	•		•	•		•	•	•	•	•	•	178
	•	382	•																•	178
•	•	1	•				L			•	•	•		•					•	179
•	•	1		•		•	L	•				•	•						•	180
•		33	•				L					•		•					•	180
	•	291		•													•		•	181
•	•	1	•				L			•		•		•	•			•	•	182
	•	1	•		•		L	•		•	•	•							•	182
	•	1	•				L					•							•	183
	•	1	•		•		L					•						•	•	183
		1				•	L	•				•	•						•	184
	•	2	•		•	•	L	•		•	•	•							•	184
	•	1	•				L					•				•			•	185
	•	2	•			•	L	•				•				•			•	185
	•	1	•			•	L	•	•	•	•	•						•	•	186
	•	1	•			•	L					•				•				186
•	•	2	•			•	L	•	•		•	•							•	187
		1	•		•	•	N	•	•	•						•	•	•	•	187
	•	2	•		•	•	L	•	•			•		•	•	•			•	188
	•	5	•	•		•	L	•	•	•		•		•	•	•			•	188
•		1	•				L					•				•			•	188
	•	1	•				L					•						•	•	189
	•	155	•	•	•		L	•				•		•	•	•			•	190
	•	1	•				L	•				•				•			•	193
		1	•		•	•				•						•			•	193
•	•	1	•				L					•						•	•	194
	•	1	•				L	•	•	•		•				•			•	194
	•	33	•				L	•	•	•		•		•	•	•	•	•	•	194
		1	•				L	•	•			•							•	195
	•	1	•	•			L	•	•			•		•					•	196
		1		•			L					•				•			•	196
	•	2	•	•			L					•		•			•		•	197
	•	1	•				L			•		•		•	•				•	198
	•	1		•			L	•	•			•				•			•	196
		1		•		•	L	•				•		•	•	•	•		•	199
•	•	1	•	•		•	L					•				•			•	199
	•	1	•	•			L		•			•						•	•	200
•	•	1	•				L				•	•		•	•		•		•	200
		1			•	L	•					•			•	•	•	•	•	201

		Nat. High Street	Reg. High Street	Ind. Merchant	Wine Club	Supermarket
HR	Howard Ripley Fine French Wines			•		
WRB	William Robbs					•
CAR	C A Rookes Wine Merchants			•		
RTW	The Rose Tree Wine Co			•		
WRU	William Rush			•		
R&I	Russell & McIver Ltd			•		
SAC	Le Sac a Vin			•		
SAF	Safeway	•				•
SB	Sainsbury Bros			•		
JS	J Sainsbury Plc	•				•
SC	Sandgate Cellars			•		
SAN	Sandiway Wine Co			•		
SPS	Sapsford Wines			•		
SWB	Satchells			•		
ASH	Ashley Scott			•	•	
SEB	Sebastapol Wines			•		
SK	Seckford Wines			•		
SEL	Selfridges					
SHV	Sherborne Vintners			•		
SAS	Sherston Wine Company (St Albans)			•		
AS	Andre Simon Wine Shops Ltd			•		
SV	Smedley Vintners			•		
HAS	H Allen Smith			•		
SOL	La Solitude			•		
SPR	Spar UK Ltd					•
FSW	Frank E Stainton			•		
SUM	Summerlee Wines Ltd			•		
DWL	Sunday Times Wine Club				•	
SUP	Supergrape Ltd			•		
T&W	T & W Wines			•		
TAL	Talbot Wines			•		
TAN	Tanners Wines Ltd		•	•		
TO	Tesco					•
TW	Thames Wines Sellers			•	•	
TH	Thresher Wine Shops	•				
TRE	Tremaynes			•		
UBC	Ubiquitous Chip Ltd			•		
U	Unwins Wine Merchants		•			
V&C	Valvona & Crolla Ltd			•		

Wine W'House	By The Bottle	No. of Branches	Credit Cards	Own Charge Card	Account Facilities	Mail Order	Delivery	Coll. Discount	Cellerage	Invest. Advice	En Primeur	Free Glass Loan	Glass Loan	Ice	Party Planning	Gift Mailing	Books	In-Store Tastings	Tutored Tastings	Page No.
		1			•	•	L			•	•	•			•				•	201
	•	1	•	•	•	•	L					•					•		•	201
•	•	1			•		L			•	•	•		•	•	•	•	•	•	202
	•	1	•		•		L			•	•	•			•	•	•	•	•	202
		1	•				L					•							•	203
		1					L			•	•	•			•	•			•	203
	•	5	•		•		L			•	•	•		•		•		•	•	203
	•	312	•									•							•	204
•	•	3	•		•		L	•				•							•	206
	•	300										•					•			205
		1	•				L					•			•				•	206
		1			•		L					•				•	•		•	207
		1				•	L							•					•	207
	•	1	•		•	•	L			•	•	•			•	•			•	207
		1			•	•	L			•	•	•				•	•		•	208
•		1	•				L	•			•	•				•	•		•	208
•		1	•				L			•	•	•				•	•		•	209
	•	1	•	•	•		L					•				•	•		•	209
		1			•	•	L					•	•		•				•	210
	•	1	•				L					•			•	•	•		•	210
	•	3	•				L	•		•	•	•			•	•		•	•	211
•		1	•				L			•	•	•			•	•	•		•	211
	•	2	•			•	L					•				•		•	•	211
	•	1	•				L	•				•					•		•	212
	•	2000							•									•	•	212
	•	1	•			•	L			•	•	•			•	•	•		•	212
	•	1	•		•		L			•	•	•			•	•	•		•	213
		1			•	•				•	•	•						•		213
	•	1	•		•		L			•	•	•			•	•		•		214
	•	1	•			•	L			•	•	•				•	•		•	214
	•	2	•		•		L					•				•		•	•	215
	•	6	•		•	•	L	•		•	•	•			•			•	•	215
	•	370	•									•						•	•	216
		1			•	•	L			•	•			•	•	•			•	217
	•	462	•				L					•			•	•	•		•	218
	•	1	•				L	•		•		•			•			•	•	219
	•	1	•				L			•	•	•	•						•	219
	•	300	•				L	•				•				•			•	220
	•	1	•			•	•	N	•		•		•			•	•		•	221

		Nat. High Street	Reg. High Street	Ind. Merchant	Wine Club	Supermarket
HVW	Helen Verdcourt			•		
VW	Victoria Wine	•				
LV	La Vigneronne			•		
VIL	Village Wines			•		
VLW	Villeneuve Wines Ltd			•		
VER	Vinceremos Wines					
VR	Vintage Roots			•		
ALV	A L Vose & Co Ltd			•		
W	Waitrose Ltd					•
PWA	Peter Warburton Wines			•		
WAW	Waterloo Wine Co Ltd			•		
WAC	Waters of Coventry Ltd			•		
WES	Wessex Wines			•		
WOC	Whitesides of Clitheroe Ltd			•		
WTL	Whittalls Wines			•		
WDW	Windrush Wines Ltd			•		
WE	The Wine Emporium Ltd			•		
WR	Wine Rack	•				
WSC	The Wine Schoppen Ltd			•		
WSO	The Wine Society			•	•	
WTR	The Wine Treasury			•		
WCE	Winecellars			•		
WRK	Wineraks			•		
WIN	The Winery			•		
WFP	Wines from Paris			•		
WNS	Winos Wine Shop			•		
MAW	M & A Winter			•		
WIZ	Wizard Wine Warehouses plc			•		
WRW	The Wright Wine Co			•		
PWY	Peter Wylie Fine Wines			•		
YAP	Yapp Bros plc			•		

Wine W'House	By The Bottle	No. of Branches	Credit Cards	Own Charge Card	Account Facilities	Mail Order	Delivery	Coll. Discount	Cellerage	Invest. Advice	En Primeur	Free Glass Loan	Glass Loan	Ice	Party Planning	Gift Mailing	Books	In-Store Tastings	Tutored Tastings	Page No.
		1			•	•	L			•	•	•				•			•	221
	•	800	•			•					•					•			•	222
	•	1	•			•	L	•	•	•	•					•		•	•	223
•		1	•		•	•	L			•	•	•				•	•	•	•	224
	•	1	•		•	•	L	•	•		•			•	•	•	•	•	•	224
		1	•		•	•	L	•			•					•		•		225
		1	•		•	•	N	•								•				225
		1	•		•		L				•					•			•	225
	•	95									•			•	•					226
		1			•		L				•				•					226
		1	•				L			•		•			•	•	•		•	227
	•	1	•		•	•	L				•	•				•			•	227
		1	•				L	•			•				•	•	•	•	•	227
	•	1	•		•	•	L				•				•	•		•	•	228
•		1	•		•	•	L			•	•	•		•		•			•	229
		1	•		•		N			•	•	•							•	229
•		1	•		•		L	•	•	•	•	•			•	•		•	•	230
	•	78	•		•		L				•	•		•	•	•		•	•	230
•		2	•		•	•	L	•	•	•	•	•			•	•		•	•	232
•		1	•		•	•	L	•	•	•	•				•	•			•	232
		1			•					•										233
	•	1	•		•	•	N	•				•			•	•		•	•	233
	•	2	•				L		•			•			•	•		•	•	234
	•	1	•		•		L		•			•				•		•	•	235
		1	•		•	•	L	•		•		•			•	•	•	•	•	235
	•	1	•		•	•	L				•	•			•	•	•	•	•	235
	•	1	•		•		L	•	•		•	•			•	•		•	•	236
•	•	13	•		•	•	L				•	•			•	•	•	•	•	236
	•	1	•				L			•		•			•	•		•	•	237
	•	1	•		•	•	L	•	•		•						•			237
•	•	1	•		•	•	L	•		•		•			•	•	•	•	•	238

		Bordeaux	Burgundy	Rhone	Loire	Alsace
ABB	Abbey Cellars					
AHC	Ad Hoc Wines	•	•	•		
WA	William Addison (Newport) Ltd					
ADN	Adnams	•	•	•	•	
DAL	David Alexander	•				
AMW	Amey's Wines					
JAR	John Armit Wines	•	•			
LAV	Les Amis du Vin					
AKC	Arriba Kettle & Co				•	
A	Asda Stores Limited					
AUC	Australian Wine Centre					
AV	Averys of Bristol	•	•			
BH	B H Wines					
NB	Nigel Baring & Co Ltd					
BWS	The Barnes Wine Shop					
AB	Augustus Barnett Limited					
BAT	The Battersea Wine Company					
BFI	Bedford Fine Wines Ltd					
BEN	Bennetts					
BSN	Benson Fine Wines Ltd					
BKW	Berkeley Wines					
BBR	Berry Bros & Rudd	•				
BI	Bibendum Wine Ltd	•	•	•		
BIN	Bin 89 Wine Warehouse					
BND	Bin Ends					
BLW	Blayneys					
BTH	Booths (of Preston)	•				
BOO	Booths (of Stockport)					
BD	Bordeaux Direct					
BGC	Borg Castel					
B&B	Bottle & Basket					
BNK	The Bottleneck					
BOS	Bottles		•			
BU	Bottoms Up					
BRO	The Broad Street Wine Co.					
BUD	Budgens				•	
BWI	Bute Wines		•			
BUT	The Butlers Wine Cellar	•	•	•	•	•
ABY	Anthony Byrne Fine Wines Ltd	•	•	•	•	•

		Bordeaux	Burgundy	Rhone	Loire	Alsace
DBY	D Byrne & Co					
CAC	Cachet Wines	•				•
CWI	A Case of Wine					
CVR	The Celtic Vintner Ltd		•		•	
CDV	Champagne de Villages		•		•	
CPL	Chaplin & Son	•				
CHP	Chateau Pleck	•	•	•	•	
CFW	Christchurch Fine Wine Co	•	•	•	•	•
CIW	City Wines					
CWW	Classic Wine Warehouses Ltd	•	•			•
CNL	Connollys (Wine Merchants) Ltd					
C&B	Corney & Barrow Ltd	•	•			
CWM	Cornwall Wine Merchants Ltd					
CGW	The Cote Green Wines Ltd					
CWS	Co-op					
CUM	Cumbrian Cellar					
D	Davisons Wine Merchants	•	•			
DLM	Del Monico Wines Ltd					
ROD	Rodney Densem Wines					
DWS	Direct Wine Shipments					
PD	Peter Dominic					
DX	Drinkx plc	•	•			
EE	Eaton Elliot Fine Wines					
ECK	Eckington Wines					
EP	Eldridge Pope & Co	•	•		•	•
EBA	Ben Ellis & Assocs Ltd	•	•			
EVI	Evingtons					
PEY	Philip Eyres Wine Merchants	•				
FAR	Farr Vintners Ltd	•	•	•		
AF	Alex Findlater & Co					
LEF	Le Fleming Wines					
JFR	John Frazier					
FWC	Fulham Road Wine Centre					
FUL	Fuller Smith & Turner	•	•			
G	Gateway					
GON	T.F. Gauntley Ltd		•	•	•	
GEL	Gelston Castle Fine Wines	•	•			
MG	Matthew Gloag & Son	•		•		
G&M	Gordon & Macphail					

Champagne	French Reg.	Germany	Spain	Portugal	Italy	Australia	New Zealand	California	Other U.S.	South America	South Africa	England	Sherry	Port	Madeira	Organic	Fine/Old Wines	Malt Whisky	Half Bottles	Page No.
						•												•		136
						•														138
	•	•	•		•	•	•									•				138
	•		•										•						•	139
•																				140
													•	•				•	•	140
														•			•			141
•		•												•		•	•		•	141
	•									•										141
•			•			•												•	•	142
	•					•												•	•	142
														•			•			143
																				144
														•				•		144
																				143
						•												•		144
						•	•							•						145
																				146
																	•			146
																				146
																				147
•							•													147
																				148
		•																		148
	•	•												•			•		•	149
																				149
						•								•	•		•	•		150
		•							•								•			151
													•	•	•		•			151
						•														152
																				152
																				153
																	•			154
•	•																			154
																				155
				•							•						•			156
		•																		156
							•						•	•			•			157
																				157

		Bordeaux	Burgundy	Rhone	Loire	Alsace
GI	Grape Ideas					
GEW	Great English Wines					
GNW	Great Northern Wine Co	•	•			
GRT	Great Western Wine Co Ltd					
PTR	Peter Green				•	•
TGB	The Grog Blossom					•
PGR	Patrick Grubb Selections					
HLV	Halves Ltd					
HAM	Hampton Wine Co	•	•	•	•	•
HFV	Harcourt Fine Wines		'			
HPD	Harpenden Wines	•		•	•	
GHS	Gerard Harris Fine Wines					
ROG	Roger Harris Wines					
HAR	Harrods Ltd	•				
RHV	Richard Harvey Wines					
HV	John Harvey & Sons	•				
HFW	Haughton Fine Wines					
HHC	Haynes Hanson & Clarke	•	•		•	
H&H	Hector & Honorez Wines Ltd		•	•	•	•
HW	Hedley Wright					
HEM	The Hermitage					
H&D	Hicks & Don Ltd	•		•	•	
HBV	High Breck Vintners	•			•	•
HBR	Hilbre Wines Co Ltd					
GHL	George Hill of Loughborough					
JEH	J E Hogg	•				•
RHW	Rodney Hogg Wines					
HOL	Holland Park Wine Co				•	
HOP	Hopton Wines	•	•		•	
HOT	House of Townend					
HUN	Hungerford Wine Co	•	•	•		
H	Hunters Food and Wine Ltd					
HYN	Hynard Hughes & Co Ltd					
JCK	JC Karn & Sons				•	
JOB	Jeroboams			•	•	
SHJ	SH Jones & Co Ltd	•	•	•	•	
J&B	Justerini & Brooks	•	•	•		
K&B	King & Barnes					
L&W	Lay & Wheeler	•	•	•	•	•

Champagne	French Reg.	Germany	Spain	Portugal	Italy	Australia	New Zealand	California	Other U.S.	South America	South Africa	England	Sherry	Port	Madeira	Organic	Fine/Old Wines	Malt Whisky	Half Bottles	Page No.
																				157
												•								158
	•					•	•	•												158
																				159
			•			•	•			•			•				•	•		160
•		•				•	•	•					•					•		160
																				161
																			•	161
	•			•							•	•	•	•						161
		•										•								162
				•							•			•						162
																	•			163
	•																		•	163
•													•	•			•	•		164
	•																			165
													•	•						164
		•				•	•									•				165
•								•												166
	•																		•	167
										•										167
																				168
	•	•				•							•				•			169
																				169
																				169
																				170
		•			•								•					•	•	170
																				171
																				171
•																	•			172
													•							172
																	•			173
							•													173
													•							174
							•													176
•							•												•	174
															•					175
														•			•	•	•	175
																				176
•	•	•				•	•	•	•				•	•					•	177

		Bordeaux	Burgundy	Rhone	Loire	Alsace
LEA	Lea & Sandeman Co Ltd	•	•	•	•	•
LES	CRS Ltd – Leos					
LWL	London Wine Ltd					
LHV	Lorne House Vintners				•	
MWW	Majestic Wine Warehouses					
M&S	Marks & Spencer	•				
MC	The Master Cellar	•	•			
MYS	Mayor Sworder & Co Ltd					
MCL	McLeod's					
MM	Michael Menzel Wines					
MIL	Millevini					
MTL	Mitchells Wine Merchants Ltd	•	•	•		
TMW	Moffat Wine Shop					
MOR	Moreno Wines					
M&V	Morris & Verdin		•		•	
NZC	New Zealand Wine Club					
LNR	Le Nez Rouge		•		•	–
JN	James Nicholson					
N&P	Nickolls & Perks Ltd					
NIC	Nicolas	•				
NRW	Noble Rot Wine Warehouse Ltd					
NI	Nobody Inn				•	
OD	Oddbins					
OLS	The Old St Wine Co				•	
ORG	The Organic Wine Co					
PAL	Pallant Wines Ltd					
P	Parfrements					
THP	Thos Peatling	•	•			
PIM	Pimlico Dozen	•			•	
CPW	Christopher Piper Wines Ltd		•	•		
TP	Terry Platt Wine Merchant	•	•			•
POR	Portland Wine Company					
PUG	Pugsons of Buxton					
RAE	Raeburn Fine Wine		•	•	•	
RAV	Ravensbourne Wine Co Ltd					
RD	Reid Wines	•	•	•		•
REW	La Reserva Wines					
RWW	Richmond Wine Warehouse	•	•			
RWC	Rioja Wine Co Ltd					

Champagne	French Reg.	Germany	Spain	Portugal	Italy	Australia	New Zealand	California	Other U.S.	South America	South Africa	England	Sherry	Port	Madeira	Organic	Fine/Old Wines	Malt Whisky	Half Bottles	Page No.
•					•		•						•	•			•		•	178
																				178
																				179
																				180
																				180
	•																			181
			•			•								•					•	182
																				182
																			•	183
																				183
					•															184
•			•			•	•							•					•	184
																			•	185
			•								•		•							185
								•												186
							•													186
																				187
																				187
																				188
	•																•			188
																				188
						•	•					•							•	189
•	•				•									•					•	190
														•			•			193
		•															•			193
																				194
				•			•							•						194
		•				•	•							•			•			194
	•																			195
	•																		•	196
	•						•													196
																				197
	•																			198
								•											•	196
																				199
				•														•	•	199
			•																	200
•																	•			200
		•	•	•										•						201

		Bordeaux	Burgundy	Rhone	Loire	Alsace
HR	Howard Ripley Fine French Wines		•			
WRB	William Robbs					
CAR	C A Rookes Wine Merchants					
RTW	The Rose Tree Wine Co	•	•		•	
WRU	William Rush		•			
R&I	Russell & McIver Ltd	•	•	•	•	•
SAC	Le Sac a Vin		•			
SAF	Safeway	•				
SB	Sainsbury Bros					
JS	J Sainsbury Plc					
SC	Sandgate Cellars					
SAN	Sandiway Wine Co					
SPS	Sapsford Wines				•	
SWB	Satchells	•				
ASH	Ashley Scott					
SEB	Sebastapol Wines			•	•	•
SK	Seckford Wines	•	•			
SEL	Selfridges					
SHV	Sherborne Vintners					
SAS	Sherston Wine Company (St Albans)	•	•	•	•	•
AS	Andre Simon Wine Shops Ltd					
SV	Smedley Vintners					
HAS	H Allen Smith					
SOL	La Solitude	•	•			
SPR	Spar UK Ltd					
FSW	Frank E Stainton					
SUM	Summerlee Wines Ltd	•	•	•	•	•
DWL	Sunday Times Wine Club					
SUP	Supergrape Ltd					
T&W	T & W Wines	•	•	•		•
TAL	Talbot Wines					
TAN	Tanners Wines Ltd					
TO	Tesco					
TW	Thames Wines Sellers			•		
TH	Thresher Wine Shops	•				•
TRE	Tremaynes					
UBC	Ubiquitious Chip Ltd	•	•	•		
U	Unwins Wine Merchants	•				
V&C	Valvona & Crolla Ltd					

		Bordeaux	Burgundy	Rhone	Loire	Alsace
HVW	Helen Verdcourt			•		
VW	Victoria Wine					
LV	La Vigneronne			•	•	•
VIL	Village Wines	•	•			
VLW	Villeneuve Wines Ltd					
VER	Vinceremos Wines					
VR	Vintage Roots					
ALV	A L Vose & Co Ltd					
W	Waitrose Ltd					
PWA	Peter Warburton Wines		•			
WAW	Waterloo Wine Co Ltd				•	•
WAC	Waters of Coventry Ltd					
WES	Wessex Wines					
WOC	Whitesides of Clitheroe Ltd					
WTL	Whittalls Wines	•	•	•	•	
WDW	Windrush Wines Ltd		•			
WE	The Wine Emporium Ltd					
WR	Wine Rack	•				•
WSC	The Wine Schoppen Ltd					
WSO	The Wine Society	•	•	•		
WTR	The Wine Treasury					
WCE	Winecellars					
WRK	Wineraks					•
WIN	The Winery	•				
WFP	Wines from Paris					
WNS	Winos Wine Shop					
MAW	M & A Winter	•	•			
WIZ	Wizard Wine Warehouses plc					
WRW	The Wright Wine Co					
PWY	Peter Wylie Fine Wines	•	•			
YAP	Yapp Bros plc			•	•	•

Champagne	French Reg.	Germany	Spain	Portugal	Italy	Australia	New Zealand	California	Other U.S.	South America	South Africa	England	Sherry	Port	Madeira	Organic	Fine/Old Wines	Malt Whisky	Half Bottles	Page No.
																				221
										•										222
	•		•							•			•	•	•		•		•	223
		•																		224
																				224
																•				225
																•				225
																				225
																				226
																				226
	•					•	•													227
																				227
																				227
•						•		•							•				•	228
														•			•			229
	•				•			•	•											229
																				230
	•						•						•	•	•					230
		•																		232
															•		•	•		232
								•												233
					•															233
																				234
•					•	•		•											•	235
																				235
																				235
•														•			•	•		236
																				236
													•					•	•	237
•														•	•		•			237
																				238

Quality ranges from 1–10, from the worst to the greatest respectively. Please note that these marks are all generalisms – good producers make good wine in bad years and bad producers can make even good years into a disaster.

	BORDEAUX RED	BORDEAUX WHITE-SWEET	BURGUNDY RED	BURGUNDY WHITE	RHONE RED	GERMANY WHITE	ITALY RED	SPAIN RIOJA	AUSTRALIA WHITE	AUSTRALIA RED	CALIFORNIA RED	PORT
1990	8△	9△	8△	9△	8△	9△	8△	8△	9△	9△	7△	8△
1989	9△	9△	8△	9△	7△	9▲	7△	8△	6▲	6△	7△	6△
1988	8△	9△	9△	8△	8△	8▲	9△	6△	8▲	8△	7△	5△
1987	6△	5△	7▲	7●	6△	7▲	7△	7△	8●	8●	8△	6△
1986	8△	8△	8△	8▲	7△	7▲	7△	6▲	7●	8△	8▲	5△
1985	8△	7△	9▲	7▲	8▲	8▲	10●	7▲	8●	8▲	9▲	10△
1984	5▲	3△	6●	7▲	6●	5●	5●	5●	8●	8▲	8▲	4●
1983	8△	9△	7▲	6●	9▲	9▲	9▲	7●		7●	6●	9△
1982	9△	4●	5●	6●	7●	7●	5▽	8●	9▲	8●	7●	7△
1981	8●	6△	4▽	8●	6●	6▽	7●	8●			6▽	5●
1980	5●	5●	8●	6▲	6●	5▲	7▲	5▽			7▼	8▲
1979	7▲	7●	7●	8●	7●	6▽	8▼	4▽			7▼	7△
1978	8▲	4●	8●	8●	10▲	3▽	7▼	8▼				8▲
1977	4▼	2●	4▽	6●	4▼	4▼	7▼	3▼				10△
1976	6●	8●	7▼	5▼	7▲	8●		7▽				7▲
1975	7●	8●	2▽	5▽	3▽	8●	6▽	8▼				7●
1974	4▽	★	3▽	4▽	4▽	★	6▼	4▽				4▼
1973	3▽	3▼	3▽	4▽	5●	★	4▽	8▼				
1972	3▽	★	8●	8▼	5●	★	3▽	3▽				
1971	6▼	8●	9●	8▼	9●	10▼	8▼	4▽				
1970	8●	6●	6▼	6▼	7●	★	8▼	9▼				9▲
1969	★	3▼	8▼	8▼	8●	★	7▽	7▽				
1968	★	★	★	★	★	★	6▼	8▼				
1967	5▼	7●	5▽	5▼	7▼	★	7▼	6▼				7▼
1966	7●	4▼	7▼	7▽	8▼	★	4▽	7▽				9●
1965	★	★	★	★	★	★	★	★				
1964	★	★	8▼	9▼	8▼	★	8▽	9▽				
1963	★	★	★	★	★	★	★	★				10●
1962	6▼	8●	6▽	8▽	8●	★	★	★				
1961	8●	7●	★	★	★	★	★	★				
1960	★	★	★	★	★	★	★	★				8▼
1959	7▼	★	★	★	★	★	★	★				

△ Still needs keeping
▲ Can be drunk but will improve
● Drinking now
▼ Should be drunk soon
▽ Probably over the hill
★ Bad year/don't buy/past it

Reproduced by kind permission of *WINE* magazine

INDEX TO WINES

Wines that appear in bold type are particularly recommended. Those that appear printed in red are the *Guide*'s Wines of the Year.